OBTAINING THE
GRACE OF CHRIST

OBTAINING THE GRACE OF CHRIST

BOOK THIRD

INSTITUTES OF THE CHRISTIAN RELIGION

JOHN CALVIN

A New Translation by Henry Beveridge, Esq.

BRIDGE
LOGOS

Alachua, Florida 32615

Bridge-Logos
Alachua, FL 32615 USA

Obtaining the Grace of Christ
by John Wesley

Translation by Henry Beveridge, Esq.

Printed in the United States of America.

Library of Congress Catalog Card Number: 2013941979
International Standard Book Number 978-1-61036-002-9

Unless otherwise indicated, Scripture quotations in this book are from the *King James Version* of the Bible.

VP 06-06-13

General Index of Chapters

BOOK THIRD

THE MODE OF OBTAINING THE GRACE OF CHRIST. THE BENEFITS IT CONFERS AND THE EFFECTS RESULTING FROM IT

Foreword

To read John Calvin is to study the work of some of the finest minds and sharpest pens in Christendom. Calvin was extremely well read and drew heavily from the writings of Turtullian, Origen, the Apostles, Saint Augustine, and Bernard, to name only a few. Befitting his training as an attorney and his passion as a Christian, Calvin devoted years to writing and rewriting his *Institutes of the Christian Religion*, deftly weaving the ideas of his predecessors with his own into a brilliant case for reformation.

That other scholars have enjoined this discussion is no surprise. In the spirit of this partnership of elite brothers that has spanned centuries, the biography of John Calvin in this volume was written by John Foxe (1516-1587), author of *Foxe's Book of Martyrs*. At the end of his piece, we have included some insights from Calvin's personal friends to give you insight into the character of this very human man. Additionally, Charles Haddon Spurgeon (1850-1892), author of *Morning by Morning* and *Evening by Evening*, contributes his treatise, *A Defense of Calvinism*.

We have maintained as much of the original vocabulary as we dare. Calvin wrote in a time when books were rare and owned by only a few. Since Calvin's day, and with the ever widening availability of books and other written media, our culture has developed a distinction between the spoken word and the written word. Their styles are sharply different, with rules that govern each. But Calvin and his contemporaries had no concept of "written" word. That would evolve with readers over the next several centuries. Their work was "spoken" word put to paper. As a consequence, it tends to be oratory in style, filled with flourish and flare. To further complicate the matter of unfamiliar style, Calvin was a Frenchman who wrote in Latin. The work we have today has been translated with careful intention of honoring Calvin's words. If, as a present-day reader, you get tangled up in an occasional sentence that seems to meander maddeningly through a peppering of punctuation marks, merely read it out loud. You will become clear about the meaning, and moreover, you will "hear" Calvin as he thunders. We beg your indulgence, and assure you that the occasional challenge is well worth the result.

Welcome to the mind of Calvin.

The Original Translator's Preface

PREFIXED TO THE FOURTH EDITION 1581
AND REPRINTED VERBATIM IN ALL THE
SUBSEQUENT EDITIONS.
T[HOMAS] N[ORTON], THE TRANSLATOR
TO THE READER.

Good reader, here is now offered you, the fourth time printed in English, M. Calvin's book of the Institutes of the Christian Religion; a book of great labor to the author, and of great profit to the Church of God. M. Calvin first wrote it when he was a young man, a book of small volume, and since that season he has at sundry times published it with new increases, still protesting at every edition himself to be one of those qui scribendo proficiunt, et proficiendo scribunt, which with their writing do grow in profiting, and with their profiting do proceed in writing. At length having, in many [of] his other works, traveled about exposition of sundry books of the Scriptures, and in the same finding occasion to discourse of sundry common-places and matters of doctrine, which being handled according to the occasions of the text that were offered him, and not in any other method, were not so ready for the reader's use, he therefore entered into this purpose to enlarge this book of Institutions, and therein to treat of all those titles and commonplaces largely, with this intent, that whensoever any occasion fell in his other books to treat of any such cause, he would not newly amplify his books of commentaries and expositions therewith, but refer his reader wholly to this storehouse and treasure of that sort of divine learning. As age and weakness grew upon him, so he hastened his labor; and, according to his petition to God, he in manner ended his life with his work, for he lived not long after.

So great a jewel was meet to be made most beneficial, that is to say, applied to most common use. Therefore, in the very beginning of the Queen's Majesty's most blessed reign, I translated it out of Latin into English for the commodity of the Church of Christ, at the special request of my dear friends of worthy memory, Reginald Wolfe and Edward Whitchurch, the one her Majesty's printer for the Hebrew, Greek, and Latin tongues, the other her Highness' printer of the books of Common Prayer. I performed my work in the house of my said friend, Edward Whitchurch, a man well known of upright heart and dealing, an ancient zealous gospeller, as plain and true a friend as ever I knew living, and as desirous to do anything to common good, especially by the advancement of true religion.

At my said first edition of this book, I considered how the author thereof had of long time purposely labored to write the same most exactly, and to pack great plenty of matter in small room of words; yea, and those so circumspectly and precisely ordered, to avoid the cavillations of such as for enmity to the truth therein contained would gladly seek and abuse all advantages which might be found by any oversight in penning of it, that the sentences were thereby become so full as nothing might well be added without idle superfluity, and again so highly pared, that nothing could be diminished without taking away some necessary substance of matter therein expressed.

This manner of writing, beside the peculiar terms of arts and figures, and the difficulty of the matters themselves, being throughout interlaced with the school men's controversies, made a great hardness in the author's own book, in that tongue wherein otherwise he is both plentiful and easy, insomuch that it sufficeth not to read him once, unless you can be content to read in vain. This consideration encumbered me with great doubtfullness for the whole order and frame of my translation. If I should follow the words, I saw that of necessity the hardness in the translation must needs be greater than was in the tongue wherein it was originally written. If I should leave the course of words, and grant myself liberty after the natural manner of my own tongue, to say that in English which I conceived to be his meaning in Latin, I plainly perceived how hardly I might escape error, and on the other side, in this matter of faith and religion, how perilous it was to err. For I durst not presume to warrant myself to have his meaning without his words. And they that knew what it is to translate well and faithfully, especially in matters of religion, do know that not the only grammatical construction of words sufficeth, but the very building and order to observe all advantages of vehemence or grace, by placing or accent of words, maketh much to the true setting forth of a writer's mind.

In the end, I rested upon this determination, to follow the words so near as the phrase of the English tongue would suffer me. Which purpose I so performed, that if the English book were printed in such paper and letter as the Latin is, it should not exceed the Latin in quantity. Whereby, beside all other commodities that a faithful translation of so good a work may bring, this one benefit is moreover provided for such as are desirous to attain some knowledge of the Latin tongue (which is, at this time, to be wished in many of those men for whose profession this book most fitly serveth), that they shall not find any more English than shall suffice to construe the Latin withal, except in such few places where the great difference of the phrases of the languages enforced me: so that, comparing the one with the other, they shall both profit in good matter, and furnish themselves with understanding of that speech, wherein the greatest treasures of knowledge are disclosed.

In the doing hereof, I did not only trust mine own wit or ability, but examined my whole doing from sentence to sentence throughout the whole book with conference and overlooking of such learned men, as my translation being allowed by their Judgment, I did both satisfy mine own conscience that I had done truly, and their approving of it might be a good warrant to the reader that nothing should herein be delivered him but sound, unmingled, and uncorrupted doctrine, even in such sort as the author himself had first framed it. All that I wrote, the grave, learned, and virtuous man, M. David Whitehead (whom I name with honorable remembrance), did, among others, compare with the Latin, examining every sentence throughout the whole book. Beside all this, I privately required many, and generally all men with whom I ever had any talk of this matter, that if they found anything either not truly translated, or not plainly Englished, they would inform me thereof, promising either to satisfy them or to amend it. Since which time, I have not been advertised by any man of anything, which they would require to be altered. Neither had I myself, by reason of my profession, being otherwise occupied, any leisure to peruse it. And that is the cause, why not only at the second and third time, but also at this impression, you have no change at all in the work, but altogether as it was before.

Indeed, I perceived many men well-minded and studious of this book, to require a table for their ease and furtherance. Their honest desire I have fulfilled in the second edition, and have added thereto a plentiful table, which is also here inserted, which I have translated out of the Latin, wherein the principal matters discoursed in this book are named by their due titles in order of alphabet, and under every title is set forth a brief sum of the whole doctrine taught in this book concerning the matter belonging to that title or common-place; and therewith is added the book, chapter, and section or division of the chapter, where the same doctrine is more largely expressed and proved. And for the readier finding thereof, I have caused the number of the chapters to be set upon every leaf in the book, and quoted the sections also by their due numbers with the usual figures of algorism. And now at this last publishing, my friends, by whose charge it is now newly imprinted in a Roman letter and smaller volume, with divers other Tables which, since my second edition, were gathered by M. Marlorate, to be translated and here added for your benefit.

Moreover, whereas in the first edition the evil manner of my scribbling hand, the interlining of my copy, and some other causes well known among workmen of that faculty, made very many faults to pass the printer, I have, in the second impression, caused the book to be composed by the printed copy, and corrected by the written; whereby it must needs be that it was much more truly done than the other was, as I myself do know above three hundred faults amended. And now at this last printing, the composing after a printed copy bringeth some ease, and the diligence used about the correction having been right faithfully looked unto, it cannot be but much more truly set forth. This also is performed, that the volume being smaller, with a letter fair and legible, it is of more easy price, that it may be of more common use, and so to more large communicating of so great a treasure to those that desire Christian knowledge for instruction of their faith, and guiding of their duties. Thus, on the printer's behalf and mine, your ease and commodity (good readers) provided for. Now resteth your own diligence, for your own profit, in studying it.

To spend many words in commending the work itself were needless; yet thus much I think, I may both not unruly and not vainly say, that though many great learned men have written books of common-places of our religion, as Melancthon, Sarcerius, and others, whose works are very good and profitable to the Church of God, yet by the consenting Judgment of those that understand the same, there is none to be compared to this work of Calvin, both for his substantial sufficiency of doctrine, the sound declaration of truth in articles of our religion, the large and learned confirmation of the same, and the most deep and strong confutation of all old and new heresies; so that (the Holy Scriptures excepted) this is one of the most profitable books for all students of Christian divinity. Wherein (good readers), as I am glad for the glory of God, and for your benefit, that you may have this profit of my travel, so I beseech you let me have this use of your gentleness, that my doings may be construed to such good end as I have meant them; and that if anything mislike you by reason of hardness, or any other cause that may seem to be my default, you will not forthwith condemn the work, but read it after; in which doing you will find (as many have confessed to me that they have found by experience) that those things which at the first reading shall displease you for hardness, shall be found so easy as so hard matter would suffer, and, for the most part, more easy than some other phrase which should with greater looseness and smoother sliding away deceive your understanding. I confess, indeed, it is not finely and pleasantly written, nor carrieth with it such delightful grace of speech as some great wise men have bestowed upon some foolisher things, yet it containeth sound truth set forth with faithful plainness, without wrong done to the author's meaning; and so, if you accept and use it, you shall not fail to have great profit thereby, and I shall think my labor very well employed.

Thomas Norton.

The Printers to the Readers

hereas some men have thought and reported it to be [very great negligence in us for that we have so long kept back from you this,] being so profitable a work for you, namely before the master J[ohnne] Dawes had translated it and delivered it into our hands more than a twelvemonth past: you shall understand for our excuse in that behalf, that we could not well imprint it sooner. For we have been by diverse necessary causes constrained with our earnest entreatance to procure an other frebe or oures to translate it whole again. This translation, we trust, you shall well allow. For it hath not only been faithfully done by the translator himself, but also hath been wholly perused by such men, whose ingement and credit all the godly learned in England well know I estheme. But since it is now come forth, we pray you accept it, and see it. If any faults have passed us by oversight, we beseech you let us have your patience, as you have had our diligence.

The Institutes of the Christian Religion, written in Latin by M. John Calvin, and translated into English according to the Author's last edition, with sundry Tables to find the principal matters entreated of in this book, and also the declaration of places of Scripture therein expounded, by Thomas Norton. Whereunto there are newly added in the margen of the book, notes containing in briefs the substance of the matter handled in each Section.

Originally printed at London by Arnold Hatfield, for Bonham Norton. 1599

Prefactory Address

TO HIS MOST CHRISTIAN MAJESTY,
THE MOST MIGHTY AND ILLUSTRIOUS MONARCH,
FRANCIS, KING OF THE FRENCH, HIS SOVEREIGN;
JOHN CALVIN PRAYS PEACE AND SALVATION IN CHRIST.

Sire, when I first engaged in this work, nothing was further from my thoughts than to write what should afterwards be presented to your Majesty. My intention was only to furnish a kind of rudiment, by which those who feel some interest in religion might be trained to true godliness. And I toiled at the task chiefly for the sake of my countrymen, the French multitudes of whom I perceived to be hungering and thirsting after Christ, while very few seemed to have been duly imbued with even a slender knowledge of him. That this was the object, which I had in view, is apparent from the work itself, which is written in a simple and elementary form adapted for instruction.

But when I perceived that the fury of certain bad men had risen to such a height in your realm, that there was no place in it for sound doctrine, I thought it might be of service if I were in the same work both to give instruction to my countrymen, and also lay before your Majesty a Confession from which you may learn what the doctrine is that so inflames the rage of those madmen who are this day, with fire and sword, troubling your kingdom. For I fear not to declare that what I have here given may be regarded as a summary of the very doctrine, which, they shout, ought to be punished with confiscation, exile, imprisonment, and flames, as well as exterminated by land and sea.

Indeed, I am aware of how, in order to render our cause as hateful to your Majesty as possible, they have filled your ears and mind with atrocious insinuations; but you will be pleased, of your clemency, to reflect that neither in word nor deed could there be any innocence, were it sufficient merely to accuse. When anyone with the view of exciting prejudice observes that this doctrine, of which I am endeavoring to give your Majesty an account, has been condemned by the suffrages of all the estates, and was long ago stabbed again and again by partial sentences of courts of law, he undoubtedly says nothing more than that it has sometimes been violently oppressed by the power and faction of adversaries, and sometimes fraudulently and insidiously overwhelmed by lies, cavils, and calumny. While a cause is unheard, it is violence to pass sanguinary sentences against it; it is fraud to charge it, contrary to its deserts, with sedition and mischief.

That no one may suppose we are unjust in thus complaining, you yourself, most illustrious Sovereign, can bear us witness with what lying calumnies it is daily traduced in your presence, as aiming at nothing else than to wrest the scepters of kings out of their hands, to overturn all tribunals and seats of justice, to subvert all order and government, to disturb the peace and quiet of society, to abolish all laws, to destroy the distinctions of rank and property, and, in short, to turn all things upside down. And yet, that which you hear is but the smallest portion of what is said; for among the common people are disseminated certain horrible insinuations—insinuations which, if well founded, would justify the whole world in condemning the doctrine with its authors to a thousand fires and gibbets. Who can wonder that the popular hatred is inflamed against it, when credit is given to those most iniquitous accusations? See why all ranks unite with one accord in condemning our persons and our doctrine!

Carried away by this feeling, those who sit in judgment merely give utterance to the prejudices, which they have imbibed at home, and who think they have duly performed their part if they do not order punishment to be inflicted on anyone until convicted, either on his own confession, or on legal evidence. But of what crime convicted? "Of that condemned doctrine," is the answer. But with what justice condemned? The very essence of the defense was not to abjure the doctrine itself, but to maintain its truth. On this subject, however, not a whisper is allowed!

Justice, then, most invincible Sovereign, entitles me to demand that you will undertake a thorough investigation of this cause, which has hitherto been tossed about in any kind of way, and handled in the most irregular manner, without any order of law, and with passionate heat rather than judicial gravity. Let it not be imagined that I am here framing my own private defense with the view of obtaining a safe return to my native land. Though I cherish towards it the feelings, which become me as a man, still, as matters now are, I can be absent from it without regret. The cause, which I plead, is the common cause of all the godly, and therefore the very cause of Christ—a cause which, throughout your realm, now lies in despair—torn and trampled upon in all kinds of ways, and that more through the tyranny of certain Pharisees than any sanction from yourself. But it matters not to inquire how the thing is done; the fact that it is done cannot be denied. For so far have the wicked prevailed, that the truth of Christ, if not utterly routed and dispersed, lurks as if it were ignobly buried; while the poor Church, either wasted by cruel slaughter or driven into exile or intimidated and terror—struck, scarcely ventures to breathe. Still her enemies press on with their wonted rage and fury over the ruins, which they have made, strenuously assaulting the wall, which is already giving way. Meanwhile, no man comes forth to offer his protection against such furies. Any who would be thought most favorable to the truth, merely talk of pardoning the error and imprudence of ignorant men, for so those modest personages speak: giving the name of *error and imprudence* to that which they know to be the infallible truth of God, and of *ignorant men* to those whose intellect they see that Christ has not despised, seeing he has deigned to entrust them with the mysteries of his heavenly wisdom. Thus, all are ashamed of the Gospel.

Your duty, most serene Prince, is to not shut either your ears or mind against a cause involving such mighty interests as these: how the glory of God is to be maintained on the earth inviolate, how the truth of God is to preserve its dignity, how the kingdom of Christ is to continue amongst us compact and secure. The cause is worthy of your ear, worthy of your investigation, worthy of your throne.

The characteristic of a true sovereign is to acknowledge that in the administration of his kingdom, he is a minister of God. He, who does not make his reign subservient to the divine glory, acts the part not of a king, but a robber. He, moreover, deceives himself who anticipates long prosperity to any kingdom, which is not ruled by the scepter of God—that is, by his divine word. For the heavenly oracle is infallible which has declared, "where there is no vision the people perish" (Proverbs 29:18).

Let not a contemptuous idea of our insignificance dissuade you from the investigation of this cause. We, indeed, are perfectly conscious how poor and abject we are: in the presence of God we are miserable sinners, and in the sight of men most despised—we are, if you will, the mere dregs and off—scouting of the world, or worse, if worse can be named: so that before God there remains nothing of which we can glory save only his mercy, by which, without any merit of our own, we are admitted to the hope of eternal salvation: and before men not even this much remains, since we can glory only in our infirmity, a thing which, in the estimation of men, it is the greatest ignominy even tacitly to confess. But our doctrine must stand sublime above all the glory of the world, and invincible by all its power, because it is not ours, but that of the living God and his Anointed, whom the Father has appointed King, that he may rule from sea to sea, and from the rivers even to the ends of the earth; and so rule as to smite the whole earth and its strength of iron and brass, its splendor of gold and silver, with the mere rod of his mouth, and break them in pieces like a potter's vessel; according to the magnificent predictions of the prophets respecting his kingdom (Daniel 2:34, Isaiah 11:4, Psalm 2:9).

Our adversaries, indeed, clamorously maintain that our appeal to the word of God is a mere pretext—that we are, in fact, its worst corrupters. How far this is not only malicious calumny, but also shameless effrontery, you will be able to decide of your own knowledge by reading our Confession. Here, however, it may be necessary to make some observations which may dispose, or at least assist, you to read and study it with attention.

When Paul declared that all prophecy ought to be according to the analogy of faith (Romans 12:6), he laid down the surest rule for determining the meaning of Scripture. Let our doctrine be tested by this rule, and our victory is secure. For what accords better and more aptly with faith than to acknowledge ourselves divested of all virtue that we may be clothed by God, devoid of all goodness, that we may be filled by him; the slaves of sin, that he may give us freedom; blind, that he may enlighten; lame, that he may cure; and feeble, that he may sustain us; to strip ourselves of all ground of glorying, that he alone may shine forth glorious, and we be glorified in him? When these things and others to the same effect are said by us, they interpose and querulously complain, that in this way we overturn some blind light of nature, fancied preparations, free will, and works meritorious of eternal salvation, with their own supererogation also; because they cannot bear that the entire praise and glory of all goodness, virtue, justice, and wisdom should remain with God. But we read not of any having been blamed for drinking too much of the fountain of living water; on the contrary, those are severely reprimanded who "have hewed them out cisterns, broken cisterns, that can hold no water" (Jeremiah 2:13). Again, what more agreeable to faith than to feel assured that God is a propitious Father when Christ is acknowledged as a brother and propitiator, than confidently to expect all prosperity and gladness from Him, whose ineffable love towards us was such that He "spared not his own Son, but delivered him up for us all" (Romans 8:32), than to rest in the sure hope of salvation and eternal life whenever Christ, in whom such treasures are hid, is conceived to have been given by the Father? Here they attack us, and loudly maintain that this sure confidence is not free from arrogance and presumption. But as nothing is to be presumed of ourselves, so all things are to be presumed of God; nor are we stripped of vainglory for any other reason than that we may learn to glory in the Lord. Why go further? Take but a cursory view, most valiant King, of all the parts of our cause, and count us of all wicked men the most iniquitous, if you do not discover plainly, that "therefore we both labor and suffer reproach because we trust in the living God" (1 Timothy 4:10); because we believe it to be "life eternal" to know "the only true God, and Jesus Christ," whom he has sent (John 17:3). For this hope some of us are in bonds, some beaten with rods, some made a gazing—stock, some proscribed, some most cruelly tortured, some obliged to flee; we are all pressed with straits, loaded with dire execrations, lacerated by slanders, and treated with the greatest indignity.

Look now to our adversaries (I mean the priesthood, at whose beck and pleasure others ply their enmity against us), and consider with me for a little by what zeal they are actuated. The true religion which is delivered in the Scriptures, and which all ought to hold, they readily permit both themselves and others to be ignorant of, to neglect and despise; and they deem it of little moment what each man believes concerning God and Christ, or disbelieves, provided he submits to the judgment of the Church with what they call implicit faith; nor are they greatly concerned though they should see the glow of God dishonored by open blasphemies, provided not a finger is raised against the primacy of the Apostolic See and the authority of holy mother Church. Why, then, do they war for the mass, purgatory, pilgrimage, and similar follies, with such fierceness and acerbity, that though they cannot prove one of them from the word of God, they deny godliness can be safe without faith in these things—faith drawn out, if I may so express it, to its utmost stretch? Why? Just because their belly is their God, and their kitchen their religion, and they believe that if these were away they would not only not be Christians, but not even men. For although some wallow in luxury, and others feed on slender crusts, still they all live by the same pot, which without that fuel might not only cool, but altogether freeze. He, accordingly, who is most anxious about his stomach, proves the fiercest champion of his faith. In short, the object on which all to a man are bent, is to keep their kingdom safe or their belly filled; not one gives even the smallest sign of sincere zeal.

Nevertheless, they cease not to assail our doctrine, and to accuse and defame it in what terms they may, in order to render it either hated or suspected. They call it new, and of recent birth; they carp at it as doubtful and uncertain; they bid us tell by what miracles it has been confirmed; they ask if it be fair to receive it against the consent of so many holy Fathers and the most ancient custom; they urge us to confess either that it is schismatical in giving battle to the Church, or that the Church must have been without life during the many centuries in which nothing of the kind was heard. Lastly, they say there is little need of argument, for its quality may be known by its fruits: namely, the large number of sects, the many seditious disturbances, and the great licentiousness, which it has produced. No doubt, it is a very easy matter for them, in presence of an ignorant and credulous multitude, to insult over an undefended cause; but were an opportunity of mutual discussion afforded, that acrimony which they now pour out upon us in frothy torrents, with as much license as impunity, would assuredly boil dry.

1 First, in calling it new, they are exceedingly injurious to God, whose sacred word deserved not to be charged with novelty. To them, indeed, I very little doubt it is new, as Christ is new, and the Gospel new; but those who are acquainted with the old saying of Paul, that Christ Jesus "died for our sins, and rose again for our justification" (Romans 4:25), will not detect any novelty in us. That it long lay buried and unknown is the guilty consequence of man's impiety; but now when, by the kindness of God, it is restored to us, it ought to resume its antiquity just as the returning citizen resumes his rights.

2 It is owing to the same ignorance that they hold it to be doubtful and uncertain; for this is the very thing of which the Lord complains by his prophet, "The ox knoweth his owner, and the ass his master's crib; but Israel doth not know, my people doth not consider" (Isaiah 1:3). But however they may sport with its uncertainty, had they to seal their own doctrine with their blood, and at the expense of life, it would be seen what value they put upon it. Very different is our confidence—a confidence that is not appalled by the terrors of death, and therefore not even by the judgment—seat of God.

3 In demanding miracles from us, they act dishonestly. For we have not coined some new gospel, but retain the very one the truth of which is confirmed by all the miracles which Christ and the apostles ever wrought. But they have a peculiarity, which we have not—they can confirm their faith by constant miracles down to the present day! Way rather, they allege miracles, which might produce wavering in minds otherwise well disposed; they are so frivolous and ridiculous, so vain and false. But were they even exceedingly wonderful, they could have no effect against the truth of God, whose name ought to be hallowed always, and everywhere, whether by miracles, or by the natural course of events. The deception would

perhaps be more specious if Scripture did not admonish us of the legitimate end and use of miracles. Mark tells us (Mark 16:20) that the signs which followed the preaching of the apostles were wrought in confirmation of it; so Luke also relates that the Lord "gave testimony to the word of his grace, and granted signs and wonders to be done" by the hands of the apostles (Acts 14:3). Very much to the same effect are those words of the apostle, that salvation by a preached gospel was confirmed, "The Lord bearing witness with signs and wonders, and with divers miracles" (Hebrews 2:4). Those things that we are told are seals of the gospel, shall we pervert to the subversion of the gospel? What was destined only to confirm the truth, shall we misapply to the confirmation of lies? The proper course, therefore, is, in the first instance, to ascertain and examine the doctrine, which is said by the Evangelist to precede; then after it, has been proved, but not until then, it may receive confirmation from miracles. But the mark of sound doctrine given by our Savior himself is its tendency to promote the glory not of men, but of God (John 7:18, 8:50). Our Savior having declared this to be test of doctrine, we are in error if we regard as miraculous, works, which are used for any other purpose than to magnify the name of God. And it becomes us to remember that Satan has his miracles, which, although they are tricks rather than true wonders, are still such as to delude the ignorant and unwary. Magicians and enchanters have always been famous for miracles, and miracles of an astonishing description have given support to idolatry: these, however, do not make us converts to the superstitions either of magicians or idolaters. In old times, too, the Donatists used their power of working miracles as a battering ram, with which they shook the simplicity of the common people. We now give to our opponents the answer, which Augustine then gave to the Donatists, "The Lord put us on our guard against those wonder—workers, when he foretold that false prophets would arise, who, by lying signs and divers wonders, would, if it were possible, deceive the very elect" (Matthew 24:24). Paul, too, gave warning that the reign of antichrist would be "with all power, and signs, and lying wonders" (2 Thessalonians 2:9).

But our opponents tell us that their miracles are wrought not by idols, not by sorcerers, not by false prophets, but by saints: as if we did not know it to be one of Satan's wiles to transform himself "into an angel of light" (2 Corinthians 11:14). The Egyptians, in whose neighborhood Jeremiah was buried, anciently sacrificed and paid other divine honors to him. Did they not make an idolatrous abuse of the holy prophet of God? And yet, in recompense for so venerating his tomb, they thought that they were cured of the bite of serpents. What, then, shall we say but that it has been, and always will be, a most just punishment of God, to send on those who do not receive the truth in the love of it, "strong delusion, that they should believe a lie?" (2 Thessalonians 2:11). We, then, have no lack of miracles, sure miracles, that cannot be gainsaid; but those to which our opponents lay claim are mere delusions of Satan, inasmuch as they draw off the people from the true worship of God to vanity.

4 It is slanderous to represent us as opposed to the Fathers (I mean the ancient writers of a purer age), as if the Fathers were supporters of their impiety. Were the contest to be decided by such authority (to speak in the most moderate terms), the better part of the victory would be ours. While there is much that is admirable and wise in the writings of those Fathers, and while in some things it has fared with them as with ordinary men; these pious sons, forsooth, with the peculiar acuteness of intellect, and judgment, and soul, which belongs to them, adore only their slips and errors, while those things which are well said they either overlook, or disguise, or corrupt; so that it may be truly said their only care has been to gather dross among gold. Then, with dishonest clamor, they assail us as enemies and despisers of the Fathers. So far are we from despising them, that if this were the proper place, it would give us no trouble to support the greater part of the doctrines, which we now hold by their suffrages. Still, in studying their writings, we have endeavored to remember (1 Corinthians 3:21-23), that all things are ours, to serve, not lord it over us, but that we axe Christ's only, and must obey him in all things without exception. He who does not draw this distinction will not have any fixed principles in religion; for those holy men were ignorant of many things, are often opposed to each other, and are sometimes at variance with themselves.

It is not without cause (remark our opponents) we are thus warned by Solomon, "Remove not the ancient landmarks which thy fathers have set" (Proverbs 22:28). But the same rule applies not to the measuring of fields and the obedience of faith. The rule applicable to the latter is, "Forget also thine own people, and thy father's house" (Psalm 45:10). But if they are so fond of allegory, why do they not understand the apostles, rather than any other class of Fathers, to be meant by those whose landmarks it is unlawful to remove? This is the interpretation of Jerome, whose words they have quoted in their canons. But as regards those to whom they apply the passage, if they wish the landmarks to be fixed, why do they, whenever it suits their purpose, so freely overleap them?

Among the Fathers there were two, the one of whom said, "Our God neither eats nor drinks, and therefore has no need of chalices and salvers;" and the other, "Sacred rites do not require gold, and things which are not bought with gold, please not by gold." They step beyond the boundary; therefore, when in sacred matters they are so much delighted with gold, driver, ivory, marble, gems, and silks, that unless everything is overlaid with costly show, or rather insane luxury, they think God is not duly worshipped.

It was a Father, who said, "He ate flesh freely on the day on which others abstained from it, because he was a Christian." They overleap the boundaries, therefore, when they doom to perdition every soul that, during Lent, shall have tasted flesh.

There were two Fathers, the one of whom said, "A monk not laboring with his own hands is no better than a violent man and a robber;" and the other, "Monks, however assiduous they may be in study, meditation, and prayer, must not live by others." This boundary, too, they transgressed, when they placed lazy gormandizing monks in dens and stews, to gorge themselves on other men's substance.

It was a Father, who said, "It is a horrid abomination to see in Christian temples a painted image either of Christ or of any saint." Nor was this pronounced by the voice era single individual; but an Ecclesiastical Council also decreed, "Let nothing that is worshipped be depicted on walls." Very far are they from keeping within these boundaries when they leave not a corner without images.

Another Father counseled, "That after performing the office of humanity to the dead in their burial, we should leave them at rest." These limits they burst through when they keep up a perpetual anxiety about the dead.

It is a Father, who testified, "That the substance of bread and wine in the Eucharist does not cease but remains, just as the nature and substance of man remains united to the Godhead in the Lord Jesus Christ." This boundary they pass in pretending that, as soon as the words of our Lord are pronounced, the substance of bread and wine ceases and is transubstantiated into body and blood.

They were Fathers, who, as they exhibited only one Eucharist to the whole Church, and kept back from it the profane and flagitious; so they, in the severest terms, censured all those who, being present, did not communicate How far have they removed these landmarks, in filling not churches only, but also private houses, with their masses, admitting all and sundry to be present, each the more willingly the more largely he pays, however wicked and impure he may be—not inviting anyone to faith in Christ and faithful communion in the sacraments, but rather vending their own work for the grace and merits of Christ!

There were two Fathers, the one of whom decided that those were to be excluded altogether from partaking of Christ's sacred supper, who, contented with communion in one kind, abstained from the other; while the other Father strongly contends that the blood of the Lord ought not to be denied to the Christian people, who, in confessing him, are enjoined to shed their own blood. These landmarks, also, they removed, when, by an unalterable law, they ordered the very thing, which the former Father punished with excommunication, and the latter condemned for a valid reason.

It was a Father, who pronounced it rashness in an obscure question, to decide in either way without clear and evident authority from Scripture. They forgot this landmark when they enacted so many constitutions, so many canons, and so many dogmatic decisions, without sanction from the word of God.

It was a Father, who reproved Montanus, among other heresies, for being the first who imposed laws of fasting. They have gone far beyond this landmark also in enjoining fasting under the strictest laws.

It was a Father, who denied that the ministers of the Church should be interdicted from marrying, and pronounced married life to be a state of chastity; and there were other Fathers, who assented to his decision. These boundaries they overstepped in rigidly binding their priests to celibacy.

It was a Father who thought that Christ only should be listened to, from its being said, "Hear him," and that regard is due not to what others before us have said or done, but only to what Christ, the head of all, has commanded. This landmark they neither observe themselves nor allow to be observed by others, while they subject themselves and others to any master whatever, rather than Christ.

There is a Father, who contends that the Church ought not to prefer herself to Christ, who always judges truly, whereas ecclesiastical judges, who are but men, are generally deceived. Having burst through this barrier also, they hesitate not to suspend the whole authority of Scripture on the judgment of the Church.

All the Fathers with one heart execrated, and with one mouth protested against, contaminating the word of God with subtleties of sophists, and involving it in the brawls of dialecticians. Do they keep within these limits when the sole occupation of their lives is to entwine and entangle the simplicity of Scripture with endless disputes, and worse than sophistical jargon? So much so, that were the Fathers to rise from their graves, and listen to the brawling art which bears the name of speculative theology, there is nothing they would suppose it less to be than a discussion of a religious nature.

But my discourse would far exceed its just limits were I to show, in detail, how petulantly those men shake off the yoke of the Fathers, while they wish to be thought their most obedient sons. Months, nay, years would fail me; and yet so deplorable and desperate is their effrontery, that they presume to chastise us for overstepping the ancient landmarks!

5 Then, again, it is to no purpose they call us to the bar of custom. To make everything yield to custom would be to do the greatest injustice. Were the judgments of mankind correct, custom would be

regulated by the good. But it is often far otherwise in point of fact; for, whatever the many are seen to do, forthwith obtains the force of custom. But human affairs have scarcely ever been so happily constituted as that the better course pleased the greater number. Hence, the private vices of the multitude have generally resulted in public error, or rather that common consent in vice which these worthy men would have to be law. Anyone with eyes may perceive that it is not one flood of evils, which has deluged us; that many fatal plagues have invaded the globe; that all things rush headlong; so that either the affairs of men must be altogether despaired of, or we must not only resist, but boldly attack prevailing evils. The cure is prevented by no other cause than the length of time during which we have been accustomed to the disease. But be it so that public error must have a place in human society, still, in the kingdom of God, we must look and listen only to his eternal truth, against which no series of years, no custom, no conspiracy, can plead prescription. Thus Isaiah formerly taught the people of God, "Say ye not, A confederacy, to all to whom this people shall say, A confederacy;" i.e. do not unite with the people in an impious consent; "neither fear ye their fear, nor be afraid. Sanctify the Lord of hosts himself; and let him be your fear, and let him be your dread" (Isaiah 8:12). Now, therefore, let them, if they will, object to us both past ages and present examples; if we sanctify the Lord of hosts, we shall not be greatly afraid. Though many ages should have consented to like ungodliness, He is strong who taketh vengeance to the third and fourth generation; or the whole world should league together in the same iniquity. He taught experimentally what the end is of those who sin with the multitude, when He destroyed the whole human race with a flood, saving Noah with his little family, who, by putting his faith in Him alone, "condemned the world" (Hebrews 11:7). In short, depraved custom is just a kind of general pestilence in which men perish not the less that they fall in a crowd. It would be well, moreover, to ponder the observation of Cyprian: that those who sin in ignorance, though they cannot be entirely exculpated, seem, however, to be, in some sense, excusable; whereas those who obstinately reject the truth, when presented to them by the kindness of God, have no defense to offer.

6 Their dilemma does not push us so violently as to oblige us to confess, either that the Church was a considerable time without life, or that we have now a quarrel with the Church. The Church of Christ assuredly has lived, and will live, as long as Christ shall reign at the right hand of the Father. By his hand it is sustained, by his protection defended, by his mighty power preserved in safety. For what he once undertook he will undoubtedly perform, he will be with iris people always, "even to the end of the world" (Matthew 28:20). With the Church we wage no war, since, with one consent, in common with the whole body of the faithful, we worship and adore one God, and Christ Jesus the Lord, as all the pious have always adored him. But they themselves err not a little from the truth in not recognizing any church but that which they behold with the bodily eye, and in endeavoring to circumscribe it by limits, within which it cannot be confined.

The hinges on which the controversy turns are these: first, in their contending that the form of the Church is always visible and apparent; and, secondly, in their placing this form in the see of the Church of Rome and its hierarchy. We, on the contrary, maintain, both that the Church may exist without any apparent form, and, moreover, that the form is not ascertained by that external splendor which they foolishly admire, but by a very different mark, namely, by the pure preaching of the word of God, and the due administration of the sacraments. They make an outcry whenever the Church cannot be pointed to with the finger. But how oft was it the fate of the Church among the Jews to be so defaced that no comeliness appeared? What do we suppose to have been the splendid form when Elijah complained that he was left alone? (1 Kings 19:14). How long after the advent of Christ, did it lie hid without form? How often since has it been so oppressed by wars, seditions, and heresies, that it was nowhere seen in splendor? Had they lived at that time, would they have believed there was any Church? But Elijah learned that there remained seven thousand men, who had not bowed the knee to Baal; nor ought we to doubt that Christ has always reigned on earth ever since he ascended to heaven. Had the faithful at that time required some discernible form, must they not have forthwith given way to despondency? And, indeed, Hilary accounted it a very great fault in his day that men were so possessed with a foolish admiration of Episcopal dignity as not to perceive the deadly hydra lurking under that mask. His words are, "One advice I give: Beware of Antichrist; for, unhappily, a love of walls has seized you; unhappily, the Church of God which you venerate exists in houses and buildings; unhappily, under these you find the name of peace. Is it doubtful that in these Antichrist will have his seat? Safer to me are mountains, and woods, and lakes, and dungeons, and whirlpools; since in these prophets, dwelling or immersed, did prophesy."

And what is it at the present day that the world venerates in its horned bishops, unless that it imagines those who are seen presiding over celebrated cities to be holy prelates of religion? Away, then, with this absurd mode of judging! Let us rather reverently admit that, as God alone knows who are his, so he may sometimes withdraw the external manifestation of his Church from the view of men. This, I allow, is a fearful punishment, which God sends on the earth; but if the wickedness of men so deserves, why do we strive to oppose the just vengeance of God? It was thus that God, in past ages, punished the ingratitude of men; for after they had refused to obey his truth, and had extinguished his light, he allowed them, when blinded by sense, both to be deluded by lying vanities and plunged in thick darkness, so that no face of a true Church appeared. Meanwhile, however, though his own people were dispersed and concealed amidst errors and darkness, he saved them from destruction. No wonder; for he knew how to preserve them even in the confusion of Babylon and the flame of the fiery furnace.

But as to the wish that the form of the Church should be ascertained by some kind of vain pomp, how perilous it is I will briefly indicate, rather than explain, that I may not exceed all bounds. What they say is, that the Pontiff, who holds the Apostolic See, and the priests who are anointed and consecrated by him, provided they have the insignia of fillets and miters, represent the Church, and ought to be considered as in the place of the Church, and therefore cannot err. Why so? Because they are pastors of the Church, and consecrated to the Lord. And were not Aaron and other prefects of Israel pastors? But Aaron and his sons, though already set apart to the priesthood, erred notwithstanding when they made the calf (Exodus 32:4). Why, according to this view, should not the four hundred prophets who lied to Ahab represent the Church? (1 Kings 22:11), etc.). The Church, however, stood on the side of Micaiah. He was alone, indeed, and despised, but from his mouth, the truth proceeded. Did not the prophets also exhibit both the name and face of the Church, when, with one accord, they rose up against Jeremiah, and with menaces boasted of it as a thing impossible that the law should perish from the priest, or counsel from the wise, or the word from the prophet? (Jeremiah 19:18). In opposition to the whole body of the prophets, Jeremiah is sent alone to declare from the Lord (Jeremiah 4:9), that a time would come when the law would perish from the priest, counsel from the wise, and the word from the prophet. Was not like splendor displayed in that council when the chief priests, scribes, and Pharisees assembled to consult how they might put Jesus to death? Let them go, then, and cling to the external mask, while they make Christ and all the prophets of God schismatics, and, on the other hand, make Satan's ministers the organs of the Holy Spirit!

But if they are sincere, let them answer me in good faith, —in what place, and among whom, do they think the Church resided, after the Council of Basle degraded and deposed Eugenius from the popedom, and substituted Amadeus in his place? Do their utmost, they cannot deny that that Council was legitimate as far as regards external forms, and was summoned not only by one Pontiff, but by two. Eugenius, with the whole herd of cardinals and bishops who had joined him in plotting the dissolution of the Council, was there condemned of contumacy, rebellion, and schism. Afterwards, however, aided by the favor of princes, he got back his popedom safe. The election of Amadeus, duly made by the authority of a general holy synod, went to smoke; only he himself was appeased with a cardinal's cap, like a piece of offal thrown to a barking dog. Out of the lap of these rebellious and contumacious schismatics proceeded all future popes, cardinals, bishops, abbots, and presbyters. Here they are caught, and cannot escape. For, on which party will they bestow the name of Church? Will they deny it to have been a general Council, though it lacked nothing as regards external majesty, having been solemnly called by two bulls, consecrated by the legate of the Roman See as its president, constituted regularly in all respects, and continuing in possession of all its honors to the last? Will they admit that Eugenius, and his whole train, through whom they have all been consecrated, were schismatic? Let them, then, either define the form of the Church differently, or, however numerous they are, we will hold them all to be schismatics in having knowingly and willingly received ordination from heretics. But had it never been discovered before that the Church is not tied to external pomp, we are furnished with a lengthened proof in their own conduct, in proudly vending themselves to the world under the specious title of Church, notwithstanding that they are the deadly pests of the Church. I speak not of their manners and of those tragic atrocities with which their whole life teems, since it is said that they are Pharisees who should be heard, not imitated. By devoting some portion of your leisure to our writings, you will see, not obscurely, that their doctrine—the very doctrine to which they say it is owing that they are the Church—is a deadly murderer of souls, the firebrand, ruin, and destruction of the Church.

7 Lastly, they are far from candid when they invidiously number up the disturbances, tumults, and disputes, which the preaching of our doctrine has brought in its train, and the fruits which, in many instances, it now produces; for the doctrine itself is undeservedly charged with evils which ought to be ascribed to the malice of Satan. It is one of the characteristics of the divine word, that whenever it appears, Satan ceases to slumber and sleep. This is the surest and most unerring test for distinguishing it from false doctrines, which readily betray themselves, while they are received by all with willing ears, and welcomed by an applauding world. Accordingly, for several ages, during which all things were immersed in profound darkness, almost all mankind were mere jest and sport to the god of this world, who, like any Sardanapalus, idled and luxuriated undisturbed. For what else could he do but laugh and sport while in tranquil and undisputed possession of his kingdom? But when light beaming from above somewhat dissipated the darkness—when the strong man arose and aimed a blow at his kingdom—then, indeed, he began to shake off his wonted torpor, and rush to arms. And first he stirred up the hands of men, that by them he might violently suppress the dawning

truth; but when this availed him not, he turned to snares, exciting dissensions and disputes about doctrine by means of his Catabaptists, and other portentous miscreants, that he might thus obscure, and, at length, extinguish the truth. And now be persists in assailing it with both engines, endeavoring to pluck up the true seed by the violent hand of man, and striving, as much as in him lies, to choke it with his tares, that it may not grow and bear knit. But it will be in vain, if we listen to the admonition of the Lord, who long ago disclosed his wiles, that we might not be taken unawares, and armed us with full protection against all his machinations. But how malignant to throw upon the word of God itself the blame either of the seditions which wicked men and rebels, or of the sects which impostors stir up against it! The example, however, is not new. Elijah was asked if it had been he, who troubled Israel. Christ was seditious, according to the Jews; and the apostles were charged with the crime of popular commotion. What else do those who, in the present day, impute to us all the disturbances, tumults, and contentions, which break out against us? Elijah, however, has taught us our answer (1 Kings 18:17, 18). It is not we who disseminate errors or stir up tumults, but they who resist the mighty power of God.

But while this single answer is sufficient to rebut the rash charges of these men, it is necessary, on the other hand, to consult for the weakness of those who take the alarm at such scandals, and not infrequently waver in perplexity. But that they may not fall away in this perplexity, and forfeit their good degree, let them know that the apostles in their day experienced the very things, which now befall us. There were then unlearned and unstable men who, as Peter tells us (2 Peter 3:16), wrested the inspired writings of Paul to their own destruction. There were despisers of God, who, when they heard that sin abounded in order that grace might more abound, immediately inferred, "We will continue in sin that grace may abound" (Romans 6:1); when they heard that believers were not under the law, but under grace, forthwith sung out, "We will sin because we are not under the law, but under grace" (Romans 6:15). There were some who charged the apostle with being the minister of sin. Many false prophets entered in privately to pull down the churches, which he had reared. Some preached the gospel through envy and strife, not sincerely (Philippians

1:15)—maliciously even—thinking to add affliction to his bonds. Elsewhere the gospel made little progress. All sought their own, not the things which were Jesus Christ's. Others went back like the dog to his vomit, or the sow that was washed to her wallowing in the mire. Great numbers perverted their spiritual freedom to carnal licentiousness. False brethren crept in to the imminent danger of the faithful. Among the brethren themselves various quarrels arose. What, then, were the apostles to do? Were they either to dissemble for the time, or rather lay aside and abandon that gospel which they saw to be the seed—bed of so many strifes, the source of so many perils, the occasion of so many scandals? In straits of this kind, they remembered that "Christ was a stone of stumbling, and a rock of offense," "set up for the fall and rising again of many," and "for a sign to be spoken against" (Luke 2:34); and, armed with this assurance, they proceeded boldly through all perils from tumults and scandals. It becomes us to be supported by the same consideration, since Paul declares that it is a never failing characteristic of the gospel to be a "savor of death unto death in them that perish" (2 Corinthians 2:16), although rather destined to us for the purpose of being a savor of life unto life, and the power of God for the salvation of believers. This we should certainly experience it to be, did we not by our ingratitude corrupt this unspeakable gift of God, and turn to our destruction what ought to be our only saving defense.

But to return, Sire. Be not moved by the absurd insinuations with which our adversaries are striving to frighten you into the belief that nothing else is wished and aimed at by this new gospel (for so they term it), than opportunity for sedition and impunity for all kinds of vice. Our Go is not the author of division, but of peace; and the Son of God, who came to destroy the works of the devil, is not the minister of sin. We, too, are undeservedly charged with desires of a kind for which we have never given even the smallest suspicion. We, forsooth, meditate the subversion of kingdoms; we, whose voice was never heard in faction, and whose life, while passed under you, is known to have been always quiet and simple; even now, when exiled from our home, we nevertheless cease not to pray for all prosperity to your person and your kingdom. We, forsooth, are aiming after an unchecked indulgence in vice, in whose manners, though there is much to be blamed, there is nothing which deserves such an imputation; nor (thank God) have we profited so little in the gospel that our life may not be to these slanderers an example of chastity, kindness, pity, temperance, patience, moderation, or any other virtue. It is plain, indeed, that we fear God sincerely, and worship him in truth, since, whether by life or by death, we desire his name to be hallowed; and hatred herself has been forced to bear testimony to the innocence and civil integrity of some of our people on whom death was inflicted for the very thing which deserved the highest praise. But if any, under pretext of the gospel, excite tumults (none such have as yet been detected in your realm), if any use the liberty of the grace of God as a cloak for licentiousness (I know of numbers who do), there are laws and legal punishments by which they may be punished up to the measure of their deserts—only, in the mean time, let not the gospel of God be evil spoken of because of the iniquities of evil men.

Sire, That you may not lend too credulous an ear to the accusations of our enemies, their virulent injustice has been set before you at sufficient length; I fear even more than sufficient, since this preface has grown almost to the bulk of a full apology. My object, however, was not to frame a defense, but only with a view to the hearing of our cause, to mollify your mind, now indeed turned away and estranged from us—I add, even inflamed against us—but whose good will, we are confident, we should regain, would you but once, with calmness and composure, read this our Confession, which we desire your Majesty to accept instead of a defense. But if the whispers of the malevolent so possess your ear, that the accused are to have no opportunity of pleading their cause; if those vindictive furies, with your connivance, are always to rage with bonds, scourging, torture, maiming, and burnings, we, indeed, like sheep doomed to slaughter, shall be reduced to every extremity; yet so that, in our patience, we will possess our souls, and wait for the strong hand of the Lord, which, doubtless, will appear in its own time, and show itself armed, both to rescue the poor from affliction, and also take vengeance on the despisers, who are now exulting so securely.

Most illustrious King, may the Lord, the King of kings, establish your throne in righteousness, and your scepter in equity.

Epistle to the Reader

[Prefixed to the last edition, revised by the author.]

In the First Edition of this work, having not the least expectation of the success which God, in his boundless goodness, has been pleased to give it, I had, for the greater part, performed my task in a perfunctory manner (as is usual in trivial undertakings); but when I understood that it had been received, by almost all the pious with a favor which I had never dared to ask, far less to hope for, the more I was sincerely conscious that the reception was beyond my deserts, the greater I thought my ingratitude would be, if, to the very kind wishes which had been expressed towards me, and which seemed of their own accord to invite me to diligence, I did not endeavor to respond, at least according to my humble ability. This I attempted not only in the Second Edition, but in every subsequent one the work has received some improvement. But though I do not regret the labor previously expended, I never felt satisfied until the work was arranged in the order in which it now appears. Now I trust it will approve itself to the Judgment of all my readers. As a clear proof of the diligence with which I have labored to perform this service to the Church of God, I may be permitted to mention, that last winter, when I thought I was dying of quartan ague, the more the disorder increased, the less I spared myself, in order that I might leave this book behind me, and thus make some return to the pious for their kind urgency. I could have wished to give it sooner, but it is soon enough if good enough. I shall think it has appeared in good time when I see it more productive of benefit than formerly to the Church of God. This is my only wish.

And truly it would fare ill with me if, not contented with the approbation of God alone, I were unable to despise the foolish and perverse censures of ignorant as well as the malicious and unjust censures of ungodly men. For although, by the blessing of God, my most ardent desire has been to advance his kingdoms and promote the public good, —although I feel perfectly conscious, and take God and his angels to witness, that ever since I began to discharge the office of teacher in the Church, my only object has been to do good to the Church, by maintaining the pure doctrine of godliness, yet I believe there never was a man more assailed, stung, and torn by calumny [as well by the declared enemies of the truth of God, as by many worthless persons who have crept into his Church—as well by monks who have brought forth their frocks from their cloisters to spread infection wherever they come, as by other miscreants not better than they]. After this letter to the reader was in the press, I had undoubted information that, at Augsburg, where the Imperial Diet was held, a rumor of my defection to the papacy was circulated, and entertained in the courts of the princes more readily than might have been expected. This, forsooth, is the return made me by those who certainly are aware of numerous proofs of my constancy—proofs which, while they rebut the foul charge, ought to have defended me against it, with all humane and impartial judges. But the devil, with all his crew, is mistaken if he imagines that, by assailing me with vile falsehoods, he can either cool my zeal, or diminish my exertions. I trust that God, in his infinite goodness, will enable me to persevere with unruffled patience in the course of his holy vocation. Of this, I give the pious reader a new proof in the present edition.

I may further observe, that my object in this work has been, so to prepare and train candidates for the sacred office, for the study of the sacred volume, that they may both have an easy introduction to it, and be able to prosecute it with unfaltering step; for, if I mistake not, I have given a summary of religion in all its parts, and digested it in an order which will make it easy for anyone, who rightly comprehends it, to ascertain both what he ought chiefly to look for in Scripture, and also to what head he ought to refer whatever is contained in it. Having thus paved the way, as it will be unnecessary, in any Commentaries on Scripture which I may afterwards publish, to enter into long discussions of doctrinal points, and enlarge on commonplaces, I will compress them into narrow compass. In this way much trouble and fatigue will be spared to the pious reader, provided he comes prepared with a knowledge of the present work as an indispensable prerequisite. The system here followed being set forth as in a mirror in all my Commentaries, I think it better to let it speak for itself than to give any verbal explanation of it.

Farewell, kind reader: if you derive any benefit from my labors, aid me with your prayers to our heavenly Father.

Geneva, 1st *August* 1559.

The zeal of those whose cause I undertook,
Has swelled a short defense into a book.

"I profess to be one of those who, by profiting, write, and by writing profit." —*Augustine*, Epist. 7.

The Rev. Dr. Wisner, in his late discourse at Plymouth, on the anniversary of the landing of the Pilgrims, made the following assertion:

"Much as the name of Calvin has been scoffed at and loaded with reproach by many sons of freedom, there is not an historical proposition more susceptible of complete demonstration than this, that no man has lived to whom the world is under greater obligations for the freedom it now enjoys, than John Calvin."

✢

An Account of the Life of
John Calvin

by John Foxe

excerpted from *The Foxe's Book of Martyrs*

The reformer John Calvin was born in France at Noyon in Picardy, July 10, 1509. He was instructed in grammar in Paris under Maturinus Corderius, and studied philosophy in the College of Montaign under a Spanish professor.

Young John's father noticed his son's marks of early piety (particularly in his reprehensions of the vices of his companions), reared him for the church, and got him presented on May 21, 1521, to the chapel of Notre Dame de la Gesine in the Church of Noyon. In 1527, John was presented to the rectory of Marseville, which he exchanged in 1529 for the rectory of Point l'Eveque near Noyon. His father afterward changed his resolution and would have him study law. John readily consented. By that time, through reading the Scriptures, he had grown to dislike the superstitions of popery. He gladly resigned the chapel in 1534. He made a great progress in law, and improved no less in the knowledge of divinity by his private studies. At Bourges he studied Greek under the direction of Professor Wolmar.

His father's death called him back to Noyon, where he stayed only a short time before he ventured on to Paris. It was there that he furnished materials for a speech delivered by Nicholas Cop, rector of the University of Paris. The speech greatly displeased the Sorbonne and the parliament, and gave rise to a persecution against the Protestants in general and Calvin in particular. He narrowly escaped being taken in the College of Forteret, and was forced to flee to Xaintonge after having had the honor of being introduced to the queen of Navarre, who had raised this first storm against the Protestants.

Calvin returned to Paris in 1534. This year the reformed met with severe treatment. He determined that he would have to leave France, particularly after publishing a treatise against those who believed that departed souls are in a kind of sleep. He retired to Basel, where he studied Hebrew: at this time he published his *Institutions of the Christian Religion*; a work well adapted to spread his fame, though he himself was desirous of living in obscurity. It is dedicated to the French king, Francis I.

Calvin next wrote an apology for the Protestants who were burned for their religion in France. After the publication of this work, Calvin went to Italy to pay a visit to the duchess of Ferrara, a lady of eminent piety, by whom he was very kindly received.

From Italy he returned to France, and having settled his private affairs, proposed to go to Strassburg or Basel with his sole surviving brother, Antony Calvin. The roads were not safe because of the war. The exception was a road that ran through the duke of Savoy's territories. The Calvin brothers chose that road. "This was a particular direction of Providence," says Bayle, "It was his destiny that he should settle at Geneva, and when he was wholly intent upon going farther, he found himself detained by an order from heaven, if I may so speak."

At Geneva, Calvin therefore was obliged to comply with the choice, which the consistory and magistrates made of him, with the consent of the people: to be one of their ministers and a professor of divinity. He wanted to serve only as a professor of divinity, but in the end he was obliged to take both offices upon him in August 1536. The year following, he made all the people declare, upon oath, their assent to the confession of faith, which contained a renunciation of popery. He next intimated that he could not submit to a regulation, that the canton of Berne had made. The syndics of Geneva summoned an assembly of the people, and it was ordered that Calvin, Farel, and another minister should leave the town in a few days for refusing to administer the Sacrament.

Calvin retired to Strassburg and established a French church in that city, of which he was the first minister. He was also appointed to be professor of divinity there. Meanwhile the people of Geneva entreated him so earnestly to return to them that at last he consented, and arrived September 13, 1541, to the great satisfaction both of the people and the magistrates. The first thing he did after his arrival was to establish a form of church discipline, and a consistorial jurisdiction, invested with power of inflicting censures and canonical punishments, as far as excommunication, inclusively.

It has long been the delight of both infidels and some professed Christians, when they wish to bring odium upon the opinions of Calvin, to refer to his participation in the death of Michael Servetus. Those who are unable to overthrow his opinions use this as a conclusive argument against his whole system. A certain class of reasoners use, "Calvin burned Servetus! Calvin burned Servetus!" as good proof that the doctrine of the Trinity is not true, that divine sovereignty is against Scripture, and that Christianity a cheat.

We have no wish to palliate any act of Calvin's, which is manifestly wrong. All his proceedings in relation to the unhappy affair of Servetus, we think, cannot be defended. Still it should be remembered that the true principles of religious toleration were very little understood in the time of Calvin. All the other reformers then living approved of Calvin's conduct. Even the gentle and amiable Melancthon expressed himself in relation to this affair in the following manner. In a letter addressed to Bullinger, he says, "I have read your statement respecting the blasphemy of Servetus, and praise your piety and judgment; and am persuaded that the Council of Geneva has done right in putting to death this obstinate man, who would never have ceased his blasphemies. I am astonished that any one can be found to disapprove of this proceeding." Farel expressly says, "Servetus deserved a capital punishment." Bucer did not hesitate to declare, "Servetus deserved something worse than death."

The truth is, although Calvin had some hand in the arrest and imprisonment of Servetus, he was unwilling that he should be burned at all. "I desire," said he, "that the severity of the punishment should be remitted.... We endeavored to commute the kind of death, but in vain."

"By wishing to mitigate the severity of the punishment," said Farel to Calvin, "you discharge the office of a friend towards your greatest enemy."

"That Calvin was the instigator of the magistrates that Servetus might be burned," says Turritine, "historians neither anywhere affirm, nor does it appear from any considerations. Nay, it is certain, that he, with the college of pastors, dissuaded from that kind of punishment."

It has been often asserted that Calvin possessed so much influence with the magistrates of Geneva that he might have obtained the release of Servetus had he not wanted his destruction. This, however, is not true. So far from it, that Calvin was himself once banished from Geneva by these very magistrates and often opposed their arbitrary measures in vain. Calvin was so against the death of Servetus that he warned him of his danger, and suffered him to remain several weeks at Geneva before he was arrested. But his language, which was then accounted blasphemous, was the cause of his imprisonment. When in prison, Calvin visited him and used every argument to persuade him to retract his horrible blasphemies without reference to his peculiar sentiments. This was the extent of Calvin's agency in this unhappy affair.

It cannot, however, be denied that in this instance, Calvin acted contrary to the kind and gracious spirit of the Gospel. It is better to drop a tear over the inconsistency of human nature and to bewail those infirmities that cannot be justified. He declared that he acted conscientiously, and publicly justified the act.

It was the opinion, that erroneous religious principles are punishable by the civil magistrate that did the mischief, whether at Geneva, in Transylvania, or in Britain. To this, rather than to Trinitarianism or Unitarianism, it ought to be imputed.

After the death of Luther, Calvin exerted great sway over the men of that notable period. He was influential in France, Italy, Germany, Holland, England, and Scotland. Two thousand one hundred and fifty reformed congregations were organized, receiving from him their preachers.

Calvin, triumphant over all his enemies, felt his death drawing near. Yet he continued to exert himself in every way with youthful energy. When about to lie down in rest, he drew up his will, saying:

I do testify that I live and purpose to die in this faith which God has given me through His Gospel, and that I have no other dependence for salvation than the free choice which is made of me by Him. With my whole heart I embrace His mercy, through which all my sins are covered, for Christ's sake, and for the sake of His death and sufferings. According to the measure of grace granted unto me, I have taught this pure, simple Word by sermons, by deeds, and by expositions of this Scripture. In all my battles with the enemies of the truth I have not used sophistry, but have fought the good fight squarely and directly.

May 27, 1564, was the day of his release and blessed journey home. He was in his fifty-fifth year.

That a man who had acquired so great a reputation and such an authority should have had but a salary of one hundred crowns, and refuse to accept more; and after living fifty-five years with the utmost frugality should leave but three hundred crowns to his heirs, including the value of his library, which sold very dear, is something so heroic, that one must have lost all feeling not to admire.

When Calvin took his leave of Strassburg, to return to Geneva, they wanted to continue to him the privileges of a freeman of their town, and the revenues of a prebend, which had been assigned to him; the former he accepted, but absolutely refused the other. He carried one of the brothers with him to Geneva, but he never took any pains to get him preferred to an honorable post, as any other possessed of his credit would have done. He took care indeed of the honor of his brother's family, by getting him freed from an adulteress, and obtaining leave to him to marry again; but even his enemies relate that he made him learn the trade of a bookbinder, which he followed all his life after.

John Calvin was buried in the cemetery of Plain Palais, and at his own request, no monument was set up to mark his grave. The exact spot is unknown to this day.

Other historians and biographers offer personal insight into John Calvin, the man.

ERNEST RENAN, educated for the Romish priesthood, but later a skeptic, pays this striking tribute to Calvin's character:

> Calvin was one of those absolute men, cast complete in one mold, who is taken in wholly at a single glance: one letter, one action, suffices for a judgment of him. There were no folds in that inflexible soul, which never knew doubt or hesitation. Careless of wealth, of titles, of honors, indifferent to pomp, modest in his life, transparently humble, sacrificing everything to the desire of making others like himself, I hardly know of a man, save Ignatius Loyola, who could match him … Lacking that vivid, deep, sympathetic ardor which was one of the secrets of Luther's success, lacking the charm, the languishing tenderness of Francis of Sales, Calvin succeeded, in an age and in a country which called for a reaction towards Christianity, simply because he was the most Christian man of his generation.

GUIZOT, the French historian, concludes his biography:

> Calvin is great by reason of his marvelous powers, his enduring labors, and the moral height and purity of his character. Earnest in faith, pure in motive, austere in his life, and mighty in his works, Calvin is one of those who deserve their great fame. Three centuries separate us from him, but it is impossible to examine his character and history without feeling, if not affection and sympathy, at least profound respect and admiration for one of the great Reformers of Europe and one of the great Christians of France.

THEODORE BEZA, Calvin's close friend, confidante, and successor, offers an intimate look at a beloved man:

> Calvin was not of large stature: his complexion was pale, and rather brown: even to his last moments his eyes were peculiarly bright, and indicative of his penetrating genius. He knew nothing of luxury in his outward life, but was fond

of the greatest neatness, as became his thorough simplicity. His manner of living was so arranged that he showed himself equally averse to extravagance and meanness. He took so little nourishment, such being the weakness of his stomach, that for many years he contented himself with one meal a day. Of sleep he had almost none. His memory was incredible; he immediately recognized, after many years, those whom he had once seen; and when he had been interrupted for several hours, in some work about which he was employed, he could immediately resume and continue it, without reading again what he had written. Of the numerous details connected with the business of his office, he never forgot even the most trifling, and this notwithstanding the multitude of his affairs.

His judgment was so acute and correct in regard to the most opposite concerns about which his advice was asked, that he often seemed to possess the gift of looking into the future. I never remember to have heard that anyone who followed his counsel went wrong. He despised fine speaking, and was rather abrupt in his language; but he wrote admirably, and no theologian of his time expressed himself so clearly, so impressively and acutely as he; and yet he labored as much as any one of his contemporaries, or of the fathers. For this fluency he was indebted to the several studies of his youth, and to the natural acuteness of his genius, which had been still further increased by the practice of dictation, so that proper and dignified expressions never failed him, whether he was writing or speaking. He never, in any wise, altered the doctrine, which he first adopted, but remained true to it to the last.

Although nature had endowed Calvin with a dignified seriousness, both in manner and character, no one was more agreeable than he in ordinary conversation. He could bear, in a wonderful manner, with the failings of others, when they sprang from mere weakness. Thus he never shamed anyone by ill-timed reproofs, or discouraged a weak brother; while, on the other hand, he never spared or overlooked willful sin. An enemy to all flattery, he hated dissimulation, especially every dishonest sentiment in reference to religion. He was therefore as powerful and strong an enemy to vices of this kind as he was a devoted friend to truth, simplicity and uprightness. His temperament was naturally choleric, and his active public life had tended greatly to increase this failing; but the Spirit of God had so taught him to moderate his anger, that no word ever escaped him unworthy of a righteous man. Still less did he ever commit aught unjust towards others. It was then only, indeed, when the question concerned religion, and when he had to contend against hardened sinners, that he allowed himself to be moved and excited beyond the bounds of moderation.

Let us take but a single glance at the history of those men who, in any part of the world, have been distinguished for their virtues, and no one will be surprised at finding that the great and noble qualities which Calvin exhibited, both in his private and public life, excited against him a host of enemies. We ought not indeed to feel any wonder that so powerful a champion of pure doctrine, and so stern a teacher of sound morals, as well at home as in the world, should be so fiercely assailed. Rather ought we to let our admiration dwell on the fact that, standing alone as he did, he was sufficiently mighty to avail himself of that strongest of weapons, the Word of God. Thus, however numerous the adversaries, whom Satan excited against him (for he never had any but such as had declared war against piety and virtue), the Lord gave His servant sufficient strength to gain the victory over all.

Having been for sixteen years a witness of his labors, I have pursued the history of his life and death with all fidelity; and I now unhesitatingly testify that every true Christian may find in this man the noble pattern of a truly Christian life and Christian death; a pattern, however, which it is as easy to calumniate as it would be difficult to follow.

John Calvin's *Magnum Opus:* The
Institutes of the Christian Religion

Various depictions of John Calvin

St. Peter's Church in Geneva.

John Calvin preaching at St. Peter's Church in Geneva.

*Left: Theodore Beza,
Calvin's close friend, and
confidante
Middle: Michael Servetus
and John Calvin debating
before the Council of Geneva.
Below: Calvin's friend,
Evangelist William Farel,
stands before the death bed
of Calvin.*

Institutes of the Christian Religion

Book Third

Book Third

THE MODE OF OBTAINING THE GRACE OF CHRIST. THE BENEFITS IT CONFERS AND THE EFFECTS RESULTING FROM IT

ARGUMENT

The two former books treated of God the Creator and Redeemer. This book, which contains a full exposition of the third part of the Apostles' Creed, treats of the mode of procuring the grace of Christ, the benefits which we derive, and the effects which follow from it, or of the operations of the Holy Spirit in regard to our salvation.

The subject is comprehended under seven principal headings, which almost all point to the same end, namely, the doctrine of faith.

I. As it is by the secret and special operation of the Holy Spirit that we enjoy Christ and all His benefits, the first chapter treats of this operation, which is the foundation of faith, new life, and all holy exercises.

II. Faith being the hand by which we embrace Christ the Redeemer, offered to us by the Holy Spirit Faith is fully considered in the second chapter.

III. In further explanation of saving faith, and the benefits derived from it, it is mentioned that true repentance always flows from true faith. The doctrine of repentance is considered generally in the third chapter, popish repentance in the fourth chapter, indulgences and purgatory in the fifth chapter. Chapters sixth to tenth are devoted to a special consideration of the different parts of true repentance—viz. mortification of the flesh and quickening of the Spirit.

IV. More clearly to show the utility of this faith and the effects resulting from it, the doctrine of justification by faith is explained in the eleventh chapter, and certain questions connected with it explained from the twelfth to the eighteenth chapters. Christian liberty, a kind of accessory to justification, is considered in the nineteenth chapter.

V. The twentieth chapter is devoted to prayer, the principal exercise of faith, and the medium or instrument through which we daily procure blessings from God.

VI. As all do not indiscriminately embrace the fellowship of Christ offered in the gospel, but those only whom the Lord favors with the effectual and special grace of His Spirit, lest any should impugn this arrangement, chapters twenty-first to twenty-fourth are occupied with a necessary and apposite discussion of the subject of election.

VII. Lastly, as the hard warfare, which the Christian is obliged constantly to wage, may have the effect of disheartening him, it is shown how it may be alleviated by meditating on the final resurrection. Hence, the subject of the resurrection is considered in the twenty-fifth chapter.

Chapter 1

THE BENEFITS OF CHRIST MADE AVAILABLE TO US BY THE SECRET OPERATION OF THE SPIRIT

The three divisions of this chapter are: I. The secret operation of the Holy Spirit, which seals our salvation, should be considered first in Christ the Mediator as our Head, sections 1 and 2. II. The titles given to the Holy Spirit show that we become members of Christ by His grace and energy, section 3. III. As the special influence of the Holy Spirit is manifested in the gift of faith, the former is a proper introduction to the latter, and thus prepares for the second chapter, section 4.

Sections

1. The Holy Spirit as the bond, which unites us with Christ. This is the result of faith produced by the secret operation of the Holy Spirit. This is obvious from Scripture.

2. In Christ, the Mediator, the gifts of the Holy Spirit are to be seen in all their fullness. To what end? Why the Holy Spirit is called the Spirit of the Father and the Son.

3. Titles of the Spirit: —A. The Spirit of adoption. B. An earnest and seal. C. Water. D. Life. E. Oil and unction. F. Fire. G. A fountain. H. The Word of God. Use of these titles.

4. Faith being the special work of the Holy Spirit, the power and efficacy of the Holy Spirit usually ascribed to it.

1 **The Holy Spirit as the bond, which unites us with Christ. This is the result of faith produced by the secret operation of the Holy Spirit. This is obvious from Scripture.**

We must now see in what way we become possessed of the blessings that God has bestowed on His only begotten Son, not for private use, but to enrich the poor and needy. And the first thing to be attended to is that so long as we are without Christ and separated from Him, nothing which He suffered and did for the salvation of the human race is of the least benefit to us. To communicate to us the blessings, which He received from the Father, He must become ours and dwell in us. Accordingly, He is called our Head, and the first-born among many brethren, while, on the other hand, we are said to be engrafted into Him and clothed with Him, all which He possesses being, as I have said, nothing to us until we become one with Him. It is true that we obtain this by faith, but since we see that not all indiscriminately embrace the offer of Christ made by the gospel, the very nature of the case teaches us to ascend higher and inquire into the secret efficacy of the Spirit. There we enjoy Christ and all his blessings.

I have already treated of the eternal essence and divinity of the Spirit (Book 1, chapter 13, sections 14,15); let us at present attend to the special point, that Christ came by water and blood, as the Spirit testifies concerning Him, that we might not lose the benefits of the salvation which he has purchased. For as there are said to be three witnesses in Heaven, the Father, the Word, and the Spirit, so there are also three on the Earth, namely, water, blood, and Spirit. It is not without cause that the testimony of the Spirit is twice mentioned, a testimony which is engraved on our hearts by way of His seal, and thus seals the cleansing and sacrifice of Christ. For which reason, also, Peter says that believers are "elect," "through sanctification of the Spirit, unto obedience and sprinkling of the blood of Jesus Christ" (1 Peter 1:2). By these words, He reminds us that if the shedding of his sacred blood is not to be in vain, our souls must be washed in it by the secret cleansing of the Holy Spirit. For which reason, also, Paul, speaking of cleansing and purification, says, "But ye are washed, but ye are sanctified, but ye are justified in the name of the Lord Jesus and by the Spirit of our God" (1 Corinthians 6:11). The whole comes to this that the Holy Spirit is the bond by which Christ effectually binds us to himself. Here we may refer to what was said in the last book concerning his anointing.

2 In Christ, the Mediator, the gifts of the Holy Spirit are to be seen in all their fullness. To what end? Why the Holy Spirit is called the Spirit of the Father and the Son.

But in order to have a clearer view of this most important subject we must remember that Christ came provided with the Holy

Spirit after a peculiar manner, namely that He might separate us from the world, and unite us in the hope of an eternal inheritance. Hence, the Spirit is called the Spirit of sanctification, because He quickens and cherishes us, not merely by the general energy which is seen in the human race, as well as other animals, but because He is the seed and root of heavenly life in us. Accordingly, one of the highest commendations that the prophets give to the Kingdom of Christ is that under it the Spirit would be poured out in richer abundance.

One of the most remarkable passages is found in Joel, "It shall come to pass afterward, that I will pour out my Spirit upon all flesh" (Joel 2:28). For although the prophet seems to confine the gifts of the Spirit to the office of prophesying, he yet intimates under a figure that God will, by the illumination of His Spirit, provide himself with disciples who had previously been altogether ignorant of heavenly doctrine. Moreover, as it is for the sake of his Son that God bestows the Holy Spirit upon us, and yet has deposited Him in all His fullness with the Son to be the minister and dispenser of His liberality, He is called at one time the Spirit of the Father, at another the Spirit of the Son: "Ye are not in the flesh but in the Spirit, if so be that the Spirit of God dwell in you. Now, if any man have not the Spirit of Christ, he is none of his" (Romans 8:9).

Hence, He encourages us to hope for complete renovation: "If the Spirit of him that raised up Jesus from the dead dwell in you, he that raised up Christ from the dead shall also quicken your mortal bodies by His Spirit that dwelleth in you" (Romans 8:11). There is no inconsistency in ascribing the glory of those gifts to the Father, inasmuch as He is the Author of them, and, at the same time, ascribing them to Christ, with whom they have been deposited, that he may bestow them on His people.

Hence, He invites all the thirsty to come unto Him and drink. (See John 7:37.) And Paul teaches that "unto everyone of us is given grace, according to the measure of the gift of Christ" (Ephesians 4:7). And we must remember that the Spirit is called the Spirit of Christ, not only inasmuch as the eternal Word of God is with the Father united with the Spirit, but also in respect of His office of Mediator; because, had He not been endued with the energy of the Spirit, he had come to us in vain. In this sense He is called the "last Adam," and said to have been sent from Heaven "a quickening Spirit" (1 Corinthians 15:45), where Paul contrasts the special life which Christ breathes into His people, that they may be one with Him with the animal life which is common even to the reprobate. In like manner, when he prays that believers may have "the grace of our Lord Jesus Christ, and the love of God," he at the same time adds, "the communion of the Holy Ghost," without which no man shall ever taste the paternal favor of God or the benefits of Christ. Thus, also, in another passage he says, "The love of God is shed abroad in our hearts by the Holy Ghost, which is given unto us" (Romans 5:5).

3 Titles of the Spirit: A. The Spirit of adoption. B. An earnest and seal. C. Water. D. Life. E. Oil and unction. F. Fire. G. A fountain. H. The Word of God. Use of these titles.

Here it will be proper to point out the titles which the Scripture bestows on the Spirit, when it treats of the commencement and entire renewal of our salvation. First, He is called the "Spirit of adoption," because He is witness to us of the free favor with which God the Father embraced us in his well-beloved and only begotten Son, so as to become our Father and give us boldness of access to Him; nay He dictates the very words, so that we can boldly cry, "Abba, Father." For the same reason, He is said to have "sealed us, and given the earnest of the Spirit in our hearts," because, as pilgrims in the world, and persons in a manner dead, He so quickens us from above as to assure us that our salvation is safe in the keeping of a faithful God.

Hence, also, the Spirit is said to be "life because of righteousness." But since it is His secret irrigation that makes us bud forth and produce the fruits of righteousness, He is repeatedly described as *water*. Thus, in Isaiah "Ho, everyone that thirsteth, come ye to the waters." Again, "I will pour water upon him that is thirsty, and floods upon the dry ground." Corresponding to this are the words of our Savior, to which I lately referred, "If any man thirst, let him come unto me and drink." Sometimes, indeed, he receives this name from his energy in cleansing and purifying, as in Ezekiel, where the Lord promises, "Then will I sprinkle you with clean water, and ye shall be clean." As those sprinkled with the Spirit are restored to the full vigor of life, He hence obtains the names of *Oil* and *Unction*.

On the other hand, as He is constantly employed in subduing and destroying the vices of our concupiscence, and inflaming our hearts with the love of God and piety, He hence receives the name of *Fire*. He is described to us as a *Fountain*, whence all heavenly riches flow to us; or as the *Hand* by which God exerts His power, because by His divine inspiration He so breathes divine life into us that we are no longer acted upon by ourselves, but ruled by His motion and agency, so that everything good in us is the fruit of His grace, while our own endowments without Him are mere darkness of mind and perverseness of heart. Already, indeed, it has been clearly shown that until our minds are intent on the Spirit, Christ is in a manner unemployed, because we view Him coldly without us, and so at a distance from us. Now we know that he is of no avail save only to those to whom He is a Head and the first-born among the brethren, to those, in fine, who are clothed with Him. To this union alone it owes that in regard to us, the Savior has not come in vain. To this is to be referred that sacred marriage, by which we become bone of his bone, and flesh of His flesh, and so one with Him (Ephesians 5:30), for it is by the Spirit alone that he unites himself to us. By the same grace and energy of the Spirit, we become His members, so that He keeps us under Him, and we in our turn possess Him.

4 Faith being the special work of the Holy Spirit, the power and efficacy of the Holy Spirit usually ascribed to it.

But as faith is His principal work, all those passages that express His power and operations are, in a great measure, referred to it only by faith that He brings us to the light of the gospel, and just as John teaches that to those who believe in Christ is given the privilege "to become the sons of God, even to them that believe in his name, which were born not of blood, nor of the will of the flesh, nor of the will of man, but of God" (John 1:12). Opposing *God* to *flesh and blood*, He declares it a supernatural gift, that those, who would otherwise remain in unbelief, receive Christ by faith. Similar to this is our Savior's reply to Peter: "Flesh and blood has not revealed it unto thee, but my Father which is in heaven" (Matthew 16:17).

These things I now briefly advert to, as I have fully considered them elsewhere. To the same effect Paul says to the Ephesians, "Ye were sealed with that Holy Spirit of promise" (Ephesians 1:13); thus showing that he is the internal Teacher, by whose agency the promise of salvation, which would otherwise only strike the air or our ears, penetrates into our minds. In like manner, he says to the Thessalonians, "God has from the beginning chosen you to salvation, through sanctification of the Spirit and belief of the truth" (2 Thessalonians 2:13); by this passage, briefly reminding us that faith itself is produced only by the Spirit. This John explains more distinctly, "We know that he abideth in us, by the Spirit which he has given us;" again, "Hereby know we that we dwell in him and he in us, because he has given us of his Spirit" (1 John 3:23; 4:13). Accordingly, to make His disciples capable of heavenly wisdom, Christ promised them "the Spirit of truth, whom the world cannot receive" (John 14:17). As His proper office, He assigns it to Him to bring to remembrance the things that he had verbally taught. Light would be offered to the blind in vain, if that Spirit of understanding did not open the intellectual eye; so that He himself may be properly termed the key by which the treasures of the heavenly kingdom are unlocked, and His illumination, the eye of the mind by which we are enabled to see.

Hence, Paul so highly commends the ministry of the Spirit (2 Corinthians 3:6), since teachers would cry aloud to no purpose, did not Christ, the internal teacher, by means of His Spirit, draw to himself those who are given Him of the Father. Therefore, as we have said that salvation is perfected in the person of Christ, so, in order to make us partakers of it, He baptizes us "with the Holy Spirit and with fire" (Luke 3:16), enlightening us into the faith of His gospel, and so regenerating us to be new creatures. Thus cleansed from all pollution, He dedicates us as holy temples to the Lord.

Chapter 2

OF FAITH. THE DEFINITION OF IT. ITS PECULIAR PROPERTIES

This chapter consists of three principal parts: I. A brief explanation of certain matters pertaining to the doctrine of faith, sections 1-14. First, of the object of faith, section 1. Second, of Implicit Faith, sections 2-6. Third, Definition of faith, section 7. Fourth, the various meanings of the term Faith, sections 8-13. II. A full exposition of the definition given in the seventh section, sections 14-40. III. A brief confirmation of the definition by the authority of an apostle. The mutual relation between faith, hope, and charity, sections 41-43.

Sections
1. A brief recapitulation of the leading points of the whole discussion. The scope of this chapter. The necessity of the doctrine of faith. This doctrine obscured by the schoolmen, who make God the object of faith, without referring to Christ. The Schoolmen refuted by various passages.
2. The dogma of implicit faith refuted. It destroys faith, which consists in a knowledge of the divine will. What this will is, and how necessary the knowledge of it is.
3. Many things are and will continue to be implicitly believed. Faith, however, consists in the knowledge of God and Christ, not in a reverence for the Church. Another refutation from the absurdities to which this dogma leads.
4. In what sense our faith may be said to be implicit. Examples in the apostles, in the holy women, and in all believers.
5. In some, faith is implicit, as being a preparation for faith. This, however, is widely different from the implicit faith of the Schoolmen.
6. The Word of God has a similar relation to faith, the Word being the source and basis of faith, and the mirror in which it beholds God. Confirmation from various passages of Scripture. Without the

23

knowledge of the Word, there can be no faith. Sum of the discussion of the Scholastic doctrine of implicit faith.

7. What faith properly has respect to in the Word of God, namely, the promise of grace offered in Christ, provided it is embraced with faith. a proper definition of faith.

8. Scholastic distinction between faith formed and unformed, refuted by a consideration of the nature of faith, which, as the gift of the Spirit, cannot possibly be disjoined from pious affection.

9. Objection from a passage of Paul. Answer to it. Error of the Schoolmen in giving only one meaning to faith, whereas it has many meanings. The testimony of faith improperly ascribed to two classes of men.

10. View to be taken of this. Who those are that believe for a time. The faith of hypocrites. With whom they may be compared.

11. Why faith is attributed to the reprobate. Objection. Answer. What perception of grace is in the reprobate. How the elect are distinguished from the reprobate.

12. Why faith is temporary in the reprobate, while being firm and perpetual in the elect. Reason in the case of the reprobate. Example. Why God is angry with His children. In what sense many are said to fall from faith.

13. Various meanings of the term faith. A. Taken for soundness in the faith. B. Sometimes restricted to a particular object. C. Signifies the ministry or testimony by which we are instructed in the faith.

14. Definition of faith explained under six principal heads. What is meant by knowledge in the definition.

15. Why this knowledge must be sure and firm. Reason drawn from the consideration of our weakness. Another reason from the certainty of the promises of God.

16. The leading point in this certainty. Its fruits. A description of the true believer.

17. An objection to this certainty. Answer. Confirmation of the answer from the example of David. This is enlarged upon from the opposite example of Ahab. Also from the uniform experience and the prayers of believers.

18. For this reason the conflict between the flesh and the Spirit in the soul of the believer described. The issue of this conflict, the victory of faith.

19. On the whole, the faith of the elect is certain and indubitable. Confirmation from analogy.

20. Another confirmation from the testimony of an Apostle, making it apparent that, though the faith of the elect is as yet imperfect, it is nevertheless firm and sure.

21. A fuller explanation of the nature of faith. A. When the believer is shaken with fear, he retakes himself to the bosom of a merciful God. B. He does not even shun God when angry, but hopes in Him. C. He does not suffer unbelief to reign in his heart. D. He opposes unbelief, and is never finally lost. E. Faith, however often assailed, at length comes off victorious.

22. Another species of fear, arising from a consideration of the judgment of God against the wicked. This also faith overcomes. Examples of this description, placed before the eyes of believers, repress presumption, and fix their faith in God.

23. Nothing contrary to this in the exhortation of the apostle to work out our salvation with fear and trembling. Fear and faith are mutually connected. Confirmation from the words of a prophet.

24. This doctrine gives no countenance to the error of those who dream of a confidence mingled with incredulity. Refutation of this error, from a consideration of the dignity of Christ dwelling in us. The argument retorted. Refutation confirmed by the authority of an apostle. What we ought to hold on this question.

25. Confirmation of the preceding conclusion by a passage from Bernard.

26. True fear caused in two ways—viz. when we are required to reverence God as a Father, and also to fear Him as Lord.

27. Objection from a passage in the Apostle John. Answer founded on the distinction between filial and servile fear.

28. How faith is said to have respect to the divine benevolence. What is comprehended under this benevolence. Confirmation from David and Paul.

29. Of the free promise which is the foundation of faith. Reason. Confirmation.

30. Faith is not divided in thus seeking a free promise in the gospel. Reason. Conclusion confirmed by another reason. 31. The Word of God, the prop and root of faith. The Word attests the divine goodness and mercy. In what sense faith has respect to the power of God. Various passages of Isaiah, inviting the godly to behold the power of God, explained. Other passages from David. We must beware of going beyond the limits prescribed by the Word, lest false zeal lead us astray, as it did with Sarah, Rebekah, and Isaac. In this way, faith is obscured, though not extinguished. We must not depart one iota from the Word of God. 32. All the promises included in Christ. Two objections answered. A third objection drawn from example. An answer explaining the faith of Naaman, Cornelius, and the Eunuch. 33. Faith revealed to our minds, and sealed on our hearts, by the Holy Spirit. A. The mind is purified to have a relish for divine truth. B. The mind is thus established in the truth by the agency of the Holy Spirit. 34. Proof of the former. A. By reason. B. By Scripture. C. By example. D. By analogy. 35. E. By the excellent qualities of faith. F. By a celebrated passage from Augustine. 36. Proof of the latter by the argument a minore ad majus. *Why the Spirit is called a seal, an earnest, and the Spirit of promise. 37. Believers sometimes shaken, but not to perish finally. They ultimately overcome their trials, and remain steadfast. Proofs from Scripture. 38. Objection of the Schoolmen. Answer. Attempt to support the objection by a passage in Ecclesiastes. Answer, explaining the meaning of the passage. 39. Another objection, charging the elect in Christ with rashness and presumption. Answer. Answer confirmed by various passages from the Apostle Paul. Also from John and Isaiah. 40. A third objection, impugning the final perseverance of the elect. Answer by an apostle. Summary of the refutation. 41. The definition of faith accords with that given by the apostle in the Hebrews. Explanation of this definition. Refutation of the scholastic error, that charity is prior to faith and hope.*

42. Hope is the inseparable attendant of true faith. Reason. Connection between faith and hope. They mutually support each other. Obvious from the various forms of temptation, that the aid of hope is necessary to establish faith.

43. The terms faith and hope are sometimes confounded. Refutation of the Schoolmen, who attribute a twofold foundation to hope—viz. the grace of God and the merit of works.

1 A brief recapitulation of the leading points of the whole discussion. The scope of this chapter. The necessity of the doctrine of faith. This doctrine obscured by the Schoolmen, who make God the object of faith, without referring to Christ. The Schoolmen refuted by various passages.

All these things will be easily understood after we have given a clearer definition of faith, to enable the readers to apprehend its nature and power. Here it is of importance to call to mind what was formerly taught: first, that since God by His Law prescribes what we ought to do, failure in any one respect subjects us to the dreadful judgment of eternal death, which it denounces.

Secondly, because it is not only difficult, but altogether beyond our strength and ability, to fulfill the demands of the Law, if we look only to ourselves and consider what is due to our merits, no ground of hope remains, but we lie forsaken of God under eternal death.

Thirdly, that there is only one method of deliverance which can rescue us from this miserable calamity—viz. when Christ the Redeemer appears, by whose hand our heavenly Father, out of His infinite goodness and mercy, has been pleased to succor us, if we with true faith embrace this mercy, and with firm hope rest in it.

It is now proper to consider the nature of this faith, by means of which those who are adopted into the family of God obtain possession of the heavenly kingdom. For the accomplishment of so great an end, it is obvious that no mere opinion or persuasion is adequate. And the greater care and diligence is necessary in discussing the true nature of faith, from the pernicious delusions that many, in the present day, labor under with regard to it. On hearing the term, great numbers think that nothing more is meant than a certain common assent to the gospel history. Nay, when the subject of faith is discussed in the schools, by simply representing God as its object and by empty speculation, they hurry wretched souls away from the right mark instead of directing them to it. For seeing that God dwells in light that is inaccessible, Christ must intervene. Hence, He calls himself "the light of the world"; and in another passage, "the way, the truth, and the life." None cometh to the Father (who is the fountain of life) except by Him; for "No man knoweth who the Father is but the Son, and he to whom the Son will reveal him." For this reason, Paul declares, "I count all things as loss for the excellency of the knowledge of Christ Jesus my Lord." In the twentieth chapter of the Acts, he states that he preached "faith towards our Lord Jesus Christ." In another passage, he introduces Christ as thus: "I have appeared unto thee for this purpose, to make thee a minister and a witness;" "...delivering thee from the people, and from the Gentiles, unto whom now I send thee;" "...that they may receive forgiveness of sins, and inheritance among them which are sanctified through faith which is in me." Paul further declares that in the person of Christ the glory of God is visibly manifested to us, or, which is the same thing, we have "the light of the knowledge of the glory of God in the face of Jesus Christ."

It is true, indeed, that faith has respect to God only; but to this we should add that it acknowledges Jesus Christ whom He has sent. God would remain far off, concealed from us, were we not irradiated by the brightness of Christ. All that the Father had, He deposited with His only begotten Son, in order that He might manifest himself in Him, and thus by the communication of blessings express the true image of his glory. Since, as has been said, that we must be led by the Spirit and thus stimulated to seek Christ, so must we also remember that the invisible Father is to be sought nowhere but in this image. For which reason Augustine, treating of the object of faith, elegantly says, "The thing to be known is, whither we are to go, and by what way;" and immediately after he infers that "the surest way to avoid all errors is to know him who is both God and man. It is to God we tend, and it is by man we go, and both of these are found only in Christ." Paul, when he preaches faith towards God, surely does not intend to overthrow what he so often inculcates—viz. that faith has all its stability in Christ. Peter most appropriately connects both, saying that by him "we believe in God" (1 Peter 1:21).

2 The dogma of implicit faith refuted. It destroys faith, which consists in a knowledge of the divine will. What this will is, and how necessary the knowledge of it is.

This evil, therefore, must, like innumerable others, be attributed to the Schoolmen, who have in a manner drawn a veil over Christ, to whom, if our eye is not directly turned, we must always wander through many labyrinths. But besides impairing and almost annihilating, faith by their obscure definition, they have invented the fiction of implicit faith, with which name they deck the grossest ignorance, and they delude the wretched populace to their great destruction. Nay, to state the fact more truly and plainly, this fiction not only buries true faith, but also entirely destroys it. Is it faith to understand nothing and merely submit your convictions implicitly to the Church? Faith consists not in ignorance, but in knowledge— knowledge not of God merely, but of the divine will. We do not obtain salvation either because we are prepared to embrace every dictate of the Church as true, or leave to the Church the province of inquiring and determining; but when we recognize God as a propitious Father through the reconciliation made by Christ, and Christ as given to us for righteousness, sanctification, and life. By this knowledge, I say, not by the submission of our understanding, we obtain an entrance into the Kingdom of Heaven. For when the apostle says, "With the heart man believeth unto righteousness; and with the mouth confession is made unto salvation" (Romans 10:10), he intimates that it is not enough to believe implicitly without understanding, or even inquiring. The thing requisite is an explicit recognition of the divine goodness, in which our righteousness consists.

3 Many things are and will continue to be implicitly believed. Faith, however, consists in the knowledge of God and Christ, not in a reverence for the Church. Another refutation from the absurdities to which this dogma leads.

I indeed deny not (so enveloped are we in ignorance) that to us very many things now are and will continue to be completely involved until we lay aside this weight of flesh, and approach nearer to the presence of God. In such cases, the fittest course is to suspend our judgment, and resolve to maintain unity with the Church. But under this pretext, to honor ignorance tempered with humility with the name of faith, is most absurd. Faith consists in the knowledge of God and Christ (John 17:3), not in reverence for the Church. And we see what a labyrinth they have formed out of this implicit faith—everything, sometimes even the most monstrous errors, being received by the ignorant as oracles without any discrimination, provided that they are prescribed to them under the name of the Church. This inconsiderate facility, though the surest precipice to destruction, is, however, excused on the ground that it believes nothing definitely, but only with the appended condition, if such is the faith of the Church. Thus, they pretend to find truth in error, light in darkness, true knowledge in ignorance. Not to dwell longer in refuting these views, we simply advise the reader to compare them with ours. The clearness of truth will itself furnish a sufficient refutation. For the question they raise is not whether there may be an implicit faith with many remains of ignorance; rather, they maintain that persons living and even indulging in a stupid ignorance duly believe, provided they assent to the authority and judgment of the Church with regard to things unknown, as if Scripture did not uniformly teach that with faith understanding is conjoined.

4 In what sense our faith may be said to be implicit. Examples in the apostles, in the holy women, and in all believers.

We grant, indeed, that so long as we are pilgrims in the world faith is implicit, not only because as yet many things are hidden from us, but also because, involved in the mists of error, we attain not to all. The highest wisdom, even of him who has attained the greatest perfection, is to go forward, and endeavor in a calm and teachable spirit to make further progress. Hence, Paul exhorts believers to wait for further illumination in any matter in which they differ from each other. (See Philippians 3:15.) And certainly, experience teaches that so long as we are in the flesh, our attainments are less than what is to be desired. In our daily reading, we fall in with many obscure passages that convict us of ignorance. With this curb, God keeps us modest, assigning to each a measure of faith that every teacher, however excellent, may still be disposed to learn. Striking examples of this implicit faith may be observed in the disciples of Christ before they were fully illuminated. We see with what difficulty they take in the first rudiments, how they hesitate in the minutest matters, how, though hanging on the lips of their Master, they make no great progress; nay, even after running to the sepulcher on the report of the women, the Resurrection of their Master appears to them to be a dream. As Christ previously bore testimony to their faith, we cannot say that they were altogether devoid of it; nay, had they not been persuaded that Christ would rise again, all their zeal would have been extinguished. Nor was it superstition that led the women to prepare spices to embalm a dead body of whose revival they had no expectation; but, although they gave credit to the words of one whom they knew to be true, yet the ignorance, which still possessed their minds, involved their faith in darkness and left them in amazement.

Hence, they are said to have believed only when, by the reality, they perceive the truth of what Christ had spoken; not that they then began to believe, but the seed of a hidden faith, which lay dead in their hearts, then burst forth in vigor. They had, therefore, a true but implicit faith, having reverently embraced Christ as the only Teacher. Then, being taught by Him, they felt assured that He was the author of salvation: in fine, believed that He had come from heaven to gather disciples and take them thither through the grace of the Father. There cannot be a more familiar proof of this than that in all men faith is always mingled with incredulity.

5 In some, faith is implicit, as being a preparation for faith. This, however, is widely different from the implicit faith of the Schoolmen.

We may also call their faith implicit, as being properly nothing else than a preparation for faith. The evangelists describe many as having believed, although they were only roused to admiration by the miracles, and went no further than to believe that Christ was the promised Messiah, without being imbued at all with evangelical doctrine. The reverence, which subdued them and made them willingly submit to Christ, is honored with the name of faith, though it was nothing but the commencement of it. Thus the nobleman who believed in the promised cure of his son, on returning home, is said by the evangelist (see John 4:53) to have again believed; that is, he had first received the words which fell from the lips of Christ as an oracular response, and thereafter submitted to His authority and received His doctrine. Although it is to be observed that he was docile and disposed to learn, yet the word believed in the former passage denotes a particular faith, and in the latter gives him a place among those disciples who had devoted themselves to Christ. Not unlike this is the example which John gives of the Samaritans who believed the women, and eagerly hastened to Christ; but, after they had heard Him, thus express themselves, "Now we believe, not because of thy saying, for we have heard him ourselves, and know that this is indeed the Christ, the Savior of the world" (John 4:42). From these passages it is obvious that even those who are not yet imbued with the first principles, provided they are disposed to obey, are called believers, not properly indeed, but inasmuch as God is pleased in kindness so highly to honor their pious feeling. But this docility, with a desire of further progress, is widely different from the gross ignorance in which those who sluggishly indulge are contented with the implicit faith of the papists. If Paul severely condemns those who are "ever learning, and never able to come to the knowledge of the truth," how much more sharply ought those to be rebuked who avowedly affect to know nothing?

6 The Word of God has a similar relation to faith, The word being the source and basis of faith, and the mirror in which it beholds God. Confirmation from various passages of Scripture. Without the knowledge of the Word, there can be no faith. Sum of the discussion of the Scholastic doctrine of implicit faith.

The true knowledge of Christ consists in receiving Him as He is offered by the Father, namely, as invested with his gospel. For, as He is appointed as the end of our faith, so we cannot directly tend towards Him, except under the guidance of the gospel. Therein are certainly unfolded to us treasures of grace. If these continued shut, Christ would profit us little. Hence, Paul makes faith the inseparable attendant of doctrine in these words, "Ye have not so learned Christ; if so be that ye have heard him, and have been taught by him, as the truth is in Jesus" (Ephesians 4:20, 21). Still, I do not confine faith to the gospel in such a sense as not to admit that enough was delivered to Moses and the prophets to form a foundation of faith; but as the Gospel exhibits a fuller manifestation of Christ, Paul justly terms it the doctrine of faith. (See 1 Timothy 4:6.) For which reason, also he elsewhere says that, by the coming of faith, the Law was abolished (see Romans 10:4), including under the expression a new and unwonted mode of teaching, by which Christ, from the period of his appearance as the great Master, gave a fuller illustration of the Father's mercy, and testified more surely of our salvation. But an easier and more appropriate method will be to descend from the general to the particular. First, we must remember that there is an inseparable relation between faith and the Word, and that these can no more be disconnected from each other than rays of light from the sun.

Hence, in Isaiah the Lord exclaims, "Hear, and your soul shall live" (Isaiah 4:3). And John points to this same fountain of faith in the following words, "These are written that ye might believe" (John 20:31). The Psalmist, also exhorting the people to faith, says, "Today, if ye will hear his voice" (Psalm 95:7), to *hear* being uniformly taken for to *believe*.

In Isaiah, the Lord distinguishes the members of the Church from strangers by this mark, "All thy children shall be taught of the Lord" (Isaiah 54:13); for if the benefit was indiscriminate, why should He address His words only to a few? Corresponding with this, the Evangelists uniformly employ the terms *believers* and *disciples* as being synonymous. This is done especially by Luke in several passages of the Acts. He even applies the term *disciple* to a woman. (See Acts 9:36). Wherefore, if faith declines in the least degree from the mark at which it ought to aim, it does not retain its nature, but becomes uncertain credulity and vague wandering of mind. The same word is the basis on which it rests and is sustained. Declining from it, it falls. Take away the Word, therefore, and no faith will remain.

We are not here discussing, whether, in order to propagate the word of God by which faith is engendered, the ministry of man is necessary (this will be considered elsewhere); but we say that the Word itself, whatever be the way in which it is conveyed to us, is a kind of mirror in which faith beholds God. In this, therefore, whether God uses the agency of man or works immediately by his own power, it is always by His Word that he manifests himself to those whom He designs to draw to himself. Hence, Paul designates faith as the obedience given to the gospel. (See Romans 1:5). Writing to the Philippians, he commends them for the obedience of faith. (See Philippians 2:17.) For faith includes not merely the knowledge that God is, but also, nay chiefly, a perception of his will toward us. It concerns us to know not only what He is in himself, but also in what character He is pleased to manifest himself to us.

We now see, therefore, that faith is the knowledge of the divine will concerning us, as ascertained from His Word. And the foundation of it is a previous persuasion of the truth of God. So long as your mind entertains any misgivings as to the certainty of the Word, its authority will either be weak and dubious, or have no authority at all. Nor is it sufficient to believe that God is true, and cannot lie or deceive, unless you feel firmly persuaded that every word from Him is sacred, inviolable truth.

7 What faith properly has respect to in the Word of God, namely, the promise of grace offered in Christ, provided it is embraced with faith. A proper definition of faith.

But since the heart of man is not brought to faith by every word of God, we must still consider what it is that faith properly has respect to in the Word. The declaration of God to Adam was, "Thou shalt surely die" (Genesis 2:17); and to Cain, "The voice of thy brother's blood crieth unto me from the ground" (Genesis 4:10); but these, so far from being fitted to establish faith, tend only to shake it. At the same time, we deny not that it is the office of faith to assent to the truth of God whenever, whatever, and in whatever way He speaks: we are only inquiring what faith can find in the Word of God to lean and rest upon. When conscience sees only wrath and indignation, how can it but tremble and be afraid? And how can it avoid shunning the God whom it thus dreads? But faith ought to seek God, not shun Him. It is evident, therefore, that we have not yet obtained a full definition of faith, it being impossible to give the name to every kind of knowledge of the divine will. Shall we, then, for "will," which is often the messenger of bad news and the herald of terror, substitute the benevolence or mercy of God? In this way, doubtless, we make a nearer approach to the nature of faith. For we are allured to seek God when told that our safety is treasured up in Him; and we are confirmed in this when He declares that He studies and takes an interest in our welfare.

Hence, there is need for the gracious promise, in which He testifies that he is a propitious Father; since there is no other way in which we can approach Him, the promise being the only thing on which the heart of man can recline. For this reason, the two things, mercy and truth, are uniformly conjoined in the Psalms as having a mutual connection with each other. For it would not avail us to know that God is true, if He did not allure us to himself in mercy.

In addition, we could not of ourselves embrace His mercy if He did not expressly offer it. "I have declared thy faithfulness and thy salvation: I have not concealed thy loving-kindness and thy truth. Withhold not thy tender mercies from me, O Lord: let thy loving-kindness and thy truth continually preserve me" (Psalm 40:10, 11). "Thy mercy, O Lord, is in the heavens; and thy faithfulness reacheth unto the clouds" (Psalm 36:5). "All the paths of the Lord are mercy and truth unto such as keep his covenant and his testimonies" (Psalm 25:10). "His merciful kindness is great toward us: and the truth of the Lord endureth forever" (Psalm 117:2). "I will praise thy name for thy loving-kindness and thy truth" (Psalm 138:2).

I need not quote what is said in the prophets, to the effect that God is merciful and faithful in His promises. It would be presumptuous to hold that God is propitious to us, had we not His own testimony, and did He not prevent us by his invitation, which leaves no doubt or uncertainty as to his will. It has already been seen that Christ is the only pledge of love, for without Him all things, both above and below, speak of hatred and wrath. We have also seen that since the knowledge of the divine goodness cannot be of much importance unless it leads us to confide in it, we must exclude a knowledge mingled with doubt—a knowledge which, so far from being firm, is continually wavering. But the human mind, when blinded and darkened, is very far from being able to rise to a proper knowledge of the divine will; nor can the heart, fluctuating with perpetual doubt, rest secure in such knowledge.

Hence, in order that the Word of God may gain full credit, the mind must be enlightened, and the heart confirmed, from some other quarter. We shall now have a full definition of faith if we say that it is a firm and sure knowledge of the divine favor toward us, founded on the truth of a free promise in Christ, revealed to our minds, and sealed on our hearts, by the Holy Spirit.

8 Scholastic distinction between formed and unformed faith, refuted by a consideration of the nature of faith, which, as the gift of the Spirit, cannot possibly be disjoined from pious affection.

But before I proceed further, it will be necessary to make some preliminary observations for removing difficulties that might otherwise obstruct the reader. First, I must refute the nugatory distinction of the Schoolmen as to formed and unformed faith. For they imagine that persons who have no fear of God, and no sense of piety, may believe all that is necessary to be known for salvation; as if the Holy Spirit were not the witness of our adoption by enlightening our hearts unto faith. Still, however, though the whole Scripture is against them, they dogmatically give the name of faith to a persuasion devoid of the fear of God. It is unnecessary to go further in refuting their definition than simply to state the nature of faith as it is declared in the Word of God. From this it will clearly appear how unskillfully and absurdly they babble, rather than discourse, on this subject. I have already done this in part, and will afterwards add the remainder in its proper place. At present, I say that nothing can be imagined to be more absurd than their fiction. They insist that faith is an assent with which any despiser of God may receive that which Scripture delivers. But we must first see whether anyone can by his own strength acquire faith, or whether the Holy Spirit, by means of it, becomes the witness of adoption.

Hence, it is childish trifling in them to inquire whether the faith formed by the supervening quality of love be the same, or a different and new faith. By talking in this style, they show plainly that they have never thought of the special gift of the Spirit; since one of the first elements of faith is reconciliation implied in man's drawing near to God. Had they duly pondered the saying of Paul, "With the heart man believeth unto righteousness" (Romans 10:10), they would cease to dream of that frigid quality. There is one consideration which ought at once to put an end to the debate—viz. that assent itself (as I have already observed, and will afterwards more fully illustrate) is more a matter of the heart than the head, of the affection than the intellect. For this reason, it is termed "the obedience of faith" (Romans 1:5), which the Lord prefers to all other service, and justly, since nothing is more precious to Him than His truth, which, as John the Baptist declares, is in a manner signed and sealed by believers. (See John 3:33.)

As there can be no doubt on the matter, we in one word conclude that they talk absurdly when they maintain that faith is formed by the addition of pious affection as an accessory to assent, since assent itself, such at least as the Scriptures describe, consists in pious affection. However, we are furnished with a still clearer argument. Faith embraces Christ as the Father offers Him: not only for justification, for forgiveness of sins and peace, but also for sanctification, and as the fountain of living waters. Therefore, it is certain that no man will ever know him aright without receiving the sanctification of the Spirit at the same time. To express the matter more plainly, faith consists in the knowledge of Christ; we cannot know Christ without the sanctification of His Spirit. Therefore, faith cannot possibly be disjoined from pious affection.

9 Objection from a passage of Paul. An answer to it. Error of the Schoolmen in giving only one meaning of faith, whereas it has many meanings. The testimony of faith improperly ascribed to two classes of men.

In their attempt to mar faith by divesting it of love, they are wont to insist on the words of Paul, "Though I have all faith, so that I could remove mountains, and have not charity, I am nothing" (1 Corinthians 13:2). But they do not consider what the faith is of which the apostle speaks. Having, in the previous chapter, discoursed on the various gifts of the Spirit (see 1 Corinthians 12:10), including diversity of tongues, miracles, and prophecy, and exhorted the Corinthians to follow the better gifts (those from which the whole body of the Church would derive greater benefit), he adds, "Yet show I unto you a more excellent way" (1 Corinthians 12:30).

All other gifts, however excellent they may be in themselves, are of no value unless they are subservient to charity. They were given for the edification of the Church, and fail of their purpose if not so applied. To prove this he adopts a division, repeating the same gifts, which he had mentioned before, but under different names. Miracles and faith are used to denote the same thing—viz. the power of working miracles. Seeing, then, that this miraculous power or faith is the particular gift of God, which a wicked man may possess and abuse, as the gift of tongues, prophecy, or other gifts, it is not strange that he separates it from charity. Their whole error lies in this, that while the term faith has a variety of meanings, overlooking this variety, they argue as if its meaning were invariably one and the same.

The passage of James, by which they endeavor to defend their error, will be elsewhere discussed (*infra*, chapter 17, section 11). In discoursing about faith, we admit that it has a variety of forms. Yet, when our object is to show what knowledge of God the wicked possess, we hold and maintain, in accordance with Scripture, that only the pious have faith. Multitudes undoubtedly believe that God is, and admit the truth of the gospel history, and the other parts of Scripture, in the same way in which they believe the records of past events, or events which they have actually witnessed. Some go even further: They regard the Word of God as an infallible oracle; they do not altogether disregard its precepts, but are moved to some degree by its threatening and promises. To such the testimony of faith is attributed, but by *catachresis*; because they do not with open impiety impugn, reject, or condemn, the Word of God, but rather exhibit some semblance of obedience.

10 The view to be taken of this. Who those are that believe for a time. The faith of hypocrites. With whom they may be compared.

But as this shadow or image of faith is of no moment, so it is unworthy of the name. How far it differs from true faith will shortly be explained at length. Here, however, we may just indicate it in passing. Simon Magus is said to have believed, though he soon after gave proof of his unbelief. (See Acts 8:13-18.) With regard to the faith attributed to him, we do not understand with some that he merely pretended a belief that had no existence in his heart. Rather, we think that, overcome by the majesty of the gospel, he yielded some kind of assent and so far acknowledged Christ to be the Author of life and salvation, as willingly to assume His name.

In like manner, in the Gospel of Luke, those in whom the seed of the Word is choked before it brings forth fruit, or in whom, from having no depth of earth, it soon withers away, are said to believe for a time. Such, we doubt not, eagerly receive the Word with a kind of relish, and have some feeling of its divine power, so as not only to impose upon men by a false semblance of faith, but even to impose upon themselves. They imagine that the reverence, which they give to the Word, is genuine piety, because they have no idea of any impiety but that which consists in open and avowed contempt. But whatever that assent may be, it by no means penetrates to the heart, so as to have a fixed seat there. Although it sometimes seems to have planted its roots, these have no life in them. The human heart has so many recesses for vanity, so many lurking places for falsehood, and is so shrouded by fraud and hypocrisy that it often deceives itself. Let those who glory in such semblances of faith know that, in this respect, they are not a whit superior to devils. The one class, indeed, is inferior to them, inasmuch as they are able without emotion to hear and understand things, the knowledge of which makes devils tremble. (See James 2:19.) The other class equals them in this, that whatever be the impression made upon them, its only result is terror and consternation.

11 Why faith is attributed to the reprobate. Objection. Answer. What perception of grace in the reprobate. How the elect are distinguished from the reprobate.

I am aware that it seems unaccountable to some that faith is attributed to the reprobate, seeing that it is declared by Paul to be one of the fruits of election. Yet the difficulty is easily solved, for though none are enlightened into faith, and truly feel the efficacy of the gospel, with the exception of those who is preordained to salvation, yet experience shows that the reprobate are sometimes affected in a way so similar to the elect that even in their own judgment, there is no difference between them.

Hence, it is not strange that a taste of heavenly gifts by the apostle and temporary faith by Christ himself are ascribed to them. Not that they truly perceive the power of spiritual grace and the sure light of faith; but the Lord, the better to convict them, and leave them without excuse, instills into their minds such a sense of His goodness as can be felt without the Spirit of adoption. Should it be objected that believers have no stronger testimony to assure them of their adoption, I answer that although there is great resemblance and affinity between the elect of God and those who are impressed for a time with a fading faith, the elect alone have that full assurance which is extolled by Paul, and by which they are enabled to cry, "Abba, Father."

Therefore, as God regenerates the elect only forever by incorruptible seed, as the seed of life once sown in their hearts never perishes, so He effectually seals in them the grace of His adoption, that it may be sure and steadfast. But in this, there is nothing to prevent an inferior operation of the Spirit from taking its course in the reprobate. Meanwhile, believers are taught to examine themselves carefully and humbly, lest carnal security creep in and take the place of assurance of faith.

We may add that reprobates never have any other than a confused sense of grace, laying hold of the shadow rather than the substance, because the Spirit properly seals the forgiveness of sins in the elect only, applying it by special faith to their use. Still it is correct that the reprobate believe God to be propitious to them, inasmuch as they accept the gift of reconciliation, though confusedly and without due discernment. They are not partakers of the same faith or regeneration with the children of God, but under a covering of hypocrisy, they seem to have a principle of faith in common with them. Nor do I even deny that God illumines their minds to this extent, that they recognize His grace; but that conviction He distinguishes from the peculiar testimony which He gives to His elect in this respect, that the reprobate never attain to the full result or to fruition. When He shows himself propitious to them, it is not as if He had truly rescued them from death, and taken them under his protection. He only gives them a manifestation of his present mercy. In the elect alone, He implants the living root of faith, so that they persevere even to the end. Thus, we dispose of the objection that if God truly displays His grace, it must endure forever. There is nothing inconsistent in this with the fact of His enlightening some with a present sense of grace, which afterwards proves evanescent.

12 Why faith is temporary in the reprobate, firm and perpetual in the elect. Reason in the case of the reprobate. Example. Why God is angry with his children. In what sense many are said to fall from faith.

Although faith is knowledge of the divine favor towards us, and a full persuasion of its truth, it is not strange that the sense of the divine love, which though akin to faith differs much from it, vanishes in those who are temporarily impressed. The will of God is, I confess, immutable, and His truth is always consistent with itself; but I deny that the reprobate ever advances so far as to penetrate to that secret revelation which Scripture reserves for the elect only. I therefore deny that they either consider His will to be immutable or steadily embrace his truth. The evidence is that they rest satisfied with an evanescent impression, just as a tree not planted deep enough may take root, but will in process of time wither away, although it may for several years not only put forth leaves and flowers, but produce fruit. In short, as by the revolt of the first man, the image of God could be effaced from his mind and soul, so there is nothing strange in His shedding some rays of grace on the reprobate, and afterwards allowing these to be extinguished. There is nothing to prevent His giving some a slight knowledge of his gospel, and imbuing others thoroughly.

Meanwhile, we must remember that however feeble and slender the faith of the elect may be, yet as the Spirit of God is to them a sure earnest and a seal of their adoption, the impression once engraved can never be effaced from their hearts, whereas the light which glimmers in the reprobate is afterwards quenched. Nor can it be said that the Spirit therefore deceives, because He does not quicken the seed, which lies in their hearts to make it ever remain incorruptible as in the elect.

I go further: seeing it is evident, from the doctrine of Scripture and from daily experience that the reprobates are occasionally impressed with a sense of divine grace, some desire of mutual love must necessarily be excited in their hearts. Thus for a time a pious affection prevailed in Saul, disposing him to love God. Knowing that he was treated with paternal kindness, he was in some degree attracted by it. But as the reprobate has no rooted conviction of the paternal love of God, so he does not in return yield the love of a son, but are led by a kind of mercenary affection. The Spirit of love was given to Christ alone, for the express purpose of conferring this Spirit upon His members. There can be no doubt that Paul's words apply only to the elect: "The love of God is shed abroad in our hearts, by the Holy Ghost which is given unto us" (Romans 5:5); namely, the love which begets that confidence in prayer.

On the other hand, we see that God is mysteriously offended with His children, though he ceases not to love them. He certainly hates them not, but He alarms them with a sense of His anger, that He may humble the pride of the flesh, arouse them from lethargy, and urge them to repentance. Hence, they, at the same instant, feel that He is angry with them or their sins, and propitious to their persons. It is not from fictitious dread that they deprecate His anger, and yet they retake themselves to him with tranquil confidence.

It hence appears that the faith of some, though not true faith, is not mere pretense. They are borne along by some sudden impulse of zeal, and erroneously impose upon themselves, sloth undoubtedly preventing them from examining their hearts with due care. Such probably was the case of those whom John describes as believing on Christ; but of whom he says, "Jesus did not commit himself unto them, because he knew all men, and needed not that any should testify of man: for he knew what was in man" (John 2:24, 25). Were it not true that many fall away from the common faith (I call it common, because there is a great resemblance between temporary and living, everduring faith), Christ would not have said to His disciples, "If ye continue in my word, then are ye my disciples indeed; and ye shall know the truth, and the truth shall make you free" (John 8:31, 32). He is addressing those who had embraced His doctrine, and urging them to progress in the faith, lest by their sluggishness they extinguish the light that they have received.

Accordingly, Paul claims faith as the peculiar privilege of the elect, intimating that many, from not being properly rooted, fall away (Titus 1:1). In the same way, in Matthew, our Savior says, "Every plant which my heavenly Father has not planted shall be rooted up" (Matthew 16:13). Some who are not ashamed to insult God and man are more grossly false. Against this class of men, who profane the faith by impious and lying pretense, James inveighs. (See James 2:14). Nor would Paul require the faith of believers to be unfeigned (see 1 Timothy 1:5), were there not many who presumptuously arrogate to themselves what they have not, deceiving others, and sometimes even themselves, with empty show. Hence, he compares a good conscience to the ark in which faith is preserved, because many have shipwrecked in regard to it by falling away.

13 Various meanings of the term faith: A. Taken for soundness in the faith. B. Sometimes restricted to a particular object. C. Signifies the ministry or testimony by which we are instructed in the faith.

It is necessary to attend to the ambiguous meaning of the term: for *faith* is often equivalent in meaning to *sound doctrine*, as in the passage that we recently quoted, and in the same epistle where Paul enjoins the deacons to hold "the mystery of the faith in a pure conscience." In like manner, he denounces the defection of certain ones from the faith. The meaning again is the same, when he says that Timothy had been brought up in the faith; and in like manner, when he says that profane babblings and oppositions of science, falsely so called, lead many away from the faith. Such persons he elsewhere calls reprobate as to the faith.

On the other hand, when he enjoins Titus, "Rebuke them sharply, that they may be sound in the faith," by soundness he means purity of doctrine, which is easily corrupted, and degenerates through the fickleness of men. And indeed, since in Christ, as possessed by faith, are "hid all the treasures of wisdom and knowledge" (Colossians 1:2-3), the term *faith* is justly extended to the whole sum of heavenly doctrine, from which it cannot be separated.

On the other hand, it is sometimes confined to a particular object, as when Matthew says of those who let down the paralytic through the roof, that Jesus saw their faith (see Matthew 9:2); and Jesus himself exclaims in regard to the centurion, "I have not found so great faith, no, not in Israel" (Matthew 8:10).

Now, it is probable that the centurion was thinking only of the cure of his son, by whom his whole soul was engrossed; but because he is satisfied with the simple answer and assurance of Christ, and does not request his bodily presence, this circumstance calls forth the eulogium on his faith. And we have lately shown how Paul uses the term faith for the gift of miracles—a gift possessed by persons who were neither regenerated by the Spirit of God, nor sincerely reverenced Him. In another passage, he uses faith for the doctrine by which we are instructed in the faith. For when he says, "that which is in part shall be done away" (1 Corinthians 13:10), there can be no doubt that reference is made to the ministry of the Church, which is necessary in our present imperfect state; in these forms of expression the analogy is obvious. But when the name of faith is improperly transferred to a false profession or lying assumption, the *catachresis* ought not to seem harsher than when the fear of God is used for vicious and perverse worship; as when it is repeatedly said in sacred history that the foreign nations, which had been transported to Samaria and the neighboring districts feared false gods and the God of Israel—in other words, confounded heaven with earth. But we have now been inquiring what the faith is, which distinguishes the children of God from unbelievers, the faith by which we invoke God the Father, by which we pass from death unto life, and by which Christ, our eternal salvation and life, dwells in us. I trust its power and nature have been explained briefly and clearly.

14 Definition of faith explained under six principal heads. What is meant by Knowledge in the definition.

Let us now again go over the parts of the definition separately: I should think that, after a careful examination of them, no doubt will remain. By knowledge, we do not mean comprehension, such as that which we have of things falling under human sense. For that knowledge is so much superior that the human mind must far surpass and go beyond itself in order to reach it. Nor even when it has reached it does it comprehend what it feels, but persuaded of what it comprehends not, it understands more from mere certainty of persuasion than it could discern of any human matter by its own capacity.

Hence, it is elegantly described by Paul as the ability "to comprehend with all saints what is the breadth, and length, and depth, and height; and to know the love of Christ, which passeth knowledge" (Ephesians 3:18, 19). His object was to intimate that what our mind embraces by faith is every way infinite, that this kind of knowledge far surpasses all understanding. But because the "mystery which has been hid from ages and from generations" is now "made manifest to the saints" (Colossians 1:26), faith is, for good reason, occasionally termed in Scripture as understanding (see Colossians 2:2); and knowledge, as by John (see 1 John 3:2), when he declares that believers know themselves to be the sons of God. And certainly, they do know, but rather as confirmed by a belief of the divine veracity than taught by any demonstration of reason. This is also indicated by Paul when he says, "Whilst we are at home in the body, we are absent from the Lord: (For we walk by faith, not by sight)" (2 Corinthians 5:6-7), thus showing that what we understand by faith is yet distant from us and escapes our view. Hence, we conclude that the knowledge of faith consists more of certainty than discernment.

15 Why this knowledge must be sure and firm. Reason drawn from the consideration of our weakness. Another reason from the certainty of the promises of God.

We add that it is sure and firm, the better to express strength and constancy of persuasion. For as faith is not contented with a dubious and fickle opinion, so neither is it contented with an obscure and ill-defined conception. The certainty that it requires must be full and decisive as is usual concerning matters ascertained and proved. So deeply rooted in our hearts is unbelief, so prone are we to it that while all confess with the lips that God is faithful, no man ever believes it without an arduous struggle. Especially when brought to the test, we by our wavering betray the vice that lurked within. Nor is it without cause that the Holy Spirit bears such distinguished testimony to the authority of God in order that it may cure the disease of which I have spoken, and induce us to give full credit to the divine promises: "The words of the Lord," says David (Psalm 12:6), "are pure words, as silver tried in a furnace of earth purified seven times." "The word of the Lord is tried: he is a buckler to all those that trust in him" (Psalm 18:30). And Solomon declares the same thing almost in the same words, "Every word of God is pure" (Proverbs 30:5).

Further quotation is superfluous, as the 119th Psalm is almost wholly occupied with this subject. Certainly, whenever God thus recommends His Word, He indirectly rebukes our unbelief, the purport of all that is said being to eradicate perverse doubt from our hearts.

There are very many also, who form such an idea of the divine mercy as yields them very little comfort. For they are harassed by miserable anxiety while they doubt whether God will be merciful to them. They think, indeed, that they are most fully persuaded of the divine mercy, but they confine it within too narrow limits. The idea they entertain is that this mercy is great and abundant, is shed upon many, is offered and ready to be bestowed upon all; but that it is uncertain whether it will reach to them individually, or rather whether they can reach to it. Thus, their knowledge stopping short leaves them only midway, not so much confirming and tranquilizing the mind as harassing it with doubt and disquietude.

Very different is that feeling of full assurance, which the Scriptures uniformly attribute to faith—an assurance that leaves no doubt that the goodness of God is clearly offered to us. This assurance we cannot have without truly perceiving its sweetness, and experiencing it in ourselves. Hence, from faith the apostle deduces confidence, and from confidence boldness. His words are, "In whom (Christ) we have boldness and access with confidence by the faith of him" (Ephesians 3:12) thus undoubtedly showing that our faith is not true unless it enables us to appear calmly in the presence of God. Such boldness springs only from confidence in the divine favor and salvation. So true is this, that the term faith is often used as equivalent to confidence.

16 The leading point in this certainty. Its fruits. A description of the true believer.

The principal hinge on which faith turns is this: We must not suppose that any promises of mercy which the Lord offers are only true outside of us, and not at all within us: we should rather make them ours by inwardly embracing them. In this way only is engendered that confidence which He elsewhere terms peace. (See Romans 5:1.) Though perhaps He rather means to make peace follow from it. This security quiets and calms the conscience in the view of the judgment of God. Without it, the conscience is necessarily vexed and almost torn with tumultuous dread, unless when it happens to slumber for a moment, forgetful both of God and of itself. Moreover, truthfully it is but for a moment. It never long enjoys that miserable obliviousness, for the memory of the divine judgment, always recurring, stings it to the quick. Only a true believer is firmly persuaded that God is reconciled and a kind Father to him, hopes everything from His kindness, and trusts the promises of the divine favor with undoubting confidence that anticipates salvation.

The apostle shows this in these words, "We are made partakers of Christ, if we hold the beginning of our confidence steadfast unto the end" (Hebrews 3:14). He thus holds that none hope well in the Lord save those who confidently glory in being the heirs of the heavenly kingdom. No man, I say, is a believer except he who trusts the security of his salvation, and confidently triumphs over the devil and death. As we are taught by the noble exclamation of Paul, "I am persuaded that neither death, nor life, nor angels, nor principalities, nor powers, nor things present, nor things to come, nor height, nor depth, nor any other creature, shall be able to separate us from the love of God, which is in Christ Jesus our Lord" (Romans 8:38). In like manner, the same apostle does not consider that the eyes of our understanding are enlightened unless we know the hope of the eternal inheritance to which we are called. (See Ephesians 1:18). Thus, he uniformly intimates throughout his writings that the goodness of God is not properly comprehended when security does not follow as its fruit.

17 An objection to this certainty. Answer. Confirmation of the answer from the example of David. This enlarged upon from the opposite example of Ahab. Also from the uniform experience and the prayers of believers.

But it will be said that this differs widely from the experience of believers, who, in recognizing the grace of God toward them, not only feel disquietude (this often happens), but sometimes tremble, overcome with terror, so violent are the temptations which assail their minds. This scarcely seems consistent with certainty of faith. It is necessary to solve this difficulty, in order to maintain the doctrine laid down above. When we say that faith must be certain and secure, we certainly speak not of an assurance which is never affected by doubt, nor a security which anxiety never assails; we rather maintain that believers have a perpetual struggle with their own distrust, and are thus far from thinking that their consciences possess a placid quiet, uninterrupted by perturbation.

On the other hand, whatever be the mode in which they are assailed, we deny that they fall off and abandon that sure confidence which they have formed in the mercy of God. Scripture does not set before us a brighter or more memorable example of faith than in David, especially if regard be had to the constant tenor of his life. And yet how far his mind was from being always at peace is declared by innumerable complaints, of which it will be sufficient to select a few. When he rebukes the turbulent movements of his soul, what else is it but a censure of his unbelief? "Why art thou cast down, my soul? In addition, why art thou disquieted in me? Hope thou in God" (Psalm 42:6). His alarm was undoubtedly a manifest sign of distrust, as if he thought that the Lord had forsaken him. In another passage, we have a fuller confession: "I said in my haste, I am cut off from before thine eyes" (Psalm 31:22). In another passage, in anxious and wretched perplexity, he debates with himself, nay, raises a question as to the nature of God: "Has God forgotten to be gracious? Has he in anger shut up his tender mercies?" (Psalm 77:9). What follows is still harsher: "I said this is my infirmity; but I will remember the years of the right hand of the Most High." As if desperate, he adjudges himself to destruction. He not only confesses that he is agitated by doubt, but as if he had fallen in the contest, leaves himself nothing in reserve, God having deserted him, and made the hand which was wont to help him the instrument of his destruction. Wherefore, after having been tossed among tumultuous waves, it is not without reason he exhorts his soul to return to her quiet rest (Psalm 116:7). And yet (what is strange) amid those commotions, faith sustains the believer's heart, and truly acts the part of the palm tree, which supports any weights laid upon it, and rises above them; thus David, when he seemed to be overwhelmed, ceased not by urging himself forward to ascend to God.

However, he, anxiously contending with his own infirmity, has recourse to faith, and is already in a great measure victorious. This we may infer from the following passage, and others similar to it: "Wait on the Lord: be of good courage, and he shall strengthen thine heart: wait, I say, on the Lord" (Psalm 27:14). He accuses himself of timidity, and repeating the same thing twice, confesses that he is always exposed to agitation. Still he is not only dissatisfied with himself for so feeling, but earnestly labors to correct it. Were we to take a nearer view of his case, and compare it with that of Ahaz, we should find a great difference between them. Isaiah is sent to relieve the anxiety of an impious and hypocritical king, and addresses him in these terms: "Take heed, and be quiet; fear not," etc. (Isaiah 7:4). How did Ahab act? As has already been said, his heart was shaken as a tree is shaken by the wind: though he heard the promise, he ceased not to tremble. This, therefore, is the proper hire and punishment of unbelief, so to tremble as in the day of trial to turn away from God, who gives access to himself only by faith.

On the other hand, believers, though weighed down and almost overwhelmed with the burden of temptation, constantly rise up, though not without toil and difficulty; hence, feeling conscious of their own weakness, they pray with the prophet, "Take not the word of truth utterly out of my mouth" (Psalm 119:43). By these words, we are taught that they at times become dumb, as if their faith were overthrown, and yet that they do not withdraw or turn their backs, but persevere in the contest, and by prayer stimulate their sluggishness, so as not to fall into stupor by giving way to it.

18 For this reason the conflict between the flesh and the Spirit in the soul of the believer described. The issue of this conflict, the victory of faith.

To make this intelligible, we must return to the distinction between flesh and spirit, to which we have already referred, and which here becomes most apparent. The believer finds within himself two principles: the one filling him with delight in recognizing the divine goodness, the other filling him with bitterness under a sense of his fallen state; the one leading him to recline on the promise of the gospel, the other alarming him by the conviction of his iniquity; the one making him exult with the anticipation of life, the other making him tremble with the fear of death. This diversity is owing to imperfection of faith, since we are never so well in the course of the present life as to be entirely cured of the disease of distrust, and completely replenished and engrossed by faith. Hence, those conflicts: the distrust cleaving to the remains of the flesh rising up to assail the faith enlisting in our hearts. But if in the believer's mind certainty is mingled with doubt, must we not always be carried back to the conclusion that faith consists not of a sure and clear, but only of an obscure and confused understanding of the divine will in regard to us? By no means. Though we are distracted by various thoughts, it does not follow that we are immediately divested of faith. Though we are agitated and carried to and fro by distrust, we are not immediately plunged into the abyss; though we are shaken, we are not therefore driven from our place. The invariable issue of the contest is that faith in the long run surmounts the difficulties by which it was beset and seemed to be endangered.

19 On the whole, the faith of the elect is certain and indubitable Conformation from analogy.

The whole, then, comes to this: As soon as the minutest particle of faith is instilled into our minds, we begin to behold the face of God placid, serene, and propitious; far off, indeed, but still so distinctly as to assure us that there is no delusion in it. In proportion to the progress we afterwards make (and the progress ought to be uninterrupted), we obtain a nearer and surer view, the very continuance making it more familiar to us. Thus we see that a mind illumined with the knowledge of God is at first involved in much ignorance—ignorance, however, which is gradually removed. Still this partial ignorance or obscure discernment does not prevent that clear knowledge of the divine favor, which holds the first and principal part in faith. For as one shut up in a prison, where from a narrow opening he receives the rays of the sun indirectly and in a manner divided, though deprived of a full view of the sun, has no doubt of the source from which the light comes, and is benefited by it. So it is with believers, while bound with the fetters of an earthly body and though surrounded on all sides with much obscurity, are so far illumined by any slender light that beams upon them and displays the divine mercy as to feel secure.

20 Another confirmation from the testimony of an apostle, king it apparent that, though the faith of the elect is as yet imperfect, it is nevertheless firm and sure.

The Apostle elegantly refers to both in different passages. When he says, "We know in part, and we prophesy in part;" and "Now we see through a glass darkly" (1 Corinthians 13:9, 12), he intimates how very minute a portion of divine wisdom is given to us in the present life. Those expressions do not simply indicate that faith is imperfect so long as we groan under a weight of flesh, and that the necessity of being constantly engaged in learning is due to our imperfection. At the same time, he reminds us that by our feeble and narrow capacities, we cannot comprehend a subject of boundless extent. This Paul affirms of the whole Church, each individual being retarded and impeded by his own ignorance from making so near an approach as would be wished. He elsewhere shows that the foretaste we obtain from any minute portion of faith is certain, and by no means fallacious. He affirms that, "We all, with open face beholding as in a glass the glory of the Lord, are changed into the same image, from glory to glory, even as by the Spirit of the Lord" (2 Corinthians 3:18).

In such degrees of ignorance, much doubt and trembling are necessarily implied, especially because our heart is by its own natural bias prone to unbelief. To this we must add the temptations, which, various in kind and infinite in number, are always violently assailing us. In particular, conscience itself, burdened with an incumbent load of sins, at one time complains and groans, at another accuses itself; at one time murmurs in secret, at another openly rebels. Therefore, whether adverse circumstances betoken the wrath of God, or conscience finds the subject and matter within itself, unbelief thence draws weapons and engines to put faith to flight. The aim of all its efforts is to make us think that God is adverse and hostile to us, and thus, instead of hoping for any assistance from Him, to make us dread Him as a deadly foe.

21 A fuller explanation of the nature of faith. A. When the believer is shaken with fear, he retakes himself to the bosom of a merciful God. B. He does not even shun God when angry, but hopes in Him. C. He does not suffer unbelief to reign in his heart. D. He opposes unbelief, and is never finally lost. E. Faith, however often assailed, at length comes off victorious.

To withstand these assaults, faith arms and fortifies itself with the Word of God. When the temptation suggested is that God is an enemy because He afflicts, faith replies that while He afflicts He is merciful, His chastening proceeds more from love than anger. To the thought that God is the avenger of wickedness, it opposes the pardon ready to be bestowed on all offenses whenever the sinner takes himself to the divine mercy. Thus the pious mind, however much it may be agitated and torn, at length rises superior to all difficulties, and allows not its confidence in the divine mercy to be destroyed. Nay, rather, the disputes that exercise and disturb it tend to establish this confidence. A proof of this is that the saints, when the hand of God lies heaviest upon them, still lodge their complaints with Him, and continue to invoke Him, when to all appearance He is least disposed to hear. But of what use was it to lament before Him if they had no hope of solace? They never would invoke Him did they not believe that he is ready to assist them. Thus the disciples, while reprimanded by their Master for the weakness of their faith in crying out that they were perishing, still implored his aid (Matthew 8:25). And He, in rebuking them for their want of faith, does not disown them or class them with unbelievers, but urges them to shake off the vice. Therefore, as we have already said, we again maintain that faith remaining fixed in the believer's breast never can be eradicated from it.

However, it may seem shaken and bent in this direction or in that, its flame is never so completely quenched as not at least to lurk under the embers. In this way, it appears that the Word, which is an incorruptible seed, produces fruit similar to itself. Its germ never withers away utterly and perishes. The saints cannot have a stronger ground for despair than to feel that, according to present appearances, the hand of God is armed for their destruction; and yet Job thus declares the strength of his confidence: "Though he slay me, yet will I trust in him."

The truth is that unbelief reigns not in the hearts of believers, but only assails them from without; does not wound them mortally with its darts, but annoys them, or, at the utmost, gives them a wound, which can be healed. Faith, as Paul (declares (see Ephesians 6:16), is our shield, which receiving these darts, either wards them off entirely, or at least breaks their force, and prevents them from reaching the vitals. Hence, when faith is shaken, it is just as when, by the violent blow of a javelin, a soldier standing firm is forced to step back and yield a little; and again, when faith is wounded, it is as if the shield were pierced, but not perforated by the blow. The pious mind will always rise, and be able to say with David, "Yea, though I walk through the valley of the shadow of death, I will fear no evil: for thou art with me" (Psalm 23:4).

Doubtless, it is a terrific thing to walk in the darkness of death, and it is impossible for believers, however great their strength may be, not to shudder at it; but since the prevailing thought is that God is present and providing for their safety, the feeling of security overcomes that of fear. As Augustine says, whatever be the engines that the devil erects against us, as he cannot gain the heart where faith dwells, he is cast out. Thus, if we may judge by the event, not only do believers come off safe from every contest so as to be ready, after a short repose, to descend again into the arena, but the saying of John, in his Epistle, is fulfilled, "This is the victory that overcometh the world, even our faith" (1 John 5:4). It is not said that it will be victorious in a single fight, or a few, or some one assault, but that it will be victorious over the whole world, though it should be a thousand times assailed.

22 Another species of fear, arising from a consideration of the judgment of God against the wicked. This also faith overcomes. Examples of this description, placed before the eyes of believers, repress presumption and fix their faith in God.

There is another species of fear and trembling, which, so far from impairing the security of faith, tends rather to establish it: when believers, reflecting that the examples of the divine vengeance on the ungodly are a kind of beacon warning them not to provoke the wrath of God by similar wickedness, keep anxious watch; or when believers, taking a view of their own inherent wretchedness, learn their entire dependence on God, without whom they feel themselves to be fleeting and evanescent as the wind. For when the apostle sets before the Corinthians the scourges which the Lord in ancient times inflicted on the people of Israel, that they might be afraid of subjecting themselves to similar calamities, he does not in any degree destroy the ground of their confidence; he only shakes off their carnal torpor which suppresses faith, but does not strengthen it. Nor when he takes occasion from the case of the Israelites to exhort, "Let him that thinketh he standeth take heed lest he fall" (1 Corinthians 10:12), he does not bid us waver, as if we had no security for our steadfastness: he only removes arrogance and rash confidence in our strength, telling the Gentiles not to presume because the Jews had been cast off, and they had been admitted to their place. (See Romans 11:20.)

In that passage, indeed, he is not addressing believers only, but also hypocrites, who gloried merely in external appearance. Nor is he addressing individuals: by contrasting the Jews and Gentiles, he first shows that the rejection of the former was a just punishment of their ingratitude and unbelief, and then exhorts the latter to beware lest pride and presumption deprive them of the grace of adoption which had lately been transferred to them. For as in that rejection of the Jews there still remained some who were not excluded from the covenant of adoptions so there might be some among the Gentiles who, possessing no true faith, were only puffed up with vain carnal confidence, and so abused the goodness of God to their own destruction. Though you should hold that the words were addressed to elect believers, no inconsistency will follow. It is one thing, in order to prevent believers from indulging vain confidence, to repress the temerity which, from the remains of the flesh, sometimes gains upon them, and it is another thing to strike terror into their consciences, and prevent them from feeling secure in the mercy of God.

23 Nothing contrary to this in the exhortation of the apostle to work out our salvation with fear and trembling. Fear and faith mutually connected. Confirmation from the words of a Prophet.

Then, when he bids us work out our salvation with fear and trembling, all he requires is that we accustom ourselves to think very meanly of our own strength, and confide in the strength of the Lord. For nothing stimulates us so strongly to place all our confidence and assurance on the Lord as self-diffidence, and the anxiety produced by a consciousness of our calamitous condition. In this sense are we to understand the words of the Psalmist: "I will come into thy house in the multitude of thy mercy: and in thy fear will I worship toward thy holy temples" (Psalm 5:7). Here he appropriately unites confident faith, leaning on the divine mercy with religious fear, which of necessity we must feel whenever coming into the presence of the divine majesty we are made aware by its splendor of the extent of our own impurity. Truly also does Solomon declare: "Happy is the man that feareth alway; but he that hardeneth his heart falleth into mischief" (Proverbs 28:14). The fear he speaks of is that which renders us more cautious, not that which produces despondency, the fear that is felt when the mind confounded in itself resumes its equanimity in God, downcast in itself, takes courage in God, distrusting itself, breathes confidence in God. Hence, there is nothing inconsistent in believers being afraid, and at the same time possessing secure consolation as they alternately behold their own vanity, and direct their thoughts to the truth of God.

How, it will be asked, can fear and faith dwell in the same mind? Just in the same way as sluggishness and anxiety can so dwell. The ungodly court a state of lethargy that the fear of God may not annoy them; and yet the judgment of God so urges that they cannot gain their desire. In the same way, God can train His people in humility, and curb them by the bridle of modesty, while yet fighting bravely. From the context, it is plain that this was the apostle's meaning, since he states, as the ground of fear and trembling, that it is God who works in us to will and to do of his good pleasure. In the same sense we must understand the words of the prophet, "The children of Israel"... "shall fear the Lord and his goodness in the latter days" (Hosea 3:5). For not only does piety beget reverence of God, but the sweet attractiveness of grace inspires a man, though desponding of himself, at once with fear and admiration, making him feel his dependence on God, and submit humbly to His power.

24 This doctrine gives no countenance to the error of those who dream of a confidence mingled with incredulity. Refutation of this error, from a consideration of the dignity of Christ dwelling in us. The argument retorted. Refutation confirmed by the authority of an apostle. What we ought to hold on this question.

Here, however, we give no countenance to that most pestilential philosophy which some semi-papists are at present beginning to broach in corners. Unable to defend the gross doubt inculcated by the Schoolmen, they have recourse to another fiction, that they may compound a mixture of faith and unbelief. They admit that whenever we look to Christ, we are furnished with full ground for hope; but as we are ever unworthy of all the blessings, which are offered us in Christ, they will have us to fluctuate and hesitate in the view of our unworthiness. In short, they give conscience a position between hope and fear, making it alternate, by successive turns, to the one and the other.

Hope and fear, again, they place in complete contrast, —the one falling as the other rises, and rising as the other falls. Thus Satan, finding the devices by which he was wont to destroy the certainty of faith too manifest to be now of any avail, is endeavoring, by indirect methods, to undermine it. But what kind of confidence is that which is always supplanted by despair? They tell you, if you look to Christ salvation is certain; if you return to yourself, damnation is certain. Therefore, your mind must be alternately ruled by diffidence and hope, as if we were to imagine Christ standing at a distance, and not rather dwelling in us. We expect salvation from Him—not because He stands aloof from us, but because engrafting us into His body he not only makes us partakers of all His benefits, but also of himself. Therefore, I thus give this retort to the argument: If you look to yourself, damnation is certain: but since Christ has been communicated to you with all His benefits, so that all which is His is made yours, you become a member of Him, and hence one with him. His righteousness covers your sins—His salvation extinguishes your condemnation; He interposes with His worthiness, and so prevents your unworthiness from coming into the view of God. Thus it truly is. It will never do to separate Christ from us or us from Him; but we must, with both hands, keep firm hold of that alliance by which He has riveted us to himself.

This the apostle teaches us: "The body is dead because of sin; but the spirit is life because of righteousness" (Romans 8:10). According to the frivolous trifling of these objectors, he ought to have said, Christ indeed has life in himself, but you, as you are sinners, remain liable to death and condemnation. Very different is his language. He tells us that the condemnation that we deserve is annihilated by the salvation of Christ. To confirm this, he employs the argument to which I have referred—viz. that Christ is not external to us, but dwells in us; and not only unites us to himself by an undivided bond of fellowship, but by a wondrous communion brings us daily into closer connection until He becomes altogether one with us.

And yet I deny not, as I lately said, that faith occasionally suffers certain interruptions when, by violent assault, its weakness is made to bend in this direction or in that; and its light is buried in the thick darkness of temptation. Still happen what may, faith ceases not to long after God.

25 Confirmation of the preceding conclusion by a passage from Bernard.

The same doctrine is taught by Bernard when he treats professedly on this subject in his *Fifth Homily on the Dedication of the Temple*: "By the blessing of God, sometimes meditating on the soul, methinks, I find in it two contraries. When I look at it as it is in itself and of itself, the truest thing I can say of it is that it has been reduced to nothing. What need is there to enumerate each of its miseries? how burdened with sin, obscured with darkness, ensnared by allurements, teeming with lusts, ruled by passion, filled with delusions, ever prone to evil, inclined to every vice; lastly, full of ignominy and confusion. If all its righteousness, when examined by the light of truth, is but as filthy rags (see Isaiah 64:6), what must we suppose its unrighteousness to be? "If, therefore, the light that is in thee be darkness, how great is that darkness?" (Matthew 6:23).

What then? Man doubtless has been made subject to vanity—man here has been reduced to nothing—man is nothing. Yet how is he whom God exalts utterly nothing? How is he nothing to whom a divine heart has been given? Let us breathe again, brethren. Although we are nothing in our hearts, perhaps something of us may lurk in the heart of God. O Father of mercies! O Father of the miserable! How plantest thou thy heart in us? Where thy heart is, there is thy treasure also. But how are we thy treasure if we are nothing? All nations before thee are as nothing. Observe, *before* thee, not *within* thee. Such are they in the judgment of thy truth, but not such concerning thy affection. Thou callest the things which be not as though they were; and they are not, because thou callest them "things that be not" and yet they are because thou callest them. For though they are not as to themselves, yet they are with thee according to the declaration of Paul: "Not of works, but of him that calleth" (Romans 9:11). He then goes on to say that the connection is wonderful in both points of view. Certainly, things that are connected together do not mutually destroy each other. This he explains more clearly in his conclusion in the following terms: "If, in both views, we diligently consider what we are—in the one view our nothingness, in the other our greatness—I presume our glorying will seem restrained; but perhaps it is rather increased and confirmed, because we glory not in ourselves, but in the Lord. Our thought is, if He determined to save us we shall be delivered; and here we begin again to breathe. However, ascending to a loftier height, let us seek the city of God, let us seek the Temple, let us seek our home, let us seek our spouse. I have not forgotten myself when, with fear and reverence, I say, we are! We are in the heart of God. We are, by His dignifying, not by our own dignity."

26 True fear caused in two ways—viz. when we are required to reverence God as a Father, and also to fear him as Lord.

Moreover, the fear of the Lord, which is uniformly attributed to all the saints, and which, in one passage, is called "the beginning of wisdom," in another *wisdom* itself, although it is one, proceeds from a twofold cause. God is entitled to the reverence of a Father and a Lord. Hence, he who desires duly to worship Him will study to act the part of both an obedient son and a faithful servant.

The obedience paid to God as a Father He by His prophet terms *honor*; the service performed to Him as a master he terms *fear*. "A son honoreth his father, and a servant his master. If then I be a father, where is mine honor? And if I be a master, where is my fear?"

However, while He thus distinguishes between the two, it is obvious that He at the same time confounds them. The fear of the Lord, therefore, may be defined reverence mingled with honor and fear. It is not strange that the same mind can entertain both feelings; for he who considers with himself what kind of a Father God is to us, will see sufficient reason, even were there no hell, why the thought of offending Him should seem more dreadful than any death. But so prone is our carnal nature to indulgence in sin, that, in order to curb it in every way, we must also give place to the thought that all iniquity is abomination to the Master under whom we lie; that those who, by wicked lives, provoke His anger, will not escape his vengeance.

27 Objection from a passage in the Apostle John. Answer founded on the distinction between filial and servile fear.

There is nothing repugnant to this in the observation of John: "There is no fear in love; but perfect love casteth out fear: because fear has torment"(1 John 4:18). He is speaking of the fear of unbelief, between which and the fear of believers there is a wide difference. The wicked do not fear God from any unwillingness to offend him, provided they could do so with impunity; but knowing that He is armed with power for vengeance, they tremble in dismay on hearing of His anger. In addition, they thus dread His anger, because they think it is impending over them, and they every moment expect it to fall upon their heads.

However, believers, as has been said, dread the offense even more than the punishment. They are not alarmed by the fear of punishment, as if it were impending over them, but are rendered the more cautious of doing anything to provoke it. Thus the apostle, addressing believers, says, "Let no man deceive you with vain words; for because of these things, the wrath of God cometh upon the children of disobedience" (Ephesians 5:6; Colossians 3:6). He does not threaten that wrath will descend upon them; but he admonishes them, while they think how the wrath of God is prepared for the wicked, on account of the crimes which he had enumerated, not to run the risk of provoking it. It seldom happens that mere threatening should have the effect of arousing the reprobate; nay, becoming more callous and hardened when God thunders verbally from Heaven, they obstinately persist in their rebellion. It is only when actually smitten by His hand that they are forced, whether they will or not, to fear. This fear the sacred writers term *servile*, and oppose to the free and voluntary fear, which becomes sons. Some, by a subtle distinction, have introduced an intermediate species, holding that that forced and servile fear sometimes subdues the mind, and leads spontaneously to proper fear.

28 How faith is said to have respect to the divine benevolence. What comprehended under this benevolence. Confirmation from David and Paul.

The divine favor to which faith is said to have respect, we understand to include in it the possession of salvation and eternal life. For if, when God is propitious, no good thing can be wanting to us, we have ample security for our salvation when we are assured of His love. "Turn us again, O God, and cause thy face to shine," says the prophet, "and we shall be saved" (Psalm 80:3). Hence, the Scriptures make the sum of our salvation to consist in the removal of all enmity, and our admission into favor; thus intimating that when God is reconciled all danger is past, and everything good will befall us. Wherefore, faith apprehending the love of God has the promise both of the present and the future life, and ample security for all blessings (See Ephesians 2:14.) The nature of this must be ascertained from the word. Faith does not promise us length of days, riches, and honors (the Lord not having been pleased that any of these should be appointed us); but is contented with the assurance that however poor we may be in regard to present comforts, God will never fail us. The chief security lies in the expectation of future life, which is placed beyond doubt by the Word of God. Whatever be the miseries and calamities that await the children of God in this world, they cannot make His favor cease from being complete happiness.

Hence, when we were desirous to express the sum of blessedness, we designated it by the favor of God, from which, as their source, all kinds of blessings flow. In addition, we may observe throughout the Scriptures that they refer us to the love of God, not only when they treat of our eternal salvation, but of any blessing whatever. For which reason David sings that the lovingkindness of God experienced by the pious heart is sweeter and more to be desired than life itself. (See Psalm 63:3.) In short, if we have every earthly comfort to a wish, but are uncertain whether we have the love or the hatred of God, our felicity will be cursed, and therefore miserable. However, if God lifts on us the light of His fatherly countenance, our very miseries will be blessed, inasmuch as they will become helps to our salvation. Thus Paul, after bringing together all kinds of adversity, boasts that they cannot separate us from the love of God; and in his prayers he uniformly begins with the grace of God as the source of all prosperity. In like manner, to all the terrors which assail us, David opposes merely the favor of God: "Yea, though I walk through the valley of the shadow of death, I will fear no evil: for thou art with me" (Psalm 23:4). And we feel that our minds always waver until, contented with the grace of God, we in it seek peace, and feel thoroughly persuaded of what is said in the Psalm, "Blessed is the nation whose God is the Lord, and the people whom he has chosen for his own inheritance" (Psalm 33:12).

29 Of the free promise which is the foundation of faith. Reason Confirmation.

Free promise we find the foundation of faith, because in it faith properly consists. For though it holds that God is always true, whether in ordering or forbidding, promising or threatening; though it obediently receives His commands, observes His prohibitions, and gives heed to His threatening; yet it properly begins with promise, continues with it, and ends with it. It seeks life in God, life that is not found in commands or the denunciations of punishment, but in the promise of mercy. And this promise must be gratuitous; for a conditional promise, which throws us back upon our works, promises life only insofar as we find it existing in ourselves. Therefore, if we would not have faith to waver and tremble, we must support it with the promise of salvation, which is offered by the Lord spontaneously and freely, from a regard to our misery rather than our worth.

Hence, the apostle bears this testimony to the gospel, that it is the word of faith. (See Romans 10:8.) This he concedes not either to the precepts or the promises of the Law, since there is nothing which can establish our faith, but that free embassy by which God reconciles the world to himself.

Hence, he often uses faith and the gospel as correlative terms, as when he says that the ministry of the Gospel was committed to him for "obedience to the faith;" that "it is the power of God unto salvation to everyone that believeth;" that "therein is the righteousness of God revealed from faith to faith" (Romans 1:5, 16, 17). No wonder: for because the Gospel is "the ministry of reconciliation" (2 Corinthians 5:18), there is no other sufficient evidence of the divine favor, such as faith requires knowing. Therefore, when we say that faith must rest on a free promise, we deny not that believers accept and embrace the Word of God in all its parts, but we point to the promise of mercy as its special object. Believers, indeed, ought to recognize God as the judge and avenger of wickedness; and yet mercy is the object to which they properly look, since He is exhibited to their contemplation as "good and ready to forgive," "plenteous in mercy," "slow to anger," "good to all," and shedding "his tender mercies over all his works." (See Psalm 86:5; 103:8; 145:8, 9.)

30 Faith not divided in thus seeking a Free Promise in the Gospel Reason. Conclusion confirmed by another reason.

I stay not to consider the rabid objections of Pighius, and others like-minded, who inveigh against this restriction, as rending faith, and laying hold of one of its fragments. I admit, as I have already said, that the general object of faith (as they express it) is the truth of God, whether He threatens or gives hope of His favor. Accordingly, the apostle attributes it to faith in Noah, that he feared the destruction of the world, when as yet it was not seen. (See Hebrews 11:17.)

If fear of impending punishment was a work of faith, threatening ought not to be excluded in defining it. This is indeed true; but we are unjustly and calumniously charged with denying that faith has respect to the whole Word of God. We only mean to maintain these two points: that faith is never decided until it attains to a free promise; and that the only way in which faith reconciles us to God is by uniting us with Christ. Both are deserving of notice. We are inquiring after a faith, which separates the children of God from the reprobates, believers from unbelievers. Shall every man, then, who believes that God is just in what He commands, and true in what He threatens, be on that account classed with believers? Very far from it. Faith, then, has no firm footing until it stands in the mercy of God. Then what end have we in view in discoursing of faith? Is it not that we may understand the way of salvation? But how can faith be saving, unless it grafts us into the Body of Christ? There is no absurdity, therefore, when, in defining it, we thus press its special object, and, by way of distinction, add to the generic character the particular mark, which distinguishes the believer from the unbeliever. In short, the malicious have nothing to carp at in this doctrine, unless they are to bring the same censure against the Apostle Paul, who specially designates the Gospel as "the word of faith" (Romans 10:8).

31 The Word of God, the prop and root of faith. The Word attests the divine goodness and mercy. In what sense faith has respect to the power of God. Various passages of Isaiah, inviting the godly to behold the power of God, explained. Other passages from David. We must beware of going beyond the limits prescribed by the Word, lest false zeal lead us astray, as it did Sarah, Rebekah, and Isaac. In this way, faith is obscured, though not extinguished. We must not depart one iota from the Word of God.

Hence, again we infer, as has already been explained, that faith has no less need of the Word than the fruit of a tree has of a living root; because, as David testifies, none can hope in God but those who know His name. (See Psalm 9:10). This knowledge, however, is not left to every man's imagination, but depends on the testimony which God himself gives to His goodness. The same Psalmist confirms this in another passage, "Thy salvation according to thy word" (Psalm 119:41). Again, "Save me," "I hoped in thy word" (Psalm 119:146; 147). Here we must attend to the relation of faith to the Word, and to salvation as its consequence. Still, however, we exclude not the power of God. If faith cannot support itself in the view of this power, it never will give Him the honor, which is due.

Paul seems to relate a trivial or very ordinary circumstance with regard to Abraham, when he says that he believed that God, who had given him the promise of a blessed seed, was able also to perform it. (See Romans 4:21.) And in like manner, in another passage, he says of himself, "I know whom I have believed, and am persuaded that he is able to keep that which I have committed unto him against that day" (2 Timothy 1:12). But let anyone consider with himself how he is always assailed with doubts in regard to the power of God, and he will readily perceive that those who duly magnify it have made no small progress in faith. We all acknowledge that God can do whatsoever He pleases; but while every temptation, even the most trivial, fills us with fear and dread, it is plain that we derogate from the power of God by attaching less importance to His promises than to Satan's threatening against them.

This is the reason that Isaiah, when he would impress on the hearts of the people the certainty of faith, discourses so magnificently of the boundless power of God. He often seems, after beginning to speak of the hope of pardon and reconciliation, to digress and unnecessarily take a long and circuitous course. He describes how wonderfully God rules the fabric of Heaven and Earth with the whole course of nature. Yet, he introduces nothing that is not appropriate to the occasion, because unless the power of God, to which all things are possible, is presented to our eye, our ears malignantly refuse admission to the Word or set no just value upon it. We may add that an effectual power is here meant; for piety, as it has elsewhere been seen, always makes a practical application of the power of God; in particular, keeps those works in view in which He has declared himself to be a Father.

Hence, the frequent mention in Scripture of redemption, from which the Israelites might learn that He who had once been the author of salvation would be its perpetual guardian. By his own example, David also reminds us that the benefits, which God has bestowed privately on any individual, tend to confirm his faith for the time to come. Nay, when God seems to have forsaken us, we ought to extend our view further, and take courage from His former favors. As is said in another Psalm, "I remember the days of old: I meditate on all thy works" (Psalm 143:5). Again "I will remember the works of the Lord; surely I will remember thy wonders of old" (Psalm 77:11). But because all our conceptions of the power and works of God are evanescent without the Word, we are not rash in maintaining that there is no faith until God presents us with clear evidence of His grace.

Here, however, a question might be raised as to the view to be taken of Sarah and Rebekah, both of whom, impelled as it would seem by zeal for the faith, went beyond the limits of the Word. Sarah, in her eager desire for the promised seed, gave her maid to her husband. That she sinned in many respects is not to be denied; but the only fault to which I now refer is her being carried away by zeal, and not confining herself within the limits prescribed by the Word. It is certain, however, that her desire proceeded from faith. Rebekah, again, divinely informed of the election of her son Jacob, procures the blessing for him by a wicked stratagem; deceives her husband, who was a witness and minister of divine grace; forces her son to lie; and corrupts divine truth by various frauds and impostures. In fine, by exposing His promise to scorn, she does all in her power to make it of no effect. Yet, this conduct, however vicious and reprehensible, was not devoid of faith. She must have overcome many obstacles before she obtained so strong a desire of that which, without any hope of earthly advantage, was full of difficulty and danger. In the same way, we cannot say that the holy patriarch Isaac was altogether void of faith, in that, after he had been similarly informed of the honor transferred to the younger son, he still continues his predilection in favor of his first-born, Esau.

These examples certainly show that error is often mingled with faith; and yet that when faith is real, it always obtains the preeminence. For as the particular error of Rebekah did not render the blessing of no effect, neither did it nullify the faith, which generally ruled in her mind, and was the principle and cause of that action. In this, nevertheless, Rebekah showed how prone the human mind is to turn aside whenever it gives itself the least indulgence. Though defect and infirmity obscure faith, they do not extinguish it. Still, they admonish us how carefully we ought to cling to the Word of God, and at the same time, confirm what we have taught—viz. that faith gives way when not supported by the Word, just as the minds of Sarah, Isaac, and Rebekah would have lost themselves in devious paths, had not the secret restraint of providence kept them obedient to the Word.

32 All the promises included in Christ. Two objections answered. A third objection drawn from example. Answer explaining the faith of Naaman, Cornelius, and the eunuch.

On the other hand, we have good ground for comprehending all the promises in Christ, since the apostle comprehends the whole gospel under the knowledge of Christ, and declares that all the promises of God are in Him yea and amen. The reason for this is obvious. Every promise which God makes is evidence of His goodwill. This is invariably true, and is not inconsistent with the fact, that the large benefits, which the divine liberality is constantly bestowing on the wicked, are preparing them for heavier judgment. As they neither think that these proceed from the hand of the Lord nor acknowledge them as His (or if they do so acknowledge them, never regard them as proofs of His favor), they are in no respect more instructed thereby in His mercy than brute beasts, which, according to their condition, enjoy the same liberality, and yet never look beyond it.

Still it is true, that by rejecting the promises generally offered to them, they subject themselves to severer punishment. For though it is only when the promises are received in faith that their efficacy is manifested, still their reality and power are never extinguished by our infidelity or ingratitude. Therefore, when the Lord by His promises invites us not only to enjoy the fruits of his kindness, but also to meditate upon them, He at the same time declares His love. Thus, we are brought back to our statement, that every promise is a manifestation of the divine favor toward us. Now, without controversy, God loves no man out of Christ. He is the beloved Son, in whom the love of the Father dwells, and from whom it afterwards extends to us.

Thus, Paul says, "In whom he has made us accepted in the Beloved" (Ephesians 1:6). It is by His intervention, therefore, that love is diffused to reach us. Accordingly, in another passage, the apostle calls Christ "our peace" (Ephesians 2:14), and represents him as the bond by which the Father is united to us in paternal affection. (See Romans 8:3). It follows that whenever any promise is made to us, we must turn our eyes toward Christ. Hence, with good reasons Paul declares that in him all the promises of God are confirmed and completed. (See Romans 15:8.)

Some examples are brought forward as repugnant to this view. When Naaman the Syrian made inquiry of the prophet as to the true mode of worshiping God, we cannot (it is said) suppose that he was informed of the Mediator, and yet he is commended for his piety. (See 2 Kings 5:17-19.) Nor could Cornelius, a Roman heathen, be acquainted with what was not known to all the Jews, and at best known obscurely. And yet, his alms and prayers were acceptable to God. (See Acts 10:31.) The prophet by his answer approved of the sacrifices of Naaman. In both, this must have been the result of faith. In like manner, the eunuch to whom Philip was sent, had he not been endued with some degree of faith, never would have incurred the fatigue and expense of a long and difficult journey to obtain an opportunity to worship. (See Acts 8:27, 31:) And yet we see how, when interrogated by Philip, he betrays his ignorance of the Mediator.

I admit that, in some respect, their faith was not explicit either as to the person of Christ, or the power and office assigned Him by the Father. Still it is certain that they were imbued with principles, which might give some, though a slender foretaste of Christ. This should not be thought strange, for the eunuch would not have hastened from a distant country to Jerusalem to an unknown God; nor could Cornelius, after having once embraced the Jewish religion, have lived so long in Judea without becoming acquainted with the rudiments of sound doctrine.

In regard to Naaman, it is absurd to suppose that Elisha, while he gave him many minute precepts, said nothing of the principal matter. Therefore, although their knowledge of Christ may have been obscure, we cannot suppose that they had no such knowledge at all. They used the sacrifices of the Law, and must have distinguished them from the spurious sacrifices of the Gentiles, by the end to which they referred—viz. Christ.

33 Faith revealed to our minds and sealed on our hearts by the Holy Spirit. A. The mind is purified to have a relish for divine truth. B. The mind is thus established in the truth by the agency of the Holy Spirit.

A simple external manifestation of the Word ought to be amply sufficient to produce faith, if our blindness and perverseness did not prevent this. But such is the proneness of our mind to vanity that it can never adhere to the truth of God, and such its dullness, that it is always blind even in His light. Hence, without the illumination of the Spirit, the Word has no effect; and hence it is obvious that faith is something higher than human understanding. Nor were it sufficient for the mind to be illumined by the Spirit of God unless the heart also were strengthened and supported by his power. Here the Schoolmen go completely astray, dwelling entirely in their consideration of faith, on the bare, simple assent of the understanding, and altogether overlooking confidence and security of heart.

Faith is the special gift of God in both ways—in purifying the mind to give it a relish for divine truth, and afterwards in establishing it therein. For the Spirit does not merely originate faith, but gradually increases it, until by its means He conducts us into the heavenly kingdom. "That good thing which was committed unto thee," says Paul, "keep by the Holy Ghost which dwelleth in us" (2 Timothy 1:14).

In what sense Paul says (see Galatians 3:2) that the Spirit is given by the hearing of faith, may be easily explained. If there were only a single gift of the Spirit, He, who is the author and cause of faith, could not, without absurdity, be said to be its effect. But after celebrating the gifts with which God adorns His church, and by successive additions of faith, leads it to perfection, there is nothing strange in His ascribing to faith the very gifts which faith prepares us for receiving. It seems to some paradoxical when it is said that none can believe Christ except those to whom it is given, but this is partly because they do not observe how recondite and sublime heavenly wisdom is, or how dull the mind of man is in discerning divine mysteries. It is partly because they pay no regard to that firm and stable constancy of heart, which is the chief part of faith.

34 Proof of the former. A. By reason. B. By Scripture. C. By example. D. By analogy.

Paul argues, "What man knoweth the things of a man, save the spirit of man which is in him? Even so the things of God knoweth no man but the Spirit of God" (1 Corinthians 2:11). If in regard to divine truth we hesitate even as to those things which we see with the bodily eye, how can we be firm and steadfast in regard to those divine promises which neither the eye sees nor the mind comprehends? Here human discernment is so defective and lost that the first step of advancement in the school of Christ is to renounce it. (See Matthew 11:25; Luke 10:21.) As a veil interposed, it prevents us from beholding divine masteries, which are revealed only to babes. "Flesh and blood" does not reveal them (See Matthew 16:17.) "The natural man receiveth not the things of the Spirit of God: for they are foolishness unto him; neither can he know them, for they are spiritually discerned" (1 Corinthians 2:14). The supplies of the Holy Spirit are therefore necessary. His agency is here the only strength. "For who has known the mind of the Lord? Or who has been his counselor?" (Romans 11:34); but "The Spirit searcheth all things, yea, the deep things of God" (1 Corinthians 2:10). Thus it is that we attain to the mind of Christ: "No man can come to me, except the Father which has sent me draw him: and I will raise him up at the last day." "Every man therefore that has heard, and learned of the Father, cometh unto me. Not that any man has seen the Father, save he which is of God, he has seen the Father" (John 6:44, 45, 46).

Therefore, as we cannot possibly come to Christ unless drawn by the Spirit, so when we are drawn, we are both in mind and spirit exalted far above our own understanding. For the soul, when illumined by Him, receives a new eye, enabling it to contemplate heavenly mysteries by the splendor of which it was previously dazzled. Thus, indeed, it is only when the human intellect is irradiated by the light of the Holy Spirit that it begins to have a taste of those things, which pertain to the Kingdom of God; previously it was too stupid and senseless to have any relish for them. Hence, our Savior, when clearly declaring the mysteries of the Kingdom to the two disciples, makes no impression until he opens their minds to understand the Scriptures (See Luke 24:27, 45.)

Hence, also, though He had taught the apostles with His own divine lips, it was still necessary to send the Spirit of truth to instill into their minds the same doctrine, which they had heard with their ears. The Word is, in regard to those to whom it is preached, like the sun, which shines upon all, but is of no use to the blind. In this matter we are all naturally blind; and hence the Word cannot penetrate our minds unless the Spirit, that internal teacher, by His enlightening power makes an entrance for it.

35 E. By the excellent qualities of faith. F. By a celebrated passage from Augustine.

Having elsewhere shown more fully, when treating of the corruption of our nature, how little able men are to believe (Book 2, chapters 2, 3), I will not fatigue the reader by again repeating it. Let it suffice to observe that the spirit of faith is used by Paul as being synonymous with the very faith which we receive from the Spirit, but which we do not have naturally. (See 2 Corinthians 4:13.) Accordingly, he prays for the Thessalonians, "that our God would count you worthy of this calling, and fulfill all the good pleasure of his goodness, and the work of faith with power" (2 Thessalonians 1:2). Here, by designating faith to be the work of God, and distinguishing it by way of epithet, appropriately calling it His *good pleasure*, he declares that it is not of man's own nature; and not contented with this, he adds that it is an illustration of divine power. In addressing the Corinthians, when he tells them that faith stands not "in the wisdom of man, but in the power of God" (1 Corinthians 2:4), he is no doubt speaking of external miracles; but as the reprobate are blinded when they behold them, he also includes that internal seal of which he elsewhere makes mention.

Moreover, the better to display His liberality in this most excellent gift, God does not bestow it upon all promiscuously, but, by special privilege, He imparts it to whomever He will. To this effect, we have already quoted passages of Scripture, as to which Augustine, their faithful expositor, exclaims, "Our Savior, to teach that faith in Him is a gift, not a merit, says, No man can come to me, except the Father, which has sent me, draw him, (John 6:44). It is strange when two persons hear, the one despises, and the other ascends. Let him who despises impute it to himself; let him who ascends not arrogate it to himself." In another passage he asks, "Wherefore is it given to the one, and not to the other? I am not ashamed to say, This is one of the deep things of the cross. From some unknown depth of the judgments of God, which we cannot scrutinize, all our ability proceeds. I see that I am able; but how I am able, I see not—this far only I see that it is of God. But why the one, and not the other? This is too great for me: it is an abyss, a depth of the cross. I can cry out with wonder; not discuss and demonstrate." The whole comes to this, that Christ, when He produces faith in us by the agency of His Spirit, at the same time engrafts us into His body, that we may become partakers of all blessings.

36 Proof of the latter by the argument a minore ad majus. Why the Spirit is called a seal, an earnest, and the Spirit of promise.

The next thing necessary is that what the mind has imbibed be transferred into the heart. The Word is not received in faith when it merely flutters in the brain, but when it has taken deep root in the heart, and has become an invincible bulwark to withstand and repel all the assaults of temptation. But if the illumination of the Spirit is the true source of understanding in the intellect, much more manifest is his agency in the confirmation of the heart; inasmuch as there is more distrust in the heart than blindness in the mind; and it is more difficult to inspire the soul with security than to imbue it with knowledge. Hence, the Spirit performs the part of a seal, sealing upon our hearts the very promises, the certainty of which was previously impressed upon our minds. It also serves as an earnest in establishing and confirming these promises. Thus the apostle says, "In whom also, after that ye believed, ye were sealed with that Holy Spirit of promise, which is the earnest of our inheritance" (Ephesians 1:13, 14). You see how he teaches that the hearts of believers are stamped with the Spirit as with a seal, and calls it the Spirit of promise, because it ratifies the gospel to us. In like manner, he says to the Corinthians, "God has also sealed us, and given the earnest of the Spirit in our hearts" (2 Corinthians 1:22). Again, when speaking of a full and confident hope, he founds it on the "earnest of the Spirit" (2 Corinthians 5:5).

37 Believers sometimes shaken, but not to perish finally. They ultimately overcome their trials, and remain steadfast. Proofs from Scripture.

I am not forgetting what I formerly said, and experience brings daily to remembrance—viz. that faith is subject to various doubts, so that the minds of believers are seldom at rest, or at least are not always tranquil. Still, whatever be the engines by which they are shaken, they either escape from the whirlpool of temptation or remain steadfast in their place. Faith finds security and protection in the words of the Psalm, "God is our refuge and strength, a very present help in trouble; therefore will not we fear, though the earth be removed, and the mountains be carried into the midst of the sea" (Psalm 46:1, 2). This delightful tranquility is elsewhere described: "I laid me down and slept; I awaked, for the Lord sustained me" (Psalm 3:5). Not that David was uniformly in this joyful frame; but as far as the measure of his faith made him sensible of the divine favor, he glories in intrepidly despising everything that could disturb his peace of mind. Hence, the Scripture, when it exhorts us to faith, bids us be at peace. In Isaiah it is said, "In quietness and in confidence shall be your strength" (Isaiah 30:15); and in the Psalm, "Rest in the Lord, and wait patiently for him." Corresponding to this is the passage in the Hebrews, "Ye have need of patience," etc (Hebrews 10:36).

38 Objection of the Schoolmen. Answer. Attempt to support the objection by a passage in Ecclesiastes. Answer, explaining the meaning of the passage.

Hence, we may judge how pernicious is the Scholastic dogma, that we can have no stronger evidence of the divine favor toward us than moral conjecture, according as each individual deems himself not unworthy of it. Doubtless, if we are to determine by our works in what way the Lord stands affected towards us, I admit that we cannot even get the length of a feeble conjecture: but since faith should accord with the free and simple promise, there is no room left for ambiguity. With what kind of confidence, pray, shall we be armed if we reason in this way—God is propitious to us, provided we deserve it by the purity of our lives? But since we have reserved this subject for discussion in its proper place, we shall not prosecute it further at present, especially seeing it is already plain that nothing is more adverse to faith than conjecture, or any other feeling akin to doubt. Nothing can be worse than their perversion of the passage of Ecclesiastes, which is ever in their mouths: "No man knoweth either love or hatred by all that is before them" (Ecclesiastes 9:1). I do not insist that the passage is erroneously rendered in the common version. Even a child cannot fail to perceive what Solomon's meaning is—viz. that "All things come alike to all" "to him that sacrificeth, and to him that sacrificeth not." God does not always declare His love to those on whom He bestows uninterrupted prosperity, nor his hatred against those whom He afflicts. And it tends to prove the vanity of the human intellect, that it is so completely in the dark as to matters, which it is of the highest importance to know. Thus Solomon had said a little before, "That which befalleth the sons of men befalleth beasts; even one thing befalleth them: as the one dieth, so dieth the other" (Ecclesiastes 3:19). Would not anyone be deemed insane to imply that we hold the immortality of the soul by conjecture merely? Are those then sane who cannot obtain any certainty of the divine favor, because the carnal eye is now unable to discern it from the present appearance of the world?

39 Another objection, charging the elect in Christ with rashness and presumption. Answer. Answer confirmed by various passages from the Apostle Paul. Also from John and Isaiah.

But, they say, it is rash and presumptuous to pretend to have an undoubted knowledge of the divine will. I would grant this, did we hold that we were able to subject the incomprehensible counsel of God to our feeble intellect. But when we simply say with Paul, "We have received not the spirit of the world, but the Spirit which is of God; that we might know the things that are freely given to us of God" (1 Corinthians 2:12), what can they oppose to this, without offering insult to the Spirit of God? But if it is a sacrilege to charge the revelation, which He has given us with falsehood, or uncertainty, or ambiguity, how can we be wrong in maintaining its certainty? But they still exclaim that there is great temerity in our presuming to glory in possessing the Spirit of God. Who could believe that these men, who desire to be thought the masters of the world, could be so stupid as to err thus grossly in the very first principles of religion? To me, indeed, it would be incredible, did not their own writings make it manifest.

Paul declares that those only are the sons of God who are led by His Spirit (see Romans 8:14); these men would have those who are the sons of God be led by their own and void of the divine Spirit. He tells us that we call God our Father in terms dictated by the Spirit, who alone bears witness with our spirit that we are the sons of God (see Romans 8:16); they, though they forbid us not to invoke God, withdraw the Spirit, by whose guidance He is duly invoked. He declares that those only are the servants of Christ who are led by the Spirit of Christ (Romans 8:9); they imagine a Christianity, which has no need of the Spirit of Christ. He holds out the hope of a blessed resurrection to those only who feel His Spirit dwelling in them (see Romans 8:11); they imagine hope when there is no such feeling. But perhaps they will say that they deny not the necessity of being endued with the Spirit, but only hold it to be the part of modesty and humility not to recognize it.

What, then, does Paul mean, when he says to the Corinthians, "Examine yourselves whether ye be in the faith: prove your own selves. Know ye not your own selves, that Jesus Christ is in you, except ye be reprobates?" (2 Corinthians 13:5). John, moreover, says, "Hereby we know that he abideth in us by the Spirit which he has given us" (1 John 3:24). And what else is it than to bring the promises of Christ into doubt, when we would be deemed servants of Christ without having His Spirit, whom He declared that He would pour out on all His people? (Isaiah 44:3).

What! Do we not insult the Holy Spirit, when we separate faith, which is His peculiar work, from himself? These being the first rudiments of religion, it is the most wretched blindness to charge Christians with arrogance for presuming to glory in the presence of the Holy Spirit—a glorying without which Christianity itself does not exist. The example of these men illustrates the truth of our Savior's declaration, that his Spirit "the world cannot receive, because it seeth him not, neither knoweth him; but ye know him, for he dwelleth with you, and shall be in you" (John 14:17).

39 Another objection, charging the elect in Christ with rashness and presumption. Answer. Answer confirmed by various passages from the Apostle Paul. Also from John and Isaiah.

That they may not attempt to undermine the certainty of faith in one direction only, they attack it in another—viz. that though it be lawful for the believer, from his actual state of righteousness, to form a judgment as to the favor of God, the knowledge of final perseverance still remains in suspense. An admirable security, indeed, is left us, if, for the present moment only, we can judge from moral conjecture that we are in grace, but know not how we are to be tomorrow! Very different is the language of the apostle: "I am persuaded that neither death, nor life, nor angels, nor principalities, nor powers, nor things present, nor things to come, nor height, nor depth, nor any other creature, shall be able to separate us from the love of God, which is in Christ Jesus our Lord" (Romans 8:38). They endeavor to evade the force of this by frivolously pretending that the apostle had this assurance by special revelation. They are too well caught thus to escape; for in that passage he is treating not of his individual experience, but of the blessings which all believers in common derive from faith. Then Paul in another passage alarms us by the mention of our weakness and inconstancy, "Let him that thinketh he standeth take heed lest he fall" (1 Corinthians 10:12). True but this he says not to inspire us with terror, but that we may learn to humble ourselves under the mighty hand of God, as Peter explains. (See 1 Peter 5:6.) Then how preposterous is it to limit the certainty of faith to a point of time, seeing it is the property of faith to pass beyond the whole course of this life, and stretch forward to a future immortality? Therefore, since believers owe it to the favor of God, that, enlightened by His Spirit, they, through faith, enjoy the prospect of heavenly life; there is so far from an approach to arrogance in each glorying, that anyone ashamed to confess it, instead of testifying modesty or submission, rather betrays extreme ingratitude, by maliciously suppressing the divine goodness.

40 A third objection, impugning the final perseverance of the elect. Answer by an apostle. Summary of the refutation.

Since the nature of faith could not be better or more clearly evinced than by the substance of the promise on which it leans as its proper foundation, and without which it immediately falls or rather vanishes away, we have derived our definition from it—a definition, however, not at all at variance with that definition or description, which the apostle accommodates to his discourse, when he says that faith is "The substance of things hoped for, the evidence of things not seen" (Hebrews 11:1). By interpreting the Greek term as, "substance," he means a kind of prop on which the pious mind rests and leans. Interpreted this way, he says that faith is a kind of certain and secure possession of those things that are promised to us by God, unless we prefer interpreting the Greek word for substance as "confidence."

I have no objection to this, though I am more inclined to adopt the other interpretation, which is more generally accepted. Again, to intimate that until the last day, when the books will be opened (see Daniel 7:10; Revelation 20:12), the things pertaining to our salvation are too lofty to be perceived by our senses, seen by our eyes, or handled by our hands, and that in the meantime there is no possible way in which these can be possessed by us, unless we can transcend the reach of our own intellect, and raise our eyes above all worldly objects; in short, surpass ourselves, he adds that this certainty of possession relates to things which are only hoped for, and therefore not seen. For as Paul says (Romans 8:24), "A hope that is seen is not hope," that we "hope for that we see not." When he calls it the evidence or proof, or, as Augustine repeatedly renders it, the conviction of things not present, the Greek term being "substance," it is the same as if he had called it the appearance of things not apparent, the sight of things not seen, the clearness of things obscure, the presence of things absent, the manifestation of things hid.

The mysteries of God (and to this class belong the things which pertain to our salvation) cannot be discerned in themselves, or, as it is expressed, in their own nature; but we behold them only in His Word, of the truth of which we ought to be as firmly persuaded as if we held that everything which it says were done and completed. But how can the mind rise to such a perception and foretaste of the divine goodness, without being at the same time wholly inflamed with love for God? The abundance of joy which God has treasured up for those who fear Him cannot be truly known without making a most powerful impression. He who is thus once affected is raised and carried entirely towards Him.

Hence, it is not strange that no sinister, perverse heart ever experiences this feeling, by which, transported to Heaven itself, we are admitted to the most hidden treasures of God, and the holiest recesses of His kingdom, which must not be profaned by the entrance of a heart that is impure. For what the Schoolmen say as to the priority of love to faith and hope is a mere dream, since it is faith alone that first engenders love. How much better is Bernard who wrote, "The testimony of conscience, which Paul calls 'the rejoicing' of believers, I believe to consist in three things. It is necessary, first of all, to believe that you cannot have remission of sins except by the indulgence of God; secondly, that you cannot have any good work at all unless He also give it; lastly, that you cannot by any works merit eternal life unless it also be freely given." Shortly after he adds, "These things are not sufficient, but are a kind of commencement of faith; for while believing that your sins can only be forgiven by God, you must also hold that they are not forgiven until persuaded by the testimony of the Holy Spirit that salvation is treasured up for us; that as God pardons sins, and gives merits, and after merits rewards, you cannot halt at that beginning." But these and other topics will be considered in their own place; let it suffice at present to understand what faith is.

41 The definition of faith accords with that given by the apostle in the Hebrews. Explanation of this definition. Refutation of the scholastic error, that charity is prior to faith and hope.

Wherever this living faith exists, it must have the hope of eternal life as its inseparable companion, or rather must of itself beget and manifest it; where it is wanting, however clearly and elegantly we may discourse of faith, it is certain we have it not. For if faith is a firm persuasion of the truth of God—a persuasion that it can never be false, never deceive, and never be in vain, then those who have received this assurance must at the same time expect that God will perform His promises. In their conviction, these are true, so that in one word, "hope" is nothing more than the expectation of those things which faith previously believes to have been truly promised by God.

Thus, faith believes that God is true; hope expects that in due season He will manifest his truth. Faith believes that He is our Father;

hope expects that He will always act the part of a Father towards us. Faith believes that eternal life has been given to us; hope expects that it will one day be revealed. Faith is the foundation on which hope rests; hope nourishes and sustains faith. For as no man can expect anything from God without previously believing His promises, so, on the other hand, the weakness of our faith, which might grow weary and fall away, must be supported and cherished by patient hope and expectation. For this reason Paul justly says, "We are saved by hope" (Romans 8:24). For while hope silently waits for the Lord, it restrains faith from hastening on with too much precipitation, confirms it when it might waver in regard to the promises of God or begin to doubt their truth, refreshes it when it might be fatigued, and extends its view to the final goal, so as not to allow it to give up in the middle of the course, or at the very outset.

In short, by constantly renovating and reviving, it is always furnishing more vigor for perseverance. On the whole, how necessary the reinforcements of hope are to establish faith will better appear if we reflect on the numerous forms of temptation by which those who have embraced the Word of God are assailed and shaken. First, the Lord often keeps us in suspense, by delaying the fulfillment of His promises much longer than we could wish. Here the office of hope is to perform what the prophet enjoins, "Though it tarry, wait for it" (Habakkuk 2:3). Sometimes He not only permits faith to grow languid, but also even openly manifests His displeasure. Here there is still greater necessity for the aid of hope, that we may be able to say with another prophet, "I will wait upon the Lord that hideth his face from the house of Jacob, and I will look for him" (Isaiah 8:17).

Scoffers also rise up, as Peter tells us, and ask, "Where is the promise of his coming? For since the fathers fell asleep, all things continue as they were from the beginning of the creation" (2 Peter 3:4). Nay, the world and the flesh insinuate the same thing. Here faith must be supported by the patience of hope, and fixed on the contemplation of eternity, considering that "One day is with the Lord as a thousand years, and a thousand years as one day" (2 Peter 3:8; Psalm 90:4).

42 Hope the inseparable attendant of true faith. Reason. Connection between faith and hope. Mutually support each other. Obvious from the various forms of temptation, that the aid of hope is necessary to establish faith.

On account of this connection and affinity, the Scripture sometimes confounds the two terms faith and hope. For when Peter says that we are "...kept by the power of God through faith until salvation, ready to be revealed in the last times" (1 Peter 1:5), he attributes to faith what more properly belongs to hope. And not without cause, since we have already shown that hope is nothing else than the food and strength of faith. Sometimes the two are joined together, as in the same epistles "That your faith and hope might be in God" (1 Peter 1:21). Paul, again, in the Epistle to the Philippians, from hope deduces expectation (see Philippians 1:20), because in hoping patiently we suspend our wishes until God manifests His own time. The whole of this subject may be better understood from the tenth chapter of the Epistle to the Hebrews, to which I have already referred. Paul, in another passage, though not in strict propriety of speech, expresses the same thing in these words, "For we through the Spirit wait for the hope of righteousness by faith" (Galatians 5:5); that is, after embracing the testimony of the gospel as to a love that is free, we wait until God openly manifests what is now only an object of hope.

It is now obvious how absurdly Peter Lombard lays down a double foundation of hope—viz. the grace of God and the merit of works. Hope cannot have any other object than faith has. But we have already shown clearly that the only object of faith is the mercy of God, to which, to use the common expression, it must look with both eyes. But it is worthwhile to listen to the strange reason, which he adduces. If you presume, says he, to hope for anything without merit, it should not be called hope, but presumption. Who, dear reader, does not execrate the gross stupidity, which calls it rashness, and presumption to confide in the truth of God? The Lord desires us to expect everything from His goodness and yet these men tell us, it is presumption to rest in it. O teacher, worthy of the pupils, whom you found in these insane, raving schools! Because, by the oracles of God, sinners are enjoined to entertain the hope of salvation, let us willingly presume so far on His truth as to cast away all confidence in our works, and trusting in His mercy, venture to hope. He who has said, "According to your faith be it unto you" (Matthew 9:29), will never deceive.

Chapter 3

REGENERATION BY FAITH. OF REPENTANCE

This chapter is divided into five parts. I. The title of the chapter seems to promise a treatise on faith, but the only subject here considered is repentance, the inseparable attendant of faith. And, first, various opinions on the subject of repentance are stated, sections 1-4. II. An exposition of the orthodox doctrine of repentance, sections 5-9. III. Reasons why repentance must be prolonged to the last moment of life, section 10-14. IV. Of the fruits of repentance, or its object and tendency, sections 15-20. V. The source whence repentance proceeds, sections 21-24. Of the sin against the Holy Spirit, and the impenitence of the reprobate, section 25.

Sections

1. Connection of this chapter with the previous one and the subsequent chapters. Repentance follows faith, and is produced by it. Reason. Error of those who take a contrary view.

2. Their First Objection. Answer. In what sense the origin of repentance is ascribed to faith. Cause of the erroneous idea that faith is produced by repentance. Refutation of it. The hypocrisy of monks and Anabaptists in assigning limits to repentance exposed.

3. A second opinion concerning repentance considered.

4. A third opinion, assigning two forms to repentance, a legal and an evangelical. Examples of each.

5. The orthodox doctrine of repentance. A. Faith and repentance to be distinguished, not confounded or separated. B. A consideration of the name. C. A definition of the thing, or what repentance is. Doctrine of the prophets and apostles.

6. Explanation of the definition. This consists of three parts. Repentance (first part) is a turning of our life unto God. This is described and enlarged upon.

7. *Repentance (second part) produced by fear of God. Hence, the mention of divine judgment by the prophets and apostles. Example. Exposition of the second branch of the definition from a passage in Paul. Why the fear of God is the first part of repentance.*

8. *Repentance (third part) consists in the mortification of the flesh and the quickening of the Spirit. These are required by the Prophets. They are explained separately.*

9. *How this mortification and quickening are produced. Repentance is just a renewal of the divine image in us. It is not completed in a moment, but extends to the last moment of life.*

10. *Reasons why repentance must so extend. Augustine's opinion as to concupiscence in the regenerate examined. A passage of Paul, which seems to confirm that opinion.*

11. *Answer. Confirmation of the answer by the apostle himself. Another confirmation from a precept of the Law. Conclusion.*

12. *Exception, that those desires only are condemned, which are repugnant to the order of God. Desires not condemned insofar as they are natural, but insofar as they are inordinate. This held by Augustine.*

13. *Passages from Augustine to show that this was his opinion. Objection from a passage in James.*

14. *Another objection of the Anabaptists and libertines to the continuance of repentance throughout the present life. An answer disclosing its impiety. Another answer, founded on the absurdities to which it leads. A third answer, contrasting sincere Christian repentance with the erroneous view of the objectors. Conformation from the example and declaration of an apostle.*

15. *Of the fruits of repentance. Carefulness. Excuse. Indignation. Fear. Desire. Zeal. Revenge. Moderation to be observed, as most sagely counseled by Bernard.*

16. *Internal fruits of repentance. A. Piety towards God. B. Charity towards man. C. Purity of life. How carefully these fruits are commended by the prophets. External fruits of repentance. Bodily exercises too much commended by ancient writers. Twofold excess in regard to them.*

17. Delusion of some who consider these external exercises as the chief part of repentance. Why received in the Jewish church. The legitimate use of these exercises in the Christian Church.

18. The principal part of repentance consists in turning to God. Confession and acknowledgment of sins. What their nature should be. Distinction between ordinary and special repentance. Use of this distinction.

19. End of repentance. Its nature is shown by the preaching of John Baptist, our Savior, and His apostles. The sum of this preaching.

20. Christian repentance terminates with the end of our life.

21. Repentance has its origin in the grace of God, as communicated to the elect, whom God is pleased to save from death. The hardening and final impenitence of the reprobate. A passage of an apostle as to voluntary reprobates gives no countenance to the Novatians.

22. Of the sin against the Holy Ghost. The true definition of this sin as proved and explained by Scripture. Who they are that sin against the Holy Spirit. Examples: A. The Jews resisting Stephen. B. The Pharisees. Definition confirmed by the example of Paul.

23. Why that sin is unpardonable. The paralogism of the Novatians in wresting the words of the apostle examined. Two passages from the same apostle.

24. First objection to the above doctrine. Answer. Solution of a difficulty founded on the example of Esau and the threatening of a prophet. Second objection.

25. Third objection, founded on the seeming approval of the feigned repentance of the ungodly, as Ahab. Answer. Confirmation from the example of Esau. Why God bears for a time with the ungodly, pretending repentance. Exception.

1 **Connection of this chapter with the previous one and the subsequent chapters. Repentance follows faith, and is produced by it. Reason. Error of those who take a contrary view.**

Although we have already in some measure shown how faith possesses Christ, and gives us the enjoyment of His benefits, the subject would still be obscure were we not to add an exposition of the effects resulting from it. For good reason, the sum of the gospel is made to consist in repentance and forgiveness of sins; and, therefore, where these two heads are omitted, any discussion concerning faith will be meager and defective, and indeed almost useless. Now, since Christ confers upon us, and we obtain by faith, both free reconciliation and newness of life, reason and order require that I should here begin to treat of both. The shortest transition, however, will be from faith to repentance for repentance being properly understood it will better appear how a man is justified freely by faith alone, and yet that holiness of life, *real* holiness, as it is called, is inseparable from the free imputation of righteousness. That repentance not only always follows faith, but is produced by it, ought to be without controversy. Since pardon and forgiveness are offered by the preaching of the gospel in order that the sinner—delivered from the tyranny of Satan, the yoke of sin, and the miserable bondage of iniquity—may pass into the Kingdom of God, it is certain that no man can embrace the grace of the gospel without retaking himself from the errors of his former life into the right path, and making it his whole study to practice repentance. Those who think that repentance precedes faith instead of flowing from it, or being produced by it, as the fruit by the tree, have never understood its nature, and are moved to adopt that view on insufficient grounds.

2 Their first objection. Answer. In what sense the origin of repentance is ascribed to faith. Cause of the erroneous idea that faith is produced by repentance. Refutation of it. The hypocrisy of monks and Anabaptists in assigning limits to repentance exposed.

Christ and John, it is said, in their discourses, first exhort the people to repentance, and then add that the kingdom of heaven is at hand. (See Matthew 3:2; 4:17.) Such, too, is the message, which the apostles received and such the course which Paul followed, as is narrated by Luke. (See Acts 20:21.) But clinging superstitiously to the juxtaposition of the syllables, they attend not to the coherence of meaning in the words. For when our Lord and John began their preaching thusly, "Repent, for the kingdom of heaven is at hand" (Matthew 3:2), do they not deduce repentance because of the offer of grace and promise of salvation? The force of the words, therefore, is the same as if it were said, "As the kingdom of heaven is at hand, for that reason repent." For Matthew, after relating that John so preached, says that therein was fulfilled the prophecy concerning the voice of one crying in the desert, "Prepare ye the way of the Lord, make straight in the desert a highway for our God" (Isaiah 40:3). That voice is ordered to commence with consolation and glad tidings. Still, when we attribute the origin of repentance to faith, we do not dream of some period of time in which faith is to give birth to it: we only wish to show that a man cannot seriously engage in repentance unless he knows that he is of God.

However, no man is truly persuaded that he is of God until he has embraced His offered favor. These things will be more clearly explained as we proceed. Some are perhaps misled by this, that not a few are subdued by terror of conscience, or disposed to obedience before they have been imbued with knowledge, nay, before they have had any taste of the divine favor. This is that initial fear which some writers class among the virtues, because they think it approximates to true and genuine obedience. But we are not here considering the various modes in which Christ draws us to himself or prepares us for the study of piety. All I say is, that no righteousness can be found where the Spirit, whom Christ received in order to communicate it to His members, reigns not.

Then, according to the passage in the Psalms, "There is forgiveness with thee, that thou mayest be feared" (Psalm 130:4), and no man will ever reverence God who does not trust that God is propitious to him, no man will ever willingly set himself to observe the Law who is not persuaded that his services are pleasing to God. The indulgence of God in tolerating and pardoning our iniquities is a sign of paternal favor. This is also clear from the exhortation in Hosea, "Come, and let us return unto the Lord: for he has torn, and he will heal us; he has smitten, and he will bind us up" (Hosea 6:1) The hope of pardon is employed as a stimulus to prevent us from becoming reckless in sin. But there is no semblance of reason in the absurd procedure of those who, that they may begin with repentance, prescribe to their neophytes certain days during which they are to exercise themselves in repentance, and after these are elapsed, admit them to communion in gospel grace.

I allude to great numbers of Anabaptists, those of them especially who please themselves on being spiritual, and their associates, the Jesuits, and others of the same stamp. Such are the fruits, produced by their giddy spirits: that repentance, which in every Christian man lasts as long as life, is completed in a few short days with them.

3 A second opinion concerning repentance considered.

Certain learned men, who lived long before the present days and were desirous to speak simply and sincerely according to the rule of Scripture, held that repentance consists of two parts: mortification and quickening. By mortification they meant grief of soul and terror, produced by a conviction of sin and a sense of the divine judgment. For when a man is brought to a true knowledge of sin, he begins truly to hate and detest sin. He also is sincerely dissatisfied with himself, confesses that he is lost and undone, and wishes he were different from what he is.

Moreover, when he is touched with some sense of the divine justice (for the one conviction immediately follows the other), he lies terror-struck and amazed, humbled and dejected, and he desponds and despairs. This, which they regarded as the first part of repentance, they usually termed *contrition*. By "quickening" they mean the comfort which is produced by faith, as when a man prostrated by a consciousness of sin and smitten with the fear of God. Afterwards, he beholds His goodness, and the mercy, grace, and salvation obtained through Christ, looks up, begins to breathe, takes courage, and passes from death unto life. I admit that these terms, when rightly interpreted, aptly enough express the power of repentance; only I cannot assent to their using the term *quickening*, for the joy that the soul feels after being calmed from perturbation and fear is not quickened. It more properly means that desire of pious and holy living, which springs from the new birth, as if it were said that the man dies to himself, that he may begin to live unto God.

4 A third opinion, assigning two forms to repentance, a legal and an evangelical. Examples of each.

Others, seeing that the term is used in Scripture in different senses, have set down two forms of repentance, and, in order to distinguish them, have called the one legal repentance: The sinner, stung with a sense of his sin and overwhelmed with fear of the divine anger, remains in that state of perturbation and is unable to escape from it.

The other is evangelical repentance. The sinner, though grievously downcast in himself, looks up and sees in Christ the cure for his wound, the solace of his terror, and the haven of rest from his misery. They give Cain, Saul, and Judas as examples of legal repentance. Scripture, in describing their repentance, means that they perceived the heinousness of their sins and dreaded the divine anger, but, thinking only of God as a judge and avenger, were overwhelmed by the thought. Their repentance, therefore, was nothing better than a kind of threshold into hell, into which having entered even in the present life, they began to endure the punishment inflicted by the presence of an offended God. Examples of evangelical repentance we see in all those who, first stung with a sense of sin, but afterwards raised and revived by confidence in the divine mercy, turned unto the Lord. Hezekiah was frightened on receiving the message of his death, but praying with tears, and beholding the divine goodness, regained his confidence. The Ninevites were terrified at the fearful announcement of their destruction; but clothing themselves in sackcloth and ashes, they prayed, hoping that the Lord might relent and avert His anger from them. David confessed that he had sinned greatly in numbering the people, but added, "Now, I beseech thee O Lord, take away the iniquity of thy servant." When rebuked by Nathan, he acknowledged the crime of adultery, and humbled himself before the Lord; but he, at the same time, looked for pardon.

Similar was the repentance of those who, stung to the heart by the preaching of Peter, yet trusted in the divine goodness, and added, "Men and brethren, what shall we do?" Similar was the case of Peter himself, who indeed wept bitterly, but ceased not to hope.

5 The orthodox doctrine of repentance. A. Faith and repentance to be distinguished, not confounded or separated. B. A consideration of the name. C. A definition of what repentance is. Doctrine of the prophets and apostles.

Though all this is true, the term *repentance* (insofar as I can ascertain from Scripture) must be differently taken. For in comprehending faith under repentance, they are at variance with what Paul says in the Acts, as to his "testifying both to the Jews and also to the Greeks, repentance toward God, and faith toward our Lord Jesus Christ" (Acts 20:21). Here he mentions faith and repentance as two different things. What then? Can true repentance exist without faith? By no means. But although they cannot be separated, they ought to be distinguished. As there is no faith without hope, and yet faith and hope are different, so repentance and faith, though constantly linked together, are only to be united, not confounded.

I am aware that under the term *repentance* is comprehended the whole work of turning to God, of which not the least important part is faith; but in what sense this is done will be perfectly obvious when its nature and power shall have been explained. The term repentance is derived in the Hebrew from "conversion," or turning again; and in the Greek from a change of mind and purpose; nor it inappropriate to both derivations, for it is substantially this, that withdrawing from ourselves we turn to God, and laying aside the old, we put on a new mind. Wherefore, it seems to me, that repentance may be not inappropriately defined as being real conversion of our life unto God, proceeding from a sincere and serious fear of God, and consisting in the mortification of our flesh and the old man, and the quickening of the Spirit. In this sense are to be understood all those addresses in which the prophets first, and the apostles afterwards, exhorted the people of their time to repent. The great object for which they labored was to fill them with confusion for their sins and dread of the divine judgment, that they might fall down and humble themselves before Him whom they had offended, and, with true repentance, retake themselves to the right path. Accordingly, they use indiscriminately in the same sense, the expressions turning (or returning) to the Lord, and repenting (doing repentance). Whence, also, the sacred history describes it as repentance towards God, when men who disregarded Him and continued in their lusts begin to obey His Word, and are prepared to go whithersoever He may call them. And John Baptist and Paul, under the expression, bringing forth fruits meet for repentance, described a course of life exhibiting and bearing testimony, in all its actions, to such a repentance.

6 Explanation of the definition. This consists of three parts. Repentance (first part) is a turning of our life unto God. This is described and enlarged upon.

But before proceeding further, it will be proper to give a clearer exposition of the definition which we have adopted. There are three things, then, that are principally to be considered. First, in the conversion of the life to God, we require a transformation not only in external works, but also in the soul itself, which is able only after it has put off its old habits to bring forth fruits conformable to its renovation. The prophet, intending to express this, enjoins those whom he calls to repentance to make them "a new heart and a new spirit" (Ezekiel 18:31).

Hence, Moses, on several occasions, when he would show how the Israelites were to repent and turn to the Lord, told them that it must be done with the whole heart, and the whole soul (a mode of expression of frequent recurrence in the prophets), and by terming it the circumcision of the heart, points to the internal affections. But there is no passage better fitted to teach us the genuine nature of repentance than the following: "If thou wilt return, O Israel, saith the Lord, return unto me." "Break up your fallow ground, and sow not among thorns. Circumcise yourselves to the Lord, and take away the foreskins of your heart" (Jeremiah 4:1-4). See how he declares to them that it will be of no avail to commence the study of righteousness unless impiety shall first have been eradicated from their inmost heart. He reminds them that they have to do with God, and can gain nothing by deceit, because He hates a double heart. For this reason Isaiah derides the preposterous attempts of hypocrites, who zealously aimed at an external repentance by the observance of ceremonies, but in the meanwhile cared not "to loose the bands of wickedness, to undo the heavy burdens, and to let the oppressed go free." (See Isaiah 5:6.) In these words, he admirably shows wherein the acts of unfeigned repentance consist.

7 Repentance (the second part) is produced by fear of God. Hence, the mention of divine judgment by the prophets and apostles. Example. Exposition of the second branch of the definition from a passage in Paul. Why the fear of God is the first part of repentance.

The second part of our definition is that repentance proceeds from a sincere fear of God. Before the mind of the sinner can be inclined to repentance, he must be aroused by the thought of divine judgment. However, when his mind has grasped the thought that God will one day ascend His to His tribunal to take an account of all words and actions, it will not allow him to rest or have one moment's peace. The thought will perpetually urge him to adopt a different plan of life, that he may be able to stand securely at that judgment-seat.

Hence, the Scripture, when exhorting us to repentance, often introduces the subject of judgment, as in Jeremiah, "Lest my fury come forth like fire, and burn that none can quench it, because of the evil of your doings" (Jeremiah 4:4). Paul, in his discourse to the Athenians says, "The times of this ignorance God winked at; but now commandeth all men everywhere to repent: because he has appointed a day in the which he will judge the world in righteousness" (Acts 17:30-31).

The same thing is repeated in several other passages. Sometimes God is declared a judge, from the punishments already inflicted, thus leading sinners to reflect that worse awaits them if they do not quickly repent. There is an example of this in the 29th chapter of Deuteronomy. As repentance begins with dread and hatred of sin, the apostle sets down godly sorrow as one of its causes. (See 2 Corinthians 7:10.) By godly sorrow, he means when we not only tremble at the punishment, but also hate and abhor the sin, because we know it is displeasing to God. It is not strange that this should be, for unless we are stung to the quick, the sluggishness of our carnal nature cannot be corrected; nay, no degree of pungency would suffice for our stupor and sloth, did not God lift the rod and strike deeper.

There is, moreover, a rebellious spirit, which must be broken as with hammers. The stern threatening which God employs is extorted from Him by our depraved dispositions. For while we are asleep it would be in vain to allure us by soothing measures. Passages to this effect are found everywhere, and I need not quote them. But there is another reason that the fear of God lies at the root of repentance—viz. that though the lives of men are virtuous and they are lauded in the world, still if they do not bear reference to God, they are mere abominations in Heaven. Why? It is the principal part of righteousness to render to God that service and honor of which He is impiously defrauded whenever it is not our express purpose to submit to His authority.

8 Repentance (the third part) consists in the mortification of the flesh and the quickening of the Spirit. These are required by the prophets. They are explained separately.

We must now explain the third part of the definition, and show what is meant when we say that repentance consists of two parts—viz. the mortification of the flesh, and the quickening of the

Spirit. The prophets, in accommodation to a carnal people, express this in simple and homely terms, but clearly, when they say, "Depart from evil, and do good" (Psalm 34:14). "Wash you, make you clean, put away the evil of your doings from before mine eyes; cease to do evil; learn to do well; seek judgment; relieve the oppressed ..." etc. (Isaiah 1:16, 17). In dissuading us from wickedness, they demand the entire destruction of the flesh, which is full of perverseness and malice. It is a most difficult and arduous achievement to renounce ourselves and lay aside our natural disposition. For the flesh must not be thought to be destroyed unless everything that we have of our own is abolished. But because all the desires of the flesh are enmity against God (see Romans 8:7), the first step to the obedience of His law is the renouncement of our own nature. Renovation is afterwards manifested by the fruits produced by it—viz. justice, judgment, and mercy. Since it would be not sufficient duly to perform such acts, were not the mind and heart previously endued with sentiments of justice, judgment, and mercy, this is done when the Holy Spirit, instilling his holiness into our souls, so inspired them with new thoughts and affections, that they may justly be regarded as new. Indeed, as we are naturally averse to God, unless we practice self-denial, we shall never tend to that which is right. Hence, we are so often enjoined to put off the old man, to renounce the world and the flesh, to forsake our lusts, and to be renewed in the spirit of our mind. Moreover, the very word, "mortification" reminds us of how difficult it is to forget our former nature. We infer that we cannot be trained to the fear of God and learn the first principles of piety unless we are violently smitten with the sword of the Spirit and annihilated, as if God were declaring that to be ranked among His sons, there must be a destruction of our ordinary nature.

9 How this mortification and quickening are produced. Repentance is just a renewal of the divine image in us. It is not completed in a moment, but it extends to the last moment of life.

Both of these we obtain by union with Christ. For if we have true fellowship in His death, our old man is crucified by His power, and the body of sin becomes dead, so that the corruption of our original nature is never again in full vigor. (See Romans 6:5, 6.) If we are partakers in His resurrection, we are raised up by means of it to newness of life, which conforms us to the righteousness of God. In one word, then, by repentance I understand regeneration, the only aim of which is to form in us anew the image of God, which was sullied, and all but effaced by the transgression of Adam. So the apostle teaches when he says, "We all with open face beholding as in a glass the glory of the Lord, are changed into the same image from glory to glory, as by the Spirit of the Lord." Again, "Be renewed in the spirit of your minds" and "put ye on the new man, which after God is created in righteousness and true holiness." Again, "Put ye on the new man, which is renewed in knowledge after the image of him that created him." Accordingly through the blessing of Christ we are renewed by that regeneration into the righteousness of God from which we had fallen through Adam, the Lord being pleased in this manner to restore the integrity of all whom He appoints to the inheritance of life. This renewal, indeed, is not accomplished in a moment, a day, or a year. By uninterrupted, sometimes even slow, progress, God abolishes the remains of carnal corruption in His elect, cleanses them from pollution, and consecrates them as His temples. He restores all their inclinations to real purity, so that during their whole lives, they may practice repentance and know that death is the only termination to this warfare. The greater is the effrontery of an impure, raving apostate named Staphylus, who pretends that I confound the condition of the present life with the celestial glory, when, after Paul, I make the image of God to consist in righteousness and true holiness; as if in every definition it would be not necessary to take the thing defined in its integrity and perfection.

It is not denied that there is room for improvement but what I maintain is that the nearer anyone approaches in resemblance to God, the more does the image of God appear in him. That believers may attain to it, God assigns repentance as the goal towards which they must keep running during the whole course of their lives.

10 Reasons why repentance must so extend. Augustine's opinion as to concupiscence in the regenerate examined. A passage of Paul, which seems to confirm that opinion.

By regeneration the children of God are delivered from the bondage of sin, but not as if they had already obtained full possession of freedom, and no longer felt any annoyance from the flesh. Materials for an unremitting contest remain, that they may be exercised, and not only exercised, but may better understand their weakness. All writers of sound judgment agree in this, that, in the regenerate man, there is still a spring of evil which is perpetually sending forth desires that allure and stimulate him to sin. They also acknowledge that the saints are still so liable to the disease of concupiscence, that, though opposing it, they cannot avoid being always prompted and incited to lust, avarice, ambition, or other vices.

It is unnecessary to spend much time in investigating the sentiments of ancient writers. Augustine alone may suffice, as he has collected all their opinions with great care and fidelity. Any reader who is desirous to know the sense of antiquity may obtain it from him. There is this difference apparently between him and us, that while he admits that believers, so long as they are in the body, are so liable to concupiscence that they cannot but feel it, he does not venture to give this disease the name of sin. He is contented with giving it the name of infirmity, and says, that it only becomes sin when either external act or consent is added to conception or apprehension; that is, when the will yields to the first desire. We again regard it as sin whenever man is influenced in any degree by any desire contrary to the Law of God; nay, we maintain that the very gravity, which begets in us such desires, is sin. Accordingly, we hold that there is always sin in the saints until they are freed from their mortal frame, because depraved concupiscence resides in their flesh, and is at variance with rectitude. Augustine himself does not always refrain from using the name of sin, as when he says, "Paul gives the name of sin to that carnal concupiscence from which all sins arise. This in regard to the saints loses its dominion in this world, and is destroyed in heaven." In these words, he admits that believers, as far as they are liable to carnal concupiscence, are chargeable with sin.

11 Answer. Confirmation of the answer by the apostle himself Another confirmation from a precept of the Law. Conclusion.

When it is said that God purifies His Church, so as to be "holy and without blemish" (Ephesians 5:26, 27), that He promises this cleansing by means of baptism, and performs it in his elect, I understand that reference is made to the guilt rather than to the matter of sin. In regenerating His people, God indeed accomplishes this much for them; He destroys the dominion of sin by supplying the agency of the Spirit, which enables them to come off victorious from the contest. Sin, however, though it ceases to reign, ceases not to dwell in them. Accordingly, though we say that the old man is crucified, and the law of sin is abolished in the children of God (see Romans 6:6), the remains of sin survive not to have dominion, but to humble them under a consciousness of their infirmity. We admit that these remains, just as if they had no existence, are not imputed, but we, at the same time, contend that it is owing to the mercy of God that the saints are not charged with the guilt which would otherwise make them sinners before God. It will not be difficult for us to confirm this view, seeing that we can support it by clear passages of Scripture.

How can we express our view more plainly than Paul does in Romans 7:6? We have elsewhere shown and Augustine by solid reasons proves that Paul is there speaking in the person of a regenerated man. I say nothing as to his use of the words "evil" and "sin." However those who object to our view may quibble on these words, can any man deny that aversion to the Law of God is an evil and that hindrance to righteousness is sin? In short, who will not admit that there is guilt where there is spiritual misery? But all these things Paul affirms of this disease. Again, the Law furnishes us with a clear demonstration by which the whole question may be quickly disposed of. We are enjoined to love God with all our heart, all our soul, and all our strength. Since all the faculties of our soul ought thus to be engrossed with the love of God, it is certain that the commandment is not fulfilled by those who receive the smallest desire into their heart, or admit into their minds any thought whatever which may lead them away from the love of God to vanity. What then? Is it not through the faculties of mind that we are assailed with sudden motions, that we perceive sensual, or form conceptions of mental objects? Since these faculties give admission to vain and wicked thoughts, do they not show that to that extent they are devoid of the love of God? He, then, who admits not that all the desires of the flesh are sins, and that that disease of concupiscence, which they call a stimulus, is a fountain of sin, must of necessity deny that the transgression of the Law is sin.

12 Exception, that those desires only are condemned, which are repugnant to the order of God. Desires not condemned insofar as natural, but insofar as inordinate. This view is held by Augustine.

If anyone thinks it absurd thus to condemn all the desires by which man is naturally affected, because they have been implanted by

God, the author of nature, we answer that we by no means condemn those appetites that God so implanted in the mind of man at his first creation, that they cannot be eradicated without destroying human nature itself, but only the violent, lawless movements which war with the order of God. However, as in consequence of the corruption of nature, all our faculties are so vitiated and corrupted that a perpetual disorder and excess is apparent in all our actions, and as the appetites cannot be separated from this excess, we maintain that they are vicious. Or to give the substance in fewer words, we hold that all human desires are evil and charge them with sin not in as far as they are natural, but because they are inordinate, and inordinate because nothing pure and upright can proceed from a corrupt and polluted nature. Nor does Augustine depart from this doctrine in reality so much as in appearance. From an excessive dread of the invidious charge with which the Pelagians assailed him, he sometimes refrains from using the term sin in this sense; but when he says, "The law of sin remaining in the saints, the guilt only is taken away," he shows clearly enough that his view is not very different from ours.

13 Passages from Augustine to show that this was his opinion Objection from a passage in James.

We will produce some other passages to make it more apparent what his sentiments were. In his second book against Julian, he says, "This law of sin is both remitted in spiritual regeneration and remains in the mortal flesh; remitted, because the guilt is forgiven in the sacrament by which believers are regenerated, and yet remains, inasmuch as it produces desires against which believers fight." Again, "Therefore the law of sin (which was in the members of this great apostle also) is forgiven in baptism, not ended." Again, "The law of sin, the guilt of which, though remaining, is forgiven in baptism, Ambrose called iniquity, for it is iniquitous for the flesh to lust against the Spirit." Again, "Sin is dead in the guilt by which it bound us; and until it is cured by the perfection of burial, though dead it rebels." In the fifth book he says still more plainly, "As blindness of heart is the sin by which God is not believed; and the punishment of sin, by which a proud heart is justly punished; and the cause of sin, when through the error of a blinded heart any evil is committed, so the lust of the flesh, against which the good Spirit wars, is also sin, because disobedient to the authority of the mind; and the punishment of sin, because the recompense rendered for disobedience; and the cause of sin, consenting by revolt or springing up through contamination." He here without ambiguity calls it sin, because the Pelagian heresy being now refuted, and the sound doctrine confirmed, he was less afraid of slanderous accusation. Thus, also, in his forty-first homily on John, where he speaks his own sentiments without controversy, he says, 'If with the flesh you serve the law of sin, do what the apostle himself says, "Let not sin, therefore, reign in your mortal body, that ye should obey it in the lusts thereof' (Romans 6:12). He does not say, 'Let it not be,' but 'Let it not reign.' As long as you live there must be sin in your members, but at least let its dominion be destroyed; do not what it orders." Those who maintain that concupiscence is not sin are wont to found their belief on the passage of James, "Then, when lust has conceived, it bringeth forth sin" (James 1:15). But this is easily refuted: for unless we understand him as speaking only of wicked works or actual sins, even a wicked inclination will not be accounted as sin. But from his calling crimes and wicked deeds the fruits of lust, and also giving them the name of sins, it does not follow that the lust itself is not an evil, and in the sight of God deserving of condemnation.

14 Another objection of the Anabaptists and Libertines to the continuance of repentance throughout the present life. An answer disclosing its impiety. Another answer, founded on the absurdities to which it leads. A third answer, contrasting sincere Christian repentance with the erroneous view of the objectors. Conformation from the example and declaration of an apostle.

Some Anabaptists in the present age mistake some indescribable sort of frenzied excess for the regeneration of the Spirit, holding that the children of God are restored to a state of innocence, and, therefore, need to give themselves no anxiety about curbing the lust of the flesh; that they have the Spirit for their guide, and under His agency they never err. It would be incredible that the human mind could proceed to such insanity, did they not openly and exultingly give utterance to their dogma. It is indeed monstrous, and yet it is just, that those who have resolved to turn the Word of God into a lie should thus be punished for their blasphemous audacity. Is it indeed true, that all distinction between base and honorable, just and unjust, good and evil, virtue and vice is abolished? The distinction, they say, is from the curse of the old Adam, and from this we are exempted by Christ. There will be no difference, then, between whoredom and chastity, sincerity and craft, truth and falsehood, justice and robbery. Away with vain fear! They say that the Spirit will not bid you do anything that is wrong, provided you sincerely and boldly leave yourself to His agency. Who is not amazed at such monstrous doctrines? Yet, this philosophy is popular with those who, blinded by insane lusts, have thrown off common sense. But what kind of Christ, pray, do they fabricate? What kind of Spirit do they belch forth? We acknowledge one Christ, and His one Spirit, whom the prophets foretold and the gospel proclaims as actually manifested, but we hear nothing of this kind respecting Him. That Spirit is not the patron of murder, adultery, drunkenness, pride, contention, avarice, and fraud, but the author of love, chastity, sobriety, modesty, peace, moderation, and truth. He is not a Spirit of giddiness, rushing rashly and precipitately, without regard to right and wrong, but full of wisdom and understanding, by which He can duly distinguish between justice and injustice. He instigates not to lawless and unrestrained licentiousness, but, discriminating between lawful and unlawful, teaches temperance and moderation.

But why dwell longer in refuting that brutish frenzy? To Christians, the Spirit of the Lord is not a turbulent phantom that they have produced by dreaming or have received ready-made by others. On the contrary, they religiously seek the knowledge of Him from Scripture, where two things are taught concerning Him.

First, He is given to us for sanctification, that He may purge us from all iniquity and defilement and bring us to the obedience of divine righteousness, an obedience which cannot exist unless the lusts to which these men would give loose reins are tamed and subdued.

Secondly, although purged by His sanctification, we are still beset by many vices and much weakness, so long as we are enclosed in the prison of the body. Thus it is, that placed at a great distance from perfection, we must always be endeavoring to make some progress, and daily struggling with the evil by which we are entangled. Hence, too, it follows that shaking off sloth and security, we must be intently vigilant, so as not to be taken unawares in the snares of our flesh unless, indeed, we presume to think that we have made greater progress than the apostle, who was buffeted by a messenger of Satan, in order that his strength might be perfected in weakness, and who gives in his own person a true, not a fictitious representation, of the strife between the Spirit and the flesh. (See 2 Corinthians 12:7, 9; Romans 7:6.)

15 Of the fruits of repentance. Carefulness. Excuse. Indignation Fear. Desire. Zeal. Revenge. Moderation to be observed, as most sagely counseled by Bernard.

The apostle, in his description of repentance (see 2 Corinthians 7:2), enumerates seven causes, effects, or parts belonging to it, and that on the best grounds. These are carefulness, excuse, indignation, fear, desire, zeal, and revenge. It should not excite surprise that I venture not to determine whether they ought to be regarded as causes or effects; both views may be maintained. They may also be called affections conjoined with repentance; but as Paul's meaning may be ascertained without entering into any of these questions, we shall be contented with a simple exposition.

He says then that godly sorrow produces *carefulness*. He who is really dissatisfied with himself for sinning against his God, is, at the same time, stimulated to care and attention, that he may completely disentangle himself from the chains of the devil, and keep a better guard against his snares, so as not afterwards to lose the guidance of the Holy Spirit, or be overcome by security. Next comes excuse, which in this place means not defense in which the sinner, to escape the judgment of God, either denies his fault or extenuates it, but apologizes, which trusts more to intercession than to the goodness of the cause. Just as children, not altogether abandoned, acknowledge and confess their errors, yet employ deprecation. To make room for it, they testify by every means in their power that they have by no means cast off the reverence, which they owe to their parents. In short, they endeavor by excuse, not to prove themselves righteous and innocent, but only to obtain pardon.

Next follows *indignation*, under which the sinner inwardly murmurs expostulates, and is offended with himself on recognizing his perverseness and ingratitude to God. By the term "fear" is meant "trepidation" that takes possession of our minds whenever we consider both what we have deserved, and the "fearful severity of the divine anger against sinners." Accordingly, the exceeding disquietude, which we must necessarily feel, both trains us to humility and makes us more cautious for the future. But if the carefulness or anxiety, which he first mentioned is the result of fear, the connection between the two becomes obvious.

Desire seems to me to be used as equivalent to diligence in duty, and alacrity in doing service, to which the sense of our misdeeds ought to be a powerful stimulus. To this also pertains zeal, which immediately follows; for it signifies the ardor, with which we are inflamed when such goads as these are applied to us. "What have I done? Into what abyss had I fallen had not the mercy of God prevented?"

The last of all is *revenge*, for the stricter we are with ourselves, and the severer the censure we pass upon our sins, the more ground we have to hope for the divine favor and mercy. And certainly, when the soul is overwhelmed with a dread of divine judgment, it cannot but act the part of an avenger in inflicting punishment upon itself. Pious men, doubtless, feel that there is punishment in the shame, confusion, groans, self-displeasure, and other feelings produced by a serious review of their sins.

Let us remember, however, that moderation must be used, so that we may not be overwhelmed with sadness, there being nothing to which trembling consciences are more prone than to rush into despair. This, too, is one of Satan's artifices. Those whom he sees thus overwhelmed with fear, he plunges deeper and deeper into the abyss of sorrow, that they may never again rise. It is true that the fear, which ends in humility without relinquishing the hope of pardon, cannot be in excess. Yet, we must always beware, according to the apostolic injunction, of giving way to extreme dread, as this tends to make us shun God while He is calling us to himself by repentance. Wherefore, the advice of Bernard is good, "Grief for sins is necessary, but must not be perpetual. My advice is to turn back at times from sorrow and the anxious remembrance of your ways, and escape to the plain, to a calm review of the divine mercies. Let us mingle honey with wormwood, that the salubrious bitter may give health when we drink it tempered with a mixture of sweetness: while you think humbly of yourselves, think also of the goodness of the Lord."

16 Internal fruits of repentance. A. Piety towards God. B. Charity towards man. C. Purity of life. How carefully these fruits are commended by the prophets. External fruits of repentance. Bodily exercises too much commended by ancient writers. Twofold excess in regard to them.

We can now understand what are the fruits of repentance—viz. offices of piety towards God, and love towards men, general holiness and purity of life. In short, the more a man studies to conform his life to the standard of the divine law, the surer signs he gives of his repentance. Accordingly, the Spirit, in exhorting us to repentance, brings before us at one time each separate precept of the law; at another the duties of the second table; although there are also passages in which, after condemning impurity in its fountain in the heart, he afterwards descends to external marks, by which repentance is proved to be sincere. A portraiture of this I will shortly set before the eye of the reader when I come to describe the Christian life (*infra*, chapter 6).

I will not here collect the passages from the prophets, in which they deride the frivolous observances of those who labor to appease God with ceremonies, and show that they are mere mockery; or those in which they show that outward integrity of conduct is not the chief part of repentance, seeing that God looks at the heart. Anyone moderately versed in Scripture will understand by himself, without being reminded by others, that when he has to do with God, nothing is gained without beginning with the internal affections of the heart.

There is a passage of Joel that will avail not a little for the understanding of others: "Rend your heart, and not your garments" (Joel 2:13). Both are also briefly expressed by James in these words: "Cleanse your hands, ye sinners; and purify your hearts, ye double-minded" (James 4:8). Here, indeed, the accessory is set down first; but the source and principle is afterwards pointed out—viz. that hidden defilements must be wiped away and an altar erected to God in the very heart. There are, moreover, certain external exercises which we employ in private as remedies to humble us and tame our flesh, and in public, to testify our repentance. These have their origin in that revenge of which Paul speaks (see 2 Corinthians 7:2), for when the mind is distressed, it naturally expresses itself in sackcloth, groans, and tears, shuns ornament and every kind of show, and abandons all delights. Then he, who feels how great an evil the rebellion of the flesh is, tries every means of curbing it. Besides, he who considers aright how grievous a thing it is to have offended the justice of God, cannot rest until, in his humility, he has given glory to God.

Ancient writers often mention such exercises when they speak of the fruits of repentance. Although they by no means place the power of repentance in them, yet my readers must pardon me for saying what I think—they certainly seem to insist on them more than is right. Anyone who judiciously considers the matter will, I trust, agree with me that they have exceeded in two ways; first, by so strongly urging and extravagantly commending that corporal discipline, they indeed succeeded in making the people embrace it with greater zeal; but they in a manner obscured what they should have regarded as of much more serious moment. Secondly, the inflictions, which they enjoined, were considerably more rigorous than ecclesiastical mildness demands, as will be elsewhere shown.

17 Delusion of some who consider these external exercises as the chief part of Repentance. Why received in the Jewish Church. The legitimate use of these exercises in the Christian Church.

As there are some who, from the frequent mention of sackcloth, fasting, and tears, especially in Joel (2:12), think that these constitute the principal part of repentance, we must dispel their delusion. In that passage the proper part of repentance is described by the words, "Turn ye even to me with your whole heart;" "rend your heart, and not your garments." The "fasting," "weeping," and "mourning" are introduced not as invariable or necessary effects, but as special circumstances. Having foretold that most grievous disasters were impending over the Jews, he exhorts them to turn away the divine anger not only by repenting, but also by giving public signs of sorrow. For as a criminal, to excite the commiseration of the judge, appears in a supplicating posture, with a long beard, uncombed hair, and coarse clothing, so should those who are charged at the judgment-seat of God deprecate His severity in a garb of wretchedness. But, although sackcloth and ashes were perhaps more conformable to the customs of these times, yet it is plain that weeping and fasting are very appropriate in our case whenever the Lord threatens us with any defeat or calamity.

In presenting the appearance of danger, he declares that he is preparing, and, in a manner, arming himself for vengeance. Rightly, therefore, does the prophet exhort those, on whose crimes he had said a little before that vengeance was to be executed, to weeping and fasting, that is, to the mourning habit of criminals. Nor in the present day do ecclesiastical teachers act improperly when, seeing ruin hanging over the necks of their people, they call aloud on them to hasten with weeping and fasting: only they must always urge, with greater care and earnestness, "rend your hearts, and not your garments."

It is beyond doubt that fasting is not always a concomitant of repentance, but is specially destined for seasons of calamity. Hence, our Savior connects it with mourning (see Matthew 9:15) and relieves the apostles of the necessity of it until, by being deprived of His presence, they were filled with sorrow. I speak of formal fasting. For the life of Christians ought ever to be tempered with frugality and sobriety, so that the whole course of it should present some appearance of fasting. As this subject will be fully discussed when the discipline of the Church comes to be considered, I now dwell less upon it.

18 The principal part of repentance consists in turning to God Confession and acknowledgment of sins. What their nature should be. Distinction between ordinary and special repentance. Use of this distinction.

This much, however, I will add: when the word *repentance* is applied to the external profession, it is used improperly, and not in the genuine meaning, as I have explained it. For that is not so much a turning unto God as the confession of a fault accompanied with deprecation of the sentence and punishment. Thus to repent in sackcloth and ashes (see Matthew 11:21; Luke 10:13) is just to testify self-dissatisfaction when God is angry with us for having grievously offended Him. It is, indeed, a kind of public confession by which, condemning ourselves before angels and the world, we prevent the judgment of God. For Paul, rebuking the sluggishness of those who indulge in their sins, says, "If we would judge ourselves, we should not be judged" (1 Corinthians 11:31). It is not always necessary, however, openly to inform others, and make them the witnesses of our repentance. To confess privately to God is a part of true repentance that cannot be omitted. Nothing were more incongruous than that God should pardon the sins in which we are flattering ourselves, and hypocritically cloaking that he may not bring them to light. We must not only confess the sins which we daily commit, but more grievous lapses ought to carry us further, and bring to our remembrance things which seemed to have been long ago buried. Of this David sets an example before us in his own person. (See Psalm 51.) Filled with shame for a recent crime he examines himself, going back to the womb, and acknowledging that even then he was corrupted and defiled. This he does not to extenuate his fault, as many hide themselves in the crowd, and catch at impunity by involving others along with them.

Very differently does David, who ingenuously makes it an aggravation of his sin, that being corrupted from his earliest infancy he ceased not to add iniquity to iniquity. In another passage, also, he takes a survey of his past life, and implores God to pardon the errors of his youth. (See Psalm 25:7.) And, indeed, we shall not prove that we have thoroughly shaken off our stupor until, groaning under the burden, and lamenting our sad condition, we seek relief from God.

It is moreover to be observed, that the repentance which we are enjoined assiduously to cultivate, differs from that which raises from death those who had fallen more shamefully, or given themselves up to sin without restraint, or by some kind of open revolt, had thrown off the authority of God. For Scripture, in exhorting to repentance, often speaks of it as a passage from death unto life, and when relating that a people had repented, means that they had abandoned idolatry, and other forms of gross wickedness. For which reason Paul denounces woe to sinners, "who have not repented of the uncleanness, and fornication, and lasciviousness which they have committed" (2 Corinthians 12:21).

This distinction ought to be carefully observed, lest when we hear of a few individuals having been summoned to repent, we indulge in supine security, as if we had nothing to do with the mortification of the flesh; whereas, in consequence of the depraved desires that are always enticing us, and the iniquities, which are always springing from them, it must engage our unremitting care. The special repentance enjoined upon those who have gotten entangled in deadly snares and have withdrawn from the fear of God, does not abolish that ordinary repentance which the corruption of nature obliges us to cultivate during the whole course of our lives.

19 End of Repentance. Its nature is shown by the preaching of John the Baptist, our Savior, and His apostles. The sum of this preaching.

Moreover, if it is true, and nothing can be more certain, than that a complete summary of the gospel is included under these two heads—viz. repentance and the remission of sins, do we not see that the Lord justifies His people freely, and at the same time renews them to true holiness by the sanctification of His Spirit? John, the messenger sent before the face of Christ to prepare His ways, proclaimed, "Repent, for the kingdom of heaven is at hand" (Matthew 11:10; 3:2). By inviting them to repentance, he urged them to acknowledge that they were sinners, and in all respects condemned before God, that thus they might be induced earnestly to seek the mortification of the flesh, and a new birth in the Spirit. By announcing the Kingdom of God, he called for faith. By the Kingdom of God, which he declared to be at hand, he meant forgiveness of sins, salvation, life, and every other blessing we obtain in Christ; wherefore we read in the other Evangelists: "John did baptize in the wilderness, and preach the baptism of repentance for the remission of sins" (Mark 1:4; Luke 3:3). What does this mean, but that weary and oppressed with the burden of sin, they should turn to the Lord and entertain hopes of forgiveness and salvation? Thus, too, Christ began His preaching: "The kingdom of God is at hand: repent ye, and believe the Gospel" (Mark 1:10).

First, He declares that the treasures of the divine mercy were opened in Him; next, He enjoins repentance; and, lastly, He encourages confidence in the promises of God. Accordingly, when intending to give a brief summary of the whole gospel, He said that he behaved "...to suffer, and to rise from the dead the third day, and that repentance and remission of sins should be preached in his name among all nations" (Luke 24:26, 46).

In like manner, after His resurrection, the apostles preached, "Him has God exalted with his right hand, to be a Prince and a Savior, for to give repentance to Israel and forgiveness of sins" (Acts 5:31). Repentance is preached in the name of Christ, when men learn, through the doctrines of the gospel, that all their thoughts, affections, and pursuits, are corrupt and vicious; and that, therefore, if they would enter the Kingdom of God, they must be born again. Forgiveness of sins is preached when men are taught that Christ "...is made unto us wisdom, and righteousness, and sanctification, and redemption" (1 Corinthians 1:30), that on His account they are freely deemed righteous and innocent in the sight of God. Though both graces are obtained by faith (as has been shown elsewhere), yet as the goodness of God, by which sins are forgiven, is the proper object of faith, it was proper carefully to distinguish it from repentance.

20   Christian repentance terminates with our death.

Moreover, as hatred of sin, which is the beginning of repentance, first gives us access to the knowledge of Christ, who manifests himself to none but miserable and afflicted sinners—groaning, laboring, burdened, hungry, and thirsty, and pining away with grief and wretchedness. Therefore, if we would stand in Christ, we must aim at repentance, cultivate it during our whole lives, and continue it to the last. Christ came to call sinners, but to call them to repentance. He was sent to bless the unworthy, but by "turning away everyone" "from his iniquities." The Scripture is full of similar passages. Hence, when God offers forgiveness of sins, He in return usually stipulates for repentance, intimating that His mercy should induce men to repent. "Keep ye judgment," saith He, "and do justice: for my salvation is near to come." Again, "The Redeemer shall come to Zion, and unto them that turn from transgression in Jacob." Again, "Seek ye the Lord while he may be found, call ye upon him while he is near. Let the wicked forsake his way, and the unrighteous man his thoughts, and let him return unto the Lord, and he will have mercy upon him." "Repent ye, therefore, and be converted, that your sins may be blotted out." Here, however, it is to be observed, that repentance is not made a condition in such a sense as to be a foundation for meriting pardon; nay, it rather indicates the end at which they must aim if they would obtain favor, God having resolved to take pity on men for the express purpose of leading them to repent. Therefore, so long as we dwell in the prison of the body, we must constantly struggle with the vices of our corrupt nature, and so with our natural disposition.

Plato sometimes says that the life of the philosopher is to meditate on death. More truly may we say, that the life of a Christian man is constant study and exercise in mortifying the flesh, until it is certainly slain, and the Spirit of God obtains dominion in us. Wherefore, he seems to me to have made most progress who has learned to be most dissatisfied with himself. He does not, however, remain in the miry clay without going forward; but rather hastens and sighs after God, that, engrafted into both the death and the life of Christ, he may constantly meditate on repentance. Unquestionably, those who have a genuine hatred of sin cannot do otherwise: for no man ever hated sin without being previously enamored of righteousness. This view, as it is the simplest of all, seemed to me also to accord best with Scripture truth.

21 Repentance has its origin in the grace of God, as communicated to the elect, whom God is pleased to save from death. The hardening and final impenitence of the reprobate. A passage of an Apostle as to voluntary reprobates gives no countenance to the Novatians.

Moreover, that repentance is a special gift of God I trust is too well understood from the above doctrine to require any lengthened discourse. Hence, the Church extols the goodness of God, and looks on in wonder, saying, "Then has God also to the Gentiles granted repentance unto life" (Acts 11:18). Paul, enjoining Timothy to deal meekly and patiently with unbelievers, says, "If God per adventure will give them repentance to the acknowledging of the truth, and that they may recover themselves out of the snare of the devil" (2 Timothy 2:25, 26).

God indeed declares, that He would have all men to repent, and addresses exhortations in common to all; their efficacy, however, depends on the Spirit of regeneration. It was easier to create us at first, than for us by our own strength to acquire a more excellent nature. Wherefore, concerning the whole process of regeneration, it is not without cause that we are called God's "...workmanship, created in Christ Jesus unto good works, which God has before ordained that we should walk in them" (Ephesians 2:10).

Those whom God is pleased to rescue from death, He quickens by the Spirit of regeneration; not that repentance is properly the cause of salvation, but because, as already seen, it is inseparable from the faith and mercy of God; for, as Isaiah declares, "The Redeemer shall come to Zion, and unto them that turn from transgression in Jacob." This, indeed, is a standing truth, that wherever the fear of God is in vigor, the Spirit has been carrying on His saving work. Hence, in Isaiah, while believers complain and lament that they have been forsaken of God, they set down the supernatural hardening of the heart as a sign of reprobation. The apostle, also, intending to exclude apostates from the hope of salvation, states as the reason that it is impossible to renew them to repentance. (See Hebrews 6:6.) That is, God, by renewing those whom He wills not to perish, gives them a sign of paternal favor and in a manner attracts them to himself by the beams of a calm and reconciled countenance.

On the other hand, by hardening the reprobate, whose impiety is not to be forgiven, He thunders against them. This kind of vengeance the apostle denounces against voluntary apostates (see Hebrews 10:29), who, in falling away from the faith of the gospel, mock God, insultingly reject His favor, profane and trample under foot the blood of Christ, nay, as far as in them lies, crucify Him afresh. Still, he does not, as some austere persons preposterously insist, eliminate hope of pardon of voluntary sins, but shows that because apostasy is altogether without excuse, it is not strange that God is inexorably rigorous in punishing sacrilegious contempt thus shown to Him.

In the same epistle, he says, "It is impossible for those who were once enlightened, and have tasted of the heavenly gift, and were made partakers of the Holy Ghost, and have tasted the good word of God, and the powers of the world to come, if they shall fall away to renew them again to repentance, seeing they crucify the Son of God afresh, and put him to an open shame" (Hebrews 7:4-6). And in another passage, "If we sin willingly, after that we have received the knowledge of the truth, there remaineth no more sacrifice for sins, but a certain fearful looking for of judgment" (Hebrews 11:25, 26). There are other passages, from a misinterpretation of which the Novatians of old extracted materials for their heresy; so much so, that some good men taking offense at their harshness, have deemed the epistle altogether spurious, though it truly savors in every part of it of the apostolic spirit. But as our dispute is only with those who receive the epistle, it is easy to show that those passages give no support to their error.

First, the apostle must of necessity agree with his Master, who declares that, "All manner of sin and blasphemy shall be forgiven unto men, but the blasphemy against the Holy Ghost shall not be forgiven unto men," "…neither in this world, neither in the world to come" (Matthew 12:31; Luke 12:10). We must hold that this was the only exception, which the apostle recognized, unless we would set him in opposition to the grace of God. Hence, it follows, that pardon is denied to no sin except one, which proceeding from desperate fury cannot be ascribed to infirmity, and plainly shows that the man guilty of it is possessed by the devil.

22 Of the sin against the Holy Ghost. The true definition of this sin as proved and explained by Scripture. Who they are that sin against the Holy Spirit. Examples: —A. The Jews resisting Stephen. B. The Pharisees. Definition confirmed by the example of Paul.

Here, however, it is proper to consider what the dreadful iniquity is which is not to be pardoned. The definition which Augustine somewhere gives—viz. that it is obstinate perverseness, with distrust of pardon, continued until death—scarcely agrees with the words of Christ, that it shall not be forgiven in this world. For either this is said in vain, or it may be committed in this world. But if Augustine's definition is correct, the sin is not committed unless persisted in until death. Others say that the sin against the Holy Spirit consists in envying the grace conferred upon a brother; but I know not on what it is founded. Here, however, let us give the true definition, which, when once it is established by sound evidence, will easily overturn all the others by itself. I say therefore that he sins against the Holy Spirit who, while so constrained by the power of divine truth that he cannot plead ignorance, yet deliberately resists, and that merely for the sake of resisting. For Christ, in explanation of what he had said, immediately adds, "Whosoever speaketh a word against the Son of man, it shall be forgiven him; but whosoever speaketh against the Holy Ghost, it shall not be forgiven him" (Matthew 12:31). And Matthew uses the term "spirit of blasphemy" for blasphemy against the Spirit. How can anyone insult the Son, without at the same time attacking the Spirit? In this way: Those who in ignorance assail the unknown truth of God, and yet are so disposed that they would be unwilling to extinguish the truth of God when it is manifested to them, or utter one word against Him whom they knew to be the Lord's Anointed, sin against the Father and the Son. Thus, there are many in the present day who have the greatest abhorrence to the doctrine of the gospel, and yet, if they knew it to be the doctrine of the gospel, would be prepared to venerate it with their whole heart.

But those who are convinced in conscience that what they repudiate and impugn is the Word of God, and yet cease not to impugn it, are said to blaspheme against the Spirit, inasmuch as they struggle against the illumination, which is the work of the Spirit. Such were some of the Jews, who, when they could not resist the Spirit speaking by Stephen, yet were bent on resisting. (See Acts 6:10.) There can be no doubt that many of them were carried away by zeal for the Law; but it appears that there were others who maliciously and impiously raged against God himself, that is, against the doctrine which they knew to be of God. Such, too, were the Pharisees, on whom our Lord denounced woe. To depreciate the power of the Holy Spirit, they defamed Him by the name of Beelzebub. (See Matthew 9:3, 4; 12:24.) The spirit of blasphemy, therefore, is, when a man audaciously, and of set purpose, rushes forth to insult his divine name. This Paul intimates when he says, "but I obtained mercy, because I did it ignorantly in unbelief;" otherwise he had deservedly been held unworthy of the grace of God. If ignorance joined with unbelief made him obtain pardon, it follows, that there is no room for pardon when knowledge is added to unbelief.

23 Why that sin unpardonable. The paralogism of the Novatians in wresting the words of the apostle examined. Two passages from the same Apostle.

If you attend properly, you will perceive that the apostle speaks not of one particular lapse or two, but of the universal revolt by which the reprobate renounces salvation. It is not strange that God should be implacable to those whom John, in his epistle, declares not to have been of the elect, from whom they went out. (See 1 John 2:19.) For he is directing his discourse against those who imagined that they could return to the Christian religion though they had once revolted from it. To divest them of this false and pernicious opinion, he says, as is most true, that those who had once knowingly and willingly cast off fellowship with Christ, had no means of returning to it.

It is not, however, so cast off by those who merely, by the dissoluteness of their lives, transgress the Word of the Lord, but by those who avowedly reject His whole doctrine. There is a paralogism in the expression *casting off* and *sinning*. *Casting off*, as interpreted by the Novatians, is when anyone, notwithstanding of being taught by the Law of the Lord not to steal or commit adultery, refrains not from theft or adultery.

On the contrary, I hold that there is a tacit antithesis, in which all the things, contrary to those which had been said, must be held to be repeated, so that the thing expressed is not some particular vice, but universal aversion to God, and (so to speak) the apostasy of the whole man. Therefore, when he speaks of those falling away,

"...who were once enlightened, and have tasted of the heavenly gift, and were made partakers of the Holy Ghost, and have tasted of the good word of God, and the powers of the world to come," we must understand that he refers to those who, with deliberate impiety, have quenched the light of the Spirit, tasted of the heavenly Word and spurned it, alienated themselves from the sanctification of the Spirit, and trampled under foot the word of God and the powers of a world to come. The better to show that this was the species of impiety intended, he afterwards expressly adds the term *willfully*. For when he says, "If we sin willfully, after that we have received the knowledge of the truth, there remaineth no more sacrifice for sins," he does not deny that Christ is a perpetual victim to expiate the transgressions of saints (this the whole epistle distinctly proclaims in explaining the priesthood of Christ), but he says that there remains no other sacrifice after this one is abandoned. In addition, it is abandoned when the truth of the Gospel is professedly abjured.

24 First objection to the above doctrine. Answer. Solution of a difficulty founded on the example of Esau and the threatening of a Prophet. Second objection.

To some it seems harsh and at variance with the divine mercy, utterly to deny forgiveness to any who retake themselves to it. This is easily disposed of. It is not said that pardon will be refused if they turn to the Lord, but it is altogether denied that they can turn to repentance, inasmuch as for their ingratitude they are struck by the just judgment of God with eternal blindness. There is nothing contrary to this in the application, which is afterwards made of the example of Esau, who tried in vain, by crying and tears, to recover his lost birthright; nor in the denunciation of the prophet, "They cried, and I would not hear." Such modes of expression do not denote true conversion or calling upon God, but that anxiety with which the wicked, when in calamity, are compelled to see what they before securely disregarded—viz. that nothing can avail but the assistance of the Lord. This, however, they do not so much implore as lament the loss of. Hence, all that the prophet means by crying, and the apostle by tears, is the dreadful torment which stings and excruciates the wicked in despair. It is of consequence carefully to observe this: for otherwise God would be inconsistent with himself when He proclaims through the prophet that, "If the wicked will turn from all his sins that he has committed,"—"he shall surely live, he shall not die" (Ezekiel 18:21, 22). And (as I have already said) it is certain that the mind of man cannot be changed for the better unless by His preventing grace. The promise as to those who call upon Him will never fail; but the names of conversion and prayer are improperly given to that blind torment by which the reprobate are distracted when they see that they must seek God if they would find a remedy for their calamities, and yet shun to approach him.

25 Third objection, founded on the seeming approval of the feigned repentance of the ungodly, as Ahab. Answer. Confirmation from the example of Esau. Why God bears for a time with the ungodly, pretending repentance. Exception.

But as the apostle declares that God is not appeased by feigned repentance, it is asked how Ahab obtained pardon and averted the punishment denounced against him (1 Kings 21:28, 29), seeing, it appears, he was only amazed on the sudden, and afterwards continued his former course of life. He, indeed, clothed himself in sackcloth, covered himself with ashes, laid on the ground, and (as the testimony given to him bears) humbled himself before God. It was a small matter to rend his garments while his heart continued obstinate and swollen with wickedness, and yet we see that God was inclined to mercy. I answer that though hypocrites are thus occasionally spared for a time, the wrath of God still lies upon them, and that they are thus spared not so much on their own account as for a public example. For what did Ahab gain by the mitigation of his punishment except that he did not suffer it alive on the Earth? The curse of God, though concealed, was fixed on His house, and he himself went to eternal destruction.

We may see the same thing in Esau. (See Genesis 27:38, 39.) For though he met with a refusal, a temporal blessing was granted to his tears. But as, according to the declaration of God, the spiritual inheritance could be possessed only by one of the brothers, when Jacob was selected instead of Esau, that event excluded him from the divine mercy. Still, there was given to him, as a man of a groveling nature, this consolation: that he should be filled with the fullness of the Earth and the dew of Heaven. And this, as I lately said, should be regarded as done for the example of others, so that we may learn to apply our minds and exert ourselves with greater alacrity in the way of sincere repentance.

There cannot be the least doubt that God will be ready to pardon those who turn to him truly and with the heart, seeing that His mercy extends even to the unworthy, though they bear marks of His displeasure. In this way also, we are taught how dreadful the judgment is which awaits all the rebellious who with audacious brow and iron heart make it their sport to despise and disregard the divine threatening. God in this way often stretched forth His hand to deliver the Israelites from their calamities, though their cries were pretended, and their minds double and perfidious, as he himself complains in the Psalms, that they immediately returned to their former course. (See Psalm 78:36, 37.) But He designed thus by kindness and forbearance to bring them to true repentance, or leave them without excuse. Yet, by remitting the punishment for a time, He does not lay himself under any perpetual obligation. He rather at times rises with greater severity against hypocrites, and doubles their punishment, that it may thereby appear how much hypocrisy displeases him. But, as I have observed, He gives some examples of His inclination to pardon, that the pious may thereby be stimulated to amend their lives, and the pride of those who petulantly kick against the pricks be more severely condemned.

Chapter 4

PENITENCE, AS EXPLAINED IN THE SOPHISTICAL JARGON OF THE SCHOOLMEN, WIDELY DIFFERENT FROM THE PURITY REQUIRED BY THE GOSPEL. OF CONFESSION AND SATISFACTION

The divisions of this chapter are: I. The orthodox doctrine of repentance being already expounded, the false doctrine is refuted in the present chapter; a general summary survey being at the same time taken of the doctrine of the Schoolmen, sections 1, 2. II. Its separate parts are afterwards examined. Contrition, sections 2 and 3. Confession, sections 4-20. Sanctification, from section 20 to the end of the chapter.

Sections

1. Errors of the Schoolmen in delivering the doctrine of repentance. A. Errors in defining it. Four different definitions considered. B. Absurd division. C. Vain and puzzling questions. D. Mode in which they entangle themselves.

2. The false doctrine of the Schoolmen necessary to be refuted. Of contrition. Their view of it examined.

3. True and genuine contrition.

4. Auricular confession. Whether or not of divine authority. Arguments of Canonists and Schoolmen. Allegorical argument founded on Judaism. Two answers. Reason that Christ sent the lepers to the priests.

5. Another allegorical argument. Answer.

6. A third argument from two passages of Scripture. These passages expounded.

7. Confession proved not to be of divine authority. The use of it free for almost twelve hundred years after Christ. Its nature. When enacted into a law. Confirmation from the history of the Church. A representation of the ancient auricular confession still existing among the papists, to bear judgment against them. *Confession abolished in the Church of Constantinople.*

8. *This mode of confession disapproved by Chrysostom, as shown by many passages.*

9. *False confession being thus refuted, the confession enjoined by the Word of God is considered. Mistranslation in the old version. Proof from Scripture that confession should be directed to God alone.*

10. *Effect of secret confession thus made to God. Another kind of confession made to men.*

11. *Two forms of the latter confession—viz. public and private. Public confession, either ordinary or extraordinary. Use of each. Objection to confession and public prayer. Answer.*

12. *Private confession of two kinds. A. On our own account. B. On account of our neighbor. Use of the former. Great assistance to be obtained from faithful ministers of the Church. Mode of procedure. Caution to be used.*

13. *The use of the latter recommended by Christ. What is comprehended under it. Scripture sanctions no other method of confession.*

14. *The power of the keys exercised in these three kinds of confession. The utility of this power in regard to public confession and absolution. Caution to be observed.*

15. *Popish errors respecting confession. A. In enjoining on all the necessity of confessing every sin. B. Fictitious keys. C. Pretended mandate to loose and bind. D. To whom the office of loosing and binding is committed.*

16. *Refutation of the first error, from the impossibility of so confessing, as proved by the testimony of David.*

17. *Refuted further from the testimony of conscience. Impossible to observe this most rigid obligation. Necessarily leads to despair or indifference. Confirmation of the preceding remarks by an appeal to conscience.*

18. *Another refutation of the first error from analogy. Sum of the whole refutation. Third refutation, laying down the surest rule of confession. Explanation of the rule. Three objections answered.*

19. *Fourth objection—viz. that auricular confession does no harm and is even useful. Answer, unfolding the hypocrisy, falsehood, impiety, and monstrous abominations of the patrons of this error.*

Scripture, and the uniform experience of the Church. Distinction between the reprobate and the elect in regard to punishment.

33. Second distinction. The punishment of the reprobates a commencement of the eternal punishment awaiting them; that of the elect designed to bring them to repentance. This is confirmed by passages of Scripture and of the Fathers.

34. Two uses of this doctrine to the believer. In affliction, he can believe that God, though angry, is still favorable to him. In the punishment of the reprobate, he sees a prelude to their final doom.

35. Objection, as to the punishment of David, answered. Why all men here are subjected to chastisement.

36. Objections, founded on five other passages, answered.

37. Answer continued.

38. Objection, founded on passages in the Fathers. Answer, with passages from Chrysostom and Augustine.

39. These satisfactions had reference to the peace of the Church, and not to the throne of God. The Schoolmen have perverted the meaning of some absurd statements by obscure monks.

1 Errors of the Schoolmen in delivering the doctrine of repentance. A. Errors in defining it. Four different definitions considered. B. Absurd division. C. Vain and puzzling questions. D. Mode in which they entangle themselves.

I come now to an examination of what the scholastic Sophists teach concerning repentance. This I will do as briefly as possible; for I leave no intention to take up every point, lest this work, which I am desirous to frame as a compendium of doctrine, should exceed all bounds. They have managed to envelop a matter, otherwise not much involved, in so many perplexities, that it will be difficult to find an outlet if once you get plunged but a little way into their mire. And, first, in giving a definition, they plainly show they never understood what repentance means. For they fasten on some expressions in the writings of the Fathers which are very far from expressing the nature of repentance. For instance, that to *repent* is to deplore past sins and not commit what is to be deplored. Again that it is to bewail past evils and not to sin to do what is to be bewailed. Again that it is a kind of grieving revenge, punishing in itself what it grieves to have committed. Again, that it is sorrow of heart and bitterness of soul for the evils, which the individual has committed, or to which he has consented. Supposing we grant that these things were well said by the Fathers (though, if one were inclined to dispute, it would be not difficult to deny it), they were not, however, said with the view of describing repentance but only of exhorting penitents not again to fall into the same faults from which they had been delivered.

However, if all descriptions of this kind are to be converted into definitions, there are others, which have as good a title to be added. For instance, the following sentence of Chrysostom: "Repentance is a medicine for the cure of sin, a gift bestowed from above, an admirable virtue, a grace surpassing the power of laws." Moreover, the doctrine, which they afterwards deliver, is somewhat worse than their definition. For they are so keenly bent on external exercises, that all you can gather from immense volumes is, that repentance is a discipline, and austerity, which serves partly to subdue the flesh, partly to chasten and punish sins, regarding internal renovation of mind, bringing with it true amendment of life there is a strange silence. No doubt, they talk much of contrition and attrition, torment the soul with many scruples, and involve it in great trouble and anxiety; but when they seem to have deeply wounded the heart, they cure all its bitterness by a slight sprinkling of ceremonies.

Repentance thus shrewdly defined, they divide into contrition of the heart, confession of the mouth, and satisfaction of works. This is not more logical than the definition, though they would be thought to have spent their whole lives in framing syllogisms. But if anyone argues from the definition (a mode of argument prevalent with dialecticians) that a man may weep over his past sins and not commit things that cause weeping, may bewail past evils and not commit things that are to be bewailed, may punish what he is grieved for having committed, even though he does not confess it with the mouth, how will they defend their division? For if he may be a true penitent and not confess, repentance can exist without confession. If they answer, that this division refers to repentance regarded as a sacrament, or is to be understood of repentance in its most perfect form, which they do not comprehend in their definitions, the mistake does not rest with me: let them blame themselves for not defining more purely and clearly.

When any matter is discussed, I certainly am dull enough to refer everything to the definition as the hinge and foundation of the whole discussion. But granting that this is a license, which masters have, let us now survey the different parts in their order. In omitting as frivolous several things, which they vend with solemn brow as mysteries, I do it not from ignorance. It would be not very difficult to dispose of all those points, which they pride themselves on their acuteness and subtlety in discussing, but I consider it a sacred duty not to trouble the reader to no purpose with such absurdities. It is certainly easy to see from the questions, which they move and agitate, and in which they miserably entangle themselves, that they are dealing with things they know not. Of this nature are the following: Whether repentance of one sin is pleasing to God, while there is an obstinate adherence to other sins. Again, whether punishments divinely indicted are available for satisfaction. Again, whether repentance can be several times repeated for mortal sins, whereas they grossly and wickedly define that daily repentance has to do with none but venial sins.

In like manner, with gross error, they greatly torment themselves with a saying of Jerome, that repentance is a second plank after shipwreck. Herein they show that they have never awakened from brutish stupor, to obtain a distant view of the thousandth part of their sins.

2 The false doctrine of the Schoolmen necessary to be refuted. Of contrition. Their view of it examined.

I would have my readers observe that the dispute here relates not to a matter of no consequence; but to one of the most important of all—viz. the forgiveness of sins. For while they require three things in repentance—viz. compunction of heart, confession of the mouth, and satisfaction of work—they at the same time teach that these are necessary to obtain the pardon of sins. If there is anything in the whole compass of religion, which it is of importance to us to know, this certainly is one of the most important—viz. to perceive and rightly hold by what means, what rule, what terms, with what facility or difficulty, forgiveness of sins may be obtained. Unless our knowledge here is clear and certain, our conscience can have no rest at all, no peace with God, no confidence or security, but is continually trembling, fluctuating, boiling, and distracted; it dreads, hates, and shuns the presence of God.

But if forgiveness of sins depends on the conditions to which they bind it, nothing can be more wretched and deplorable than our situation. *Contrition* they represent as the first step in obtaining pardon; and they exact it as due, that is, full and complete: meanwhile, they decide not when one may feel secure about having performed this contrition in due measure. I admit that we are bound strongly and incessantly to urge every man bitterly to lament his sins, and thereby stimulate himself more and more to dislike and hate them. For this is the "repentance to salvation not to be repented of" (2 Corinthians 7:10). But when such bitterness of sorrow is demanded as may correspond to the magnitude of the offense and be weighed in the balance with confidence of pardon, miserable consciences are sadly perplexed and tormented when they see that the contrition due for sin is laid upon them. Yet, they have no measure of what is due, to enable them to determine that they have made full payment. If they say we are to do what in us lies, we are always brought back to the same point, for when will any man venture to promise himself that he has done his utmost in bewailing sin? Therefore, when consciences, after a lengthened struggle and long contests with themselves, find no haven in which they may rest, as a means of alleviating their condition in some degree, they extort sorrow and wring out tears in order to perfect their contrition.

3 True and genuine contrition.

If they say that this is calumny on my part, let them come forward and point out a single individual who, by this doctrine of contrition, has not either been driven to despair, or has not, instead of true, opposed pretended fear to the justice of God. We have elsewhere observed that forgiveness of sins never can be obtained without repentance, because none but the afflicted and those wounded by a consciousness of sins can sincerely implore the mercy of God.

But we, at the same time, added that repentance cannot be the cause of the forgiveness of sins. We also did away with that torment of souls—the dogma that it must be performed as due. Our doctrine was that the soul looked not to its own compunction or its own tears, but fixed both eyes on the mercy of God alone. Only we observed that those who labor and are heavy laden are called by Christ, seeing he was sent "to preach good tidings to the meek" "to bind up the broken-hearted; to proclaim liberty to the captives, and the opening of the prison to them that are bound" "to comfort all that mourn."

Hence, the Pharisees were excluded, because, full of their own righteousness, they acknowledged not their own poverty; and despisers, because, regardless of the divine anger, they sought no remedy for their wickedness. Such persons neither labor nor are heavy laden, are not broken-hearted, bound, nor in prison. But there is a great difference between teaching that forgiveness of sins is merited by full and complete contrition (which the sinner never can give), and instructing him to hunger and thirst after the mercy of God—that recognizing his wretchedness, his turmoil, weariness, and captivity, you may show him where he should seek refreshment, rest, and liberty, and teach him in his humility to give glory to God.

4 Auricular confession. Whether or not of divine authority. Arguments of Canonists and Schoolmen. Allegorical argument founded on Judaism. Two answers. Reason that Christ sent the lepers to the priests.

Confession has ever been a subject of keen contest between the Canonists and the Scholastic theologians; the former contending that confession is of divine authority—the latter insisting, on the contrary, that it is merely enjoined by ecclesiastical constitution. In this contest, the theologians, who have corrupted and violently wrested every passage of Scripture they have quoted in their favor, have displayed great effrontery. And when they saw that even thus they could not gain their object, those who wished to be thought particularly acute had recourse to the evasion that confession is of divine authority in regard to the substance, but that it afterwards received its form from positive enactment. Thus the silliest of these quibblers refer the citation to divine authority, from its being said, "Adam, where art thou?" (Genesis 3:9, 12); and the exception from Adam having replied as if excepting, "The women whom thou gavest to be with me," etc., but say that the form of both was appointed by civil law. Let us see by what arguments they prove that this confession, formed or unformed, is a divine commandment. The Lord, they say, sent the lepers to the priests. (See Matthew 8:4.) What? Did He send them to confession? Who ever heard that the Levitical priests were appointed to hear confession? Here they resort to allegory. The priests were appointed by the Mosaic Law to discern between leper and leper, and sin is spiritual leprosy; therefore, it belongs to the priests to decide about this.

Before I answer I would ask, in passing, why, if this passage makes them judges of spiritual leprosy, they claim the cognizance of natural and carnal leprosy. This, forsooth, is not to play upon Scripture! The Law gives the cognizance of leprosy to the Levitical priests: let us usurp this to ourselves. Sin is spiritual leprosy: let us also have cognizance of sin. I now give my answer: There being a change of the priesthood, there must of necessity be a change of the Law. All the sacerdotal functions were transferred to Christ, and in him fulfilled and ended. (See Hebrews 7:12.) To Him alone, therefore, all the rights and honors of the priesthood have been transferred. If they are so fond then of hunting out allegories, let them set Christ before them as the only priest, and place full and universal jurisdiction on His tribunal; this we will readily admit. Besides, there is an incongruity in their allegory: it classes a merely civil enactment among ceremonies. Why, then, does Christ send the lepers to the priests? Lest the priests should be charged with violating the Law, which ordained that the person cured of leprosy should present himself before the priest, and be purified by the offering of a sacrifice, He orders the lepers who had been cleansed to do what the Law required. "Go and show thyself to the priest, and offer for thy cleansing according as Moses commanded for a testimony unto them" (Luke 5:17). And assuredly, this miracle would be a testimony to them: they had pronounced them lepers; they now pronounce them cured. Whether they would or not, they are forced to become witnesses to the miracles of Christ. Christ allows them to examine the miracle, and they cannot deny it: yet, as they still quibble, they have need of a testimony.

So it is elsewhere said, "This Gospel of the kingdom shall be preached in all the world, for a witness unto all nations" (Matthew 24:14). Again, "Ye shall be brought before governors and kings for my sake, for a testimony against them and the Gentiles" (Matthew 10:18); that is, in order that, in the judgment of God they might be more convicted.

But if they prefer taking the view of Chrysostom, he shows that this was done by Christ for the sake of the Jews also, that he might not be regarded as a violator of the Law. But we are ashamed to appeal to the authority of any man in a matter so clear, when Christ declares that He left the legal right of the priests entire, as professed enemies of the Gospel, who were always intent on making a clamor if their mouths were not stopped. Wherefore, let the popish priests, in order to retain this privilege, openly make common cause with those whom it was necessary to restrain, by forcible means, from speaking evil of Christ. For there is here no reference to His true ministers.

5 Another allegorical argument. Answer.

They draw their second argument from the same fountain, I mean from the same allegory, as if allegories were of much avail in confirming any doctrine. However, indeed, let them avail, if those, which I am able to produce, are not more specious than theirs are. They say, then, that the Lord, after raising Lazarus, commanded His disciples to "loose him and let him go" (John 11:44). Their first statement is untrue. We nowhere read that the Lord said this to the disciples, and it is much more probable that He spoke to the Jews who were standing by, that from there being no suspicion of fraud the miracle might be more manifest, and His power might be the more conspicuous from his raising the dead without touching him, by a mere word. In the same way, I understand that our Lord, to leave no ground of suspicion to the Jews, wished them to roll back the stone, feel the stench, perceive the sure signs of death, see him rise by the mere power of a word. And this is the view of Chrysostom. But granting that it was said to the disciples, what can they gain by it? That the Lord gave the apostles the power of loosing? How much more aptly and dexterously might we allegorize and say that by this symbol, the Lord designed to teach His followers to loose those whom He raises. That is, not to bring to remembrance the sins which He himself had forgotten, not to condemn as sinners those whom He had acquitted, not still to upbraid those whom He had pardoned, not to be stern and severe in punishing, while He himself was merciful and ready to forgive. Certainly, nothing should more incline us to pardon than the example of the Judge who threatens that He will be inexorable to the rigid and inhumane. Let them go now and vend their allegories.

6 A third argument from two passages of Scripture. These passages expounded.

They now come to closer quarters, while they support their view by passages of Scripture, which they think are clearly in their favor. Those who came to John's baptism confessed their sins, and James bids us to confess our sins one to another. (See James 5:16.) It is not strange that those who wished to be baptized confessed their sins. It has already been mentioned that John preached the baptism of repentance; he baptized with water unto repentance. Whom then could he baptize, but those who confessed that they were sinners? Baptism is a symbol of the forgiveness of sins, and who could be admitted to receive the symbol but sinners acknowledging themselves as such? They, therefore, confessed their sins, that they might be baptized. Nor without good reason does James enjoin us to confess our sins one to another. But if they would attend to what immediately follows, they would perceive that this gives them little support. The words are, "Confess your sins one to another, and pray one for another." He joins together mutual confession and mutual prayer. If, then, we are to confess to priests only, we are also to pray for them only. What? It would even follow from the words of James that priests alone can confess. In saying that we are to confess mutually, he must be addressing those only who can hear the confession of others. He says, it is to be done *mutually, by turns*, or, if they prefer it, *reciprocally*. But those only can confess reciprocally who are fit to hear confession. This being a privilege, which they bestow upon priests only, we also leave them the office of confessing to each other.

Have done then with such frivolous absurdities, and let us receive the true meaning of the apostle, which is plain and simple. First, we are to deposit our infirmities in the breasts of each other, with the view of receiving mutual counsel, sympathy, and comfort; and, secondly, mutually conscious of the infirmities of our brethren, we are to pray to the Lord for them. Why then quote James against us who so earnestly insist on acknowledgment of the divine mercy? No man can acknowledge the mercy of God without previously confessing his own misery. Nay, we pronounce every man to be anathema who does not confess himself a sinner before God, before His angels, before the Church; in short, before all. "The Scripture has concluded all under sin," "that every mouth may be stopped, and all the world may become guilty before God," that God alone may be justified and exalted. (See Galatians 3:22; Romans 3:9, 19.)

7 The rite of confession proved not to be of divine authority. The use of it has been free for almost twelve hundred years after

Christ. Its nature. When enacted into a law. Confirmation from the history of the Church. A representation of the ancient auricular confession still existing among the Papists, to bear judgment against them. Confession abolished in the Church of Constantinople.

I wonder at their effrontery in venturing to maintain that the confession of which they speak is of divine authority. We admit that the use of it is very ancient, but we can easily prove that at one time it was free. It certainly appears, from their own records that no law or constitution respecting it was enacted before the days of Innocent III. Surely if there had been a more ancient law they would have fastened on it, instead of being satisfied with the decree of the Council of Lateral, and so making themselves ridiculous even to children. In other matters, they hesitate not to coin fictitious decrees, which they ascribe to the most ancient councils, that they may blind the eyes of the simple by veneration for antiquity. In this instance, it has not occurred to them to practice this deception, and hence, themselves being witnesses, three centuries have not yet elapsed since the bridle was put, and the necessity of confession imposed by Innocent III. And to say nothing of the time, the mere barbarism of the terms used destroys the authority of the Law. For when these worthy fathers enjoin that every person of *both sexes* (utriusque sexus) must once a year confess his sins to his own priest, men of wit humorously object that the precept binds hermaphrodites only, and has no application to anyone who is either a male or a female. A still grosser absurdity has been displayed by their disciples, who are unable to explain what is meant by one's own priest (proprius sacerdos).

Let all the hired ravers of the pope babble as they may. We hold that Christ is not the author of this law, which compels men to enumerate their sins; nay, that twelve hundred years elapsed after the Resurrection of Christ before any such law was made, and that consequently, this tyranny was not introduced until piety and doctrine were extinct, and pretended pastors had usurped to themselves unbridled license.

There is clear evidence in historians and other ancient writers, to show that this was a politic discipline introduced by bishops, not a law enacted by Christ or the apostles.

Out of many, I will produce only one passage, which will be no obscure proof. Sozomen relates that this constitution of the bishops was carefully observed in the Western churches, but especially at Rome; thus intimating that it was not the universal custom of all churches. He also says that one of the presbyters was specially appointed to take charge of this duty. This abundantly confutes their falsehood as to the keys being given to the whole priesthood indiscriminately for this purpose, since the function was not common to all the priests, but specially belonged to the one priest whom the bishop had appointed to it. He it was (the same who at present in each of the cathedral churches has the name of penitentiary) who had cognizance of offenses, which were more heinous, and required to be rebuked for the sake of example. He afterwards adds that the same custom existed at Constantinople until a certain matron, while pretending to confess, was discovered to have used it as a cloak to cover her intercourse with a deacon. In consequence of that crime, Nectarius, the bishop of that church—a man famous for learning and sanctity—abolished the custom of confessing.

Here, then, let these asses prick up their ears. If auricular confession was a divine law, how could Nectarius have dared to abolish or remodel it? Nectarius, a holy man of God, approved by the suffrage of all antiquity, will they charge with heresy and schism? With the same vote, they will condemn the church of Constantinople, in which Sozomen affirms that the custom of confessing was not only disguised for a time, but also even in his own memory abolished. Nay, let them charge with defections not only Constantinople but also all the Eastern churches, which (if they say true) disregarded an inviolable law enjoined on all Christians.

8 This mode of confession disapproved by Chrysostom, as shown by many passages.

This abrogation is clearly attested in so many passages by Chrysostom, who lived at Constantinople, and was himself prelate of the church, that it is strange they can venture to maintain the contrary. "Tell your sins," says he, "that you may efface them: if you blush to tell another what sins you have committed, tell them daily in your soul. I say not, tell them to your fellow servant who may upbraid you, but tell them to God who cures them. Confess your sins upon your bed, that your conscience may there daily recognize its iniquities." Again, "Now, however, it is not necessary to confess before witnesses; let the examination of your faults be made in your own thought: let the judgment be without a witness: let God alone see you confessing." Again, "I do not lead you publicly into the view of your fellow servants; I do not force you to disclose your sins to men; review and lay open your conscience before God. Show your wounds to the Lord, the best of physicians, and seek medicine from him. Show to him who upbraids not, but cures most kindly." Again, "Certainly tell it not to man lest he upbraid you. Nor must you confess to your fellow servant, who may make it public; but show your wounds to the Lord, who takes care of you, who is kind and can cure." He afterwards introduces God speaking thus: "I oblige you not to come into the midst of a theatre, and have many witnesses; tell your sins to me alone in private, that I may cure the ulcer." Shall we say that Chrysostom, in writing these and similar passages, carried his presumption so far as to free the consciences of men from those chains with which they are bound by the divine law? By no means; but knowing that it was not at all prescribed by the Word of God, he dares not exact it as necessary.

9 False confession being thus refuted, the confession enjoined by the Word of God is considered. Mistranslation in the old version. Proof from Scripture that confession should be directed to God alone.

But that the whole matter may be more plainly unfolded, we shall first honestly state the nature of confession as delivered in the Word of God, and thereafter subjoin their inventions—not all of them indeed (who could drink up that boundless sea?) but those only which contain summary of their secret confession. Here I am grieved to mention how frequently the old interpreter has rendered the word *confess* instead of *praise*, a fact notorious to the most illiterate, were it not fitting to expose their effrontery in transferring to their tyrannical edict what was written concerning the praises of God. To prove that confession has the effect of exhilarating the mind, they obtrude the passage in the Psalm, "With the voice of joy and praise" (Vulgate, *confessionis*) (Psalm 42:4). But if such a metamorphosis is valid, anything may be made of anything. But, as they have lost all shame, let pious readers reflect how, by the just vengeance of God, they have been given over to a reprobate mind, that their audacity may be the more detestable. If we are disposed to acquiesce in the simple doctrine of Scripture, there will be no danger of our being misled by such glosses.

There one method of confessing is prescribed; since it is the Lord who forgives, forgets, and wipes away sins, to Him let us confess them, that we may obtain pardon. He is the physician; therefore let us show our wounds to Him. He is hurt and offended; let us ask peace of Him. He is the discerner of the heart, and knows all one thoughts; let us hasten to pour out our hearts before Him. He it is, in fine, who invites sinners; let us delay not to draw near to Him. "I acknowledge my sin unto thee," says David, "and mine iniquity have I not hid. I said, I will confess my transgressions unto the Lord; and thou forgavest the iniquity of my sin" (Psalm 32:5). Another specimen of David's confessions is as follows: "Have mercy upon me, O God, according to thy loving kindness" (Psalm 51:1). The following is Daniel's confession: "We have sinned, and have committed iniquity, and have done wickedly, and have rebelled, even by departing from thy precepts and thy judgments" (Daniel 9:5). Other examples everywhere occur in Scripture: the quotation of them would almost fill a volume. "If we confess our sins," says John, "he is faithful and just to forgive us our sins" (1 John 1:9). To whom are we to confess? To Him surely, that is, we are to fall down before him with a grieved and humbled heart, and sincerely accusing and condemning ourselves, seek forgiveness of His goodness and mercy.

10 Effect of secret confession thus made to God. Another kind of confession made to men.

Be who has adopted this confession from the heart and, as in the presence of God, will doubtless have a tongue ready to confess whenever there is occasion among men to publish the mercy of God. He will not be satisfied to whisper the secret of his heart for once into the ear of one individual, but will often, and openly, and in the hearing of the whole world, ingenuously make mention both of his own ignominy, and of the greatness and glory of the Lord. In this way David, after Nathan accused him, being stung in his conscience, confesses his sin before God and men. "I have sinned unto the Lord," says he (see 2 Samuel 12:13); that is, I have now no excuse, no evasion; all must judge me a sinner; and that which I wished to be secret with the Lord must also be made manifest to men. Hence, the secret confession, which is made to God, is followed by voluntary confession to men, whenever that is conducive to the divine glory or our humiliation. For this reason the Lord anciently enjoined the people of Israel that they should repeat the words after the priest, and make public confession of their iniquities in the Temple; because he foresaw that this was a necessary help to enable each one to form a just idea of himself. And it is proper that by confession of our misery, we should manifest the mercy of our God both among ourselves and before the whole world.

11 Two forms of the latter confession—viz. public and private. Public confession either ordinary or extraordinary. Use of each. Objection to confession and public prayer. Answer.

It is proper that this mode of confession should both be ordinary in the Church, and be specially employed on extraordinary occasions, when the people in common happen to have fallen into any fault. Of this latter description, we have an example in the solemn confession, which the whole people made under the authority and guidance of Ezra and Nehemiah. (See Nehemiah 1:6, 7.) For their long captivity, the destruction of the Temple, and suppression of their religion, having been the common punishment of their defection, they could not make meet acknowledgment of the blessing of deliverance without previous confession of their guilt. And it matters not, though in one assembly it may sometimes happen that a few are innocent, because the members of a languid and sickly body cannot boast of soundness. Nay, it is scarcely possible that these few have not contracted some taint and so bear part of the blame. Therefore, as often as we are afflicted with pestilence, or war, or famine, or any other calamity whatsoever, if it is our duty to retake ourselves to mourning, fasting, and other signs of guiltiness, confession also, on which all the others depend, is not to be neglected. That ordinary confession which the Lord has moreover expressly commended, no sober man, who has reflected on its usefulness, will venture to disapprove. Because in every sacred assembly, we stand in the view of God and angels, in what way should our service begin except in acknowledging our own unworthiness? But this you will say is done in every prayer; for as often as we pray for pardon, we confess our sins. I admit it. But if you consider how great is our carelessness or drowsiness or sloth, you will grant me that it would be a salutary ordinance if the Christian people were exercised in humiliation by some formal method of confession. For though the ceremony, which the Lord enjoined on the Israelites, belonged to the tutelage of the

Law, yet the thing itself belongs in some respect to us also. And, indeed, in all well ordered churches, in observance of a useful custom, the minister, each Lord's Day, frames a formula of confession in his own name and that of the people, in which he makes a common confession of iniquity, and supplicates pardon from the Lord. In short, by this key a door of prayer is opened privately for each and publicly for all.

12 Private confession of two kinds. A. On our own account. B. On account of our neighbor. Use of the former. Great assistance to be obtained from faithful ministers of the Church. Mode of procedure. Caution to be used.

Two other forms of private confession are approved by Scripture. The one is made on our own account, and to it reference is made in the passage in James, "Confess your sins one to another" (James 5:16); for the meaning is that by disclosing our infirmities to each other, we are to obtain the aid of mutual counsel and consolation. The other is to be made for the sake of our neighbor, to appease and reconcile him if by our fault he has been in any respect injured.

In the former, although James, by not specifying any particular individual into whose bosom we are to unburden our feelings, leaves us the free choice of confessing to any member of the church who may seem fittest; yet, as for the most part, pastors are to be supposed better qualified than others, our choice ought chiefly to fall upon them.

The ground of preference is that the Lord, by calling them to the ministry, points them out as the persons by whose lips we are to be taught to subdue and correct our sins, and derive consolation from the hope of pardon. For as the duty of mutual admonition and correction is committed to all Christians, but is specially enjoined on ministers, so while we ought all to console each other mutually and confirm each other in confidence in the divine mercy, we see that ministers, to assure our consciences of the forgiveness of sins, are appointed to be the witnesses and sponsors of it, so that they are themselves said to forgive sins and loose souls. (See Matthew 16:19; 18:18.) When you hear this attributed to them, reflect that it is for your use.

Let every believer, therefore, remember that if in private he is so agonized and afflicted by a sense of his sins that he cannot obtain relief without the aid of others, it is his duty not to neglect the remedy which God provides for him—viz. to have recourse for relief to a private confession to his own pastor, and for consolation privately implore the assistance of him whose business it is, both in public and private, to solace the people of God with gospel doctrine. But we are always to use moderation, lest in a matter as to which God prescribes no certain rule, our consciences be burdened with a certain yoke.

Hence, it follows first that confession of this nature ought to be free, so as not to be exacted of all, but only recommended to those who feel that they have need of it. Secondly, even those who use it according to their necessity must neither be compelled by any precept, nor artfully induced to enumerate all their sins, but only insofar as they shall deem it for their interest, that they may obtain the full benefit of consolation. Faithful pastors, as they would both eschew tyranny in their ministry, and superstition in the people, must not only leave this liberty to churches, but also defend and strenuously vindicate it.

13 The use of the latter recommended by Christ. What is comprehended under it. Scripture sanctions no other method of confession.

Of the second form of confession, our Savior speaks in Matthew. "If thou bring thy gift to the altar, and there remember that thy brother has ought against thee; leave there thy gift before the altar; first be reconciled to thy brother, and then come and offer thy gift" (Matthew 5:23, 24). Thus love, which has been interrupted by our fault, must be restored by acknowledging and asking pardon for the fault. Under this head is included the confession of those who by their sin have given offense to the whole Church (*supra*, section 10). For if Christ attaches so much importance to the offense of one individual, that He forbids the sacrifice of all who have sinned in any respect against their brethren, until by due satisfaction they have regained their favor, how much greater reason is there that he, who by some evil example has offended the Church should be reconciled to it by the acknowledgment of his fault? Thus, the member of the church of Corinth was restored to communion after he had humbly submitted to correction. (See 2 Corinthians 2:6.) This form of confession existed in the ancient Christian church, as Cyprian relates: "They practice repentance," says he, "for a proper time, then they come to confession, and by the laying on of the hands of the bishop and clergy, are admitted to communion." Scripture knows nothing of any other form or method of confessing, and it belongs not to us to bind new chains upon consciences, which Christ most strictly prohibits from being brought into bondage. Meanwhile, that the flock present themselves before the pastor whenever they would partake of the Holy Supper, I am so far from disapproving, that I am most desirous it should be everywhere observed. For both those whose conscience is hindered may thence obtain singular benefit, and those who require admonition thus afford an opportunity for it, provided always no countenance is given to tyranny and superstition.

14 The power of the keys exercised in these three kinds of confession. The utility of this power in regard to public confession and absolution. Caution is to be observed.

The *power of the keys* has place in the three following modes of confession: either when the whole Church, in a formal acknowledgment of its defects, supplicates pardon; or when a private individual, who has given public offense by some notable delinquency, testifies his repentance; or when he who from disquiet of conscience needs the aid of his minister, acquaints him with his infirmity. With regard to the reparation of offense, the case is different. For though in this also provision is made for peace of conscience, yet the principal object is to suppress hatred, and reunite brethren in the bond of peace. But the benefit of which I have spoken is by no means to be despised, that we may the more willingly confess our sins. For when the whole Church stands at the bar of God, confesses her guilt, and finds her only refuge in the divine mercy, it is no common or light solace to have an ambassador of Christ present, invested with the mandate of reconciliations by whom she may hear her absolution pronounced. Here the utility of the keys is justly commended when that embassy is duly discharged with becoming order and reverence. In like manner, when he who has become an alien from the Church receives pardon, and is thus restored to brotherly unity, how great is the benefit of understanding that he is pardoned by those to whom Christ said, "Whose soever sins ye remit, they are remitted unto them" (John 20:23). Nor is private absolution of less benefit or efficacy when asked by those who stand in need of a special remedy for their infirmity. It often happens that he who hears general promises which are intended for the whole congregation of the faithful, nevertheless remains somewhat in doubts, and is still disquieted in mind, as if his own remission were not yet obtained. Should this individual lay open the secret wound of his soul to his pastor, and hear these words of the gospel specially addressed to him, "Son, be of good cheer, thy sins be forgiven thee" (Matthew 9:2), his mind will feel secure and escape from the trepidation with which it was previously agitated. But when we treat of the keys, we must always beware of dreaming of any power apart from the preaching of the gospel.

This subject will be more fully explained when we come to treat of the government of the Church (Book 4, chapters 11, 12). There we shall see that whatever privilege of binding and loosing Christ has bestowed on His Church is annexed to the Word. This is especially true with regard to the ministry of the keys, the whole power of which consists in this, that the grace of the gospel is publicly and privately sealed on the minds of believers by means of those whom the Lord has appointed; and the only method in which this can be done is by preaching.

15 Popish errors respecting confession. A. In enjoining on all the necessity of confessing every sin. B. Fictitious keys. C. Pretended mandate to loose and bind. D. To whom the office of loosing and binding is committed.

What say the Roman theologians? That all persons of both sexes, as soon as they shall have reached the years of discretion, must, once a year at least, confess all their sins to their own priest; that the sin is not discharged unless the resolution to confess has been firmly conceived; that if this resolution is not carried into effect when an opportunity offers, there is no entrance into Paradise; that the priest, moreover, has the power of the keys, by which he can loose and bind the sinner; because the declaration of Christ is not in vain: "Whatsoever ye shall bind on earth shall be bound in heaven" (Matthew 18:18).

Concerning this power, however, they wage a fierce war among themselves. Some say there is only one key essentially—viz. the power of binding and loosing; that knowledge, indeed, is requisite for the proper use of it, but only as an accessory, not as essentially inherent in it. Others seeing that this gave too unrestrained license, have imagined two keys—viz. discernment and power. Others, again, because the license of priests was curbed by such restraint, have forged other keys (*infra*, section 21), the authority of discerning to be used in defining, and the power to carry their sentences into execution; and to these they add knowledge as a counselor. This binding and loosing, however, they do not venture to interpret simply, to forgive and wipe away sins, because they hear the Lord proclaiming by the prophet, "I, even I, am the Lord; and beside me there is no savior." "I, even I, am he that blotteth out thy transgressions" (Isaiah 43:11, 25).

But they say it belongs to the priest to declare who are bound or loosed, and whose sins are remitted or retained; to declare, moreover, either by confession, when he absolves and retains sins, or by sentence, when he excommunicates or admits to communion in the sacraments.

Lastly, perceiving that the knot is not yet untied, because it may always be objected that persons are often undeservedly bound and loosed, and, therefore, not bound or loosed in Heaven; as their ultimate resource, they answer that the conferring of the keys must be taken with limitations because Christ has promised that the sentence of the priest, properly pronounced, will be approved at His judgment-seat according as the bound or loosed ask what they have merited.

They say, moreover, that those keys which are conferred by bishops at ordination were given by Christ to all priests, but that the free use of them is with those only who discharge ecclesiastical functions; that with priests excommunicated or suspended, the keys themselves indeed remain, but they are tied and rusty. Those who speak thus may justly be deemed modest and sober compared with others, who on a new anvil have forged new keys, by which they say that the treasury of Heaven is locked up: these we shall afterwards consider in their own place (chapter 5, section 2).

16 Refutation of the first error, from the impossibility of so confessing, as proved by the testimony of David.

To each of these views I will briefly reply. As to their binding the souls of believers by their laws, whether justly or unjustly, I say nothing at present, as it will be seen at the proper place. But their enacting it as a law, that all sins are to be enumerated; their denying that sin is discharged except under the condition that the resolution to confess has been firmly conceived. Their pretense that there is no admission into Paradise if the opportunity of confession has been neglected, are things, which it is impossible to bear. Are all sins to be enumerated? But David, who, I presume, had honestly pondered with himself as to the confession of his sins, exclaimed, "Who can understand his errors? Cleanse thou me from secret faults" (Psalm 19:12); and in another passage, "Mine iniquities are gone over my head: as a heavy burden they are too heavy for me" (Psalm 38:4). He knew how deep was the abyss of our sins, how numerous the forms of wickedness, how many heads the hydra carried, how long a tail it drew. Therefore, he did not sit down to make a catalogue, but from the depth of his distress he cried unto the Lord, "I am overwhelmed, and buried, and sore vexed; the gates of hell have encircled me: let thy right hand deliver me from the abyss into which I am plunged, and from the death which I am ready to die." Who can now think of a computation of his sins when he sees David's inability to number his?

17 Refuted further from the testimony of conscience. Impossible to observe this most rigid obligation. Necessarily leads to despair or indifference. Confirmation of the preceding remarks by an appeal to conscience.

By this ruinous procedure, the souls of those who were affected with some sense of God have been most cruelly racked. First, they retook themselves to calculation, proceeding according to the formula given by the Schoolmen, and dividing their sins into boughs, branches, twigs, and leaves; then they weighed the qualities, quantities, and circumstances; and in this way, for some time, matters proceeded. But after they had advanced farther, when they looked around, nothing was seen except sea and sky; no road, no harbor. The longer the space they ran over, a longer still met the eye; nay, lofty mountains began to rise, and there seemed no hope of escape; none at least until after long wanderings. They were thus brought to a dead halt, until at length the only issue was found in despair. Here these cruel murderers, to ease the wounds, which they had made, applied certain fomentations. Everyone was to do his best. But new cares again disturbed, nay, new torments excruciated their souls. "I have not spent enough of time; I have not exerted myself sufficiently: many things I have omitted through negligence: forgetfulness proceeding from want of care is not excusable." Then new drugs were supplied to alleviate their pains. "Repent of your negligence; and provided it is not done supinely, it will be pardoned." All these things, however, could not heal the wound, being not so much alleviations of the sore as poison besmeared with honey, that its bitterness might not at once offend the taste, but penetrate to the vitals before it could be detected. The dreadful voice, therefore, was always heard pealing in their ears, "Confess all your sins," and the dread thus occasioned could not be pacified without sure consolation.

Here let my readers consider whether it is possible to take an account of the actions of a whole year, or even to collect the sins committed in a single day, seeing every man's experience convinces him that at evening, in examining the faults of that single day, memory gets confused, so great is the number and variety presented. I am not speaking of dull and heartless hypocrites, who, after ruminating on three or four of their grosser offenses, think the work finished; but of the true worshipers of God, who, after they have performed their examination, feeling themselves overwhelmed, still add the words of John: "If our heart condemn us, God is greater than our heart, and knoweth all things" (1 John 3:20); and, therefore, tremble at the thought of that Judge whose knowledge far surpasses our comprehension.

18 Another refutation of the first error from analogy. Sum of the whole refutation. Third refutation, laying down the surest rule of confession. Explanation of the rule. Three objections answered.

Though a good part of the world rested in these soothing suggestions by which this fatal poison was somewhat tempered, it was not because they thought that God was satisfied, or they had quite satisfied themselves; it was rather like an anchor cast out in the middle of the deep, which for a little interrupts the navigation, or a weary, worn-out traveler, who lies down by the way. I give myself no trouble in proving the truth of this fact. Everyone can be his own witness. I will mention generally, what the nature of this law is.

First, the observance of it is simply impossible; and hence its only results to destroy, condemn, confound, to plunge into ruin and despair.

Secondly, by withdrawing sinners from a true sense of their sins, it makes them hypocritical, and ignorant of both God and themselves. For, while they are wholly occupied with the enumeration of their sins, they lose sight of that lurking hydra, their secret iniquities, and internal defilements, the knowledge of which would have made them sensible of their misery. But the surest rule of confession is, to acknowledge and confess our sins to be an abyss so great as to exceed our comprehension.

On this rule we see the confession of the publican was formed, "God be merciful to me, a sinner" (Luke 18:13); as if he had said, "How great, how very great a sinner, how utterly sinful I am! The extent of my sins I can neither conceive nor express. Let the depth of thy mercy engulf the depth of sin!" What! You will say, are we not to confess every single sin? Is no confession acceptable to God but that which is contained in the words, "I am a sinner"? Nay, our endeavor must rather be, as much as in us lies, to pour out our whole heart before the Lord. Nor are we only in one word to confess ourselves sinners, but truly and sincerely to acknowledge ourselves as such; to feel with our whole soul how great and various the pollutions of our sins are; confessing not only that we are impure, but what the nature of our impurity is, its magnitude and its extent; not only that we are debtors, but what the debts are which burden us, and how they were incurred; not only that we are wounded, but how numerous and deadly are the wounds. When thus recognizing himself, the sinner shall have poured out his whole heart before God, let him seriously and sincerely reflect that a greater number of sins remain, and that their recesses are too deep for him thoroughly to penetrate. Accordingly, let him exclaim with David, "Who can understand his errors? cleanse thou me from secret faults" (Psalm 19:12).

But when the Schoolmen affirm that sins are not forgiven, unless the resolution to confess has been firmly conceived, and that the gate of Paradise is closed on him who has neglected the opportunity of confessing when offered, far be it from us to concede this to them.

The remission of sins is not different now from what it has ever been. In all the passages in which we read that sinners obtained forgiveness from God, we read not that they whispered into the ear of some priest. Indeed, they could not then confess, as priests were not then confessionaries, nor did the confessional itself exist. And for many ages afterwards, this mode of confession, by which sins were forgiven on this condition, was unheard of. But not to enter into a long discussion, as if the matter were doubtful, the Word of God, which abideth forever, is plain, "When the wicked shall turn away from all his sins that he has committed, and keep all my statutes, and do that which is lawful and right, he shall surely live, he shall not die" (Ezekiel 18:21). He who presumes to add to this declaration binds not sins, but the mercy of God.

When they contend that judgment cannot be given unless the case is known, the answer is easy, that they usurp the right of judging, being only self-created judges. And it is strange, how confidently they lay down principles, which no man of sound mind will admit. They give out, that the office of binding and loosing has been committed to them, as a kind of jurisdiction annexed to the right of inquiry. That the jurisdiction was unknown to the apostles their whole doctrine proclaims. Nor does it belong to the priest to know for certainty whether or not a sinner is loosed, but to Him from whom acquittal is asked, since he who only hears can ever know whether or not the enumeration is full and complete. Thus, there would be no absolution, without restricting it to the words of him who is to be judged.

We may add that the whole system of loosing depends on faith and repentance, two things that no man can know of another, to pronounce sentence. It follows, therefore, that the certainty of binding and loosing is not subjected to the will of an earthly judge, because the minister of the Word, when he duly executes his office, can only acquit conditionally, when, for the sake of the sinner, he repeats the words, "Whose soever sins ye remit;" lest he should doubt of the pardon, which, by the command and voice of God, is promised to be ratified in Heaven.

19 Fourth objection—viz. that auricular confession does no harm, and is even useful. Answer, unfolding the hypocrisy, falsehood, impiety, and monstrous abominations of the patrons of this error.

It is not strange, therefore, that we condemn that auricular confession, as a thing pestilent in its nature, and in many ways injurious to the Church and desire to see it abolished. But if the thing were in itself indifferent, yet, seeing it is of no use or benefit, and has given occasion to so much impiety, blasphemy, and error, who does not think that it ought to be immediately abolished? They enumerate some of its uses, and boast of them as very beneficial, but they are either fictitious or of no importance.

One thing they specially commend that the blush of shame in the penitent is a severe punishment, which makes him more cautious for the future, and anticipates divine punishment, by his punishing himself. As if a man was not sufficiently humbled with shame when brought under the cognizance of God at His supreme tribunal. Admirable proficiency—if we cease to sin because we are ashamed to make one man acquainted with it, and blush not at having God as the witness of our evil conscience!

The assertion, however, as to the effect of shame, is most unfounded, for we may everywhere see that there is nothing which gives men greater confidence and license in sinning than the idea, that after making confession to priests, they can *wipe their lip, and say, I have not done it*. And not only do they during the whole year become bolder in sin, but, secure against confession for the remainder of it, they never sigh after God, never examine themselves, but continue heaping sins upon sins, until, as they suppose, they get rid of them all at once. And when they have got rid of them, they think they are unburdened of their load, and imagine they have deprived God of the right of judging, by giving it to the priest; have made God forgetful, by making the priest conscious.

Moreover, who is glad when he sees the day of confession approaching? Who goes with a cheerful mind to confess, and does not rather, as if he were dragged to prison with a rope about his neck, go unwillingly, and struggling against it? With the exception, perhaps, of the priests themselves, who take a fond delight in the mutual narrative of their own misdeeds, as a kind of merry tale.

I will not pollute my page by retailing the monstrous abominations with which auricular confession teems; I only say that if that holy man did not act unadvisedly when for one rumor of whoredom he banished confession from his church, or rather from the memory of his people, the innumerable acts of prostitution, adultery, and incest, which it produces in the present day, warn us of the necessity of abolishing it.

20 Refutation of the second error. A. Priests not successors of the Apostles. B. They do not have the Holy Spirit, who alone is arbiter of the keys.

As to the pretence of the confessionaries respecting the power of the keys, and their placing in it, so to speak, the sum and substance of their kingdom, we must see what force it ought to have. Were the keys, then (they ask), given without a cause? Was it said without a cause, "Whatsoever ye shall bind on earth shall be bound in heaven, and whatsoever ye shall loose on earth shall be loosed in heaven" (Matthew 18:18)?

Do we make void the word of Christ? I answer that there was a weighty reason for giving the keys, as I lately explained, and will again show at greater length when I come to deal with Excommunication (Book Fourth, chapter 12). But what if I should cut off the handle for all such questions with one sword—viz. that priests are neither vicars nor successors of the apostles? But that also will be elsewhere considered (Book 4, chapter 6).

Now, at the very place where they are most desirous to fortify themselves, they erect a battering ram, by which all their own machinations are overthrown. Christ did not give His apostles the power of binding and loosing before He endued them with the Holy Spirit. I deny, therefore, that any man, who has not previously received the Holy Spirit, is competent to possess the power of the keys. I deny that anyone can use the keys, unless the Holy Spirit precedes, teaching and dictating what is to be done. They pretend, indeed, that they have the Holy Spirit, but by their works they deny Him, unless, indeed, we are to suppose that the Holy Spirit is some vain thing of no value, as they certainly do feign, but we will not believe them. With this engine, they are completely overthrown; whatever be the door of which they boast of having the key, we must always ask,whether they have the Holy Spirit, who is arbiter and ruler of the keys? If they reply that they have, we must again ask whether or not the Holy Spirit can err. This they will not venture to say distinctly, although by their doctrine they indirectly insinuate it.

Therefore, we must infer that no priestlings have the power of the keys, because they everywhere and indiscriminately loose what the Lord was pleased should be bound, and bind what He has ordered to be loosed.

21 Refutation of the third error. They are ignorant of the command and promise of Christ. By abandoning the Word of God, they run into innumerable absurdities.

When they see themselves convicted on the clearest evidence, of loosing and binding worthy and unworthy without distinction, they lay claim to power without knowledge. And although they dare not deny that knowledge is requisite for the proper use, they still affirm that the power itself has been given to bad administrators. This, however, is the power, "Whatsoever ye shall bind on earth shall be bound in heaven, and whatsoever ye shall loose on earth shall be loosed in heaven." Either the promise of Christ must be false, or those, who are endued with this power, bind and loose properly. There is no room for the evasion, that the words of Christ are limited, according to the merits of him who is loosed or bound. We admit that none can be bound or loosed but those who are worthy of being bound or loosed.

But the preachers of the gospel and the Church have the Word by which they can measure this worthiness. By this Word, preachers of the gospel can promise forgiveness of sins to all who are in Christ by faith, and can declare a sentence of condemnation against all, and upon all, who do not embrace Christ. In this Word the Church declares that "neither fornicators, nor idolaters, nor adulterers," "nor thieves, nor covetous, nor drunkards, nor revilers, nor extortioners shall inherit the kingdom of God" (1 Corinthians 6:9, 10). Such it binds in sure fetters. By the same Word it looses and consoles the penitent.

But what kind of power is it, which knows not what is to be bound or loosed? You cannot bind or loose without knowledge. Why, then, do they say that they absolve by authority given to them, when absolution is uncertain? As regards us, this power is merely imaginary, if it cannot be used. Now, I hold either that there is no use or one so uncertain as to be virtually no use at all. For when they confess that a good part of the priests do not use the keys duly, and that power without the legitimate use is ineffectual, who is to assure me that the one by whom I am loosed is a good dispenser of the keys? But if he is a bad one, what better has he given me than this nugatory dispensation, What is to be bound or loosed in you I know not, since I have not the proper use of the keys; but if you deserve it, I absolve you? As much might be done, I say not by clergy (since they would scarcely listen to such a statement), but by the Turk or the devil. For it is just to say, I have not the Word of God, the sure rule for loosing, but authority has been given me to absolve you, if you deserve it.

We see, therefore, what their object was, when they defined (see section 16) the keys as authority to discern and power to execute; and said that knowledge is added as a counselor, and counsels the proper use their object was to reign libidinously and licentiously, without God and His Word.

22 Objection to the refutation of the third error. Answers, reducing the Papists to various absurdities.

Should anyone object, first, that the lawful ministers of Christ will be no less perplexed in the discharge of their duty, because the absolution, which depends on faith, will always be equivocal; and, secondly, that sinners will receive no comfort at all, or cold comfort, because the minister, who is not a fit judge of their faith, is not certain of their absolution, we are prepared with an answer. They say that no sins are remitted by the priest, but such sins as he is cognizant of; thus, according to them, remission depends on the judgment of the priest, and unless he accurately discriminates as to who are worthy of pardon, the whole procedure is null and void. In short, the power of which they speak is a jurisdiction annexed to examination, to which pardon and absolution are restricted. Here no firm footing can be found, nay, there is a profound abyss; because, where confession is not complete, the hope of pardon also is defective; next, the priest himself must necessarily remain in suspense, while he knows not whether the sinner gives a faithful enumeration of his sins; lastly, such is the rudeness and ignorance of priests, that the greater part of them are in no respect fitter to perform this office than a cobbler to cultivate the fields, while almost all the others have good reason to suspect their own fitness.

Hence, the perplexity and doubt as to the popish absolution, from their choosing to found it on the person of the priest, and not on his person only, but on his knowledge, so that he can only judge regarding what is laid before him as investigated and ascertained. Now, what would be the answer if any should ask these good doctors whether the sinner is reconciled to God when some sins are remitted? I know not what answer they could give, unless that they should be forced to confess that whatever the priest pronounces with regard to the remission of sins which have been enumerated to him will be unavailing, so long as others are not exempted from condemnation. On the part of the penitent, again, it is hence obvious in what a state of pernicious anxiety his conscience will be held, because, while he leans on what they call the discernment of the priest, he cannot come to any decision from the Word of God. From all these absurdities, the doctrine, which we deliver, is completely free. For absolution is conditional, allowing the sinner to trust that God is propitious to him, provided he sincerely seeks expiation in the sacrifice of Christ, and accepts the grace that is offered to him. Thus, he cannot err who, in the capacity of a herald, promulgates what has been dictated to him from the Word of God.

The sinner, again, can receive a clear and sure absolution when, in regard to embracing the grace of Christ, the simple condition annexed is in terms of the general rule of our Master himself, a rule impiously spurned by the Papacy, "According to your faith be it unto you" (Matthew 9:29).

23 Refutation of the fourth error. A. Petitio principii. B. Inversion of ecclesiastical discipline. Three objections answered.

The absurd jargon, which they make of the doctrine of Scripture concerning the power of the keys, I have promised to expose elsewhere; the proper place will be in discussing the government of the Church (Book 4, chapter 12). Meanwhile, let the reader remember how absurdly they wrest to auricular and secret confession what was said by Christ partly of the preaching of the gospel, and partly of excommunication. Wherefore, when they object that the power of loosing was given to the apostles, and that this power priests exercise by remitting sins acknowledged to them, it is plain that the principle which they assume is false and frivolous: for the absolution which is subordinate to faith is nothing else than an evidence of pardon, derived from the free promise of the gospel, while the other absolution, which depends on the discipline of the Church, has nothing to do with secret sins; but is more a matter of example for the purpose of removing the public offense given to the Church.

As to their diligence in searching up and down for passages by which they may prove that it is not sufficient to confess sins to God alone, or to laymen, unless the priest takes cognizance, it is vile and disgraceful. For when the ancient fathers advise sinners to unburden themselves to their pastor, we cannot understand them to refer to a recital, which was not then in use. Then, so unfair are Lombard and others who are like-minded, that they seem intentionally to have devoted themselves to spurious books, that they might use them as a cloak to deceive the simple. They, indeed, acknowledge truly, that as forgiveness always accompanies repentance, no obstacle properly remains after the individual is truly penitent, though he may not have actually confessed; and, therefore, that the priest does not so much remit sins, as pronounce and declare that they are remitted; though in the term *declaring*, they insinuate a gross error, surrogating ceremony in place of doctrine. But in pretending that he who has already obtained pardon before God is acquitted in the face of the Church, they unseasonably apply to the special use of every individual, that which we have already said was designed for common discipline when the offense of a more heinous and notorious transgression was to be removed.

Shortly after they pervert and destroy their previous moderation, by adding that there is another mode of remission, namely, by the infliction of penalty and satisfaction, in which they arrogate to their priests the right of dividing what God has everywhere promised to us entire. While He simply requires repentance and faith, their division or exception is altogether blasphemous. For it is just as if the priest, assuming the office of tribune, were to interfere with God, and try to prevent him from admitting to his favor by his mere liberality anyone who had not previously lain prostrate at the tribunal bench, and there been punished.

24 Conclusion of the whole discussion against this fictitious confession.

The whole comes to this, when they wish to make God the author of this fictitious confession, their vanity is proved as I have shown their falsehood in expounding the few passages, which they cite. But while it is plain that men imposed the Law, I say that it is both tyrannical and insulting to God, who, in binding consciences to His Word, would have them free from human rule. Then when confession is prescribed as necessary to obtain pardon, which God wished to be free, I say that the sacrilege is altogether intolerable, because nothing belongs more peculiarly to God than the forgiveness of sins, in which our salvation consists. Moreover, I have shown that this tyranny was introduced when the world was sunk in shameful barbarism. Besides, I have proved that the Law is pestiferous, inasmuch as when the fear of God exists, it plunges men into despair, and when there is security soothing itself with vain flattery, it blunts it the more. Lastly, I have explained that all the mitigations, which they employ, have no other tendency than to entangle, obscure, corrupt the pure doctrine, and cloak their iniquities with deceitful colors.

25 Of satisfaction, to which the Sophists assign the third place in repentance. Errors and falsehoods. These views opposed by the terms: A. Forgiveness. B. Free forgiveness. C. God destroying iniquities. D. By and because of Christ. No need of our satisfaction.

In repentance, they assign the third place to satisfaction, all their absurd talk as to which can be refuted in one word. They say it is not sufficient for the penitent to abstain from past sins and change his conduct for the better, unless he satisfies God for what he has done; and that there are many helps by which we may redeem sins, such as tears, fasting oblations, and offices of charity; that by them the Lord is to be propitiated; by them the debts due to divine justice are to be paid; by them our faults are to be compensated; by them pardon is to be deserved: for though in the riches of His mercy He has forgiven the guilt, he yet, as a just discipline, retains the penalty, and that this penalty must be bought off by satisfaction. The sum of the whole comes to this: that we indeed obtain pardon of our sins from the mercy of God, but still by the intervention of the merit of works, by which the evil of our sins is compensated, and due satisfaction made to divine justice.

To such false views I oppose the free forgiveness of sins, one of the doctrines most clearly taught in Scripture.

First, what is forgiveness but a gift of mere liberality? A creditor is not said to forgive when he declares by granting a discharge that the money has been paid to him; but when, without any payment, through voluntary kindness, he expunges the debt. And why is the term *gratis* (free) afterwards added, but to take away all idea of satisfaction? With what confidence, then, do they still set up their satisfactions, which are thus struck down as with a thunderbolt? What? When the Lord proclaims by Isaiah, "I, even I, am he that blotteth out thy transgressions for mine own sake, and will not remember thy sins," does He not plainly declare that the cause and foundation of forgiveness is to be sought from His goodness alone?

Besides, when the whole of Scripture bears this testimony to Christ, that through His name the forgiveness of sins is to be obtained (Acts 10:43), does it not plainly exclude all other names? How then do they teach that it is obtained by the name of satisfaction? Let them not deny that they attribute this to satisfactions, though they bring them in as subsidiary aids. For when Scripture says, *by the name of Christ*, it means that we are to bring nothing, pretend nothing of our own, but lean entirely on the recommendation of Christ.

Thus, Paul, after declaring that "God was in Christ reconciling the world unto himself, not imputing their trespasses unto them," immediately adds the reason and the method, "For he has made him to be sin for us who knew no sin" (2 Corinthians 5:19, 20).

26 Objection, confining the grace and efficacy of Christ within narrow limits. Answers by both John the Evangelist and John the Baptist. Consequence of these answers.

But with their usual perverseness, they maintain that both the forgiveness of sins and reconciliation take place at once when we are received into the favor of God through Christ in baptism; that in lapses after baptism we must rise again by means of satisfactions; that the blood of Christ is of no avail unless insofar as it is dispensed by the keys of the Church. I speak not of a matter as to which there can be any doubt; for this impious dogma is declared in the plainest terms, in the writings not of one or two, but of the whole Schoolmen.

Their master, after acknowledging, according to the doctrine of Peter, that Christ "bare our sins in his own body on the tree" (1 Peter 2:24), immediately modifies the doctrine by introducing the exception, that in baptism all the temporal penalties of sin are relaxed; but that after baptism they are lessened by means of repentance, the cross of Christ and our repentance thus cooperating together. St. John speaks very differently, "If any man sin, we have an advocate with the Father, Jesus Christ the righteous; and he is the propitiation for our sins." "I write unto you, little children, because your sins are forgiven you for his name's sake" (1 John 2:1, 2, 12). He certainly is addressing believers, and while setting forth Christ as the propitiation for sins, shows them that there is no other satisfaction by which an offended God can be propitiated or appeased.

He does not say that God was once reconciled to you by Christ; now, seek other methods. but he makes Him a perpetual advocate, who always, by His intercession, reinstates us in His Fathered favor—a perpetual propitiation by which sins are expiated. For what was said by another, John will ever hold true, "Behold the Lamb of God, which taketh away the sins of the world" (John 1:29).

He, I say, took them away, and no other; that is, since He alone is the Lamb of God, He alone is the offering for our sins; He alone is expiation; He alone is satisfaction. For though the right and power of pardoning properly belongs to the Father, when He is distinguished from the Son, as has already been seen, Christ is here exhibited in another view, as transferring to himself the punishment due to us, and wiping away our guilt in the sight of God. Whence it follows that we could not be partakers of the expiation accomplished by

Christ, were He not possessed of that honor of which those who try to appease God by their compensations seek to rob Him.

27 Two points violated by the fiction of satisfaction. First, the honor of Christ is impaired. Secondly, the conscience cannot find peace. Objection, confining the forgiveness of sins to Catechumen is refuted.

Here it is necessary to keep two things in view: that the honor of Christ be preserved entire and unimpaired, and that the conscience, assured of the pardon of sin, may have peace with God. Isaiah says that the Father "has laid on him the iniquity of us all;" that "with his stripes we are healed" (Isaiah 53:5, 6). Peter, repeating the same thing, in other words says that he, "...bare our sins in his own body on the tree" (1 Peter 2:24). Paul's words are, "God sending his own Son in the likeness of sinful flesh, and for sin condemned sin in the flesh," "being made a curse for us" (Romans 8:3; Galatians 3:13); in other words, the power and curse of sin was destroyed in His flesh when He was offered as a sacrifice, on which the whole weight of our sins was laid, with their curse and execration, with the fearful judgment of God, and condemnation to death. Here there is no mention of the vain dogma, that after the initial cleansing no man experiences the efficacy of Christ's passion in any other way than by means of satisfying penance, we are directed to the satisfaction of Christ alone for every fall.

Now call to mind their pestilential dogma: that the grace of God is effective only in the first forgiveness of sins, but if we afterwards fall, our works cooperate in obtaining the second pardon. If these things are so, do the properties above attributed to Christ remain entire? How immense the difference between the two propositions— that our iniquities were laid upon Christ, that in His own person He might expiate them, and that they are expiated by our works; that Christ is the propitiation for our sins, and that God is to be propitiated by works. Then, in regard to pacifying the conscience, what pacification will it be to be told that sins are redeemed by satisfactions? How will it be able to ascertain the measure of satisfaction? It will always doubt whether God is propitious; it will always fluctuate, always tremble.

Those who rest satisfied with petty satisfactions form too contemptible an estimate of the justice of God, and little consider the grievous heinousness of sin, as shall afterwards be shown. Even were we to grant that they can buy off some sins by due satisfaction, still what will they do while they are overwhelmed with so many sins that not even a hundred lives, though wholly devoted to the purpose, could suffice to satisfy for them?

We may add that all the passages in which the forgiveness of sins is declared refer not only to catechumens, but also to the regenerate children of God, to those who have long been nursed in the bosom of the Church. That embassy which Paul so highly extols, "We pray you in Christ's stead, be ye reconciled to God" (2 Corinthians 5:20), is not directed to strangers, but to those who had been regenerated long before. Setting satisfactions altogether aside, he directs us to the cross of Christ. Thus, when he writes to the Colossians that Christ had "made peace through the blood of his cross," "to reconcile all things unto himself," he does not restrict it to the moment at which we are received into the Church but extends it to our whole course. This is plain from the context, where he says that in him, "We have redemption by his blood, even the forgiveness of sins" (Colossians 1:14). It is needless to collect more passages, as they are ever occurring.

28 Objection, founded on the arbitrary distinction between venial and mortal sins. This distinction is insulting to God and repugnant to Scripture. Answer, showing the true distinction with regard to venial sin.

Here they take refuge in the absurd distinction that some sins are *venial* and others *mortal*; that for the latter a weighty satisfaction is due, but that the former are purged by easier remedies; by the Lord's Prayer, the sprinkling of holy water, and the absolution of the Mass. Thus, they insult and trifle with God. Yet, though they have the terms venial and mortal sin continually in their mouths, they have not yet been able to distinguish one from the other, except by making impiety and impurity of heart to be venial sin.

We, on the contrary, taught by the Scripture standard of righteousness and unrighteousness, declare that "The wages of sin is death;" and that "The soul that sinneth, it shall die" (Romans 6:23; Ezekiel 18:20). The sins of believers are venial, not because they do not merit death, but because by the mercy of God there is "now no condemnation to those which are in Christ Jesus," their sin being not imputed, but effaced by pardon.

I know how unjustly they calumniate this our doctrine, for they say it is the paradox of the Stoics concerning the equality of sins. But we shall easily convict them out of their own mouths. I ask them whether, among those sins that they hold to be mortal, they acknowledge a greater and a lesser. If so, it cannot follow, as a matter of course, that all sins, which are mortal, are equal. Since Scripture declares that the wages of sin is death, that obedience to the law is the way to life, the transgression of it the way to death, —they cannot evade this conclusion. In such a mass of sins, therefore, how will they find an end to their satisfactions? If the satisfaction for one sin requires one day, while preparing it, they involve themselves in more sins, because no man, however righteous, passes one day without falling repeatedly. While they prepare themselves for their satisfactions, number, or rather numbers without number, will be added. Confidence in satisfaction being thus destroyed, what more would they have? How do they still dare to think of satisfying?

29 Objection, founded on a distinction between guilt and the punishment of it. Answer, illustrated by various passages of Scripture. Admirable saying of Augustine.

They endeavor, indeed, to disentangle themselves, but it is impossible. They pretend a distinction between penalty and guilt, holding that the guilt is forgiven by the mercy of God; but that, though the guilt is remitted, the punishment which divine justice requires to be paid remains. Satisfactions then properly relate to the remission of the penalty. How ridiculous this levity is! They now confess that the remission of guilt is gratuitous; and yet they are always telling as to merit it by prayers and tears, and other preparations of every kind. Still the whole doctrine of Scripture regarding the remission of sins is diametrically opposed to that distinction.

But although I think I have already done more than enough to establish this, I will subjoin some other passages, by which these slippery snakes will be so caught as to be afterwards unable to writhe even the tips of their tails: "Behold, the days come, saith the Lord, that I will make a new covenant with the house of Israel, and with the house of Judah." "I will forgive their iniquity, and I will remember their sin no more" (Jeremiah 31:31, 34). What this means we learn from another prophet, when the Lord says, "When the righteous turneth away from his righteousness"; "all his righteousness that he has done shall not be mentioned." "Again, when the wicked man turneth away from his wickedness that he has committed, and does that which is lawful and right, he shall save his soul alive" (Ezekiel 18:24, 27).

When he declares that he will not remember righteousness, the meaning is that he will take no account of it to reward it. In the same way, not to remember sins is not to bring them to punishment. The same thing is denoted in other passages, by casting them behind His back, blotting them out as a cloud, casting them into the depths of the sea, not imputing them, hiding them.

By such forms of expression, the Holy Spirit has explained His meaning not obscurely, if we would lend a willing ear. Certainly if God punishes sins, He imputes them; if He avenges, He remembers; if He brings them to judgment, He has not hid them; if He examines, he has not cast them behind His back; if He investigates, He has not blotted them out like a cloud; if He exposes them, he has not thrown them into the depths of the sea. In this way Augustine clearly interprets: "If God has covered sins, he willed not to advert to them; if he willed not to advert, he willed not to animadvert; if he willed not to animadvert, he willed not to punish: he willed not to take knowledge of them, he rather willed to pardon them. Why then did he say that sins were hid? Just that they might not be seen. What is meant by God seeing sins but punishing them?" But let us hear from another prophetical passage on what terms the Lord forgives sins: "Though your sins be as scarlet, they shall be white as snow; though they be red like crimson, they shall be as wool" (Isaiah 1:18). In Jeremiah again we read: "In those days, and in that time, saith the Lord, the iniquity of Israel shall be sought for, and there shall be none; and the sins of Judah, they shall not be found: for I will pardon them whom I reserve" (Jeremiah 50:20).

Would you briefly comprehend the meaning of these words? Consider what, on the contrary, is meant by these expressions: "That transgression is sealed up in a bag"; "That the iniquity of Ephraim is bound up; his sin is hid"; that "the sin of Judah is written with a pen of iron, and with the point of a diamond." If they mean, as they certainly do, that vengeance will be recompensed, there can be no doubt that, by the contrary passages, the Lord declares that He renounces all thought of vengeance. Here I must entreat the reader not to listen to any glosses of mine, but only to give some deference to the Word of God.

30 Answer, founded on a consideration of the efficacy of Christ's death, and the sacrifices under the Law. Our true satisfaction.

What, pray, did Christ perform for us if the punishment of sin is still exacted? For when we say that He "bare our sins in his own body on the tree" (1 Peter 2:24), all we mean is that He endured the penalty and punishment which was due to our sins. This is more significantly declared by Isaiah, when he says that the "...chastisement [or correction] of our peace was upon him" (Isaiah 53:5). But what is the correction of our peace, unless it is the punishment due to our sins, and to be paid by us before we could be reconciled to God, had He not become our substitute? Thus, you clearly see that Christ bore the punishment of sin, that He might thereby exempt His people from it. And whenever Paul makes mention of the redemption procured by Him, he does not simply mean *redemption*, as it is commonly understood, but the very *price* and satisfaction of redemption. For which reason, he also says that Christ gave himself (as a ransom) for us. "What is propitiation with the Lord, Augustine wrote, but sacrifice? And what is sacrifice but that which was offered for us in the death of Christ?"

But we have our strongest argument in the injunctions of the Mosaic Law as to expiating the guilt of sin. The Lord does not there appoint this or that method of satisfying, but requires the whole compensation to be made by sacrifice, though He at the same time enumerates all the rites of expiation with the greatest care and exactness. How is it that He does not at all enjoin works as the means of procuring pardon, but only requires sacrifices for expiation, unless it would be His purpose thus to testify that this is the only kind of satisfaction by which His justice is appeased? For the sacrifices which the Israelites then offered were not regarded as human works, but were estimated by their anti-type, that is, the sole sacrifice of Christ.

The kind of compensation which the Lord receives from us is elegantly and briefly expressed by Hosea: (here is remission) "Take with you words, and turn to the Lord: say unto him, Take away all iniquity, and receive us graciously." "So will we render the calves of our lips," here is satisfaction (Hosea 14:2). I know that they have still a more subtle evasion, by making a distinction between eternal and temporal punishment; but as they define temporal punishment to be any kind of infliction with which God visits either the body or the soul, eternal death only excepted, this restriction avails them little. The passages, which we have quoted above, say expressly that the terms on which God receives us into favor are these—viz. he remits all the punishment, which we deserved by pardoning our guilt. And whenever David or the other prophets ask pardon for their sins, they deprecate punishment. Nay, a sense of the divine justice impels them to this. On the other hand, when they promise mercy from the Lord, they usually discourse of punishments and the forgiveness of them. Assuredly, when the Lord declares in Ezekiel that He will put an end to the Babylonish captivity, not "For your sakes, O house of Israel, but for mine holy name's sake" (Ezekiel 36:22), He sufficiently demonstrates that both are gratuitous. In short, if Christ frees us from guilt, the punishment consequent upon guilt must cease with it.

31 An objection, perverting six passages of Scripture. Preliminary observations concerning a twofold judgment on the part of God. A. For punishment. B. For correction.

But since they also arm themselves with passages of Scripture, let us see what the arguments are which they employ. David, they say, when upbraided by Nathan the prophet for adultery and murder, receives pardon of the sin. Yet, by the death of the son born of adultery is afterwards punished. (See 2 Samuel 12:13, 14.) Such punishments, which were to be inflicted after the remission of the guilt, we are taught to ransom by satisfactions. For Daniel exhorted Nebuchadnezzar: "Break off thy sins by righteousness, and thine iniquities by showing mercy to the poor" (Daniel 4:27). And Solomon says, "By mercy and truth iniquity is purged" (Proverbs 16:6); and again, "Love covereth all sins" (Proverbs 10:12). This sentiment is confirmed by Peter. (See 1 Peter 4:8.) Also in Luke, our Lord says of the woman that was a sinner, "Her sins, which are many, are forgiven; for she loved much" (Luke 7:47). How perverse and preposterous the judgment they ever form of the doings of God! Had they observed, what certainly they ought not to have overlooked, that there are two kinds of divine judgment, they would have seen in the correction of David a very different form of punishment from that which must be thought to be designed for vengeance.

Since it in no slight degree concerns us to understand the purpose of God in the chastisements by which He reacts to our sins and how much they differ from the exemplary punishments, which He indignantly inflicts on the wicked and the reprobates, I think it will not be improper briefly to glance at it. For the sake of distinction, we may call the one kind of judgment *punishment*, the other *chastisement*. In judicial punishment, God is to be understood as taking vengeance on His enemies by displaying His anger against them, confounding, scattering, and annihilating them. By divine punishment, properly so called, let us then understand punishment accompanied with indignation. In judicial chastisement, He is offended, but not in wrath; He does not punish by destroying or striking down as with a thunderbolt.

Hence, it is not properly punishment or vengeance, but correction and admonition. The one is the act of a judge, the other of a father. When the judge punishes a criminal, he responds to the crime by demanding the penalty. When a father corrects his son sharply, it is not to avenge, but rather to teach him and make him more cautious for the future. Chrysostom in his writings employs a simile, which is somewhat different, but the same in purport. He says, "A son is whipt, and a slave is whipt, but the latter is punished as a slave for his offense; the former is chastised as a free-born son, standing in need of correction." The correction of the latter is designed to prove and amend him, that of the former is scourging and punishment.

32 Two distinctions arise hence. Objection, that God is often angry with His elect. Answer, God in afflicting His people, does not take His mercy from them. This is confirmed by His promise, by Scripture, and the uniform experience of the Church. Distinction between the reprobate and the elect in regard to punishment.

To have a short and clear view of the whole matter, we must make two distinctions. First, whenever the infliction is designed to avenge, then the curse and wrath of God displays themselves. This is never the case with believers. On the contrary, the chastening of God carries His blessing with it and is an evidence of love, as Scripture teaches. This distinction is plainly marked throughout the Word of God. All the calamities, which the wicked suffer in the present life, are depicted to us as a kind of anticipation of the punishment of hell. In these, they already see, as from a distance, their eternal condemnation, and so far are they from being thereby reformed, or deriving any benefit, that by such preludes they are rather prepared for the fearful doom, which finally awaits them. The Lord chastens His servants sore, but does not give them over unto death. (See Psalm 118:18.) When afflicted, they acknowledge it is good for them, that they may learn his statutes (Psalm 119:71). But as we everywhere read that the saints received their chastisements with placid mind, so inflictions of the latter kind they always most earnestly deprecated. "O Lord, correct me," says Jeremiah, "but with judgment; not in thine anger, lest thou bring me to nothing. Pour out thy fury upon the heathen that know thee not, and upon the families that call not on thy name" (Jeremiah 10:24-25). David says, "O Lord, rebuke me not in thine anger, neither chasten me in thy hot displeasure" (Psalm 6:1).

There is nothing inconsistent with this in its being repeatedly said that the Lord is angry with his saints when He chastens them for their sins. (See Psalm 38:7.) In like manner, we read in Isaiah, "And in that day thou shalt say, O Lord, I will praise thee: though thou wast angry with me, thine anger is turned away, and thou comfortedst me" (Isaiah 12:1). Likewise, in Habakkuk, "In wrath remember mercy" (Habakkuk 3:2); and in Micah, "I will bear the indignation of the Lord, because I have sinned against him" (Micah 7:9). Here we are reminded not only that those who are justly punished gain nothing by murmuring, but also that believers obtain a mitigation of their pain by reflecting on the divine intention. For the same reason, He is said to profane His inheritance, and yet we know that He will never profane it. The expression refers not to the counsel or purpose of God in punishing, but to the keen sense of pain endured by those who are visited with any measure of divine severity.

The Lord not only chastens His people with a slight degree of austerity, but sometimes so wounds them that they seem to themselves on the very eve of perdition. He thus declares that they have deserved His anger, and it is fitting so to do, that they may be dissatisfied with themselves for their sins, may be more careful in their desires to appease God, and anxiously hasten to seek His pardon; still, at this very time, He gives clearer evidence of his mercy than of his anger.

He who cannot deceive has declared that the covenant made with us in our true Solomon stands fast and will never be broken, "If his children forsake my law, and walk not in my judgments; if they break my statutes, and keep not my commandments; then will I visit their transgressions with the rod, and their iniquity with stripes. Nevertheless, my loving-kindness will I not utterly take from him, nor suffer my faithfulness to fail" (Psalm 89:31-34). To assure us of this mercy, He says that the *rod* with which He will chastise the posterity of Solomon will be the "rod of men," and "the stripes of the children of men" (2 Timothy 7:14).

While by these terms he denotes moderation and levity, he, at the same time, intimates that those who feel the hand of God opposed to them cannot but tremble and be confounded. How much regard He has to this levity in chastening His Israel he shows by the prophet, "Behold, I have refined thee, but not with silver; I have chosen thee in the furnace of affliction" (Isaiah 48:10). Although He tells them that they are chastisements with a view to purification, He adds that even these are so tempered, that they are not to be too much crushed by them. And this is very necessary, for the more a man reveres God, and devotes himself to the cultivation of piety, the more tender he is in bearing his anger. (See Psalm 90:11.)

Reprobates, though they groan under the lash, yet because they weigh not the true cause, but rather turn their backs, as well upon their sins as upon the divine judgment, become hardened in their stupor; or, because they murmur and kick, and so rebel against their Judge, their infatuated violence fills them with frenzy and madness. Believers, again, admonished by the rod of God, immediately begin to reflect on their sins, and, struck with fear and dread, retake themselves as suppliants to implore mercy. Did not God mitigate the pains by which wretched souls are excruciated, they would give way a hundred times, even at slight signs of his anger.

33 Second distinction. The punishment of the reprobates a commencement of the eternal punishment awaiting them; that of the elect designed to bring them to repentance. This is confirmed by passages of Scripture and of the Fathers.

The second distinction is that when the reprobates are brought under the lash of God, they begin in a manner to pay the punishment due to His justice; and though their refusal to listen to these proofs of the divine anger will not escape with impunity, still they are not punished with the view of bringing them to a better mind, but only to teach them by dire experience that God is a Judge and avenger. The sons of God are beaten with rods, not that they may pay the punishment due to their faults, but that they may thereby be led to repent. Accordingly, we perceive that they have more respect to the future than to the past. I prefer giving this in the words of Chrysostom rather than my own: "His object in imposing a penalty upon us, is not to inflict punishment on our sins but to correct us for the future." So also Augustine, "The suffering at which you cry is medicine, not punishment; chastisement, not condemnation. Do not drive away the rod, if you would not be driven away from the inheritance. Know, brethren, that the whole of that misery of the human race, under which the world groans, is a medicinal pain, not a penal sentence."

It seemed proper to quote these passages, lest anyone should think the mode of expression, which I have used to be novel or uncommon. To the same effect are the indignant terms in which the Lord expostulates with His people, for their ingratitude in obstinately despising all His infliction. In Isaiah He says, "Why should ye be stricken any more? Ye will revolt increasingly. The whole head is sick and the whole heart faint" (Isaiah 1:5, 6). But as such passages abound in the prophets, it is sufficient briefly to have shown that the only purpose of God in punishing His Church is to subdue her to repentance. Thus, when he rejected Saul from the kingdoms he punished in vengeance (see 1 Samuel 15:23); when He deprived David of his child, He chastised for amendment (see 2 Samuel 12:18). In this sense Paul is to be understood when he says, "When we are judged, we are chastened of the Lord, that we should not be condemned with the world" (1 Corinthians 11:32); that is, while we, as sons of God, are afflicted by our heavenly Father's hand, it is not punishment to confound, but only chastisement to train us.

On this subject, Augustine is plainly with us. For he shows that the punishments with which men are equally chastened by God are to be variously considered; because the saints after the forgiveness of their sins have struggles and exercises, the reprobates without forgiveness are punished for their iniquity. Enumerating the punishments inflicted on David and other saints, he says that it was designed by thus humbling them to prove and exercise their piety. The passage in Isaiah in which it is said, "Speak ye comfortably to Jerusalem, and cry unto her, that her warfare is accomplished that her iniquity is pardoned; for she has received of the Lord's hands double for all her sins" (Isaiah 40:2), does not prove that the pardon of sin depends on freedom from punishment.

It is just as if He had said, "Sufficient punishment has now been exacted; as for their number and heinousness you have long been oppressed with sorrow and mourning; it is time to send you a message of complete mercy, that your minds may be filled with joy on feeling me to be a Father." For God there assumes the character of a father who repents even of the just severity with which he has treated his son.

34 Two uses of this doctrine to the believer. In affliction he can believe that God, though angry, is still favorable to him. In the punishment of the reprobates, He sees a prelude to their final doom.

These are the thoughts with which the believer ought to be provided in the bitterness of affliction, "The time is come that judgment must begin at the house of God," "the city which is called by my name" (1 Peter 4:17; Jeremiah 25:29). What could the sons of God do if they thought that the severity which they feel was vengeance? He, who smitten by the hand of God, thinks that God is a judge inflicting punishment, cannot conceive of Him except as being angry and at enmity with him; cannot but detest the rod of God as a curse and a condemnation; in short, he can never persuade himself that he is loved by God, while he feels that He is still disposed to inflict punishment upon him.

He only profits under the divine chastening who considers that God, though offended with his sins, is still propitious and favorable toward him. Otherwise, the feeling must necessarily be what the Psalmist complains that he had experienced, "Thy wrath lieth hard upon me, and thou hast afflicted me with all thy waves." Also what Moses says, "For we are consumed by thine anger, and by thy wrath we are troubled. Thou hast set our iniquities before thee, our secret sins in the light of thy countenance. For all our days are passed away in thy wrath; we spend our years as a tale that is told" (Psalm 90:7-9). On the other hand, David speaking of fatherly chastisements, to show how believers are more assisted than oppressed by them, thus sings, "Blessed is the man whom thou chastenest, O Lord, and teachest him out of thy law; that thou mayest give him rest from the days of adversity, until the pit be dug for the wicked" (Psalm 94:12, 13).

It is certainly a sore temptation, when God, sparing unbelievers and overlooking their crimes, appears more rigid towards His own people. Hence, to solace them, He adds the admonition of the Law, which teaches them that their salvation is consulted when they are brought back to the right path, whereas the wicked are borne headlong in their errors, which ultimately lead to the pit. It matters not whether the punishment is eternal or temporary. For disease, pestilence, famine, and war, are curses from God, as much as even the sentence of eternal death, whenever their tendency is to operate as instruments of divine wrath and vengeance against the reprobate.

35 Objection, as to the punishment of David, answered. Why all men here subjected to chastisement.

All, if I mistake not, now see what view the Lord had in chastening David, namely, to prove that murder and adultery are most offensive to God, and to manifest this offensiveness in a beloved and faithful servant, that David himself might be taught never again to dare to commit such wickedness; still, however, it was not a punishment designed in payment of a kind of compensation to God. In the same way are we to judge of that other correction in which the Lord subjects His people to a grievous pestilence for the disobedience of David in forgetting himself so far as to number the people. He indeed freely forgave David the guilt of his sin; but because it was necessary, both as a public example to all ages and also to humble David himself not to allow such an offense to go unpunished, He chastened him most sharply with His whip. We ought also to keep this in view in the universal curse of the human race. For since after obtaining grace we still continue to endure the miseries denounced to our first parent as the penalty of transgression, we ought thereby to be reminded, how offensive to God is the transgression of His law, that thus humbled and dejected by a consciousness of our wretched condition, we may aspire more ardently to true happiness.

But it would be most foolish in anyone to imagine that we are subjected to the calamities of the present life for the guilt of sin. This seems to me to have been Chrysostom's meaning when he said, "If the purpose of God in inflicting punishment is to bring those persisting in evil to repentance, when repentance is manifested punishment would be superfluous." Wherefore, as He knows what the disposition of each requires, He treats one with greater harshness and another with more indulgence. Accordingly, when He wishes to show that He is not excessive in exacting punishment, He upbraids a hard-hearted and obstinate people, because, after being smitten, they continued in sin. (See Jeremiah 5:3.) In the same sense, he complains, "Ephraim is a cake not turned" (Hosea 7:8), because chastisement did not make a due impression on their minds, and, correcting their vices, make them fit to receive pardon. Surely he who thus speaks shows that as soon as anyone repents He will be ready to receive him, and that the rigor which He exercises in chastising faults is wrung from Him by our perverseness, since we should prevent Him by a voluntary correction. Such, however, being the hardness and rudeness of all hearts, that they stand universally in need of castigation, our infinitely wise Parent has seen it meet to exercise all without exception, during their whole lives, with chastisement.

It is strange how they fix their eyes so intently on the one example of David, and are not moved by the many examples in which they might have beheld the free forgiveness of sins. The publican is said to have gone down from the temple justified. (See Luke 18:14.) No punishment follows. Peter obtained the pardon of his sin. (See Luke 22:61.) "We read of his tears," says Ambrose, "we read not of satisfaction." To the paralytic it is said, "Son, be of good cheer; thy sins be forgiven thee" (Matthew 9:2). No penance is enjoined. All the acts of forgiveness mentioned in Scripture are gratuitous. The rule ought to be drawn from these numerous examples, rather than from one example, which contains a kind of specialty.

36 Objections, founded on five other passages, answered.

Daniel, in exhorting Nebuchadnezzar to break off his sins by righteousness and his iniquities by showing mercy to the poor (see Daniel 4:27), meant not to intimate that righteousness and mercy are able to propitiate God and redeem from punishment (far be it from us to suppose that there ever was any other *ransom* than the blood of Christ); but the breaking off referred to in that passage has reference to man rather than to God. It is as if he had said, O king, you have exercised an unjust and violent domination, you have oppressed the humble, spoiled the poor, treated your people harshly and unjustly; instead of unjust exaction, instead of violence and oppression, now practice mercy and justice.

In like manner, Solomon says that love covers a multitude of sins, not, however, with God, but among men. For the whole verse stands thus, "Hatred stirreth up strifes; but love covereth all sins" (Proverbs 10:12). Here, after his manner, he contrasts the evils produced by hatred with the fruits of charity. Those who hate are incessantly biting, carping at, upbraiding, lacerating each other, making everything a fault; but those who love mutually conceal each other's faults, wink at many, forgive many not that the one approves the vices of the other, but tolerates and cures by admonishing, rather than exasperates by assailing.

That the passage is quoted by Peter (see 1 Peter 4:8) in the same sense we cannot doubt, unless we would charge him with corrupting or craftily wresting Scripture. When it is said that "by mercy and truth iniquity is purged" (Proverbs 16:6), the meaning is not that by them compensation is made to the Lord, so that He being thus satisfied remits the punishment which He would otherwise have exacted; but intimation is made after the familiar manner of Scripture, that those who, forsaking their vices and iniquities turn to the Lord in truth and piety will find Him propitious. It is as if he had said that the wrath of God is calmed, and His judgment is at rest, whenever we rest from our wickedness. But, indeed, it is not the cause of pardon that is described, but rather the mode of true conversion; just as the prophets frequently declare that it is in vain for hypocrites to offer God fictitious rites instead of repentance, seeing that His delight is in integrity and the duties of charity.

In like manner, also, the author of the Epistle to the Hebrews, commending kindness and humanity, reminds us "with such sacrifices God is well pleased" (Hebrews 13:16). And indeed when Christ, rebuking the Pharisees because they were intent merely on the outside of the cup and platter, they neglected purity of heart, enjoins them, in order that they may be clean in all respects, to give alms. Does He exhort them to give satisfaction thereby? He only tells them what the kind of purity is which God requires. Of this mode of expression, we have treated elsewhere. (See Matthew 23:25; Luke 11:39-41.)

37 Answer continued.

In regard to the passage in Luke (Luke 7:36), no man of sober judgment, who reads the parable there employed by our Lord, will raise any controversy with us. The Pharisee thought that the Lord did not know the character of the woman whom He had so easily admitted to His presence. For he presumed that He would not have admitted her if He had known what kind of a sinner she was; and from this he inferred that one who could be deceived in this way was not a prophet. Our Lord, to show that she was not a sinner, inasmuch as she had already been forgiven, spoke this parable: "There was a certain creditor which had two debtors; the one owed five hundred pence, and the other fifty. And when they had nothing to pay, he frankly forgave them both. Tell me, therefore, which of them will love him most?" The Pharisee answers: "I suppose that he to whom he forgave most." Then our Savior rejoins: "Her sins, which are many, are forgiven; for she loved much."

By these words it is plain that He does not make love the cause of forgiveness, but the proof of it. The similitude is borrowed from the case of a debtor to whom a debt of five hundred pence had been forgiven. It is not said that the debt is forgiven because he loved much, but that he loved much because it was forgiven. The similitude ought to be applied in this way: You think this woman is a sinner, but you ought to have acknowledged her as not a sinner, in respect that her sins have been forgiven her. Her love ought to have been to you a proof of her having obtained forgiveness, that love being an expression of gratitude for the benefit received. It is an argument *a posteriori*, by which something is demonstrated by the results produced by it.

Our Lord plainly attests that the ground on which she had obtained forgiveness, when he says, "Thy faith has saved thee." By faith, therefore, we obtain forgiveness; by love, we give thanks, and bear testimony to the lovingkindness of the Lord.

38 Objection, founded on passages in the Fathers. Answer, with passages from Chrysostom and Augustine.

I am little moved by the numerous passages in the writings of the Fathers relating to satisfaction. I see indeed that some (I will frankly say almost all whose books are extant) have either erred in this matter, or spoken too roughly and harshly, but I cannot admit that they were so rude and unskillful as to write these passages in the sense in which they are read by our new "satisfactionaries." Chrysostom somewhere says, "When mercy is implored, interrogation ceases; when mercy is asked, judgment rages not; when mercy is sought, there is no room for punishment; where there is mercy, no question is asked; where there is mercy, the answer gives pardon." However much these words may be twisted, they can never be reconciled with the dogmas of the Schoolmen. In the book *De Dogmatibus Ecclesiasticis*, which is attributed to Augustine, you read in chapter 54, "The satisfaction of repentance is to cut off the causes of sins, and not to indulge an entrance to their suggestions." From this it appears that the doctrine of satisfaction, said to be paid for sins committed, was everywhere derided in those ages; for here, the only satisfaction referred to is caution, abstinence from sin for the future.

I am unwilling to quote what Chrysostom says about God requiring nothing more of us than to confess our faults before Him with tears, as similar sentiments abound in both his writings and those of others. Augustine indeed calls works of mercy remedies for obtaining forgiveness of sins; but lest anyone should stumble at the expression, he himself, in another passage, obviates the difficulty. "The flesh of Christ," says he, "is the true and only sacrifice for sins— not only for those which are all effaced in baptism, but those into which we are afterwards betrayed through infirmity, and because of which the whole Church daily cries, "Forgive us our debts" (Matthew 6:12). And they are forgiven by that special sacrifice."

39 These satisfactions had reference to the peace of the Church, and not to the throne of God. The Schoolmen have perverted the meaning of some absurd statements by obscure monks.

By satisfaction, however, they, for the most part, meant not compensation to be paid to God, but the public testimony, by which those who had been punished with excommunication and wished again to be received into communion, assured the Church of their repentance. For those penitents were enjoined certain fasts and other things, by which they might prove that they were truly, and from the heart, weary of their former life, or rather might obliterate the remembrance of their past deeds. In this way they were said to give satisfaction, not to God, but to the Church. Augustine expressed the same thing in a passage that is found in his *Enchiridion ad Laurentium*. From that ancient custom the satisfactions and confessions now in use took their rise. It is indeed a viperish progeny, not even a vestige of the better form now remaining.

I know that ancient writers sometimes speak harshly; nor do I deny, as I lately said, that they have perhaps erred; but dogmas, which were tainted with a few blemishes now that they have fallen into the unwashed hands of those men, are altogether defiled. And if we were to decide the contest by authority of the Fathers, what kind of Fathers are those whom they obtrude upon us? A great part of those, from whom Lombard their Coryphaeus framed his centos, are extracted from the absurd dreams of certain monks passing under the names of Ambrose, Jerome, Augustine, and Chrysostom. On the present subject almost all his extracts are from the book of Augustine, *De Paenitentia*, a book absurdly compiled by some rhapsodist, alike from good and bad authors—a book which indeed bears the name of Augustine, but which no person of the least learning would deign to acknowledge as his.

Wishing to save my readers trouble, they will pardon me for not searching minutely into all their absurdities. For me, it would be not very laborious, and might gain some applause, to give a complete exposure of dogmas, which have hitherto been vaunted as mysteries; but as my object is to give useful instruction, I desist.

Chapter 5

OF THE MODES OF SUPPLEMENTING
SATISFACTION—VIZ. INDULGENCES
AND PURGATORY

Divisions of the chapter: I. A summary description and refutation of popish indulgences, sections 1, 2. II. Confutation by Leo and Augustine. Answer to two objections urged in support of them, sections 3, 4. A profane love of filthy lucre on the part of the pope. The origin of indulgences unfolded, section 5. III. An examination of popish purgatory. Its horrible impiety, section 6. An explanation of five passages of Scripture by which Sophists endeavor to support that dream, sections 7, 8. Sentiments of the ancient theologians concerning purgatory, section 10.

Sections

1. The dogma of satisfaction, the parent of indulgences. Vanity of both. The reason for it. Evidence of the avarice of the pope and the Romish clergy; also of the blindness with which the Christian world was smitten.

2. View of indulgences given by the Sophists. Their true nature. Refutation of them. Refutation confirmed by seven passages of Scripture.

3. Confirmed also by the testimony of Leo, a Roman bishop, and by Augustine. Attempts of the popish doctors to establish the monstrous doctrine of indulgences, and even support it by apostolical authority. First answer.

4. Second answer to the passage of an apostle adduced to support the dogma of indulgences. Answer confirmed by a comparison with other passages and from a passage in Augustine, explaining the apostle's meaning. Another passage from the same apostle confirming this view.

5. *The pope's profane thirst for filthy lucre exposed. The origin of indulgences.*

6. *Examination of the fictitious purgatory of the Papists. A. From the nature of the thing itself. B. From the authority of God. C. From the consideration of the merit of Christ, which is destroyed by this fiction. Purgatory, what it is. D. From the impiety teeming from this fountain.*

7. *Exposition of the passages of Scripture quoted in support of purgatory. A. Of the unpardonable sin, from which it is inferred that there are some sins afterwards to be forgiven. B. Of the passage as to paying the last farthing.*

8. *C. The passage concerning the bending of the knee to Christ by things under the Earth. D. The example of Judas Maccabaeus in sending an oblation for the dead to Jerusalem.*

9. *E. Of the fire which shall try every man's work. The sentiment of the ancient theologians. Answer, containing* a reductio ad absurdum. *Confirmation by a passage of Augustine. The meaning of the apostle. What is to be understood by fire. A clear exposition of the metaphor. The day of the Lord. How those who suffer loss are saved by fire.*

10. *The doctrine of purgatory ancient, but refuted by a more ancient apostle. It is not supported by ancient writers, by Scripture, or solid argument. Introduced by custom and a zeal not duly regulated by the* Word of God. *Ancient writers, such as Augustine, speak doubtfully in commending prayer for the dead. At all events, we must hold to the* Word of God, *which rejects this fiction. A vast difference between the more ancient and the more modern builders of purgatory. This is shown by comparing them.*

1 The dogma of satisfaction the parent of indulgences. Vanity of both. The reason for it. Evidence of the avarice of the pope and the Romish clergy: also of the blindness with which the Christian world was smitten.

From this dogma of satisfaction that of indulgences takes its rise. For the pretense is that what is wanting to our own ability is hereby supplied; and they go to the insane length of defining them to be a dispensation of the merits of Christ and the martyrs which the pope makes by his bulls. Though they are fitter for the flower hellebore than for argument, and it is scarcely worthwhile to refute these frivolous errors, which, already battered down, begin of their own accord to grow antiquated, and totter to their fall. Yet, as a brief refutation it may be useful to some of the unlearned, I will not omit it. Indeed, the fact that indulgences have so long stood safe and with impunity, and wantoned with so much fury and tyranny, may be regarded as a proof into how deep a night of ignorance mankind were for some ages plunged. They saw themselves insulted openly, and without disguise, by the pope and his bull-bearers; they saw the salvation of the soul being made the subject of a lucrative traffic, salvation taxed at a few pieces of money, and nothing given gratuitously; they saw what was squeezed from them in the form of oblations basely consumed on strumpets, pimps and gluttony. The loudest trumpeters of indulgences being the greatest despisers. They saw the monster stalking abroad, and every day luxuriating with greater license, and that without end. New bulls were being constantly issued, and new sums were extracted. Still, indulgences were received with the greatest reverence, worshiped, and bought. Even those who saw more clearly deemed them pious frauds, by which, even in deceiving, some good was gained. Now, at length, that a considerable portion of the world has begun to rethink themselves, indulgences grow cool, and gradually even begin to freeze, preparatory to their final extinction.

2 View of indulgences given by the Sophists. Their true nature. Refutation of them. Refutation confirmed by seven passages of Scripture.

But since very many who see the vile imposture, theft, and rapine (with which the dealers in indulgences have hitherto deluded and sported with us) are not aware of the true source of the impiety, it may be proper to show not only what indulgences truly are, but also that they are polluted in every part. They give the name of *treasury of the Church* to the merits of Christ, the holy postles, and Martyrs. They pretend, as I have said that the radical custody of the granary has been delivered to the Roman bishop, to whom the dispensation of these great blessings belongs in such a sense, that he can both exercise it by himself, and delegate the power of exercising it to others. Hence, we have from the pope at one time plenary indulgences, at another for certain years, from the cardinals for a hundred days, and from the bishops for forty. These, to describe them truly, are a profanation of the blood of Christ, and a delusion of Satan, by which the Christian people are led away from the grace of God and the life, which is in Christ, and turned aside from the true way of salvation.

For how could the blood of Christ be more shamefully profaned than by denying its sufficiency for the remission of sins, for reconciliation and satisfaction, unless its defects, as if it were dried up and exhausted, are supplemented from some other quarter?

Peter's words are: "To him give all the prophets witness, that through his name whosoever believeth in him shall receive remission of sins" (Acts 10:43); but indulgences bestow the remission of sins through Peter, Paul, and the martyrs. "The blood of Jesus Christ his Son cleanseth us from all sin," says John (1 John 1:7). Indulgences make the blood of the martyrs an ablution of sins. "He has made him to be sin (*i.e.* a satisfaction for sin) for us who knew no sin," says Paul (see 2 Corinthians 5:21), "that we might be made the righteousness of God in him." Indulgences make the satisfaction of sin to depend on the blood of the martyrs. Paul exclaimed and testified to the Corinthians, that Christ alone was crucified and died for them. (See 1 Corinthians 1:13.) Indulgences declare that Paul and others died for us. Paul elsewhere says that Christ purchased the Church with His own blood. (See Acts 20:28.)

Indulgences assign another purchase to the blood of martyrs. "By one offering he has perfected forever them that are sanctified," says the apostle (Hebrews 10:14). Indulgences, on the other hand, insist that sanctification, which would otherwise be insufficient, is perfected by martyrs. John says that all the saints "...have washed their robes, and made them white in the blood of the Lamb" (Revelation 7:14). Indulgences tell us to wash our robes in the blood of saints.

3 Confirmed also by the testimony of Leo, a Roman bishop, and by Augustine. Attempts of the popish doctors to establish the monstrous doctrine of indulgences, and even support it by Apostolical authority. First answer.

There is an admirable passage in opposition to their blasphemies in Leo, a Roman bishop. "Although the death of many saints was precious in the sight of the Lord (see Psalms 116:15), yet no innocent man's slaughter was the propitiation of the world. The just received crowns did not give them; and the fortitude of believers produced examples of patience, not gifts of righteousness: for their deaths were for themselves; and none by his final end paid the debt of another, except Christ our Lord, in whom alone all are crucified—all dead, buried, and raised up." This sentiment, as it was of a memorable nature, he has elsewhere repeated. Certainly one could not desire a clearer confutation of this impious dogma.

Augustine introduces the same sentiment: "Although brethren die for brethren, yet no martyr's blood is shed for the remission of sins: this Christ did for us, and in this conferred upon us not what we should imitate, but what should make us grateful." Again, in another passage: "As he alone became the Son of God and the Son of man, that he might make us to be with himself sons of God, so he alone, without any ill desert, undertook the penalty for us, that through him we mighty without good desert, obtain undeserved favor."

Indeed, as their whole doctrine is a patchwork of sacrilege and blasphemy, this is the most blasphemous of the whole. Let them acknowledge whether or not they hold the following dogmas: That the martyrs, by their death, performed more to God, and merited more than was necessary for themselves, and that they have a large surplus of merits which may be applied to others; that in order that this great good may not prove superfluous, their blood is mingled with the blood of Christ, and out of both is formed the treasury of the Church, for the forgiveness and satisfaction of sins; and that in this sense we must understand the words of Paul: "Who now rejoice in my sufferings, and fill up that which is behind of the afflictions of Christ in my flesh for his body's sake, which is the Church" (Colossians 1:24).

What is this but merely to leave the name of Christ, and at the same time make Him a vulgar saintling, who can scarcely be distinguished in the crowd? He alone ought to be preached, alone held forth, alone named, alone looked to, whenever the subject considered is the obtaining of the forgiveness of sins, expiation, and sanctification. But let us hear their propositions. That the blood of martyrs may not be shed without fruit, it must be employed for the common good of the Church. Is it so? Was there no fruit in glorifying God by death? In sealing His truth with their blood? In testifying, by contempt of the present life, that they looked for a better? In confirming the faith of the Church, and at the same time disabling the pertinacity of the enemy by their constancy? But thus it is. They acknowledge no fruit if Christ is the only propitiation, if He alone died for our sins, if He alone was offered for our redemption.

Nevertheless, they say, Peter and Paul would have gained the crown of victory though they had died in their beds a natural death. But as they contended to blood, it would not accord with the justice of God to leave their doing so barren and unfruitful. It is as if God were unable to augment the glory of His servants in proportion to the measure of his gifts. The advantage derived in common by the Church is great enough, when, by their triumphs, she is inflamed with zeal to fight.

4 Second answer to the passage of an apostle adduced to support the dogma of indulgences. Answer confirmed by a comparison with other passages and from a passage in Augustine, explaining the apostle's meaning. Another passage from the same apostle confirming this view.

How maliciously they wrest the passage in which Paul says that he supplies in his body that which was lacking in the sufferings of Christ! (See Colossians 1:23.) That defect or supplement refers not to the work of redemption, satisfaction, or expiation, but to those afflictions with which the members of Christ, in other words, all believers, behave to be exercised, so long as they are in the flesh. He says, therefore, that part of the sufferings of Christ remains—viz. that what He suffered in himself He daily suffers in His members. Christ so honors us as to regard and count our afflictions as His own.

By the additional words—for *the Church*, Paul means not for the redemptions reconciliation, or satisfaction, of the Church, but for her edification and progress. As he elsewhere says, "I endure all things for the elect's sakes, that they may also obtain the salvation which is in Christ Jesus with eternal glory" (2 Timothy 2:10). He also writes to the Corinthians: "Whether we be afflicted, it is for your consolation and salvation, which is effectual in the enduring of the same sufferings which we also suffer" (2 Corinthians 1:6). In the same place, he immediately explains his meaning by adding that he was made a minister of the Church, not for redemption, but according to the dispensation, which he received to preach the Gospel of Christ. But if they still desire another interpreter, let them hear Augustine: "The sufferings of Christ are in Christ alone, as in the head; in Christ and the Church as in the whole body. Hence, Paul, being one member, says, "I fill up in my body that which is behind of the sufferings of Christ." Therefore, O hearers, whoever you be, if you are among the members of Christ whatever you suffer from those who are not members of Christ, was lacking to the sufferings of Christ." He elsewhere explains the end of the sufferings of the apostles undertaken for Christ: "Christ is my door to you, because ye are the sheep of Christ purchased by his blood: acknowledge your price, which is not paid by me, but preached by me." He afterwards adds, "As he laid down his life, so ought we to lay down our lives for the brethren, to build up peace and maintain faith."

Far be it from us to imagine that Paul thought anything was wanting to the sufferings of Christ in regard to the complete fullness of righteousness, salvation, and life, or that he wished to make any addition to it, after showing so clearly and eloquently that the grace of Christ was poured out in such rich abundance as far to exceed all the power of sin. (See Romans 5:15.) All saints have been saved by it alone, not by the merit of their own life or death, as Peter distinctly testifies. (See Acts 15:11.) It is an insult to God and His Anointed to place the worthiness of any saint in anything, save the mercy of God alone. But why dwell longer on this, as if the matter were obscure, when to mention these monstrous dogmas is to refute them?

5 The pope's profane thirst for filthy lucre exposed. The origin of indulgences.

Moreover, to say nothing of these abominations, who taught the pope to enclose the grace of Jesus Christ in lead and parchment, grace which the Lord is pleased to dispense by the word of the gospel? Undoubtedly either the Gospel of God or indulgences must be false. That Christ is offered to us in the gospel with all the abundance of heavenly blessings, with all His merits, all His righteousness, wisdom, and grace, without exception, Paul bears witness when he says, "Now then we are ambassadors for Christ, as though God did beseech you by us: we pray you in Christ's stead, be ye reconciled to God. For he has made him to be sin for us, who knew no sin; that we might be made the righteousness of God in him" (2 Corinthians 5:20, 21). And what is meant by the fellowship of Christ, which according to the same apostle (see 1 Corinthians 1:9) is offered to us in the gospel, all believers know. On the contrary, indulgences, bringing forth some portion of the grace of God from the armory of the pope, fix it to lead, parchment, and a particular place, but sever it from the Word of God. When we inquire into the origin of this abuse, it appears to have arisen from this, that when in old times the satisfactions imposed on penitents were too severe to be borne, those who felt themselves burdened beyond measure by the penance imposed, petitioned the Church for relaxation. The remission so given was called indulgence. But as they transferred satisfactions to God, and called them compensations by which men redeem themselves from the justice of God, they in the same way transferred indulgences, representing them as expiatory remedies, which free us from merited punishment. The blasphemies to which we have referred have been feigned with so much effrontery that there is not the least pretext for them.

6 Examination of the fictitious purgatory of the papists. A. From the nature of the thing itself. B. From the authority of God. C. From the consideration of the merit of Christ, which is destroyed by this fiction. Purgatory, what it is. D. From the impiety teeming from this fountain.

Their purgatory cannot now give us much trouble, since with this ax we have struck it, thrown it down, and overturned it from its very foundations. I cannot agree with some who think that we ought to dissemble in this matter, and make no mention of purgatory, from which (as they say) fierce contests arise, and very little edification can be obtained. I myself would think it right to disregard their follies did they not tend to serious consequences. But since purgatory has been reared on many, and is daily propped up by new blasphemies; since it produces many grievous offenses, assuredly it is not to be connived at, however it might have been disguised for a time, that without any authority from the Word of God, it was devised by prying audacious rashness, that credit was procured for it by fictitious revelations, the wiles of Satan, and that certain passages of Scripture were ignorantly wrested to its support. Although the Lord bears not that human presumption should thus force its way to the hidden recesses of His judgments; although He has issued a strict prohibition against neglecting His voice, and making inquiry to the dead (see Deuteronomy 18:11), and permits not His Word to be so erroneously contaminated.

Let us grant, however, that all this might have been tolerated for a time as a thing of no great moment; yet when the expiation of sins is sought elsewhere than in the blood of Christ, and satisfaction is transferred to others, silence is most perilous. We are bound, therefore, to raise our voice to its highest pitch, and cry aloud that purgatory is a deadly device of Satan; that it makes void the cross of Christ; that it offers intolerable insult to the divine mercy; that it undermines and overthrows our faith. For what is this purgatory but the satisfaction for sin paid after death by the souls of the dead?

Hence, when this idea of satisfaction is refuted, purgatory itself is forthwith completely overturned. But if it is perfectly clear, from what was lately said that the blood of Christ is the only satisfaction, expiation, and cleansing for the sins of believers, what remains but to hold that purgatory is mere blasphemy, horrid blasphemy against Christ? I say nothing of the sacrilege by which it is daily defended, the offenses, which it begets in religion, and the other innumerable evils, which we see teeming forth from that fountain of impiety.

7 Exposition of the passages of Scripture quoted in support of purgatory. A. Of the unpardonable sin, from which it is inferred that there are some sins afterwards to be forgiven. B. Of the passage as to paying the last farthing.

It may be worthwhile to wrench out of their hands those passages of Scripture on which it is their wont falsely and iniquitously to fasten. When the Lord declares that the sin against the Holy Ghost will not be forgiven in either this world or the world to come, He thereby intimates (they say) that there is a remission of certain sins hereafter. But who does not see that the Lord speaks of the guilt of sin? But if this is so, what has it to do with their purgatory, seeing they deny not that the guilt of those sins, the punishment of which is there expiated, is forgiven in the present life? Lest, however, they should still object, we shall give a plainer solution.

Since it was the Lord's intention to cut off all hope of pardon from this wickedness, He did not consider it enough to say that it would never be forgiven, but in the way of amplification employed a division by which He included both the judgment which every man's conscience pronounces in the present life and the final judgment which will be publicly pronounced at the resurrection. It is as if He had said, "Beware of this malignant rebellion, as you would of instant destruction; for he who of set purpose endeavors to extinguish the offered light of the Spirit, shall not obtain pardon either in this life, which has been given to sinners for conversion, or on the last day when the angels of God shall separate the sheep from the goats, and the heavenly kingdom shall be purged of all that offends." The next passage they produce is the parable in Matthew: "Agree with thine adversary quickly, whiles thou art in the way with him; lest at any time the adversary deliver thee to the judge, and the judge deliver thee to the officer, and thou be cast into prison. Verily, I say unto thee, Thou shalt by no means come out thence, until thou hast paid the uttermost earthing" (Matthew 5:25, 26). If in this passage the judge means God, the adversary the devil, the officer an angel, and the prison purgatory, I give in at once. But if every man sees that Christ there intended to show to how many perils and evils those expose themselves who obstinately insist on their utmost right, instead of being satisfied with what is fair and equitable that He might thereby the more strongly exhort His followers to concord, where, I ask, are we to find their purgatory?

8 C. The passage concerning the bending of the knee to Christ by things under the Earth. D. The example of Judas Maccabaeus in sending an oblation for the dead to Jerusalem.

They seek an argument in the passage in which Paul declares that all things shall bow the knee to Christ, "...things in heaven, and things in earth, and things under the earth" (Philippians 2:10). They take it for granted that by "things under the earth," cannot be meant those who are doomed to eternal damnation, and that the only remaining conclusion is that they must be souls suffering in purgatory. They would not reason very ill if, by the bending of the knee, the apostle designated true worship; but since he simply says that Christ has received a dominion to which all creatures are subject, what prevents us from understanding those "under the earth" to mean the devils, who shall certainly appear before the judgment-seat of God, there to recognize their Judge with fear and trembling? In this way, Paul himself elsewhere interprets the same prophecy: "We shall all stand before the judgment-seat of Christ. For it is written, 'As I live, saith the Lord, every knee shall bow to me, and every tongue shall confess to God'" (Romans 14:10, 11). But we cannot in this way interpret what is said in the Apocalypse: "Every creature which is in heaven, and on the earth, and under the earth, and such as are in the sea, heard I saying, Blessing, and honor, and glory, and power, be unto him that sitteth upon the throne, and unto the Lamb, forever and ever" (Revelation 5:13).

This I readily admit, but what kinds of creatures do they suppose are here enumerated? It is certain that both irrational and inanimate creatures are comprehended. All, then, which is affirmed, is that every part of the universe, from the highest pinnacle of Heaven to the very center of the Earth, each in its own way proclaims the glory of the Creator.

To the passage, which they produce from the history of the Maccabees (1 Maccabees 12:43), I will not deign to reply, lest I should seem to include that work among the canonical books. But Augustine holds it to be canonical. First, with what degree of confidence? "The Jews," says he, "do not hold the book of the Maccabees as they do the Law, the prophets, and the Psalms, to which the Lord bears testimony as to his own witnesses, saying, Ought not all things which are written in the Law, and the Psalms, and the Prophets, concerning me be fulfilled? (Luke 24:44). But it has been received by the Church not uselessly, if it be read or heard with soberness."

Jerome, however, unhesitatingly affirms that it is of no authority in establishing doctrine; and from the ancient little book, *De Expositione Symboli*; which bears the name of Cyprian, it is plain that it was in no estimation in the ancient Church. And why do I here contend in vain? It is as if the author himself did not sufficiently show what degree of deference is to be paid him, when in the end he asks pardon for anything less properly expressed. (See 2 Maccabees 15:38.) He, who confesses that his writings stand in need of pardon, certainly proclaims that they are not oracles of the Holy Spirit. We may add that the piety of Judas is commended for no other reason than for having a firm hope of the final resurrection, in sending his oblation for the dead to Jerusalem. For the writer of the history does not represent what he did as furnishing the price of redemption, but merely that they might be partakers of eternal life with the other saints who had fallen for their country and religion. The act, indeed, was not free from superstition and misguided zeal; but it is mere fatuity to extend the legal sacrifice to us, seeing we are assured that the sacrifices then in use ceased on the advent of Christ.

9 E. Of the fire which shall try every man's work. The sentiment of the ancient theologians. Answer, containing a reductio ad absurdum. Confirmation by a passage of Augustine. The meaning of the apostle. What to be understood by fire. A clear exposition of the metaphor. The day of the Lord. How those who suffer loss are saved by fire.

But, it seems, they find in Paul an invincible support, which cannot be so easily overthrown. His words are, "Now if any man build upon this foundation gold, silver, precious stones, wood, hay, stubble; every man's work shall be made manifest: for the day shall declare it, because it shall be revealed by fire; and the fire shall try every man's work of what sort it is. If any man's work shall be burnt, he shall suffer loss: but he himself shall be saved; yet so as by fire" (1 Corinthians 3:12-15). What fire (they ask) can that be but the fire of purgatory, by which the defilements of sin are wiped away, in order that we may enter pure into the Kingdom of God? But most of the Fathers give it a different meaning—viz. the tribulation or cross by which the Lord tries His people, that they may not rest satisfied with the defilements of the flesh. This is much more probable than the fiction of a purgatory. I do not, however, agree with them, for I think I see a much surer and clearer meaning to the passage. But, before I produce it, I wish they would answer me, whether they think the apostle and all the saints have to pass through this purgatorial fire? I am aware they will say no, for it would be too absurd to hold that purification is required by those whose superfluous merits they dream of as applicable to all the members of the Church. But this the apostle affirms, for he says, not that the works of certain persons, but the works of all will be tried. And this is not my argument, but that of Augustine, who thus impugns that interpretation. And (what makes the thing more absurd) he says, not that they will pass through fire for certain works, but that even if they should have edified the Church with the greatest fidelity, they will receive their reward after their works shall have been tried by fire.

First, we see that the apostle used a metaphor when he gave the names of wood, hay, and stubble to doctrines of man's device. The ground of the metaphor is obvious—viz. that as wood when it is put into the fire is consumed and destroyed, so neither will those doctrines be able to endure when they come to be tried.

Moreover, everyone sees that the trial is made by the Spirit of God. Therefore, in following the thread of the metaphor and adapting its parts properly to each other, He gave the name of fire to the examination of the Holy Spirit. For, just as silver and gold, the nearer they are brought to the fire, give stronger proof of their genuineness and purity, so the Lord's truth, the more thoroughly it is submitted to spiritual examination, has its authority the better confirmed. As hay, wood, and stubble, when the fire is applied to them, are suddenly consumed, so the inventions of man, not founded on the Word of God, cannot stand the trial of the Holy Spirit, but forthwith give way and perish.

If spurious doctrines are compared to wood, hay, and stubble, because, like wood, hay, and stubble, they are burned by fire and fitted for destruction, though the actual destruction is only completed by the Spirit of the Lord, it follows that the Spirit is that fire by which they will be proved. This proof Paul calls the *day of the Lord*; using a term that is common in Scripture. For the day of the Lord is said to take place whenever He in some way manifests His presence to men, His face being specially said to shine when His truth is manifested.

It has now been proved that Paul has no idea of any other fire than the trial of the Holy Spirit. But how are those who suffer the loss of their works saved by fire? This it will not be difficult to understand, if we consider of what kind of persons he speaks. For he designates them builders of the Church, who, retaining the proper foundation, build different materials upon it; that is, who, not abandoning the principal and necessary articles of faith, err in minor and less perilous matters, mingling their own fictions with the Word of God.

Such, I say, must suffer the loss of their work by the destruction of their fictions. They themselves, however, are saved, yet so as by fire; that is, not that their ignorance and delusions are approved by the Lord, but they are purified from them by the grace and power of the Holy Spirit. All those, accordingly, who have tainted the golden purity of the divine Word with the pollution of purgatory, must necessarily suffer the loss of their work.

10 The ancient doctrine of purgatory refuted by a more ancient apostle. Not supported by ancient writers, by Scripture, or solid argument. Introduced by custom and a zeal not duly regulated by the Word of God. Ancient writers, as Augustine, speak doubtfully in commending prayer for the dead. At all events, we must hold by the Word of God, which rejects this fiction. There is vast difference between the more ancient and the more modern builders of purgatory. This is shown by comparing them.

But the observance of it in the Church is of the highest antiquity. This objection is disposed of by Paul, when, including even his own age in the sentence, he declares that all who in building the Church have laid upon it something not conformable to the foundation, must suffer the loss of their work. When, therefore, my opponents object that it has been the practice for thirteen hundred years to offer prayers for the dead, I, in return, ask them, by what word of God, by what revelation, by what example was it done? For here not only are passages of Scripture wanting, but also in the examples of all the saints of whom we read, nothing of the kind is seen. We have numerous and sometimes long narratives of their mourning and sepulchral rites, but not one word is said of prayers. But the more important the matter was, the more they ought to have dwelt upon it. Even those who in ancient times offered prayers for the dead saw that they were not supported by the command of God and legitimate example. Why then did they presume to do it? I hold that herein they suffered the common lot of man, and therefore maintain that what they did is not to be imitated. Believers ought not to engage in any work without a firm conviction of its propriety, as Paul enjoins (see Romans 14:23); and this conviction is expressly requisite in prayer. It is to be presumed, however, that they were influenced by some reason; they sought a solace for their sorrow, and it seemed cruel not to give some attestation of their love to the dead, when in the presence of God. All know by experience how natural it is for the human mind thusly to feel.

Received custom, too, was a kind of torch by which the minds of many were inflamed. We know that among all the Gentiles and in all ages certain rites were paid to the dead. Although Satan deluded foolish mortals by these impostures, yet the means of deceiving were borrowed from a sound principle—viz. that death is not destruction, but a passage from this life to another. And there can be no doubt that superstition itself always left the Gentiles without excuse before the judgment-seat of God, because they neglected to prepare for that future life which they professed to believe. Thus, that Christians might not seem worse than heathens, they felt ashamed of paying no office to the dead, as if they had been utterly annihilated.

Hence, their ill-advised assiduity, because they thought they would expose themselves to great disgrace, if they were slow in providing funeral feasts and oblations. What was thus introduced by perverse rivalry, always received new additions, until the highest holiness of the papacy consisted in giving assistance to the suffering dead. But far better and more solid comfort is furnished by Scripture when it declares, "Blessed are the dead that die in the Lord;" and adds the reason, "for they rest from their labors" (Revelation 14:13). We ought not to indulge our love so far as to set up a perverse mode of prayer in the Church. Surely, every person possessed of the least prudence easily perceives that whatever we meet with on this subject in ancient writers was in deference to public custom and the ignorance of the vulgar.

I admit they were themselves also carried away into error, the usual effect of rash credulity being to destroy the judgment. Meanwhile the passages themselves show that when they recommended prayer for the dead it was with hesitation.

Augustine relates in his *Confessions*, that his mother, Monica, earnestly entreated to be remembered when the solemn rites at the altar were performed; doubtless an old woman's wish, which her son did not bring to the test of Scripture, but from natural affection wished others to approve. His book, *De Cura pro Mortals Agenda, on Showing Care for the Dead*, is so full of doubt that its coldness may well extinguish the heat of a foolish zeal. Should anyone, in pretending to be a patron of the dead, deal merely in probabilities, the only effect will be to make those indifferent who were formerly solicitous.

The only support of this dogma is that as a custom of praying for the dead prevailed, the duty ought not to be despised. But granting that ancient ecclesiastical writers deemed it a pious thing to assist the dead, the rule which can never deceive is always to be observed—viz. that we must not introduce anything of our own into our prayers, but must keep all our wishes in subordination to the Word of God, because it belongs to Him to prescribe what He wishes us to ask.

Now, since the whole Law and gospel do not contain one syllable which countenances the right of praying for the dead, it is a profanation of prayer to go one step further than God enjoins. But lest our opponents boast of sharing their error with the ancient Church, I say that there is a wide difference between the two. The latter made a commemoration of the dead, that they might not seem to have cast off all concern for them; but they, at the same time, acknowledged that they were doubtful as to their state; assuredly they made no such assertion concerning purgatory, as implied that they did not hold it to be uncertain.

The former insist that their dream of purgatory shall be received without question as an article of faith. The latter sparingly and in a perfunctory manner only commended their dead to the Lord, in the communion of the holy supper. The former are constantly urging the care of the dead, and by their importunate preaching of it, make out that it is to be preferred to all the offices of charity. But it would not be difficult for us to produce some passages from ancient writers, which clearly overturn all those prayers for the dead, which were then in use.

Such is the passage of Augustine, in which he shows that the resurrection of the flesh and eternal glory is expected by all, but that rest which follows death is received by everyone who is worthy of it when he dies. Accordingly, he declares that all the righteous, not less than the apostles, prophets, and martyrs, immediately after death enjoy blessed rest. If such is their condition, what, I ask, will our prayers contribute to them? I say nothing of those grosser superstitions by which they have fascinated the minds of the simple; and yet they are innumerable, and most of them so monstrous, that they cannot cover them with any cloak of decency. I say nothing, moreover, of those most shameful trafficking, which they plied as they listed while the world was stupefied. For I would never come to an end if I were to do so, and, without enumerating them, the pious reader will here find enough to establish his conscience.

Chapter 6

THE LIFE OF A CHRISTIAN MAN. SCRIPTURAL ARGUMENTS EXHORTING TO IT

This and the four following chapters discuss the Life of the Christian and are so arranged as to admit of being classed under two principal heads.

First, it must be held to be a universally acknowledged point, that no man is a Christian who does not feel some special love for righteousness, chapter 6. Secondly, in regard to the standard by which every man ought to regulate his life, although it seems to be considered in chapter 7 only, yet the three following chapters also refer to it. They show that the Christian has two duties to perform. First, the observance being so arduous, he needs the greatest patience. Hence, chapter 8 treats professedly of the utility of the cross, and chapter 9 invites the reader to meditation on the future life. Lastly, chapter 10 clearly shows, as in no small degree conducive to this end, how we are to use this life and its comforts without abusing them.

This sixth chapter consists of two parts: I. Connection between this treatise on the Christian life and the doctrine of regeneration and repentance. Arrangement of the treatise, sections 1-3. II. Extremes to be avoided: first, false Christians denying Christ by their works condemned, section 4, and second, Christians should not despair, though they have not attained perfection, provided they make daily progress in piety and righteousness.

Sections

1. Connection between this chapter and the doctrine of regeneration. Necessity of the doctrine concerning the Christian life. The brevity of this treatise. The method of it. Plainness and unadorned simplicity of the Scripture system of morals.

2. Two divisions. First, Personal holiness. A. Because God is holy. B. Because of our communion with His saints.

3. *Second division, relating to our redemption. Admirable moral system of Scripture. Five special inducements or exhortations to a Christian life.*

4. *False Christians who are opposed to this life censured A. They have not truly learned Christ. B. The gospel is not the guide of their words or actions. C. They do not imitate Christ the Master. D. They would separate the Spirit from his word.*

5. *Christians ought not to grow despondent, provided that: A. They take the Word of God for their guide. B. Sincerely cultivate righteousness. C. Walk, according to their capacity, in the ways of the Lord. D. Make some progress. E. Persevere.*

1 Connection between this chapter and the doctrine of regeneration. Necessity of the doctrine concerning the Christian Life. The brevity of this treatise. The method of it. The plainness and unadorned simplicity of the Scripture system of morals.

We have said that the object of regeneration is to bring the life of believers into concord and harmony with the righteousness of God and so confirm the adoption, which has received them as sons. But although the Law comprehends within it that new life by which the image of God is restored in us, yet, as our sluggishness stands greatly in need both of helps and incentives, it will be useful to collect out of Scripture a true account of this reformation lest any who have a heartfelt desire of repentance should in their zeal go astray.

Moreover, I am aware that, in undertaking to describe the life of the Christian, I am entering on a large and extensive subject, one which, when fully considered in all its parts, is sufficient to fill a large volume. We see the length to which the Fathers, in treating of individual virtues, extend their exhortations. This they do, not from mere loquaciousness; for whatever the virtue which you undertake to recommend, your pen is spontaneously led by the copiousness of the matter so to amplify, that you seem not to have discussed it properly if you have not done it at length.

My intention, however, in the plan of life which I now propose to give, is not to extend it so far as to treat of each virtue specially and expatiate in exhortation. This must be sought in the writings of others, and particularly in the homilies of the Fathers. For me it will be sufficient to point out the method by which a pious man may be taught how to frame his life aright, and briefly lay down some universal rule by which he may not improperly regulate his conduct. I shall one day possibly find time for more ample discourse, [or leave others to perform an office for which I am not so fit. I have a natural love of brevity, and, perhaps, any attempt of mine at copiousness would not succeed. Even if I could gain the highest applause by being more wordy, I would scarcely be disposed to attempt it], while the nature of my present work requires me to glance at simple doctrine with as much brevity as possible.

As philosophers have certain definitions of rectitude and honesty, from which they derive particular duties and the whole train of virtues; so in this respect Scripture is not without order, but presents a most beautiful arrangement, one which is every way much more certain than that of philosophers. The only difference is that they, under the influence of ambition, constantly affect an exquisite perspicuity of arrangement, which may serve to display their genius, whereas the Spirit of God, teaching without affectation, is not so perpetually observant of exact method, and yet by observing it at times sufficiently intimates that it is not to be neglected.

2 Two divisions. First, Personal holiness. A. Because God is holy. B. Because of our communion with His saints.

The Scripture system of which we speak aims chiefly at two objects. The former is that the love of righteousness, to which we are by no means naturally inclined, may be instilled and implanted into our minds. The latter is (see chapter 7) to prescribe a rule, which will prevent us while in the pursuit of righteousness from going astray. It has numerous admirable methods of recommending righteousness. Many have been already pointed out in different parts of this work; but we shall here also briefly refer to some of them. With what better foundation can it begin than by reminding us that we must be holy, because "God is holy" (see Leviticus 19:1; 1 Peter 1:16)? For when we were scattered abroad like lost sheep, wandering through the labyrinth of this world, He brought us back again to His own fold.

When mention is made of our union with God, let us remember that holiness must be the bond; not that by the merit of holiness we come into communion with Him (we ought rather first to cleave to Him, in order that, pervaded with His holiness, we may follow whither He calls), but because it greatly concerns His glory not to have any fellowship with wickedness and impurity. Wherefore He tells us that this is the end of our calling, the end to which we ought ever to have respect, if we would answer the call of God. For to what end were we rescued from the iniquity and pollution of the world into which we were plunged, if we allow ourselves, during our whole lives, to wallow in them? Besides, we are at the same time admonished that if we would be regarded as the Lord's people, we must inhabit the holy city of Jerusalem (see Isaiah rev. 8, *et alibi*); which, as He hath consecrated it to himself, it would be impious for its inhabitants to profane by impurity. Hence, the expressions, "Who shall abide in thy tabernacle? Who shall dwell in thy holy hill? He that walketh uprightly, and worketh righteousness" (Psalm 15:1, 2; 24:3, 4); for the sanctuary in which He dwells certainly ought not to be like an unclean stall.

3 Second division, relating to our redemption. Admirable moral system of Scripture. Five special inducements or exhortations to a Christian life.

The better to arouse us, it exhibits God the Father, who, as He hath reconciled us to himself in his Anointed, has impressed His image upon us, to which He would have us to be conformed. (See Psalm 5:4.) Come, then, and let them show me a more excellent system among philosophers, who think that they only have a moral philosophy duly and orderly arranged. They, when they would give excellent exhortations to virtue, can only tell us to live agreeably to nature. Scripture derives its exhortations from the true source, when it not only enjoins us to regulate our lives with a view to God, its Author to whom it belongs, but after showing us that we have degenerated from our true origin—viz. the law of our Creator, adds that Christ, through whom we have returned to favor with God, is set before us as a model, the image of which our lives should express.

What do you require that is more effectual than this? Nay, what do you require beyond this? If the Lord adopts us for His sons on the condition that our life be a representation of Christ, the bond of our adoption—then, unless we dedicate and devote ourselves to righteousness, we not only, with the utmost perfidy, revolt from our Creator, but also abjure the Savior himself. Then, from an enumeration of all the blessings of God, and each part of our salvation, it finds materials for exhortation.

Ever since God exhibited himself to us as a Father, we must be convicted of extreme ingratitude if we do not in turn exhibit ourselves as His sons. Ever since Christ purified us by the laver of His blood and communicated this purification by baptism, it would ill become us to be defiled with new pollution. Ever since He engrafted us into His body, we, who are His members, should anxiously beware of contracting any stain or taint. Ever since He who is our Head ascended to Heaven, it is befitting in us to withdraw our affections from the Earth, and with our whole soul aspire to Heaven. Ever since the Holy Spirit dedicated us as temples to the Lord, we should make it our endeavor to show forth the glory of God, and guard against being profaned by the defilement of sin. Ever since our soul and body were destined to heavenly incorruptibility and an unfading crown, we should earnestly strive to keep them pure and uncorrupted against the day of the Lord.

These, I say, are the surest foundations of a well-regulated life, and you will search in vain for anything resembling them among philosophers, who, in their commendation of virtue, never rise higher than the natural dignity of man.

4 False Christians who are opposed to this life are censured. A. They have not truly learned Christ. B. The gospel is not the guide of their words or actions. C. They do not imitate Christ, the Master. D. They would separate the Spirit from His Word.

This is the place to address those who, having nothing of Christ but the name and sign, would yet be called Christians. How dare they boast of this sacred name? None have intercourse with Christ but those who have acquired the true knowledge of him from the gospel. The apostle denies that any man truly has learned Christ who has not learned to put off "the old man, which is corrupt according to the deceitful lusts, and put on Christ" (Ephesians 4:22). They are, therefore, convicted of falsely and unjustly pretending knowledge of Christ, whatever be the volubility and eloquence with which they can talk of the gospel. Doctrine is not an affair of the tongue, but of the life. It is not apprehended by the intellect and memory merely, like other branches of learning, but is received only when it possesses the whole soul and finds its seat and habitation in the inmost recesses of the heart. Let them, therefore, either cease to insult God, by boasting that they are what they are not, or let them show themselves not unworthy disciples of their divine Master. To the doctrine in which our religion is contained we have given the first place, since by it our salvation commences; but it must be transfused into the breast, and pass into the conduct, and so transform us into itself, as not to prove unfruitful. If philosophers are justly offended, and banish from their company with disgrace those who, while professing an art, which ought to be the mistress of their conduct, convert it into mere loquacious sophistry, with how much better reason shall we detest those flimsy Sophists who are contented to let the gospel play upon their lips, when, from its efficacy, it ought to penetrate the inmost affections of the heart, fix its seat in the soul, and pervade the whole man a hundred times more than the frigid discourses of philosophers?

5 Christians ought not to become despondent: provided: A. They take the Word of God for their guide. B. Sincerely cultivate righteousness. C. Walk, according to their capacity, in the ways of the Lord. D. Make some progress. E. Persevere.

I insist not that the life of the Christian shall breathe nothing but the perfect gospel, though this is to be desired, and ought to be attempted. I insist not so strictly on evangelical perfection, as to refuse to acknowledge as a Christian any man who has not attained it. In this way all would be excluded from the Church, since there is no man who is not far removed from this perfection, while many, who have made but little progress, would be undeservedly rejected. What then? Let us set this before our eye as the end at which we ought constantly to aim. Let it be regarded as the goal towards which we are to run. For you cannot divide the matter with God, undertaking part of what His Word enjoins, and omitting parts at your pleasure. For, in the first place, God uniformly recommends integrity as the principal part of His worship, meaning by integrity real singleness of mind, devoid of gloss and fiction, and to this is opposed a double mind; it is as if it had been said that the spiritual commencement of a good life is when the internal affections are sincerely devoted to God in the cultivation of holiness and justice. But seeing that, in this earthly prison of the body, no man is supplied with strength sufficient to hasten in his course with due alacrity, while the greater number are so oppressed with weakness, that hesitating, and halting, and even crawling on the ground, they make little progress, let everyone of us go as far as his humble ability enables him and prosecute the journey once begun. No one will travel so badly as not daily to make some degree of progress. This, therefore, let us never cease to do, that we may daily advance in the way of the Lord; and let us not despair because of the slender measure of success. However little the success may correspond with our wish, our labor is not lost when today is better than yesterday, provided with true singleness of mind we keep our aim, and aspire to the goal, not speaking flattering things to ourselves, nor indulging our vices, but making it our constant endeavor to become better, until we attain to goodness itself. If, during the whole course of our life, we seek and follow, we shall at length attain it, when relieved from the infirmity of flesh we are admitted to full fellowship with God.

Chapter 7

A SUMMARY OF THE CHRISTIAN LIFE.
OF SELF-DENIAL

The divisions of the chapter are: I. The rule which permits us not to go astray in the study of righteousness requires two things—viz. that man, abandoning his own will, should devote himself entirely to the service of God; whence it follows, that we must seek not our own things, but the things of God, sections 1, 2. II. A description of this renovation or Christian life taken from the epistle to Titus, and accurately explained under certain special heads, section 3 to end.

Sections

1. Consideration of the second general division in regard to the Christian life. Its beginning and sum. A twofold respect. First, we are not our own. Respect to both the fruit and the use. Unknown to philosophers, who have placed reason on the throne of the Holy Spirit.

2. Second, since we are not our own, we must seek the glory of God and obey His will. Self-denial is recommended to the disciples of Christ. He who neglects it is deceived either by pride or hypocrisy, and rushes on destruction.

3. Three things that need to be followed, and two to be shunned in life. Impiety and worldly lusts to be shunned. Sobriety, justice, and piety to be followed. An inducement to right conduct.

4. Self-denial the sum of Paul's doctrine. Its difficulty. Qualities in us which make it difficult. Cures for these qualities. A. Ambition to be suppressed. B. Humility to be embraced. C. Candor to be esteemed. D. Mutual charity to be preserved. E. Modesty to be sincerely cultivated.

5. The advantage of our neighbor is to be promoted. Here self-denial most necessary and yet most difficult. Here a double remedy.

A. The benefits bestowed upon us are for the common benefit of the Church. B. We ought to do all we can for our neighbor. This illustrated by analogy from the members of the human body. This duty of charity is founded on the divine command.

6. Charity ought to have for its attendants patience and kindness. We should consider the image of God in our neighbors, especially in those who are of the household of faith. Hence, a fourfold consideration which refutes all objections. A common objection refuted.

7. The Christian life cannot exist without charity. Remedies for the vices opposed to charity. A. Mercy. B. Humility. C. Modesty. D. Diligence. E. Perseverance.

8. Self-denial, in respect to God, should lead to equanimity and tolerance. A. We are always subject to God. B. We should shun avarice and ambition. C. We should expect all prosperity from the blessing of God, and entirely depend on Him.

9. We ought not to desire wealth or honors without the divine blessing, nor follow the arts of the wicked. We ought to cast all our care upon God, and never envy the prosperity of others.

10. We ought to commit ourselves entirely to God. The necessity of this doctrine. Various uses of affliction. Heathen abuse and corruption.

1 **Consideration of the second general division in regard to the Christian life. Its beginning and sum. A twofold respect. First, we are not our own. Respect to both the fruit and the use. Unknown to philosophers, who have placed reason on the throne of the Holy Spirit.**

Although the Law of God contains a perfect rule of conduct that is admirably arranged, it has seemed proper to our divine Master to train His people by a more accurate method, to the rule which is enjoined in the Law; and the leading principle in the method is that it is the duty of believers to present their "bodies a living sacrifice, holy and acceptable unto God, which is their reasonable service" (Romans 12:1). Hence, He draws the exhortation: "Be not conformed to this world: but be ye transformed by the renewing of your mind, that ye may prove what is that good, and acceptable, and perfect will of God."

The great point, then, is that we are consecrated and dedicated to God, and, therefore, should not henceforth think, speak, design, or act, without a view to His glory. What He hath made sacred cannot, without signal insult to Him, be applied to profane use. But if we are not our own, but the Lord's, it is plain both what error is to be shunned, and to what end the actions of our lives ought to be directed. We are not our own; therefore, neither is our own reason or will to rule our acts and counsels. We are not our own; therefore, let us not make it our end to seek what may be agreeable to our carnal nature. We are not our own; therefore, as far as possible, let us forget ourselves and the things that are ours.

On the other hand, we are God's; let us, therefore, live and die to him. (See Romans 14:8.) We are God's; therefore, let His wisdom and will preside over all our actions. We are God's; to Him, then, as the only legitimate end, let every part of our life be directed. O how great the proficiency of him who, taught that he is not his own, has withdrawn the dominion and government of himself from his own reason that he may give them to God! For as the surest source of destruction to men is to obey themselves, so the only haven of safety is to have no other will, no other wisdom, than to follow the Lord wherever He leads.

Let this, then, be the first step: to abandon ourselves and devote the whole energy of our minds to the service of God. By service, I mean not only that which consists in verbal obedience, but also that by which the mind, divested of its own carnal feelings, implicitly obeys the call of the Spirit of God.

This transformation (which Paul calls *the renewing of the mind*, see Romans 12:2; Ephesians 4:23), though it is the first entrance to life, was unknown to all the philosophers. They give the government of man to reason alone, thinking that reason alone is to be listened to; in short, they assign to reason the sole direction of the conduct. But Christian philosophy bids reason to give place and to yield complete submission to the Holy Spirit, so that the man himself no longer lives, but Christ lives and reigns in him. (See Galatians 2:20.)

2 Second, since we are not our own, we must seek the glory of God and obey His will. Self-denial is recommended to the disciples of Christ. He who neglects it is deceived either by pride or hypocrisy, and rushes on to destruction.

Hence, follows the other principle that we are not to seek our own, but the Lord's will, and act with a view to promote His glory. Great is our proficiency, when, almost forgetting ourselves, certainly postponing our own reason, we faithfully make it our study to obey God and His commandments. For when Scripture enjoins us to lay aside private regard to ourselves, it not only divests our minds of an excessive longing for wealth or power or human favor, but also eradicates all ambition and thirst for worldly glory, and other more secret pests. The Christian ought, indeed, to be so trained and disposed as to consider that during his whole life he has to do with God. For this reason, as he will bring all things to the disposal and estimate of God, so he will religiously direct his whole mind to Him. For he who has learned to look to God in everything he does is at the same time diverted from all vain thoughts. This is that self-denial, which Christ so strongly enforces on His disciples from the very outset (see Matthew 16:24), which, as soon as it takes hold of the mind, leaves no place either, first, for pride, show, and ostentation; or, secondly, for avarice, lust, luxury, effeminacy, or other vices which are engendered by self-love.

On the contrary, wherever it reigns not, the foulest vices are indulged in without shame; or, if there is some appearance of virtue, it is vitiated by a depraved longing for applause. Show me, if you can, an individual who, unless he has renounced himself in obedience to the Lord's command, is disposed to do good for its own sake. Those who have not so renounced themselves have followed virtue at least for the sake of praise.

The philosophers who have contended most strongly that virtue is to be desired on its own account, were so inflated with arrogance as to make it apparent that they sought virtue for no other reason than as a ground for indulging in pride. So far, therefore, is God from being delighted with these hunters after popular applause with their swollen breasts, that He declares they have received their reward in this world. (See Matthew 6:2.) And He says that harlots and publicans are nearer the kingdom of heaven than they. (See Matthew 21:31.)

We have not yet sufficiently explained how great and numerous are the obstacles by which a man is impeded in the pursuit of rectitude, so long as he has not renounced himself. The old saying is true: There is a world of iniquity treasured up in the human soul. Nor can you find any other remedy for this than to deny yourself, renounce your own reason, and direct your whole mind to the pursuit of those things which the Lord requires of you, and which you are to seek only because they are pleasing to Him.

3 **Three things that need to be followed, and two to be shunned in life. Impiety and worldly lusts to be shunned. Sobriety, justice, and piety to be followed. An inducement to right conduct.**

In another passage, Paul gives a brief, indeed, but more distinct account of each of the parts of a well-ordered life: "The grace of God that bringeth salvation hath appeared to all men, teaching us that, denying ungodliness and worldly lusts, we should live soberly, righteously, and godly in this present world looking for that blessed hope, and the glorious appearance of the great God and our Savior Jesus Christ; who gave himself for us, that he might redeem us from all iniquity, and purify to himself a peculiar people, zealous of good works" (Titus 2:11-14). After holding forth the grace of God to animate us and pave the way for His true worship, he removes the two greatest obstacles which stand in the way—viz. ungodliness, to which we are by nature too prone, and worldly lusts, which are of still greater extent.

Under *ungodliness*, he includes not merely superstition, but everything at variance with the true fear of God. *Worldly lusts* are equivalent to the lusts of the flesh. Thus, he enjoins us, in regard to both tables of the Law, to lay aside our own mind and renounce whatever our own reason and will dictate. Then he reduces all the actions of our lives to three branches sobriety, righteousness, and godliness. *Sobriety* undoubtedly denotes as well chastity and temperance as the pure and frugal use of temporal goods and patient endurance of want. *Righteousness* comprehends all the duties of equity in everyone his due. Next follows *godliness*, which separates us from the pollutions of the world, and connects us with God in true holiness.

These, when connected together by an indissoluble chain, constitute complete perfection. But as nothing is more difficult than to bid adieu to the will of the flesh, subdue, nay, abjure our lusts, devote ourselves to God and our brethren, and lead an angelic life amid the pollutions of the world, Paul, to set our minds free from all entanglements, recalls us to the hope of a blessed immortality, justly urging us to contend, because as Christ has once appeared as our Redeemer, so on His final advent He will give full effect to the salvation obtained by Him. And in this way he dispels all the allurements which becloud our path, and prevent us from aspiring as we ought to heavenly glory; nay, He tells us that we must be pilgrims in the world, that we may not fail of obtaining the heavenly inheritance.

4 Self-denial—the sum of Paul's doctrine. Its difficulty. Qualities in us, which make it difficult. Cures for these qualities. A. Ambition to be suppressed. B. Humility to be embraced. C. Candor to be esteemed. D. Mutual charity to be preserved. E. Modesty to be sincerely cultivated.

Moreover, we see by these words that self-denial has respect partly to men and partly (more especially) to God (section 8-10). For when Scripture enjoins us, in regard to our fellowmen, to prefer them in honor to ourselves, and sincerely labor to promote their advantages (see Romans 12:10; Philippians 2:3), He gives us commands which our mind is utterly incapable of obeying until its natural feelings are suppressed. For so blindly do we all rush in the direction of self-love that everyone thinks he has a good reason for exalting himself and despising all others in comparison. If God has bestowed on us something not to be repented of, trusting to it, we immediately become elated, and not only swell, but almost burst with pride.

The vices with which we abound we both carefully conceal from others, and flatteringly represent to ourselves as minute and trivial, nay, sometimes hug them as virtues. When the same qualities which we admire in ourselves are seen in others, even though they should be superior, we, in order that we may not be forced to yield to them, maliciously lower and carp at them; in like manner, in the case of vices, not contented with severe and keen criticism, we studiously exaggerate them.

Hence, the insolence with which each, as if exempted from the common lot, seeks to exalt himself above his neighbor, confidently and proudly despising others, or at least looking down upon them as his inferiors. The poor man yields to the rich, the plebeian to the noble, the servant to the master, the unlearned to the learned, and yet everyone inwardly cherishes some idea of his own superiority. Thus, each, flattering himself, sets up a kind of kingdom in his breast; the arrogant, to satisfy themselves, pass censure on the minds and manners of other men, and when contention arises, the full venom is displayed. Many bear about with them some measure of mildness so long as all things go smoothly and lovingly with them, but how few are there who, when stung and irritated, preserve the same tenor of moderation? For this there is no other remedy than to pluck up by the roots those most noxious pests, self-love and love of victory. This the doctrine of Scripture does. For it teaches us to remember that the endowments which God has bestowed upon us are not our own, but His free gifts, and that those who plume themselves upon them betray their ingratitude. "Who maketh thee to differ," saith Paul, "and what hast thou that thou didst not receive? Now if thou didst receive it, why dost thou glory, as if thou hadst not received it?" (1 Corinthians 4:7).

Then by a diligent examination of our faults, let us keep ourselves humble. Thus while nothing will remain to swell our pride, there will be much to subdue it. Again, we are enjoined, whenever we behold the gifts of God in others, so to reverence and respect the gifts, as also to honor those in whom they reside. God, having been pleased to bestow honor upon them, it would ill become us to deprive them of it. Then we are told to overlook their faults, not, indeed, to encourage by flattering them, but not because of them to insult those whom we ought to regard with honor and goodwill. In this way, with regard to all with whom we have intercourse, our behavior will be not only moderate and modest, but also courteous and friendly. The only way by which you can ever attain to true meekness, is to have your heart imbued with a humble opinion of yourself and respect for others.

5 The advantage of our neighbor is to be promoted. Here self-denial most necessary and yet most difficult. Here a double remedy. A. The benefits bestowed upon us are for the common benefit of the Church. B. We ought to do all we can for our neighbor. This is illustrated by analogy from the members of the human body. This duty of charity is founded on the divine command.

How difficult it is to perform the duty of seeking the good of our neighbor! Unless you leave off all thought of yourself and in a manner cease to be yourself, you will never accomplish it. How can you exhibit those works of charity which Paul describes unless you renounce yourself, and become wholly devoted to others? "Charity [says he, 1 Corinthians 13:4] suffereth long, and is kind; charity envieth not;

charity vaunteth not itself, is not puffed up, doth not behave itself unseemly, seeketh not her own, is not easily provoked," etc.

Were it the only thing required of us to seek not our own, nature would not have the least power to comply: she so inclines us to love ourselves only that she will not easily allow us carelessly to pass by ourselves and our own interests that we may watch over the interests of others, nay, spontaneously to yield our own rights and resign them to another. But Scripture, to conduct us to this, reminds us that whatever we obtain from the Lord is granted on the condition of our employing it for the common good of the Church, and that, therefore, the legitimate use of all our gifts is a kind and liberal communication of them with others.

There cannot be a surer rule, nor a stronger exhortation to the observance of it, than when we are taught that all the endowments which we possess are divine deposits entrusted to us for the very purpose of being distributed for the good of our neighbor. But Scripture proceeds still further when it likens these endowments to the different members of the body. (See 1 Corinthians 12:12.) No member has its function for itself, or applies it for its own private use, but transfers it to its fellow-members; nor does it derive any other advantage from it than that which it receives in common with the whole body. Thus, whatever the pious man can do, he is bound to do for his brethren, not consulting his own interest in any other way than by striving earnestly for the common edification of the Church.

Let this, then, be our method of showing goodwill and kindness, considering that, in regard to everything which God has bestowed upon us, and by which we can aid our neighbor, we are His stewards, and are bound to give account of our stewardship; moreover, that the only right mode of administration is that which is regulated by love. In this way, we shall not only unite the study of our neighbor's advantage with a regard to our own, but also make the latter subordinate to the former. And lest we should have omitted to perceive that this is the law for duly administering every gift which we receive from God, He of old applied that law to the minutest expressions of His own kindness. He commanded the first fruits to be offered to Him as an attestation by the people that it was impious to reap any advantage from goods not previously consecrated to Him. (See Exodus 22:29; 23:19.) But if the gifts of God are not sanctified to us until we have with our own hand dedicated them to the Giver, it must be a gross abuse that does not give signs of such dedication.

It is in vain to contend that you cannot enrich the Lord by your offerings. Though, as the Psalmist says, "Thou art my Lord: my goodness extendeth not unto thee," yet you can extend it "to the saints that are in the earth" (Psalm 16:2, 3); and, therefore, a comparison is drawn between sacred oblations and alms, as now corresponding to the offerings under the Law.

6 Charity ought to have for its attendants patience and kindness. We should consider the image of God in our neighbors, especially in those who are of the household of faith. Hence, a fourfold consideration which refutes all objections. A common objection refuted.

Moreover, that we may not become weary in well-doing (as would otherwise forthwith and infallibly be the case), we must add the other quality in the apostle's enumeration, "Charity suffereth long, and is kind, is not easily provoked" (1 Corinthians 13:4). The Lord enjoins us to do good to all without exception, though the greater part, if estimated by their own merit, are most unworthy of it. But Scripture subjoins a most excellent reason, when it tells us that we are not to look to what men in themselves deserve, but to attend to the image of God, which exists in all, and to which we owe all honor and love. But in those who are of the household of faith, the same rule is to be more carefully observed, inasmuch as that image is renewed and restored in them by the Spirit of Christ. Therefore, whoever be the man that is presented to you as needing your assistance, you have no ground for declining to give it to him. Say he is a stranger. The Lord has given him a mark, which ought to be familiar to you: for which reason he forbids you to despise your own flesh. (See Galatians 6:10.) Say he is mean and of no consideration. The Lord points him out as one whom He has distinguished by the luster of His own image. (See Isaiah 58:7.) Say that no ties of duty bind you to him. The Lord has substituted him into his own place, that in him you may recognize the many great obligations under which the Lord has laid you to himself. Say that he is unworthy of your least exertion on his account; but the image of God, by which he is recommended to you, is worthy of yourself and all your exertions. But if he not only merits no good, but also has provoked you by injury and mischief, still this is no good reason that you should not embrace him in love, and visit him with offices of love. He has deserved very differently from me you will say. But what has the Lord deserved? Whatever injury he has done you, when he enjoins you to forgive him, he certainly means that it should be imputed to himself. In this way only we attain to what is not to say difficult but altogether against nature, to love those that hate us, render good for evil, and blessing for cursing, remembering that we are not to reflect on the wickedness of men, but look to the image of God in them, an image which, covering and obliterating their faults, should by its beauty and dignity allure us to love and embrace them.

7 Christian life cannot exist without charity. Remedies for the vices opposed to charity. A. Mercy. B. Humility. C. Modesty. D. Diligence. E. Perseverance.

We shall thus succeed in mortifying ourselves if we fulfill all the duties of charity. Those duties, however, are not fulfilled by the mere discharge of them, though none is omitted, unless it is done from a pure feeling of love. For it may happen that one may perform every one of these offices, insofar as the external act is concerned, and be far from performing them aright. For you see some who would be thought very liberal, and yet accompany everything they give with insult, by the haughtiness of their looks, or the violence of their words. And to such a calamitous condition have we come in this unhappy age, that most men almost never give alms without contempt and insult. Such conduct ought not to have been tolerated even among the heathen, but from Christians something more is required than to carry cheerfulness in their looks, and give attractiveness to the discharge of their duties by courteous language.

First, they should put themselves in the place of him whom they see in need of their assistance, and pity his misfortune, as if they felt and bore it, so that a feeling of pity and humanity should incline them to assist him just as they would themselves. He who is thus minded will give assistance to his brethren, and not only not taint his acts with arrogance or upbraiding but will neither look down upon the brother to whom he does a kindness, as one who needed his help, or keep him in subjection as under obligation to him, just as we do not insult a diseased member when the rest of the body labors for its recovery, nor think it under special obligation to the other members, because it has required more exertion than it has returned. A communication of offices between members is not regarded as at all gratuitous, but rather as the payment of that which, being due by the law of nature, it would be monstrous to deny. For this reason, he who has performed one kind of duty will not think himself thereby discharged, as is usually the case when a rich man, after contributing some of his substance, delegates remaining burdens to others as if he had nothing to do with them. Everyone should rather consider that however great he is, he owes himself to his neighbors, and that the only limit to his beneficence is the failure of his means. The extent of these should regulate that of his charity.

8 Self-denial, in respect to God, should lead to equanimity and tolerance. A. We are always subject to God. B. We should shun avarice and ambition. C. We should expect all prosperity from the blessing of God and entirely depend on Him.

The principal part of self-denial, that which, as we have said, has reference to God, let us again consider more fully. Many things have already been said with regard to it, which it would be superfluous to repeat; and, therefore, it will be sufficient to view it as forming us to equanimity and endurance.

First, then, in seeking the convenience or tranquility of the present life, Scripture calls us to resign ourselves and all we have to the disposal of the Lord, to give Him the affections of our heart, that He may tame and subdue them. We have a frenzied desire, an infinite eagerness, to pursue wealth and honor, intrigue for power, accumulate riches, and collect all those frivolities which seem conducive to luxury and splendor. On the other hand, we have a remarkable dread, a remarkable hatred of poverty, mean birth, and a humble condition, and feel the strongest desire to guard against them. Hence, in regard to those who frame their life after their own counsel, we see how restless they are in mind, how many plans they try, to what fatigues they submit, in order that they may gain what avarice or ambition desires, or, on the other hand, escape poverty and meanness.

To avoid similar entanglements, the course which Christian men must follow is this: first, they must not long for, or hope for, or think of any kind of prosperity apart from the blessing of God; on it they must cast themselves, and there safely and confidently recline. For, however much the carnal mind may seem sufficient for itself when in the pursuit of honor or wealth, it depends on its own industry and zeal, or is aided by the favor of men it is certain that all this is nothing, and that neither intellect nor labor will be of the least avail, except insofar as the Lord prospers both. On the contrary, His blessing alone makes a way through all obstacles and brings everything to a joyful and favorable issue. Secondly, though without this blessing we may be able to acquire some degree of fame and opulence (as we daily see wicked men loaded with honors and riches), yet since those on whom the curse of God lies do not enjoy the least particle of true happiness, whatever we obtain without His blessing must turn out ill. Surely, men ought not to desire what adds to their misery.

9 We ought not to desire wealth or honors without the divine blessing, nor follow the arts of the wicked. We ought to cast all our care upon God, and never envy the prosperity of others.

Therefore, if we believe that all prosperous and desirable success depends entirely on the blessing of God, and that when it is wanting all kinds of misery and calamity await us, it follows that we should not eagerly contend for riches and honors, trusting to our own dexterity and assiduity, or leaning on the favor of men, or confiding in any empty imagination of fortune; but should always have respect to the Lord, that under His auspices we may be conducted to whatever lot He has provided for us.

First, the result will be that instead of rushing on regardless of right and wrong, by wiles and wicked arts, and with injury to our neighbors, to catch at wealth and seize upon honors, we will only follow such fortune as we may enjoy with innocence. Who can hope for the aid of the divine blessing amid fraud, rapine, and other iniquitous arts? As this blessing attends him only who thinks purely and acts uprightly, so it calls off all who long for it from sinister designs and evil actions.

Secondly, a curb will be laid upon us, restraining a too eager desire of becoming rich or an ambitious striving after honor. How can anyone have the effrontery to expect that God will aid him in accomplishing desires at variance with his word? What God with his own lips pronounces cursed, never can be prosecuted with his blessing.

Lastly, if our success is not equal to our wish and hope, we shall, however, be kept from impatience and detestation of our condition, whatever it be, knowing that so to feel is to murmur against God, at whose pleasure riches and poverty, contempt and honors, are dispensed. In short, he who leans on the divine blessing in the way which has been described, will not, in the pursuit of those things which men are wont most eagerly to desire, employ wicked arts which he knows would avail him nothing; nor when anything prosperous befalls him will he impute it to himself and his own diligence, or industry, or fortune, instead of ascribing it to God as its author. If, while the affairs of others flourish, his make little progress, or even go backward, he will bear his humble lot with greater equanimity and moderation than any irreligious man does the moderate success which only falls short of what he wished; for he has a solace in which he can rest more tranquilly than at the very summit of wealth or power, because he considers that his affairs are ordered by the Lord in the manner most conducive to his salvation. This, we see, is the way in which David was affected, who, while he follows God and gives up himself to His guidance, declares, "Neither do I exercise myself in great matters, or in things too high for me. Surely I have behaved and quieted myself as a child that is weaned of his mother" (Psalm 131:1, 2).

10 We ought to commit ourselves entirely to God. The necessity of this doctrine. Various uses of affliction. Heathen abuse and corruption.

Nor is it in this respect only that pious minds ought to manifest this tranquility and endurance; it must be extended to all the accidents to which this present life is liable. He alone, therefore, has properly denied himself, who has resigned himself entirely to the Lord, placing all the course of his life entirely at his disposal. Happen what may, he whose mind is thus composed will deem neither himself wretched nor murmur against God because of his lot. How necessary this disposition is will appear, if you consider the many accidents to which we are liable. Various diseases always attack us: at one time pestilence rages; at another we are involved in all the calamities of war. Frost and hail, destroying the promise of the year, cause sterility, which reduces us to penury; wife, parents, children, and relatives are carried off by death; our house is destroyed by fire.

These are the events which make men curse their life, detest the day of their birth, execrate the light of Heaven, even censure God, and (as they are eloquent in blasphemy) charge Him with cruelty and injustice. The believer must in these things also contemplate the mercy and truly paternal indulgence of God. Accordingly, should he see his house by the removal of kindred reduced to solitude even then he will not cease to bless the Lord; his thought will be, still the grace of the Lord, which dwells within my house, will not leave it desolate. If his crops are blasted, mildewed, or cut off by frost, or struck down by hail, and he sees famine before him, he will not, however, despond or murmur against God, but maintain his confidence in Him; "We thy people, and sheep of thy pasture, will give thee thanks forever" (Psalm 79:13); He will supply me with food, even in the extreme of sterility. If he is afflicted with disease, the sharpness of the pain will not so overcome him, as to make him break out with impatience, and expostulate with God; but recognizing justice and lenity in the rod, will patiently endure.

In short, whatever happens, knowing that it is ordered by the Lord, he will receive it with a placid and grateful mind, and will not contumaciously resist the government of Him, at whose disposal he has placed himself and all that he has. Especially let the Christian breast eschew that foolish and most miserable consolation of the heathen, who, to strengthen their mind against adversity, imputed it to fortune, at which they deemed it absurd to feel indignant, as fortune was aimless and rash and blindly wounded the good equally with the bad. On the contrary, the rule of piety is that the hand of God is the ruler and arbiter of the fortunes of all, and, instead of rushing on with thoughtless violence, dispenses good and evil with perfect regularity.

Chapter 8

OF BEARING THE CROSS—ONE BRANCH OF SELF-DENIAL

The four divisions of this chapter are: I. The nature of the cross, its necessity and dignity, sections 1, 2. II. The manifold advantages of the cross described, sections 3-6. III. The form of the cross, the most excellent of all, and yet it by no means removes all sense of pain, sections 7, 8. IV. A description of warfare under the cross, and of true patience (not that of philosophers), after the example of Christ, sections 9-11.

Sections

1. What the cross is. By whom, and on whom, and for what cause it is imposed. Its necessity and dignity.

2. The cross is necessary. A. To humble our pride. B. To make us apply to God for aid. Example of David.

3. To give us experience of God's presence. C. Manifold uses of the cross. (A) Produces patience, hope, and firm confidence in God, gives us victory and perseverance. Faith is invincible.

4. (B). Frames us to obedience. Example of Abraham. This training is very useful.

5. The cross is necessary to subdue the wantonness of the flesh. This is portrayed by an apposite simile. Various forms of the cross.

6. (C). God permits our infirmities, and corrects our past faults, that He may keep us in obedience. This is confirmed by a passage from Solomon and an apostle.

7. Singular consolation under the cross, when we suffer persecution for righteousness. Some parts of this consolation.

8. This form of the cross is most appropriate to believers and should be borne willingly and cheerfully. This cheerfulness is not unfeeling hilarity, but, while groaning under the burden, it waits patiently for the Lord.

9. *A description of this conflict. Opposed to the vanity of the Stoics. Illustrated by the authority and example of Christ.*

10. *Proved by the testimony and uniform experience of the elect. Also by the special example of the Apostle Peter. The nature of the patience required of us.*

11. *Distinction between the patience of Christians and philosophers. The latter pretend a necessity, which cannot be resisted. The former hold forth the justice of God and His care of our safety. A full exposition of this difference.*

1 **What the cross is. By whom, and on whom, and for what cause it is imposed. Its necessity and dignity.**

The pious mind must ascend still higher, namely, whither Christ calls His disciples, when He says that every one of them must "take up his cross" (Matthew 16:24). Those whom the Lord has chosen and honored with His intercourse must prepare for a hard, laborious, troubled life, a life full of many and various kinds of evils; it being the will of our heavenly Father to exercise His people in this way while putting them to the proof. Having begun this course with Christ the first-born, He continues it towards all His children. For though that Son was dear to Him above others, the Son in whom He was "well pleased," yet we see that far from being treated gently and indulgently, we may say that not only was He subjected to a perpetual cross while He dwelt on Earth, but His whole life was nothing else than a kind of perpetual cross. The apostle assigns the reason, "Though he was a Son, yet learned he obedience by the things which he suffered" (Hebrews 5:8).

Why, then, should we exempt ourselves from that condition to which Christ our Head behooved to submit; especially since He submitted on our account that He might in His own person exhibit a model of patience? Wherefore, the Apostle declares that all the children of God are destined to be conformed to Him. Hence, it affords us great consolation in hard and difficult circumstances, which men deem evil and adverse, to think that we are holding fellowship with the sufferings of Christ; that, as He passed to celestial glory through a labyrinth of many woes, so we too are conducted thither through various tribulations. For, in another passage, Paul himself thus speaks, "We must through much tribulation enter the kingdom of God" (Acts 14:22); and again, "That I may know him, and the power of his resurrection, and the fellowship of his sufferings, being made conformable unto his death" (Romans 8:29). How powerfully should it soften the bitterness of the cross to think that the more we are afflicted with adversity, the surer we are made of our fellowship with Christ, by communion with whom our sufferings are not only blessed to us, but tend greatly to the furtherance of our salvation.

2 The cross is necessary. A. To humble our pride. B. To make us apply to God for aid. Example of David.

We may add that the only thing which made it necessary for our Lord to undertake to bear the cross, was to testify and prove his obedience to the Father, whereas there are many reasons, which make it necessary for us to live constantly under the cross. Feeble as we are by nature, and prone to ascribe all perfection to our flesh, unless we receive ocular demonstration of our weakness, we readily estimate our virtue above its proper worth, and doubt not that, whatever happens, it will stand unimpaired and invincible against all difficulties. Hence, we indulge a stupid and empty confidence in the flesh, and then trusting to it, wax proud against the Lord himself, as if our own faculties were sufficient without his grace.

This arrogance cannot be better repressed than when He proves to us by experience, not only how great our weakness, but also our frailty is. Therefore, He visits us with disgrace or poverty or bereavement or disease, or other afflictions. Feeling altogether unable to support them, we forthwith, as far as regards ourselves, give way, and thus humbled we learn to invoke His strength, which alone can enable us to bear up under a weight of affliction. Nay, even the holiest of men, however well aware that they stand not in their own strength, but by the grace of God, would feel too secure in their own fortitude and constancy were they not brought to a more thorough knowledge of themselves by the trial of the cross.

This feeling gained even upon David, "In my prosperity, I said, I shall never be moved. Lord, by thy favor thou hast made my mountain to stand strong: thou didst hide thy face, and I was troubled" (Psalm 30:6, 7). He confesses that in prosperity his feelings were dulled and blunted, so that, neglecting the grace of God, on which alone he ought to have depended, he leaned toward himself, and promised himself perpetuity. If it so happened to this great prophet, who of us should not fear and study caution? Though in tranquility they flatter themselves with the idea of greater constancy and patience, yet, humbled by adversity, they learn the deception. Believers, I say, warned by such proofs of their diseases, make progress in humility, and, divesting themselves of a depraved confidence in the flesh, betake themselves to the grace of God, and, when they have so betaken themselves, experience the presence of the divine power in which is ample protection.

3 To give us experience of God's presence. C. Manifold uses of the cross. (A) Produces patience, hope, and firm confidence in God, gives us victory and perseverance. Faith is invincible.

This Paul teaches when he says that tribulation worketh patience, and patience experience. God has promised that He will be with believers in tribulation, and they feel the truth of the promise; while supported by His hand, they endure patiently. This they could never do by their own strength. Patience, therefore, gives the saints an experimental proof that God in reality furnishes the aid which He has promised whenever there is need.

Hence, their faith is confirmed, for it would be very ungrateful not to expect that in future the truth of God will be, as they have already found it, firm and constant. We now see how many advantages are at once produced by the cross. Overturning the overweening opinion we form of our own virtue and detecting the hypocrisy in which we delight, it removes our pernicious carnal confidence, teaching us, when thus humbled, to recline on God alone, so that we neither are oppressed nor despondent. Then victory is followed by hope, inasmuch as the Lord, by performing what He has promised, establishes His truth about the future.

Were these the only reasons, it is surely plain how necessary it is for us to bear the cross. It is of no little importance to be rid of your self-love, and made fully conscious of your weakness; so impressed with a sense of your weakness as to learn to distrust yourself—to distrust yourself so as to transfer your confidence to God, reclining on Him with such heartfelt confidence as to trust in his aid and continue invincible to the end, standing by His grace so as to perceive that He is true to His promises, and so assured of the certainty of his promises as to be strong in hope.

4 (B). Frames us to obedience. Example of Abraham. This training is very useful.

Another end which the Lord has in afflicting His people is to try their patience, and train them in obedience—not that they can yield obedience to him except insofar as He enables them; but He is pleased thus to attest and display striking proofs of the graces which He has conferred upon His saints, lest they should remain within unseen and unemployed. Accordingly, by bringing forward openly the strength and constancy of endurance with which He has provided His servants, he is said to try their patience. Hence, the expressions that God tempted Abraham (see Genesis 21:1, 12) and made proof of his piety by not declining to sacrifice his only son.

Hence, too, Peter tells us that our faith is proved by tribulation, just as gold is tried in a furnace of fire. But who will say it is not expedient that the most excellent gift of patience, which the believer has received from his God, should be applied to uses by being made sure and manifest? Otherwise men would never value it according to its worth. But if God himself, to prevent the virtues which He has conferred upon believers from lurking in obscurity, nay, lying useless and perishing, does right in supplying materials for calling them forth, there is the best reason for the afflictions of the saints, since without them their patience could not exist.

I say that by the cross they are also trained to obedience, because they are thus taught to live not according to their own wish, but at the disposal of God. Indeed, did all things proceed as they wish they would not know what it is to follow God. Seneca mentions that there was an old proverb when anyone was exhorted to endure adversity, "*Follow God,*" thereby intimating, that men truly submitted to the yoke of God only when they gave their back and hand to His rod. But if it is most right that we should in all things prove our obedience to our heavenly Father, and certainly we ought not to decline any method by which He trains us to obedience.

5 The cross is necessary to subdue the wantonness of the flesh. This is portrayed by an apposite simile. Various forms of the cross.

Still, however, we see not how necessary that obedience is, unless we at the same time consider how prone our carnal nature is to shake off the yoke of God whenever it has been treated with some degree of gentleness and indulgence. It just happens to it as with refractory horses, which, if kept idle for a few days at hack and manger, become ungovernable, and no longer recognize the rider, whose command they implicitly obeyed before. And we invariably become what God complains of in the people of Israel—waxing gross and fat, we kick against Him who reared and nursed us. (See Deuteronomy 32:15.)

The kindness of God should allure us to ponder and love His goodness, but since such is our malignity, that we are invariably corrupted by His indulgence, it is more than necessary for us to be restrained by discipline from breaking forth into such petulance. Thus, lest we become emboldened by an over-abundance of wealth; lest elated with honor, we grow proud; lest inflated with other advantages of body, or mind, or fortune, we grow insolent, the Lord himself interferes as He sees to be expedient by means of the cross, subduing and curbing the arrogance of our flesh, and that in various ways, as the advantage of each requires. For as we do not all equally labor under the same disease, so we do not all need the same difficult cure. Hence, we see that all are not exercised with the same kind of cross. While the heavenly Physician treats some more gently, in the case of others He employs harsher remedies, His purpose being to provide a cure for all. Still none is left free and untouched, because He knows that all, without a single exception, are diseased.

6 (C). God permits our infirmities, and corrects our past faults, that He may keep us in obedience. This is confirmed by a passage from Solomon and an apostle.

We may add that our most merciful Father requires not only to prevent our weakness, but often to correct our past faults, that He may keep us in due obedience. Therefore, whenever we are afflicted, we ought immediately to call to mind our past life. In this way we will find that the faults, which we have committed, are deserving of such castigation. Yet, the exhortation to patience is not to be founded chiefly on the acknowledgment of sin. For Scripture supplies a far better consideration when it says that in adversity "we are chastened of the Lord, that we should not be condemned with the world" (1 Corinthians 11:32). Therefore, in the very bitterness of tribulation we ought to recognize the kindness and mercy of our Father, since even then He ceases not to further our salvation. For He afflicts, not that He may ruin or destroy, but rather that He may deliver us from the condemnation of the world. Let this thought lead us to what Scripture elsewhere teaches: "My son, despise not the chastening of the Lord; neither be weary of his correction: For whom the Lord loveth he correcteth; even as a father the son in whom he delighteth" (Proverbs 3:11, 12).

When we perceive our Father's rod, is it not our part to behave as obedient docile sons rather than to rebelliously imitate desperate men, who are hardened in wickedness? God dooms us to destruction, if He does not by correction call us back when we have fallen off from Him, so that it is truly said, "If ye be without chastisement," "then are ye bastards, and not sons" (Hebrews 12:8).

We are most perverse then if we cannot bear Him while He is manifesting his goodwill toward us, and the care which He takes of our salvation. Scripture states not the difference between believers and unbelievers is, that the latter, as the slaves of inveterate and deep-seated iniquity, only become worse and more obstinate under the lash, whereas the former, like freeborn sons, turn to repentance. Now, therefore, choose your class. But as I have already spoken of this subject, it is sufficient to have here briefly adverted to it.

7 Singular consolation under the cross, when we suffer persecution for righteousness. Some parts of this consolation.

There is singular consolation, moreover, when we are persecuted for righteousness' sake. For our thought should then be, how high the honor which God bestows upon us in distinguishing with by the special badge of His soldiers. By suffering persecution for righteousness' sake, I mean not only striving for the defense of the gospel, but for the defense of righteousness in any way. Whether, therefore, in maintaining the truth of God against the lies of Satan or defending the good and innocent against the injuries of the bad we are obliged to incur the offense and hatred of the world, so as to endanger life, fortune, or honor, let us not grieve or decline so far to spend ourselves for God; let us not think ourselves wretched in those things in which He has pronounced us blessed. (See Matthew 5:10.)

Poverty, indeed considered in itself, is misery; so are exile, contempt, imprisonment, and ignominy: in fine, death itself is the last of all calamities. But when the favor of God breathes upon is, none of these things will turn us from our happiness. Let us then be contented with the testimony of Christ rather than with the false estimate of the flesh, and then, after the example of the apostles, we will rejoice in being "counted worthy to suffer shame for his name" (Acts 5:41). Why? If, while conscious of our innocence, we are deprived of our substance by the wickedness of man, we are, no doubt, humanly speaking, reduced to poverty; but in truth our riches in Heaven are increased. If driven from our homes, we have a more welcome reception into the family of God; if vexed and despised, we are more firmly rooted in Christ; if stigmatized by disgrace and ignominy, we have a higher place in the Kingdom of God; and if we are slain, entrance is thereby given us to eternal life. The Lord having set such a price upon us, let us be ashamed to estimate ourselves at less than the shadowy and evanescent allurements of the present life.

8 This form of the cross is most appropriate to believers and should be borne willingly and cheerfully. This cheerfulness is not unfeeling hilarity, but, while groaning under the burden, it waits patiently for the Lord.

Since by these and similar considerations, Scripture abundantly solaces us for the ignominy or calamities which we endure in defense of righteousness, we are very ungrateful if we do not willingly and cheerfully receive them at the hand of the Lord, especially since this form of the cross is the most appropriate to believers, being that by which Christ desires to be glorified in us, as Peter also declares. (See 1 Peter 4:11, 14.) But as to ingenuous natures, it is more bitter to suffer disgrace than a hundred deaths; Paul expressly reminds us that not only persecution, but also disgrace await us, "Because we trust in the living God" (1 Timothy 4:10). So in another passage he bids us, after his example, to walk "...by evil report and good report" (2 Corinthians 6:8).

The cheerfulness required, however, does not imply a total insensibility to pain. The saints could show no patience under the cross if they were not both tortured with pain and grievously molested. Were there no hardship in poverty, no pain in disease, no sting in ignominy, no fear in death, where would be the fortitude and moderation in enduring them? But while every one of these, by its inherent bitterness, naturally vexes the mind, the believer in this displays his fortitude, that though fully sensible of the bitterness and laboring grievously, he still withstands and struggles boldly; in this displays his patience, that though sharply stung, he is however curbed by the fear of God from breaking forth into any excess; in this displays his alacrity, that though pressed with sorrow and sadness, he rests satisfied with spiritual consolation from God.

9 A description of this conflict. Opposed to the vanity of the Stoics. Illustrated by the authority and example of Christ.

This conflict which believers maintain against the natural feeling of pain while they study moderation and patience, Paul elegantly describes in these words: "We are troubled on every side, yet not distressed; we are perplexed, but not in despair; persecuted, but not forsaken; cast down, but not destroyed" (2 Corinthians 4:8, 9).

You see that to bear the cross patiently is not to have your feelings altogether blunted and to be absolutely insensible to pain, according to the absurd description which the Stoics of old gave of their hero as one who, divested of humanity, was affected in the same way by adversity and prosperity, grief and joy; or rather, like a stone, was not affected by anything. And what did they gain by that sublime wisdom? They exhibited a shadow of patience, which never did and never can exist among men. Nay, rather by aiming at a too exact and rigid patience, they banished it altogether from human life. Now, also, we have among Christians a new kind of Stoics, who hold it vicious to not only groan and weep, but also even to be sad and anxious.

These paradoxes are usually started by indolent men who, employing themselves more in speculation than in action, can do nothing else for us than beget such paradoxes. But we have nothing to do with that iron philosophy which our Lord and Master condemned—not only in word, but also by His own example. For He both grieved and shed tears for His own and others' woes. Nor did He teach His disciples differently: "Ye shall weep and lament, but the world shall rejoice" (John 16:20). And lest anyone should regard this as vicious, He expressly declares, "Blessed are they that mourn" (Matthew 5:4). And no wonder. If all tears are condemned, what shall we think of our Lord himself, whose "Sweat was great drops of blood falling down to the ground?" (Luke 22:44; Matthew 26:38). If every kind of fear is a mark of unbelief, what place shall we assign to the dread, which, it is said, in no slight degree amazed him; if all sadness is condemned, how shall we justify Him when he confesses, "My soul is exceeding sorrowful, even unto death?"

10 Proved by the testimony and uniform experience of the elect. Also by the special example of the Apostle Peter. The nature of the patience required of us.

I wished to make these observations to keep pious minds from despair, lest, from feeling it impossible to divest themselves of the natural feeling of grief, they might altogether abandon the study of patience. This must necessarily be the result with those who convert patience into stupor, and a brave and firm man into a block. Scripture gives saints the praise of endurance when, though afflicted by the hardships they endure, they are not crushed; though they feel bitterly, they are at the same time filled with spiritual joy; though pressed with anxiety, they breathe exhilarated by the consolation of God. Still there is a certain degree of repugnance in their hearts, because natural sense shuns and dreads what is adverse to it, while pious affection, even through these difficulties, tries to obey the divine will. This repugnance the Lord expressed when He thus addressed Peter: "Verily, verily, I say unto thee, When thou wast young, thou girdedst thyself and walkedst whither thou wouldst; but when thou shalt be old, thou shalt stretch forth thy hands, and another shall gird thee; and carry thee whither thou wouldest not" (John 21:18).

It is not probable, indeed, that when it became necessary to glorify God by death He was driven to it unwilling and resisting; had it been so, little praise would have been due to His martyrdom. Though He obeyed the divine ordination with the greatest alacrity of heart, yet, as He had not divested himself of humanity, he was distracted by a double will. When he thought of the bloody death which He was to die, struck with horror, He would willingly have avoided it: on the other hand, when He considered that it was God who called Him to it, His fear was vanquished and suppressed, and he met death cheerfully.

It must, therefore, be our study, if we would be disciples of Christ, to imbue our minds with such reverence and obedience to God as may tame and subjugate all affections contrary to His appointment. In this way, whatever be the kind of cross to which we are subjected, we shall in the greatest straits firmly maintain our patience. Adversity will have its bitterness and sting us. When afflicted with disease, we shall groan and be disquieted, and long for health; pressed with poverty, we shall feel the stings of anxiety and sadness, feel the pain of ignominy, contempt, and injury, and pay the tears due to nature at the death of our friends: but our conclusion will always be, "The Lord so willed it; therefore, let us follow His will." Nay, amid the pungency of grief, among groans and tears, this thought will necessarily suggest itself and incline us cheerfully to endure the things for which we are so afflicted.

11 Distinction between the patience of Christians and philosophers. The latter pretend a necessity, which cannot be resisted. The former hold forth the justice of God and His care of our safety. A full exposition of this difference.

But since the chief reason for enduring the cross has been derived from a consideration of the divine will, in a few words we must explain wherein lies the difference between philosophical and Christian patience. Indeed, very few of the philosophers advanced so far as to perceive that the hand of God tries us by means of affliction and that we ought in this matter to obey God. The only reason which they adduce is that *so it must be*. But is not this just to say that we must yield to God, because it is in vain to contend against Him? For if we obey God only because it is necessary, provided we can escape, we shall cease to obey Him. But what Scripture calls us to consider in the will of God is very different, namely, first justice and equity, and then a regard to our own salvation.

Hence, Christian exhortations to patience are of this nature. Whether poverty or exile or imprisonment or contumely or disease or bereavement, or any such evil affects us, we must think that none of them happens except by the will and providence of God; moreover, that everything He does is in the most perfect order. What! Do not our numberless daily faults deserve to be chastised more severely and with a heavier rod than His mercy lays upon us? Is it not most right that our flesh should be subdued and be accustomed to the yoke, so as not to rage and wanton as it lists? Are not the justice and the truth of God worthy of our suffering on their account? But if the equity of God is undoubtedly displayed in affliction, we cannot murmur or struggle against them without iniquity.

We no longer hear the frigid cant, "Yield," because it is necessary, but a living and energetic precept; "Obey," because it is unlawful to resist; bear patiently, because impatience is rebellion against the justice of God. Then, as that only seems to us attractive which we perceive to be for our own safety and advantage, here also our heavenly Father consoles us by the assurance that in the very cross with which He afflicts us He provides for our salvation. But if it is clear that tribulations are salutary to us, why should we not receive them with calm and grateful minds? In bearing them patiently we are not submitting to necessity but resting satisfied with our own good. The effect of these thoughts is that to whatever extent our minds are contracted by the bitterness which we naturally feel under the cross; to the same extent will they be expanded with spiritual joy. Hence, thanksgiving arises, which cannot exist unless joy is felt. But if the praise of the Lord and thanksgiving can emanate only from a cheerful and gladdened breast, and there is nothing which ought to interrupt these feelings in us, it is clear how necessary it is to temper the bitterness of the cross with spiritual joy.

Chapter 9

OF MEDITATING ON THE FUTURE LIFE

The three divisions of this chapter: I. The principal use of the cross is that it in various ways accustoms us to despise the present, and excites us to aspire to the future life, sections 1, 2. II. In withdrawing from the present life, we must neither shun it nor feel hatred for it but desiring the future life, gladly quit the present at the command of our sovereign Master, sections 3, 4. III. Our infirmity in dreading death described. The correction and safe remedy, section 6.

Sections
1. The design of God in afflicting His people. A. To accustom us to despise the present life. Our infatuated love of it. Afflictions employed as the cure. B. To lead us to aspire to heaven.

2. Excessive love of the present life prevents us from duly aspiring to the other. Hence, the disadvantages of prosperity. Blindness of human judgment. Our philosophizing on the vanity of life only of momentary influence. The necessity of the cross.

3. The present life is an evidence of the divine favor to his people; and, therefore, it is not to be detested. On the contrary, it should call forth thanksgiving. The crown of victory in Heaven after the contest on Earth.

4. Weariness of the present life; how it is to be tempered. The believer's estimate of life. Comparison of the present and the future life. How far the present life should be hated.

5. Christians should not tremble at the fear of death. Two reasons. Objection. Answer. Other reasons.

6. Reasons continued. Conclusion.

1 The design of God in afflicting His people. A. To accustom us to despise the present life. Our infatuated love of it. Afflictions employed as the cure. B. To lead us to aspire to Heaven.

Whatever the kind of tribulation with which we are afflicted may be, we should always consider the end of it to be that we may be trained to despise the present and thereby stimulated to aspire to the future life. For since God well knows how strongly we are inclined by nature to a slavish love of this world, in order to prevent us from clinging too strongly to it, He employs the fittest reason for calling us back and shaking off our lethargy. Every one of us, indeed, would be thought to aspire and aim at heavenly immortality during the whole course of life. For we would be ashamed in no respect to excel the above lower animals, whose condition would not be at all inferior to ours had we not a hope of immortality beyond the grave. But when you attend to the plans, wishes, and actions of each, you see nothing in them but the Earth.

Hence, our stupidity—our minds being dazzled with the glare of wealth, power, and honors, that they can see no further. The heart also, engrossed with avarice, ambition, and lust, is weighed down and cannot rise above them.

In short, the whole soul, ensnared by the allurements of the flesh, seeks its happiness on the Earth. To meet this disease, the Lord makes His people sensible of the vanity of the present life by a constant proof of its miseries. Thus, that they may not promise themselves deep and lasting peace in it, He often allows them to be assailed by war, tumult, or rapine, or to be disturbed by other injuries. That they may not long with too much eagerness after fleeting and fading riches or rest in those which they already possess, He reduces them to want, or, at least, restricts them to a moderate allowance—at one time by exile, at another by sterility, at another by fire, or by other means. That they may not indulge too complacently in the advantages of married life, he vexes them by the misconduct of their partners, humbles them by the wickedness of their children, or afflicts them by bereavement. But if in all these He is indulgent to them, lest they should either swell with vainglory or be elated with confidence by diseases and dangers He sets palpably before them how unstable and evanescent are all the advantages competent to mortals.

We duly profit by the discipline of the cross when we learn that this life, estimated in itself, is restless, troubled, in numberless ways, wretched, and plainly in no respect happy; that what are estimated its blessings are uncertain, fleeting, vain, and vitiated by a great a mixture of evil. From this we conclude that all we have to seek or hope for here is contest; that when we think of the crown, we must raise our eyes to Heaven. For we must hold that our mind never rises seriously to desire and aspire after the future, until it has learned to despise the present life.

2 Excessive love of the present life prevents us from duly aspiring to the other. Hence, the disadvantages of prosperity. Blindness of human judgment. Our philosophizing on the vanity of life is only of momentary influence. The necessity of the cross.

There is no medium between the two things; the Earth must either be worthless in our estimation, or keep us enslaved by an intemperate love of it. Therefore, if we have any regard for eternity, we must carefully strive to unencumber ourselves of these fetters. Moreover, since the present life has many enticements to allure us and great semblance of delight, grace, and sweetness to soothe us, it is of great consequence to us to be now and then called off from its fascinations. For what, pray, would happen, if we here enjoyed an uninterrupted course of honor and felicity, when even the constant stimulus of affliction cannot arouse us to a due sense of our misery? Human life is like smoke or a shadow; this is not only known to the learned; there is not a more trite proverb among the vulgar. Considering it a fact most useful to be known, they have recommended it in many well-known expressions.

Still there is no fact which we ponder less carefully or less frequently remember. We form all our plans just as if we had fixed our immortality on the Earth. If we see a funeral or walk among graves, as the image of death is then present to the eye, I admit we philosophize admirably on the vanity of life. We do not indeed always do so, for those things often have no effect upon us at all. But, at the best, our philosophy is momentary. It vanishes as soon as we turn our back, and leaves not the vestige of remembrance behind; in short, it passes away, just like the applause of a theater at some pleasant spectacle. Forgetful not only of death, but also of mortality itself, as if no rumor of it had ever reached us, we indulge in supine security as expecting a terrestrial immortality.

Meanwhile, if anyone breaks in with the proverb, that man is the creature of a day, we indeed acknowledge its truth, but, so far from giving heed to it, the thought of perpetuity still keeps hold of our minds. Who, then, can deny that it is of the highest importance to us all, not to be admonished by words, but convinced by all possible experience of the miserable condition of our earthly life; since even when convinced, we scarcely cease to gaze upon it with vicious, stupid admiration, as if it contained within itself the sum of all that is good? But if God finds it necessary so to train us, it must be our duty to listen to Him when He calls and shakes us from our torpor, that we may hasten to despise the world and aspire with our whole heart to the future life.

3 The present life is an evidence of the divine favor to His people; and therefore, it is not to be detested. On the contrary, it should call forth thanksgiving. The crown of victory in Heaven after the contest on Earth.

Still, the contempt, which believers should train themselves to feel for the present life, must not be of a kind to beget hatred of it or ingratitude to God. This life, though abounding in all kinds of wretchedness, is justly classed among divine blessings, which are not to be despised. Wherefore, if we do not recognize the kindness of God in it, we are chargeable with no little ingratitude towards Him. To believers, especially, it ought to be a proof of divine benevolence, since it is wholly destined to promote their salvation. Before openly exhibiting the inheritance of eternal glory, God is pleased to manifest himself to us as a Father by minor proofs—viz. the blessings that He daily bestows upon us. Therefore, while this life serves to acquaint us with the goodness of God, shall we disdain it as if it did not contain one particle of good?

We ought, therefore, to feel and be affected towards it in such a manner as to place it among those gifts of the divine benignity, which are by no means to be despised. Were there no proofs in Scripture (they are most numerous and clear), yet nature herself exhorts us to return thanks to God for having brought us forth into light, granted us the use of it, and bestowed upon us all the means necessary for its preservation. And there is a much higher reason when we reflect that here we are in a manner prepared for the glory of the heavenly kingdom. For the Lord hath ordained that those who are ultimately to be crowned in Heaven must maintain a previous warfare on the earth, that they may not triumph before they have overcome the difficulties of war and obtained the victory.

Another reason is that we here begin to experience in various ways a foretaste of the divine benignity, in order that our hope and desire may be whetted for its full manifestation. When once we have concluded that our earthly life is a gift of the divine mercy, of which, agreeably to our obligation, it behooves us to have a grateful remembrance, we shall then properly descend to consider its most wretched condition, and thus escape from that excessive fondness for it, to which, as I have said, we are naturally prone.

4 Weariness of the present life; how it is to be tempered. The believer's estimate of life. Comparison of the present and the future life. How far the present life should be hated.

In proportion as this improper love diminishes, our desire of a better life should increase. I confess, indeed, that a most accurate opinion was formed by those who thought that the best thing was not to be born, the next best to die early. For, being destitute of the light of God and of true religion, what could they see in it that was not of dire and evil omen? Nor was it unreasonable for those who felt sorrow and shed tears at the birth of their kindred to keep holiday at their deaths. But this they did without profit; because, devoid of the true doctrine of faith, they saw not how that which in itself is neither happy nor desirable turns to the advantage of the righteous and, hence, their opinion is issued in despair.

Let believers, then, in forming an estimate of this mortal life, and perceiving that in itself it is nothing but misery, make it their aim to exert themselves with greater alacrity and less hindrance in aspiring to the future and eternal life.

When we contrast the two, the former may not only be securely neglected, but, in comparison to the latter, be disdained and contemned. If Heaven is our country, what can the Earth be but a place of exile? If departure from the world is entrance into life, what is the world but a sepulcher, and what is residence in it but immersion in death? If to be freed from the body is to gain full possession of freedom, what is the body but a prison? If it is the very summit of happiness to enjoy the presence of God, is it not miserable to want it? "Whilst we are at home in the body, we are absent from the Lord" (2 Corinthians 5:6).

Thus, when the earthly life is compared with the heavenly life, it may undoubtedly be despised and trampled under foot. We ought never, indeed, to regard it with hatred, except as far as it keeps us subject to sin; and even this hatred ought not to be directed against life itself. At all events, we must stand so affected towards it in regard to weariness or hatred as, while longing for its termination, to be ready at the Lord's will to continue in it, keeping far from everything such as murmuring and impatience. For it is as if the Lord had assigned us a post, which we must maintain until He recalls us. Paul, indeed, laments his condition, in being still bound with the fetters of the body and sighs earnestly for redemption. (See Romans 7:24.) Nevertheless, he declared that, in obedience to the command of God, he was prepared for both courses, because he acknowledges it as his duty to God to glorify his name whether by life or by death, while it belongs to God to determine what is most conducive to His glory. (See Philippians 1:20-24.) Wherefore, if it becomes us to live and die to the Lord, let us leave the period of our life and death at his disposal. Still let us ardently long for death, constantly meditate upon it, and in comparison with future immortality, let us despise life, and, because of the bondage of sin, long to renounce it whenever it shall so please the Lord.

5 Christians should not tremble at the fear of death. Two reasons. Objection. Answer. Other reasons.

But, most strange to say, many who boast of being Christians, instead of thus longing for death, are so afraid of it that they tremble at the very mention of it as a thing ominous and dreadful. We cannot wonder, indeed, that our natural feelings should be somewhat shocked at the mention of our dissolution. But it is altogether intolerable that the light of piety should not be so powerful in a Christian breast as with greater consolation to overcome and suppress that fear. For if we reflect that this, our tabernacle, unstable, defective, corruptible, fading, pining, and putrid, is dissolved in order that it may forthwith be renewed in sure, perfect, incorruptible, and heavenly glory, will not faith compel us eagerly to desire what nature dreads? If we reflect that by death we are recalled from exile to inhabit our native country, a heavenly country, shall this give us no comfort? But everything longs for permanent existence. I admit this, and therefore contend that we ought to look to future immortality, where we may obtain that fixed condition, which nowhere appears on the earth. For Paul admirably enjoins believers to hasten cheerfully to death, not because they "…would be unclothed, but clothed upon" (2 Corinthians 5:2).

Shall the lower animals and inanimate creatures themselves, even wood and stone, as being conscious of their present vanity, long for the final resurrection, that they may with the sons of God be delivered from vanity? (See Romans 8:19.) Shall we, endued with the light of intellect, and more than intellect, enlightened by the Spirit of God, when our essence is in question, rise no higher than the corruption of this Earth? But it is not my purpose, nor is this the place, to plead against this great perverseness.

At the outset, I declared that I had no wish to engage in a diffuse discussion of commonplaces. My advice to those whose minds are thus timid is to read the short treatise of Cyprian De Mortalitate, unless it is more in line with their deserts to send them to the philosophers, that by inspecting what they say on the contempt of death, they may begin to blush. This, however let us hold as fixed, that no man has made much progress in the school of Christ who does not look forward with joy to the day of death and the final resurrection (see 2 Timothy 4:18; Titus 2:13), for Paul distinguishes all believers by this mark. The usual course of Scripture is to direct us there whenever it would furnish us with an argument for substantial joy. "Look up," says our Lord, "and lift up your heads: for your redemption draweth nigh" (Luke 21:28).

Is it reasonable, I ask, that what He intended to have a powerful effect in stirring us up to alacrity and exultation should produce nothing but sadness and consternation? If it is so, why do we still glory in him as our Master? Therefore, let us come to a sounder mind, and how repugnant so ever the blind and stupid longing of the flesh may be, let us doubt not to desire the advent of the Lord not in wish only, but with earnest sighs, as the most propitious of all events. He will come as a Redeemer to deliver us from an immense abyss of evil and misery and lead us to the blessed inheritance of His life and glory.

6 Reasons continued. Conclusion.

Thus, indeed, it is; the whole body of the faithful, so long as they live on the Earth, must be like sheep for the slaughter in order that they may be conformed to Christ their Head. (See Romans 8:36.) Most deplorable, therefore, would their situation be did they not, by raising their mind to Heaven, become superior to all that is in the world and rise above the present aspect of affairs. (See 1 Corinthians 15:19.)

On the other hand, when once they have raised their head above all earthly objects, though they see the wicked flourishing in wealth and honor, and enjoying profound peace, indulging in luxury and splendor, and reveling in all kinds of delights, though they should moreover be wickedly assailed by them, suffer insult from their pride, be robbed by their avarice, or assailed by any other passion, they will have no difficulty in bearing up under these evils. They will turn their eye to that day (see Isaiah 25:8; Revelation 7:17), on which the Lord will receive His faithful servants, wipe away all tears from their eyes, clothe them in a robe of glory and joy, feed them with the ineffable sweetness of His pleasures, exalt them to share with Him in His greatness; and admit them to a participation in His happiness.

But the wicked who may have flourished on the Earth, He will cast forth in extreme ignominy, will change their delights into torments, their laughter and joy into wailing and gnashing of teeth, their peace into the gnawing of conscience, and punish their luxury with unquenchable fire. He will also place their necks under the feet of the godly, whose patience they abused. For, as Paul declares, "It is a righteous thing with God to recompense tribulation to them that trouble you; and to you who are troubled rest with us, when the Lord Jesus shall be revealed from heaven" (2 Thessalonians 1:6, 7).

This, indeed, is our only consolation; deprived of it, we must either give way to despondency, or resort to our destruction to the vain solace of the world. The Psalmist confesses, "My feet were almost gone: my steps had well nigh slipt: for I was envious at the foolish when I saw the prosperity of the wicked" (Psalm 73:3, 4); and he found no resting-place until he entered the sanctuary, and considered the latter end of the righteous and the wicked. To conclude in one word, the cross of Christ, then, only triumphs in the breasts of believers over the devil and the flesh, sin and sinners, when their eyes are directed to the power of His resurrection.

Chapter 10

HOW TO USE THE PRESENT LIFE
AND THE COMFORTS OF IT

The divisions of this chapter are: I. The necessity and usefulness of this doctrine. Extremes to be avoided, if we would rightly use the present life and its comforts, sections 1, 2. II. One of these extremes—viz. the intemperance of the flesh—to be carefully avoided. Four methods of doing so described in order, sections 3-6.

Sections

1. The necessity of this doctrine. Use of the goods of the present life. Extremes to be avoided: A. Excessive austerity. B. Carnal intemperance and lasciviousness.

2. God, by creating so many mercies, consulted not only for our necessities, but also for our comfort and delight. Confirmation from a passage in the Psalms and from experience.

3. Excessive austerity, therefore, is to be avoided. So also must the wantonness of the flesh. A. The creatures invite us to know, love, and honor the Creator. B. This is not done by the wicked, who only abuse these temporal mercies.

4. All earthly blessings are to be despised in comparison to the heavenly life. Aspiration after this life is destroyed by an excessive love of created objects. First, intemperance.

5. Second, impatience and immoderate desire. Remedy of these evils. The creatures assigned to our use. Man still accountable for the use he makes of them.

6. God requires us in all our actions to look to His calling. Use of this doctrine. It is full of comfort.

1 The necessity of this doctrine. Use of the goods of the present life. Extremes to be avoided. A. Excessive austerity. B. Carnal intemperance and lasciviousness.

By such rudiments we are well instructed at the same time by Scripture in the proper use of earthly blessings, a subject that, in forming a scheme of life, is by no mean to be neglected. For if we are to live, we must use the necessary supports of life; nor can we even shun those things which seem more subservient to delight than to necessity. We must, therefore, observe a mean, that we may use them with a pure conscience, whether for necessity or for pleasure. This the Lord prescribes by His Word, when He tells us that to His people the present life is a kind of pilgrimage by which they hasten to the heavenly kingdom. If we are only to pass through the earth, there can be no doubt that we are to use its blessings only insofar as they assist our progress rather than retard it.

Accordingly, Paul, not without cause, admonishes us to use this world without abusing it, and to buy possessions as if we were selling them. (See 1 Corinthians 7:30, 31.) But as this is a slippery place, and there is great danger of falling on either side, let us fix our feet where we can stand safely.

There have been some good and holy men who, when they saw intemperance and luxury perpetually carried to excess, if not strictly curbed and were desirous to correct so pernicious an evil, imagined that there was no other method than to allow man to use corporeal goods only insofar as they were necessities: a counsel pious indeed, but unnecessarily austere, for it does the very dangerous thing of binding consciences in closer fetters than those in which they are bound by the Word of God. Moreover, necessity, according to them, was abstinence from everything, which could be wanted, so that they held it scarcely lawful to make any addition to bread and water. Others were still more austere, as is related of Cratetes the Theban, who threw his riches into the sea, because he thought that unless he destroyed them they would destroy him. Many also in the present day, while they seek a pretext for carnal intemperance in the use of external things and at the same time would pave the way for licentiousness, assume for granted what I by no means concede that this liberty is not to be restrained by any modification, but that it is to be left to every man's conscience to use them as far as he thinks lawful.

I indeed confess that here consciences neither can nor ought to be bound by fixed and definite laws; but that Scripture having laid down general rules for the legitimate uses we should keep within the limits which they prescribe.

2 God, by creating so many mercies, consulted not only for our necessities, but also for our comfort and delight. Confirmation from a passage in the Psalms and from experience.

Let this be our principle, that we err not in the use of the gifts of providence when we refer them to the end for which their Author made and destined them, since He created them for our good, and not for our destruction. No man will keep the true path better than he who shall have this end carefully in view. Now, then, if we consider for what end He created food, we shall find that He consulted not only for our necessity, but also for our enjoyment and delight. Thus, in clothing, the end was, in addition to necessity, comeliness, and honor; and in herbs, fruits, and trees, besides their various uses, gracefulness of appearance and sweetness of smell. Were it not so, the prophet would not enumerate among the mercies of God, "… wine that maketh glad the heart of man, and oil to make his face to shine" (Psalm 104:15).

The Scriptures would not mention, in commendation of His benignity, that He had given such things to men. The natural qualities of things themselves demonstrate to what end and how far they may be lawfully enjoyed. Has the Lord adorned flowers with all the beauty, which spontaneously presents itself to the eye, and the sweet odor, which delights the sense of smell, and shall it be unlawful for us to enjoy that beauty and this odor? What? Has He not so distinguished colors as to make some more agreeable than others? Has He not given qualities to gold, silver, ivory, and marble, thereby rendering them precious above other metals or stones? In short, has He not given many things a value without having any necessary use?

3 Excessive austerity, therefore, to be avoided. So also must the wantonness of the flesh. A. The creatures invite us to know, love, and honor the Creator. B. This is not done by the wicked, who only abuse these temporal mercies.

Have done, then, with that inhuman philosophy which, in allowing no use of the creatures but for necessity, not only maliciously deprives us of the lawful fruit of the divine beneficence, but also cannot be realized without depriving man of all his senses, and reducing him to a block. But, on the other hand, let us with no less care guard against the lusts of the flesh, which, if not kept in order, break through all bounds, and are, as I have said, advocated by those who, under pretense of liberty, allow themselves every sort of license.

First one restraint is imposed when we hold that the object of creating all things was to teach us to know their author, and feel grateful for His indulgence. Where is the gratitude, if you so gorge or stupefy yourself with feasting and wine as to be unfit for offices of piety or the duties of your calling? Where is the recognition of God, if the flesh, boiling forth in lust through excessive indulgences infects the mind with its impurity, to lose the discernment of honor and rectitude? Where is thankfulness to God for clothing, if on account of sumptuous raiment we both admire ourselves and disdain others? If, from a love of show and splendor, we pave the way for immodesty? Where is our recognition of God, if the glare of these things captivates our minds?

For many are so devoted to luxury in all their senses that their minds lie buried: many are so delighted with marble, gold, and pictures that they become marble-hearted—are changed into metal and made like painted figures. The kitchen, with its savory smells, so engrosses them that they have no spiritual savor. The same thing may be seen in other matters. Wherefore, it is plain that there is here great necessity for curbing licentious abuse, and conforming to the rule of Paul, "Make not provision for the flesh to fulfill the lusts thereof" (Romans 13:14). Where too much liberty is given to them, they break forth without measure or restraint.

4 All earthly blessings are to be despised in comparison to the heavenly life. Aspiration after this life is destroyed by an excessive love of created objects. First, intemperance.

There is no surer or quicker way of accomplishing this than by despising the present life and aspiring to celestial immortality. Hence, two rules arise: first, "It remaineth, that both they that have wives be as though they had none," "And they that use this world, as not abusing it" (1 Corinthians 7:29, 31).

Secondly, we must learn to be no less placid and patient in enduring penury than moderate in enjoying abundance. He who makes it his rule to use this world as if he used it not, not only cuts off all gluttony in regard to meat and drink and all effeminacy, ambition, pride, excessive shows, and austerity in regard to his table, his house, and his clothes, but removes every care and affection which might withdraw or hinder him from aspiring to the heavenly life, and cultivating the interest of his soul. It was well said by Cato: Luxury causes great care and produces great carelessness with regard to virtue. There is an old proverb: Those who are much occupied with the care of the body usually give little care to the soul. Therefore while the liberty of the Christian in external matters is not to be tied down to a strict rule, it is, however, subject to this law—he must indulge as little as possible; on the other hand, it must be his constant aim not only to curb luxury, but to cut off all show of superfluous abundance and carefully beware of converting a help into an hindrance.

5 Second, impatience and immoderate desire. Remedy of these evils. The creatures assigned to our use. Man is still accountable for the use he makes of them.

Another rule is that those in narrow and slender circumstances should learn to bear their wants patiently, that they might not become immoderately desirous of things, the moderate use of which implies no small progress in the school of Christ. For in addition to the many other vices which accompany a longing for earthly good, he who is impatient under poverty usually betrays the contrary disease in abundance. By this I mean that he who is ashamed of a sordid garment will be vainglorious of a splendid one; he who is not contented with a slender meal feels annoyed at the want of a more luxurious supper, and will intemperately abuse his luxury if he obtains it; he who has a difficulty and is dissatisfied in submitting to a private and humble condition will be unable to refrain from pride if he attains to honor. Let it be the aim of all who have any unfeigned desire for piety to learn after the example of the apostle, "Both to be full and to be hungry, both to abound and to suffer need" (Philippians 4:12).

Scripture, moreover, has a third rule for modifying the use of earthly blessings. We have already referred to it when considering the offices of charity. For it declares that they have all been given us by the kindness of God, and appointed for our use under the condition of being regarded as trusts, of which we must one day give account. We must, therefore, administer them as if we constantly heard the words sounding in our ears, "Give an account of your stewardship."

At the same time, let us remember by whom the account is to be taken—viz. by him who, while he so highly commends abstinence, sobriety, frugality, and moderation, abominates luxury, pride, ostentation, and vanity; who approves of no administration but that which is combined with charity, who with his own lips has already condemned all those pleasures which withdraw the heart from chastity and purity, or darken the intellect.

6 God requires us in all our actions to look to His calling. The use of this doctrine. It is full of comfort.

The last thing to be observed is that the Lord enjoins every one of us, in all the actions of life, to have respect to our own calling. He knows the boiling restlessness of the human mind, the fickleness with which it is borne hither and thither, its eagerness to hold opposites at one time in its grasp its ambition. Therefore, lest all things should be thrown into confusion by our folly and rashness, He has assigned distinct duties to each in the different modes of life. And that no one may presume to overstep his proper limits, He has distinguished the different modes of life by the name of callings.

Every man's mode of life, therefore, is a kind of station that is assigned to him by the Lord, that he may not be always driven about at random. So necessary is this distinction that all our actions are thereby estimated in His sight, and often in a very different way from that in which human reason or philosophy would estimate them. There is no more illustrious deed even among philosophers than to free one's country from tyranny, and yet the private individual who stabs the tyrant is openly condemned by the voice of the heavenly Judge.

But I am unwilling to dwell on particular examples; it is enough to know that in everything the call of the Lord is the foundation and beginning of right action. He who does not act with reference to it will never in the discharge of duty keep the right path. He will sometimes be able, perhaps, to give the semblance of something laudable, but whatever it may be in the sight of man, it will be rejected before the throne of God; besides, there will be no harmony in the different parts of his life.

Hence, he only who directs his life to this end will have it properly framed; because free from the impulse of rashness, he will not attempt more than his calling justifies, knowing that it is unlawful to overleap the prescribed bounds. He who is obscure will not decline to cultivate a private life, that he may not desert the post at which God has placed him. Again, in all our cares, toils, annoyances, and other burdens, it will be no small alleviation to know that all these are under the superintendence of God. The magistrate will more willingly perform his office and the father of a family confine himself to his proper sphere. Everyone in his particular mode of life will, without repining, suffer its inconveniences, cares, uneasiness, and anxiety, persuaded that God has laid on the burden. This, too, will afford admirable consolation, that in following your proper calling no work will be so mean and sordid as not to have a splendor and value in the eye of God.

Chapter 11

OF JUSTIFICATION BY FAITH. BOTH THE NAME AND THE REALITY DEFINED

In this chapter and the seven which follow, the doctrine of justification by faith is expounded, and opposite errors refuted. The following may be regarded as the arrangement of these chapters: —Chapter 11 states the doctrine, and the four subsequent chapters, by destroying the righteousness of works, confirm the righteousness of faith, each in the order which appears in the respective titles of these chapters. In Chapter 12 the doctrine of justification is confirmed by a description of perfect righteousness; in Chapter 13 by calling attention to two precautions; in Chapter 14 by a consideration of the commencement and progress of regeneration in the regenerate; and in Chapter 15 by two very pernicious effects which constantly accompany the righteousness of works. The three other chapters are devoted to refutation Chapter 16 disposes of the objections of opponents Chapter 17 replies to the arguments drawn from the promises of the Law or the gospel Chapter 18 refutes what is said in support of the righteousness of faith from the promise of reward.

There are three principal divisions in the Eleventh Chapter: I. The terms used in this discussion are explained, sections 1-4. II. Osiander's dream as to essential righteousness is impugned, sections 5-13. III. The righteousness of faith is established in opposition to the righteousness of works.

Sections

1. Connection between the doctrine of justification and that of regeneration. The knowledge of this is doctrine very necessary for two reasons.

2. For the purpose of facilitating the exposition of it, the terms are explained. A. What it is to be justified in the sight of God. B. To be justified by works. C. To be justified by faith. Definition.

3. Various meanings of the term "justification." A. To give praise to God and truth. B. To make a vain display of righteousness. C. To impute righteousness by faith, by and on account of Christ. Confirmation from an expression of Paul and another of our Lord.

4. Another confirmation from a comparison with other expressions in which justification means free righteousness before God through faith in Jesus Christ. A. Acceptance. B. Imputation of righteousness. C. Remission of sins. D. Blessedness. E. Reconciliation with God. F. Righteousness by the obedience of Christ.

5. The second part of the chapter. Osiander's dream as to essential righteousness refuted. A. Osiander's argument: Answer. B. Osiander's second argument: Answer. Third argument: Answer.

6. Necessity of this refutation. Fourth argument: Answer. Confirmation: Another answer. Fifth and sixth arguments and answers.

7. Seventh and eighth arguments.

8. Ninth argument: Answer.

9. Tenth argument: Answer.

10. In what sense Christ is said to be our righteousness. Eleventh and twelfth arguments and answers.

11. Thirteenth and fourteenth arguments: Answers. An exception by Osiander. Imputed and begun righteousness to be distinguished. Osiander confounds them. Fifteenth argument: Answer.

12. Sixteenth argument, a dream of Osiander: Answer. Other four arguments and answers. Conclusion of the refutation of Osiander's errors.

13. Last part of the chapter. Refutation of the Sophists, pretending a righteousness compounded partly of faith and partly of works.

14. Sophistical evasion by giving the same name to different things: Two answers.

15. Second evasion: Two answers. First answer. Pernicious consequences resulting from this evasion.

16. Second answer, showing wherein, according to Scripture, that justification consists.

17. In the explanation of this doctrine of justification, two passages of Scripture are produced.

18. Another passage of Scripture.

19. Third evasion. Papist objection to the doctrine of justification by faith alone: Three answers. Fourth evasion: Three answers.

20. Fifth evasion, founded on the application of the term "righteousness" to good works, and also on their reward: Answer, confirmed by the invincible argument of Paul. Sixth evasion: Answer.

21. Osiander and the Sophists being thus refuted, the accuracy of the definition of justification by faith is established.

22. Definition confirmed. A. By passages of Scripture. B. By the writings of the ancient fathers.

23. Man justified by faith, not because by it he obtains the Spirit, and is thus made righteous, but because by faith he lays hold of the righteousness of Christ. An objection removed. An example of the doctrine of justification by faith from the works of Ambrose.

1 Connection between the doctrine of justification and that of regeneration. The knowledge of this doctrine is very necessary for two reasons.

I trust I have now sufficiently shown how man's only resource for escaping from the curse of the Law, and recovering salvation lies in faith, and also what the nature of faith is, what the benefits which it confers are, and what the fruits it produces are. The whole may be thus summed up: Christ is given to us by the kindness of God. This is apprehended and possessed by faith, by means of which we obtain in particular a twofold benefit: first, being reconciled by the righteousness of Christ, God becomes, instead of a Judge, an indulgent Father; and, secondly, being sanctified by His Spirit, we aspire to integrity and purity of life. This second benefit—viz. regeneration, appears to have been already sufficiently discussed. On the other hand, the subject of justification was discussed more cursorily, because it seemed of more consequence first to explain that the faith by which alone, through the mercy of God, we obtain free justification, is not destitute of good works; and also to show the true nature of these good works on which this question partly turns. The doctrine of Justification is now to be fully discussed, and discussed under the conviction, that as it is the principal ground on which religion must be supported, so it requires greater care and attention. For unless you understand first of all what your position is before God, and what the judgment which he passes upon you, you have no foundation on which your salvation can be laid, or on which piety towards God can be reared. The necessity of thoroughly understanding this subject will become more apparent as we proceed with it.

2 For the purpose of facilitating the exposition of it, the terms are explained. A. What it is to be justified in the sight of God. B. To be justified by works. C. To be justified by faith. Definition.

Lest we should stumble at the very threshold (this we should do were we to begin the discussion without knowing what the subject is), let us first explain the meaning of the expressions, *to be justified in the sight of God, and to be justified by faith or by works*. A man is said to be justified in the sight of God when in the judgment of God, he is deemed to be righteous and is accepted on account of his righteousness; for as iniquity is abominable to God, so neither can the sinner find grace in His sight, so far as he is and so long as he is regarded as a sinner. Hence, wherever sin is, there also are the wrath and vengeance of God. He, on the other hand, is justified who is regarded not as a sinner, but as righteous. As such, he stands acquitted at the judgment-seat of God, where all sinners are condemned. As an innocent man, when charged before an impartial judge, who decides according to his innocence, is said to be justified by the judge, as a man is said to be justified by God when, removed from the catalogue of sinners, he has God as the witness and assertor of his righteousness. In the same manner, a man will be said to be *justified by works*, if in his life, there can be found a purity and holiness, which merits an attestation of righteousness at the throne of God, or if by the perfection of his works, he can answer and satisfy the divine justice. On the contrary, a man will be *justified by faith* when, excluded from the righteousness of works, he by faith lays hold of the righteousness of Christ, and clothed in it, appears in the sight of God not as a sinner, but as righteous. Thus, we simply interpret justification as the acceptance with which God receives us into His favor as if we were righteous; and we say that this justification consists in the forgiveness of sins and the imputation of the righteousness of Christ. (See section 21 and 23.)

3 Various meanings of the term "justification." A. To give praise to God and truth. B. To make a vain display of righteousness. C. To impute righteousness by faith by and on account of Christ. Confirmation from an expression of Paul and another of our Lord.

In confirmation of this, there are many clear passages of Scripture. First, it cannot be denied that this is the proper and most usual signification of the term. But it is too tedious to collect all the passages, and compare them with each other, so let it suffice to have called the reader's attention to the fact. By so doing he will easily convince himself of its truth. I will only mention a few passages in which the justification of which we speak is expressly handled. First, when Luke relates that all the people that heard Christ "justified God" (Luke 7:29), and when Christ declares that "Wisdom is justified of all her children" (Luke 7:35), Luke means not that they conferred righteousness, which always dwells in perfection with God, although the whole world should attempt to wrest it from Him, nor does Christ mean that the doctrine of salvation is made just. It is thus its own nature, but both modes of expression are equivalent to attributing due praise to God and His doctrine.

On the other hand, when Christ upbraids the Pharisees for justifying themselves (see Luke 16:15), He means not that they acquired righteousness by acting properly, but that they ambitiously courted a reputation for righteousness of which they were destitute. Those who are acquainted with Hebrew understand the meaning better, for in that language the name of wicked is given not only to those who are conscious of wickedness, but to those who receive the sentence of condemnation. Thus, when Bathsheba says, "I and my son Solomon shall be counted offenders," she does not acknowledge a crime, but complains that she and her son will be exposed to the disgrace of being numbered among reprobates and criminals. (See 1 Kings 1:21.)

It is, indeed, plain from the context that the term, even in Latin, must be thus understood—viz. *relatively* and does not denote any quality. In regard to the use of the term with reference to the present subject, when Paul speaks of the Scripture, "Foreseeing that God would justify the heathen through faith" (Galatians 3:8), what other meaning can you give it than That [God] imputes righteousness by faith? Again, when he says, "that he (God) might be just, and the justifier of him who believeth in Jesus" (Romans 3:26), what can the meaning be, if not that God, in consideration of their faith, frees them from the condemnation which their wickedness deserves? This appears still more plainly at the conclusion, when he exclaims, "Who shall lay anything to the charge of God's elect? It is God that justifieth. Who is he that condemneth? It is Christ that died, yea rather, that is risen again, who is even at the right hand of God, who also maketh intercession for us" (Romans 8:33, 34). For it is just as if he had said, "Who shall accuse those whom God has acquitted? Who shall condemn those for whom Christ pleads?" To *justify*, therefore, is nothing else than to acquit from the charge of guilt, as if innocence were proved. Hence, when God justifies us through the intercession of Christ, He does not acquit us on a proof of our own innocence, but by an imputation of righteousness, so that, though not righteous in ourselves, we are deemed righteous in Christ.

Thus, it is said in Paul's discourse in the Book of Acts, "Through this man is preached unto you the forgiveness of sins; and by him all that believe are justified from all things from which ye could not be justified by the law of Moses" (Acts 13:38, 39). You see that after remission of sins, justification is set down by way of explanation; you see plainly that it is used for acquittal; you see how it cannot be obtained by the works of the Law; you see that it is entirely through the interposition of Christ; you see that it is obtained by faith; you see, in fine, that satisfaction intervenes, since it is said that we are justified from our sins by Christ. Thus, when the Publican is said to have gone down to his house "justified" (see Luke 18:14), it cannot be held that he obtained this justification by any merit of works. All that is said is that after obtaining the pardon of sins, he was regarded in the sight of God as righteous. He was justified, therefore, not by any approval of works, but by gratuitous acquittal on the part of God. Hence, Ambrose elegantly terms the confession of sins "legal justification."

4 Another confirmation from a comparison with other expressions in which justification means free righteousness before God through faith in Jesus Christ. A. Acceptance. B. Imputation of righteousness. C. Remission of sins. D. Blessedness. E. Reconciliation with God. F. Righteousness by the obedience of Christ.

Without saying more about the term, we shall have no doubt as to the thing meant if we attend to the description which is given of it. Paul certainly designates justification by the term *acceptance*, when he says to the Ephesians, "Having predestinated us

230

unto the adoption of children by Jesus Christ to himself, according to the good pleasure of his will, to the praise of the glory of his grace, wherein he has made us accepted in the Beloved" (Ephesians 1:5, 6). His meaning is the very same as where he elsewhere says, "Being justified freely by his grace" (Romans 3:24). In the fourth chapter of the Epistle to the Romans, he first terms it the *imputation* of righteousness and hesitates not to place it in forgiveness of sins: "Even as David also describeth the blessedness of the man unto whom God imputeth righteousness without works, saying, Blessed are they whose iniquities are forgiven," etc. (Romans 4:6-8). There, indeed, he is not speaking of a part of justification, but of the whole. He declares, moreover, that a definition of it was given by David, when he pronounced him *blessed* who has obtained the *free* pardon of his sins. Whence it appears that this righteousness of which he speaks is simply opposed to judicial guilt. But the most satisfactory passage on this subject is that in which he declares the sum of the Gospel message to be reconciliation to God, who is pleased, through Christ, to receive us into favor by not imputing our sins. (See 2 Corinthians 5:18-21.)

Let my readers carefully weigh the whole context. For Paul shortly after adding, by way of explanation, in order to designate the mode of reconciliation, that Christ who knew no sin was made sin for us, undoubtedly understands by reconciliation nothing else than justification. Nor, indeed, could it be said, as he elsewhere does, that we are made righteous "by the obedience" of Christ (Romans 5:19), were it not that we are deemed righteous in the sight of God in him and not in ourselves.

5 The second part of the chapter. Osiander's dream as to essential righteousness refuted. A. Osiander's argument: Answer. B. Osiander's second argument: Answer. Third argument: Answer.

But as Osiander has introduced a kind of monstrosity termed *essential righteousness*, by which, although he designed not to abolish free righteousness, he involves it in darkness, and by that darkness, deprives pious minds of a serious sense of divine grace, before I pass to other matters, it may be proper to refute this delirious dream. And, first, the whole speculation is mere empty curiosity. He, indeed, heaps together many passages of Scripture Showing that Christ is one with us, and we likewise one with him, a point which needs no proof; but he entangles himself by not attending to the bond of this unity. The explanation of all difficulties is easy to us, who hold that we are united to Christ by the secret agency of His Spirit, but he had formed some idea akin to that of the Manichees, desiring to transfuse the divine essence into men. Hence, his other notion, that Adam was formed in the image of God, because even before the Fall, Christ was destined to be the model of human nature. But as I study brevity, I will confine myself to the matter in hand. He says that we are one with Christ. This we admit, but still we deny that the essence of Christ is confounded with ours. Then we say that he absurdly endeavors to support his delusions by means of this principle: that Christ is our righteousness, because He is the eternal God, the fountain of righteousness, and the very righteousness of God.

My readers will pardon me for now only touching on matters which method requires me to defer to another place. But although he pretends that, by the term "essential righteousness," he merely means to oppose the sentiment that we are reputed righteous on account of Christ, he, however, clearly shows that not contented with that righteousness, which was procured for us by the obedience and sacrificial death of Christ, he maintains that we are substantially righteous in God by an infused essence as well as quality. For this is the reason that he so vehemently contends that, not only Christ, but also the Father and the Spirit dwell in us. The fact I admit to be true, but still I maintain it is wrested by him. He ought to have attended to the mode of dwelling—viz. that the Father and the Spirit are in Christ; and as in Him the fullness of the Godhead dwells, so in him we possess God entire. Hence, whatever he says separately concerning the Father and the Spirit has no other tendency than to lead away the simple from Christ. Then he introduces a substantial mixture, by which God, transfusing himself into us, makes us a part of himself. Our being made one with Christ by the agency of the Spirit, He being the head and we the members, he regards as almost nothing unless His essence is mingled with us.

But, as I have said, in the case of the Father and the Spirit, he more clearly betrays his views—namely, that we are not justified by the mere grace of the Mediator, and that righteousness is not simply or entirely offered to us in His person, but that we are made partakers of divine righteousness when God is essentially united to us.

6 Necessity of this refutation. Fourth argument: Answer. Confirmation: Another answer. Fifth and sixth arguments and answers.

Had he only said, that Christ by justifying us becomes ours by an essential union, and that He is our head not only insofar as He is man, but that as the essence of the divine nature is diffused into us, he might indulge his dreams with less harm, and, perhaps, it would be less necessary to contest the matter with him; but since this principle is like a cuttle-fish, which, by the ejection of dark and inky blood, conceals its many tails, if we would not knowingly and willingly allow ourselves to be robbed of that righteousness which alone gives us full assurance of our salvation, we must strenuously resist. For, in the whole of this discussion, the noun *righteousness* and the verb *to justify*, are extended by Osiander to two parts; to be justified being not only to be reconciled to God by a free pardon, but also to be made just; and righteousness being not a free imputation, but the holiness and integrity which the divine essence dwelling in us inspires. And he vehemently asserts (see Section 8) that Christ is himself our righteousness, not as far as He, by expiating sins, appeased the Father, but because He is the eternal God and life.

To prove the first point—viz. that God justifies not only by pardoning but by regenerating, he asks, whether He leaves those whom He justifies as they were by nature, making no change upon their vices? The answer is very easy: as Christ cannot be divided into parts, so the two things, justification and sanctification, which we perceive to be united together in Him, are inseparable. Whomsoever, therefore, God receives into his favor, He presents with the Spirit of adoption, whose agency forms them anew into His image. But if the brightness of the sun cannot be separated from its heat, are we therefore to say, that the Earth is warmed by light and illumined by heat? Nothing can be more apposite to the matter in hand than this simile. The sun by its heat quickens and fertilizes the earth; by its rays it enlightens and illumines it. Here is a mutual and undivided connection, and yet reason itself prohibits us from transferring the peculiar properties of the one to the other. In the confusion of a twofold grace, which Osiander obtrudes upon us, there is a similar absurdity. Because those whom God freely regards as righteous, He in fact renews to the cultivation of righteousness, Osiander confounds that free acceptance with this gift of regeneration, and contends that they are one and the same.

But Scriptures, while combining both, classe them separately, that they may better display the manifold grace of God. Nor is Paul's statement superfluous, that Christ is made unto us "righteousness and sanctification" (1 Corinthians 1:30). And whenever he argues from the salvation procured for us, from the paternal love of God and the grace of Christ, that we are called to purity and holiness, he plainly intimates, that to be justified is something else than to be made new creatures. Osiander, on coming to Scripture, corrupts every passage which he quotes. Thus when Paul says, "To him that worketh not, but believeth on him that justifieth the ungodly, his faith is counted for righteousness," he expounds *justifying* as *making just*. With the same rashness, he perverts the whole of the fourth chapter of the Romans. He hesitates not to give a similar gloss to the passage which I lately quoted, "Who shall lay anything to the charge of God's elect? It is God that justifieth." Here it is plain that guilt and acquittal simply are considered, and that the apostle's meaning depends on the antithesis. Therefore, his futility is detected in both his argument and his quotations for support from Scripture. He is not a whit sounder in discussing the term "righteousness," when it is said, that faith was imputed to Abraham for righteousness after he had embraced Christ (who is the righteousness of God and God himself) and was distinguished by excellent virtues. Hence, it appears that he viciously converts two things which are perfect into one that is corrupt. For the righteousness which is there mentioned pertains not to the whole course of life; or rather, the Spirit testifies, that though Abraham greatly excelled in virtue and by long perseverance in it had made so much progress, the only way in which he pleased God was by receiving the grace which was offered by the promise in faith. From this it follows, that, as Paul justly maintains, there is no room for works in justification.

7 Seventh and eighth arguments.

When he objects that the power of justifying exists not in faith, considered in itself, but only as receiving Christ, I willingly admit it. For did faith justify of itself, or (as it is expressed) by its own intrinsic virtue, as it is always weak and imperfect, its efficacy would be partial, and thus our righteousness, being maimed, would give us only a portion of salvation. We, indeed, imagine nothing of the kind, but say that, properly speaking, God alone justifies. The same thing we likewise transfer to Christ, because He was given to us for righteousness, while we compare faith to a kind of vessel, because we are incapable of receiving Christ, unless we are emptied and come with open mouth to receive His grace.

Hence, it follows, that we do not withdraw the power of justifying from Christ, when we hold that, before His righteousness, He himself is received by faith. Still, however, I admit not the tortuous figure of the Sophist, that faith is Christ, as if a vessel of clay were a treasure, because gold is deposited in it. Yet, this is no reason that faith, though in itself of no dignity or value, should not justify us by giving Christ; just as such a vessel filled with coin may give wealth. I say, therefore, that faith, which is only the instrument for receiving justification, is ignorantly confounded with Christ, who is the material cause, as well as the author and minister of this great blessing. This disposes of the difficulty—viz. how the term *faith* is to be understood when treating of justification.

8 Ninth argument: Answer.

Osiander goes still further in regard to the mode of receiving Christ, holding that by the ministry of the external Word the internal word is received; that he may thus lead us away from the priesthood of Christ and His office of Mediator to His eternal divinity. We, indeed, do not divide Christ, but hold that he who, reconciling us to God in His flesh, bestowed righteousness upon us, is the eternal Word of God; and that He could not perform the office of Mediator, nor acquire righteousness for us, if He were not the eternal God. Osiander will have it, that as Christ is God and man, he was made our righteousness in respect not of His human nature but of His divine nature. But if this is a peculiar property of the Godhead, it will not be peculiar to Christ, but common to him with the Father and the Spirit, since their righteousness is one and the same. Thus, it would be incongruous to say that that which existed naturally from eternity was made ours. But granting that God was made unto us righteousness, what are we to make of Paul's interposed statement, that He was so made by God? This certainly is peculiar to the office of Mediator, for although He contains in himself the divine nature, yet He receives his own proper title, that He may be distinguished from the Father and the Spirit. But he makes a ridiculous boast of a single passage of Jeremiah in which it is said, that Jehovah will be our righteousness. (See Jeremiah 23:6; 33:16.) But all he can extract from this is that Christ, who is our righteousness, was God manifest in the flesh. We have elsewhere quoted from Paul's discourse, that God purchased the Church with His own blood. (See Acts 20:28.)

Were anyone to infer from this that the blood by which sins were expiated was divine, and of a divine nature, who could endure so foul a heresy? But Osiander, thinking that he has gained the whole cause by this childish cavil, swells, exults, and stuffs whole pages with his bombast, whereas the solution is simple and obvious—viz. that Jehovah, when made of the seed of David, was indeed to be the righteousness of believers, but in what sense Isaiah declares, "By his knowledge shall my righteous servant justify many" (Isaiah 53:11). Let us observe that it is the Father who speaks. He attributes the office of justifying to the Son, and adds the reason: because He is "righteous." He places the method or *medium* (as it is called) in the doctrine by which Christ is known. For the word is more properly to be understood in a passive sense.

Hence, I infer, first, that Christ was made righteousness when He assumed the form of a servant; secondly, that He justified us by His obedience to the Father; and, accordingly that He does not perform this for us in respect of His divine nature, but according to the nature of the dispensation laid upon Him. For though God alone is the fountain of righteousness, and the only way in which we are righteous is by participation with Him, yet, as by our unhappy revolt we are alienated from His righteousness, it is necessary to descend to this lower remedy, that Christ may justify us by the power of His death and resurrection.

9 Tenth argument: Answer.

If he objects that this work by its excellence transcends human nature, and, therefore can only be ascribed to the divine nature; I concede the former point, but maintain that on the latter he is ignorantly deluded. For although Christ could neither purify our souls by His own blood, nor appease the Father by His sacrifice, nor acquit us from the charge of guilt, nor, in short, perform the office of priest unless He had been very God, because no human ability was equal to such a burden, it is however certain that He performed all these things in His human nature.

If it is asked, in what way we are justified? Paul answers, *by the obedience of Christ*. Did he obey in any other way than by assuming the form of a servant? We infer, therefore, that righteousness was manifested to us in His flesh. In like manner, in another passage (which I greatly wonder that Osiander does not blush repeatedly to quote), he places the fountain of righteousness entirely in the incarnation of Christ, "He has made him to be sin for us who knew no sin, that we might be made the righteousness of God in him" (2 Corinthians 5:21).

Osiander in turgid sentences lays hold of the expression, *righteousness of God*, and shouts victory! As if he had proved it his own phantom of essential righteousness, though the words have a very different meaning—viz. that we are justified through the expiation made by Christ. That the righteousness of God is used for the righteousness which is approved by God, should be known to mere novices, as in John, the praise of God is contrasted with the praise of men. (See John 12:43.)

I know that by the righteousness of God is sometimes meant that of which God is the author, and which He bestows upon us; but here the only thing that is meant is that, being supported by the expiation of Christ, we are able to stand at the tribunal of God, sound readers perceive without any observation of mine. The word is not of so much importance, provided Osiander agrees with us in this, that we are justified by Christ in respect that He was made an expiatory victim for us. This He could not be in His divine nature. For which reason also, when Christ would seal the righteousness and salvation, which He brought to us, he holds forth the sure pledge of it in His flesh. He indeed calls himself "living bread," but, in explanation of the mode, adds, "My flesh is meat indeed, and my blood is drink indeed" (John 6:55).

The same doctrine is clearly seen in the sacraments; which, though they direct our faith to the whole, not to a part of Christ, yet, at the same time, declare that the materials of righteousness and salvation reside in His flesh, not that the mere man of himself justifies or quickens, but that God was pleased, by means of a Mediator, to manifest His own hidden and incomprehensible nature.

Hence, I often repeat that Christ has been in a manner set before us as a fountain, whence we may draw what would otherwise lie without use in that deep and hidden abyss which streams forth to us in the person of the Mediator. In this way and in this meaning, I deny not that Christ, as He is God and man, justifies us; that this work is common also to the Father and the Holy Spirit; in fine, that the righteousness of which God makes us partakers is the eternal righteousness of the eternal God, provided effect is given to the clear and valid reasons to which I have adverted.

10 In what sense Christ is said to be our righteousness. Eleventh and twelfth arguments and answers.

Moreover, lest by his cavils he deceive the unwary, I acknowledge that we are devoid of this incomparable gift until Christ becomes ours. Therefore, to that union of the Head and members, the residence of Christ in our hearts, in fine, the mystical union, we assign the highest rank; Christ, when He becomes ours, making us partners with Him in the gifts with which He was endued. Hence, we do not view Him as at a distance and without us, but as we have put Him on, and been engrafted into His body, He deigns to make us one with himself, and, therefore, we glory in having a fellowship of righteousness with Him.

This disposes of Osiander's calumny, that we regard faith as righteousness, as if we were robbing Christ of His rights when we say, that, destitute in ourselves, we draw near to Him by faith, to make way for His grace, that He alone may fill us. But Osiander, spurning this spiritual union, insists on a gross mixture of Christ with believers; and, accordingly, to excite prejudice, gives the name of Zuinglians to all who subscribe not to his fanatical heresy of essential righteousness, because they do not hold that, in the supper, Christ is eaten substantially.

For my part, I count it the highest honor to be thus assailed by a haughty man, devoted to his own impostures, though he assails not me only, but writers of known reputation throughout the world, and whom it became him modestly to venerate. This, however, does not concern me, as I plead not my own cause, and plead the more sincerely that I am free from every sinister feeling. In insisting so vehemently on essential righteousness, and an essential inhabitation of Christ within us, his meaning is, first, that God, by a gross mixture, transfuses himself into us, as he pretends that there is a carnal eating in the supper; and, secondly that by instilling His own righteousness into us, He makes us really righteous with himself since, according to him, this righteousness is as well God himself as the probity or holiness or integrity of God is.

I will not spend much time in disposing of the passages of Scripture which he adduces, and which, though used in reference to the heavenly life, he wrests to our present state. Peter says that through the knowledge of Christ "...are given unto us exceeding great and precious promises, that by them ye might be partakers of the divine nature" (2 Peter 1:4); as if we now were what the gospel promises we shall be at the final advent of Christ; nay, John reminds us, "When he shall appear we shall be like him, for we shall see him as he is" (1 John 3:2). I only wished to give my readers a slender specimen of Osiander; it being my intention to decline the discussion of his frivolities, not because there is any difficulty in disposing of them, but because I am unwilling to annoy the reader with superfluous labor.

11 Thirteenth and fourteenth arguments: Answers. An exception by Osiander. Imputed and begun righteousness to be distinguished. Osiander confounds them. Fifteenth argument: Answer.

But more poison lurks in the second branch when he says that we are righteous together with God. I think I have already sufficiently proved, that although the dogma were not so pestiferous, yet because it is frigid and jejune and falls by its own vanity, it must justly be disrelished by all sound and pious readers. But it is impossible to tolerate the impiety, which, under the pretence of twofold righteousness, undermines our assurance of salvation, and hurrying us into the clouds, tries to prevent us from embracing the gift of expiation in faith, and invoking God with quiet minds. Osiander derides us for teaching that to be *justified* is a forensic term, because it behooves us to be in reality just: there is nothing also to which he is more opposed than the idea of our being justified by a free imputation. Say, then, if God does not justify us by acquitting and pardoning, what does Paul mean when he says, "God was in Christ reconciling the world unto himself, not imputing their trespasses unto them"? "He made him to be sin for us who knew no sin; that we might be made the righteousness of God in him" (2 Corinthians 5:19, 21).

Here I learn, first, that those who are reconciled to God are regarded as righteous: then the method is stated, God justifies by pardoning; and, hence, in another place, justification is opposed to accusation (see Romans 8:33); this antithesis clearly demonstrates that the mode of expression is derived from forensic use. And, indeed, no man, moderately verdant in the Hebrew tongue (provided he is also of sedate brain), is ignorant that this phrase thus took its rise, and thereafter derived its tendency and force. Now, then, when Paul says that David "describeth the blessedness of the man unto whom God imputeth righteousness without works, saying, Blessed are they whose iniquities are forgiven" (Romans 4:6, 7; Psalm 32:1), let Osiander say whether this is a complete or only a partial definition. He certainly does not adduce the Psalmist as a witness that pardon of sins is a part of righteousness, or concurs with something else in justifying, but he includes the whole of righteousness in gratuitous forgiveness, declaring those to be blessed "whose iniquities are forgiven, and whose sins are covered," and "to whom the Lord will not impute sin." He estimates and judges of his happiness from this that in this way he is righteous not in reality, but by imputation.

Osiander objects that it would be insulting to God and contrary to His nature to justify those who remain wicked. But it ought to be remembered, as I already observed, that the gift of justification is not separated from regeneration, though the two things are distinct. But as it is too well known by experience, that the remains of sin always exist in the righteous, it is necessary that justification should be something very different from reformation to newness of life. This latter God begins in His elect, and carries on during the whole course of life, gradually and sometimes slowly, so that if placed at his judgment-seat they would always deserve a sentence of death. He justifies not partially, but freely, so that they can appear in the heavens as if they are clothed with the purity of Christ. No portion of righteousness could pacify the conscience. It must be decided that we are pleasing to God, as being, without exception, righteous in His sight.

Hence, it follows that the doctrine of justification is perverted and completely overthrown whenever doubt is instilled into the mind, confidence in salvation is shaken, and free and intrepid prayer is retarded; yea, whenever rest and tranquility with spiritual joy are not established. Hence, Paul argues against objectors, that, "If the inheritance be of the law, it is no more of promise" (Galatians 3:18), that in this way faith would be made vain; for if respect be had to works, it fails; the holiest of men in that case finding nothing in which they can confide.

This distinction between justification and regeneration (Osiander confounding the two, calls them a twofold righteousness) is admirably expressed by Paul. Speaking of his real righteousness or the integrity bestowed upon him (which Osiander terms his essential righteousness), he mournfully exclaims, "O wretched man that I am! Who shall deliver me from the body of this death?" (Romans 7:24); but retaking himself to the righteousness which is founded solely on the mercy of God, he breaks forth, thus magnificently, into the language of triumph: "Who shall lay anything to the charge of God's elect? It is God that justifieth." "Who shall separate us from the love of Christ? Shall tribulation, or distress, or persecution, or famine, or nakedness, or peril, or sword?" (Romans 8:33, 35).

He clearly declares that the only righteousness for him is that which alone suffices for complete salvation in the presence of God, so that that miserable bondage, the consciousness of which made him a little before lament his lot, derogates not from his confidence and is no obstacle in his way. This diversity is well known, and indeed is familiar to all the saints who groan under the burden of sin, and yet with victorious assurance, rise above all fears.

Osiander's objection as to its being inconsistent with the nature of God falls back upon himself; for though he clothes the saints with a twofold righteousness as with a coat of skins, he is, however, forced to admit, that without forgiveness no man is pleasing to God. If this be so, let him at least admit, that with reference to what is called the proportion of imputation, those are regarded as righteous who are not so in reality. But how far shall the sinner extend this gratuitous acceptance, which is substituted in the room of righteousness? Will it amount to the whole pound, or will it be only an ounce? He will remain in doubt, vibrating to this side and to that, because he will be unable to assume to himself as much righteousness as will be necessary to give confidence. It is well that he who would prescribe a law to God is not the judge in this cause. But this saying will ever stand true, "That thou mightest be justified when thou speakest, and be clear when thou judges" (Psalm 51:4). What arrogance to condemn the supreme Judge when He acquits freely and try to prevent the response from taking affect: "I will have mercy on whom I will have mercy."

Yet, the intercession of Moses, which God calmed by this answer, was not for pardon to some individual, but to all alike, by wiping away the guilt to which all were liable. And we, indeed, say that the lost are justified before God by the burial of their sins; for (as He hates sin) He can only love those whom He justifies. But herein is the wondrous method of justification, that, clothed with the righteousness of Christ, they dread not the judgment of which they are worthy, and while they justly condemn themselves, are yet deemed righteous out of themselves.

12 Sixteenth argument, a dream of Osiander: Answer. Other four arguments and answers. Conclusion of the refutation of Osiander's errors.

I must admonish the reader carefully to attend to the mystery, which he boasts he is unwilling to conceal from them. For after contending with great prolixity that we do not obtain favor with God through the mere imputation of the righteousness of Christ, because (to use his own words) it would be impossible for God to hold those as righteous who are not so, he at length concludes that Christ was given to us for righteousness, in respect not of his human, but of his divine nature; and though this can only be found in the person of the Mediator, it is, however, the righteousness not of man, but of God. He does not now twist his rope of two righteousnesses, but plainly deprives the human nature of Christ of the office of justifying. It is worthwhile to understand what the nature of his argument is. It is said in the same passage that Christ is made unto us *wisdom* (1 Corinthians 1:30); but this is true only of the eternal Word, and, therefore, it is not the man Christ that is made *righteousness*. I answer, that the only begotten Son of God was indeed His eternal wisdom, but that this title is applied to Him by Paul in a different way—viz. because "In him are hid all the treasures of wisdom and righteousness" (Colossians 2:3). That, therefore, which he had with the Father he manifested to us; and thus Paul's expression refers not to the essence of the Son of God, but to our use, and is fitly applied to the human nature of Christ; for although the light shone in darkness before He was clothed with flesh, yet He was a hidden light until He appeared in human nature as the *Sun of Righteousness*, and hence He calls himself the *light of the world*.

It is also foolishly objected by Osiander that justifying far transcends the power of both men and angels, since it depends not on the dignity of any creature, but on the ordination of God. Were angels to attempt to give satisfaction to God, they could have no success, because they are not appointed for this purpose, it being the peculiar office of Christ, who "…has redeemed us from the curse of the law, being made a curse for us" (Galatians 3:13). Those who deny that Christ is our righteousness, in respect to His divine nature, are wickedly charged by Osiander with leaving only a part of Christ, and (what is worse) with making two Gods; because, while admitting that God dwells in us, they still insist that we are not justified by the righteousness of God. For though we call Christ the Author of life, inasmuch as He endured death that He might destroy him who had the power of death (Hebrews 2:14), we do not thereby rob Him of this honor, in His whole character, as God manifested in the flesh. We only make a distinction as to the manner in which the righteousness of God comes to us and is enjoyed by us—a matter as to which Osiander shamefully erred. We deny not that that which was openly exhibited to us in Christ flowed from the secret grace and power of God; nor do we dispute that the righteousness, which Christ confers upon us, is the righteousness of God, and proceeds from Him. What we constantly maintain is that our righteousness and life are in the death and resurrection of Christ.

I say nothing of that absurd accumulation of passages with which, without selection or common understanding, he has loaded his readers, in endeavoring to show that whenever mention is made of righteousness, this essential righteousness of His should be understood, as when David implores help from the righteousness of God. This David does more than a hundred times, and as often Osiander hesitates not to pervert his meaning. Not a whit more solid is his objection that the name of righteousness is rightly and properly applied to that by which we are moved to act aright, but that it is God only who works in us both to will and to do. (See Philippians 2:13.) For we deny not that God by His Spirit forms us anew to holiness and righteousness of life, but we must first see whether He does this of himself, immediately, or by the hand of his Son, with whom he has deposited all the fullness of the Holy Spirit, that out of His own abundance He may supply the wants of His members. When, although righteousness comes to us from the secret fountain of the Godhead, it does not follow that Christ, who sanctified himself in the flesh on our account, is our righteousness in respect of His divine nature. (See John 17:19.) Not less frivolous is his observation, that the righteousness with which Christ himself was righteous was divine; for had not the will of the Father impelled Him, He could not have fulfilled the office assigned Him.

For although it has been elsewhere said that all the merits of Christ flow from the mere good pleasure of God, this gives no countenance to the phantom by which Osiander fascinates both his own eyes and those of the simple. For who will allow him to infer that because God is the source and commencement of our righteousness, we are essentially righteous, and the essence of the divine righteousness dwells in us? In redeeming us, says Isaiah, "He (God) put on righteousness as a breastplate, and an helmet of salvation upon his head" (Isaiah 59:17), was this to deprive Christ of the armor, which He had given Him, and prevent Him from being a perfect Redeemer? All that the prophet meant was that God borrowed nothing from an external quarter, that in redeeming us He received no external aid. The same thing is briefly expressed by Paul in different terms when he says that God set him forth "to declare his righteousness for the remission of sins." This is not the least repugnant to his doctrine: in another place, that "By the obedience of one shall many be made righteous" (Romans 5:19). In short, everyone who, by the entanglement of twofold righteousness, prevents miserable souls from resting entirely on the mere mercy of God, mocks Christ by putting on Him a crown of plaited thorns.

13 Last part of the chapter. Refutation of the Sophists pretending a righteousness compounded partly of faith and partly of works.

But since a great part of mankind imagine, righteousness compounded of faith and works, let us here show that there is so wide a difference between justification by faith and by works, that the establishment of the one necessarily overthrows the other. The apostle says, "Yea doubtless, and I count all things but loss for the excellency of the knowledge of Christ Jesus my Lord: for whom I have suffered the loss of all things, and do count them but dung, that I may win Christ, and be found in him, not having mine own righteousness, which is of the law, but that which is through the faith of Christ, the righteousness which is of God by faith" (Philippians 3:8, 9). You here see a comparison of contraries, and an intimation that everyone who would obtain the righteousness of Christ must renounce his own. Hence, he elsewhere declares the cause of the rejection of the Jews to have been, that "They being ignorant of God's righteousness, and going about to establish their own righteousness, have not submitted themselves unto the righteousness of God" (Romans 10:3).

If we destroy the righteousness of God by establishing our own righteousness, then, in order to obtain His righteousness, our own must be entirely abandoned. This also he shows, when he declares that boasting is not excluded by the Law, but by faith. (See Romans 3:27.) Hence, it follows, that so long as the smallest portion of our own righteousness remains, we have still some ground for boasting.

Now if faith utterly excludes boasting, the righteousness of works cannot in any way be associated with the righteousness of faith. This meaning is so clearly expressed in the fourth chapter to the Romans as to leave no room for cavil or evasion. "If Abraham were justified by works he has whereof to glory"; and then it is added, "But not before God" (Romans 4:2). The conclusion, therefore, is that works did not justify him. He then employs another argument from contraries—viz. when *reward* is paid to works, it is done *of debt*, not *of grace*; but the righteousness of faith is of grace: therefore, it is not of the merit of works. Away, then, with the dream of those who invent righteousness compounded of faith and works.

14 Sophistical evasion by giving the same name to different things: Two answers.

The Sophists, who delight in sporting with Scripture and in empty cavils, think they have a subtle evasion when they expound *works* to mean, such as unregenerated men do literally, and by the effect of free will, without the grace of Christ, and deny that these have any reference to spiritual works. Thus, according to them, man is justified by faith as well as by works, provided these are not his own works, but gifts of Christ and fruits of regeneration; Paul's only object in so expressing himself being to convince the Jews, that in trusting to their own strength they foolishly arrogated righteousness to themselves, whereas it is bestowed upon us by the Spirit of Christ alone, and not by studied efforts of our own nature. But they observe not that in the antithesis between legal and gospel righteousness, which Paul elsewhere introduces, all kinds of works, with whatever name adorned, are excluded (Galatians 3:11, 12). For he says that the righteousness of the Law consists in obtaining salvation by doing what the Law requires, but that the righteousness of faith consists in believing that Christ died and rose again. (See Romans 10:5-9.) Moreover, we shall afterwards see, at the proper place, that the blessings of sanctification and justification, which we derive from Christ, are different. Hence, it follows that not even spiritual works are taken into account when the power of justifying is ascribed to faith. And, indeed, the passage above quoted, in which Paul declares that Abraham had no ground of glorying before God, because he was not justified by works, ought not to be confined to a literal and external form of virtue, or to the effort of free will. The meaning is that though the life of the patriarch had been spiritual and almost angelic, yet he could not have procured justification before God by the merit of works.

15 Second evasion: Two answers. First answer. Pernicious consequences resulting from this evasion.

The Schoolmen treat the matter somewhat more grossly by mingling their preparations with it; and yet the others instill into the simple and unwary a no less pernicious dogma, when, under cover of the Spirit and grace, they hide the divine mercy, which alone can give peace to the trembling soul. We, indeed, hold with Paul, that God justifies those who fulfill the Law, but because we are all far from observing the Law, we infer that the works, which should be most effectual to justification, are of no avail to us, because we are destitute of them.

In regard to vulgar papists or Schoolmen, they are here doubly wrong, both in calling faith assurance of conscience while waiting to receive from God the reward of merits, and in interpreting divine grace to mean not the imputation of gratuitous righteousness, but the assistance of the Spirit in the study of holiness. They quote from an apostle: "He that comes to God must believe that he is, and that he is the rewarder of them that diligently seek him" (Hebrews 11:6). But they observe not what the method of seeking is. Then in regard to the term *grace*, it is plain from their writings that they labor under a delusion. For Lombard holds, Christ gives that justification to us in two ways. "First," says he, "the death of Christ justifies us when by means of it the love by which we are made righteous is excited in our hearts; and, secondly, when by means of it sin is extinguished—sin by which the devil held us captive, but by which he cannot now procure our condemnation." You see here that the chief office of divine grace in our justification he considers to be its directing us to good works by the agency of the Holy Spirit. He intended, no doubt, to follow the opinion of Augustine, but he follows it at a distance, and even wanders far from a true imitation of him both obscuring what was clearly stated by Augustine, and making what in him was less pure more corrupt.

The Schools have always gone from worse to worse, until at length, in their downward path, they have degenerated into a kind of Pelagianism. Even the sentiment of Augustine, or at least his mode of expressing it, cannot be entirely approved of. For although he is admirable in stripping man of all merit of righteousness, and transferring the whole praise of it to God, yet he classes the grace by which we are regenerated to newness of life under the head of sanctification.

16 **Second answer, showing wherein, according to Scripture, Justification consists.**

Scripture, when it treats of justification by faith, leads us in a very different direction. Turning away our view from our own works, it bids us look only to the mercy of God and the perfection of Christ. The order of justification which it sets before us is this: first, God of His mere gratuitous goodness is pleased to embrace the sinner in whom he sees nothing that can move him to mercy but wretchedness, because he sees him altogether naked and destitute of good works. He, therefore, seeks the cause of kindness in himself, that thus he may affect the sinner by a sense of his goodness, and induce him, in distrust of his own works, to cast himself entirely upon his mercy for salvation. This is the meaning of faith by which the sinner comes into the possession of salvation, when, according to the doctrine of the gospel, he perceives that he is reconciled by God; when, by the intercession of Christ, he obtains the pardon of his sins, and is justified; and, though renewed by the Spirit of God, considers that, instead of leaning on his own works, he must look solely to the righteousness which is treasured up for him in Christ. When these things are weighed separately, they will clearly explain our view, though they may be arranged in a better order than that in which they are here presented. But it is of little consequence, provided they are so connected with each other as to give us a full exposition and solid confirmation of the whole subject.

17 **In explanation of this doctrine of justification, two passages of Scripture produced.**

ere, it is proper to remember the relation, which we previously established between faith and the gospel; faith being said to justify because it receives and embraces the righteousness offered in the Gospel. By the very fact of its being said to be offered by the gospel, all consideration of works is excluded. This Paul repeatedly declares, and in two passages, in particular, most clearly demonstrates. In the Epistle to the Romans, comparing the Law and the Gospel, he says, "Moses describeth the righteousness which is of the law, that the man which does those things shall live by them. But the righteousness which is of faith speaketh on this wise, If thou shalt confess with thy mouth the Lord Jesus, and shalt believe in thine heart that God has raised him from the dead, thou shalt be saved" (Romans 10:5, 6, 9).

Do you see how he makes the distinction between the Law and the gospel to be, that the former gives justification to works, whereas the latter bestows it freely without any help from works? This is a notable passage, and may free us from many difficulties if we understand that the justification, which is given us by the gospel, is free from any terms of Law. It is for this reason he more than once places the promise in diametrical opposition to the Law. "If the inheritance be of the law, it is no more of promise" (Galatians 3:18).

Expressions of similar import occur in the same chapter. Undoubtedly the Law also has its promises; and, therefore, between them and the Gospel promises there must be some distinction and difference, unless we are to hold that the comparison is inept. And in what can the difference consist unless in this, that the promises of the gospel are gratuitous and founded on the mere mercy of God, whereas the promises of the Law depend on the condition of works? But let no pester here allege that only the righteousness which men would obtrude upon God of their own strength and free will is repudiated; since Paul declares, without exception, that the Law gained nothing by its commands, being such as none, not only of mankind in general, but none even of the most perfect, are able to fulfill.

Love assuredly is the chief commandment in the Law, and since the Spirit of God trains us to love, it cannot but be a cause of righteousness in us, though that righteousness even in the saints is defective, and therefore of no value as a ground of merit.

18 Another passage of Scripture.

he second passage is, "That no man is justified by the law in the sight of God, it is evident: for, The just shall live by faith.

And the law is not of faith: but, The man that does them shall live in them" (Galatians 3:11, 12; Habukkuk 2:4). How could the argument hold unless it is true that works are not to be taken into account, but are to be altogether separated? The Law, he says, is different from faith. Why? Because to obtain justification by it, works are required; and hence it follows, that to obtain justification by the gospel they are not required. From this statement, it appears that those who are justified by faith are justified independent of, nay, in the absence of, the merit of works, because faith receives that righteousness which the gospel bestows. But the gospel differs from the Law in this, that it does not confine justification to works, but places it entirely in the mercy of God.

In like manner, Paul contends, in the Epistle to the Romans, that Abraham had no ground of glorying, because faith was imputed to him for righteousness (see Romans 4:2); and he adds in confirmation, that the proper place for justification by faith is where there are no works to which reward is due. "To him that worketh is the reward not reckoned of grace, but of debt." What is given to faith is gratuitous, this being the force of the meaning of the words, which he there employs. Shortly after he adds, "Therefore it is of faith, that it might be by grace" (Romans 4:16); and hence infers that the inheritance is gratuitous because it is procured by faith. How so but just because faith without the aid of works leans entirely on the mercy of God? And in the same sense, doubtless, he elsewhere teaches, that the righteousness of God without the Law was manifested, being witnessed by the Law and the prophets (see Romans 3:21); for excluding the Law, he declares that it is not aided by works, that we do not obtain it by working, but are destitute when we draw near to receive it.

19 Third evasion. Catholic objection to the doctrine of Justification by faith alone: Three answers. Fourth evasion: Three answers.

The reader now perceives with what fairness the Sophists of the present day cavil at our doctrine, when we say that a man is justified by faith alone. (See Romans 4:2.) They dare not deny that *he is justified by faith*, seeing Scripture so often declares it; but as the word *alone* is nowhere expressly used they will not tolerate its being added. Is it so? What answer, then, will they give to the words of Paul when he contends that righteousness is not of faith unless it is gratuitous? How can it be gratuitous, and yet by works? By what cavils, moreover, will they evade his declaration in another place, that in the Gospel the righteousness of God is manifested? (See Romans 1:17.) If righteousness is manifested in the gospel, it is certainly not a partial or mutilated, but a full and perfect righteousness.

The Law, therefore, has no part in its and their objection to the exclusive word *alone* as not only unfounded, but as obviously absurd. Does he not plainly enough attribute everything to faith alone when he disconnects it with works? What, I would ask is meant by the expressions, "The righteousness of God without the law is manifested;" "Being justified freely by his grace;" "Justified by faith without the deeds of the law?" (Romans 3:21, 24, 28). Here they have an ingenious subterfuge, one which, though not of their own devising but taken from Origen and some ancient writers, is most childish. They pretend that the works excluded are ceremonial, not moral works. Such profit do they make by their constant wrangling, that they possess not even the first elements of logic. Do they think the apostle was raving when he produced, in proof of his doctrine, these passages? "The man that does them shall live in them" (Galatians 3:12). "Cursed is everyone that continueth not in all things that are written in the book of the law to do them" (Galatians 3:10). Unless they are themselves raving, they will not say that life was promised to the observers of ceremonies, and the curse denounced only against the transgressors of them.

If these passages are to be understood of the moral law, there cannot be a doubt that moral works also are excluded from the power of justifying. To the same effect are the arguments, which he employs. "By the deeds of the law there shall no flesh be justified in his sight: for by the law is the knowledge of sin" (Romans 3:20). "The law worketh wrath,"(Romans 4:15), and, therefore, not righteousness. "The law cannot pacify the conscience," and therefore cannot confer righteousness. "Faith is imputed for righteousness," and, therefore, righteousness is not the reward of works, but is given without being due. Because "we are justified by faith," boasting is excluded. "Had there been a law given which could have given life, verily righteousness should have been by the law. But the Scripture has concluded all under sin, that the promise by faith of Jesus Christ might be given to them that believe" (Galatians 3:21, 22). Let them maintain, if they dare, that these things apply to ceremonies, and not to morals, and the very children will laugh at their effrontery. The true conclusion, therefore, is that the whole Law is spoken of when the power of justifying is denied to it.

20 Fifth evasion, founded on the application of the term "righteousness" to good works, and also on their reward: Answer, confirmed by the invincible argument of Paul. Sixth evasion: Answer.

Should anyone wonder why the apostle, not contented with having named works, employs this addition, the explanation is easy. However highly works may be estimated, they have their whole value more from the approbation of God than from their own dignity. For who will presume to plume himself before God on the righteousness of works, unless insofar as He approves of them? Who will presume to demand of Him a reward except as far as He has promised it? It is owing entirely to the goodness of God that works are deemed worthy of the honor and reward of righteousness; and, therefore, their whole value consists in this, that by means of them we endeavor to manifest obedience to God. Wherefore, in another passage, the apostle, to prove that Abraham could not be justified by works, declares, "That the covenant, that was confirmed before of God in Christ, the law, which was four hundred and thirty years after, cannot disannul, that it should make the promise of none effect" (Galatians 3:17).

The unskillful would ridicule the argument that there could be righteous works before the promulgation of the Law, but the apostle, knowing that works could derive this value solely from the testimony and honor conferred on them by God, takes it for granted that, before the Law, they had no power of justifying. We see why he expressly terms them works of the Law when he would deny the power of justifying to them—viz. because it was only with regard to such works that a question could be raised; although he sometimes, without addition, excepts all kinds of works whatever, as when on the testimony of David he speaks of the man to whom the Lord imputeth righteousness without works. (See Romans 4:5, 6.) No cavils, therefore, can enable them to prove that the exclusion of works is not general. In vain do they lay hold of the frivolous subtlety, that the *faith alone* by which we are justified, "*worketh by love*," and that love, therefore, is the foundation of justification.

We, indeed, acknowledge with Paul that the only faith which justifies is that which works by love (Galatians 3:6); but love does not give it its justifying power. Nay, its only means of justifying consists in its bringing us into communication with the righteousness of Christ. Otherwise, the whole argument on which the apostle insists with so much earnestness, would fall. "To him that worketh is the reward not reckoned of grace, but of debt. But to him that worketh not, but believeth on him that justifieth the ungodly, his faith is counted for righteousness." Could he express more clearly than in this word, that there is justification in faith only where there are no works to which reward is due, and that faith is imputed for righteousness only when righteousness is conferred freely without merit?

21 Osiander and the Sophists being thus refuted, the accuracy of the definition of justification by faith is established.

Let us now consider the truth of what was said in the definition— viz. that justification by faith is reconciliation with God, and that this consists solely in the remission of sins. We must always return to the axioms that the wrath of God lies upon all men so long as they continue to be sinners. This is elegantly expressed by Isaiah in these words: "Behold, the Lord's hand is not shortened, that it cannot save; neither his ear heavy, that it cannot hear: but your iniquities have separated between you and your God, and your sins have hid his face from you, that he will not hear" (Isaiah 59:1, 2).

We are told here that sin is a separation between God and man that His countenance is turned away from the sinner and that it cannot be otherwise, since, to have any intercourse with sin is repugnant to His righteousness. Hence, the apostle shows that man is at enmity with God until he is restored to favor by Christ. (See Romans 5:8-10.) When the Lord, therefore, admits him to union, he is said to justify him, because he can neither receive him into favor, nor unite him to himself without changing his condition from that of a sinner into that of a righteous man. We add that this is done by remission of sins. For if those whom the Lord has reconciled to himself are estimated by works, they will still prove to be in reality sinners, while they ought to be pure and free from sin.

It is evident, therefore, that the only way in which those whom God embraces are made righteous is by having their pollutions wiped away by the remission of sins, so that this justification may be termed in one word the remission of sins.

22 Definition confirmed. A. By passages of Scripture. B. By the writings of the ancient fathers.

Both of these become perfectly clear from the words of Paul: "God was in Christ reconciling the world unto himself, not imputing their trespasses unto them; and has committed unto us the word of reconciliation." He then subjoins the sum of his embassy: "He has made him to be sin for us who knew no sin; that we might be made the righteousness of God in him" (2 Corinthians 5:19-21). He here uses righteousness and reconciliation indiscriminately, to make us understand that the one includes the other. The mode of obtaining this righteousness he explains to be that our sins are not imputed to us. Wherefore, you cannot henceforth doubt how God justifies us when you hear that He reconciles us to himself by not imputing our faults. In the same manner, in the Epistle to the Romans, he proves, by the testimony of David, that righteousness is imputed without works, because he declares the man to be blessed "...whose transgression is forgiven, whose sin is covered," and "... unto whom the Lord imputeth not iniquity" (Romans 4:6; Psalm 32; 1, 2). There he undoubtedly uses blessedness for righteousness; and, as he declares that it consists in forgiveness of sins, there is no reason that we should define it otherwise. Accordingly, Zacharias, the father of John the Baptist, sings that the knowledge of salvation consists in the forgiveness of sins. (See Luke 1:77.) The same course was followed by Paul when, in addressing the people of Antioch, he gave them a summary of salvation. Luke states that he concluded in this way: "Through this man is preached unto you the forgiveness of sins, and by him all that believe are justified from all things from which ye could not be justified by the law of Moses" (Acts 13:38, 39).

Thus, the apostle connects forgiveness of sins with justification in such a way as to show that they are altogether the same; and, hence, he properly argues that justification, which we owe to the indulgence of God, is gratuitous. Nor should it seem an unusual mode of expression to say that believers are justified before God not by works, but by gratuitous acceptance, seeing it is frequently used in Scripture and sometimes also by ancient writers. Thus, Augustine says: "The righteousness of the saints in this world consists more in the forgiveness of sins than the perfection of virtue." To this corresponds the well-known sentiment of Bernard: "Not to sin is the righteousness of God, but the righteousness of man is the indulgence of God." He previously asserts that Christ is our righteousness in absolution, and, therefore, that those only are just who have obtained pardon through mercy.

23 Man justified by faith, not because by it he obtains the Spirit, and is thus made righteous, but because by faith he lays hold of the righteousness of Christ. An objection removed. An example of the doctrine of justification by faith from the works of Ambrose.

Hence, also, it is proved that it is entirely by the intervention of Christ's righteousness that we obtain justification before God. This is equivalent to saying that man is not just in himself, but that the righteousness of Christ is communicated to him by imputation, while he is strictly deserving of punishment. Thus vanishes the absurd dogma that man is justified by faith, inasmuch as it brings him under the influence of the Spirit of God by whom he is rendered righteous. This is so repugnant to the above doctrine that it never can be reconciled with it. There can be no doubt that he who is taught to seek righteousness out of himself does not previously possess it in himself. This is most clearly declared by the apostle when he says that he who knew no sin was made an expiatory victim for sin, that we might be made the righteousness of God in him. (See 2 Corinthians 5:21.) You see that our righteousness is not in ourselves, but in Christ; that the only way in which we become possessed of it is by being made partakers with Christ, since with Him we possess all riches. There is nothing repugnant to this in what He elsewhere says: "God sending his own Son in the likeness of sinful flesh, and for sin condemned sin in the flesh: that the righteousness of the law might be fulfilled in us" (Romans 8:3, 4). Here the only fulfillment to which he refers is that which we obtain by imputation.

Our Lord Jesus Christ communicates His righteousness to us, and so by some wondrous ways insofar as pertains to the justice of God it transfuses its power into us. That this was the apostle's view is abundantly clear from another sentiment which he had expressed a little before: "As by one man's disobedience many were made sinners, so by the obedience of one shall many be made righteous" (Romans 5:19). To declare that we are deemed righteous solely because the obedience of Christ is imputed to us as if it were our own is just to place our righteousness in the obedience of Christ. Wherefore, Ambrose appears to me to have most elegantly adverted to the blessing of Jacob as an illustration of this righteousness, when he says that as he who did not merit the birthright in himself personated his brother, put on his garments, which gave forth a most pleasant odor, and thus introduced himself to his father that he might receive a blessing to his own advantage, though under the person of another, so we conceal ourselves under the precious purity of Christ, our first-born brother, that we may obtain an attestation of righteousness from the presence of God.

The words of Ambrose are, "Isaac's smelling the odor of his garments, perhaps means that we are justified not by works, but by faith, since carnal infirmity is an impediment to works, but errors of conduct are covered by the brightness of faith, which merits the pardon of faults." And so, indeed, it is; for in order to appear in the presence of God for salvation, we must send forth that fragrant odor, having our vices covered and buried by His perfection.

Chapter 12

NECESSITY OF CONTEMPLATING THE JUDGMENT-SEAT OF GOD, IN ORDER TO BE SERIOUSLY CONVINCED OF THE DOCTRINE OF GRATUITOUS JUSTIFICATION

The divisions of this chapter are: I. A consideration of the righteousness of God overturns the righteousness of works, as is plain from passages of Scripture, and the confession and example of the saints, sections 1-3. II. The same effect produced by a serious examination of the conscience, and a constant citation to the divine tribunal, sections 4 and 5. III. Hence, arises in the hearts of the godly, not hypocrisy, or a vain opinion of merit, but true humility. This illustrated by the authority of Scripture and the example of the Publican, sections 6 and 7. IV. Conclusion—arrogance and security must be discarded, every man throwing an impediment in the way of the divine goodness in proportion as he trusts to himself.

Sections

1. Source of error on the subject of justification. Sophists speak as if the question were to be discussed before some human tribunal. It relates to the majesty and justice of God. Hence, nothing accepted without absolute perfection. Passages confirming this doctrine. If we descend to the righteousness of the Law, the curse immediately appears.

2. Source of hypocritical confidence. Illustrated by a simile. Exhortation. Testimony of Job, David, and Paul.

3. Confession of Augustine and Bernard.

4. Another engine overthrowing the righteousness of works—viz. A serious examination of the conscience, and a comparison between the perfection of God and the imperfection of man.

5. How it is that we so indulge this imaginary opinion of our own works. The proper remedy to be found in a consideration of the majesty of God and our own misery. A description of this misery.

6. *Christian humility consists in laying aside the imaginary idea of our own righteousness, and trusting entirely to the mercy of God, apprehended by faith in Christ. This humility is described. Proved by passages of Scripture.*

7. *The parable of the Publican explained.*

8. *Arrogance, security, and self-confidence must be renounced. General rule, or summary of the above doctrine.*

1 **Source of error on the subject of justification. Sophists speak as if the question were to be discussed before some human tribunal. It relates to the majesty and justice of God. Hence, nothing accepted without absolute perfection. Passages confirming this doctrine. If we descend to the righteousness of the Law, the curse immediately appears.**

Although the perfect truth of the above doctrine is proved by clear passages of Scripture, yet we cannot clearly see how necessary it is, before we bring distinctly into view the foundations on which the whole discussion ought to rest. First, then, let us remember that the righteousness which we are considering is not that of a human, but of a heavenly tribunal; and so beware of employing our own little standard to measure the perfection, which is to satisfy the justice of God.

It is strange with what rashness and presumption this is commonly defined. Nay, we see that none talk more confidently, or, so to speak, more blusteringly, of the righteousness of works than those whose diseases are most palpable and blemishes most apparent. This they do because they reflect not on the righteousness of Christ, which, if they had the slightest perception of it, they would never treat with so much insult. It is certainly undervalued, if not recognized to be so perfect that nothing can be accepted that is not in every respect entire and absolute, and tainted by no impurity; such indeed as never has been and never will be found in man. It is easy for any man, within the precincts of the schools, to talk of the sufficiency of works for justification; but when we come into the presence of God there must be a truce to such talk.

The matter is there discussed in earnest, and is no longer a theatrical logomachy. Hither must we turn our minds if we would inquire to any purpose concerning true righteousness; the question must be: How shall we answer the heavenly Judge when He calls us to account? Let us contemplate that Judge, not as our own unaided intellect conceives of Him, but as He is portrayed to us in Scripture (see especially the Book of Job), with a brightness which obscures the stars, a strength which melts the mountains, an anger which shakes the Earth, a wisdom which takes the wise in their own craftiness, a purity before which all things become impure, a righteousness to which not even angels are equal (so far is it from making the guilty innocent), a vengeance which, once kindled burns to the lowest hell. (See Exodus 34:7; Nahum 1:3; Deuteronomy 32:22.) Let Him, I say, sit in judgment on the actions of men, and who will feel secure in sitting himself before His throne? "Who among us," says the prophets "shall dwell with the devouring fire? Who among us shall dwell with everlasting burnings? He that walketh righteously and speaketh uprightly," etc. (Isaiah 33:14, 15). Let whoso will come forth. Nay, the answer shows that no man can. For, on the other hand, we hear the dreadful voice: "If thou, Lord, shouldst mark our iniquities, O Lord, who shall stand?" (Psalm 130:3). All must immediately perish, as Job declares, "Shall mortal man be more just than God? Shall a man be more pure than his Maker? Behold, he put no trust in his servants; and his angels he charged with folly: How much less in them that dwell in houses of clay, whose foundation is in the dust, which are crushed before the moth? They are destroyed from morning to evening" (Job 4:17-20). Again, "Behold, he putteth no trust in his saints; yea, the heavens are not clean in his sight. How much more abominable and filthy is man, which drinketh iniquity like water?" (Job 15:15, 16).

I confess, indeed, that in the Book of Job reference is made to a righteousness of a more exalted description than the observance of the Law. It is of importance to attend to this distinction; for even could a man satisfy the Law, he could not stand the scrutiny of that righteousness which transcends all our thoughts. Hence, although Job was not conscious of offending, he is still dumb with astonishment, because he sees that God could not be appeased even by the sanctity of angels, were their works weighed in that supreme balance. But to advert no further to this righteousness, which is incomprehensible, I only say, that if our life is brought to the standard of the written law, we are lethargic indeed if we are not filled with dread at the many maledictions which God has employed for the purpose of arousing us, and among others, the following general one: "Cursed be he that confirmeth not all the words of this law to do them" (Deuteronomy 27:26). In short, the whole discussion of this subject will be insipid and frivolous, unless we sit ourselves before the heavenly Judge, and anxious for our acquittal, voluntarily humble ourselves, confessing our nothingness.

2 Source of hypocritical confidence. Illustrated by a simile. Exhortation. Testimony of Job, David, and Paul.

Thus then must we raise our eyes that we may learn to tremble instead of vainly exulting. It is easy, indeed, when the comparison is made among men, for everyone to plume himself on some quality, which others ought not to despise; but when we rise to God, that confidence instantly falls and dies away. The case of the soul with regard to God is very analogous to that of the body in regard to the visible firmament. The bodily eye, while employed in surveying adjacent objects, is pleased with its own perspicacity; but when directed to the sun, being dazzled and overwhelmed by the refulgence, it becomes no less convinced of its weakness than it formerly was of its power in viewing inferior objects. Therefore, lest we deceive ourselves by vain confidence, let us recollect that even though we deem ourselves equal or superior to other men, this is nothing to God, by whose judgment the decision must be given.

But if our presumption cannot be tamed by these considerations, He will answer us as He did the Pharisees, "Ye are they which justify yourselves before men; but God knoweth your hearts: for that which is highly esteemed among men is abomination in the sight of God" (Luke 16:15). Go now and make a proud boast of your righteousness among men, while God in heaven abhors it. But what are the feelings of the servants of God, of those who are truly taught by His Spirit? "Enter not into judgment with thy servant; for in thy sight shall no man living be justified" (Psalm 143:2). Another, though in a sense somewhat different, says, "How should man be just with God? If he will contend with him he cannot answer him one of a thousand" (Job 9:2, 3). Here we are plainly told what the righteousness of God is, namely, a righteousness which no human works can satisfy, which charges us with a thousand sins, while not one sin can be excused. Of this righteousness Paul, that chosen vessel of God, had formed a just idea, when he declared, "I know nothing by myself, yet am I not hereby justified" (1 Corinthians 4:4).

3 Confession of Augustine and Bernard.

Such examples exist not in the sacred volume only; all pious writers show that their sentiment was the same. Thus, Augustine says, "Of all pious men groaning under this burden of corruptible flesh, and the infirmities of this life, the only hope is that we have one Mediator, Jesus Christ the righteous, and that He intercedes for our sins." What do we hear? If this is their only hope, where is their confidence in works? When he says *only*, he leaves no other.

Bernard says, "And, indeed, where have the infirm firm security and safe rest, but in the wounds of the Savior? Hold it, then, the more securely, the more powerful He is to save. The world frowns, the body presses, the devil lays snares: I fall not, because I am founded on a firm rock. I have sinned a grievous sin: conscience is troubled, but it shall not be overwhelmed, for I will remember the wounds of the Lord." He afterwards concludes, "My merit, therefore, is the compassion of the Lord; plainly I am not devoid of merit so long as He is not devoid of commiseration. But if the mercies of the Lord are many, equally many are my merits. Shall I sing of my own righteousness? O Lord, I will make mention of thy righteousness alone. That righteousness is mine also, being made mine by God." Again, in another passage, "Man's whole merit is to place his whole hope in him who makes the whole man safe." In like manner, reserving peace to himself, he leaves the glory to God: "Let thy glory remain unimpaired: it is well with me if I have peace; I altogether abjure boasting, lest if I should usurp what is not mine, I lose also what is offered." He says still more plainly in another place: "Why is the Church solicitous about merits? God purposely supplies her with a firmer and more secure ground of boasting. There is no reason for asking by what merits may we hope for blessings, especially when you hear in the prophet, 'Thus saith the Lord God, I do not this for your sakes, O house of Israel, but for mine holy name's sake' (Ezekiel 36:22, 32).

"It is sufficient for merit to know that merits suffice not, but as it is sufficient for merit not to presume on merit, so to be without merits is sufficient for condemnation." The free use of the term merits for good works must be pardoned to custom. Bernard's purpose was to alarm hypocrites, who turned the grace of God into licentiousness, as he shortly after explains: "Happy the church which neither wants merit without presumption, nor presumption without merit. It has ground to presume, but not merit. It has merit, merit to deserve, not presume. Is not the absence of presumption itself a merit? He, therefore, to whom the many mercies of the Lord furnish ample grounds of boasting, presumes the more securely that he presumes not."

4 Another engine overthrowing the righteousness of works—viz. A serious examination of the conscience and a comparison between the perfection of God and the imperfection of man.

Thus, indeed, it is. Aroused consciences, when they have to do with God, feel this to be the only asylum in which they can breathe safely. For if the stars which shine most brightly by night lose their brightness on the appearance of the sun, what do we think will be the case with the highest purity of man when contrasted with the purity of God? For the scrutiny will be most strict, penetrating to the most hidden thoughts of the heart. As Paul says, it "…will bring to light the hidden things of darkness and will make manifest the counsels of the heart" (1 Corinthians 4:5); it will compel the reluctant and dissembling conscience to bring forward everything, even things, which have now escaped our memory. The devil, aware of all the iniquities which he has induced us to perpetrate, will appear as the accuser; the external show of good works, the only thing now considered, will then be of no avail; the only thing demanded will be the true intent of the will.

Hence, hypocrisy, not only that by which a man, though consciously guilty before God, affects to make an ostentatious display before man, but that by which each imposes upon himself before God (so prone are we to soothe and flatter ourselves), will fall confounded, no matter how much it may now swell with pride and presumption. Those who do not turn their thoughts to this scene may be able for the moment calmly and complacently to rear up righteousness for themselves; but this the judgment of God will immediately overthrow, just as great wealth amassed in a dream vanishes the moment we awake.

Those who, as in the presence of God, inquire seriously into the true standard of righteousness, will certainly find that all the works of men, if estimated by their own worth, are nothing but vileness and pollution, that what is commonly deemed justice is with God mere iniquity; what is deemed integrity is pollution; what is deemed glory is ignominy.

5 How it is that we so indulge this imaginary opinion of our own works. The proper remedy to be found in a consideration of the majesty of God and our own misery. A description of this misery.

Let us not decline to descend from this contemplation of the divine perfection, to look into ourselves without flattery or blind self-love. It is not strange that we are so deluded in this matter, seeing none of us can avoid that pestilential self-indulgence, which, as Scripture proclaims, is naturally inherent in all: "Every way of a man is right in his own eyes," says Solomon (Proverbs 21:2). And again, "All the ways of a man are clean in his own eyes" (Proverbs 16:2). What then? Does this hallucination excuse him? No, indeed, as Solomon immediately adds, "The Lord weigheth the spirits;" that is, while man flatters himself by wearing an external mask of righteousness, the Lord weighs the hidden impurity of the heart in His balance. Seeing, therefore, that nothing is gained by such flattery, let us not voluntarily delude ourselves with regard to our own destruction.

To examine ourselves properly, our conscience must be called to the judgment-seat of God. His light is necessary to disclose the secret recesses of wickedness, which otherwise lie too deeply hidden. Then only shall we clearly perceive what the value of our works is; that man, so far from being just before God, is but rottenness and a worm, abominable and vain, drinking in "iniquity like water." For "who can bring a clean thing out of an unclean? Not one" (Job 14:5). Then we shall experience the truth of what Job said of himself: "If I justify myself, mine own mouth shall condemn me: if I say I am perfect, it shall prove me perverse" (Job 9:20).

Nor does the complaint, which the prophet made concerning Israel, apply to one age only. It is true of every age, that "All we like sheep have gone astray; we have turned everyone to his own way" (Isaiah 53:6). Indeed, he there comprehends all to whom the gift of redemption was to come. And the strictness of the examination ought to be continued until it has completely alarmed us, and in that way prepared us for receiving the grace of Christ. For he is deceived who thinks himself capable of enjoying it, until he has laid aside all loftiness of mind. There is a well-known declaration, "God resisteth the proud, but giveth grace to the humble" (1 Peter 5:5).

6 Christian humility consists in laying aside the imaginary idea of our own righteousness, and trusting entirely to the mercy of God,

apprehended by faith in Christ. This humility described. Proved by passages of Scripture.

But what means is there of humbling ourselves, if we do not make way for the mercy of God by our utter indigence and destitution? For I call it not humility, so long as we think there is any good remaining in us. Those who have joined the two things, to think humbly of ourselves before God and yet hold our own righteousness in some estimation, have hitherto taught a pernicious hypocrisy. For if we confess to God contrary to what we feel, we wickedly lie to Him; but we cannot feel as we ought without seeing that everything like a ground of boasting is completely crushed. Therefore, when you hear from the prophets, "Thou wilt save the afflicted people; but wilt bring down high looks" (Psalm 18:27), consider, first, that there is no access to salvation unless all pride is laid aside and true humility embraced; secondly, that that humility is not a kind of moderation by which you yield to God some article of your right. (Thus, men are called humble in regard to each other when they neither conduct themselves haughtily nor insult over others, though they may still entertain some consciousness of their own excellence), but that it is the unfeigned submission of a mind overwhelmed by a serious conviction of its want and misery. Such is the description everywhere given by the Word of God.

When in Zephaniah the Lord speaks, "I will take away out of the midst of thee them that rejoice in thy pride, and thou shalt no more be haughty because of my holy mountain. I will also leave in the midst of thee an afflicted and poor people, and they shall trust in the name of the Lord" (Zephaniah 3:11, 12), does He not plainly show who are the humble—viz. those who lie afflicted by knowledge of their poverty? On the contrary, He describes the proud as rejoicing (*exultantes*), such being the mode in which men usually express their delight in prosperity. To the humble, whom He designs to save, He leaves nothing but hope in the Lord.

Thus, also, in Isaiah, "To this man will I look, even to him that is poor and of a contrite spirit, and trembleth at my word" (Isaiah 66:2). Again, "Thus saith the high and lofty One that inhabiteth eternity, whose name is Holy; I dwell in the high and holy place, with him also that is of a contrite and humble spirit, to revive the spirit of the humble, and to revive the heart of the contrite ones" (Isaiah 57:15). By the term *contrition*, which you so often hear, understand a wounded heart, which, humbling the individual to the Earth, allows him not to rise. With such contrition must your heart be wounded, if you would, according to the declaration of God, be exalted with the humble. If this is not your case, you shall be humbled by the mighty hand of God to your shame and disgrace.

7 The parable of the Publican explained.

Our divine Master, not confining himself to words, has by a parable set before us, as in a picture, a representation of true humility. He brings forward a Publican, who standing afar off, and not daring to lift up his eyes to Heaven, smites upon his breast, laments aloud, and exclaims, "God be merciful to me a sinner" (Luke 18:13). Let us not suppose that he gives the signs of a fictitious modesty when he dares not come near or lift up his eyes to Heaven, but smiting upon his breast, confesses himself a sinner, let us know that these are the evidences of his internal feeling. With him, our Lord contrasts the Pharisee, who thanks God, "I am not as other men are, extortioners, unjust, adulterers, or even as this publican. I fast twice in the week, I give tithes of all that I possess." In this public confession, he admits that the righteousness, which he possesses, is the gift of God; but because of his confidence that he is righteous, he departs from the presence of God unaccepted and abominated. The Publican, acknowledging his iniquity, is justified.

Hence, we may see how highly our humility is valued by the Lord: our breast cannot receive His mercy until it is deprived completely of all opinion of its own worth. When such an opinion is entertained, the door of mercy is shut. That there might be no doubt on this matter, the mission on which Christ was sent into the world by His Father was "to preach good tidings to the meek," "to bind up the broken-hearted, to proclaim liberty to the captives, and the opening of the prison to them that are bound; to proclaim the acceptable year of the Lord, and the day of vengeance of our God; to comfort all that mourn; to appoint unto them that mourn in Zion to give unto them beauty for ashes, the oil of joy for mourning, the garment of praise for the spirit of heaviness" (Isaiah 61:1-3). In fulfillment of that mission, the only persons whom He invites to share in His beneficence are the "weary and heavy laden." In another passage He says, " I am not come to call the righteous, but sinners to repentance" (Matthew 11:28; 9:13).

8 Arrogance, security, and self-confidence, must be renounced. General rule, or summary of the above doctrine.

Therefore, if we would make way for the call of Christ, we must put far from us all arrogance and confidence. The former is produced by a foolish persuasion of self-righteousness when a man thinks that he has something in himself, which deservedly recommends him to God; the latter may exist without any confidence in works. For many sinners, intoxicated with the pleasures of vice, think not of the judgment of God. Lying stupefied by a kind of lethargy, they aspire not to the offered mercy. It is not less necessary to shake off torpor of this description than every kind of confidence in ourselves, in order that we may haste to Christ unencumbered, and while hungry and empty be filled with His blessings. Never shall we have sufficient confidence in Him unless utterly distrustful of ourselves; never shall we take courage in Him until we first despond of ourselves; never shall we have full consolation in Him until we cease to have any in ourselves. When we have entirely discarded all self-confidence, and trust solely in the certainty of His goodness, we are fit to apprehend and obtain the grace of God.

"When" (as Augustine says), "forgetting our own merits, we embrace the gifts of Christ, because if He should seek for merits in us we should not obtain His gifts." With this, Bernard admirably accords, comparing the proud who presume in the least on their merits, to unfaithful servants, who wickedly take the merit of a favor merely passing through them, just as if a wall were to boast of producing the ray, which it receives through the window. Not to dwell longer here, let us lay down this short but sure and general rule, that he is prepared to reap the fruits of the divine mercy who has thoroughly emptied himself, I say not of righteousness (he has none), but of a vain and blustering show of righteousness; for to whatever extent any man rests in himself, to the same extent he impedes the beneficence of God.

Chapter 13

TWO THINGS TO BE OBSERVED IN GRATUITOUS JUSTIFICATION

The divisions of this chapter are: I. The glory of God and peace of conscience, both secured by gratuitous justification. An insult to the glory of God to glory in ourselves and seek justification out of Christ, whose righteousness, apprehended by faith, is imputed to all the elect for reconciliation and eternal salvation, sections 1, 2. II. Peace of conscience cannot be obtained in any other way than by gratuitous justification. This is fully proved, section 3-5.

Sections
1. The glory of God remains untarnished, when He alone is acknowledged to be just. This is proved from Scripture.
2. Those who glory in themselves glory against God. Objection. Answer, confirmed by the authority of Paul and Peter.
3. Peace of conscience is obtained by free justification only. Testimony of Solomon, of conscience itself, and the Apostle Paul, who contends that faith is made vain if righteousness comes by the Law.
4. The promise is confirmed by faith in the mercy of Christ. This is confirmed by Augustine and Bernard, is in accordance with what has been above stated, and is illustrated by clear predictions of the prophets.
5. Further demonstration by an apostle. Refutation of a sophism.

1 **The glory of God remains untarnished, when He alone is acknowledged to be just. This is proved from Scripture.**

Here, two ends must be kept especially in view, namely, that the glory of God be maintained unimpaired, and that our consciences, in the view of His tribunal, be secured in peaceful rest and calm tranquility. When the question relates to righteousness, we see how often and how anxiously Scripture exhorts us to give the whole praise of it to God. Accordingly, the apostle testifies that the purpose of the Lord in conferring righteousness upon us in Christ was to demonstrate his own righteousness. The nature of this demonstration he immediately subjoins—viz. "That he might be just, and the justifier of him which believeth in Jesus" (Romans 3:25).

Observe that the righteousness of God is not sufficiently displayed, unless He alone is held to be righteous and freely communicates righteousness to the undeserving. For this reason, it is His will that "Every mouth may be stopped, and all the world may become guilty before God" (Romans 3:19). For so long as a man has anything, however small, to say in his own defense, so long he deducts somewhat from the glory of God. Thus, we are taught in Ezekiel how much we glorify His name by acknowledging our iniquity: "Then shall ye remember your ways and all your doings, wherein ye have been defiled; and ye shall loathe yourselves in your own sight, for all your evils that ye have committed. And ye shall know that I am the Lord, when I have wrought with you for my name's sake, not according to your wicked ways, nor according to your corrupt doings" (Ezekiel 20:43, 44). If part of the true knowledge of God consists in being oppressed by a consciousness of our own iniquity, and in recognizing Him as doing good to those who are unworthy of it, why do we attempt, to our great injury, to steal from the Lord even one particle of the praise of unmerited kindness?

In like manner, when Jeremiah exclaims, "Let not the wise man glory in his wisdom, neither let the mighty man glory in his might, let not the rich man glory in his riches: but let him that glorieth glory" in the Lord (Jeremiah 9:23, 24), does he not intimate that the glory of the Lord is infringed when man glories in himself? To this purpose, indeed, Paul accommodates the words when he says that all the parts of our salvation are treasured up with Christ, that we may glory only in the Lord. (See 1 Corinthians 1:29.) For he intimates, that whosoever imagines he has anything of his own, rebels against God, and obscures His glory.

2 Those who glory in themselves glory against God. Objection. Answer, confirmed by the authority of Paul and Peter.

Thus, indeed, it is: we never truly glory in Him until we have utterly discarded our own glory. Therefore, it must be regarded as a universal proposition, that whoso glories in himself glories against God. Paul, indeed, considers that the whole world is not made subject to God until every ground of glorying has been withdrawn from men. (See Romans 3:19.) Accordingly, Isaiah, when he declares, "In the Lord shall all the seed of Israel be justified," adds, "and shall glory" (Isaiah 45:25), as if he had said that the elect are justified by the Lord, in order that they may glory in Him and in none else. The way in which we are to glory in the Lord He had explained in the preceding verse, "Unto me every knee shall bow, every tongue shall swear;" "Surely, shall one say, in the Lord have I righteousness and strength, even to him shall men come."

Observe, that the thing required is not simple confession, but confession confirmed by an oath, that it might not be imagined that any kind of fictitious humility might suffice. And let no man here allege that he does not glory, when without arrogance he recognizes his own righteousness; such recognition cannot take place without generating confidence, nor such confidence without begetting boasting.

Let us remember, therefore, that in the whole discussion concerning justification the great thing to be attended to is that God's glory be maintained entire and unimpaired, since as the apostle declares, it was in demonstration of His own righteousness that He shed His favor upon us; it was, "That he might be just, and the justifier of him which believeth in Jesus" (Romans 3:26). Hence, in another passage, having said that the Lord conferred salvation upon us, in order that He might show forth the glory of His name (Ephesians 1:6), he afterwards, as if repeating the same thing, adds, "By grace are ye saved through faith; and that not of yourselves: it is the gift of God: not of works, lest any man should boast" (Ephesians 2:8). And Peter, when he reminds us that we are called to the hope of salvation, "That ye should show forth the praises of him who has called you out of darkness into his marvelous light" (1 Peter 2:9), doubtless intends thus to proclaim in the ears of believers only the praises of God, that they may bury in profound silence all arrogance of the flesh. The sum is that man cannot claim a single particle of righteousness to himself, without at the same time detracting from the glory of the divine righteousness.

3 Peace of conscience is obtained by free justification only. The testimony of Solomon, of conscience itself, and the Apostle Paul, who contends that faith is made vain if righteousness comes by the Law.

If we now inquire in what way the conscience can be quieted as in the view of God, we shall find that the only way is by having righteousness bestowed upon us freely by the gift of God. Let us always remember the words of Solomon, "Who can say I have made my heart clean, I am free from my sin?" (Proverbs 20:9). Undoubtedly there is not one man who is not covered with infinite pollutions. Let the most perfect man descend into his own conscience and bring his actions to account, and what will the result be? Will he feel calm and quiescent, as if all matters were well arranged between himself and God; or will he not rather be stung with dire torment, when he sees that the ground of condemnation is within him if his works estimate him? Conscience, when it beholds God, either must have sure peace with His justice, or be beset by the terrors of hell. We gain nothing, therefore, by discoursing about righteousness, unless we hold it to be righteousness that is stable enough to support our souls before the tribunal of God.

When the soul is able to appear intrepidly in the presence of God, and receive His sentence without dismay, then only let us know that we have found a righteousness that is not fictitious. It is not, therefore, without cause that the apostle insists on this matter. I prefer giving it in his words rather than my own: "If they which are of the law be heirs, faith is made void, and the promise made of no effect" (Romans 4:14). He first infers that faith is made void if the promise of righteousness has respect to the merit of our works, or depends on the observance of the Law.

Never could anyone rest securely in it, for never could he feel fully assured that he had fully satisfied the Law, and it is certain that no man ever fully satisfied it by works. Not to go far for proof of this, everyone who will use his eyes aright may be his own witness. Hence, it appears how deep and dark the abyss is into which hypocrisy plunges the minds of men, when they indulge so securely as without hesitation to oppose their flattery to the judgment of God, as if they were relieving him from his office as judge.

Very different is the anxiety which fills the breasts of believers, who sincerely examine themselves. Every mind, therefore, would first begin to hesitate and at length to despair, while each determined for itself with how great a load of debt it was still oppressed, and how far it was from coming up to the enjoined condition. Thus, then, faith would be oppressed and extinguished. To have faith is not to fluctuate, to vary, to be carried up and down, to hesitate, remain in suspense, vacillate, in fine, to despair; it is to possess sure certainty and complete security of mind, to have whereon to rest and fix your foot.

4 The promise is confirmed by faith in the mercy of Christ. This is confirmed by Augustine and Bernard, is in accordance with what has been above stated, and is illustrated by clear predictions of the prophets.

Paul, moreover, adds that the promise itself would be rendered null and void. For, if its fulfillment depends on our merits when pray, will we be able to come the length of meriting the favor of God? Nay, the second clause is a consequence of the former, since the promise will not be fulfilled unless to those who put faith in it. Faith, therefore failing, no power will remain in the promise. "Therefore it is of faith, that it might be by grace, to the end the promise might be sure to all the seed" (Romans 4:16). It was abundantly confirmed when made to rest on the mercy of God alone, for mercy and truth are united by an indissoluble tie; that is, whatever God has mercifully promised he faithfully performs. Thus, David, before he asks for salvation according to the Word of God, first places the source of it in His mercy. "Let, I pray thee, thy merciful kindness be for my comfort, according to thy word unto thy servant" (Psalm 119:76). And justly, for nothing but mere mercy induces God to promise. Here, then, we must place, and firmly fix our whole hope, paying no respect to our works, and asking no assistance from them.

And lest you should suppose that there is anything novel in what I say, Augustine also enjoins us so to act. "Christ," says he, "will reign forever among His servants. This God has promised, God has spoken; if this is not enough, God has sworn. Therefore, as the promise stands firm, not in respect of our merits, but in respect of his mercy, no one ought to tremble in announcing that of which he cannot doubt." Thus Bernard also, "Who can be saved? Ask the disciples of Christ." He replies, "With men it is impossible, but not with God."

This is our whole confidence, this is our only consolation, this is the whole ground of our hope, but being assured of the possibility, what are we to say as to his willingness? Who knows whether he is deserving of love or hatred? (See Ecclesiastes 9:1.) "Who has known the mind of the Lord that he may instruct him?" (1 Corinthians

21:16). Here it is plain; faith must come to our aid. Here we must have the assistance of truth in order that the secret purpose of the Father regarding us may be revealed by the Spirit, and the Spirit testifying may persuade our hearts that we are the sons of God.

But let Him persuade by calling and justifying freely by faith; in these there is a kind of transition from eternal predestination to future glory." Let us thus briefly conclude: Scripture indicates that the promises of God are not surer unless they are apprehended with full assurance of conscience; it declares that wherever there is doubt or uncertainty, the promises are made void; on the other hand, that they can only waver and fluctuate if they depend on our works. Therefore, either our righteousness must perish, or without any consideration of our works, place must be given to faith alone, whose nature it is to prick up the ear, and shut the eye; that is, to be intent on the promise only, to give up all ideas of any dignity or merit in man. Thus is fulfilled the celebrated prophecy of Zechariah: "I will remove the iniquity of that land in one day. In that day, saith the Lord of hosts, shall ye call every man his neighbor under the vine, and under the fig-tree" (Zechariah 3:9, 10). Here the prophet intimates that the only way in which believers can enjoy true peace, is by obtaining the remission of their sins.

For we must attend to this peculiarity in the prophets, that when they discourse on the Kingdom of Christ, they set forth the external mercies of God as types of spiritual blessings. Hence, Christ is called *the Prince of Peace, and our peace*, (Isaiah 9:6; Ephesians 2:14), because He calms all the agitations of conscience. If the method is asked, we must come to the sacrifice by which God was appeased, for no man will ever cease to tremble, until he holds that God is propitiated solely by that expiation in which Christ endured His anger. In short, peace must be sought nowhere but in the agonies of Christ our Redeemer.

5 Further demonstration by an apostle. The refutation of a sophism.

But why employ a more obscure testimony? Paul uniformly declares that the conscience can have no peace or quiet joy until it is held that we are justified by faith. And he at the same time declares whence this certainty is derived—viz. when "the love of God is shed abroad in our hearts by the Holy Ghost" (Romans

5:5); as if he had said that our souls cannot have peace until we are fully assured that we are pleasing to God. Hence, he elsewhere exclaims in the person of believers in general, "Who shall separate us from the love of Christ?" (Romans 8:35). Until we have reached that haven, the slightest breeze will make us tremble, but so long as the Lord is our Shepherd, we shall walk without fear in the valley of the shadow of death. (See Psalms 23.) Thus those who pretend that justification by faith consists in being regenerated and made just by living spiritually, have never tasted the sweetness of grace in trusting that God will be propitious.

Hence, also, they know no more of praying aright than do the Turks or any other heathen people. For, as Paul declares, faith is not true, unless it suggests and dictates the delightful name of Father; nay, unless it open our mouths and enable us to cry freely, "Abba, Father." This he expresses more clearly in another passage, "In whom we have boldness and access with confidence by the faith of him" (Ephesians 3:12). This, certainly, is not obtained by the gift of regeneration, which, as it is always defective in the present state, contains within it many grounds of doubt. Wherefore, we must have recourse to this remedy; we must hold that the only hope which believers have of the heavenly inheritance is, that being grafted into the Body of Christ, they are justified freely. For, in regard to justification, faith is merely passive, bringing nothing of our own to procure the favor of God, but receiving from Christ everything we want.

Chapter 14

THE BEGINNING OF JUSTIFICATION. IN WHAT SENSE IT IS PROGRESSIVE

To illustrate what has been already said, and show what kind of righteousness man can have during the whole course of his life, mankind is divided into four classes. I. First class considered, sections 1-6. II. Second and third classes considered together, sections 7, 8. III. Fourth class considered, section 9 to end.

Sections

1. Men are either idolatrous, profane, hypocritical, or regenerate. Idolaters are void of righteousness, full of unrighteousness, and hence in the sight of God altogether wretched and undone.

2. Still here is a great difference in the characters of men. This difference is manifested. A. In the gifts of God. B. In the distinction between honorable and base. C. In the blessings of the present life.

3. All human virtue, no matter how praiseworthy it may appear, is corrupted. A. By impurity of heart. B. By the absence of a proper nature.

4. By the want of Christ, without whom there is no life.

5. The natural condition of man as described by Scripture. All men are dead in sins before regeneration.

6. Passages of Scripture to this effect. Vulgar error confounding the righteousness of works with the redemption purchased by Christ.

7. The second and third classes of men, comprehending hypocrites and Christians in name only. Every action of theirs deserves condemnation. Passage from Haggai. Objection. Answer.

8. Other passages. Quotations from Augustine and Gregory.

9. The fourth class—viz. the regenerate. Though guided by the Spirit, corruption adheres to all they do, especially when brought to the bar of God.

10. *One fault sufficient to efface all former righteousness. Hence, they cannot possibly be justified by works.*

11. *In addition to the two former arguments, a third is adduced against the Sophists, to show that whatever be the works of the regenerate, they are justified solely by faith and the free imputation of Christ's righteousness.*

12. *Sophism of the Schoolmen in opposition to the above doctrine. Answer.*

13. *Answer explained. Refutation of the fiction of partial righteousness and compensation by works of supererogation. This fiction necessarily falls with that of satisfaction.*

14. *Statement of our Savior—viz. that after we have done all, we are still unprofitable servants.*

15. *Objection founded on Paul's boasting. Answer, showing the apostle's meaning. Other answers, stating the general doctrine out of Chrysostom. Third answer, showing that supererogation is the merest vanity.*

16. *Fourth answer, showing how Scripture dissuades us from all confidence in works. Fifth answer, showing that we have no grounds for boasting.*

17. *Sixth answer, showing, in regard to four different classes, that works have no part in procuring our salvation. A. The efficient cause is the free love of the Father. B. The material cause is Christ acquiring righteousness for us. C. The instrumental cause is faith. D. The final cause is the display of the divine justice and praise of the divine goodness.*

18. *A second objection, founded on the glorying of saints. An answer, explaining these modes of expression. How the saints feel in regard to the certainty of salvation. The opinion they have of their own works as in the sight of God.*

19. *Another answer—viz. that the elect, by this kind of glorying, refer only to their adoption by the Father as proved by the fruits of their calling. The order of this glorying. Its foundation, structure, and parts.*

20. *Conclusion. The saints neither attribute anything to the merits of works nor derogate in any degree from the righteousness which they obtain in Christ. Confirmation from a passage of Augustine, in*

which he gives two reasons why no believer will presume to boast before God of his works.

21. A third objection—viz. that the good works of believers are the causes of divine blessings. Answer. There are inferior causes, but these depend on free justification, which is the only true cause why God blesses us. These modes of expression designate the order of sequence rather than the cause.

1 Men are either idolatrous, profane, hypocritical, or regenerate. Idolaters are void of righteousness, full of unrighteousness, and hence in the sight of God altogether wretched and undone.

In further illustration of the subject, let us consider what kind of righteousness man can have during the whole course of his life, and for this purpose let us make a fourfold division. Mankind, either endued with no knowledge of God, is sunk in idolatry; or, initiated in the sacraments, but by the impurity of their lives denying Him whom they confess with their mouths, are Christians in name only; or they are hypocrites, who with empty glosses hide the iniquity of the heart; or they are regenerated by the Spirit of God, and aspire to true holiness. In the first place, when men are judged by their natural endowments, not an iota of good will be found from the crown of the head to the sole of the foot, unless we are to charge Scripture with falsehood, when it describes all the sons of Adam by such terms as these: "The heart is deceitful above all things, and desperately wicked." "The imagination of man's heart is evil from his youth." "The Lord knoweth the thoughts of man that they are vanity." "They are all gone aside: they are altogether become filthy; there is none that does good, no, not one." In short, that they are *flesh,* under which name are comprehended all those works which are enumerated by Paul: adultery, fornication, uncleanness, lasciviousness, idolatry, witchcraft, hatred, variance, emulation, wrath, strife, seditions, heresies, envy, murders, drunkenness, revelry, and all kinds of pollution and abominations which it is possible to imagine. Such, then, is the worth on which men are to plume themselves. But if any among them possess an integrity of manners, which presents some semblance of sanctity among men, yet because we know that God regards not the outward appearance, we must penetrate to the very source of action, if we would see how far works avail for righteousness. We must, I say, look within, and see from what affection of the heart these works proceed. This is a very wide field of discussion, but as the matter may be explained in few words, I will use as much brevity as I can.

2 Still a great difference in the characters of men. This difference is manifested. A. In the gifts of God. B. In the distinction between honorable and base. C. In the blessings of the present life.

First, then, I deny not that whatever excellent endowments appear in unbelievers are divine gifts. Nor do I set myself so much in opposition to common sense, as to contend that there was no difference between the justice, moderation, and equity of Titus and Trojan, and the rage, intemperance, and cruelty of Caligula, Nero, and Domitian; between the continence of Vespasian, and the obscene lusts of Tiberius; and (not to dwell on single virtues and vices) between the observance of law and justice and the contempt of them. So great is the difference between justice and injustice that it may be seen even where the former is only a lifeless image. For what order would remain in the world if we were to confound them?

Hence, this distinction between honorable and base actions God has not only engraved on the minds of each, but also often confirms in the administration of His providence. For we see how He visits those who cultivate virtue with many temporal blessings. Not that that external image of virtue in the least degree merits His favor, but He is pleased thus to show how much He delights in true righteousness, since He does not leave even the outward semblance of it to go unrewarded. Hence, it follows, as we lately observed, that those virtues, or rather images of virtues of whatever kind, are divine gifts, since there is nothing in any degree praiseworthy which proceeds not from Him.

3 All human virtue, how no matter how praiseworthy it may appear, is corrupted. A. By impurity of heart. B. By the absence of a proper nature.

Still the observation of Augustine is true, that all who are strangers to the true God, however excellent they may be deemed on account of their virtues, are more deserving of punishment than of reward, because, by the pollution of their hearts, they contaminate the pure gifts of God. For though they are instruments of God to preserve human society by justice, continence, friendship, temperance, fortitude, and prudence, yet they execute these good works of God in the worst manner, because they are kept from acting ill, not by a sincere love of goodness, but merely by ambition or self-love or some other sinister affection. Seeing, then, that these actions are polluted as in their very source, by impurity of heart, they have no better title to be classed among virtues than vices, which impose upon us by their affinity or resemblance to virtue. In short, when we remember that the object at which righteousness always aims is the service of God, whatever is of a different tendency deservedly forfeits the name. Hence, as they have no regard to the end, which the divine wisdom prescribes, although from the performance the act seems good, yet from the perverse motive it is sin. Augustine, therefore, concludes that all the Fabriciuses, the Scipios, and Catos, in their illustrious deeds, sinned in, that, wanting the light of faith, they did not refer them to the proper end, and that, therefore, there was no true righteousness in them, because duties are estimated not by acts but by motives.

4 By the want of Christ, without whom there is no life.

Besides, if it is true, as John says, that there is no life without the Son of God (see 1 John 5:12), those who have no part in Christ, whoever they be, whatever they do or devise, are hastening on, during their whole career, to destruction and the judgment of eternal death. For this reason, Augustine says, "Our religion distinguishes the righteous from the wicked, by the law, not of works but of faith, without which works which seem good are converted into sins." He finely expresses the same idea in another passage, when he compares the zeal of such men to those who in a race mistake the course. He who is off the course, the more swiftly he runs is the more distant from the goal and, therefore, the more unhappy. It is better to limp in the way than run out of the way.

Lastly, as there is no sanctification without union with Christ, it is evident that they are bad trees which are beautiful and fair to look upon, and may even produce fruit sweet to the taste, but are still very far from good. Hence, we easily perceive that everything which man thinks, designs, and performs, before he is reconciled to

God by faith, is cursed, and not only of no avail for justification, but merits certain damnation. In addition, why do we talk of this as if it were doubtful, when it has already been proved by the testimony of an apostle, that "Without faith it is impossible to please God?" (Hebrews 11:6).

5 The natural condition of man as it is described by Scripture. All men are dead in sins before regeneration.

But the proof will be still clearer if divine grace is set in opposition to the natural condition of man. For Scripture everywhere proclaims that God finds nothing in man to induce Him to show kindness, but that He prevents Him by free liberality. What can a dead man do to obtain life? But when He enlightens us with the knowledge of himself, He is said to raise us from the dead and make us new creatures. (See John 5:25.) On this ground we see that the kindness of God toward us is often commended, especially by the apostle: "God," says he, "who is rich in mercy, for his great love wherewith he loved us, even when we were dead in sins, has quickened us together with Christ" (Ephesians 2:4). In another passage, when treating of the general call of believers under the type of Abraham, he says, "God quickeneth the dead, and calleth those things which be not as though they were" (Romans 4:17).

If we are nothing, what, pray, can we do? Wherefore, in the Book of Job the Lord sternly represses all arrogance in these words, "Who has prevented me, that I should repay him? Whatsoever is under the whole heaven is mine" (Job 41:11). Paul explaining this sentence, applies it in this way, "Let us not imagine that we bring to the Lord anything but the mere disgrace of want and destitution (Romans 11:35). Wherefore, in the passage above quoted, to prove that we attain to the hope of salvation, not by works but only by grace, he affirms that "we are his workmanship, created in Christ Jesus unto good works, which God has before ordained that we should walk in them" (Ephesians 2:10); it is as if he had said, Who of us can boast of having challenged God by his righteousness, seeing our first power to act aright is derived from regeneration? For, as we are formed by nature, sooner shall oil be extracted from stone than good works from us."

It is truly strange how man, convicted of such ignomiy, dares still to claim anything as his own. Let us acknowledge, therefore, with that chosen vessel, that God "...has called us with an holy calling, not according to our works, but according to his own purpose and grace;" and "...that the kindness and love of God our Savior toward men appeared not by works of righteousness which we have done, but according to his mercy he saved us"; that being justified by his grace, we might become the heirs of everlasting life. (See 2 Timothy 1:9; Titus 3:4, 5.) By this confession we strip man of every particle of righteousness, until by mere mercy he is regenerated unto the hope of eternal life, since it is not true to say we are justified by grace, if works contribute in any degree to our justification. The apostle undoubtedly had not forgotten himself in declaring that justification is gratuitous, seeing he argues in another place, that if works are of any avail, "Grace is no more grace" (Romans 11:6). And what else does our Lord mean, when He declares, "I am not come to call the righteous, but sinners to repentance?" (Matthew 9:13). If sinners alone are admitted, why do we seek admission by means of fictitious righteousness?

6 Passages of Scripture to this effect. Vulgar error confounding the righteousness of works with the redemption purchased by Christ.

The thought is always recurring to me, that I am in danger of insulting the mercy of God by laboring with so much anxiety to maintain it, as if it were doubtful or obscure. Such, however, is our malignity in refusing to concede to God what belongs to Him until most strongly urged that I am obliged to insist at greater length. But as Scripture is clear enough on this subject, I shall contend in its words rather than my own. Isaiah, after describing the universal destruction of the human race, finely subjoins the method of restitution. "The Lord saw it, and it displeased him that there was no judgment. And he saw that there was no man, and wondered that there was no intercessor: therefore his arm brought salvation unto him; and his righteousness, it sustained him" (Isaiah 59:15, 16). Where is our righteousness, if the prophet says truly, that no man in recovering salvation gives any assistance to the Lord?

Thus another prophet, introducing the Lord as treating concerning the reconciliation of sinners, says, "I will betroth thee unto me forever; yea, I will betroth thee unto me in righteousness, and in judgment, and in loving-kindness, and in mercies." "I will have mercy upon her that had not obtained mercy" (Hosea 2:19, 23). If a covenant of this kind, evidently forming our first union with God, depends on mercy, there is no foundation left for our righteousness. And, indeed, I would fain know, from those who pretend that man meets God with some righteousness of works, whether they imagine there is any kind of righteousness, save that which is acceptable to Him. If it were insane to think so, can anything agreeable to God proceed from His enemies, whom He abominates with all their deeds? Truth declares that we are all the avowed and inveterate enemies of God until we are justified and admitted to his friendship. (See Romans 5:5; Colossians 1:21.) If justification is the beginning of love, how can the righteousness of works precede it?

Hence, John, to put down the arrogant idea, carefully reminds us that God first loved us. (See 1 John 4:10.) The Lord had formerly taught the same thing by his Prophet: "I will love them freely: for mine anger is turned away from him" (Hosea 14:4). Assuredly, works do not influence Him if His love turns to us spontaneously. But the rude and vulgar idea entertained is, that we did not merit the interposition of Christ for our redemption, but that we are aided by our works in obtaining possession of it. On the contrary, though we may be redeemed by Christ, still, until we are engrafted into union with him by the calling of the Father, we are darkness, the heirs of death, and the enemies of God. For Paul declares that we are not purged and washed from our impurities by the blood of Christ until the Spirit accomplishes that cleansing in us. (See 1 Corinthians 6:11.)

Peter, intending to say the same thing, declares that the sanctification of the Spirit avails "unto obedience and sprinkling of the blood of Jesus Christ" (1 Peter 1:2). If the sprinkling of the blood of Christ by the Spirit gives us purification, let us not think that, before this sprinkling, we are anything but sinners without Christ. Let us, therefore, hold it as certain, that the beginning of our salvation is a resurrection from death unto life, because, when it is given us on behalf of Christ to believe on him (Philippians 1:29), then only do we begin to pass from death unto life.

7 **The second and third classes of men, comprehending hypocrites and Christians in name only. Every action of theirs deserves condemnation. Passage from Haggai. Objection. Answer.**

Under this head the second and third class of men noted in the above division is comprehended. Impurity of conscience proves that yet the Spirit of God regenerates neither of these classes. And, again, their not being regenerated proves their want of faith. Whence it is clear that they are not yet reconciled, not yet justified, since it is only by faith that these blessings are obtained. What can sinners, alienated from God, produce save that which is abominable in His sight? Such, however, is the stupid confidence entertained by all the wicked, and especially by hypocrites, that however conscious that their whole heart teems with impurity, they yet deem any spurious works which they may perform as worthy of the approbation of God.

Hence, the pernicious consequence that, though convicted of wicked and impious minds, they cannot be induced to confess that they are devoid of righteousness. Even acknowledging themselves to be unrighteous, because they cannot deny it, they yet arrogate to themselves some degree of righteousness. This vanity the Lord admirably refutes by the prophet: "Ask now the priests concerning the law, saying, If one bear holy flesh in the skirt of his garment, and with his skirt do touch bread, or pottage, or wine, or oil, or any meat, shall it be holy? And the priests answered and said, No. Then said Haggai, If one that is unclean by a dead body touches any of these, shall it be unclean? And the priests answered and said, It shall be unclean. Then answered Haggai, and said, So is this people, and so is this nation before me, saith the Lord; and so is every work of their hands; and that which they offer there is unclean" (Haggai 2:11-14).

I wish these sentiments could obtain full credit with us, and be deeply fixed on our memories. For there is no man, however wicked the whole tenor of his life may be, who will allow himself to be convinced of what the Lord here so clearly declares. As soon as any person, even the most wicked, has performed some one duty of the Law, he hesitates not to impute it to himself for righteousness; but the Lord declares that no degree of holiness is thereby acquired, unless the heart has previously been made pure. And not contented with this, he declares that all the works performed by sinners are contaminated by impurity of heart. Let us cease then to give the name of righteousness to works, which the mouth of the Lord condemns as polluted. How well is this shown by that elegant similitude? It might be objected, that what the Lord has commanded is inviolably holy. But He, on the contrary, replies that it is not strange that those things which are sanctified in the Law are contaminated by the impurity of the wicked, the unclean hand profaning that which is sacred by handling it.

8 Other passages. Quotations from Augustine and Gregory.

The same argument is admirably followed out by Isaiah: "Bring no more vain oblations; incense is an abomination unto me; the new moons and Sabbaths, the calling of assemblies, I cannot away with; it is iniquity, even the solemn meeting. Your new moons and your appointed feasts my foul hateth: they are a trouble unto me; I am weary to bear them. And when ye spread forth your hands I will hide mine eyes from you; yea, when ye make many prayers, I will not hear: your hands are full of blood. Wash you, make you clean; put away the evil of your doings from before mine eyes" (Isaiah 1:13-16, compared with chapter 58). What is meant by the Lord thus nauseating the observance of His law? Nay, indeed, He does not repudiate anything relating to the genuine observance of the law, the beginning of which is as He uniformly declares the sincere fear of his name. When this is wanting, all the services which are offered to Him, are not only nugatory but also vile and abominable.

Let hypocrites now go, and while keeping depravity wrapped up in their hearts, study to lay God under obligation by their works. In this way, they will only offend Him increasingly. "The sacrifice of the wicked is an abomination to the Lord; but the prayer of the upright is his delight" (Proverbs 15:8). We hold it, therefore, as indubitable, indeed it should be notorious to all tolerably verdant with Scriptures that the most splendid works performed by men, who are not yet truly sanctified, are so far from being righteousness in the sight of the Lord, that He regards them as sins. And, therefore, it is taught with perfect truth, that no man procures favor with God by means of works, but that, on the contrary, works are not pleasing to God unless the person has previously found favor in His sight. Here we should carefully observe the order which Scripture sets before us.

Moses says, "The Lord had respect unto Abel and to his offering" (Genesis 4:4). Observe how he says that the Lord was propitious (had respect) to Abel, before He had respect to his works. Wherefore, purification of heart ought to precede, in order that God may graciously accept the works performed by us: for the saying of Jeremiah is always true, "O Lord, are not thine eyes upon the truth?" (Jeremiah 5:3). Moreover, the Holy Spirit declared by the mouth of Peter, that it is by faith alone that the heart is purified. (See Acts 15:9.) Hence, it is evident that the primary foundation is in true and living faith.

9 The fourth class—viz. the regenerate. Though guided by the Spirit, corruption adheres to all they do, especially when brought to the bar of God.

Let us now see what kind of righteousness belongs to those persons whom we have placed in the fourth class. We admit that when God reconciles us to himself by the intervention of the righteousness of Christ, and bestowing upon us the free pardon of sins regards us as righteous, His goodness is at the same time conjoined with mercy, so that he dwells in us by means of His Holy Spirit, by whose agency the lusts of our flesh are every day more and more mortified while we ourselves are sanctified; that is consecrated to the Lord for true purity of life, our hearts being trained to the obedience of the Law. It thus becomes our leading desire to obey His will, and in all things advance His glory only. Still, however while we walk in the ways of the Lord, under the guidance of the Holy Spirit, lest we should become unduly elated, and forget ourselves, we still have remains of imperfection which serve to keep us humble: "There is no man that sinneth not," saith Scripture (1 Kings 8:46). What righteousness, then, can men obtain by their works?

First, I say that the best thing which can be produced by them is always tainted and corrupted by the impurity of the flesh and has some mixture of dross in it. Let the holy servant of God, I say, select from the whole course of his life the action which he deems most excellent, and let him ponder it in all its parts; he will doubtless find in it something that savors of the rottenness of the flesh, since our alacrity in well-doing is never what it ought to be, but our course is always retarded by much weakness. Although we see theft the stains by which the works of the righteous are blemished, are by no means unapparent, still, granting that they are the minutest possible, will they give no offense to the eye of God, before which even the stars are not clean? We thus see that even saints cannot perform one work, which, if judged on its own merits, is not deserving of condemnation.

10 One fault is sufficient to efface all former righteousness. Hence, they cannot possibly be justified by works.

Even were it possible for us to perform works absolutely pure, yet one sin is sufficient to efface and extinguish all remembrance of former righteousness, as the prophet says. (See Ezekiel 18:24.)

With this James agrees, "Whosoever shall keep the whole law, and yet offend in one point, is guilty of all" (James 2:10). And since this mortal life is never entirely free from the taint of sin, whatever righteousness we could acquire would always be corrupted, overwhelmed, and destroyed by subsequent sins, so that it could not stand the scrutiny of God, or be imputed to us for righteousness. In short, whenever we treat of the righteousness of works, we must look not to the legal work but to the command. Therefore, when the Law seeks righteousness, it is in vain to produce one or two single works; we must show an uninterrupted obedience. God does not (as many foolishly imagine) impute that forgiveness of sins once for all, as righteousness; so that having obtained the pardon of our past life we may afterwards seek righteousness in the Law. This was only to mock and delude us by the entertainment of false hopes. For since perfection is altogether unattainable by us, so long as we are clothed with flesh, and the Law denounces death and judgment against all who have not yielded a perfect righteousness, there will always be grounds to accuse and convict us unless the mercy of God interposes, and always absolves us by the constant remission of sins. Wherefore the statement, which we set out, is always true, if we are estimated by our own worthiness, in everything that we think or devise, with all our studies and endeavors, we deserve death and destruction.

11 In addition to the two former arguments, a third adduced against the Sophists, to show that whatever be the works of the regenerate, they are justified solely by faith and the free imputation of Christ's righteousness.

We must strongly insist on these two things: That no believer ever performed one work which, if tested by the strict judgment of God, could escape condemnation; and, moreover, that were this granted to be possible (though it is not), yet the act being vitiated and polluted by the sins of which it is certain that the author of it is guilty, it is deprived of its merit. This is the cardinal point of the present discussion. There is no controversy between us and the sounder Schoolmen as to the beginning of justification. They admit that the sinner, freely delivered from condemnation, obtains justification, and that by forgiveness of sins; but under the term justification they comprehend the renovation by which the Spirit forms us anew to the obedience of the Law; and in describing the righteousness of the regenerate man, maintain that being once reconciled to God by means of Christ, he is afterwards deemed righteous by his good works, and is accepted in consideration of them.

The Lord, on the contrary, declares that he imputed Abraham's faith for righteousness (see Romans 4:3), not at the time when he was still a worshipper of idols, but after he had been many years distinguished for holiness. Abraham had long served God with a pure heart, and performed that obedience of the Law, which a mortal man is able to perform: yet his righteousness still consisted in faith.

Hence, we infer, according to the reasoning of Paul, that it was *not of works*. In like manner when the prophet says, "The just shall live by his faith" (Habakkuk 2:4), he is not speaking of the wicked and profane, whom the Lord justifies by converting them to the faith: his discourse is directed to believers, and life is promised to them by faith. Paul also removes every doubt, when in confirmation of this sentiment he quotes the words of David, "Blessed is he whose transgression is forgiven, whose sin is covered" (Psalm 32:1). It is certain that David is not speaking of the ungodly but of believers such as he was, because he was giving utterance to the feelings of his own mind. Therefore, we must have this blessedness not once only, but must hold it fast during our whole lives.

Moreover, the message of free reconciliation with God is not promulgated for one or two days, but is declared perpetual in the Church. (See 2 Corinthians 5:18, 19.) Hence, believers have not even to the end of life any other righteousness than that which is there described. Christ ever remains a Mediator to reconcile the Father to us, and there is a perpetual efficacy in His death—viz. ablution, satisfaction, and expiation; in short, perfect obedience, by which all our iniquities are covered. In the Epistle to the Ephesians, Paul says not that the beginning of salvation is of grace but, "by grace are ye saved, ...not of works, lest any man should boast" (Ephesians 2:8, 9).

12 Sophism of the Schoolmen in opposition to the above doctrine. Answer.

The subterfuges by which the Schoolmen here endeavor to escape will not disentangle them. They say that good works are not of such intrinsic worth as to be sufficient to procure justification, but it is owing to accepting grace that they have this effect. Then because they are forced to confess that here the righteousness of works is always imperfect, they grant that so long as we are in this life we stand in need of the forgiveness of sin in order to supply the deficiency of works, but that the faults which are committed are compensated by works of supererogation. I answer that the grace which they call accepting, is nothing else than the free goodness with which the Father embraces us in Christ when He clothes us with the innocence of Christ and accepts it as ours, so that in consideration of it He regards us as holy, pure, and innocent. For the righteousness of Christ (as it alone is perfect, so it alone can stand the scrutiny of God) must be given to us, and as a surety represent us judicially. Provided with this righteousness, we constantly obtain the remission of sins through faith. Our imperfection and impurity, covered with this purity, are not imputed but are buried, so as not to come under judgment until the hour arrives when the old man is destroyed and is plainly extinguished in us, the divine goodness shall receive us into beatific peace with the new Adam, there to await the day of the Lord, on which, being clothed with incorruptible bodies, we shall be translated to the glory of the heavenly kingdom.

13 Answer explained. Refutation of the fiction of partial righteousness, and compensation by works of supererogation. This fiction necessarily falls with that of satisfaction.

If these things are so, it is certain that our works cannot in themselves make us agreeable and acceptable to God, and even cannot please God, except insofar as being covered with the righteousness of Christ, we thereby please Him and obtain forgiveness of sins. God has not promised life as the reward of certain works, but only declares, "Which if a man do, he shall live in them" (Leviticus 18:5), denouncing the well-known curse against all who do not continue in all things that are written in the Book of the Law to do them. In this way the fiction of a partial righteousness is completely refuted, the only righteousness acknowledged in Heaven being the perfect observance of the Law. There is nothing more solid in their dogma of compensation by means of works of supererogation. For must they not always return to the proposition, which has already been disproved—viz. that he who observes the Law in part is so far justified by works? This, which no man of sound judgment will concede to them, they are not ashamed to take for granted. The Lord having so often declared that He recognizes no justification by works unless they be works by which the Law is perfectly fulfilled, how perverse is it, while we are devoid of such works, to endeavor to secure some ground of glorying to ourselves; that is not to yield it entirely to God, by boasting of some kind of fragments of works, and trying to supply the deficiency by other satisfactions? Satisfactions have already been so completely disposed of that we ought never again even to dream of them.

Here all I say is that those who thus trifle with sin do not at all consider how execrable it is in the sight of God; if they did, they would assuredly understand that all the righteousness of men collected into one heap would be inadequate to compensate for a single sin. For we see that by one sin man was so cast off and forsaken by God, that he at the same time lost all power of recovering salvation. He was, therefore, deprived of the power of giving satisfaction. Those who flatter themselves with this idea will never satisfy God, who cannot possibly accept or be pleased with anything that proceeds from his enemies. But all to whom He imputes sin are enemies, and, therefore, our sins must be covered and forgiven before the Lord will have respect to any of our works. From this it follows that the forgiveness of sins is gratuitous, and those who introduce the idea of satisfaction wickedly insult this forgiveness. Let us, therefore, follow the example of the apostle, "Forgetting those things which are behind, and reaching forth unto those things which are before, I press toward the mark for the prize of the high calling of God in Jesus Christ" (Philippians 3:13, 14).

14 Statement of our Savior—viz. that after we have done all, we are still unprofitable servants.

How can boasting in works of supererogation agree with the command that has been given to us: "When ye shall have done all those things which are commanded you, say, We are unprofitable servants: we have done that which was our duty to do?" (Luke 17:10). To say or speak in the presence of God is not to feign or lie, but to declare what we hold as certain. Our Lord, therefore, enjoins us sincerely to feel and consider with ourselves that we do not perform gratuitous duties, but pay Him service which is due. And truly. For the obligations of service under which we lie are so numerous that we cannot discharge them though all our thoughts and members were devoted to the observance of the Law; and, therefore, when He says,

"When ye shall have done all those things which are commanded you," it is just as if He had said that all the righteousness of men would not amount to one of these things. Seeing, then, that everyone is very far distant from that goal, how can we presume to boast of having accumulated more than is due? It cannot be objected that a person, though failing in some measure in what is necessary, may yet in intention go beyond what is necessary. For it must ever be held that in whatever pertains to the worship of God, or to charity, nothing can ever be thought of that is not comprehended under the Law. But if it is part of the Law, let us not boast of voluntary liberality in matters of necessary obligation.

15 Objection founded on Paul's boasting. Answer, showing the Apostle's meaning. Other answers, stating the general doctrine out of Chrysostom. Third answer, showing that supererogation is the merest vanity.

On this subject, they ceaselessly allege the boast of Paul, that among the Corinthians he spontaneously renounced a right which, if he had otherwise chosen, he might have exercised. (See 1 Corinthians 9:15.) Thus, not only paying what he owed them in duty, but gratuitously bestowing upon them more than duty required. They ought to have attended to the reason there expressed, that his object was to avoid giving offense to the weak. For wicked and deceitful workmen employed this pretense of kindness that they might procure favor for their pernicious dogmas, and excite hatred against the gospel, so that it was necessary for Paul either to peril the doctrine of Christ, or to thwart their schemes.

Now, if it is a matter of indifference to a Christian whether or not he cause a scandal when it is in his power to avoid it, then I admit that the apostle performed a work of supererogation to his Master; but if the thing which he did was justly required in a prudent minister of the gospel, then I say he did what he was bound to do. In short, even when no such reason appears, yet the saying of Chrysostom is always true, that everything, which we have is held on the same condition as the private property of slaves; it is always due to our Master. Christ does not disguise this in the parable, for He asks in regard to the master who, on return from his labor, requires his servant to gird himself and serve him, "Does he thank that servant because he did the things that were commanded him? I trow not"

(Luke 17:9). But possibly the servant was more industrious than the master would have ventured to exact. Be it so; still, he did nothing to which his condition as a servant did not bind him, because his utmost ability is his master's. I say nothing as to the kind of supererogation on which these men would plume themselves before God. They are frivolities, which he never commanded, which he approves not, and will not accept when they come to give in their account. The only sense in which we admit works of supererogation is that expressed by the prophet when he says, "Who has required this at your hand?" (Isaiah 1:12). But let them remember what is elsewhere said of them: "Wherefore do ye spend money for that which is not bread? and your labor for that which satisfieth not?" (Isaiah 55:2).

It is, indeed, an easy matter for these indolent rabbis to carry on such discussions while sitting in their soft chairs under the shade, but when the supreme Judge shall sit on His tribunal, all these blustering dogmas will behave to disappear. This I say was the true question: not what we can fable and talk in schools and corners, but what ground of defense we can produce at His judgment-seat.

16 Fourth answer, showing how Scripture dissuades us from all confidence in works. Fifth answer, showing that we have no ground of boasting.

In this matter, the minds of men must be especially guarded against two pestiferous dogmas—viz. against putting any confidence in the righteousness of works or ascribing any glory to them. From all such confidence the Scriptures uniformly dissuade us when they declare that our righteousness is offensive in the sight of God unless it derives a sweet odor from the purity of Christs that it can have no other effect than to excite the divine vengeance unless sustained by His indulgent mercy. Accordingly, the only thing they leave to us is to deprecate our Judge with that confession of David: "Enter not into judgment with thy servant: for in thy sight shall no living be justified" (Psalm 143:2). And when Job says, "If I be wicked, woe unto me: and if I be righteous, yet will I not lift up my head" (Job 10:15). Although he refers to that spotless righteousness of God, before which even angels are not clean, he, however shows, that when brought to the bar of God's judgement all that mortals can do is to stand dumb. He does not merely mean that he chooses rather to give way spontaneously than to risk a contest with the divine severity, but that he was not conscious of possessing any righteousness that would not fall the very first moment it was brought into the presence of God.

Confidence being banished, all glorying must necessarily cease. For who can attribute any merit of righteousness to works, which instead of giving confidence, only make us tremble in the presence of God? We must, therefore, come to what Isaiah invites us: "In the Lord shall all the seed of Israel be justified, and shall glory" (Isaiah 45:25); for it is most true, as he elsewhere says, that we are, "The planting of the Lord, that he might be glorified" (Isaiah 61:3). Our soul, therefore, will not be duly purified until it ceases to have any confidence, or feel any exultation in works. Foolish men are puffed up to this false and lying confidence by the erroneous idea that the cause of their salvation is found in works.

17 Sixth answer, showing, in regard to four different classes, that works have no part in procuring our salvation. A. The efficient cause is the free love of the Father. B. The material cause is Christ acquiring righteousness for us. C. The instrumental cause is faith. D. The final cause the display of the divine justice and praise of the divine goodness.

But if we attend to the four kinds of causes, which philosophers bring under our view in regard to effects, we shall find that not one of them is applicable to works as a cause of salvation. The efficient cause of our eternal salvation the Scripture uniformly proclaims to be the mercy and free love of the heavenly Father towards us; the material cause to be Christ, with the obedience by which He purchased righteousness for us and what can the formal or instrumental cause be but faith? John includes the three-in-one sentence when he says, "God so loved the world, that he gave his only begotten Son, that whosoever believeth in him should not perish but have everlasting life" (John 3:16).

The apostle, moreover, declares that the final cause is the demonstration of the divine righteousness and the praise of His goodness. There also he distinctly mentions the other three causes, for he thus speaks to the Romans: "All have sinned, and come short of the glory of God, being justified freely by his grace" (Romans 3:23, 24). You have here the head and primary source—God has embraced us with free mercy. The next words are, "Through the redemption that is in Christ Jesus." This is the material cause by which righteousness is procured for us. "Whom God has set forth to be a propitiation through faith." Faith is thus the instrumental cause by which righteousness is applied to us. He lastly subjoins the final cause when he says, "To declare at this time his righteousness; that he might be just, and the justifier of him that believeth in Jesus." And to show, by the way, that this righteousness consists in reconciliation, he says that Christ was "...set forth to be a propitiation." Thus, also, in the Epistle to the Ephesians, he tells us that we are received into the favor of God by mere mercy; that this is done by the intervention of Christ; that it is apprehended by faith; the end of all being that the glory of the divine goodness may be fully displayed.

When we see that all the parts of our salvation thus exist without us, what ground can we have for glorying or confiding in our works? As to neither the efficient nor the final cause can the most sworn enemies of divine grace raise any controversy with us unless they would abjure the whole of Scripture. In regard to the material or formal cause they make a gloss, as if they held that our works divide the merit with faith and the righteousness of Christ. But here also Scripture reclaims, simply affirming that Christ is both righteousness and life, and that the blessing of justification is possessed by faith alone.

18 A second objection is founded on the glorying of saints. An answer, explaining these modes of expression. How the saints feel in regard to the certainty of salvation. The opinion they have of their own works as in the sight of God.

When the saints repeatedly confirm and console themselves with the remembrance of their innocence and integrity, and sometimes even abstain not from proclaiming them, it is done in two ways: either because by comparing their good cause with the bad cause of the ungodly, they thence feel secure of victory, not so much from commendation of their own righteousness, as from the just and merited condemnation of their adversaries; or because, reviewing themselves before God, even without any comparison with others, the purity of their conscience gives them some comfort and security.

The former reason will afterwards be considered (chapter 17, section 14, and chapter 20, section 10); let us now briefly show, in regard to the latter, how it accords with what we have above said, that we can have no confidence in works before the bar of God, that we cannot glory in any opinion of their worth. The accordance lies here, that when the point considered is the constitution and foundation of salvation, believers, without paying any respect to works, direct their eyes to the goodness of God alone. Nor do they turn to it only in the first instance, as to the commencement of blessedness, but rest in it as the completion. Conscience being thus founded, built up, and established, is further established by the consideration of works, inasmuch as they are proofs of God dwelling and reigning in us. Since, then, this confidence in works has no place unless you have previously fixed your whole confidence on the mercy of God, it should not seem contrary to that on which it depends. Wherefore, when we exclude confidence in works, we merely mean that the Christian mind must not turn back to the merit of works as an aid to salvation, but must dwell entirely on the free promise of justification.

But we forbid no believer to confirm and support this faith by the signs of the divine favor towards him. For if when we call to mind the gifts which God has bestowed upon us, they are like rays of the divine countenance, by which we are enabled to behold the highest light of His goodness; much more is this the case with the gift of good works, which shows that we have received the Spirit of adoption.

19 Another answer—viz. that the elect, by this kind of glorying, refer only to their adoption by the Father as proved by the fruits of their calling. The order of this glorying. Its foundation, structure, and parts.

When believers, therefore, feel their faith is strengthened by a consciousness of integrity and entertain sentiments of exultation, it is just because the fruits of their calling convince them that the Lord has admitted them to a place among His children. Accordingly, when Solomon says, "In the fear of the Lord is strong confidence" (Proverbs 14:26), and when the saints sometimes beseech the Lord to hear them, because they walked before His face in simplicity and integrity (Genesis 24:10; 2 Kings 20:3), these expressions apply not to laying the foundation of a firm conscience, but are of force only when taken *a posteriori*. For there is no where such a fear of God as can give full security, and the saints are always conscious that any integrity which they may possess is mingled with many remains of the flesh. But as the fruits of regeneration furnish them with a proof of the Holy Spirit dwelling in them, experiencing God to be a Father in a matter of so much moment, they are strengthened in no slight degree to wait for His assistance in all their necessities. Even this they could not do, had they not previously perceived that the goodness of God is sealed to them by nothing but the certainty of the promise. Should they begin to estimate it by their good works, nothing will be weaker or more uncertain; works, when estimated by themselves, no less proving the divine displeasure by their imperfection than His goodwill by their incipient purity.

In short, while proclaiming the mercies of the Lord, they never lose sight of His free favor, with all its "…breadth and length, and depth and height," testified by Paul (see Ephesians 3:18); as if he had said, "Whithersoever the believer turns, however loftily he climbs, however far and wide his thoughts extend, he must not go further than the love of Christ, but must be wholly occupied in meditating upon it, as including in itself all dimensions. Accordingly, he declares that it "passeth knowledge," that "to know the love of Christ" is to "be filled with all the fullness of God" (Ephesians 3:19). In another passage, where he glories that believers are victorious in every contest, he adds the reason, "Through him that loved us" (Romans 8:37).

20 Conclusion. The saints neither attribute anything to the merits of works, nor derogate in any degree from the righteousness which they obtain in Christ. Confirmation from a passage of Augustine, in which he gives two reasons why no believer will presume to boast before God of his works.

We now see that believers have no such confidence in works as to attribute any merit to them (since they regard them only as divine gifts, in which they recognize His goodness, and signs of calling, in which they discern their election); nor such confidence as to derogate in any respect from the free righteousness of Christ; since on this it depends and without this cannot subsist. The same thing is briefly but elegantly expressed by Augustine when he says, "I do not say to the Lord, Despise not the works of my hands; I have sought the Lord with my hands, and have not been deceived. But I commend not the works of my hands, for I fear that when thou examinest them thou wilt find more faults than merits. This only I say, this asks this desire, Despise not the works of thy hands. See in me thy work, not mine. If thou seest mine, thou condemnest; if thou seest thine own, thou crownest. Whatever good works I have are of thee." He gives two reasons for not venturing to boast of his works before God: first, that if he has any good works, he does not see in them anything of his own; and, secondly, that these works are overwhelmed by a multitude of sins. Whence it is, that the conscience derives from them more fear and alarm than security. Therefore, the only way in which he desires God to look at any work, which he may have done aright, is that he may therein see the grace of his calling, and perfect the work, which he has begun.

21 A third objection—viz. that the good works of believers are the causes of divine blessings. Answer. There are inferior causes, but these depend on free justification, which is the only true cause why God blesses us. These modes of expression designate the order of sequence rather than the cause.

Moreover, when the Scripture intimates that the good works of believers are causes as to why the Lord does them good, we must still understand the meaning so as to hold unshaken what has previously been said—viz. that the efficient cause of our salvation is placed in the love of God the Father; the material cause in the obedience of the Son; the instrumental cause in the illumination of the Spirit, that is, in faith; and the final cause in the praise of the divine goodness. In this, however, there is nothing to prevent the Lord from embracing works as inferior causes. But how so? In this way: Those whom in mercy He has destined for the inheritance of eternal life, He, in His ordinary administration, introduces to the possession of it by means of good works. What precedes in the order of administration is called the cause of what follows. For this reason, he sometimes makes eternal life a consequent of works; not because it is to be ascribed to them, but because those whom He has elected He justifies, that He may at length glorify (Romans 8:30); He makes the prior grace to be a kind of cause, because it is a kind of step to that which follows. But whenever the true cause is to be assigned, he enjoins us not to take refuge in works, but to keep our thoughts entirely fixed on the mercy of God "The wages of sin is death; but the gift of God is eternal life" (Romans 6:23). Why, as He contrasts life with death, does He not also contrast righteousness with sin? Why, when setting down sin as the cause of death, does He not also set down righteousness as the cause of life? The antithesis which would otherwise be complete is somewhat marred by this variation; but the apostle employed the comparison to express the fact that death is due to the deserts of men, but that life was treasured up solely in the mercy of God.

In short, by these expressions, the order rather than the cause is noted. The Lord, adding grace to grace, takes occasion from a former to add a subsequent, so that He may omit no means of enriching His servants. Still, in following out His liberality, He would have us always look to free election as its source and beginning. For although He loves the gifts which He daily bestows upon us, inasmuch as they proceed from that fountain, still our duty is to hold fast by that gratuitous acceptance, which alone can support our souls; and so to connect the gifts of the Spirit, which He afterwards bestows, with their primary cause, as in no degree to detract from it.

Chapter 15

THE BOASTED MERIT OF WORKS SUBVERSIVE BOTH OF THE GLORY OF GOD IN BESTOWING RIGHTEOUSNESS AND OF THE CERTAINTY OF SALVATION

The divisions of this chapter are: I. To the doctrine of free justification is opposed the question, Whether or not works merit favor with God, section 1. This question answered, sections 2 and 3. II. An exposition of certain passages of Scripture produced in support of the erroneous doctrine of merit, sections 4 and 5. III. Sophisms of Semipelagian Schoolmen refuted, sections 6 and 7. IV. Conclusion, proving the sufficiency of the orthodox doctrine, section 8.

Sections

1. After a brief recapitulation, the question of Whether or not good works merit favor with God is considered.

2. First answer, fixing the meaning of the term "Merit." This term is improperly applied to works, but it is used in a good sense, as by Augustine, Chrysostom, Bernard.

3. A second answer to the question. First by a negative, then by a concession. In the rewarding of works what is to be attributed to God and what is to be attributed to man. Why good works please God and are advantageous to those who do them. The ingratitude of seeking righteousness by works. This is shown by a double similitude.

4. First objection taken from Ecclesiasticus. Second objection from the Epistle to the Hebrews. Two answers to both objections. A weak distinction is refuted.

5. A third and most complete answer, calling us back to Christ as the only foundation of salvation. How Christ is our righteousness. Whence it is manifest that we have all things in Christ and He has nothing in us.

6. *We must abhor the sophistry which destroys the merit of Christ, in order to establish that of man. This impiety is refuted by clear passages of Scripture.*

7. *Errors, of the younger Sophists extracted from Lombard. Refuted by Augustine. Also refuted by Scripture.*

8. *Conclusion, showing that the foundation which has been laid is sufficient for doctrine, exhortation, and comfort. Summary of the orthodox doctrine of justification.*

1 After a brief recapitulation, the question of whether or not good works merit favor with God is considered.

The principal point in this subject has been now explained Justification, if dependent upon works, cannot possibly stand in the sight of God therefore, it must depend solely on the mercy of God and communion with Christ, and, therefore, on faith alone. But let us carefully attend to the point on which the whole subject hinges, lest we are entangled in the common delusion, not only of the vulgar, but also of the learned. For the moment the question is raised as to the justification by faith or works; they run off to those passages, which seem to ascribe some merit to works in the sight of God, just as if justification by works were proved whenever it is proved that works have any value with God. Above, we have clearly shown that justification by works consists only in a perfect and absolute fulfillment of the Law, and that, therefore, no man is justified by works unless he has reached the summit of perfection, and cannot be convicted of even the smallest transgression. But there is another and a separate question: Though works by no means suffice to justify, do they not merit favor with God?

2 First answer, fixing the meaning of the term "merit." This term is improperly applied to works, but it is used in a good sense, as by Augustine, Chrysostom, Bernard.

First, I must premise with regard to the term "merit," that he, whoever he was, that first applied it to human works, viewed in reference to the divine tribunal, consulted very ill for the purity of the faith. I willingly abstain from disputes about words, but I could wish that Christian writers had always observed this soberness—that when there was no occasion for it, they had never thought of using terms that are foreign to the Scriptures—terms which might produce much offense, but very little fruit.

I ask what need was there to introduce the word "merit," when the value of works might have been fully expressed by another term, and without offense? The quantity of offense contained in it the word shows to its great loss. It is certain that, being a high-sounding term, it can only obscure the grace of God, and inspire men with pernicious pride. I admit that ancient ecclesiastical writers used it, and I wish they had not by the abuse of one term furnished posterity with matter for heresy, although in some passages they themselves show that they had no wish to injure the truth.

For Augustine says, "Let human merits, which perished by Adam, here be silent, and let the grace of God reign by Jesus Christ." Again, "The saints ascribe nothing to their merits; everything will they ascribe solely to thy mercy, O God." Again, "And when a man sees that whatever good he has he has not of himself, but of his God, he sees that everything in him which is praised is not of his own merits, but of the divine mercy." Do you see how he denies man the power of acting aright and thus lays merit prostrate? Chrysostom says, "If any works of ours follow the free calling of God, they are return and debt; but the gifts of God are grace and beneficence, and great liberality." But to say nothing more of the name, let us attend to the thing.

I formerly quoted a passage from Bernard: "As it is sufficient for merit not to presume on merit, so to be without merit is sufficient for condemnation." He immediately adds an explanation which softens the harshness of the expression, when he says, "Hence, be careful to have merits; when you have them, know that they were given; hope for fruit from the divine mercy, and you have escaped all the perils of poverty, ingratitude, and presumption. Happy the Church which neither wants merit without presumption, nor presumption without merit." A little before he had abundantly shown that he used the words in a sound sense, saying, "Why is the Church anxious about merits? God has furnished her with a firmer and surer ground of boasting. God cannot deny himself; He will do what He has promised. Thus, there is no reason for asking by what merits may we hope for blessings; especially when you hear, 'Thus saith the Lord God; I do not this for your sakes, O house of Israel, but for mine holy name's sake' (Ezekiel 36:22). It suffices for merit to know that merits suffice not."

3 A second answer to the question. First by a negative, then by a concession. In the rewarding of works what is to be attributed to God, and what is to be attributed to man. Why good works please God and are advantageous to those who do them. The ingratitude of seeking righteousness by works. This is shown by a double similitude.

What all our works can merit Scripture shows when it declares that they cannot stand the view of God, because they are full of impurity; it next shows what the perfect observance of the Law (if it can anywhere be found) will merit when it enjoins, "So likewise ye, when ye shall have done all those things which are commanded you, say, We are unprofitable servants, we have done that which was our duty to do" (Luke 17:10); because we make no free offering to God, but only perform due service by which no favor is deserved. Yet, those good works, which the Lord has bestowed upon us, He counts as ours also, and declares that they are not only acceptable to Him, but that He will recompense them. It is ours in return to be animated by this great promise, and to keep up our courage, that we may not grow weary in well doing, but feel duly grateful for the great kindness of God.

There cannot be a doubt that everything in our works which deserves praise is owing to divine grace, and that there is not a particle of it which we can properly ascribe to ourselves. If we truly and seriously acknowledge this, not only confidence, but also every idea of merit vanishes. I say we do not, like the Sophists, share the praise of works between God and man, but we keep it entire and unimpaired for the Lord. All we assign to man is that by his impurity he pollutes and contaminates the very works which were good. Some stain always pollutes the most perfect thing, which proceeds from man. Should the Lord, therefore, bring to judgment the best of human works, He would indeed behold His own righteousness in them; but He would also behold man's dishonor and disgrace. Thus, good works please God and are not without fruit to their authors, since, by way of recompense, they obtain more ample blessings from God, not because they so deserve, but because the divine benignity is pleased of itself to set this value upon them. Such, however, is our malignity, that not contented with this liberality on the part of God, which bestows rewards on works that do not deserve them at all, we with profane ambition maintain that that which is entirely due to the divine munificence is paid to the merit of works.

Here I appeal to every man's common sense. If one, who by another's liberality, possesses the usufruct of a field, rear up a claim to the property of it, does he not by his ingratitude, deserve to lose the possession formerly granted? In like manner, if a slave, who has been manumitted, conceals his humble condition of freedman, and gives out that he was freeborn, does he not deserve to be reduced to his original slavery? A benefit can only be legitimately enjoyed when we neither arrogate more to ourselves than has been given, nor defraud the author of it his due praise; nay, rather, when we so conduct ourselves as to make it appear that the benefit conferred still in a manner resides with him who conferred it. But if this is the moderation to be observed towards men, let everyone reflect and consider for himself what is due to God.

4 First objection taken from Ecclesiasticus. Second objection from the Epistle to the Hebrews. Two answers to both objections. A weak distinction is refuted.

I know that the Sophists abuse some passages in order to prove that the Scriptures use the term *merit* with reference to God. They quote a passage from Ecclesiasticus: "Mercy will give place to every man according to the merit of his works" (Ecclesiasticus 16:14); and from the Epistle to the Hebrews: "To do good and communicate forget not; for with such sacrifices God is well pleased" (Hebrews 13:16). I now renounce my right to repudiate the authority of Ecclesiasticus; but I deny that the words of Ecclesiasticus, whoever the writer may have been, are faithfully quoted. The Greek translates as follows: "He will make room for all mercy: for each shall find according to his works." That this is the genuine reading, and has been corrupted in the Latin version, is plain, both from the very structure of the sentence and from the previous context.

In the Epistle to the Hebrews there is no room for their quibbling on one little word, for in the Greek the apostle simply says that *such sacrifices are pleasing* and acceptable to God. This alone should amply suffice to quell and beat down the insolence of our pride, and prevent us from attaching value to works beyond the rule of Scripture. It is the doctrine of Scripture, moreover, that our good works are constantly covered with numerous stains by which God is justly offended and made angry against us, so far are they from being able to conciliate Him, and call forth His favor towards us;

and yet because of His indulgence, He does not examine them with the utmost strictness; He accepts them just as if they were most pure and, therefore, rewards them, though undeserving, with innumerable blessings, both present and future.

For I admit not the distinction laid down by otherwise learned and pious men, that good works merit the favors which are conferred upon us in this life, whereas eternal life is the reward of faith only. The recompense of our toils, and crown of our contest, our Lord almost uniformly places in Heaven. On the other hand, to attribute to the merit of works, to deny it to grace, that we are loaded with other gifts from the Lord, is contrary to the doctrine of Scripture. For though Christ says, "Unto everyone that has shall be given;" "thou hast been faithful over a few things, I will make thee ruler over many things" (Matthew 25:29, 21), He, at the same time, shows that all additional gifts to believers are of His free benignity: "Ho, everyone that thirsteth, come ye to the waters, and he that has no money, come ye, buy, and eat: yea, come, buy wine and milk, without money and without price" (Isaiah 55:1). Therefore, every help to salvation bestowed upon believers, and blessedness itself, are entirely the gifts of God, and yet in both the Lord testifies that He takes account of works, since to manifest the greatness of His love toward us, He thus highly honors not ourselves only, but the gifts, which He has bestowed upon us.

5 A third and most complete answer, calling us back to Christ as the only foundation of salvation. How Christ is our righteousness. Whence it is manifest that we have all things in Christ and He has nothing in us.

Had these points been duly handled and digested in past ages, never could so many tumults and dissensions have arisen. Paul says that in the architecture of Christian doctrine, it is necessary to retain the foundation which he had laid with the Corinthians, "Other foundation can no man lay than that which is laid, which is Jesus Christ" (1 Corinthians 3:11). What, then, is our foundation in Christ? Is it that He begins salvation and leaves us to complete it? Is it that He only opened up the way and left us to follow it in our own strength? By no means, but as Paul had a little before declared, it is to acknowledge that He has been given us for righteousness. No man, therefore, is well-founded in Christ who has not entire righteousness in Him, since the apostle says not that He was sent to assist us in procuring, but was himself to be our righteousness.

Thus, it is said that God "has chosen us in him before the foundation of the world," not according to our merit, but "according to the good pleasure of his will;" that in Him, "We have redemption through His blood, even the forgiveness of sins;" that peace has been made "through the blood of his cross;" that we are reconciled by his blood; that, placed under His protection, we are delivered from the danger of finally perishing; that thus engrafted into Him we are made partakers of eternal life and hope for admission into the Kingdom of God. Nor is this all. Being admitted to participation in Him, though we are still foolish, He is our wisdom; though we are still sinners, He is our righteousness; though we are unclean, He is our purity; though we are weak, unarmed, and exposed to Satan, yet ours is the power which has been given Him in heaven and in Earth, to bruise Satan under our feet and burst the gates of hell (Matthew 28:18); though we still bear about with us a body of death, He is our life; in short, all things of His are ours, we have all things in Him, and he has nothing in us. On this foundation, I say, we must be built, if we would grow up into a holy temple in the Lord.

6 We must abhor the sophistry, which destroys the merit of Christ, in order to establish that of man. This impiety is refuted by clear passages of Scripture.

For a long time the world has been taught very differently. A kind of good works called *moral* has been found out, by which men are rendered agreeable to God before they are engrafted into Christ; as if Scripture spoke falsely when it says, "He that has the Son has life, and he that has not the Son of God has not life" (1 John 5:12). How can they produce the materials of life if they are dead? Is there no meaning in it being said that "Whatsoever is not of faith is sin?" (Romans 14:23); or can good fruit be produced from a bad tree? What have these most pestilential Sophists left to Christ on which to exert His virtue? They say that He merited for us the first grace, that is, the occasion of meriting, and that it is our part not to let slip the occasion thus offered. Oh, the daring effrontery of impiety! Who would have thought that men professing the name of Christ would thus strip Him of his power and all but trample Him under foot? The testimony uniformly borne to Him in Scripture is that whosoever believes in Him is justified; the doctrine of these men is that the only benefit which proceeds from Him is to open up a way for each to justify himself. I wish they could get a taste of what is meant by these passages: "He that hath the Son hath life." "He that heareth my word, and believeth in him that sent me is passed from death unto life." Whosoever believeth in Him "is passed from death unto life." "Being justified freely by his grace, through the redemption that is in Christ Jesus." "He that keepeth his commandments dwelleth in him, and he in him." God "has raised us up together, and made us sit together in heavenly places in Christ." "Who has delivered us from the power of darkness, and has translated us into the kingdom of his dear Son."

There are similar passages without number. Their meaning is not, that by faith in Christ an opportunity is given us of procuring justifications or acquiring salvation, but that both are given us. Hence, as soon as you are engrafted into Christ by faith, you are made a son of God, an heir of Heaven, a partaker of righteousness, a possessor of life, and (the better to manifest the false tenets of these men) you have not obtained an opportunity of meriting, but all the merits of Christ, since they are communicated to you.

7 Errors of the younger Sophists extracted from Lombard. Refuted by Augustine. Also by Scripture.

I n this way, the schools of Sorbonne, the parents of all heresies, have deprived us of justification by faith, which lies at the root of all godliness. They confess, indeed, that men are justified by a formed faith, but they afterwards explain this to mean that of faith they have good works which avail to justification, so that they almost seem to use the term faith in mockery, because they were unable, without incurring great obloquy, to pass it in silence, seeing it is so often repeated by Scripture. Yet, not contented with this, they, by the praise of good works, transfer to man what they steal from God. And seeing that good works give little ground for exultation, and are not even properly called merits, if they are regarded as the fruits of divine grace, they derive them from the power of freewill; in other words they extract oil out of stone. They deny not that the principal cause is in grace, but they contend that there is no exclusion of free will through which all merit comes. This is the doctrine not only of the later Sophists, but of Lombard, their Pythagoras, who, in comparison with them, may be called sound and sober. It was surely strange blindness while he had the words of Augustine so often in his mouth, not to see how cautiously he guarded against ascribing a single particle of praise to man because of good works.

Above, when treating of freewill, we quoted some passages from him to this effect and similar passages frequently occur in his writings, as when he forbids us ever to boast of our merits, because they themselves also are the gifts of God, and when he says that all our merits are only of grace, are not provided by our sufficiency, but are entirely the production of grace, etc.

It is less strange that Lombard was blind to the light of Scripture, in which it is obvious that he had not been a very successful student. Still, there cannot be a stronger declaration against him and his disciples than the words of the apostles, who, after interdicting all Christians from glorying, subjoin the reason that glorying is unlawful: "For we are his workmanship, created in Christ Jesus unto good works, which God has before ordained that we should walk in them" (Ephesians 2:10). Seeing, then, that no good proceeds from us unless insofar as we are regenerated—and our regeneration is without exception wholly of God—there is no ground for claiming for ourselves one iota in good works.

Lastly, while these men constantly inculcate good works, they, at the same time, train the conscience in such a way as to prevent it from venturing to confide that works will render God favorable and propitious. We, on the contrary, without any mention of merit, give singular comfort to believers when we teach them that in their works they please, and doubtless are accepted of God. Nay, here we even insist that no man shall attempt or enter upon any work without faith, that is, unless he previously had a firm conviction that it will please God.

8 Conclusion, showing that the foundation, which has been laid, is sufficient for doctrine, exhortation, and comfort. Summary of the orthodox doctrine of justification.

Wherefore, let us never on any account allow ourselves to be drawn away one nail's breadth from that only foundation. After it is laid, wise architects build upon it rightly and in order. For whether there is need of doctrine or exhortation, they remind us that "...for this purpose the Son of God was manifested, that he might destroy the works of the devil;" that "whosoever is born of God does not commit sin;" that "the time past of our life may suffice us to have wrought the will of the Gentiles;" that the elect of God are vessels of mercy, appointed "to honor," purged, "sanctified, and meet for the Master's use, and prepared unto every good work." The whole is expressed at once, when Christ thus describes His disciples, "If any man will come after me, let him deny himself, and take up his cross daily, and follow me." He who has denied himself has cut off the root of all evils so as no longer to seek his own; he who has taken up his cross has prepared himself for all meekness and endurance.

The example of Christ includes this and all offices of piety and holiness. He obeyed his Father even unto death; His whole life was spent in doing the works of God; His whole soul was intent on the glory of his Father; He laid down His life for the brethren; He did good to His enemies, and He prayed for them. And when there is need of comfort, it is admirably afforded in these words: "We are troubled on every side, yet not distressed; we are perplexed, but not in despair; persecuted but not forsaken; cast down, but not destroyed; always bearing about in the body the dying of the Lord Jesus, that the life also of Jesus might be made manifest in our body." "For if we be dead with him we shall also live with him; if we suffer, we shall also reign with him;" by means of "the fellowship of his sufferings, being made conformable unto his death;" the Father having predestinated us "to be conformed to the image of his Son, that he might be the first-born among many brethren."

Hence it is that "Neither death, nor life, nor angels, nor principalities, nor powers, nor things present, nor things to come, nor height, nor depth, nor any other creature, shall be able to separate us from the love of God which is in Christ Jesus our Lord;" nay, rather all things will work together for our good. See how it is that we do not justify men before God by works, but say that all who are of God are regenerated and made new creatures, so that they pass from the kingdom of sin into the kingdom of righteousness. In this way they make their calling sure, and, like trees, are judged by their fruits.

Chapter 16

REFUTATION OF THE CALUMNIES BY WHICH IT IS ATTEMPTED TO THROW ODIUM ON THIS DOCTRINE

The divisions of this chapter are: I. The calumnies of the papists against the orthodox doctrine of justification by faith are reduced to two classes. The first class, with its consequences is refuted, sections 1-3. II. The second class, which is dependent on the first, refuted in the last section.

Sections

1. Calumnies of the papists. That we destroy good works and give encouragement to sin. Refutation of the first calumny. A. Character of those who censure us. B. Justification by faith establishes the necessity of good works.

2. Refutation of a consequent of the former calumny—viz. that men are dissuaded from well-doing when we destroy merit. Two modes of refutation. First mode confirmed by many invincible arguments.

3. The apostles make no mention of merit, when they exhort us to good works. On the contrary, excluding merit, they refer us entirely to the mercy of God. Another mode of refutation.

4. Refutation of the second calumny and of an inference from it,—viz. that obtaining righteousness is made too easy when it is made to consist in the free remission of sins.

1 Calumnies of the papists. That we destroy good works, and give encouragement to sin. Refutation of the first calumny. A. Character of those who censure us. B. Justification by faith establishes the necessity of good works.

Our last sentence may refute the impudent calumny of certain ungodly men, who charge us, first, with destroying good works and leading men away from the study of them when we say that men are not justified and do not merit salvation by works; and, secondly, with making the means of justification too easy, when we say that it consists in the free remission of sins, and thus alluring men to sin to which they are already too much inclined. These calumnies, I say, are sufficiently refuted by that one sentence; however, I will briefly reply to both. The allegation is that justification by faith destroys good works.

I will not describe what kind of zealots for good works the persons are who thus charge us. We leave them as much liberty to bring the charge, as they take license to taint the whole world with the pollution of their lives. They pretend to lament that when faith is so highly extolled, works are deprived of their proper place. But what if they are rather ennobled and established? We dream not of a faith which is devoid of good works, nor of a justification which can exist without them; the only difference is, that while we acknowledge that faith and works are necessarily connected, we, however, place justification in faith, not in works. How this is done is easily explained, if we turn to Christ only, to whom our faith is directed, and from whom it derives all its power. Why, then, are we justified by faith? Because by faith we apprehend the righteousness of Christ, which alone reconciles us to God. This faith, however, you cannot apprehend without at the same time apprehending sanctification, for Christ "...is made unto us wisdom, and righteousness, and sanctification, and redemption" (1 Corinthians 1:30). Christ, therefore, justifies no man without also sanctifying him. A perpetual and inseparable tie conjoins these blessings. Those He enlightens by His wisdom, He redeems; whom He redeems, He justifies; whom He justifies, He sanctifies. But as the question relates only to justification and sanctification, to them let us confine ourselves.

Though we distinguish between them, they are both inseparably comprehended in Christ. Would you, then, obtain justification in Christ? You must previously possess Christ. But you cannot possess Him without being made a partaker of His sanctification: for Christ cannot be divided. Since the Lord, therefore, does not grant us the enjoyment of these blessings without bestowing himself, He bestows both at once, but never the one without the other. Thus, it appears how true it is that we are justified not without, and yet not by works, since in the participation of Christ, by which we are justified, is contained not less sanctification than justification.

2 Refutation of a consequent of the former calumny—viz. that men are dissuaded from well-doing when we destroy merit. Two modes of refutation. First mode confirmed by many invincible arguments.

It is also most untrue that men's minds are withdrawn from the desire of well-doing when we deprive them of the idea of merit. Here, by the way, the reader must be told that those men absurdly infer merit from reward, as I will afterwards more clearly explain. They thus infer, because ignorant of the principle that God gives no less a display of His liberality when He assigns reward to works, than when He bestows the faculty of well-doing. This topic it will be better to defer to its own place. At present, let it be sufficient merely to advert to the weakness of their objection. This may be done in two ways. For, first, they are altogether in error when they say that unless a hope of reward is held forth, no regard will be had to the right conduct of life. For if all that men do when they serve God is to look to the reward and hire out or sell their labor to Him, little is gained; He desires to be freely worshipped, freely loved. I say He approves the worshipper who, even if all hope of reward were cut off, would cease not to worship Him.

Moreover, when men are to be urged, there cannot be a stronger stimulus than that derived from the end of our redemption and calling, such as the Word of God employs when it says that it would be the height of impiety and ingratitude not to "love him who first loved us;" that by "the blood of Christ" our conscience is purged "from dead works to serve the living God;" that it would be impious sacrilege in anyone to count "the blood of the covenant, wherewith he was sanctified, an unholy thing;" that we have been "delivered out of the hands of our enemies," that we "might serve him without fear, in holiness and righteousness before him, all the days of our life;" that being "made free from sin," we "become the servants of righteousness;" "that our old man is crucified with him," in order that we might rise to newness of life. Again, "If ye then be risen with Christ [as becomes his members], seek those things which are above," living as pilgrims in the world and aspiring to Heaven, where our treasure is.

"The grace of God has appeared to all men, bringing salvation, teaching us that, denying ungodliness and worldly lusts, we should live soberly, righteously, and godly in this present world; looking for that blessed hope, and the glorious appearing of the great God and our Savior Jesus Christ." "For God has not appointed us to wrath, but to obtain salvation through our Lord Jesus Christ." "Know ye not that ye are the temples of the Holy Spirit," which it would be impious to profane? "Ye were sometimes darkness, but now are ye light in the Lord: walk as the children of light." "God has not called us unto uncleanness, but unto holiness." "For this is the will of God, even your sanctification, that ye should abstain" from all illicit desires: ours is a "holy calling," and we respond not to it except by purity of life. "Being then made free from sin, ye became the servants of righteousness." Can there be a stronger argument in eliciting us to charity than that of John?

"If God so loved us, we ought also to love one another." "In this the children of God are manifest, and the children of the devil: whosoever does not righteousness is not of God, neither he that loveth not his brother." Similar is the argument of Paul, "Know ye not that your bodies are the members of Christ?" "For as the body is one, and has many members, and all the members of that one body being many, are one body, so also is Christ." Can there be a stronger incentive to holiness than when we are told by John, "Every man that has this hope in him purifieth himself; even as he is pure?" and by Paul, "Having, therefore, these promises, dearly beloved, cleanse yourselves from all filthiness of the flesh and spirit;" or when we hear our Savior hold forth himself as an example to us that we should follow His steps?

3 The apostles make no mention of merit when they exhort us to good works. On the contrary, excluding merit, they refer us entirely to the mercy of God. Another mode of refutation.

I have given these few passages merely as a specimen; were I to go over them all, I should form a large volume. All the apostles abound in exhortations, admonitions, and rebukes, for training the man of God to every good work, and that without any mention of merit. Nay, rather their chief exhortations are founded on the fact, that without any merit of ours, our salvation depends entirely on the mercy of God. Thus Paul, who during a whole epistle had maintained that there was no hope of life for us, save in the righteousness of Christ, when he comes to exhortations beseeches us by the mercy which God has bestowed upon us. (See Romans 12:1.) And, indeed, this one reason ought to have been sufficient, that God may be glorified in us. But if any are not so ardently desirous to promote the glory of God, still the remembrance of His kindness is most sufficient to incite them to do good. But those men, because, by introducing the idea of merit, they perhaps extract some forced and servile obedience of the Law, falsely allege, that as we do not adopt the same course, we have no means of exhorting to good works. As if God were well-pleased with such services when He declares that He loves a cheerful giver and forbids anything to be given Him grudgingly or of necessity. (See 2 Corinthians 9:7.)

I say not that I would reject that or omit any kind of exhortation, which Scripture employs—its object being not to leave any method of animating us untried. For it states that the recompense which God will render to everyone is *according to his deeds*; but, first, I deny that that is the only, or, in many instances, the principal motive; and, secondly, I admit not that it is the motive with which we are to begin.

Moreover, I maintain that it gives not the least countenance to those merits, which these men are always preaching. This will afterwards be seen. Lastly, there is no use in this recompense, unless we have previously embraced the doctrine that we are justified solely by the merits of Christ as apprehended by faith, and not by any merit of works, because only those by whom this doctrine has been previously imbibed can fitly prosecute the study of piety. This is beautifully intimated by the Psalmist when he thus addresses God, "There is forgiveness with thee, that thou mayest be feared" (Psalm 130:4). For he shows that the worship of God cannot exist without acknowledging His mercy, on which it is founded and established. This is specially deserving of notice, as showing us not only that the beginning of the due worship of God is confidence in His mercy; but that the fear of God (which papists will have to be meritorious) cannot be entitled to the name of merit, for this reason, that it is founded on the pardon and remission of sins.

4 Refutation of the second calumny and of an inference from it, viz. that obtaining righteousness is made too easy, when it is made to consist in the free remission of sins.

But the most futile calumny of all is that men are invited to sin when we affirm that the pardon in which we hold that justification consists is gratuitous. Our doctrine is that justification is a thing of such value that it cannot be put into the balance with any good quality of ours; and, therefore, could never be obtained unless it would be gratuitous: moreover, that it is gratuitous to us, but not also to Christ, who paid so dearly for it; namely His own most sacred blood, out of which there was no price of sufficient value to pay what was due to the justice of God. When men are thus taught, they are reminded that it is owing to no merit of theirs that the shedding of that most sacred blood is not repeated every time they sin.

Moreover, we say that our pollution is so great that it can never be washed away, save in the fountain of His pure blood. Must not those who are thus addressed conceive a greater horror of sin than if it were said to be wiped off by a sprinkling of good works? If they have any reverence for God, how can they, after being once purified, avoid shuddering at the thought of again wallowing in the mire, and as much as in them lies, troubling and polluting the purity of this fountain? "I have washed my feet" (says the believing soul in the Song of Solomon 5:3), "how shall I defile them?"

It is now plain which of the two makes the forgiveness of sins of less value, and derogates from the dignity of justification. They pretend that God is appeased by their frivolous satisfactions, in other words, by mere dross. We maintain that the guilt of sin is too heinous to be so frivolously expiated; that the offense is too grave to be forgiven to such valueless satisfactions; and, therefore, that forgiveness is the prerogative of Christ's blood alone. They say that righteousness, wherever it is defective, is renewed and repaired by works of satisfaction. We think it too precious to be balanced by any compensation of works, and, therefore, in order to restore it, recourse must be had solely to the mercy of God. For the other points relating to the forgiveness of sins, see the following chapter.

Chapter 17

THE PROMISES OF THE LAW AND THE GOSPEL RECONCILED

In the following chapter, the arguments of Sophists, who would destroy or impair the doctrine of justification by faith, are reduced to two classes. The former is general, the latter is special, and it contains some arguments peculiar to itself. I. The first class, which is general, and in a manner contains the foundation of all the arguments, draws an argument from the promises of the Law. This is considered from sections 1-3. II. The second class following from the former, and containing special proofs. An argument drawn from the history of Cornelius explained, sections 4, 5. III. A full exposition of those passages of Scripture, which represent God as showing mercy and favor to the cultivators of righteousness, section 6. IV. A third argument from the passages, which distinguish good works by the name of righteousness, and declare that men are justified by them, sections 7, 8. V. The adversaries of justification by faith placed in a dilemma. Their partial righteousness refuted, sections 9, 10. VI. A fourth argument, setting the Apostle James in opposition to Paul considered, sections 11, 12. VII. Answer to a fifth argument, that, according to Paul, not the hearers, but the doors of the Law are justified, section 13. VIII. Consideration of a sixth argument, drawn from those passages in which believers boldly submit their righteousness to the judgment of God and ask Him to decide according to it, section 14. IX. Examination of the last argument, drawn from passages which ascribe righteousness and life to the ways of believers, section 15.

Sections

1. Brief summary of Chapters 15 and 16. Why justification is denied to works. Argument of opponents founded on the promises of the Law. The substance of this argument. Answer. Those who would be justified before God must be exempted from the power of the law. How this is done.

2. Confirmation of the answer ab impossibili, and from the testimony of an Apostle and of David.

3. Answer to the objection, by showing why these promises were given. Refutation of the sophistical distinction between the intrinsic value of works, and their valued parts.

4. Argument from the history of Cornelius. Answer, by distinguishing between two kinds of acceptance. Former kind. Sophistical objection refuted.

5. Latter kind. Plain from this distinction that Cornelius was accepted freely before his good works could be accepted. Similar explanations to be given of the passage in which God is represented as merciful and propitious to the cultivators of righteousness.

6. Exposition of these passages. Necessary to observe whether the promise is legal or evangelical. The legal promise always made under the condition that we "do," the evangelical under the condition that we "believe."

7. Argument from the passages, which distinguish good works by the name of righteousness, and declare that man is justified by them. Answer to the former part of the argument respecting the name. Why the works of the saints are called works of righteousness. Distinction to be observed.

8. Answer to the second part of the argument—viz. that man is justified by works. Works of no avail by themselves; we are justified by faith only. This kind of righteousness defined. Whence the value set on good works.

9. Answer confirmed and fortified by a dilemma.

10. In what sense the partial imperfect righteousness of believers is accepted. Conclusion of the refutation.

11. Argument founded on the Epistle of James. First answer. One apostle cannot be opposed to another. Second answer. Third answer, from the scope of James. A double paralogism in the term "faith." In James, that faith is said not to justify is a mere empty opinion; in Paul, it is the instrument by which we apprehend Christ our righteousness.

12. Another paralogism on the word justify. Paul speaks of the cause, James of the effects, of justification. Sum of the discussion.

13. Argument founded on Romans 2:13. Answer, explaining the apostle's meaning. Another argument, containing a reduction ad impossibili. Why Paul used the argument.

14. An argument founded on the passages in which believers confidently appeal to their righteousness. Answer, founded on a consideration of two circumstances. A. They refer only to a special cause. B. They claim righteousness in comparison with the wicked.

15. Last argument from those passages, which ascribe righteousness and life to the ways of believers. Answer. This proceeds from the paternal kindness of God. What is meant by the perfection of saints.

1 Brief summary of Chapters 15 and 16. Why justification is denied to works. Argument of opponents founded on the promises of the Law. The substance of this argument. Answer. Those who would be justified before God must be exempted from the power of the Law. How this is done.

Let us now consider the other arguments, which Satan by his satellites invents to destroy or impair the doctrine of justification by faith. I think we have already put it out of the power of our calumniators to treat us as if we were the enemies of good works—justification being denied to works not in order that no good works may be done or that those which are done may be denied to be good; but only that we may not trust or glory in them, or ascribe salvation to them. Our only confidence and boasting, our only anchor of salvation is that Christ the Son of God is ours, and that we are in Him sons of God and heirs of the heavenly kingdom, being called, not by our worth, but the kindness of God, to the hope of eternal blessedness. But since, as has been said, they assail us with other engines, let us now proceed to demolish them also.

First, they recur to the legal promises, which the Lord proclaimed to the observers of the Law, and they ask us whether we hold them to be null or effectual. Since it would be absurd and ridiculous to say they are null, they take it for granted that they have some efficacy. Hence, they infer that we are not justified by faith only. For the Lord thus speaks: "Wherefore it shall come to pass, if ye hearken to these judgments, and keep and do them, that the Lord thy God shall keep unto thee the covenant and the mercy which he sware unto thy fathers; and he will love thee, and bless thee and multiply thee" (Deuteronomy 7:12, 13). Again, "If ye thoroughly amend your ways and your doings; if ye thoroughly execute judgment between a man and his neighbor; if ye oppress not the stranger, the fatherless, and the widow, and shed not innocent blood in this place, neither walk after other gods to your hurt: then will I cause you to dwell in this place, in the land that I gave to your fathers, forever and ever" (Jeremiah 7:5-7). It would be to no purpose to quote a thousand similar passages, which, as they are not different in meaning, are to be explained on the same principle. In substance, Moses declares that in the Law is set down "a blessing and a curse," life and death (Deuteronomy 11:26); and hence they argue, either that that blessing is become inactive and unfruitful, or that justification is not by faith only. We have already shown, that if we cleave to the Law we are devoid of every blessing, and have nothing but the curse denounced on all transgressors.

The Lord does not promise anything except to the perfect observers of the Law; and none such are anywhere to be found. The results, therefore, are that the whole human race is convicted by the law, and exposed to the wrath and curse of God: to be saved from this they must escape from the power of the Law and be brought out of bondage into freedom, not that carnal freedom which indisposes us for the observance of the Law, tends to licentiousness, and allows our passions to wanton unrestrained with loosened reins; but that spiritual freedom which consoles and raises up the alarmed and smitten conscience, proclaiming its freedom from the curse and condemnation under which it was formerly held bound. This freedom from subjection to the Law, this manumission, if I may so express it, we obtain when by faith we apprehend the mercy of God in Christ, and are thereby assured of the pardon of sins, with a consciousness of which the Law stung and tortured us.

2 Confirmation of the answer ab impossibili, and from the testimony of an apostle and of David.

For this reason, the promises offered in the Law would all be null and ineffectual, did not God in his goodness send the gospel to our aid, since the condition on which they depend, and under which only they are to be performed—viz. the fulfillment of the law, will never be accomplished. Still, however the aid which the Lord gives consists not in leaving part of justification to be obtained by works, and in supplying part out of His indulgence, but in giving us Christ as in himself alone the fulfillment of righteousness. For the apostle, after premising that he and the other Jews, aware that "a man is not justified by the works of the law," had "believed in Jesus Christ," adds as the reason, not that they might be assisted to make up the sum of righteousness by faith in Christ, but that they "might be justified by the faith of Christ, and not by the works of the law" (Galatians 2:16).

If believers withdraw from the Law to faith, that in the latter they may find the justification, which they see, is not in the former, they certainly disclaim justification by the Law. Therefore, whose will, let him amplify the rewards which are said to await the observer of the Law, provided he at the same time understands, that owing to our depravity, we derive no benefit from them until we have obtained another righteousness by faith. Thus David after making mention of the reward, which the Lord has prepared for His servants (Psalm 25 almost throughout), immediately descends to an acknowledgment of sins, by which the reward is made void. In Psalm 19, also, he loudly extols the benefits of the Law; but immediately exclaims, "Who can understand his errors? Cleanse thou me from secret faults" (Psalm 19:12). This passage perfectly accords with the former, when, after saying, "The paths of the Lord are mercy and truth unto such as keep his covenant and his testimonies," he adds, "For thy name's sake, O Lord, pardon mine iniquity: for it is great" (Psalm 25:10, 11). Thus, too, we ought to acknowledge that the favor of God is offered to us in the Law, provided by our works we could deserve it, but that it never actually reaches us through any such desert.

3 Answer to the objection, by showing why these promises were given. Refutation of the sophistical distinction between the intrinsic value of works, and their value er parts.

What then? Were the promises given that they might vanish away without fruit? I lately declared that this is not my opinion. I say, indeed, that their efficacy does not extend to us so long as they have respect to the merit of works, and, therefore, that, considered in themselves, they are in some sense abolished. Hence, the apostle shows that the celebrated promise, "Ye shall therefore keep my statutes and my judgments: which if a man do, he shall live in them" (Leviticus 18:5; Ezekiel 20:10), will, if we stop at it, be of no avail, and will profit us not a whit more than if it were not given, being inaccessible even to the holiest servants of God, who are all far from fulfilling the Law, being encompassed with many infirmities. But when the gospel promises are substituted, promises which announce the free pardon of sins, the result is not only that our persons are accepted of God, but His favor also is shown to our works, and that not only in respect that the Lord is pleased with them, but also because He visits them with the blessings which were due by agreement to the observance of His law.

I admit, therefore, that the works of the faithful are rewarded with the promises, which God gave in His law to the cultivators of righteousness and holiness; but in this reward, we should always attend to the cause, which procures favor to works. This cause, then, appears to be threefold.

First, God turning His eye away from the works of His servants which merit reproach more than praise, embraces them in Christ, and by the intervention of faith alone reconciles them to himself without the aid of works.

Secondly, the works not being estimated by their own worth, He, by His fatherly kindness and indulgence, honors so far as to give them some degree of value.

Thirdly, He extends His pardon to them, not imputing the imperfection by which they are all polluted, and would deserve to be regarded as vices rather than virtues.

Hence, it appears how much Sophists were deluded in thinking they admirably escaped all absurdities when they said, that works are able to merit salvation, not from their intrinsic worth, but according to agreement, the Lord having, in His liberality, set this high value upon them. But, meanwhile, they observed not how far the works which they insisted on regarding as meritorious must be from fulfilling the condition of the promises, were they not preceded by a justification founded on faith alone and on forgiveness of sins—a forgiveness necessary to cleanse even good works from their stains. Accordingly, of the three causes of divine liberality to which it is owing that good works are accepted, they attended only to one: the other two, though the principal causes, they suppressed.

4 Argument from the history of Cornelius. Answer, by distinguishing between two kinds of acceptance. Former kind. Sophistical objection refuted.

They quote the saying of Peter as given by Luke in the Acts, "Of a truth I perceive that God is no respecter of persons: but in every nation he that feareth him, and worketh righteousness, is accepted with him" (Acts 10:34, 25). Hence, they infer as a thing which seems to them beyond a doubt, that if man by right conduct procures the favor of God, his obtaining salvation is not entirely the gift of God. Nay, that when God in His mercy assists the sinner, he is inclined to mercy by works.

There is no way of reconciling the passages of Scripture, unless you observe that man's acceptance with God is twofold. As man is by nature, God finds nothing in him, which can incline him to mercy, except merely big wretchedness. If it is clear then that man, when God first interposes for him, is naked and destitute of all good, and, on the other hand, loaded and filled with all kinds of evil, for what quality, pray, shall we say that he is worthy of the heavenly kingdom? Where God thus clearly displays free mercy, have done with that empty imagination of merit.

Another passage in the same book—viz. where Cornelius hears from the lips of an angel, "Thy prayer and thine alms are come up for a memorial before God" (Acts 10:4), is miserably wrested to prove that man is prepared by the study of good works to receive the favor of God. Cornelius being endued with true wisdom, in other words, with the fear of God, must have been enlightened by the Spirit of wisdom, and being an observer of righteousness, must have been sanctified by the same Spirit; righteousness being, as the apostle testifies, one of the most certain fruits of the Spirit (Galatians 5:5). Therefore, all those qualities by which he is said to have pleased God he owed to divine grace: so far was he from preparing himself by his own strength to receive it. Indeed, not a syllable of Scripture can be produced which does not accord with the doctrine, that the only reason why God receives man into His favor is because He sees that he is in every respect lost when left to himself; lost, if He does not display His mercy in delivering him. We now see that in thus accepting, God looks not to the righteousness of the individual, but merely manifests the divine goodness towards miserable sinners, who are altogether undeserving of this great mercy.

5 Latter kind. Plain from this distinction that Cornelius was accepted freely before his good works could be accepted. Similar

explanations to be given of the passage in which God is represented as merciful and propitious to the cultivators of righteousness.

But after the Lord has withdrawn the sinner from the abyss of perdition and set him apart for himself by means of adoption, having begotten him again and formed him to newness of life, He embraces him as a new creature, and bestows the gifts of His Spirit. This is the acceptance to which Peter refers, and by which believers, after their calling, are approved by God, even in respect of works. For the Lord cannot but love and delight in the good qualities, which He produces in them by means of His Spirit. But we must always bear in mind, that the only way in which men are accepted of God in respect of works is that whatever good works He has conferred upon those whom He admits to favor, He by an increase of liberality honors with His acceptance. For whence their good works, but just that the Lord, having chosen them as vessels of honor, is pleased to adorn them with true purity? And how are their actions deemed good as if there was no deficiency in them, but just that their merciful Father indulgently pardons the spots and blemishes which adhere to them?

In one word, the only meaning of acceptance in this passage is that God accepts and takes pleasure in His children, in whom He sees the traces and lineaments of His own countenance. We have else here said that regeneration is a renewal of the divine image in us. Since God, therefore, whenever He beholds His own face, justly loves it and holds it in honor, the life of believers, when formed to holiness and justice, is said, not without cause, to be pleasing to Him. But because believers, while encompassed with mortal flesh, are still sinners, and their good works only begun savor of the corruption of the flesh, God cannot be propitious either to their persons or their works, unless He embraces them more in Christ than in themselves. In this way are we to understand the passages in which God declares that He is clement and merciful to the cultivators of righteousness. Moses said to the Israelites, "Know, therefore, that the Lord thy God, he is God, the faithful God, which keepeth covenant and mercy with them that love him and keep his commandments, to a thousand generations."

These words afterwards became a common form of expression among the people. Thus, Solomon in his prayer at the dedication says, "Lord God of Israel, there is no God like thee, in heaven above, or on earth beneath, who keepest covenant and mercy with thy servants that walk before thee with all their heart" (1 Kings 8:23). The same words are repeated by Nehemiah (Nehemiah 1:5). As the Lord in all covenants of mercy stipulates on His part for integrity and holiness of life in His servants (Deuteronomy 29:18), lest His goodness might be held in derision, or anyone, puffed up with exultation in it, might speak flatteringly to his soul while walking in the depravity of his heart, so He is pleased that in this way those whom He admits to communion in the covenant should be kept to their duty.

Still, however, the covenant was gratuitous at first, and such it ever remains. Accordingly, while David declares, "According to the cleanness of my hands has he recompensed me," yet does he not omit the fountain to which I have referred; "He delivered me, because he delighted in me" (2 Samuel 22:20, 21). In commending the goodness of his cause, he derogates in no respect from the free mercy, which takes precedence of all the gifts of which it is the origin.

6 Exposition of these passages. It is necessary to observe whether the promise is legal or evangelical. The legal promise always made under the condition that we "do," the evangelical under the condition that we "believe."

Here, by the way, it is of importance to observe how those forms of expression differ from legal promises. By legal promises, I mean not those which lie scattered in the books of Moses (for there many Evangelical promises occur), but those which properly belong to the legal dispensation. All such promises, by whatever name they may be called, are made under the condition that the reward is to be paid on the things commanded being done. But when it is said that the Lord keeps a covenant of mercy with those who love Him, the words rather demonstrate what kind of servants those are who have sincerely entered into the covenant, than express the reason why the Lord blesses them. The nature of the demonstration is this: As the end for which God bestows upon us the gift of eternal life is, that He may be loved, feared, and worshipped by us, so the end of all the promises of mercy contained in Scripture justly is that we may reverence and serve their Author. Therefore, whenever we hear that he does good to those who observe His law, let us remember that the sons of God are designated by the duty, which they ought perpetually to observe, that His reason for adopting us is that we may reverence Him as a Father.

Hence, if we would not deprive ourselves of the privilege of adoption, we must always strive in the direction of our calling. On the other hand, however, let us remember, that the completion of the divine mercy depends not on the works of believers, but that God himself fulfill the promise of salvation to those who by right conduct correspond to their calling, because He recognizes the true badges of sons in those only who are directed to good by His Spirit. To this we may refer what is said of the members of the Church, "Lord, who shall abide in thy tabernacle? Who shall dwell in thy holy hill? He that walketh uprightly, and worketh righteousness, and speaketh the truth in his heart," etc. (Psalm 15:1, 2). Again, in Isaiah, "Who among us shall dwell with the devouring fire? Who among us shall dwell with everlasting burnings? He that walketh righteously," etc. (Isaiah 33:14, 15). For the thing described is not the strength with which believers can stand before the Lord, but the manner in which our most merciful Father introduces them into His fellowship and defends and confirms them therein. For, as He detests sin and loves righteousness, so those whom He unites to himself He purifies by His Spirit, that he may render them conformable to himself and to his kingdom.

Therefore, if it is asked, what is the first cause, which gives the saints free access to the Kingdom of God and a firm and permanent footing in it? The answer is easy. The Lord in His mercy once adopted and ever defends them. But if the question relates to the manner, we must descend to regeneration, and the fruits of it, as enumerated in the fifteenth Psalm.

7 Argument from the passages, which distinguish good works by the name of righteousness, and declare that man is justified by them. Answer to the former part of the argument respecting the name. Why the works of the saints are called works of righteousness. Distinction to be observed.

There seems much more difficulty in those passages, which distinguish good works by the name of righteousness and declare that man is justified by them. The passages of the former class are very numerous, as when the observance of the commandments is termed justification or righteousness. Of the other classes, we have a description in the words of Moses, "It shall be our righteousness, if we observe to do all these commandments" (Deuteronomy 6:25). But if you object, that it is a legal promise, which, having an impossible condition annexed to it, proves nothing, there are other passages to which the same answer cannot be made; for instance, "If the man be poor," "thou shalt deliver him the pledge again when the sun goes down:" "and it shall be righteousness unto thee before the Lord thy God" (Deuteronomy 24:13). Likewise the words of the prophet, "Then stood up Phinehas, and executed judgment: and so the plague was stayed. And that was counted unto him for righteousness unto all generations forevermore" (Psalm 106:30, 31). Accordingly, the Pharisees of our day think they have here full scope for exultation. For, as we say, that when justification by faith is established, justification by works falls; they argue on the same principle If there is a justification by works, it is false to say that we are justified by faith only.

When I grant that the precepts of the Law are termed righteousness, I do nothing strange: for they are so in reality. I must, however, inform the reader that the Septuagint, not very appropriately has interpreted the Hebrew word, "edicts," as the Greek "justifications."

But I readily give up any dispute as to the word. Nor do I deny that the Law of God contains a perfect righteousness. For although we are debtors to do all the things which it enjoins, and, therefore, even after a full obedience, are unprofitable servants; yet, as the Lord has deigned to give it the name of righteousness, it is not ours to take from it what He has given. We readily admit, therefore, that the perfect obedience of the Law is righteousness, and the observance of any precept a part of righteousness, the whole substance of righteousness being contained in the remaining parts. But we deny that any such righteousness ever exists.

Hence, we discard the righteousness of the Law, not as being in itself maimed and defective, but because of the weakness of our flesh, it nowhere appears. Then Scripture does not merely call the precepts of the Law righteousness, it also gives this name to the works of the saints, as when it states that Zacharias and his wife "...were both righteous before God, walking in all the commandments and ordinances of the Lord blameless" (Luke 1:6). Surely, when it thus speaks, it estimates works more according to the nature of the Law than their own proper character. And here, again, I must repeat the observation, which I lately made, that the Law is not to be ascertained from a careless translation of the Greek interpreter. Still, as Luke chose not to make any change on the received version, I will not contend for this.

The things contained in the Law God enjoined upon man for righteousness, but that righteousness we attain not unless by observing the whole Law: every transgression whatever destroys it. While, therefore, the Law commands nothing but righteousness, if we look to itself, everyone of its precepts is righteousness: if we look to the men by whom they are performed, being transgressors in many things, they by no means merit the praise of righteousness for one work, and that a work which, through the imperfection adhering to it, is always in some respect vicious.

8 Answer to the second part of the argument—viz. that man is justified by works. Works of no avail by themselves; we are justified by faith only. This kind of righteousness defined. Whence the value is set on good works.

I come to the second class (section 1, 7, ad init.), in which the chief difficulty lies. Paul finds nothing stronger to prove justification by faith than that which is written of Abraham, that he "...believed God, and it was counted unto him for righteousness" (Romans 4:3; Galatians 3:6). Therefore, when it is said that the achievement of Phinehas "was counted unto him for righteousness" (Psalm 106:30, 31), we may argue that what Paul contends for respecting faith applies also to works. Our opponents, accordingly, as if the point were proved, set it down that, though we are not justified without faith, it is not by faith only; our justification is completed by works. Here I beseech believers, as they know that the true standard of righteousness must be derived from Scripture alone, to consider with me seriously and religiously how Scripture can be reconciled with that view.

Paul, knowing that justification by faith was the refuge of those who wanted righteousness of their own, confidently infers that all who are justified by faith are excluded from the righteousness of works. But, as it is clear that this justification is common to all believers, he with equal confidence infers that no man is justified by works; nay, more, that justification is without any help from works. But it is one thing to determine the power works have in themselves, and another to determine what place they are to hold after justification by faith has been established. If a price is to be put upon works according to their own worth, we hold that they are unfit to appear in the presence of God: that man, accordingly, has no works in which he can glory before God, and that hence, deprived of all aid from works, he is justified by faith alone. Justification, moreover, we thus define: The sinner being admitted into communion with Christ is, for His sake, reconciled to God; when purged by His blood, he obtains the remission of sins, and clothed with righteousness, just as if it were his own, stands secure before the judgment-seat of Heaven.

Forgiveness of sins being previously given, the good works which follow have a value different from their merit, because whatever is imperfect in them is covered by the perfection of Christ, and all their blemishes and pollutions are wiped away by His purity, so as never to come under the cognizance of the divine tribunal. The guilt of all transgressions, by which men are prevented from offering God an acceptable service, being thus effaced, and the imperfection which is wont to sully even good works being buried, the good works which are done by believers are deemed righteous, or, which is the same thing, are imputed for righteousness.

9 Answer confirmed and fortified by a dilemma.

Now, should anyone state this to me as an objection to justification by faith, I would first ask him whether a man is deemed righteous for one holy work or two, while in all the other acts of his life lie is a transgressor of the Law? This would be, indeed, more than absurd. I would next ask, Whether he is deemed righteous because of many good works if he is guilty of transgression in some one part? Even this he will not venture to maintain in opposition to the authority of the Law, which pronounces, "Cursed be he that confirmeth not all the words of this law to do them" (Deuteronomy 27:26).

I would go still further and ask, whether there be any work, which may not justly be convicted of impurity or imperfection? How, then, will it appear to that eye before which even the heavens are not clean, and angels are chargeable with folly? (See Job 4:18.) Thus he will be forced to confess that no good work exists that is not defiled, both by contrary transgression and also by its own corruption, so that it cannot be honored as righteousness. But if it is certainly owing to justification by faith that works, otherwise impure, unclean, defective, unworthy of the sight, not to say of the love of God, are imputed for righteousness, why do they by boasting of this imputation aim at the destruction of that justification, but for which the boasts were vain? Are they desirous of having a viper's birth? To this their ungodly language tends. They cannot deny that justification by faith is the beginning, the foundation, the cause, the subject, the substance of works of righteousness, and yet they conclude that justification is not by faith, because good works are counted for righteousness.

Let us have done then with this frivolity, and confess the fact as it stands; if any righteousness, which works are supposed to possess, depends on justification by faith, this doctrine is not only not impaired, but on the contrary it is confirmed, its power being thereby more brightly displayed. Nor let us suppose, that after free justification works are commended, as if they afterwards succeeded to the office of justifying or shared the office with faith. For did not justification by faith always remain entire, the impurity of works would be disclosed. There is nothing absurd in the doctrine, that though man is justified by faith, he is himself not only not righteous, but the righteousness attributed to his works is beyond their own deserts.

10 In what sense the partial imperfect righteousness of believers is accepted. Conclusion of the refutation.

In this way we can admit not only that there is a partial righteousness in works (as our adversaries maintain), but also that they are approved by God as if they were perfect. If we remember on what foundation this is rested, every difficulty will be solved. The first time when a work begins to be acceptable is when it is received with pardon. And whence pardon, but just because God looks upon all that and us belongs to us as in Christ? Therefore, as we ourselves, when engrafted into Christ, appear righteous before God, because our iniquities are covered with his innocence, so our works are, and are deemed righteous, because everything otherwise defective in them being buried by the purity of Christ is not imputed. Thus, we may justly say, that not only ourselves, but our works also, are justified by faith alone. Now, if that righteousness of works, whatever it be, depends on faith and free justification, and is produced by it, it ought to be included under it and, so to speak, made subordinate to it, as the effect to its cause; so far is it from being entitled to be set up to impair or destroy the doctrine of justification. Thus Paul, to prove that our blessedness depends not on our works, but on the mercy of God, makes special use of the words of David, "Blessed is he whose transgression is forgiven, whose sin is covered;" "Blessed is the man unto whom the Lord imputeth not iniquity."

Should anyone here obtrude the numberless passages in which blessedness seems to be attributed to works, as, "Blessed is the man that feareth the Lord;" "He that has mercy on the poor, happy is he;" "Blessed is the man that walketh not in the counsel of the ungodly," and "that endureth temptation;" "Blessed are they that keep judgment," that are "pure in heart," "meek," "merciful," etc., they cannot make out that Paul's doctrine is not true. For seeing that the qualities thus extolled never all so exist in man as to obtain for him the approbation of God, it follows that man is always miserable until he is exempted from misery by the pardon of his sins. Since, then, all the kinds of blessedness extolled in the Scripture are vain so that man derives no benefit from them until he obtains blessedness by the forgiveness of sins, a forgiveness which makes way for them, it follows that this is not only the chief and highest, but the only blessedness, unless you are prepared to maintain that it is impaired by things which owe their entire existence to it.

There is much less to trouble us in the name of *righteous*, which is usually given to believers. I admit that they are so called from the holiness of their lives, but as they rather exert themselves in the study of righteousness than fulfill righteousness itself, any degree of it, which they possess, must yield to justification by faith, to which it is owing that it is what it is.

11 Argument founded on the Epistle of James. First answer. One apostle cannot be opposed to another. Second answer. Third answer, from the scope of James. A double paralogism in the term "faith." In James, the faith said not to justify is a mere empty opinion; in Paul, it is the instrument by which we apprehend Christ, our righteousness.

But they say that we have a still more serious business with James, who in express terms opposes us. For he asks, "Was not Abraham our father justified by works?" and adds, "You see then how that by works a man is justified, and not by faith only" (James 2:21, 24). What then? Will they engage Paul in a quarrel with James? If they hold James to be a servant of Christ, his sentiments must be understood as not dissenting from Christ speaking by the mouth of Paul. By the mouth of Paul, the Spirit declares that Abraham obtained justification by faith, not by works; we also teach that all are justified by faith without the works of the Law. By James, the same Spirit declares that both Abraham's justification and ours consists of works, and not of faith only.

It is certain that the Spirit cannot be at variance with himself. Where, then, will be the agreement? It is enough for our opponents, provided they can tear up that justification by faith, which we regard as fixed by the deepest roots: to restore peace to the conscience is to them a matter of no great concern.

Hence, you may see, that though they indeed carp at the doctrine of justification by faith, they meanwhile point out no goal of righteousness at which the conscience may rest. Let them triumph then as they will, so long as the only victory they can boast of is, that they have deprived righteousness of all its certainty. This miserable victory they will indeed obtain when the light of truth is extinguished, and the Lord permits them to darken it with their lies. But wherever the truth of God stands, they cannot prevail.

I deny, then, that the passage of James, which they are constantly holding up before us as if it were the shield of Achilles, gives them the slightest countenance. To make this plain, let us first attend to the scope of the apostle and then show wherein their hallucination consists. As at that time (and the evil has existed in the Church ever since) there were many who, while they gave manifest proof of their infidelity, by neglecting and omitting all the works peculiar to believers, ceased not falsely to glory in the name of faith, James here dissipates their vain confidence. His intention, therefore, is not to derogate in any degree from the power of true faith, but to show how absurdly these triflers laid claim only to the empty name, and resting satisfied with it, felt secure in unrestrained indulgence in vice. This state of matters being understood, it will be easy to see where the error of our opponents lies. They fall into a double paralogism, the one in the term *faith*, the other in the term *justifying*.

The apostle, in giving the name of *faith* to an empty opinion altogether differing from true faith, makes a concession, which derogates in no respect from his case. This he demonstrates at the outset by the words, "What does it profit, my brethren, though a man say he has faith, and have not works?" (James 2:14). He says not, "If a man *have* faith without works," but "if he say that he has."

This becomes still clearer when a little after he derides this faith as worse than that of devils, and at last when he calls it "dead." You may easily ascertain his meaning by the explanation, "Thou believest that there is one God." Surely, if all, which is contained in that faith, is a belief in the existence of God, there is no wonder that it does not justify. The denial of such a power to it cannot be supposed to derogate in any degree from Christian faith, which is of a very different description. For how does true faith justify unless by uniting us to Christ, so that being made one with Him, we may be admitted to a participation in His righteousness? It does not justify because it forms an idea of the divine existence, but because it reclines with confidence on the divine mercy.

12 Another paralogism on the word justify. Paul speaks of the cause, James of the effects, of justification. Sum of the discussion.

We have not made good our point until we dispose of the other paralogism: since James places a part of justification in works. If you would make James consistent with the other Scriptures and with himself, you must give the word *justify*, as used by him, a different meaning from what it has with Paul. In the sense of Paul, we are said to be justified when the remembrance of our unrighteousness is obliterated and we are counted righteous. Had James had the same meaning, it would have been absurd for him to quote the words of Moses, "Abraham believed God," etc. The context runs thus: "Was not Abraham our father justified by works when he had offered Isaac his son upon the altar? Seest thou how faith wrought with his works, and works made faith perfect? And the Scripture was fulfilled which says that, Abraham believed God, and it was imputed unto him for righteousness."

If it is absurd to say that the effect was before its cause, either Moses falsely declares in that passage that Abraham's faith was imputed for righteousness or Abraham, by his obedience in offering up Isaac, did not merit righteousness. Before the existence of Ishmael, who was a grown youth at the birth of Isaac, Abraham was justified by his faith. How can we say that he obtained justification by an obedience, which followed long after? Wherefore, either James erroneously inverts the proper order (this it would be impious to suppose), or he meant not to say that he was justified, as if he deserved to be deemed just. What then? It appears certain that he is speaking of the manifestation, not of the imputation of righteousness, as if he had said, That those who are justified by true faith prove their justification by obedience and good works, not by a bare and imaginary semblance of faith.

In one word, he is not discussing the mode of justification, but requiring that the justification of believers shall be operative. And, as Paul contends that men are justified without the aid of works, so James will not allow any to be regarded as justified who are destitute of good works. Due attention to the scope will thus disentangle every doubt; for the error of our opponents lies chiefly in this, that they think James is defining the mode of justification, whereas his only object is to destroy the depraved security of those who vainly pretended faith as an excuse for their contempt of good works. Therefore, let them twist the words of James as they may, they will never extract out of them more than the two propositions: That an empty phantom of faith does not justify, and that the believer, not contented with such an imagination, manifests his justification by good works.

13 Argument founded on Romans 2:13. Answer, explaining the apostles' meaning. Another argument, containing a reduction ad impossibili. Why Paul used the argument.

They gain nothing by quoting from Paul to the same effect, that "...not the hearers of the law are just before God, but the doers of the law shall be justified" (Romans 2:13). I am unwilling to evade the difficulty by the solution of Ambrose, that Paul spoke thus because faith in Christ is the fulfillment of the Law. This I regard as a mere subterfuge, and one, too, for which there is no occasion, as the explanation is perfectly obvious. The apostle's object is to suppress the absurd confidence of the Jews who gave out that they alone had a knowledge of the Law, though at the very time they were its greatest despisers. That they might not plume themselves so much on a bare acquaintance with the Law, he reminds them that when justification is sought by the law, the thing required is not the knowledge but the observance of it.

We certainly do not mean not to dispute that the righteousness of the law consists in works, and not only so, but that justification consists in the dignity and merits of works. But this proves not that we are justified by works unless they can produce someone who has fulfilled the law. That Paul had no other meaning is abundantly obvious from the context. After charging Jews and Gentiles in common with unrighteousness, he descends to particulars and says, "As many as have sinned without law shall also perish without law," referring to the Gentiles, and that "as many as have sinned in the Law shall be judged by the law," referring to the Jews.

Moreover, as they, winking at their transgressions, boasted merely of the Law, he adds most appropriately, that the Law was passed with the view of justifying not those who only heard it, but those only who obeyed it; as if he had said, "Do you seek righteousness in the Law? Do not bring forward the mere hearing of it, which is in itself of little weight, but bring works by which you may show that the Law has not been given to you in vain. "Since in these they were all deficient, it followed that they had no ground of boasting in the Law. Paul's meaning, therefore, rather leads to an opposite argument. The righteousness of the Law consists in the perfection of works, but no man can boast of fulfilling the Law by works, and, therefore, there is no righteousness by the Law.

14 An argument founded on the passages in which believers confidently appeal to their righteousness. Answer, founded on a consideration of two circumstances. A. They refer only to a special cause. B. They claim righteousness in comparison with the wicked.

They now betake themselves to those passages in which believers boldly submit their righteousness to the judgment of God, and wish to be judged accordingly, as in the following passages: "Judge me, O Lord, according to my righteousness, and according to mine integrity that is in me." Again, "Hear the right, O Lord;" "Thou hast proved mine heart; thou hast visited me in the night; thou hast tried me, and shalt find nothing." Again, "The Lord regarded me according to my righteousness; according to the cleanness of my hands has he recompensed me. For I have kept the ways of the Lord, and have not wickedly departed from my God." "I was also upright before him, and I kept myself from mine iniquity." Again, "Judge me, O Lord; for I have walked in mine integrity;" "I have not sat with vain persons; neither will I go in with dissemblers;" "Gather not my soul with sinners, nor my life with bloody men; in whose hands is mischief, and their right hand is full of bribes. But as for me, I will walk in mine integrity."

I have already spoken of the confidence, which the saints seem to derive simply from works. The passages now quoted will not occasion much difficulty, if we attend to their connection, or (as it is commonly called) special circumstances. These are of two kinds; for those who use them have no wish that their whole life should be brought to trial, so that they may be acquitted or condemned according to its tenor; all they wish is, that a decision should be given on the particular case; and even here the righteousness which they claim is not with reference to the divine perfection, but only by comparison with the wicked and profane.

When the question relates to justification, the thing required is not that the individual have a good ground of acquittal in regard to some particular matter, but that his whole life be in accordance with righteousness. But when the saints implore the divine justice in vindication of their innocence, they do not present themselves as free from fault, and in every respect blameless but while placing their confidence of salvation in the divine goodness only, and trusting that He will vindicate His poor when they are afflicted contrary to justice and equity, they truly commit to him the cause in which the innocent are oppressed. And when they sit-themselves with their adversaries at the tribunal of God, they pretend not to an innocence corresponding to the divine purity were inquiry strictly made, but knowing that in comparison of the malice, dishonesty, craft, and iniquity of their enemies, their sincerity, justice, simplicity, and purity are ascertained and approved by God, they dread not to call upon Him to judge between them. Thus when David said to Saul, "The Lord render to every man his righteousness and his faithfulness" (1 Samuel 26:23), he meant not that the Lord should examine and reward everyone according to his deserts, but he took the Lord to witness how great his innocence was in comparison to Saul's injustice.

Paul, too, when he indulges in the boast, "Our rejoicing is this, the testimony of our conscience, that in simplicity and godly sincerity, not with fleshly wisdom, but by the grace of God, we have had our conversation in the world, and more abundantly to you-ward" (2 Corinthians 1:12), means not to call for the scrutiny of God, but compelled by the calumnies of the wicked he appeals, in contradiction of all their slanders, to his faith and probity, which he knew that God had indulgently accepted. For we see how he elsewhere says, "I know nothing by myself; yet am I not hereby justified" (1 Corinthians 4:4); in other words, he was aware that the divine judgment far transcended the blind estimate of man. Therefore, however believers may, in defending their integrity against the hypocrisy of the ungodly, appeal to God as their witness and judge, still when the question is with God alone, they all with one mouth exclaim, "If thou, Lord, should mark iniquities, O Lord, who shall stand?" Again, "Enter not into judgment with thy servant; for in thy sight shall no man living be justified." Distrusting their own words, they gladly exclaim, "Thy loving-kindness is better than life" (Psalm 130:3; 143:2; 63:3).

15 Last argument from those passages, which ascribe righteousness and life to the ways of believers. Answer. This proceeds from the paternal kindness of God. What is meant by the perfection of saints.

There are other passages not unlike those quoted above, at which some may still demur. Solomon says, "The just man walketh in his integrity" (Proverbs 20:7). Again, "In the way of righteousness is life; and in the pathway thereof there is no death" (Proverbs 12:28). For this reason Ezekiel says, he that "has walked in my statutes, and has kept my judgments, to deal truly; he is just, he shall surely live" (Ezekiel 18:9, 21; 23:15). None of these declarations do we deny or obscure. But let one of the sons of Adam come forward with such integrity. If there is none, they must perish from the presence of God or retake themselves to the asylum of mercy. Still we deny not that the integrity of believers, though partial and imperfect, is a step to immortality. How so, but just that the works of those whom the Lord has assumed into the covenant of grace, He tries not by their merit, but embraces with paternal indulgence. By this, we understand not with the Schoolmen, that works derive their value from accepting grace. For their meaning is that works, otherwise unfit to obtain salvation in terms of law, are made fit for such a purpose by the divine acceptance.

On the other hand, I maintain that these works being sullied both by other transgressions and by their own deficiencies, have no other value than this, that the Lord indulgently pardons them; in other words, that the righteousness which He bestows on man is gratuitous. Here they unseasonably obtrude those passages in which the apostle prays for all perfection to believers, "To the end he may establish your hearts unblamable in holiness before God, even our Father" (1 Thessalonians 3:13, and elsewhere). These words were strongly urged by the Celestines of old, in maintaining the perfection of holiness in the present life. To this we deem it sufficient briefly to reply with Augustine, that the goal to which all the pious ought to aspire is to appear in the presence of God without spot and blemish; but, as the course of the present life is at best nothing more than progress, we shall never reach the goal until we have laid aside the body of sin, and been completely united to the Lord. If anyone choose to give the name of perfection to the saints, I shall not obstinately quarrel with him, provided he defines this perfection in the words of Augustine, "When we speak of the perfect virtue of the saints, part of this perfection consists in the recognition of our imperfection both in truth and in humility."

Chapter 18

THE RIGHTEOUSNESS OF WORKS IMPROPERLY INFERRED FROM REWARDS

There are three divisions in this chapter,—I. A solution of two general objections which are urged in support of justification by works. First, that God will render to everyone according to his works, section 1. Second, that the reward of works is called eternal, sections 2-6. II. Answer to other special objections derived from the former, and a perversion of passages of Scripture, sections 6-9. III. Refutation of the sophism that faith itself is called a work, and, therefore, justification by it is by works, section 10.

Sections

1. Two general objections. The former solved and explained. What is meant by the term working.

2. Solution of the second general objection. A. Works are not the cause of salvation. This is shown from the name and nature of inheritance. B. A striking example that the Lord rewards the works of believers with blessings which He had promised before the works were thought of.

3. First reason that eternal life is said to be the reward of works. This is confirmed by passages of Scripture. The concurrence of Ambrose. A rule to be observed. Declarations of Christ and an apostle.

4. Other four reasons. Holiness is the way to the Kingdom, not the cause of obtaining it. Proposition of the Sophists.

5. Objection that God crowns the works of His people. Three answers from Augustine. A fourth from Scripture.

6. First special objection—viz. that we are ordered to lay up treasures in Heaven. Answer, showing in what way this can be done.

7. Second objection—viz. that the righteous enduring affliction are said to be worthy of the Kingdom of Heaven. Answer. What is meant by righteousness.

8. *A third objection founded on three passages of Paul. Answer.*

9. *Fourth objection founded on our Savior's words, "If ye would enter into life, keep the commandments." Answer, giving an exposition of the passage.*

10. *Last objection—viz. that faith itself is called a work. Answer—it is not as a work that faith justifies.*

1 Two general objections. The former solved and explained. What is meant by the term working.

Let us now proceed to those passages, which affirm that God will render to everyone according to his deeds. Of this description are the following: "We must all appear before the judgment-seat of Christ; that everyone may receive the things done in his body, according to that he has done, whether it be good or bad;" "Who will render to every man according to his deeds: to them who by patient continuance in well-doing seek for glory, and honor, and immortality, eternal life;" but "tribulation and anguish upon every soul of man that does evil;" "They that have done good, unto the resurrection of life; and they that have done evil, unto the resurrection of damnation;" "Come, ye blessed of my Father;" "For I was an hungered, and ye gave me meat; I was thirsty, and ye gave me drink," etc. To these we may add the passages which describe eternal life as the reward of works, such as the following: "The recompense of a man's hands shall be rendered unto him;" "He that feareth the commandment shall be rewarded;" "Rejoice and be exceeding glad, for great is your reward in heaven;" "Every man shall receive his own rewards according to his own labor." The passages in which it is said that God will reward every man according to his works are easily disposed of. For that mode of expression indicates not the cause but the order of sequence.

Now, it is beyond a doubt that the steps by which the Lord in His mercy consummates our salvation are these, "Whom he did predestinate, them he also called; and whom he called, them he also justified; and whom he justified, them he also glorified" (Romans 8:30). But though it is by mercy alone that God admits His people to life, yet, as He leads them into possession of it by the course of good works, that He may complete His work in them in the order which He has destined, it is not strange that they are said to be crowned according to their works, since by these doubtless they are prepared for receiving the crown of immortality. Nay, for this reason they are aptly said to work out their own salvation (see Philippians 2:12), while by exerting themselves in good works, they aspire to eternal life, just as they are elsewhere told to labor for the meat which perisheth not (John 6:27), while they acquire life for themselves by believing in Christ; and yet it is immediately added that this meat "the Son of man shall give unto you."

Hence, it appears, that *working* is not at all opposed to *grace*, but refers to pursuit, and, therefore, it follows not that believers are the authors of their own salvation, or that it is the result of their works. What then? The moment they are admitted to fellowship with Christ, by the knowledge of the gospel, and the illumination of the Holy Spirit, their eternal life is begun, and then He who has begun a good work in them "will perform it until the day of Jesus Christ" (Philippians 1:6). And it is performed when in righteousness and holiness they bear a resemblance to their heavenly Father, and prove that they are not degenerate sons.

2 Solution of the second general objection. A. Works are not the cause of salvation. This is shown from the name and nature of inheritance. B. A striking example that the Lord rewards the works of believers with blessings which He had promised before the works were thought of.

There is nothing in the term *reward* to justify the inference that our works are the cause of salvation. First, let it be a fixed principle in our hearts, that the Kingdom of Heaven is not the hire of servants, but the inheritance of sons (see Ephesians 1:18); an inheritance obtained by those only whom the Lord has adopted as sons, and obtained for no other cause than this adoption, "The son of the bond-woman shall not be heir with the son of the free-woman" (Galatians 4:30). Hence, in those very passages in which the Holy Spirit promises eternal glory as the reward of works, by expressly calling it an inheritance, He demonstrates that it comes to us from some other quarter. Thus Christ enumerates the works for which He bestows Heaven as a recompense, while He is calling His elect to the possession of it, but He at the same time adds, that it is to be possessed by right of inheritance (Matthew 25:34).

Paul, too, encourages servants, while faithfully doing their duty, to hope for reward from the Lord, but adds, "of the inheritance" (Colossians 3:24). You see how in formal terms they carefully caution us to attribute eternal blessedness not to works, but to the adoption of God. Why, then, do they at the same time make mention of works? This question will be elucidated by an example from Scripture (see Genesis 15:5; 17:1). Before the birth of Isaac, Abraham had received promise of a seed in whom all the families of the Earth should be blessed; the propagation of a seed that for number should equal the stars of heaven, and the sand of the sea, etc. Many years after he prepares, in obedience to a divine message, to sacrifice his son. Having done this act of obedience, he receives the promise, "By myself have I sworn, saith the Lord, for because thou hast done this thing, and hast not withheld thy son, thine only son; that in blessing I will bless thee, and in multiplying I will multiply thy seed as the stars of the heaven, and as the sand which is upon the sea-shore, and thy seed shall possess the gate of his enemies; and in thy seed shall all the nations of the earth be blessed, because thou hast obeyed my voice" (Genesis 22:16-18). What is it that we hear? Did Abraham by his obedience merit the blessing, which had been promised to him before the precept was given? Here assuredly we see without ambiguity that God rewards the works of believers with blessings which He had given them before the works were thought of, there still being no cause for the blessings which He bestows but His own mercy.

3 The first reason eternal life is said to be the reward of works. This is confirmed by passages of Scripture. The concurrence of Ambrose. A rule to be observed. Declarations of Christ and an apostle.

And yet, the Lord does not act in vain, or delude us when He says that he renders to works what He had freely given before works. As He would have us to be exercised in good works, while aspiring to the manifestation, or, if I may so speak, the fruition of the things which He has promised, and by means of them to hasten on to the blessed hope set before us in Heaven, the fruit of the promises is justly ascribed to those things by which it is brought to maturity.

The apostle elegantly expressed both things when he told the Colossians to study the offices of charity, "...for the hope which is laid up for you in heaven, whereof ye heard before in the word of the truth of the Gospel" (Colossians 1:5). For when he says that the gospel informed them of the hope which was treasured up for them in Heaven, he declares that it depends on Christ alone, and not at all upon works. With this accords the saying of Peter, that believers "...are kept by the power of God through faith unto salvation, ready to be revealed in the last time" (1 Peter 1:5). When he says that they strive because of it, he intimates that believers must continue running during the whole course of their lives in order that they may attain it. But to prevent us from supposing that the reward which is promised becomes a kind of merit, our Lord introduced a parable, in which He represented himself as a householder, who sent all the laborers whom he met to work in his vineyard, some at the first hour of the day, others at the second, others at the third, some even at the eleventh; at evening he paid them all alike.

The interpretation of this parable is briefly and truly given by that ancient writer (whoever he was) who wrote the book *De Vocatione Gentium*, which goes under the name of Ambrose. I will give it in his words rather than my own: "By means of this comparison, our Lord represented the many various modes of calling as pertaining to grace alone, where those who were introduced into the vineyard at the eleventh hour and made equal to those who had toiled the whole day, doubtless represent the case of those whom the indulgence of God, to commend the excellence of grace, has rewarded in the decline of the day and the conclusion of life; not paying the price of labor, but shedding the riches of his goodness on those whom he chose without works; in order that even those who bore the heat of the day, and yet received no more than those who came last, may understand that they received a gift of grace, not the hire of works."

Lastly, it is also worthy of remark, that in those passages in which eternal life is called the reward of works, it is not taken simply for that communion which we have with God preparatory to a blessed immortality, when with paternal benevolence He embraces us in Christ, but for the possession, or, as it is called, the fruition of blessedness, as the very words of Christ express it, "In the world to come eternal life" (Mark 10:30), and elsewhere, "Come, ye blessed of my Father, inherit the kingdom," etc. (Matthew 25:34). For this reason also, Paul gives the name of *adoption* to that revelation of adoption which shall be made at the resurrection; and which adoption he afterwards interprets to mean, the redemption of our body (Romans 8:23). But, otherwise, as alienation from God is eternal death, so when man is received into favor by God that he may enjoy communion with him and become one with him, he passes from death unto life. This is owing to adoption alone. Although after their manner they pertinaciously urge the term *reward*, we can always carry them back to the declaration of Peter, that eternal life is the reward of faith. (See 1 Peter 1:9.)

4 Other four reasons. Holiness is the way to the Kingdom, not the cause of obtaining it. Proposition of the Sophists.

Let us not suppose, then, that the Holy Spirit, by this promise, commends the dignity of our works, as if they were deserving of such a reward. For Scripture leaves us nothing of which we may glory in the sight of God. Nay, rather its whole object is to repress, humble, cast down, and completely crush our pride. But in this way help is given to our weakness, which would immediately give way were it not sustained by this expectation, and soothed by this comfort.

First, let every man reflect for himself how hard it is not only to leave all things, but also to leave and abjure one's self. Yet, this is the training by which Christ initiates His disciples: that is, all the godly.

Secondly, He thus keeps them all their lifetime under the discipline of the cross, lest they should allow their heart to long for or confide in present good. In short, His treatment is usually such, that wherever they turn their eyes, as far as this world extends, they see nothing before them but despair; and hence Paul says, "If in this life only we have hope in Christ, we are of all men most miserable" (1 Corinthians 15:19). That they may not fail in these great straits, the Lord is present, reminding them to lift their head higher and extend their view farther, that in Him they may find a happiness which they see not in the world: to this happiness He gives the name of reward, hire, recompense, not as estimating the merit of works, but intimating that it is a compensation for their straits, sufferings, and affronts, etc. Wherefore, there is nothing to prevent us from calling eternal life a recompense after the example of Scripture, because in it the Lord brings His people from labor to quiet, from affliction to a prosperous and desirable condition, from sorrow to joy, from poverty to affluence, from ignominy to glory; in short, the exchanges all the evils which they endured for blessings. Thus there will be no impropriety in considering holiness of life as the way, not indeed the way which gives access to the glory of the heavenly kingdom; but a way by which God conducts his elect to the manifestation of that Kingdom, since His good pleasure is to glorify those whom He has sanctified. (See Romans 8:30.) Only let us not imagine that merit and hire are correlative terms, a point on which the Sophists absurdly insist, from not attending to the end to which we have adverted. How preposterous is it when the Lord calls us to one end to look to another? Nothing is clearer than that a reward is promised to good works, in order to support the weakness of our flesh by some degree of comfort; but not to inflate our minds with vainglory. He, therefore, who from merit infers reward, or weighs works and reward in the same balance, errs very widely from the end, which God has in view.

5 Objection that God crowns the works of His people. Three answers from Augustine. A fourth from Scripture.

Accordingly, when the Scripture speaks of "a crown of righteousness which God the righteous Judge shall give," "at that day" (2 Timothy 4:8), I not only say with Augustine, "To whom could the righteous Judge give the crown if the merciful Father had not given grace, and how could there have been righteousness but for the precedence of grace which justified the ungodly? How could these be paid as things due were not things not due previously given?" But I also add, how could He impute righteousness to our works, did not His indulgence hide the unrighteousness that is in them? How could He deem them worthy of reward, did He not with boundless goodness destroy what is unworthy in them?

Augustine is wont to give the name of grace to eternal life, because, while it is the recompense of works, it is bestowed by the gratuitous gifts of God. But Scripture humbles us more, and at the same time elevates us. For besides forbidding us to glory in works, because they are the gratuitous gifts of God, it tells us that they are always defiled by some degrees of impurity, so that they cannot satisfy God when they are tested by the standard of His justice, but that, lest our activity should be destroyed, they please merely by pardon. But though Augustine speaks somewhat differently from us, it is plain from his words that the difference is more apparent than real. After drawing a contrast between two individuals, the one with a holy and perfect life almost to a miracle; the other honest indeed, and of pure morals, yet not so perfect as not to leave much room for desiring better, he at length infers, "He who seems inferior in conduct, yet on account of the true faith in God by which he lives (Habakkuk 2:4), and in conformity to which he accuses himself in all his faults, praises God in all his good works, takes shame to himself, and ascribes glory to God, from whom he receives both forgiveness for his sins, and the love of well-doing, the moment he is set free from this life is translated into the society of Christ. Why, but just because of his faith? For though it saves no man without works (such faith being reprobate and not working by love), yet by means of it sins are forgiven; for the just lives by faith: without it works which seem good are converted into sins." Here he not obscurely acknowledges what we so strongly maintains, that the righteousness of good works depends on their being approved by God in the way of pardon.

6 First special objection—viz. that we are ordered to lay up treasures in Heaven. Answer, showing in what way this can be done.

In a sense similar to the above passages, our opponents quote the following: "Make to yourselves friends of the mammon of unrighteousness; that when ye fail, they may receive you into everlasting habitations" (Luke 16:9). "Charge them that are rich in this world, that they be not high-minded, nor trust in uncertain riches, but in the living God, who giveth us richly all things to enjoy: that they do good, that they be rich in good works, ready to distribute, willing to communicate; laying up in store for themselves a good foundation against the time to come, that they may lay hold on eternal life" (1 Timothy 6:17-19).

For the good works, which we enjoy in eternal blessedness, are compared to riches. I answer, that we shall never attain to the true knowledge of these passages unless we attend to the scope of the Spirit in uttering them. If it is true, as Christ says, "Where your treasure is, there will your heart be also" (Matthew 6:21), then, as the children of the world are intent on providing those things which form the delight of the present life, so it is the duty of believers, after they have learned that this life will shortly pass away like a dream, to take care that those things which they would truly enjoy be transmitted thither where their entire life is to be spent. Therefore, we must do as those who begin to remove to any place where they mean to fix their abode. As they send forward their effects, and grudge not to want them for a season, because they think the more they have in their future residence, the happier they are; so, if we think that heaven is our country, we should send our wealth there rather than retain it here, where on our sudden departure it will be lost to us. But how shall we transmit it? By contributing to the necessities of the poor, the Lord imputing to himself whatever is given to them. Hence, that excellent promise, "He that has pity on the poor lendeth to the Lord" (Proverbs 19:17; Matthew 25:40); and again, "He which soweth bountifully shall reap also bountifully" (2 Corinthians 9:6).

What we give to our brethren in the exercise of charity is a deposit with the Lord, who, as a faithful depositary, will ultimately restore it with abundant interest. Are our duties, then, of such value with God that they are as a kind of treasure placed in His hand? Who can hesitate to say so when Scripture so often and so plainly attests it? But if anyone would leap from the mere kindness of God to the merit of works, his error will receive no support from these passages. For all you can properly infer from them is the inclination on the part of God to treat us with indulgence. For, in order to animate us in well-doing, He allows no act of obedience, however unworthy of His eye, to pass unrewarded.

7 Second objection—viz. that the righteous enduring affliction are said to be worthy of the Kingdom of Heaven. Answer. What is meant by righteousness.

But they insist more strongly on the words of the apostle when, in consoling the Thessalonians under their tribulations, he tells them that these were sent, "That ye may be counted worthy of the kingdom of God, for which ye also suffer; seeing it is a righteous thing with God to recompense tribulation to them that trouble you; and to you who are troubled, rest with us, when the Lord Jesus shall be revealed from heaven with his mighty angels" (2 Thessalonians 1:6-7). The author of the Epistle to the Hebrews says, "God is not unrighteous to forget your work and labor of love, which ye have showed towards his name, in that ye have ministered to the saints, and do minister" (Hebrews 6:10). To the former passage I answer, that the worthiness spoken of is not that of merit, but as God the Father would have those whom He has chosen for sons to be conformed to Christ the first-born, and, as it behooved him first to suffer and then to enter into his glory, so we also, through much tribulation, enter the Kingdom of Heaven. Therefore, while we suffer tribulation for the name of Christ, we in a manner receive the marks with which God is wont to stamp the sheep of His flock. (See Galatians 6:17.)

Hence, we are counted worthy of the Kingdom of God, because we bear in our bodies the marks of our Lord and Master, these being the insignia of the children of God. In this sense are we to understand the passages: "Always bearing about in the body the dying of the Lord Jesus, that the life also of Jesus might be made manifest in our body" (2 Corinthians 4:10). "That I may know him and the power of his resurrection, and the fellowship of his sufferings, being made conformable unto his death" (Philippians 3:10). The reason which is subjoined is intended not to prove any merit, but to confirm our hope of the Kingdom of God; as if He had said, "As it is befitting the just judgment of God to take vengeance on your enemies for the tribulation which they have brought upon you, so it is also befitting to give you release and rest from these tribulations." The other passage, which speaks as if it were becoming the justice of God not to overlook the services of His people, and almost insinuates that it would be unjust to forget them, is to be thus explained: God, to arouse us from sloth, assures us that every labor which we undertake for the glory of His name shall not be in vain.

Let us always remember that this promise, like all other promises, will be of no avail unless it is preceded by the free covenant of mercy, on which the whole certainty of our salvation depends. Trusting to it, however, we ought to feel secure that however unworthy our services, the liberality of God will not allow them to pass unrewarded. To confirm us in this expectation, the apostle declares that God is not unrighteous; but will act consistently with the promise once given. Righteousness, therefore, refers rather to the truth of the divine promise than to the equity of paying what is due. In this sense there is a celebrated saying of Augustine, which, as containing a memorable sentiment, that holy man declined not repeatedly to employ, and which I think not unworthy of being constantly remembered: "Faithful is the Lord, who has made himself our debtor, not by receiving anything from us, but by promising us all things."

8 A third objection founded on three passages of Paul. Answer.

Our opponents also adduce the following passages from Paul: "Though I have all faith, so that I could remove mountains, and have not charity, I am nothing" (1 Corinthians 13:2). Again, "Now abideth faith, hope, charity, these three; but the greatest of these is charity" (1 Corinthians 13:13). "Above all these things put on charity, which is the bond of perfectness" (Colossians 3:14). From the two first passages, our Pharisees contend that we are justified by charity rather than by faith—charity being, as they say, the better virtue. This mode of arguing is easily disposed of. I have elsewhere shown that what is said in the first passage refers not to true faith. In the second passage we admit that charity is said to be greater than true faith, but not because charity is more meritorious, but because it is more fruitful, because it is of wider extent, of more general service, and always flourishes, whereas the use of faith is only for a time.

If we look to excellence, the love of God undoubtedly holds the first place. Of it, however, Paul does not here speak; for the only thing he insists on is that we should by mutual charity edify one another in the Lord. But let us suppose that charity is in every respect superior to faith, what man of sound judgment, nay, what man with any soundness in his brain, would argue that it, therefore, does more to justify? The power of justifying which belongs to faith consists not in its worth as a work. Our justification depends entirely on the mercy of God and the merits of Christ; when faith apprehends these, it is said to justify.

Now, if you ask our opponents in what sense they ascribe justification to charity, they will answer, "Being a duty acceptable to God, righteousness is in respect of its merit imputed to us by the acceptance of the divine goodness." Here you see how beautifully the argument proceeds. We say that faith justifies not because it merits justification for us by its own worth, but because it is an instrument by which we freely obtain the righteousness of Christ. They, overlooking the mercy of God, and passing by Christ, the sum of righteousness, maintain that we are justified by charity as being superior to faith; just as if one were to maintain that a king is fitter to make a shoe than a shoemaker is, because the king is infinitely the superior of the two. This one syllogism is ample proof that not all the schools of Sorbonne have had the slightest apprehension of what is meant by justification by faith.

Should any disputant here interpose and ask why we give different meanings to the term faith as used by Paul in passages so near each other, I can easily show that I have not slight grounds for so doing. For while those gifts which Paul enumerates are in some degree subordinate to faith and hope, because they relate to the knowledge of God, he by way of summary comprehends them all under the name of faith and hope; as if he had said, "Prophecy and tongues, and the gift of interpreting, and knowledge, are all designed to lead us to the knowledge of God. But in this life, it is only by faith and hope that we acknowledge God. Therefore, when I name faith and hope, I at the same time comprehend the whole. "Now abideth faith, hope, charity, these three." That is, however great the number of the gifts, they are all to be referred to them; but "The greatest of these is charity." From the third passage they infer, If charity is the bond of perfection, it must be the bond of righteousness, which is nothing else than perfection. First, without objecting that Paul here gives the name of perfection to proper union among the members of a rightly constituted Church and admitting that by charity we are perfected before God, what new result do they gain by it? I will always object in reply, that we never attain to that perfection unless we fulfill all the parts of charity; and will thence infer, that as all are most remote from such fulfillment, the hope of perfection is excluded.

9 Fourth objection founded on our Savior's words, "If ye would enter into life, keep the commandments." Answer, giving an exposition of the passage.

I am unwilling to discuss all the things, which the foolish Sorbonnists have rashly laid hold of in Scripture as it chanced to come in their way and throw out against us. Some of them are so ridiculous, that I cannot mention them without laying myself open to a charge of trifling. I will, therefore, conclude with an exposition of one of our Savior's expressions with which they are wondrously pleased. When the lawyer asked him, "Good Master, what good thing shall I do, that I may have eternal life," He answers, "If thou wilt enter into life, keep the commandments" (Matthew 19:16, 17). What more (they ask) would we have, when the very author of grace bids us acquire the Kingdom of Heaven by the observance of the commandments? As if it were not plain that Christ adapted His answers to the characters of those whom he addressed. Here He is questioned by a Doctor of the Law as to the means of obtaining eternal life, and the question is not put simply, but is, "What can men do to attain it?" Both the character of the speaker and his question induced our Lord to give this answer. Imbued with a persuasion of legal righteousness, the lawyer had a blind confidence in works. Then all he asked was what are the works of righteousness by which salvation is obtained? Justly, therefore, is he referred to the Law, in which there is a perfect mirror of righteousness.

We also distinctly declare that if life is sought in works, the commandments are to be observed. And the knowledge of this doctrine is necessary to Christians; for how should they retake themselves to Christ, unless they perceived that they had fallen from the path of life over the precipice of death? Or how could they understand how far they have wandered from the way of life unless they previously understand what that way is? Then only do they feel that the asylum of safety is in Christ when they see how much their conduct is at variance with the divine righteousness, which consists in the observance of the Law.

The sum of the whole is this: If salvation is sought in works, we must keep the commandments, by which we are instructed in perfect righteousness. But we cannot remain here unless we would stop short in the middle of our course; for none of us is able to keep the commandments. Being thus excluded from the righteousness of the Law, we must retake ourselves to another remedy—viz. to the faith of Christ. Wherefore, as a teacher of the Law, whom our Lord knew to be puffed up with a vain confidence in works, was here directed by Him to the Law, that he might learn he was a sinner exposed to the fearful sentence of eternal death; so others, who were already humbled with this knowledge, He elsewhere solaces with the promise of grace, without making any mention of the Law. "Come unto me, all ye that labor and are heavy laden, and I will give you rest." "Take my yoke upon you, and learn of me; for I am meek and lowly in heart: and ye shall find rest unto your souls" (Matthew 11:28, 29).

10 Last objection—viz. that faith itself is called a work. Answer— it is not as a work that faith justifies.

At length, after they have wearied themselves with perverting Scripture, they have recourse to subtleties and sophisms. One cavil is that faith is somewhere called a work (see John 6:29); hence, they infer that we are in error in opposing faith to works; as if faith, regarded as obedience to the divine will, could by its own merit procure our justification, and did not rather, by embracing the mercy of God, thereby seal upon our hearts the righteousness of Christ, which is offered to us in the preaching of the gospel.

My readers will pardon me if I stay not to dispose of such absurdities; their own weakness, without external assault, is sufficient to destroy them. One objection, however, which has some semblance of reason, it will be proper to dispose of in passing, lest it give any trouble to those less experienced. As common sense dictates that contraries must be tried by the same rule, and as each sin is charged against us as unrighteousness, so it is right (say our opponents) that each good work should receive the praise of righteousness. The answer, which some give, that the condemnation of men proceeds on unbelief alone and not on particular sins, does not satisfy me. I agree with them, indeed, that infidelity is the fountain and root of all evil; for it is the first act of revolt from God, and is afterwards followed by particular transgressions of the Law. But as they seem to hold, that in estimating righteousness and unrighteousness, the same rule is to be applied to good and bad works, in this I dissent from them. The righteousness of works consists in perfect obedience to the Law.

Hence, you cannot be justified by works unless you follow this straight line (if I may so call it) during the whole course of your life. The moment you decline from it, you have fallen into unrighteousness. Hence, it appears that righteousness is not obtained by a few works, but by an indefatigable and inflexible observance of the divine will. But the rule with regard to unrighteousness is very different. The adulterer or the thief is by one act guilty of death, because he offends against the majesty of God. The blunder of these arguers of ours lies here: they attend not to the words of James, "Whosoever shall keep the whole law, and yet offend in one point, he is guilty of all. For he that said, Do not commit adultery, said also, Do not kill," etc. (James 2:10, 11). Therefore, it should not seem absurd when we say that death is the just recompense of every sin, because each sin merits the just indignation and vengeance of God. But you reason absurdly if you infer the converse, that one good work will reconcile a man to God notwithstanding of his meriting wrath by many sins.

Chapter 19

OF CHRISTIAN LIBERTY

The three divisions of this chapter are,—I. Necessity of the doctrine of Christian liberty, section 1. The principal parts of this liberty explained, sections 2-8. II. The nature and efficacy of this liberty against the Epicureans and others who take no account whatever of the weak, sections 9 and 10. III. Of offense given and received. A lengthened and not unnecessary discussion of this subject, sections 11-16.

Sections

1. Connection of this chapter with the previous one on justification. A true knowledge of Christian liberty is useful and necessary. A. It purifies the conscience. B. It checks licentiousness. C. It maintains the merits of Christ, the truth of the Gospel, and the peace of the soul.

2. This liberty consists of three parts. First, believers renouncing the righteousness of the law, look only to Christ. Objection. Answer, distinguishing between legal and Evangelical righteousness.

3. This first part clearly established by the whole Epistle to the Galatians.

4. The second part of Christian liberty—viz. that the conscience, freed from the yoke of the Law, voluntarily obeys the will of God. This cannot be done so long as we are under the Law. Reason.

5. When freed from the rigorous exactions of the Law, we can cheerfully and with much alacrity answer the call of God.

6. Proof of this second part from an apostle. The end of this liberty.

7. Third part of liberty—viz. the free rise of things indifferent. The knowledge of this part is necessary to remove despair and superstition. Superstition described.

8. *Proof of this third part from the Epistle to the Romans. Those who observe it not only use evasion. A. Despisers of God. B. The desperate. C. The ungrateful. The end and scope of this third part.*

9. *Second part of the chapter, showing the nature and efficacy of Christian liberty, in opposition to the Epicureans. Their character described. Pretext and allegation. Use of things indifferent. Abuse detected. Mode of correcting it.*

10. *This liberty maintained in opposition to those who pay no regard to the weak. Error of this class of men refuted. A most pernicious error. Objection. Reply.*

11. *Application of the doctrine of Christian liberty to the subject of offenses. These of two kinds. Offense given. Offense received. Of offense given, a subject comprehended by few. Of Pharisaical offense, or offense received.*

12. *Who are to be regarded as weak and Pharisaical. Proved by examples and the doctrine of Paul. The just moderation of Christian liberty. The necessity of vindicating it. No regard to be paid to hypocrites. The duty of edifying our weak neighbors.*

13. *The application of the doctrine to things indifferent. The things necessary not to be omitted from any fear of offense.*

14. *Refutation of errors in regard to Christian liberty. The consciences of the godly not to be fettered by human traditions in matters of indifference.*

15. *Distinction to be made between spiritual and Civil government. These must not be confounded. How far conscience can be bound by human constitutions. Definition of conscience. Definition explained by passages from the Apostolic writings.*

16. *The relation which conscience bears to external obedience; first, in things good and evil; secondly, in things indifferent.*

1 The connection of this chapter with the previous one on justification. A true knowledge of Christian liberty is useful and necessary. A. It purifies the conscience. B. It checks licentiousness. C. It maintains the merits of Christ, the truth of the Gospel, and the peace of the soul.

We are now to treat of Christian liberty, the explanation of which certainly ought not to be omitted by anyone proposing to give a compendious summary of gospel doctrine. For it is a matter of primary necessity, one without the knowledge of which the conscience can scarcely attempt anything without hesitation, in many must demur and fluctuate, and in all proceed with fickleness and trepidation. In particular, it forms a proper appendix to justification, and is of no little service in understanding its force. Nay, those who seriously fear God will hence perceive the incomparable advantages of a doctrine which wicked scoffers are constantly assailing with their jibes; the intoxication of mind under which they labor, leaving their petulance without restraint. This, therefore, seems the proper place for considering the subject.

Moreover, though it has already been occasionally adverted to, there was an advantage in deferring the fuller consideration of it until now, for the moment any mention is made of Christian liberty lust begins to boil or insane commotions arise, if a speedy restraint is not laid on those licentious spirits by whom the best things are perverted into the worst. For they either, under pretext of this liberty shake off all obedience to God, and break out into unbridled licentiousness, or they feel indignant, thinking that all choice, order, and restraint, are abolished. What can we do when thus encompassed with straits? Are we to bid adieu to Christian liberty, in order that we may cut off all opportunity for such perilous consequences? But, as we have said, if the subject be not understood, neither Christ, nor the truth of the gospel, nor the inward peace of the soul, is properly known. Our endeavor must rather be, while not suppressing this very necessary part of doctrine, to obviate the absurd objections to which it usually gives rise.

2 This liberty consists of three parts. First, believers renouncing the righteousness of the Law, look only to Christ. Objection. Answer, distinguishing between legal and Evangelical righteousness.

Christian liberty seems to me to consist of three parts. First, the consciences of believers, while seeking the assurance of their justification before God, must rise above the Law and think no more of obtaining justification by it. For while the Law, as has already been demonstrated (supra, chapter 17, section 1), leaves not one man righteous, we are either excluded from all hope of justification, or we must be loosed from the Law, and so loosed as that no account at all shall be taken of works. For he who imagines that in order to obtain justification he must bring any degree of works whatever, cannot fix any mode or limit, but makes himself debtor to the whole Law. Therefore, laying aside all mention of the Law and all idea of works, we must in the matter of justification have recourse to the mercy of God only; turning away our regard from ourselves, we must look only to Christ. For the question is, not how we may be righteous, but how, though unworthy and unrighteous, we may be regarded as righteous. If consciences would obtain any assurance of this, they must give no place to the Law. Still, it cannot be rightly inferred from this that believers have no need of the Law. It ceases not to teach, exhort, and urge them to good, although it is not recognized by their consciences before the judgment-seat of God.

The two things are very different, and should be well and carefully distinguished. The whole lives of Christians ought to be a kind of aspiration after piety, seeing they are called unto holiness. (See Ephesians 1:4; 1 Thessalonians 4:5.) The office of the Law is to excite them to the study of purity and holiness by reminding them of their duty. For when the conscience feels anxious as to how it may have the favor of God, as to the answer it could give, and the confidence it would feel, if brought to His judgment-seat, in such a case the requirements of the Law are not to be brought forward, but Christ, who surpasses all the perfection of the Law, is alone to be held forth for righteousness.

3 This first part is clearly established by the whole Epistle to the Galatians.

On this, almost the whole subject of the Epistle to the Galatians hinges, for it can be proved from express passages that those are absurd interpreters who teach that Paul there contends only for freedom from ceremonies. Of such passages are the following: "Christ has redeemed us from the curse of the law, being made a curse for us." "Stand fast, therefore, in the liberty wherewith Christ has made us free, and be not entangled again with the yoke of bondage. Behold, I Paul say unto you, that if ye be circumcised, Christ shall profit you nothing. For I testify again to every man that is circumcised, that he is a debtor to do the whole law. Christ is become of no effect unto you, whosoever of you are justified by the law; ye are fallen from grace" (Galatians 3:13; 5:1-4). These words certainly refer to something of a higher order than freedom from ceremonies.

I confess, indeed, that Paul there treats of ceremonies, because he was contending with false apostles, who were plotting, to bring back into the Christian Church those ancient shadows of the Law, which were abolished by the advent of Christ. But, in discussing this question, it was necessary to introduce higher matters, on which the whole controversy turns.

First, because the brightness of the gospel was obscured by those Jewish shadows, he shows that in Christ we have a full manifestation of all those things, which were typified by Mosaic ceremonies.

Secondly, as those impostors instilled into the people the most pernicious opinion, that this obedience was sufficient to merit the grace of God, he insists very strongly that believers shall not imagine that they can obtain justification before God by any works, far less by those paltry observances. At the same time, he shows that by the cross of Christ they are free from the condemnation of the Law, to which otherwise all men are exposed, so that in Christ alone they can rest in full security. This argument is pertinent to the present subject (Galatians 4:5, 21, etc). Lastly, he asserts the right of believers to a liberty of conscience, a liberty that may not be restrained without necessity.

4 The second part of Christian liberty—viz. that the conscience, freed from the yoke of the Law, voluntarily obeys the will of God. This cannot be done so long as we are under the Law. Reason.

Another point, which depends on the former, is that consciences obey the Law, not as if compelled by legal necessity; but being free from the yoke of the Law itself, voluntarily obey the will of God. Being constantly in terror so long as they are under the dominion of the Law, they are never disposed promptly to obey God, unless they have previously obtained this liberty. Our meaning shall be explained more briefly and clearly by an example.

The command of the Law is, "Thou shalt love the Lord thy God with all thine heart, and with all thy soul, and with all thy might" (Deuteronomy 6:5). To accomplish this, the soul must previously be divested of every other thought and feeling, the heart purified from all its desires, all its powers collected and united on this one object. Those who, in comparison of others, have made much progress in the way of the Lord are still very far from this goal. For, although they love God in their minds, and with a sincere affection of heart, yet both are still in a great measure occupied with the lusts of the flesh, by which they are retarded and prevented from proceeding with quickened pace towards God. They indeed make many efforts, but the flesh partly enfeebles their strength, and partly binds them to itself. What can they do while they thus feel that there is nothing of which they are less capable than to fulfill the Law? They wish, aspire, endeavor, but they do nothing with the requisite perfection. If they look to the law, they see that every work, which they attempt or design, is accursed. Nor can anyone deceive himself by inferring that the work is not altogether bad, merely because it is imperfect, and, therefore, that any good which is in it is still accepted of God. For the Law demanding perfect love condemns all imperfection, unless its rigor is mitigated. Let any man, therefore, consider his work which he wishes to be thought partly good, and he will find that it is a transgression of the Law by the very circumstance of its being imperfect.

5 When freed from the rigorous exactions of the Law, we can cheerfully and with much alacrity answer the call of God.

See how our works lie under the curse of the Law if they are tested by the standard of the Law. But how can unhappy souls set themselves with alacrity to a work from which they cannot hope to gain anything in return but cursing? On the other hand, if freed from this severe exaction, or rather from the whole rigor of the Law, they hear themselves invited by God with paternal levity, they will cheerfully and alertly obey the call, and follow His guidance.

In one word, those who are bound by the yoke of the law are as servants who have certain tasks daily assigned to them by their masters. Such servants think that nothing has been done; and they dare not come into the presence of their masters until the exact amount of labor has been performed. But sons, who are treated in a more candid and liberal manner by their parents, hesitate not to offer them works that are only begun or half finished, or even with something faulty in them, trusting that their obedience and readiness of mind will be accepted, although the performance be less exact than was wished. Such should be our feelings, as we certainly trust that our most indulgent Parent will approve our services, however small they may be, and however rude and imperfect. Thus, He declares to us by the prophet, "I will spare them as a man spareth his own son that serveth him" (Malachi 3:17); where the word *spare* evidently means indulgence, or connivance at faults, while at the same time service is remembered. This confidence is necessary in no slight degree, since without it everything should be attempted in vain; for God does not regard any sock of ours as done to himself, unless truly done from a desire to serve him. But how can this be amidst these terrors, while we doubt whether God is offended or served by our work?

6 Proof of this second part from an apostle. The end of this liberty.

This is the reason that the author of the Epistle to the Hebrews ascribes to faith all the good works which the holy patriarchs are said to have performed, and estimates them merely by faith. (See Hebrews 11:2.) In regard to this liberty there is a remarkable passage in the Epistle to the Romans where Paul argues, "Sin shall not have dominion over you; for ye are not under the law, but under grace" (Romans 6:14). For after he had exhorted believers, "Let not sin therefore reign in your mortal body, that ye should obey it in the lusts thereof: Neither yield ye your members as instruments of unrighteousness unto sin; but yield yourselves unto God, as those that are alive from the dead, and your members as instruments of righteousness unto God;" they might have objected that they still bore about with them a body full of lust, that sin still dwelt in them. He, therefore, comforts them by adding, that they are freed from the Law; as if he had said, "Although you feel that sin is not yet extinguished, and that righteousness does not plainly live in you, you have no cause for fear and dejection, as if God were always offended because of the remains of sin, since by grace you are freed from the Law, and your works are not tried by its standard. Let those, however who infer that they may sin because they are not under the Law, understand that they have no right to this liberty, the end of which is to encourage us in well-doing.

7 Third part of liberty—viz. the free rise of things indifferent. The knowledge of this part is necessary to remove despair and superstition. Superstition described.

The third part of this liberty is that we are not bound before God to any observance of external things, which are in themselves indifferent, but that we are now at full liberty either to use or omit them. The knowledge of this liberty is very necessary to us; where it is wanting our consciences will have no rest, there will be no end of superstition. In the present day many think us absurd in raising a question as to the free eating of flesh, the free use of dress and holidays, and similar frivolous trifles, as they think them; but they are of more importance than is commonly supposed. For when once the conscience is entangled in the net, it enters a long and inextricable labyrinth, from which it is afterwards most difficult to escape. When a man begins to doubt whether it is lawful for him to use linen for sheets, shirts, napkins, and handkerchiefs, he will not long be secure as to hemp, and will at last have doubts as to tow; for he will revolve in his mind whether he cannot sup without napkins, or dispense with handkerchiefs. Should he deem a daintier food unlawful, he will afterwards feel uneasy for using loaf bread and common eatables, because he will think that his body might possibly be supported on a still meaner food. If he hesitates as to a more genial wine, he will scarcely drink the worst with a good conscience; at last, he will not dare to touch water if more than usually sweet and pure.

In fine, he will come to this, that he will deem it criminal to trample on a straw lying in his way. For it is no trivial dispute that is here commenced, the point in debate being, whether the use of this thing or that is in accordance with the divine will, which ought to take precedence over all our acts and counsels. Here some must be hurried into an abyss by despair, while others, despising God and casting off His fear, will not be able to make a way for themselves without ruin. When men are involved in such doubts, whatever be the direction in which they turn, everything they see must offend their conscience.

8 Proof of this third part from the Epistle to the Romans. Those who observe it not only use evasion. A. Despisers of God. B. The desperate. C. The ungrateful. The end and scope of this third part.

"I know," says Paul, "that there is nothing unclean of itself" (unclean means unholy); "but to him that esteemeth anything to be unclean, to him it is unclean" (Romans 14:14). By these words he makes all external things subject to our liberty, provided the nature of that liberty approves itself to our minds as before God. But if any superstitious idea suggests scruples, those things, which in their own nature were pure, are to us contaminated. Wherefore the apostle adds, "Happy is he that condemneth not himself in that which he alloweth. And he that doubteth is damned if he eat, because he eateth not of faith: for whatsoever is not of faith is sin" (Romans 14:22, 23). When men, amid such difficulties, proceed with greater confidence, securely doing whatever pleases them, do they not insofar revolt from God? Those who are thoroughly impressed with some fear of God, if forced to do many things repugnant to their consciences are discouraged and filled with dread. All such persons receive none of the gifts of God with thanksgiving, by which alone Paul declares that all things are sanctified for our use (1 Timothy 4:5). By thanksgiving, I understand that which proceeds from a mind recognizing the kindness and goodness of God in His gifts. For many, indeed, understand that the blessings which they enjoy are the gifts of God, and praise God in their words; but not being persuaded shalt these have been given to them, how can they give thanks to God as the Giver?

In one word, we see where this liberty tends—viz. that we are to use the gifts of God without any scruple of conscience, without any perturbation of mind, for the purpose for which He gave them: in this way our souls may both have peace with Him, and recognize his liberality towards us. For here are comprehended all ceremonies of free observance, so that while our consciences are not to be laid under the necessity of observing them, we are also to remember that, by the kindness of God, the use of them is made subservient to edification.

9 The second part of the chapter, showing the nature and efficacy of Christian liberty, in opposition to the Epicureans. Their character described. Pretext and allegation. The use of things indifferent. Abuse detected. Mode of correcting it.

It is, however, to be carefully observed that Christian liberty is in all its parts a spiritual matter, the whole force of which consists in giving peace to trembling consciences, whether they are anxious and disquieted as to the forgiveness of sins, or as to whether their imperfect works, polluted by the infirmities of the flesh, are pleasing to God, or are perplexed as to the use of things indifferent. It is, therefore, perversely interpreted by those who use it as a cloak for their lusts, that they may licentiously abuse the good gifts of God, or who think there is no liberty unless it is used in the presence of men, and, accordingly, in using it pay no regard to their weak brethren. Under this head, the sins of the present age are more numerous. For there is scarcely anyone whose means allow him to live sumptuously, who does not delight in feasting, dress, and the luxurious grandeur of his house, who wishes not to surpass his neighbor in every kind of delicacy, and does not plume himself amazingly on his splendor. And all these things are defended under the pretext of Christian liberty. They say they are things indifferent: I admit it, provided they are used indifferently. But when they are too eagerly longed for, when they are proudly boasted of, when they are indulged in luxurious profusion, things which otherwise were in themselves lawful are certainly defiled by these vices. Paul makes an admirable distinction in regard to things indifferent: "Unto the pure all things are pure: but unto them that are defiled and unbelieving is nothing pure; but even their mind and conscience is defiled" (Titus 1:15). For why is a woe pronounced upon the rich who have received their consolation? (Luke 6:24), who are full, who laugh now, who "lie upon beds of ivory and stretch themselves upon their couches;" "join house to house," and "lay field to field;" "and the harp and the viol, the tablet and pipe, and wine, are in their feasts" (Amos 6:6; Isaiah 5:8, 10). Certainly ivory and gold, and riches, are the good creatures of God, permitted, nay destined, by divine providence for the use of man; nor was it ever forbidden to laugh, or to be full, or to add new to old and hereditary possessions, or to be delighted with music, or to drink wine. This is true, but when the means are supplied to roll and wallow in luxury, to intoxicate the mind and soul with present and be always hunting after new pleasures, is very far from a legitimate use of the gifts of God. Let them, therefore, suppress immoderate desire, immoderate profusion, vanity, and arrogance, that they may use the gifts of God purely with a pure conscience. When their mind is brought to this state of soberness, they will be able to regulate the legitimate use. On the other hand, when this moderation is wanting, even plebeian and ordinary delicacies are excessive. For it is a true saying that a haughty mind often dwells in a coarse and homely garb, while true humility lurks under fine linen and purple.

Let everyone then live in his own station, poorly or moderately, or in splendor; but let all remember that the nourishment which God gives is for life, not luxury, and let them regard it as the law of Christian liberty, to learn with Paul in whatever state they are, "therewith to be content," to know "both how to be abased," and "how to abound," "to be full and to be hungry, both to abound and to suffer need" (Philippians 4:11).

10 This liberty is maintained in opposition to those who pay no regard to the weak. Error of this class of men refuted. A most pernicious error. Objection. Reply.

Very many also err in this: as if their liberty were not safe and entire, without having men to witness it, they use it indiscriminately and imprudently, and in this way often give offense to weak brethren. You may see some in the present day who cannot think they possess their liberty unless they come into possession of it by eating flesh on Friday. Their eating I blame not, but this false notion must be driven from their minds: for they ought to think that their liberty gains nothing new by the sight of men, but is to be enjoyed before God, and consists as much in abstaining as in using. If they understand that it is of no consequence in the sight of God whether they eat flesh or eggs, whether they are clothed in red or in black, this is amply sufficient. The conscience to which the benefit of this liberty was due is loosed. Therefore, though they should afterwards, during their whole life, abstain from flesh, and constantly wear one color, they are not less free. Nay, just because they are free, they abstain with a free conscience. But they err most egregiously in paying no regard to the infirmity of their brethren, with which it becomes us to bear, so as not rashly to give them offense. But it is sometimes also of consequence that we should assert our liberty before men. This I admit: yet must we use great caution in the mode, lest we should cast off the care of the weak whom God has specially committed to us.

11 The application of the doctrine of Christian liberty to the subject of offenses. These of two kinds. Offense given. Offense received. Of offense given, a subject comprehended by few. Of Pharisaical offense, or offense received.

I will here observe on offenses, what distinctions are to be made between them, what kind are to be avoided and what kind disregarded. This will afterwards enable us to determine what scope there is for our liberty among men. We are pleased with the common division into *offense given* and *offense taken*, since it has the plain sanction of Scripture, and not improperly expresses what is meant. If from unseasonable levity or wantonness, or rashness, you do anything out of order or not in its own place, by which the weak or unskillful are offended, it may be said that offense has been *given* by you, since the ground of offense is owing to your fault. And in general, offense is said to be *given* in any matter where the person from whom it has proceeded is in fault. Offense is said to be taken when a thing otherwise done, not wickedly or unseasonably, is made an occasion of offense from malevolence or some sinister feeling. For here, offense was not given, but sinister interpreters ceaselessly take offense. By the former kind, the weak only, by the latter, the ill tempered and Pharisaical are offended. Wherefore, we shall call the one the offense of the weak, the other the offense of Pharisees, and we will so temper the use of our liberty as to make it yield to the ignorance of weak brethren, but not to the austerity of Pharisees.

What is due to infirmity is fully shown by Paul in many passages. "Him that is weak in the faith receive ye." Again, "Let us not judge one another any more: but judge this rather, that no man put a stumbling-block, or an occasion to fall, in his brother's way;" and many others to the same effect in the same place, to which, instead of quoting them here, we refer the reader. The sum is, "We then that are strong ought to bear the infirmities of the weak, and not to please ourselves. Let everyone of us please his neighbor for his good to edification." Elsewhere he says, "Take heed lest by any means this liberty of yours become a stumbling-block to them that are weak." Again, "Whatsoever is sold in the shambles, that eat, asking no question for conscience sake." "Conscience, I say, not thine own, but of the other." Finally, "Give none offense, neither to the Jews nor to the Gentiles nor to the Church of God." Also in another passage, "Brethren, ye have been called into liberty, only use not liberty for an occasion to the flesh, but by love serve one another." Thus, indeed, it is: our liberty was not given us against our weak neighbors, whom charity enjoins us to serve in all things, but rather that, having peace with God in our minds, we should live peaceably among men.

What value is to be set upon the offense of the Pharisees we learn from the words of our Lord, in which He says, "Let them alone: they be blind leaders of the blind" (Matthew 15:14). The disciples had intimated that the Pharisees were offended at his words. He answers that they are to be let alone, that their offense is not to be regarded.

12 Who are to be regarded as weak and Pharisaical. Proved by examples and the doctrine of Paul. The just moderation of Christian liberty. The necessity of vindicating it. No regard to be paid to hypocrites. Duty of edifying our weak neighbors.

The matter still remains uncertain, unless we understand who are the weak and who the Pharisees: for if this distinction is destroyed, I see not how, in regard to offenses, any liberty at all would remain without being constantly in the greatest danger. But Paul seems to me to have marked out most clearly, as well by example as by doctrine, how far our liberty, in the case of offense, is to be modified or maintained. When he adopts Timothy as his companion, he circumcises him: nothing can induce him to circumcise Titus. (See Acts 16:3; Galatians 2:3.) The acts are different, but there is no difference in the purpose or intention; in circumcising Timothy, as he was free from all men, he made himself the servant of all: "Unto the Jews I became as a Jew, that I might gain the Jews; to them that are under the law, as under the law, that I might gain them that are under the law; to them that are without law, as without law (being not without law to God, but under the law to Christ), that I might gain them that are without law. To the weak became I as weak that I might gain the weak: I am made all things to all men, that I might by all means save some" (1 Corinthians 9:20-22).

We have here the proper modification of liberty, when in things indifferent it can be restrained with some advantage. What he had in view in firmly resisting the circumcision of Titus, he himself testifies when he thus writes: "But neither Titus, who was with me, being a Greek, was compelled to be circumcised: and that because of false brethren unawares brought in, who came in privily to spy out our liberty which we have in Christ Jesus, that they might bring us into bondage: to whom we gave place by subjection, no, not for an hour, that the truth of the Gospel might continue with you" (Galatians 2:3-5). We here see the necessity of vindicating our liberty when, by the unjust exactions of false apostles, it is brought into danger with weak consciences. In all cases, we must study charity, and look to the edification of our neighbor. "All things are lawful for me," says he, "but all things are not expedient; all things are lawful for me, but all things edify not. Let no man seek his own, but every man another's wealth" (1 Corinthians 10:23, 24). There is nothing plainer than this rule, that we are to use our liberty if it tends to the edification of our neighbor, but if inexpedient for our neighbor, we are to abstain from it. There are some who pretend to imitate this prudence of Paul by abstinence from liberty, while there is nothing for which they less employ it than for purposes of charity. Consulting their own ease, they would have all mention of liberty buried, though it is not less for the interest of our neighbor to use liberty for their good and edification, than to modify it occasionally for their advantage. It is the part of a pious man to think that the free power conceded to him in external things is to make him more ready in all offices of charity.

13 Application of the doctrine to things indifferent. Things necessary not to be omitted from any fear of offense.

Whatever I have said about avoiding offenses, I wish to be referred to things indifferent. Things, which are necessary to be done, cannot be omitted from any fear of offense. For as our liberty is to be made subservient to charity, so charity must in its turn be subordinate to purity of faith. Here, too, regard must be had to charity, but it must go as far as the altar; that is, we must not offend God for the sake of our neighbor. We approve not of the intemperance of those who do everything tumultuously, and would rather burst through every restraint at once than proceed step by step. But neither are those to be listened to who, while they take the lead in a thousand forms of impiety, pretend that they act thus to avoid giving offense to their neighbor, as if in the meantime they did not train the consciences of their neighbors to evil, especially when they always stick in the same mire without any hope of escape. When a neighbor is to be instructed, whether by doctrine or by example, then smooth-tongued men say that he is to be fed with milk, while they are instilling into him the worst and most pernicious opinions.

Paul says to the Corinthians, "I have fed you with milk, and not with meat" (1 Corinthians 3:2); but had there then been a popish mass among them, would he have sacrificed as one of the modes of giving them milk? By no means: milk is not poison. It is false, then, to say they nourish those whom, under a semblance of soothing, they cruelly murder. But granting that such dissimulation may be used for a time, how long are they to make their pupils drink that kind of milk? If they never grow up to be able to bear at least some gentle food, it is certain that they have never been reared on milk. Two reasons prevent me from now entering further into contest with these people, first, their follies are scarcely worthy of refutation, seeing all men of sense must nauseate them; and, secondly, having already amply refuted them in special treatises, I am unwilling to do it over again. Let my readers only bear in mind, first, that whatever be the offenses by which Satan and the world attempt to lead us away from the Law of God, we must, nevertheless, strenuously proceed in the course which He prescribes; and, secondly, that whatever dangers impend, we are not at liberty to deviate one nail's breadth from the command of God, that on no pretext is it lawful to attempt anything but what He permits.

14 Refutation of errors in regard to Christian liberty. The consciences of the godly not to be fettered by human traditions in matters of indifference.

Since by means of this privilege of liberty, which we have described, believers have derived authority from Christ, not to entangle themselves by the observance of things in which He wished them to be free, we conclude that their consciences are exempt from all human authority. For it would be unbecoming that the gratitude due to Christ for His liberal gift should perish or that the consciences of believers should derive no benefit from it. We must not regard it as a trivial matter when we see how much it cost our Savior, being purchased not with silver or gold, but with His own blood. (See 1 Peter 1:18, 19.) So that Paul hesitates not to say that Christ has died in vain, if we place our souls under subjection to men. (See Galatians 5:1, 4; 1 Corinthians 7:23.) Several chapters of the Epistle to the Galatians are wholly occupied with showing that Christ is obscured, or rather extinguished to us, unless our consciences maintain their liberty; from which they have certainly fallen, if they can be bound with the chains of laws and constitutions at the pleasure of men. But as the knowledge of this subject is of the greatest importance, so it demands a longer and clearer exposition. For the moment the abolition of human constitutions is mentioned, the greatest disturbances are excited, partly by the seditious, and partly by calumniators, as if obedience of every kind were at the same time abolished and overthrown.

15 Distinction to be made between Spiritual and Civil government. These must not be confounded. How far conscience can be bound by human constitutions. Definition of conscience. Definition explained by passages from the Apostolic writings.

Therefore, lest this prove a stumbling-block to any, let us observe that in man government is twofold: the one spiritual, by which the conscience is trained to piety and divine worship; the other civil, by which the individual is instructed in those duties which, as men and citizens, we are bold to performs. (See Book 4, chapter 10, sections 3-6.)

To these two forms are commonly given the not inappropriate names of spiritual and temporal jurisdiction, intimating that the former species has reference to the life of the soul, while the latter relates to matters of the present life, not only to food and clothing, but to the enacting of laws which require a man to live among his fellows purely honorably, and modestly. The former has its seat within the soul, the latter only regulates the external conduct. We may call the one the spiritual, the other the civil kingdom. Now, these two, as we have divided them, are always to be viewed apart from each other. When the one is considered, we should call off our minds, and not allow them to think of the other. For there exists in man a kind of two worlds, over which different kings and different laws can preside. By attending to this distinction, we will not erroneously transfer the doctrine of the gospel concerning spiritual liberty to civil order, as if in regard to external government. Christians are less subject to human laws, because their consciences are unbound before God, as if they were exempted from all carnal service, because in regard to the Spirit they are free. Again because even in those constitutions which seem to relate to the spiritual kingdom, there may be some delusion, it is necessary to distinguish between those which are to be held legitimate as being agreeable to the Word of God, and those, on the other hand, which ought to have no place among the pious.

We shall elsewhere have an opportunity of speaking of civil government. (See Book 4, chapter 20.) For the present, also, I defer speaking of ecclesiastical laws, because that subject will be more fully discussed in the Fourth Book, when we come to treat of the power of the Church. We would thus conclude the present discussion.

The question, as I have said, though not very obscure, or perplexing in itself, occasions difficulty to many, because they do not distinguish with sufficient accuracy between what is called the external *forum*, and the *forum* of conscience. What increases the difficulty is, that Paul commands us to obey the magistrate, "not only for wrath, but also for conscience sake" (Romans 13:1, 5). Whence it follows that civil laws also bind the conscience. Were this so, then what we said awhile ago, and are still to say of spiritual governments would fall.

To solve this difficulty, the first thing of importance is to understand what is meant by *conscience*. The definition must be sought in the etymology of the word. For as men, when they apprehend the knowledge of things by the mind and intellects are said to know, and hence arises the term knowledge or *science*, so when they have a sense of the divine justice added as a witness which allows them not to conceal their sins, but drags them forward as culprits to the bar of God, that sense is called *conscience*. For it stands between God and man, not suffering man to suppress what he knows in himself; but following him on even to conviction. It is this that Paul means when he says, "Their conscience also bearing witness, and their thoughts the meanwhile accusing, or else excusing one another" (Romans 2:15). Simple knowledge may exist in man, shut up; therefore, this sense, which sists man before the bar of God, is set over him as a kind of sentinel to observe and spy out all his secrets, that nothing may remain buried in darkness. Hence, the ancient proverb, "Conscience is a thousand witnesses." For the same reason Peter also employs the expression, "The answer of a good conscience" (1 Peter 3:21), for tranquility of mind; when persuaded of the grace of Christ, we boldly present ourselves before God. And the author of the Epistle to the Hebrews says that we have "...no more conscience of sins" (Hebrews 10:2), that we are held as freed or acquitted, so that sin no longer accuses us.

16 The relation which conscience bears to external obedience; first, in things good and evil; secondly, in things indifferent.

Wherefore, as works have respect to men, so conscience bears reference to God; a good conscience being nothing else than inward integrity of heart. In this sense, Paul says, "The end of the commandment is charity, out of a pure heart, and of a good consciences and of faith unfeigned" (1 Timothy 1:5). He, afterwards, in the same chapter, shows how much it differs from intellect when he speaks of "holding faith, and a good conscience, which some having put away, have made shipwreck" (1 Timothy 1:19). For by these words he intimates that it is a lively inclination to serve God, a sincere desire to live in piety and holiness. Sometimes, indeed, it is even extended to men, as when Paul testifies, "Herein do I exercise myself, to have always a conscience void of offense toward God, and toward men" (Acts 24:16). He speaks thus, because the fruits of a good conscience go forth and reach even to men. But, as I have said, properly speaking, it refers to God only. Hence, a law is said to bind the conscience, because it simply binds the individual, without looking at men, or taking any account of them. For example, God not only commands us to keep our minds chaste and pure from lust, but also prohibits all external lasciviousness or obscenity of language. My conscience is subjected to the observance of this law, though there were not another man in the world, and he who violates it sins not only by setting a bad example to his brethren, but stands convicted in his conscience before God.

The same rule does not hold in things indifferent. We ought to abstain from everything that produces offense, but with a free conscience. Thus, Paul, speaking of meat consecrated to idols, says, "If any man say unto you, This is offered in sacrifice unto idols, eat not for his sake that showed it, and for conscience sake:" "Conscience, I say, not thine own, but of the other" (1 Corinthians 10:28, 29). A believer, after being previously admonished, would sin were he still to eat meat so offered. Though abstinence, on his part, is necessary, in respect of a brother, as God prescribes it, still he ceases not to retain liberty of conscience. We see how the Law, while binding the external act, leaves the conscience unbound.

Chapter 20

OF PRAYER—A PERPETUAL EXERCISE OF FAITH. THE DAILY BENEFITS DERIVED FROM IT

The principal divisions of this chapter are,—I. Connection of the subject of prayer with the previous chapters. The nature of prayer, and its necessity as a Christian exercise, sections 1, 2. II. To whom prayer is to be offered. Refutation of an objection, which is too apt to present itself to the mind, section 3. III. Rules to be observed in prayer, sections 4-16. IV. Through whom prayer is to be made, sections 17-19. V. Refutation of an error as to the doctrine of our Mediator and Intercessor, with answers to the leading arguments urged in support of the intercession of saints, sections 20-27. VI. The nature of prayer, and some of its accidents, sections 28-33. VII. A perfect form of invocation, or an exposition of the Lord's Prayer, sections 34-50. VIII. Some rules to be observed with regard to prayer, as time, perseverance, the feeling of the mind, and the assurance of faith, sections 50-52.

Sections

1. A general summary of what is contained in the previous part of the work. A transition to the doctrine of prayer. Its connection with the subject of faith.

2. Prayer defined. Its necessity and use.

3. Objection, that prayer seems useless, because God already knows our wants. Answer, from the institution and end of prayer. Confirmation by example. Its necessity and propriety. Perpetually reminds us of our duty, and leads to meditation on divine providence. Conclusion. Prayer is a most useful exercise. This is proved by three passages of Scripture.

4. Rules to be observed in prayer. First, reverence to God. How the mind ought to be composed.

5. All giddiness of mind must be excluded, and all our feelings seriously engaged. This is confirmed by the form of lifting the hand in prayer. We must ask only insofar as God permits. To help our weakness, God gives the Spirit to be our Guide in prayer. What the office of the Spirit is in this respect. We must still pray both with the heart and the lips.

6. The second rule of prayer, a sense of our want. This rule violated, A. By perfunctory and formal prayer B. By hypocrites who have no sense of their sins. C. By giddiness in prayer. Remedies.

7. Objection, that we are not always under the same necessity of praying. Answer, we must pray always. This answer is confirmed by an examination of the dangers by which both our life and our salvation are every moment threatened. Confirmed further by the command and permission of God, by the nature of true repentance, and a consideration of impenitence. Conclusion.

8. Third rule, the suppression of all pride. Examples: Daniel, David, Isaiah, Jeremiah, and Baruch.

9. The advantage of thus suppressing pride. It leads to earnest entreaty for pardon, accompanied with humble confession and sure confidence in the divine mercy. This may not always be expressed in words. It is peculiar to pious penitents. A general introduction to procure favor to our prayers never to be omitted.

10. Objection to the third rule of prayer. Of the glorying of the saints. Answer. Confirmation of the answer.

11. Fourth rule of prayer, a sure confidence of being heard animating us to prayer. The kind of confidence required—viz. a serious conviction of our misery, joined with sure hope. From these true prayer springs. How diffidence impairs prayer. In general, faith is required.

12. This faith and sure hope are regarded by our opponents as most absurd. Their error is described and refuted by various passages of Scripture, which show that acceptable prayer is accompanied with these qualities. No repugnance between this certainty and an acknowledgment of our destitution.

13. To our unworthiness we oppose, A. The command of God. B. The promise. Rebels and hypocrites are completely condemned. Passages of Scripture confirming the command to pray.

14. Other passages respecting the promises, which belong to the pious, when they invoke God. These are realized though we are not possessed of the same holiness as other distinguished servants of God, provided we indulge no vain confidence, and sincerely betake ourselves to the mercy of God. Those who do not invoke God under urgent necessity are no better than idolaters. This concurrence of fear and confidence reconciles the different passages of Scripture, as to humbling ourselves in prayer and causing our prayers to ascend.

15. Objection founded on some examples—viz. that prayers have proved effectual, though not according to the form prescribed. Answer. Such examples, though not given for our imitation, are of the greatest use. Objection, the prayers of the faithful are sometimes not effectual. Answer confirmed by a noble passage of Augustine. Rule for right prayer.

16. The above four rules of prayer not so rigidly exacted, as that every prayer deficient in them in any respect is rejected by God. This is shown by examples. Conclusion, or summary of this section.

17. Through whom God is to be invoked—viz. Jesus Christ. This founded on a consideration of the divine majesty, and the precept and promise of God himself. God, therefore, is to be invoked only in the name of Christ.

18. From the first, all believers were heard through Him only: yet this specially restricted to the period subsequent to His ascension. The ground of this restriction.

19. The wrath of God lies on those who reject Christ as a Mediator. This excludes not the mutual intercession of saints on the Earth.

20. Refutation of errors interfering with the intercession of Christ. Christ, the Mediator of redemption; the saints, mediators of intercession. Answer confirmed by the clear testimony of Scripture and by a passage from Augustine. The nature of Christ's intercession.

21. Of the intercession of saints living with Christ in Heaven. Fiction of the papists in regard to it. Refuted. A. Its absurdity. B. It is nowhere mentioned by Scripture. C. Appeal to the conscience of the superstitious. D. Its blasphemy. Exception. Answers.

22. Monstrous errors resulting from this fiction. Refutation. Exception by the advocates of this fiction. Answer.

23. Arguments of the papists for the intercession of saints. A. From the duty and office of angels. Answer. B. From an expression of Jeremiah respecting Moses and Samuel. Answer, retorting the argument. C. The meaning of the prophet confirmed by a similar passage in Ezekiel, and the testimony of an apostle.

24. D. Fourth Papistical argument from the nature of charity, which is more perfect in the saints in glory. Answer.

25. Argument founded on a passage in Moses. Answer.

26. Argument from its being said that the prayers of saints are heard. Answer, confirmed by Scripture, and illustrated by examples.

27. Conclusion, that the saints cannot be invoked without impiety. A. It robs God of his glory. B. It destroys the intercession of Christ. C. It is repugnant to the word of God. D. It is opposed to the due method of prayer. E. It is without approved example. F. It springs from distrust. Last objection. Answer.

28. Kinds of prayer. Vows. Supplications. Petitions. Thanksgiving. The connection of these, their constant use and necessity. Particular explanation confirmed by reason, Scripture, and example. Rule as to supplication and thanksgiving.

29. The accidents of prayer—viz. private and public, constant, at stated seasons, etc. Exception in time of necessity. Prayer without ceasing. Its nature. The garrulity of papists and hypocrites refuted. The scope and parts of prayer. Secret prayer. Prayer at all places. Private and public prayer.

30. Of public places or churches in which common prayers are offered up. Right use of churches. Abuse.

31. Of utterance and singing. These are of no avail if they are not from the heart. The use of the voice refers more to public than private prayer.

32. Singing of the greatest antiquity, but not universal. How to be performed.

33. Public prayers should be in the vulgar, not in a foreign tongue. Reason, A. The nature of the Church. B. Authority of an apostle. Sincere affection always necessary. The tongue not always necessary. Bending of the knee, and uncovering of the head.

34. The form of prayer delivered by Christ displays the boundless goodness of our heavenly Father. The great comfort thereby afforded.

35. The Lord's Prayer divided into six petitions. Subdivision into two principal parts, the former referring to the glory of God, the latter to our salvation.

36. *What is implied by the use of the term Father implies, A. That we pray to God in the name of Christ alone. B. That we lay aside all distrust. C. That we expect everything that is for our good.*

37. *Objection, that our sins exclude us from the presence of him whom we have made a Judge, not a Father. Answer, from the nature of God, as described by an apostle, the parable of the prodigal son, and from the expression, Our Father. Christ the earnest, the Holy Spirit the witness of our adoption.*

38. *Why God is called generally, "Our Father."*

39. *We may pray specially for ourselves and certain others, provided we have in our mind a general reference to all.*

40. *In what sense God is said to be in Heaven. A threefold use of this doctrine for our consolation. Three cautions. Summary of the preface to the Lord's Prayer.*

41. *The necessity of the first petition as proof of our unrighteousness. What is meant by the name of God. How it is hallowed. Parts of this hallowing. A deprecation of the sins by which the name of God is profaned.*

42. *The distinction between the first and second petitions. The Kingdom of God. How it is said to come. Special exposition of this petition. It reminds us of three things. The advent of the Kingdom of God in the world.*

43. *The distinction between the second and third petitions. The will here is meant not the secret will or good pleasure of God, but that which is manifested in the Word. Conclusion of the three first petitions.*

44. *A summary of the second part of the Lord's Prayer. Three petitions. What is contained in the first. It declares the exceeding kindness of God and our distrust. What is meant by bread? Why the petition for bread precedes that for the forgiveness of sins. Why it is called ours. Why this is to be sought daily. The doctrine resulting from this petition, illustrated by an example. Two classes of men sin in regard to this petition. In what sense it is called, "Our bread." Why we ask God to give it to us.*

45. *The close connection between this and the subsequent petition. Why our sins are called debts. This petition violated, A. By those who think they can satisfy God by their own merits, or*

those of others. B. By those who dream of a perfection which makes pardon unnecessary. Why the elect cannot attain perfection in this life. Refutation of the libertine dreamers of perfection. Objection refuted. In what sense we are said to forgive those who have sinned against us. How the condition is to be understood.

46. The sixth petition is reduced to three headings. A. The various forms of temptation. The depraved conceptions of our minds. The wiles of Satan, on the right hand and on the left. B. What it is to be led into temptation. We do not ask not to be tempted of God. What is meant by evil, or the evil one. a summary of this petition. How necessary it is. Condemns the pride of the superstitious. Includes many excellent properties. In what sense God may be said to lead us into temptation.

47. The three last petitions show that the prayers of Christians ought to be public. The conclusion of the Lord's Prayer. Why the word Amen is added.

48. The Lord's Prayer contains everything that we can or ought to ask of God. Those who go beyond it sin in three ways.

49. We may, after the example of the saints, frame our prayers in different words, provided there is no difference in meaning.

50. Some circumstances that are to be observed. Of appointing special hours of prayer. What to be aimed at, and what is to be avoided. The will of God, the rule of our prayers.

51. Perseverance in prayer is especially recommended, both by precept and example. Condemnatory of those who assign to God a time and mode of hearing.

52. Of the dignity of faith, through which we always obtain, in answer to prayer, whatever is most expedient for us. The knowledge of this is most necessary.

1 A general summary of what is contained in the previous part of the work. A transition to the doctrine of prayer. Its connection with the subject of faith.

From the previous part of the work we clearly see how completely destitute man is of all good, how devoid of every means of procuring his own salvation. Hence, if he would obtain succor in his necessity, he must go beyond himself, and procure it in some other quarter. It has further been shown that the Lord kindly and spontaneously manifests himself in Christ, in whom He offers all happiness for our misery, all abundance for our want, opening up the treasures of Heaven to us, so that we may turn with full faith to His beloved Son, depend upon Him with full expectation, rest in Him, and cleave to him with full hope. This, indeed, is that secret and hidden philosophy which cannot be learned by syllogisms: a philosophy thoroughly understood by those whose eyes God has so opened as to see light in His light. (See Psalm 36:9.) But after we have learned by faith to know that whatever is necessary for us or defective in us is supplied in God and in our Lord Jesus Christ, in whom it hath pleased the Father that all fullness should dwell, that we may thence draw as from an inexhaustible fountain, it remains for us to seek and in prayer implore of Him what we have learned to be in Him.

To know God as the sovereign disposer of all good, inviting us to present our requests, and yet not to approach or ask of Him, were so far from availing us, that it would be just as if one told of a treasure, were to allow it to remain buried in the ground. Hence, the apostle, to show that a faith unaccompanied with prayer to God cannot be genuine, states this to be the order: As faith springs from the gospel, so by faith our hearts are framed to call upon the name of God. (See Romans 10:14.) And this is the very thing which he had expressed some time before—viz. that the *Spirit of adoption*, which seals the testimony of the gospel on our hearts, gives us courage to make our requests known unto God, calls forth groanings that cannot be uttered, and enables us to cry, "Abba, Father." (See Romans 8:26.) This last point, as we have hitherto only touched upon it slightly in passing, must now be treated more fully.

2 Prayer defined. Its necessity and use.

To *prayer*, then, are we indebted for penetrating to those riches, which are treasured up for us with our heavenly Father. For there is a kind of intercourse between God and men by which, having entered the upper sanctuary, they appear before Him and appeal to His promises, that when necessity requires, they may learn by experience that what they believed merely on the authority of

His Word was not in vain. Accordingly, we see that nothing is set before us as an object of expectation from the Lord which we are not enjoined to ask of Him in prayer, so true it is that prayer digs up those treasures which the Gospel of our Lord discovers to the eye of faith. The necessity and utility of this exercise of prayer no words can sufficiently express. Assuredly it is not without cause that our heavenly Father declares that our only safety is in calling upon His name, since by it we invoke the presence of His providence to watch over our interests, of His power to sustain us when weak and almost fainting, of His goodness to receive us into favor, though miserably loaded with sin; in fine, call upon him to manifest himself to us in all his perfections. Hence, admirable peace and tranquility are given to our consciences, for the straits by which we were pressed being laid before the Lord, we rest fully satisfied with the assurance that none of our evils are unknown to Him and that He is both able and willing to make the best provision for us.

3 Objection that prayer seems useless, because God already knows our wants. Answer, from the institution and end of prayer. Confirmation by example. Its necessity and propriety. Perpetually reminds us of our duty, and leads to meditation on divine providence. Conclusion. Prayer is a most useful exercise. This is proved by three passages of Scripture.

But someone will say, "Does He not know without a monitor both what our difficulties are, and what is meet for our interest, so that it seems in some measure superfluous to solicit him by our prayers, as if He were winking, or even sleeping, until aroused by the sound of our voice? Those who argue thus attend not to the end for which the Lord taught us to pray. It was not so much for His sake as for ours. He wills indeed, as is just, that due honor be paid Him by acknowledging that all which men desire or feel to be useful and pray to obtain, is derived from Him. But even the benefit of the homage, which we thus pay Him, redounds to ourselves. Hence, the holy patriarchs, the more confidently they proclaimed the mercies of God to themselves and others felt the stronger incitement to prayer. It will be sufficient to refer to the example of Elijah, who being assured of the purpose of God, had good ground for the promise of rain which he gives to Ahab, and yet prays anxiously upon his knees, and sends his servant seven times to inquire (see 1 Kings 18:42); not that he discredits the oracle, but because he knows it to be his duty to lay his desires before God, lest his faith should become drowsy or torpid. Wherefore, although it is true that while we are listless or insensible to our wretchedness, he wakes and watches for use and sometimes even assists us unasked; it is very much for our interest to be constantly supplicating Him; first, that our hearts may always be inflamed with a serious and ardent desire of seeking, loving, and serving Him, while we accustom ourselves to have recourse to Him as a sacred anchor in every necessity; secondly, that no desires, no longing whatever, of which we are ashamed to make Him the witness, may enter our minds, while we learn to place all our wishes in His sight, and thus pour out our heart before him; and, lastly, that we may be prepared to receive all His benefits with true gratitude and thanksgiving, while our prayers remind us that they proceed from His hand. Moreover, having obtained what we asked, being persuaded that He has answered our prayers, we are led to long more earnestly for His favor, and at the same time have greater pleasure in welcoming the blessings, which we perceive to have been obtained by our prayers. Lastly, use and experience confirm the thought of His providence in our minds in a manner adapted to our weakness, when we understand that He not only promises that He will never fail us, and spontaneously gives us access to approach him in every time of need, but has His hand always stretched out to assist His people, not amusing them with words, but proving himself to be a present aid. For these reasons, though our most merciful Father never slumbers nor sleeps, He very often seems to do so, that thus He may exercise us, when we might otherwise be listless and slothful, in asking, entreating, and earnestly beseeching Him to our great good. It is very absurd, therefore, to dissuade men from prayer, by pretending that Divine Providence, which is always watching over the government of the universes is in vain importuned by our supplications, when, on the contrary, the Lord himself declares, that he is "nigh unto all that call upon him, to all that call upon him in truth" (Psalm 145:18).

No better is the frivolous allegation of others: that it is superfluous to pray for things, which the Lord is ready of His own accord to bestow; since it is His pleasure that those very things, which flow from his spontaneous liberality, should be acknowledged as conceded to our prayers. This is testified by that memorable sentence in the Psalms to which many others correspond: "The eyes of the Lord are upon the righteous, and his ears are open unto their cry"

(Psalm 34:15). This passage, while extolling the care, which divine providence spontaneously exercises over the safety of believers, omits not the exercise of faith by which the mind is aroused from sloth. The eyes of God are awake to assist the blind in their necessity, but He is likewise pleased to listen to our groans, that He may give us the better proof of His love. And thus, both things are true, "He that keepeth Israel shall neither slumber nor sleep" (Psalm 121:4); and yet whenever He sees us dumb and torpid, He withdraws as if He had forgotten us.

4 Rules to be observed in prayer. First, reverence to God. How the mind ought to be composed.

Let the first rule of right prayer then be to have our heart and mind framed as becomes those who are entering into converse with God. This we shall accomplish in regard to the mind, if, laying aside carnal thoughts and cares which might interfere with the direct and pure contemplation of God, it not only be wholly intent on prayer, but also, as far as possible, be borne and raised above itself. I do not here insist on a mind so disengaged as to feel none of the gnawing of anxiety; on the contrary, it is by much anxiety that the fervor of prayer is inflamed. Thus, we see that the holy servants of God betray great anguish, not to say solicitude, when they cause the voice of complaint to ascend to the Lord from the deep abyss and the jaws of death. What I say is that all foreign and extraneous cares must be dispelled by which the mind might be driven to and fro in vague suspense, be drawn down from Heaven, and kept groveling on the Earth. When I say it must be raised above itself, I mean that it must not bring into the presence of God any of those things which our blind and stupid reason is wont to devise, nor keep itself confined within the little measure of its own vanity, but rise to a purity that is worthy of God.

5 All giddiness of mind must be excluded, and all our feelings seriously engaged. This is confirmed by the form of lifting the hand in prayer. We must ask only insofar as God permits. To help our weakness, God gives the Spirit to be our Guide in prayer. The office of the Spirit in this respect. We must still pray both with the heart and the lips.

Both things are especially worthy of notice. First, let everyone in professing to pray turn thither all his thoughts and feelings, and be not (as is usual) distracted by wandering thoughts; because nothing is more contrary to the reverence due to God than that levity which bespeaks a mind too much given to license and devoid of fear. In this matter we ought to labor the more earnestly the more difficult we experience it to be for no man is so intent on prayer as not to feel many thoughts creeping in, and either breaking off the tenor of his prayer, or retarding it by some turning or digression. Here let us consider how unbecoming it is when God admits us to familiar intercourse to abuse His great condescension by mingling things sacred and profane, reverence for Him not keeping our minds under restraint; but just as if in prayer we were conversing with one like ourselves forgetting Him and allowing our thoughts to run to and fro. Let us know, then, that none duly prepare themselves for prayer but those who are so impressed with the majesty of God that they engage in it free from all earthly cares and affections.

The ceremony of lifting up our hands in prayer is designed to remind us that we are far removed from God, unless our thoughts rise upward: as it is said in the Psalm, "Unto thee, O Lord, do I lift up my soul" (Psalm 25:1). And Scripture repeatedly uses the expression to *raise our prayer*, meaning that those who would be heard by God must not grovel in the mire.

The sum is that the more liberally God deals with us, condescendingly inviting us to unburden our cares into His bosom, the less excusable we are if this admirable and incomparable blessing does not in our estimation outweigh all other things and win our affection, that prayer may seriously engage our every thought and feeling. This cannot be unless our mind, strenuously exerting itself against all impediments, rise upward.

Our second proposition was that we are to ask only insofar as God permits. For though He bids us to pour out our hearts (Psalm 62:8), He does not indiscriminately give loose reins to foolish and depraved affections; and when He promises that He will grant believers their wish, his indulgence does not proceed so far as to submit to their caprice. In both matters, grievous delinquencies are everywhere committed. For not only do many without modesty, without reverence, presume to invoke God concerning their frivolities, but also impudently bring forward their dreams, whatever they may be, before the tribunal of God. Such is the folly or stupidity under which they labor, that they have the hardihood to obtrude upon God desires so vile, that they would blush exceedingly to impart them to their fellowmen.

Profane writers have derided and even expressed their detestation of this presumption, and yet the vice has always prevailed. Hence, as the ambitious adopted Jupiter as their patron; the avaricious, Mercury; the literary aspirants, Apollo and Minerva; the warlike, Mars; the licentious, Venus: so in the present day, as I lately observed, men in prayer give greater license to their unlawful desires than if they were telling jocular tales among their equals. God does not suffer His condescension to be thus mocked, but vindicating His own light, places our wishes under the restraint of His authority. We must, therefore, attend to the observation of John: "This is the confidence that we have in him, that if we ask anything according to his will, he heareth us" (1 John 5:14). But as our faculties are far from being able to attain to such high perfection, we must seek for some means to assist them. As the eye of our minds should be intent upon God, so the affections of our hearts ought to follow in the same course. But both fall far beneath this, or rather, they faint and fail, and are carried in a contrary direction.

To assist this weakness, God gives us the guidance of the Spirit in our prayers to dictate what is right, and regulate our affections. For seeing that "We know not what we should pray for as we ought," "the Spirit itself maketh intercession for us with groanings which cannot be uttered" (Romans 8:26), not that he actually prays or groans, but he excites in us sighs, and wishes, and confidence, which our natural powers are not at all able to conceive. Nor is it without cause that Paul gives the name of *groanings, which cannot be uttered,* to the prayers, which believers send forth under the guidance of the Spirit. For those who are truly exercised in prayer are aware that blind anxieties so restrain and perplex them, that they can scarcely find what it becomes them to utter; nay, in attempting to lisp they halt and hesitate.

Hence, it appears that to pray aright is a special gift. We do not speak thus in indulgence to our sloth, as if we were to leave the office of prayer to the Holy Spirit, and give way to that carelessness to which we are too prone. Thus, we sometimes hear the impious expression that we are to wait in suspense until He takes possession of our minds, while otherwise occupied.

Our meaning is that, weary of our own heartlessness and sloth, we are to long for the aid of the Spirit. Nor, indeed, does Paul, when he enjoins us to pray *in the Spirit* (see 1 Corinthians 14:14, 15), cease to exhort us to vigilance, intimating, that while the inspiration of the Spirit is effectual to the formation of prayer, it by no means impedes or retards our own endeavors; since in this matter God is pleased to try how efficiently faith influences our hearts.

6. Second rule of prayer, a sense of our want. This rule is violated, A. By perfunctory and formal prayer B. By hypocrites who have no sense of their sins. C. By giddiness in prayer. Remedies.

Another rule of prayer is that in asking we must always truly feel our wants, and seriously considering that we need all the things which we ask, accompany the prayer with a sincere, nay, ardent desire of obtaining them. Many repeat prayers in a perfunctory manner from a set form, as if they were performing a task to God, and though they confess that this is a necessary remedy for the evils of their condition, because it would be fatal to be left without the divine aid which they implore, it still appears that they perform the duty from custom, because their minds are meanwhile cold, and they ponder not what they ask. A general and confused feeling of their necessity leads them to pray, but it does not make them solicitous as in a matter of present consequence, that they may obtain the supply of their need.

Moreover, can we suppose anything more hateful or even more execrable to God than this fiction of asking the pardon of sins, while he who asks at the very time either thinks that he is not a sinner, or, at least, is not thinking that he is a sinner; in other words, a fiction by which God is plainly held in derision? But mankind, as I have lately said, is full of depravity, so that in the way of perfunctory service people often ask many things of God which they think come to them without His beneficence, or from some other quarter, or are already certainly in their possession.

There is another fault, which seems less heinous, but is not to be tolerated. Some murmur out prayers without meditation, their only principle being that God is to be propitiated by prayer. Believers ought to be specially on their guard never to appear in the presence of God with the intention of presenting a request unless they are under some serious impression, and are, at the same time, desirous to obtain it. Nay, although in these things, which we ask only for the glory of God, we seem not at first sight to consult for our necessity, yet we ought not to ask with less fervor and vehemence of desire. For instance, when we pray that His name be hallowed—that hallowing must, so to speak, be earnestly hungered and thirsted after.

7 Objection, that we are not always under the same necessity of praying. Answer, we must pray always. This answer is confirmed by an examination of the dangers by which both our life and our salvation are every moment threatened. It is confirmed further by the command and permission of God, by the nature of true repentance, and a consideration of impenitence. Conclusion.

If it is objected that the necessity which urges us to pray is not always equal; I admit it, and this distinction is profitably taught us by James: "Is any among you afflicted? Let him pray. Is any merry? Let him sing psalms" (James 5:13). Therefore, common sense itself dictates, that as we are too sluggish, we must be stimulated by God to pray earnestly whenever the occasion requires. This David calls a time when God "may be found" (a seasonable time); because, as he declares in several other passages, that the more hardly grievances, annoyances, fears, and other kinds of trial press us, the freer is our access to God, as if He were inviting us to himself. Still not less true is the injunction of Paul to pray "always" (Ephesians 6:18); because, however prosperously according to our view, things proceed, and however we may be surrounded on all sides with grounds of joy, there is not an instant of time during which our want does not exhort us to prayer. A man abounds in wheat and wine; but as he cannot enjoy a morsel of bread, unless by the continual bounty of God, his granaries or cellars will not prevent him from asking for daily bread. Then, if we consider how many dangers impend every moment, fear itself will teach us that no time ought to be without prayer. This, however, may be better known in spiritual matters. For when will the many sins of which we are conscious allow us to sit secure without suppliantly entreating freedom from guilt and punishment? When will temptation give us a truce, making it unnecessary to hasten for help? Moreover, zeal for the kingdom and glory of God ought not to seize us by starts, but urge us without intermission, so that every time should appear seasonable? It is not without cause, therefore, that assiduity in prayer is so often enjoined. I am not now speaking of perseverance, which shall afterwards be considered; but Scripture, by reminding us of the necessity of constant prayer, charges us with sloth, because we feel not how much we stand in need of this care and assiduity. By this rule hypocrisy and the device of lying to God are restrained, nay, altogether banished from prayer. God promises that He will be near to those who call upon Him in truth, and declares that those who seek Him with their whole hearts will find Him: those, therefore, who delight in their own pollution cannot surely aspire to him. One of the requisites of legitimate prayer is repentance.

Hence, the common declaration of Scripture, that God does not listen to the wicked; that their prayers, as well as their sacrifices, are an abomination to Him. For it is right that those who seal up their hearts should find the ears of God closed against them, that those who, by their hardheartedness, provoke His severity should find him inflexible. In Isaiah He thus threatens: "When ye make many prayers, I will not hear: your hands are full of blood" (Isaiah 1:15). In like manner, in Jeremiah, "Though they shall cry unto me, I will not hearken unto them" (Jeremiah 11:7, 8, 11); because He regards it as the highest insult for the wicked to boast of His covenant while profaning His sacred name by their whole lives. Hence, He complains in Isaiah: "This people draw near to me with their mouth, and with their lips do honor me; but have removed their heart far from men" (Isaiah 29:13). Indeed, He does not confine this to prayers alone, but declares that He abominates pretense in every part of His service. Hence, the words of James, "Ye ask and receive not because ye ask amiss, that ye may consume it upon your lusts" (James 4:3). It is true, indeed (as we shall again see in a little), that the pious, in the prayers which they utter, trust not to their own worth; still the admonition of John is not superfluous: "Whatsoever we ask, we receive of him, because we keep his commandments" (1 John 3:22); an evil conscience shuts the door against us. Hence, it follows, that none but the sincere worshippers of God pray aright, or are listened to. Let everyone, therefore, who prepares to pray feel dissatisfied with what is wrong in his condition, and assume, which he cannot do without repentance, the character and feelings of a poor suppliant.

8 The third rule, the suppression of all pride. Examples: Daniel, David, Isaiah, Jeremiah, and Baruch.

The third rule to be added is: that he who comes into the presence of God to pray must divest himself of all vainglorious thoughts, lay aside all idea of worth; in short, discard all self- confidence, humbly giving God the whole glory, lest by arrogating anything, however little, to himself, vain pride would cause Him to turn away His face. Of this submission, which casts down all haughtiness, we have numerous examples in the servants of God. The holier they are, the more humbly they prostrate themselves when they come into the presence of the Lord. Thus Daniel, on whom the Lord himself bestowed such high commendation, says, "We do not present our supplications before thee for our righteousness but for thy great mercies. O Lord, hear; O Lord, forgive; O Lord, hearken and do; defer not, for thine own sake, O my God: for thy city and thy people are called by thy name." This he does not indirectly in the usual manner, as if he were one of the individuals in a crowd: he rather confesses his guilt apart, and as a suppliant betaking himself to the asylum of pardon, he distinctly declares that he was confessing his own sin, and the sin of his people Israel. (See Daniel 9:18-20.) David also sets us an example of this humility: "Enter not into judgment with thy servant: for in thy sight shall no man living be justified" (Psalm 143:2).

In like manner, Isaiah prays, "Behold, thou art wroth; for we have sinned: in those is continuance, and we shall be saved. But we are all as an unclean thing, and all our righteousness are as filthy rags; and we all do fade as a leaf; and our iniquities, like the wind, have taken us away. And there is none that calleth upon thy name, that stirreth up himself to take hold of thee: for thou hast hid thy face from us, and hast consumed us, because of our iniquities. But now, O Lord, thou art our Father; we are the clay, and thou our potter; and we all are the work of thy hand. Be not wroth very sore, O Lord, neither remember iniquity forever: Behold, see, we beseech thee, we are all thy people" (Isaiah 64:5-9). You see how they put no confidence in anything but this: considering that they are the Lord's, they despair not of being the objects of his care.

In the same way, Jeremiah says, "O Lord, though our iniquities testify against us, do thou it for thy name's sake" (Jeremiah 14:7). For it was most truly and piously written by the uncertain author (whoever he may have been) who wrote the book which is attributed to the prophet Baruch, "But the soul that is greatly vexed, which goeth stooping and feeble, and the eyes that fail, and the hungry soul, will give thee praise and righteousness, O Lord. Therefore, we do not make our humble supplication before thee, O Lord our God, for the righteousness of our fathers, and of our kings." "Hear, O Lord, and have mercy; for thou art merciful: and have pity upon us, because we have sinned before thee" (Baruch 2:18, 19; 3:2).

9 Advantage of thus suppressing pride. It leads to earnest entreaty for pardon, accompanied with humble confession and sure confidence in the divine mercy. This may not always be expressed in words. It is peculiar to pious penitents. A general introduction to procure favor to our prayers never to be omitted.

In fine, supplication for pardon, with humble and ingenuous confession of guilt, forms both the preparation and commencement of right prayer. For the holiest of men cannot hope to obtain anything from God until he has been freely reconciled to Him. God cannot be propitious to any but those whom He pardons. Hence, it is not strange that this is the key by which believers open the door of prayer, as we learn from several passages in the Psalms. David, when presenting a request on a different subject, says, "Remember not the sins of my youth, nor my transgressions; according to thy mercy remember me, for thy goodness sake, O Lord" (Psalm 25:7). Again, "Look upon my affliction and my pain, and forgive my sins" (Psalm 25:18). Here also we see that it is not sufficient to call ourselves to account for the sins of each passing day; we must also call to mind those, which might seem to have been long before buried in oblivion. For in another passage the same prophet, confessing one grievous crime, takes occasion to go back to his very birth, "I was shapen in iniquity, and in sin did my mother conceive me" (Psalm 51:5); not to extenuate the fault by the corruption of his nature, but to accumulate the sins of his whole life, that the stricter he was in condemning himself, the more placable God might be. But although the saints do not always in express terms ask forgiveness of sins, yet if we carefully ponder those prayers as given in Scripture, the truth of what I say will readily appear; namely, that their courage to pray was derived solely from the mercy of God, and that they always began with appeasing Him. For when a man interrogates his conscience, so far is he from presuming to lay his cares familiarly before God, that if he did not trust to mercy and pardon, he would tremble at the very thought of approaching Him.

There is, indeed, another special confession. When believers long for deliverance from punishment, they at the same time pray that their sins may be pardoned; for it would be absurd to wish that the effect should be taken away while the cause remains. For we must beware of imitating foolish patients who, anxious only about curing accidental symptoms, neglect the root of the disease. Nay, our endeavor must be to have God propitious even before He attests His favor by external signs, both because this is the order which He himself chooses, and it would be of little avail to experience His kindness, did not conscience feel that He is appeased, and thus enable us to regard Him as altogether lovely. Of this, we are even reminded by our Savior's reply. Having determined to cure the paralytic, He says, "Thy sins are forgiven thee;" in other words, He raises our thoughts to the object which is especially to be desired—viz. admission into the favor of God, and then gives the fruit of reconciliation by bringing assistance to us. Besides that special confession of present guilt, which believers employ, in supplicating for pardon of every fault and punishment, that general introduction which procures favor for our prayers must never be omitted, because prayers will never reach God unless they are founded on free mercy. To this we may refer the words of John, "If we confess our sins, he is faithful and just to forgive us our sins and to cleanse us from all unrighteousness" (1 John 1:9).

Hence, under the Law it was necessary to consecrate prayers by the expiation of blood, both that they might be accepted, and that the people might be warned that they were unworthy of the high privilege until, being purged from their defilements, they founded their confidence in prayer entirely on the mercy of God.

10 Objection to the third rule of prayer. Of the glorying of the saints. Answer. Confirmation of the answer.

Sometimes, however, the saints in supplicating God, seem to appeal to their own righteousness, as when David says, "Preserve my soul; for I am holy" (Psalm 86:2). Also Hezekiah, "Remember now, O Lord, I beseech thee how I have walked before thee in truth, and with a perfect heart, and have done that which is good in thy sight" (Isaiah 38:2). All they mean by such expressions is, that regeneration declares them to be among the servants and children to whom God engages that he will show favor. We have already seen how He declares by the Psalmist that his eyes "...are upon the righteous, and his ears are open unto their cry" (Psalm 34:16) and again by the apostle, that "Whatsoever we ask of him we obtain, because we keep his commandments" (John 3:22).

In these passages, He does not fix a value on prayer, as a meritorious work, but designs to establish the confidence of those who are conscious of an unfeigned integrity and innocence, such as all believers should possess. For the saying of the blind man who had received his sight is in perfect accordance with divine truth, And God heareth not sinners (John 9:31); provided we take the term "sinners" in the sense commonly used by Scripture to mean those who, without any desire for righteousness, are sleeping secure in their sins; since no heart will ever rise to genuine prayer that does not at the same time long for holiness. Those supplications in which the saints allude to their purity and integrity correspond to such promises, that they may thus have, in their own experience, a manifestation of that which all the servants of God are made to expect. Thus, they usually use this mode of prayer when before God they compare themselves with their enemies, from whose injustice they long to be delivered by His hand. When making such comparisons, there is no wonder that they bring forward their integrity and simplicity of heart, that thus, by the justice of their cause, the Lord may be the more disposed to give them succor. We rob not the pious breast of the privilege of enjoying a consciousness of purity before the Lord, and thus feeling assured of the promises with which He comforts and supports His true worshippers, but we would have them to lay aside all thought of their own merits and found their confidence of success in prayer solely on the divine mercy.

11 Fourth rule of prayer, a sure confidence of being heard animating us to prayer. The kind of confidence required—viz. a serious conviction of our misery, joined with sure hope. From these true prayer springs. How diffidence impairs prayer. In general, faith is required.

The fourth rule of prayer is that notwithstanding of our being thus abased and truly humbled, we should be animated to pray with the sure hope of succeeding. There is, indeed, an appearance of contradiction between the two things, between a sense of the just vengeance of God and firm confidence in His favor, and yet they are perfectly accordant, if it is the mere goodness of God that raises up those who are overwhelmed by their own sins. For, as we have formerly shown (see chapter 3, section 1, 2), that repentance and faith go hand in hand, being united by an indissoluble tie, the one causing terror, the other joy, so in prayer they must both be present. This concurrence David expresses in a few words: "But as for me,

I will come into thy house in the multitude of thy mercy, and in thy fear will I worship toward thy holy temple" (Psalm 5:7). Under the goodness of God, he comprehends faith, at the same time not excluding fear; for not only does His majesty compel our reverence, but our own unworthiness also divests us of all pride and confidence and keeps us in fear.

The confidence of which I speak is not one which frees the mind from all anxiety and soothes it with sweet and perfect rest; such rest is peculiar to those who, while all their affairs are flowing to a wish are annoyed by no care, stung with no regret, agitated by no fear. But the best stimulus which the saints have to prayer is when, in consequence of their own necessities, they feel the greatest disquietude, and are all but driven to despair, until faith seasonably comes to their aid; because in such straits the goodness of God so shines upon them, that while they groan, burdened by the weight of present calamities, and tormented with the fear of greater, they yet trust to this goodness, and in this way both lighten the difficulty of endurance, and take comfort in the hope of final deliverance.

It is necessary, therefore, that the prayer of the believer should be the result of both feelings, and exhibit the influence of both; namely, that while he groans under present and anxiously dreads new evils, he should, at the same time have recourse to God, not at all doubting that God is ready to stretch out a helping hand to him. For it is not easy to say how much God is irritated by our distrust, when we ask what we expect not of His goodness.

Hence, nothing is more accordant to the nature of prayer than to lay it down as a fixed rule, that it is not to come forth at random, but is to follow in the footsteps of faith. To this principle Christ directs all of us in these words, "Therefore, I say unto you, What things soever ye desire, when ye pray, believe that ye receive them, and ye shall have them" (Mark 11:24). The same thing He declares in another passage, "All things, whatsoever ye shall ask in prayer, believing, ye shall receive" (Matthew 21:22). In accordance with this are the words of James, "If any of you lack wisdom, let him ask of God, that giveth to all men liberally, and upbraideth not, and it shall be given him. But let him ask in faith, nothing wavering" (James 1:5). He most aptly expresses the power of faith by opposing it to wavering. No less worthy of notice is his additional statement, that those who approach God with a doubting, hesitating mind, without feeling assured whether they are to be heard or not, gain nothing by their prayers. Such persons he compares to a wave of the sea, driven with the wind and tossed. Hence, in another passage he terms genuine prayer "the prayer of faith" (James 5:15). Again, since God so often declares that He will give to every man according to his faith, he intimates that we cannot obtain anything without faith.

In short, it is faith, which obtains everything that is granted to prayer. This is the meaning of Paul in the well-known passage to which dull men give too little heed, "How then shall they call upon him in whom they have not believed? And how shall they believe in him of whom they have not heard?" "So then faith cometh by hearing, and hearing by the word of God" (Romans 10:14, 17). Gradually deducing the origin of prayer from faith, he distinctly maintains that God cannot be invoked sincerely except by those to whom, by the preaching of the gospel, his mercy and willingness have been made known, nay, familiarly explained.

12 This faith and sure hope are regarded by our opponents as most absurd. Their error is described and refuted by various passages of Scripture, which show that acceptable prayer is accompanied with these qualities. No repugnance between this certainty and an acknowledgment of our destitution.

This necessity our opponents do not at all consider. Therefore, when we say that believers ought to feel firmly assured, they think we are saying the most absurd thing in the world. But if they had any experience in true prayer, they would assuredly understand that God cannot be duly invoked without this firm sense of the divine benevolence. But as no man can well perceive the power of faith, without at the same time feeling it in his heart, what profit is there in disputing with men of this character, who plainly show that they have never had more than a vain imagination? The value and necessity of that assurance for which we contend is learned chiefly from prayer. Everyone who does not see this gives proof of a very stupid conscience. Therefore, leaving those who are thus blinded, let us fix our thoughts on the words of Paul, that God can only be invoked by such as have obtained a knowledge of His mercy from the gospel and feel firmly assured that that mercy is ready to be bestowed upon them. What kind of prayer would this be? "O Lord, I am indeed doubtful whether or not thou art inclined to hear me;

but being oppressed with anxiety, I fly to thee, that if I am worthy, thou mayest assist me."

None of the saints whose prayers are given in Scripture thus supplicated. Nor are we thus taught by the Holy Spirit, who tells us to "Come boldly unto the throne of grace, that we may obtain mercy, and find grace to help in time of need" (Hebrews 4:16); and elsewhere teaches us to "…have boldness and access with confidence by the faith of Christ" (Ephesians 3:12). This confidence of obtaining what we ask, a confidence which the Lord commands, and all the saints teach by their example, we must, therefore, hold fast with both hands, if we would pray to any advantage. The only prayer acceptable to God is that which springs (if I may so express it) from this presumption of faith, and is founded on the full assurance of hope. He might have been contented to use the simple name of faith, but he adds not only confidence, but also liberty or boldness, that by this mark he might distinguish us from unbelievers, who indeed like us pray to God, but pray at random.

Hence, the whole Church thus prays, "Let thy mercy O Lord, be upon us, according as we hope in thee" (Psalms 33:22). The same condition is set down by the Psalmist in another passage, "When I cry unto thee, then shall mine enemies turn back: this I know, for God is for me" (Psalms 56:9). Again, "In the morning will I direct my prayer unto thee, and will look up" (Psalm 5:3). From these words we gather, that prayers are vainly poured out into the air unless they are accompanied with faith, in which, as from a watchtower, we may quietly wait for God. With this agrees the order of Paul's exhortation. For before urging believers to pray in the Spirit always, with vigilance and assiduity, he enjoins them to take "the shield of faith," "the helmet of salvation, and the sword of the Spirit, which is the word of God" (Ephesians 6:16-18).

Let the reader here call to mind what I formerly observed, that faith by no means fails though accompanied with a recognition of our wretchedness, poverty, and pollution. No matter how much believers may feel that they are oppressed by a heavy load of iniquity and are not only devoid of everything which can procure the favor of God for them, but justly burdened with many sins which make Him an object of dread, yet they cease not to present themselves, this feeling not deterring them from appearing in His presence, because there is no other access to Him.

Genuine prayer is not that by which we arrogantly extol ourselves before God or set a great value on anything of our own, but that by which, while confessing our guilt, we utter our sorrows before God, just as children familiarly lay their complaints before their parents. Nay, the immense accumulation of our sins should rather spur us on and incite us to prayer. Of this the Psalmist gives us an example, "Heal my soul: for I have sinned against thee" (Psalm 41:4). I confess, indeed, that these stings would prove to be mortal darts, did not God give succor; but our heavenly Father has, in ineffable kindness, added a remedy, by which, calming all perturbation, soothing our cares, and dispelling our fears, He condescendingly allures us to himself; nay, removing all doubts, not to say obstacles, makes the way smooth before us.

13 To our unworthiness we oppose, A. The command of God. B. The promise. Rebels and hypocrites are completely condemned. Passages of Scripture confirming the command to pray.

And first, indeed in enjoining us to pray, He by the very injunction convicts us of impious contumacy if we obey not. He could not give a more precise command than that which is contained in the Psalms: "Call upon me in the day of trouble,"(Psalm 50:15). But as there is no office of piety more frequently enjoined by Scripture, there is no occasion for here dwelling longer upon it. "Ask," says our divine Master, "and it shall be given you; seek, and ye shall find; knock, and it shall be opened unto you" (Matthew 7:7). Here, indeed, a promise is added to the precept, and this is necessary. For, though all confess that we must obey the precept, yet the greater part would shun the invitation of God, did He not promise that He would listen and be ready to answer. These two positions being laid down, it is certain that all who caviling allege that they are not to come to God directly, are not only rebellious and disobedient, but are also convicted of unbelief, inasmuch as they distrust the promises. There is the more occasion to attend to this, because hypocrites, under a pretense of humility and modesty, proudly contemn the precept, as well as deny all credit to the gracious invitation of God; nay, rob Him of a principal part of His worship. For when He rejected sacrifices, in which all holiness seemed then to consist, He declared that the chief thing, that which above all others is precious in his sight, is to be invoked in the day of necessity. Therefore, when He demands that which is His own and urges us to alacrity in obeying, no pretexts for doubt, how specious soever they may be, can excuse us.

Hence, all the passages throughout Scripture in which we are commanded to pray are set up before our eyes as so many banners to inspire us with confidence. It would be presumption to go forward into the presence of God, did He not anticipate us by His invitation. Accordingly, He opens up the way for us by His own voice, "I will say, It is my people: and they shall say, The Lord is my God" (Zechariah 13:9). We see how He anticipates His worshippers, and desires them to follow, and therefore we cannot fear that the melody, which He himself dictates, will prove unpleasing. Especially let us call to mind that noble description of the divine character, by trusting to which we shall easily overcome every obstacle: "O thou that hearest prayer, unto thee shall all flesh come" (Psalm 65:2).

What can be more lovely or soothing than to see God invested with a title, which assures us that nothing is more proper to His nature than to listen to the prayers of suppliants?

Hence, the Psalmist infers, that free access is given not to a few individuals, but to all men, since God addresses all in these terms, "Call upon me in the day of trouble: I will deliver thee, and thou shalt glorify me" (Psalm 50:15). David, accordingly, appeals to the promise thus given in order to obtain what he asks: "Thou, O Lord of hosts, God of Israel, hast revealed to thy servant, saying, I will build thee an house: therefore hath thy servant found in his heart to pray this prayer unto thee" (2 Samuel 7:27). Here we infer that he would have been afraid, but for the promise which emboldened him. So in another passage he fortifies himself with the general doctrine, "He will fulfill the desire of them that fear him" (Psalm 145:19). Nay, we may observe in the Psalms how the continuity of prayer is broken, and a transition is made at one time to the power of God, at another to His goodness, at another to the faithfulness of His promises.

It might seem that David, by introducing these sentiments, unseasonably mutilates his prayers; but believers well know by experience, that their ardor grows languid unless new fuel is added, and, therefore, that meditation as well on the nature as on the Word of God during prayer is by no means superfluous. Let us not decline to imitate the example of David, and introduce thoughts, which may reanimate our languid minds with new vigor.

14 Other passages respecting the promises, which belong to the pious, when they invoke God. These are realized though we are not possessed of the same holiness as other distinguished servants of God, provided we indulge no vain confidence, and sincerely betake ourselves to the mercy of God. Those who do not invoke God under urgent necessity are no better than idolaters. This concurrence of fear and confidence reconciles the different passages of Scripture, as to humbling ourselves in prayer and causing our prayers to ascend.

It is strange that these delightful promises affect us coldly, or scarcely at all, so that the generality of men prefer to wander up and down, forsaking the fountain of living waters, and hewing out to themselves broken cisterns, rather than embrace the divine liberality voluntarily offered to them. "The name of the Lord," says Solomon, "is a strong tower; the righteous runneth into it, and is safe." Joel, after predicting the fearful disaster, which was at hand, subjoins the following memorable sentence: "And it shall come to pass, that whosoever shall call on the name of the Lord shall be delivered." This we know properly refers to the course of the Gospel. Scarcely one in a hundred is moved to come into the presence of God, though he himself exclaims by Isaiah, "And it shall come to pass, that before they call, I will answer; and while they are yet speaking, I will hear." This honor He elsewhere bestows upon the whole Church in general, as belonging to all the members of Christ: "He shall call upon me, and I will answer him: I will be with him in trouble; I will deliver him, and honor him."

My intention, however, as I already observed, is not to enumerate all, but only select some admirable passages as specimens of how kindly God allures us to himself, and how extreme our ingratitude must be when with such powerful motives our sluggishness still retards us. Wherefore, let these words always resound in our ears: "The Lord is nigh unto all them that call upon him, to all that call upon him in truth" (Psalm 145:18). Likewise, those passages which we have quoted from Isaiah and Joel, in which God declares that His ear is open to our prayers, and that He is delighted as with a sacrifice of sweet savor when we cast our cares upon Him.

The special benefit of these promises we receive when we frame our prayer, not timorously or doubtingly, but when trusting to His Word, whose majesty might otherwise deter us, we are bold to call him Father, He himself deigning to suggest this most delightful name. Fortified by such invitations, it remains for us to know that we have therein sufficient materials for prayer, since our prayers depend on no merit of our own, but all their worth and hope of success are founded and depend on the promises of God, so that they need no other support, and require not to look up and down on this hand and on that. It must, therefore, be fixed in our minds, that though we equal not the lauded sanctity of patriarchs, prophets, and apostles, yet as the command to pray is common to us as well as them, and faith is common, so if we lean on the Word of God, we are in respect of this privilege their associates. For God declaring, as has already been seen, that He will listen and be favorable to all, encourages the most wretched to hope that they shall obtain what they ask; and, accordingly, we should attend to the general forms of expression, which, as it is commonly expressed, exclude none from first to last; only let there be sincerity of heart, self-dissatisfaction humility, and faith, that we may not, by the hypocrisy of a deceitful prayer, profane the name of God.

Our most merciful Father will not reject those whom He not only encourages to come, but urges in every possible way. Hence, David's method of prayer to which I lately referred: "And now, O Lord God, thou art that God, and thy words be true, and thou hast promised this goodness unto thy servant, that it may continue forever before thee" (2 Samuel 7:28). So also, in another passage, "Let, I pray thee, thy merciful kindness be for my comfort, according to thy word unto thy servant" (Psalm 119:76). And the whole body of the Israelites, whenever they fortify themselves with the remembrance of the covenant, plainly declare, that since God thus prescribes they are not to pray timorously (Genesis 32:13). In this, they imitated the example of the patriarchs, particularly Jacob, who, after confessing that he was unworthy of the many mercies, which he had received of the Lord's hand, says that he is encouraged to make still larger requests, because God had promised that He would grant them. But whatever be the pretexts which unbelievers employ, when they do not flee to God as often as necessity urges, nor seek after Him, nor implore His aid, they defraud Him of His due honor just as much as if they were fabricating to themselves new gods and idols, since in this way they deny that God is the Author of all their blessings.

On the contrary, nothing more effectually frees pious minds from every doubt, than to be armed with the thought that no obstacle should impede them while they are obeying the command of God, who declares that nothing is more grateful to Him than obedience. Hence, again, what I have previously said becomes still more clear, namely, that a bold spirit in prayer well accords with fear, reverence, and anxiety, and that there is no inconsistency when God raises up those who had fallen prostrate. In this way, forms of expression, apparently inconsistent, admirably harmonize. Jeremiah and David speak of humbly laying their supplications before God. In another passage Jeremiah says, "Let, we beseech thee, our supplication be accepted before thee, and pray for us unto the Lord thy God, even for all this remnant." On the other hand, believers are often said to *lift up prayer*. Thus, Hezekiah speaks, when asking the prophet to undertake the office of interceding. And David says, "Let my prayer be set forth before thee as incense; and the lifting up of my hands as the evening sacrifice."

The explanation is, that though believers, persuaded of the paternal love of God, cheerfully rely on His faithfulness, and have no hesitation in imploring the aid which He voluntarily offers, they are not elated with supine or presumptuous security; but climbing up by the ladder of the promises, still remain humble and abased suppliants.

15 An objection founded on some examples—viz. that prayers have proved effectual, though not according to the form prescribed. Answer. Such examples, though not given for our imitation, are of the greatest use. Objection, the prayers of the faithful are sometimes not effectual. Answer confirmed by a noble passage of Augustine. Rule for right prayer.

Here, by way of objection, several questions are raised. Scripture relates that God sometimes complied with certain prayers, which had been dictated by minds not duly calmed or regulated. It is true that the cause for which Jotham imprecated on the inhabitants of Shechem the disaster that afterwards befell them was well-founded; but still he was inflamed with anger and revenge (see Judges 9:20); and hence God, by complying with the execration, seems to approve of passionate impulses. Similar fervor also seized Samson when he prayed, "Strengthen me, I pray thee, only this once, O God, that I may be at once avenged of the Philistines for my two eyes" (Judges 16:28). For although there was some mixture of good zeal, yet his ruling feeling was a fervid, and, therefore, vicious longing for vengeance. God assents, and hence apparently it might be inferred that prayers are effectual, though not framed in conformity to the rule of the Word.

But I answer, *first*, that a perpetual law is not abrogated by singular examples; and, *secondly*, that special suggestions have sometimes been made to a few individuals, whose case thus becomes different from that of the generality of men. For we should attend to the answer, which our Savior gave to His disciples when they inconsiderately wished to imitate the example of Elias, "Ye know not what manner of spirit ye are of" (Luke 9:55). We must, however, go further and say that the wishes to which God assents are not always pleasing to Him; but He assents, because it is necessary, by way of example, to give clear evidence of the doctrine of Scripture—viz. that He assists the miserable and hears the groans of those who unjustly afflicted implore His aid; and, accordingly, He executes His judgments when the complaints of the needy, though in themselves unworthy of attention, ascend to Him. For how often, in inflicting punishment on the ungodly for cruelty, rapine, violence, lust, and other crimes, in curbing audacity and fury, and also in overthrowing tyrannical power, has He declared that He gives assistance to those who are unworthily oppressed, though they, by addressing an unknown deity, only beat the air?

There is one Psalm, which clearly teaches that prayers are not without effect, though they do not penetrate to Heaven by faith. (see Psalm 107:6, 13, 19.) This Psalm enumerates the prayers, which, by natural instinct, necessity extorts from unbelievers not less than from believers, and to which it shows by the event, that God is, notwithstanding, propitious. Is it to testify by such readiness to hear that their prayers are agreeable to Him? Nay it is, first, to magnify or display His mercy by the circumstance, that even the wishes of unbelievers are not denied; and, secondly, to stimulate His true worshippers to more urgent prayer, when they see that sometimes even the wailings of the ungodly are not without avail. This, however, is no reason that believers should deviate from the Law divinely imposed upon them, or envy unbelievers, as if they gained much in obtaining what they wished. We have observed (see chapter 3, section 25) that in this way God yielded to the feigned repentance of Ahab, that he might show how ready He is to listen to His elect when, with true contrition, they seek His favor. Accordingly, He upbraids the Jews, that shortly after experiencing His readiness to listen to their prayers, they returned to their own perverse inclinations.

It is also plain from the Book of Judges that, whenever they wept, though their tears were deceitful, they were delivered from the hands of their enemies. Therefore, as God sends His sunshine indiscriminately on the evil and on the good, so He despises not the tears of those who have a good cause, and whose sorrows are deserving of relief. Meanwhile, though He hears them, it has no more to do with salvation than the supply of food, which He gives to other despisers of his goodness.

There seems to be a more difficult question concerning Abraham and Samuel, one of whom, without any instruction from the Word of God, prayed in behalf of the people of Sodom, and the other, contrary to an express prohibition, prayed in behalf of Saul. (See Genesis 18:23; 1 Samuel 5:11.) Similar is the case of Jeremiah, who prayed that the city might not be destroyed (Jeremiah 32:16). It is true that their prayers were refused, but it seems harsh to affirm that they prayed without faith.

Modest readers will, I hope, be satisfied with this solution—viz. that leaning to the general principle on which God enjoins us to be merciful even to the unworthy, they were not altogether devoid of faith, though in this particular instance their wish was disappointed

Augustine shrewdly remarks, "How do the saints pray in faith when they ask from God contrary to what He has decreed? Namely, because they pray according to His will, not His hidden and immutable will, but that which He suggests to them, that He may hear them in another manner, as He wisely distinguishes." This is truly said: for, in his incomprehensible counsel, he so regulates events that the prayers of the saints, though involving a mixture of faith and error, are not in vain. Yet this no more sanctions imitation than it excuses the saints themselves, who I deny not exceeded due bounds. Wherefore, whenever no certain promise exists, our request to God must have a condition annexed to it. Here we may refer to the prayer of David, "Awake for me to the judgment that thou hast commanded" (Psalm 7:6); for he reminds us that he had received special instruction to pray for a temporal blessing.

16 The above four rules of prayer are not so rigidly exacted, as that every prayer deficient in them in any respect is rejected by God. This shown by examples. Conclusion, or summary of this section.

It is also important to observe that the four laws of prayer of which I have treated are not so rigorously enforced, as that God rejects the prayers in which He does not find perfect faith or repentance, accompanied with fervent zeal and wishes duly framed. We have said (see section 4), that though prayer is the familiar intercourse of believers with God, yet reverence and modesty must be observed. We must not give loose reins to our wishes, nor long for anything further than God permits; and, moreover, lest the majesty of God should be despised, our minds must be elevated to pure and chaste veneration. This no man ever performed with due perfection. For, not to speak of the generality of men, how often do David's complaints savor of intemperance? It's not that he actually means to expostulate with God, or murmur at His judgments, but failing, through infirmity, he finds no better solace than to pour his grief into the bosom of His heavenly Father. Nay, God tolerates even our stammering, and pardon is granted to our ignorance as often as anything rashly escapes us: indeed, without this indulgence, we should have no freedom to pray. But although it was David's intention to submit himself entirely to the will of God, and he prayed with no less patience than fervor, yet irregular emotions appear, nay, sometimes burst forth, emotions not a little at variance with the first law which we laid down. In particular, we may see in a clause of the thirty-ninth Psalm, how this saint was carried away by the vehemence of his grief, and unable to keep within bounds: "O spare me, that I may recover strength, before I go hence, and be no more" (Psalm 39:13). You would call this the language of a desperate man, who had no other desire than that God should withdraw and leave him to relish in his distresses. Not that his devout mind rushes into such intemperance, or that, as the reprobate are wont, he wishes to have done with God; he only complains that the divine anger is more than he can bear. During those trials, wishes often escape which are not in accordance with the rule of the Word, and in which the saints do not duly consider what is lawful and expedient.

Prayers contaminated by such faults, indeed, deserve to be rejected; yet provided the saints lament, administer self-correction and return to themselves, God pardons. Similar faults are committed in regard to the second law (as to which, see section 6), for the saints have often to struggle with their own coldness, their want and misery not urging them sufficiently to serious prayer. It often happens, also, that their minds wander, and are almost lost; hence, in this matter also there is need of pardon, lest their prayers, from being languid or mutilated, or interrupted and wandering, should meet with a refusal.

One of the natural feelings, which God has imprinted on our minds, is that prayer is not genuine unless the thoughts are turned upward. Hence, the ceremony of raising the hands, to which we have adverted, a ceremony that has been known to all ages and nations and is still in common use. But who, in lifting up his hands, is not conscious of sluggishness, the heart cleaving to the Earth? In regard to the petition for remission of sins (section 8), though no believer omits it, yet all who are truly exercised in prayer feel that they bring scarcely a tenth of the sacrifice of which David speaks, "The sacrifices of God are a broken spirit: a broken and a contrite heart, O God, thou wilt not despise" (Psalm 51:17).

Thus a twofold pardon is always to be asked; first, because they are conscious of many faults the sense of which, however, does not touch them so as to make them feel dissatisfied with themselves as they ought; and, secondly, insofar as they have been enabled to profit in repentance and the fear of God, they are humbled with just sorrow for their offenses, and pray for the remission of punishment by the judge.

The thing which most of all vitiates prayer, did not God indulgently interpose, is weakness or imperfection of faith; but it is not wonderful that this defect is pardoned by God, who often exercises His people with severe trials, as if He actually wished to extinguish their faith. The hardest of such trials is when believers are forced to exclaim, "O Lord God of hosts, how long wilt thou be angry against the prayer of thy people?" (Psalm 80:4), as if their very prayers offended Him.

In like manner, when Jeremiah says, "Also when I cry and shout, he shutteth out my prayers" (Lamentations 3:8), there cannot be a doubt that he was in the greatest perturbation. Innumerable examples of the same kind occur in the Scriptures, from which it is manifest that the faith of the saints was often mingled with doubts and fears, so that while believing and hoping, they, however, betrayed some degree of unbelief, But because they do not come so far as were to be wished, that is only an additional reason for their exerting themselves to correct their faults, that they may daily approach nearer to the perfect law of prayer, and at the same time feel into what an abyss of evils those are plunged, who, in the very cures they use, bring new diseases upon themselves; since there is no prayer which God would not deservedly disdain, did He not overlook the blemishes with which all of them are polluted.

I do not mention these things that believers may securely pardon themselves in any faults which they commit, but that they may call themselves to strict account, and thereby endeavor to surmount these obstacles; and though Satan endeavors to block up all the paths in order to prevent them from praying, they may, nevertheless, break through, being firmly persuaded that, though not disencumbered of all hindrances, their attempts are pleasing to God and their wishes are approved, provided they hasten on and keep their aim, though without immediately reaching it.

17 Through whom God is to be invoked—viz. Jesus Christ. This is founded on a consideration of the divine majesty and the precept and promise of God himself. God, therefore is to be invoked only in the name of Christ.

But since no man is worthy to come forward in his own name, and appear in the presence of God, our heavenly Father, to relieve us at once from fear and shame, with which all must feel oppressed, has given us His Son, Jesus Christ our Lord, to be our Advocate and Mediator, that under His guidance we may approach securely, confiding that with Him for our Intercessor, nothing which we ask in His name will be denied to us, as there is nothing which the Father can deny to Him. (See 1 Timothy 2:5; 1 John 2; see section 36, 37.) To this it is necessary to refer all that we have previously taught concerning faith; because, as the promise gives us Christ as our Mediator, so, unless our hope of obtaining what we ask is founded on Him, it deprives us of the privilege of prayer. For it is impossible to think of the dread majesty of God without being filled with alarm; and hence the sense of our own unworthiness must keep us far away, until Christ interposes and converts a throne of dreadful glory into a throne of grace, as the apostle teaches, that thus we can "Come boldly unto the throne of grace, that we may obtain mercy, and find grace to help in time of need" (Hebrews 4:16). And as a rule has been laid down as to prayer, as a promise has been given that those who pray will be heard, so we are specially enjoined to pray in the name of Christ, the promise being that we shall obtain what we ask in His name. "Whatsoever ye shall ask in my name," says our Savior, "that will I do; that the Father may be glorified in the Son;" "Hitherto ye have asked nothing in my name; ask, and ye shall receive, that your joy may be full" (John 14:13; 16:24).

Hence, it is incontrovertibly clear that those who pray to God in any other name than that of Christ contumaciously falsify his orders and regard His will as nothing, while they have no promise that they shall obtain. For, as Paul says, "All the promises of God in him are yea, and in him amen" (2 Corinthians 1:20), that is, they are confirmed and fulfilled in Him.

18 From the first, all believers were heard through Him only: yet this specially restricted to the period subsequent to His ascension. The ground of this restriction.

And we must carefully attend to the circumstance of time. Christ enjoins His disciples to have recourse to His intercession after He shall have ascended to Heaven: "At that day ye shall ask in my name" (John 16:26). It is certain, indeed, that from the very first all who ever prayed were heard only for the sake of the Mediator. For this reason God had commanded in the Law that the priest alone should enter the sanctuary, bearing the names of the twelve tribes of Israel on his shoulders, and as many precious stones on his breast, while the people were to stand at a distance in the outer court, and thereafter unite their prayers with the priest. Nay, the sacrifice had even the effect of ratifying and confirming their prayers. That shadowy ceremony of the Law, therefore, taught, first, that we are all excluded from the face of God, and, therefore, that there is need of a Mediator to appear in our name, and carry us on His shoulders and keep us bound upon his breast, that we may be heard in His person; and secondly, that our prayers, which, as has been said, would otherwise never be free from impurity, are cleansed by the sprinkling of His blood.

And we see that the saints, when they desired to obtain anything, founded their hopes on sacrifices, because they knew that by sacrifice all prayers were ratified: "Remember all thy offerings," says David, "and accept thy burnt sacrifice" (Psalm 20:3).

Hence, we infer that in receiving the prayers of His people from the very first, God was appeased by the intercession of Christ. Why then does Christ speak of a new period ("at that day") when the disciples were to begin to pray in His name, unless it be that this grace, being now more brightly displayed, ought also to be in higher estimation with us?

In this sense, He had said a little before, "Hitherto ye have asked nothing in my name; ask." Not that they were altogether ignorant of the office of Mediator (all the Jews were instructed in these first rudiments), but they did not clearly understand that Christ by his ascent to Heaven would be more the advocate of the Church than before. Therefore, to solace their grief for his absence by some more-than-ordinary result, He asserts His office of Advocate, and says that hitherto they had been without the special benefit which it would be their privilege to enjoy; when aided by His intercession they should invoke God with greater freedom. In this sense, the Apostle says that we have "boldness to enter into the holiest by the blood of Jesus, by a new and living way, which he hath consecrated for us" (Hebrews 10:19, 20). Therefore, the more inexcusable we are, if we do not with both hands (as it is said) embrace the inestimable gift, which is properly destined for us.

19 The wrath of God lies on those who reject Christ as a Mediator. This excludes not the mutual intercession of saints on the earth.

Moreover, since He himself is the only way and the only access by which we can draw near to God, those who deviate from this way, and decline this access, have no other remaining; His throne presents nothing but wrath, judgment, and terror. In short, as the Father has consecrated Him as our Guide and Head, those who abandon or turn aside from Him in any way endeavor, as much as in them lies, to sully and efface the stamp, which God has impressed. Christ, therefore, is the only Mediator by whose intercession the Father is rendered propitious and exorable. (See 1 Timothy 2:5.) For, though the saints are still permitted to use intercessions by which they mutually beseech God in behalf of each other's salvation, and of which the apostle makes mention (see Ephesians 6:18, 19; 1 Timothy 2:1); yet these depend on that one intercession, so far are they from derogating from it. For as the intercessions, which, as members of one body we offer up for each other, spring from the feeling of love, so they have reference to this one Head. Being thus also made in the name of Christ, what more do they than declare that no man can derive the least benefit from any prayers without the intercession of Christ? As there is nothing in the intercession of Christ to prevent the different members of the Church from offering up prayers for each other, so let it be held as a fixed principle that all the intercessions thus used in the Church must have reference to that one intercession. Nay, we must be especially careful to show our gratitude on this very account, that God pardoning our unworthiness, not only allows each individual to pray for himself, but also allows all to intercede mutually for each other. God having given a place in His Church to intercessors who would deserve to be rejected when praying privately on their own account, how presumptuous would it be to abuse this kindness by employing it to obscure the honor of Christ?

20 Refutation of errors interfering with the intercession of Christ. Christ the Mediator of redemption; the saints, mediators of intercession. The answer confirmed by the clear testimony of Scripture and by a passage from Augustine. The nature of Christ's intercession.

Moreover, the Sophists are guilty of the merest trifling when they allege that Christ is the Mediator of *redemption*, but that believers are mediators of *intercession*, as if Christ had only performed a temporary mediation, and left an eternal and imperishable mediation to His servants. Such, forsooth, is the treatment, which He receives from those who pretend only to take from Him a minute portion of honor. Very different is the language of Scripture, with whose simplicity every pious man will be satisfied, without paying any regard to those importers. For when John says, "If any man sin, we have an advocate with the Father, Jesus Christ the righteous" (1 John 2:1), does he mean merely that we once had an advocate; does he not rather ascribe to Him a perpetual intercession? What does Paul mean when he declares that, he "…is even at the right hand of God, who also maketh intercession for us"? (Romans 8:32). But when in another passage He declares that He is the only Mediator between God and man (1 Timothy 2:5), is He not referring to the supplications, which He had mentioned a little before? Having previously said that prayers were to be offered up for all men, He immediately adds, in confirmation of that statement, that there is one God, and one Mediator between God and man. Nor does Augustine give a different interpretation when he says, "Christian men mutually recommend each other in their prayers. But He, for whom none intercedes, while He himself intercedes for all, is the only true Mediator.

Though the Apostle Paul was under the head a principal member, yet because he was a member of the Body of Christ and knew that the most true and High Priest of the Church had entered not by figure into the inner veil to the Holy of Holies, but by firm and express truth into the inner sanctuary of Heaven to holiness, holiness not imaginary, but eternal, He also commends himself to the prayers of the faithful. He does not make himself a Mediator between God and the people, but asks that all the members of the Body of Christ should pray mutually for each other, since the members are mutually sympathetic: if one member suffers, the others suffer with it. Thus, the mutual prayers of all the members still laboring on the Earth ascend to the Head, who has gone before into Heaven, and in whom there is propitiation for our sins. For if Paul were a mediator, so would also the other apostles, and, thus, there would be many mediators, and Paul's statement could not stand, "There is one God, and one Mediator between God and men, the man Christ Jesus," in whom we also are one if we keep the unity of the faith in the bond of peace."

Likewise, in another passage Augustine says, "If thou requirest a priest, he is above the heavens, where He intercedes for those who on earth died for thee." Imagine not that He throws himself before His Father's knees and suppliantly intercedes for us; but we understand with the apostle, that He appears in the presence of God, and that the power of His death has the effect of a perpetual intercession for us; that having entered into the upper sanctuary, He alone continues to the end of the world to present the prayers of His people, who are standing far off in the outer court.

21 Of the intercession of saints living with Christ in Heaven. Fiction of the papists in regard to it. Refuted. A. Its absurdity. B. It is nowhere mentioned by Scripture. C. Appeal to the conscience of the superstitious. D. Its blasphemy. Exception. Answers.

In regard to the saints who, having died in the body live in Christ, if we attribute prayer to them, let us not imagine that they have any other way of supplicating God than through Christ who alone is the way, or that God accepts their prayers in any other name. Wherefore, since the Scripture calls us away from all others to Christ alone, since our heavenly Father is pleased to gather together all things in Him, it would be the extreme of stupidity, not to say madness, to attempt to obtain access by means of others, so as to be drawn away from Him without whom access cannot be obtained. But who can deny that this was the practice for several ages and is still the practice, wherever popery prevails?

To procure the favor of God, human merits are always obtruded, and very frequently, while Christ is passed by, God is supplicated in their name. I ask if this is not to transfer to them that office of sole intercession, which we have above claimed for Christ? Then what angel or devil ever announced one syllable to any human being concerning that fancied intercession of theirs? There is not a word on the subject in Scripture. What ground, then, was there for the fiction? Certainly, while the human mind thus seeks help for itself in which it is not sanctioned by the Word of God, it plainly manifests its distrust (see section 27).

But if we appeal to the consciences of all who take pleasure in the intercession of saints, we shall find that their only reason for it is that they are filled with anxiety, as if they supposed that Christ were insufficient or too rigorous. By this anxiety they dishonor Christ, and rob Him of his title of sole Mediator, a title which being given Him by the Father as His special privilege, ought not to be transferred to any other. By so doing they obscure the glory of his nativity and make void His cross; in short, they divest and defraud of due praise everything which He did or suffered, since all which He did and suffered goes to show that he is and ought to be deemed sole Mediator. At the same time, they reject the kindness of God in manifesting himself to them as a Father, for He is not their Father if they do not recognize Christ as their brother. This they plainly refuse to do if they think not that He feels for them a brother's affection; affection than which none can be more gentle or tender. Wherefore Scripture offers Him alone, sends us to Him, and establishes us in Him.

"He," says Ambrose, "is our mouth by which we speak to the Father; our eye by which we see the Father; our right hand by which we offer ourselves to the Father. Save by his intercession neither we nor any saints have any intercourse with God." If they object that the public prayers which are offered up in churches conclude with the words, *through Jesus Christ our Lord*, it is a frivolous evasion; because no less insult is offered to the intercession of Christ by confounding it with the prayers and merits of the dead, than by omitting it altogether, and making mention only of the dead. Then, in all their litanies, hymns, and prose where every kind of honor is paid to dead saints, there is no mention of Christ.

22 Monstrous errors resulting from this fiction. Refutation Exception by the advocates of this fiction. Answer.

But here stupidity has proceeded to such a length as to give a manifestation of the genius of superstition, which, when once it has shaken off the rein, is wont to wanton without limit. After men began to look to the intercession of saints, a peculiar administration was gradually assigned to each, so that, according to diversity of business, now one, now another intercessor was invoked. Then individuals adopted particular saints and put their faith in them, just as if they had been tutelar deities. Thus, not only were gods set up according to the number of the cities (the charge which the prophet brought against Israel of old, Jeremiah 2:28; 11:13), but according to the number of individuals.

But while the saints in all their desires refer to the will of God alone, look to it, and acquiesce in it, yet to assign to them any other prayer than that of longing for the arrival of the Kingdom of God, is to think of them stupidly, carnally, and even insultingly. Nothing can be further from such a view than to imagine that each, under the influence of private feeling, is disposed to be most favorable to his own worshippers. At length vast numbers have fallen into the horrid blasphemy of invoking them not merely as helping but presiding over their salvation.

See the depth to which miserable men fall when they forsake their proper station, that is, the Word of God. I say nothing of the more monstrous specimens of impiety in which, though detestable to God, angels, and men, they themselves feel no pain or shame. Prostrated at a statue or picture of Barbara or Catherine, and the like, they mutter a *Pater Noster*; and so far are their pastors from curing or curbing this frantic course, that, allured by the scent of gain, they approve and applaud it. But while seeking to relieve themselves of the odium of this vile and criminal procedure, with what pretext can they defend the practice of calling upon Eloy (Eligius) or Medard to look upon their servants, and send them help from Heaven, or the holy virgin to order her Son to do what they ask? The Council of Carthage forbade direct prayer to be made at the altar to saints. It is probable that these holy men, unable entirely to suppress the force of depraved custom, had recourse to this check, that public prayers might not be vitiated with such forms of expression as *Sancte Petre, ora pro nobis* —St. Peter, pray for us. But how much further has this devilish extravagance proceeded when men hesitate not to transfer to the dead the peculiar attributes of Christ and God?

23 Arguments of the papists for the intercession of saints. A. From the duty and office of angels. Answer. B. From

an expression of Jeremiah respecting Moses and Samuel. Answer, retorting the argument. C. The meaning of the prophet confirmed by a similar passage in Ezekiel and the testimony of an apostle.

In endeavoring to prove that such intercession derives some support from Scripture, they labor in vain. We frequently read (they say) of the prayers of angels, and not only so, but the prayers of believers are said to be carried into the presence of God by their hands. But if they would compare saints who have departed this life with angels, it will be necessary to prove that saints are ministering spirits, to whom has been delegated the office of superintending our salvation, to whom has assigned the province of guiding us in all our ways, of encompassing, admonishing, and comforting us, of keeping watch over us. All these are assigned to angels, but none of them to saints. How preposterously they confound departed saints with angels is sufficiently apparent from the many different offices by which Scripture distinguishes the one from the other. No one, unless admitted, will presume to perform the office of pleader before an earthly judge; whence then have worms such license as to obtrude themselves on God as intercessors, while no such office has been assigned them? God has been pleased to give angels the charge of our safety. Hence, they attend our sacred meetings, and the Church is to them a theater in which they behold the manifold wisdom of God. (See Ephesians 3:10.)

Those who transfer to others this office, which is peculiar to them, certainly pervert and confound the order, which has been established by God and ought to be inviolable. With similar dexterity, they proceed to quote other passages. God said to Jeremiah, "Though Moses and Samuel stood before me, yet my mind could not be toward this people" (Jeremiah 15:1). How (they ask) could he have spoken thus of the dead but because he knew that they interceded for the living?

My inference, on the contrary, is this: since it thus appears that neither Moses nor Samuel interceded for the people of Israel, there was then no intercession for the dead. For who of the saints can be supposed to labor for the salvation of the peoples while Moses who, when in life, far surpassed all others in this matter, does nothing? Therefore, if they persist in the paltry quibble, that the dead intercede for the living, because the Lord said, "*If they stood before me* (*intercesserint*), I will argue far more speciously in this way: Moses, of whom it is said, "*if he interceded*," did not intercede for the people in their extreme necessity: it is probable, therefore, that no other saint intercedes, all being far behind Moses in humanity, goodness, and paternal solicitude. Thus, all they gain by their caviling is to be wounded by the very arms with which they deem themselves admirably protected.

But it is very ridiculous to wrest this simple sentence in this manner; for the Lord only declares that He would not spare the iniquities of the people, though some Moses or Samuel, to whose prayers He had shown himself so indulgent, should intercede for them. This meaning is most clearly elicited from a similar passage in Ezekiel: "Though these three men, Noah, Daniel, and Job, were in it, they should deliver but their own souls by their righteousness, saith the Lord God" (Ezekiel 14:14). Here there can be no doubt that we are to understand the words as if it had been said, "If two of the persons named were again to come alive"; for the third was still living, namely, Daniel, who it is well known had then in the bloom of youth given an incomparable display of piety. Let us, therefore leave out those whom Scripture declares to have completed their course. Accordingly, when Paul speaks of David, he says not that by his prayers he assisted posterity, but only that he "served his own generation" (Acts 13:36).

24 D. Fourth papistical argument from the nature of charity, which is more perfect in the saints in glory. Answer.

They again object: Are those, then, to be deprived of every pious wish, who, during the whole course of their lives, breathed nothing but piety and mercy? I have no wish curiously to pry into what they do or meditate; but the probability is, that instead of being subject to the impulse of various and particular desires, they, with one fixed and immovable will, long for the Kingdom of God, which consists not less in the destruction of the ungodly than in the salvation of believers. If this be so, there cannot be a doubt that their charity is confined to the communion of Christ's body, and extends no further than is compatible with the nature of that communion. But though I grant that in this way they pray for us, they do not, however, lose their quiescence so as to be distracted with earthly cares: far less are they, therefore, to be invoked by us. Nor does it follow that such invocation is to be used because, while men are alive upon the Earth, they can mutually commend themselves to each other's prayers. It serves to keep alive a feeling of charity when they share each other's wants, and bear each other's burdens. This they do by the command of the Lord, and not without a promise; the two things of primary importance in prayer. But all such reasons are inapplicable to the dead, with whom the Lord, in withdrawing them from our society, has left us no means of intercourse (Ecclesiastes 9:5, 6), and to whom, as far as we can conjecture, he has left no means of intercourse with us. But if anyone allege that they certainly must retain the same charity for us, as they are united with us in one faith, who has revealed to us that they have ears capable of listening to the sounds of our voice, or eyes clear enough to discern our necessities? Our opponents, indeed, talk in the shade of their schools of some kind of light which beams upon departed saints from the divine countenance, and in which, as in a mirror, they, from their lofty abode, behold the affairs of men; but to affirm this with the confidence which these men presume to use, is just to desire, by means of the extravagant dreams of our own brain, and without any authority, to pry and penetrate into the hidden judgments of God, and trample upon Scripture, which so often declares that the wisdom of our flesh is at enmity with the wisdom of God, utterly condemns the vanity of our mind, and humbling our reason, bids us look only to the will of God.

25 Argument founded on a passage in Moses. Answer.

The other passages of Scripture, which they employ to defend their error, are miserably wrested. Jacob (they say) asks for the sons of Joseph, "Let my name be named on them, and the name of my fathers, Abraham and Isaac" (Genesis 48:16). First, let us see what the nature of this invocation was among the Israelites. They do not implore their fathers to bring succor to them, but they beseech God to remember His servants, Abraham, Isaac, and Jacob. Their example, therefore, gives no countenance to those who use addresses to the saints themselves. But such being the dullness of these blocks, that they comprehend not what it is to invoke the name of Jacob, nor why it is to be invoked, it is not strange that they blunder thus childishly as to the mode of doing it. The expression repeatedly occurs in Scripture. Isaiah speaks of women being called by the name of men, when they have them for husbands and live under their protection. (See Isaiah 4:1.) The calling of the name of Abraham over the Israelites consists in referring the origin of their race to him, and holding him in distinguished remembrance as their author and parent. Jacob does not do so from any anxiety to extend the celebrity of his name, but because he knows that all the happiness of his posterity consisted in the inheritance of the covenant that God had made with them. Because this would give them the sum of all blessings, he prays that they may be regarded as of his race, this being nothing else than to transmit the succession of the covenant to them. They again, when they make mention of this subject in their prayers, do not betake themselves to the intercession of the dead, but call to remembrance that covenant in which their most merciful Father undertakes to be kind and propitious to them for the sake of Abraham, Isaac, and Jacob.

How little, in other respects, the saints trusted to the merits of their fathers, the public voice of the Church declares in the prophets ,"Doubtless thou art, our Father, though Abraham be ignorant of us, and Israel acknowledge us not; thou, O Lord, art our Father, our Redeemer" (Isaiah 63:16). And while the Church thus speaks, she at the same time adds, "Return for thy servants' sake," not thinking of anything like intercession, but adverting only to the benefit of the covenant. Now, indeed, when we have the Lord Jesus, in whose hand the eternal covenant of mercy was not only made but confirmed, what better name can we bear before us in our prayers? And since those good doctors would make out by these words that the patriarchs are intercessors, I should like them to tell me why, in so great a multitude, no place whatever is given to Abraham, the father of the Church? We know well from what a crew they select their intercessors. Let them then tell me what consistency there is in neglecting and rejecting Abraham, whom God preferred to all others and raised to the highest degree of honor. The only reason is that as it was plain there was no such practice in the ancient Church, they thought proper to conceal the novelty of the practice by saying nothing of the Patriarchs: as if by a mere diversity of names they could excuse a practice at once novel and impure.

They sometimes, also, object that God is entreated to have mercy on his people "for David's sake" (Psalms 132:10). This is so far from supporting their error, that it is the strongest refutation of it. We must consider the character, which David bore. He is set apart from the whole body of the faithful to establish the covenant, which God made in his hand. Thus, regard is had to the covenant rather than to the individual. Under him as a type, the sole intercession of

Christ is asserted. But what was peculiar to David as a type of Christ is certainly inapplicable to others.

26 Argument from its being said that the prayers of saints are heard. Answer, confirmed by Scripture, and illustrated by examples.

But some seem to be moved by the fact that the prayers of saints are often said to have been heard. Why? Because they prayed. "They cried unto thee" (says the Psalmist), "and were delivered: they trusted in thee, and were not confounded" (Psalm 22:5). Let us also pray after their example, that like them we too may be heard. Those men, on the contrary, absurdly argue that none will be heard but those who have been heard already. How much better does James argue, "Elias was a man subject to like passions as we are, and he prayed earnestly that it might not rain: and it rained not on the earth by the space of three years and six months. And he prayed again and the heaven gave rain, and the earth brought forth her fruit" (James 5:17, 18). What? Does he infer that Elias possessed some peculiar privilege and that we must have recourse to him for the use of it? By no means. He shows the perpetual efficacy of a pure and pious prayer, that we may be induced in like manner to pray. For the kindness and readiness of God to hear others is malignantly interpreted, if their example does not inspire us with stronger confidence in His promise, since His declaration is not that He will incline His ear to one or two, or a few individuals, but to all who call upon His name. In this ignorance, they are the less excusable, because they seem avowedly to contemn the many admonitions of Scripture.

David was repeatedly delivered by the power of God. Was this to give that power to him, that we might be delivered on his application? Very different is his affirmation: "The righteous shall compass me about; for thou shalt deal bountifully with me" (Psalm 142:7). Again, "The righteous also shall see, and fear, and shall laugh at him" (Psalm 52:6). "This poor man cried, and the Lord heard him, and saved him out of all his troubles" (Psalm 34:6).

In the Psalms are many similar prayers in which David calls upon God to give him what he asks, for this reason—viz. that the righteous may not be put to shame, but by his example encouraged to hope. Here let one passage suffice, "For this shall everyone that is godly pray unto thee in a time when thou mayest be found" (Psalm 32:6).

This passage I have quoted the more readily, because those ravers, who employ their hireling tongues in defense of the papacy, are not ashamed to adduce it in proof of the intercession of the dead. As if David intended anything more than to show the benefit which he shall obtain from the divine clemency and condescension when he shall have been heard. In general, we must hold that the experience of the grace of God, as well towards ourselves as towards others, tends in no slight degree to confirm our faith in His promises.

I do not quote the many passages in which David sets forth the lovingkindness of God to him as a ground of confidence, as they will readily occur to every reader of the Psalms. Jacob had previously taught the same thing by his own example, "I am not worthy of the least of all thy mercies, and of all the truth which thou hast showed unto thy servant: for with my staff I passed over this Jordan; and now I am become two bands" (Genesis 32:10). He, indeed, alleges the promise, but not the promise only; for he at the same time adds the effect, to animate him with greater confidence in the future kindness of God. God is not like men who grow weary of their liberality, or whose means of exercising it become exhausted; but he is to be estimated by his own nature, as David properly does when he says, "Thou hast redeemed me, O Lord God of truth" (Psalm 31:5). After ascribing the praise of his salvation to God, he adds that he is true: for were He not ever like himself, His past favor would not be an infallible ground for confidence and prayer. But when we know that as often as He assists us, He gives us a specimen and proof of His goodness and faithfulness, there is no reason to fear that our hope will be ashamed or frustrated.

27 Conclusion, that the saints cannot be invoked without impiety. A. It robs God of His glory. B. Destroys the intercession of Christ. C. Is repugnant to the Word of God. D. Is opposed to the due method of prayer. E. Is without approved example. F. Springs from distrust. Last objection. Answer.

On the whole, since Scripture places the principal part of worship in the invocation of God (this being the office of piety which He requires of us in preference to all sacrifices), it is manifest sacrilege to offer prayer to others. Hence, it is said in the Psalm: "If we have forgotten the name of our God, or stretched out our hands to a strange god, shall not God search this out?" (Psalm 44:20, 21).

Again, since it is only in faith that God desires to be invoked, and He distinctly enjoins us to frame our prayers according to the rule of His Word: in fine, since faith is founded on the Word and is the parent of right prayer, the moment we decline from the Word, our prayers are impure. But we have already shown that if we consult the whole volume of Scripture, we shall find that God claims this honor to himself alone.

Concerning the office of intercession, we have also seen that it is peculiar to Christ, and that no prayer is agreeable to God, which He as Mediator does not sanctify. Though believers mutually offer up prayers to God in behalf of their brethren, we have shown that this derogates in no respect from the sole intercession of Christ, because all trust to that intercession in commending themselves as well as others to God. Moreover, we have shown that this is ignorantly transferred to the dead, of whom we nowhere read that they were commanded to pray for us.

The Scripture often exhorts us to offer up mutual prayers; but says not one syllable concerning the dead; nay, James tacitly excludes the dead when he combines the two things, to "confess our sins one to another, and to pray one for another" (James 5:16). Hence, it is sufficient to condemn this error, that the beginning of right prayer springs from faith, and that faith comes by the hearing of the Word of God, in which there is no mention of fictitious intercession, superstition having rashly adopted intercessors who have not been divinely appointed.

While the Scripture abounds in various forms of prayer, we find no example of this intercession, without which Papists think there is no prayer. Moreover, it is evident that this superstition is the result of distrust, because they are either not contented with Christ as an intercessor, or have altogether robbed Him of this honor. This last is easily proved by their effrontery in maintaining, as the strongest of all their arguments for the intercession of the saints, that we are unworthy of familiar access to God. This, indeed, we acknowledge to be most true, but we thence infer that they leave nothing to Christ, because they consider His intercession as nothing, unless it is supplemented by that of George and Hypolyte, and similar phantoms.

28 Kinds of prayer. Thanksgiving. Supplications. Petitions. Vows. Connection of these, their constant use and necessity.

Particular explanation is confirmed by reason, Scripture, and example. Rule as to supplication and thanksgiving.

B ut though prayer is properly confined to vows and supplications, yet so strong is the affinity between petition and thanksgiving, that both may be conveniently comprehended under one name. The forms, which Paul enumerates (see 1 Timothy 2:1), fall under the first member of this division. By prayer and supplication we pour out our desires before God, asking as well those things which tend to promote His glory and display His name, as the benefits which contribute to our advantage. By thanksgiving, we duly celebrate His kindnesses toward us, ascribing to His liberality every blessing, which enters into our lot. David accordingly includes both in one sentence, "Call upon me in the day of trouble: I will deliver thee, and thou shalt glorify me" (Psalm 50:15). Scripture, not without reason, commands us to use both continually. We have already described the greatness of our want, while experience itself proclaims the straits which press us on every side to be so numerous and so great, that all have sufficient ground to send forth sighs and groans to God without intermission, and suppliantly implore Him. For, even should they be exempt from adversity, still the holiest ought to be stimulated first by their sins, and, secondly, by the innumerable assaults of temptation, to long for a remedy.

The sacrifice of praise and thanksgiving can never be interrupted without guilt, since God never ceases to load us with favor upon favor, so as to force us to gratitude, however slow and sluggish we may be. In short, so great and widely diffused are the riches of his liberality towards us, so marvelous and wondrous the miracles which we behold on every side, that we never can want a subject and materials for praise and thanksgiving. To make this somewhat clearer: since all our hopes and resources are placed in God (this has already been fully proved), so that neither our persons nor our interests can prosper without His blessing, we must constantly submit ourselves and our all to Him. Then whatever we deliberate, speak, or do, should be deliberated, spoken, and done under His hand and will; in fine, under the hope of His assistance.

God has pronounced a curse upon all who, confiding in themselves or others, form plans and resolutions, who, without regarding His will, or invoking his aid, either plan or attempt to execute. (See James 4:14; Isaiah 30:1; 31:1.) And since, as has already been observed, he receives the honor, which is due when He is acknowledged to be the Author of all good, it follows that, in deriving all good from His hand, we ought continually to express our thankfulness. Moreover, we have no right to use the benefits, which proceed from His liberality, if we do not assiduously proclaim His praise and give Him thanks, these being the ends for which they are given. When Paul declares that every creature of God "...is sanctified by the word of God and prayers" (1 Timothy 4:5), he intimates that without the word and prayers none of them are holy and pure, *word* being used metonymically for *faith*. Hence, David, on experiencing the lovingkindness of the Lord, elegantly declares, "He hath put a new song in my mouth" (Psalm 40:3); intimating that our silence is malignant when we leave his blessings unpraised, seeing every blessing He bestows is a new ground of thanksgiving. Thus Isaiah, proclaiming the singular mercies of God, says, "Sing unto the Lord a new song" (Isaiah 42:10.) In the same sense, David says in another passage, "O Lord, open thou my lips; and my mouth shall show forth thy praise" (Psalm 51:15.) In like manner, Hezekiah and Jonah declare that they will regard it as the end of their deliverance "...to celebrate the goodness of God with songs in his temple" (Isaiah 38:20; Jonah 2:10).

David lays down a general rule for all believers in these words, "What shall I render unto the Lord for all his benefits toward me? I will take the cup of salvation, and call upon the name of the Lord" (Psalm 116:12, 13). This rule the Church follows in another Psalm, "Save us, O Lord our God, and gather us from among the heathen, to give thanks unto thy holy name, and to triumph in thy praise" (Psalm 106:47). Again, "He will regard the prayer of the destitute, and not despise their prayer. This shall be written for the generation to come: and the people which shall be created shall praise the Lord." "To declare the name of the Lord in Zion, and his praise in Jerusalem" (Psalm 102:18, 21). Nay, whenever believers beseech the Lord to do anything *for His own name's sake*, as they declare themselves unworthy of obtaining it in their own name, so they oblige themselves to give thanks, and promise to make the right use of his lovingkindness by being the heralds of it. Thus, Hosea, speaking of the future redemption of the Church, says, "Take away all iniquity, and receive us graciously; so will we render the calves of our lips" (Hosea 14:2).

Not only do our tongues proclaim the kindness of God, but also they naturally inspire us with love to him. "I love the Lord, because he hath heard my voice and my supplications" (Psalm 116:1). In another passage, speaking of the help which he had experienced, he says, "I will love thee, O Lord, my strength" (Psalm 18:1). No praise will ever please God that does not flow from this feeling of love. Nay, we must attend to the declaration of Paul, that all wishes are vicious and perverse which are not accompanied with thanksgiving. His words are, "In everything by prayer and supplication with thanksgiving let your requests be made known unto God" (Philippians 4:6). Because many, under the influence of moroseness, weariness, impatience, bitter grief and fear, use murmuring in their prayers, he enjoins us so to regulate our feelings as cheerfully to bless God even before obtaining what we ask. But if this connection ought always to subsist in full vigor between things that are almost contrary, the more sacred is the tie which binds us to celebrate the praises of God whenever He grants our requests. And, as we have already shown that our prayers, which otherwise would be polluted, are sanctified by the intercession of Christ, so the apostle, by enjoining us "...to offer the sacrifice of praise to God continually" by Christ (Hebrews 13:5), reminds us that without the intervention of his priesthood, our lips are not pure enough to celebrate the name of God.

Hence, we infer that a monstrous delusion prevails among papists, the great majority of whom wonder when Christ is called an intercessor. The reason that Paul enjoins, "Pray without ceasing; in everything give thanks" (1 Thessalonians 5:17, 18), is because he would have us with the utmost assiduity, at all times, in every place, in all things, and under all circumstances, direct our prayers to God, to expect all the things which we desire from Him, and when obtained, ascribe them to Him; thus furnishing perpetual grounds for prayer and praise.

29 The accidents of prayer—viz. private and public, constant, at stated seasons, etc. Exception in time of necessity. Prayer without ceasing. Its nature. The garrulity of papists and hypocrites refuted. The scope and parts of prayer. Secret prayer. Prayer at all places. Private and public prayer.

This assiduity in prayer, though it specially refers to the peculiar private prayers of individuals, extends also in some measure to the public prayers of the Church. These, it may be said, cannot be continual, and ought not to be made, except in the manner, which, for the sake of order, has been established by public consent. This I admit, and hence certain hours are fixed beforehand, hours which, though indifferent in regard to God, are necessary for the use of man, that the general convenience may be consulted, and all things be done in the Church, as Paul enjoins, "decently and in order" (1 Corinthians 14:40). But there is nothing in this to prevent each church from being now and then stirred up to a more frequent use of prayer and being more zealously affected under the impulse of some greater necessity. Of perseverance in prayer, which is much akin to assiduity, we shall speak towards the close of the chapter. (See section 51, 52.) This assiduity, moreover, is very different from the Greek interpretation, *vain speaking*, which our Savior has prohibited. (See Matthew 6:7.) For he does not there forbid us to pray long or frequently, or with great fervor, but warns us against supposing that we can extort anything from God by importuning Him with garrulous loquacity, as if He were to be persuaded after the manner of men.

We know that hypocrites, because they consider not that they have to do with God, offer up their prayers as pompously as if it were part of a triumphal show. The Pharisee, who thanked God that he was not as other men, no doubt proclaimed his praises before men, as if he had wished to gain a reputation for sanctity by his prayers. Hence, that *vain speaking*, which for a similar reason prevails so much in the papacy in the present day, some vainly spinning out the time by a reiteration of the same frivolous prayers, and others employing a long series of verbiage for vulgar display. This childish garrulity being a mockery of God, it is not strange that it is prohibited in the Church, in order that every feeling there expressed may be sincere, proceeding from the inmost heart.

Akin to this abuse is another, which our Savior also condemns, namely, when hypocrites for the sake of ostentation court the presence of many witnesses and would sooner pray in the marketplace than pray without applause. The true object of prayer being, as we have already said (section 4, 5), to carry our thoughts directly to God, whether to celebrate His praise or implore His aid, we can easily see that its primary seat is in the mind and heart, or rather that prayer itself is properly an effusion and manifestation of internal feeling before Him who is the searcher of hearts.

Hence (as has been said), when our divine Master was pleased to lay down the best rule for prayer, His injunction was, "Enter into thy closet, and when thou hast shut thy door, pray to thy Father which is in secret, and thy Father which seeth in secret shall reward thee openly" (Matthew 6:6). Dissuading us from the example of hypocrites, who sought the applause of men by an ambitious ostentation in prayer, He adds the better course—enter thy chamber, shut thy door and there pray. By these words (as I understand them), He taught us to seek a place of retirement which might enable us to turn all our thoughts inwards and enter deeply into our hearts, promising that God would hold converse with the feelings of our mind, of which the body ought to be the temple. He meant not to deny that it may be expedient to pray in other places also, but He shows that prayer is somewhat of a secret nature, having its chief seat in the mind, and requiring tranquility far removed from the turmoil of ordinary cares.

And hence, it was not without cause that our Lord himself, when He would engage more earnestly in prayer, withdrew into a retired spot beyond the bustle of the world. Thus we are reminded by His example that we are not to neglect those helps which enable the mind, in itself too much disposed to wander, to become sincerely intent on prayer. Meanwhile, as he abstained not from prayer when the occasion required it, though He were in the midst of a crowd, so must we, whenever there is need, lift up "pure hands" (see 1 Timothy 2:8) at all places.

Hence, we must hold that he, who declines to pray in the public meeting of the saints, knows not what it is to pray apart, in retirement, or at home. On the other hand, he who neglects to pray alone and in private, however sedulously he frequents public meetings, there gives his prayers to the wind, because he defers more to the opinion of man than to the secret judgment of God. Still, lest the public prayers of the Church should be held in contempt, the Lord anciently bestowed upon them the most honorable appellation, especially when He called the temple the *house of prayer*. (See Isaiah 56:7.) For by this expression He both showed that the duty of prayer is a principal part of His worship and that to enable believers to engage in it with one consent, His temple is set up before them as a kind of banner. A noble promise was also added, "Praise waiteth for thee, O God, in Zion: and unto thee shall the vow be performed" (Psalm 65:1). By these words the Psalmist reminds us that the prayers of the Church are never in vain, because God always furnishes His people with materials for a song of joy. But although the shadows of the Law have ceased, yet because God was pleased by this ordinance to foster the unity of the faith among us also, there can be no doubt that the same promise belongs to us—a promise which Christ sanctioned with his own lips, and which Paul declares to be perpetually in force.

30 Of public places or churches in which common prayers are offered up. The right use of churches. Abuse.

As God in His Word enjoins common prayer, so public temples are the places destined for the performance of them, and hence those who refuse to join with the people of God in this observance have no ground for the pretext, that they enter their chamber in order that they may obey the command of the Lord. For He who promises to grant whatsoever two or three assembled in His name shall ask (Matthew 18:20), declares, that He by no means despises the prayers which are publicly offered up, provided there be no ostentation, or catching at human applause, and provided there be a true and sincere affection in the secret recesses of the heart. If this is the legitimate use of churches (and it certainly is), we must, on the other hand, beware of imitating the practice that commenced some centuries ago—a practice of imagining that churches are the proper dwellings of God, where He is more ready to listen to us; or of attaching to them some kind of secret sanctity, which makes prayer there more holy. Seeing that we are the true temples of God, we must pray in ourselves if we would invoke God in His holy temple. Let us leave such gross ideas to the Jews or the heathen, knowing that we have a command to pray without distinction of place, "...in spirit and in truth" (John 4:23). It is true that by the order of God, the Temple was anciently dedicated for the offering of prayers and sacrifices, but this was at a time when the truth (which being now fully manifested, we are not permitted to confine to any material temple) lay hid under the figure of shadows. Even the Temple was not represented to the Jews as confining the presence of God within its walls, but was meant to train them to contemplate the image of the true Temple. Accordingly, both Isaiah and Stephen administer a severe rebuke to those who thought God could in any way dwell in temples made with hands. (See Isaiah 66:2; Acts 7:48.)

31 Of utterance and singing. These are of no avail if they are not from the heart. The use of the voice refers more to public than private prayer.

Hence, it is perfectly clear that neither words nor singing (if used in prayer) are of the least consequence, or avail one iota with God, unless they proceed from deep feeling in the heart. Nay, rather they provoke His anger against us if they come from the lips and throat only, since this is to abuse His sacred name, and hold His majesty in derision. This we infer from the words of Isaiah, which, though their meaning is of wider extent, go to rebuke this vice also: "Forasmuch as this people draw near me with their mouth, and with their lips do honor me, but have removed their heart far from me, and their fear toward me is taught by the precept of men: therefore, behold, I will proceed to do a marvelous work among this people, even a marvelous work and a wonder: for the wisdom of their wise men shall perish, and the understanding of their prudent men shall be hid" (Isaiah 29:13). Still, we do not condemn words or singing, but rather greatly commend them, provided the feeling of the mind goes along with them. For in this way the thought of God is kept alive on our minds, which, from their fickle and versatile nature, soon relax and are distracted by various objects, unless various means are used to support them. Besides, since the glory of God ought in a manner to be displayed in each part of our body, the special service to which the tongue should be devoted is that of singing and speaking, inasmuch as it has been expressly created to declare and proclaim the praise of God. This employment of the tongue is chiefly in the public services which are performed in the meeting of the saints. In this way the God whom we serve in one spirit and one faith, we glorify together with one voice and one mouth; and that openly, so that each may in turn receive the confession of his brother's faith, and be invited and incited to imitate it.

32 Singing is of the greatest antiquity, but it is not universal. How it is to be performed.

It is certain that the use of singing in churches (which I may mention in passing) is not only very ancient, but was also used by the apostles, as we may gather from the words of Paul, "I will sing with the spirit, and I will sing with the understanding also" (1 Corinthians 14:15). In like manner, he says to the Colossians, "Teaching and admonishing one another in psalms, and hymns, and spiritual songs, singing with grace in your hearts to the Lord" (Colossians 3:16).

In the former passage, he enjoins us to sing with the voice and the heart; in the latter, he commends spiritual songs, by which the pious mutually edify each other. That it was not a universal practice, however, is attested by Augustine, who states that the church of Milan first began to use singing in the time of Ambrose, when the orthodox faith was persecuted by Justina, the mother of Valentinian. The vigils of the people were more frequent than usual, and the practice was afterwards followed by the other Western churches. He had said a little before that the custom came from the East. He also intimates that it was received in Africa in his own time. His words are, "Hilarius, a man of tribunitial rank, assailed, with the bitterest invectives he could use, the custom which then began to exist at Carthage, of singing hymns from the Book of Psalms at the altar, either before the oblation, or when it was distributed to the people; I answered him, at the request of my brethren."

And certainly if singing is tempered to a gravity befitting the presence of God and angels, it both gives dignity and grace to sacred actions, and has a very powerful tendency to stir up the mind to true zeal and ardor in prayer. We must beware, lest our ears be more intent on the music than our minds on the spiritual meaning of the words.

Augustine confesses that the fear of this danger sometimes made him wish for the introduction of a practice observed by Athanasius, who ordered the reader to use only a gentle inflection of the voice, more akin to recitation than singing. But on again considering how many advantages were derived from singing, he inclined to the other side. If this moderation is used, there cannot be a doubt that the practice is most sacred and salutary. On the other hand, songs composed merely to tickle and delight the ear are unbecoming the majesty of the Church, and cannot but be most displeasing to God.

33 Public prayers should be in the vulgar, not in a foreign tongue. Reason, A. The nature of the Church. B. Authority of an apostle. Sincere affection always necessary. The tongue is not always necessary. The bending of the knee, and uncovering of the head.

It is also plain that public prayers are not to be couched in Greek among the Latins, nor in Latin among the French or English (as hitherto has been everywhere practiced). They are in the vulgar tongue, so that all present may understand them, since they ought to be used for the edification of the whole Church, which cannot be in the least degree benefited by a sound not understood. Those who are not moved by any reason of humanity or charity ought at least to be somewhat moved by the authority of Paul, whose words are by no means ambiguous: "When thou shalt bless with the spirit, how shall he that occupieth the room of the unlearned say, Amen, at thy giving of thanks, seeing he understandeth not what thou sayest? For thou verily givest thanks, but the other is not edified" (1 Corinthians 14:16, 17).

How, then can one sufficiently admire the unbridled license of the papists, who, while the apostle publicly protests against it, hesitate not to bawl out the most verbose prayers in a foreign tongue, prayers of which they themselves sometimes do not understand one syllable, and which they have no wish that others should understand? Different is the course which Paul prescribes, "What is it then? I will pray with the spirit, and I will pray with the understanding also; I will sing with the spirit, and I will sing with the understanding also:" meaning by the *spirit* the special gift of tongues, which some who had received it abused when they severed it from the mind, that is, the understanding.

The principle we must always hold is that in all prayer, public and private, the tongue without the mind must be displeasing to God. Moreover, the mind must be so incited, as in ardor of thought far to surpass what the tongue is able to express.

Lastly, the tongue is not even necessary to private prayer, unless insofar as the internal feeling is insufficient for incitement, or the vehemence of the incitement carries the utterance of the tongue along with it. For although the best prayers are sometimes without utterance, yet when the feeling of the mind is overpowering, the tongue spontaneously breaks forth into utterance, and our other members into gesture. Hence, that dubious muttering of Hannah (see 1 Samuel 1:13) is something similar to that which is experienced by all the saints when concise and abrupt expressions escape from them. The bodily gestures usually observed in prayer, such as kneeling and uncovering of the head (see Acts 20:36), are exercises by which we attempt to rise to higher veneration of God.

34 The form of prayer delivered by Christ displays the boundless goodness of our heavenly Father. The great comfort thereby afforded.

We must now attend not only to a surer method, but also the form of prayer, that, namely, which our heavenly Father has delivered to us by His beloved Son and in which we may recognize His boundless goodness and condescension. (See Matthew 6:9; Luke 11:2.) Besides admonishing and exhorting us to seek Him in our every necessity (as children betake themselves to the protection of their parents when oppressed with any anxiety), seeing that we were not fully aware of how great our poverty was or what was right or for our interest to ask, He has provided for this ignorance; that where our capacity failed, He has sufficiently supplied. For He has given us a form in which is set before us as in a picture everything which it is lawful to wish, everything which is conducive to our interest, everything which it is necessary to demand. From His goodness in this respect, we derive the great comfort of knowing, that as we ask almost in His words, we ask nothing that is absurd or foreign or unseasonable; nothing, in short, that is not agreeable to Him.

Plato, seeing the ignorance of men in presenting their desires to God—desires, which if granted, would often be most injurious to them, declares the best form of prayer to be that which an ancient poet has furnished: "O king Jupiter, give what is best, whether we wish it or wish it not; but avert from us what is evil even though we ask it." This heathen shows his wisdom in discerning how dangerous it is to ask of God what our own passion dictates; while, at the same time, he reminds us of our unhappy condition in not being able to open our lips before God without dangers unless His Spirit instruct us as to how to pray aright. (See Romans 8:26.) The higher value, therefore, ought we to set on the privilege, when the only begotten Son of God puts words into our lips, and thus relieves our minds of all hesitation.

35 Lord's Prayer divided into six petitions. Subdivision into two principal parts, the former referring to the glory of God, the latter to our salvation.

This form or rule of prayer is composed of *six petitions*. For I am prevented from agreeing with those who divide it into *seven* by the adversative mode of diction used by the Evangelist. He appears to have intended to unite the two members together. It is as if he had said, "Do not allow us to be overcome by temptation, but rather bring assistance to our frailty, and deliver us, that we may not fall." Ancient writers also agree with us: that which is added by Matthew as a seventh head is to be considered as explanatory of the sixth petition. Though in every part of the prayer the first place is assigned to the glory of God, still this is more especially the object of the three first petitions in which we are to look to the glory of God alone without any reference to what is called our own advantage.

The three remaining petitions are devoted to our interest and properly relate to things, which it is useful for us to ask. When we ask that the name of God may be hallowed, as God wishes to prove whether we love and serve Him freely, or from the hope of reward, we are not to think at all of our own interests; we must set His glory before our eyes, and keep them intent upon it alone. In the other similar petitions this is the only manner in which we ought to be affected. It is true that in this way our own interest is greatly promoted, because, when the name of God is hallowed in the way we ask, our own sanctification also is thereby promoted. But in regard to this advantage, we must, as I have said, shut our eyes and be in a manner blind, so as not even to see it.

Hence, when all hope of our private advantage is cut off, we still should never cease to wish and pray for this hallowing, and everything else which pertains to the glory of God. We have examples in Moses and Paul, who did not count it grievous to turn away their eyes and minds from themselves, and with intense and fervent zeal long for death, if by their loss the kingdom and glory of God might be promoted. (See Exodus 32:32; Romans 9:3.) On the other hand, when we ask for daily bread, although we desire what is advantageous for ourselves, we ought also especially to seek the glory of God, so much so that we would not ask at all unless it would be to turn to His glory. Let us now proceed to an exposition of the prayer.

OUR FATHER WHICH ART IN HEAVEN

36 What the use of the term Father implies, A. That we pray to God in the name of Christ alone. B. That we lay aside all distrust. C. That we expect everything that is for our good.

The first thing suggested at the very outset is, as we have already said (section 17-19), that all our prayers to God ought only to be presented in the name of Christ, as there is no other name which can recommend them. In calling God our Father, we certainly plead the name of Christ. For with what confidence could any man call God his Father? Who would have the presumption to arrogate to himself the honor of a son of God were we not gratuitously adopted as His sons in Christ? He, being the true Son, has been given to us as a brother, so that that which He possesses as His own by nature becomes ours by adoption, if we embrace this great mercy with firm faith. As John says, "As many as received him, to them gave he power to become the sons of God, even to them that believe in his name" (John 1:12). Hence, He both calls himself our Father and is pleased to be so called by us, by this delightful name relieving us of all distrust, since nowhere can a stronger affection be found than in a father. Hence, too, He could not have given us a stronger testimony of His boundless love than in calling us His sons. But his love towards us is so much the greater and more excellent than that of earthly parents, the further He surpasses all men in goodness and mercy. (See Isaiah 63:16.) Earthly parents, laying aside all paternal affection, might abandon their offspring; He will never abandon us. (See Psalm 27:10.) He cannot deny himself. For we have His promise, "If ye then, being evil, know how to give good gifts unto your children, how much more shall your Father which is in heaven give good things to them that ask him?" (Matthew 7:11). In like manner we read in the prophet, "Can a woman forget her sucking child, that she should not have compassion on the son of her womb? Yea, they may forget, yet will not I forget thee" (Isaiah 49:15). But if we are His sons, then, as a son cannot betake himself to the protection of a stranger and a foreigner without complaining of his father's cruelty or poverty, so we cannot ask assistance from any other quarter than from Him, unless we would upbraid Him with poverty, or want of means or cruelty and excessive austerity.

37 Objection, that our sins exclude us from the presence of Him whom we have made a Judge, not a Father. Answer, from the nature of God, as described by an apostle, the parable of the prodigal son, and from the expression, Our Father. Christ the earnest, the Holy Spirit the witness, of our adoption.

Dor let us allege that we are justly rendered timid by a consciousness of sin, by which our Father, though mild and merciful, is daily offended. For if among men, a son cannot have a better advocate to plead his cause with his father, and cannot employ a better intercessor to regain his lost favor than if he comes himself suppliant and downcast, acknowledging his fault, to implore the mercy of his father, whose paternal feelings cannot but be moved by such entreaties, what will that "Father of all mercies, and God of all comfort" do? (2 Corinthians 1:3). Will He not rather listen to the tears and groans of His children when supplicating for themselves (especially seeing as He invites and exhorts us to do so), than to any advocacy of others to whom the timid have recourse, not without some semblance of despair, because they are distrustful of their father's mildness and clemency? The exuberance of his paternal kindness he sets before us in the parable. (See Luke 15:20.) The father with open arms receives the son who had gone away from him, wasted his substance in riotous living, and in all ways grievously sinned against him. He waits not until pardon is asked in words, but, anticipating the request, recognizes him afar off, runs to meet him, consoles him, and restores him to favor.

By setting before us this admirable example of mildness in a man, He designed to show in how much greater abundance we may expect it from Him who is not only a Father, but the best and most merciful of all fathers, however ungrateful, rebellious, and wicked sons we may be, provided only we throw ourselves upon His mercy. And the better to assure us that he is such a Father if we are Christians, He has been pleased to be called not only a Father, but our Father, as if we were pleading with him after this manner: O Father, who art possessed of so much affection for thy children, and art so ready to forgive, we, thy children, approach thee and present our requests, fully persuaded that thou hast no other feelings towards us than those of a father, though we are unworthy of such a parent. But as our narrow hearts are incapable of comprehending such boundless favor, Christ is not only the earnest and pledge of our adoption, but also gives us the Spirit as a witness of this adoption, that through Him we may freely cry aloud, "Abba, Father." Whenever, therefore, we are restrained by any feeling of hesitation, let us remember to ask of Him, that He may correct our timidity, and placing us under the magnanimous guidance of the Spirit, enable us to pray boldly.

426

38 Why God is called generally Our Father.

The instruction given us, however, is not that every individual in particular is to call Him Father, but rather that we are all in common to call him Our Father. By this we are reminded of how strong the feeling of brotherly love between us ought to be, since we are all alike, by the same mercy and free kindness, the children of such a Father. For if He from whom we all obtain whatever is good is our common Father (see Matthew 23:9), everything which has been distributed to us we should be prepared to communicate to each other, as far as occasion demands. Nevertheless, if we are thus desirous, as we ought to be, to stretch out our hands and give assistance to each other, there is nothing by which we can more benefit our brethren than by committing them to the care and protection of the best of parents, since if He is propitious and favorable, nothing more can be desired. And, indeed, we owe this to our Father. For as he, who truly and from the heart loves the father of a family, extends the same love and good will to all his household, so the zeal and affection, which we feel for our heavenly Parent, it becomes us to extend towards his people, His family, and, in fine, His heritage, which He has honored so highly as to give them the appellation of the "fullness" of his only begotten Son. (See Ephesians 1:23.)

Let the Christian, then, so regulate his prayers as to make them common, and embrace all who are his brethren in Christ; not only those whom at present he sees and knows to be such, but all men who are alive upon the Earth. What God has determined with regard to them is beyond our knowledge, but to wish and hope the best concerning them is both pious and humane. Still, it becomes us to regard with special affection those who are of the household of faith, those whom the apostle has in express terms recommended to our care in everything. (See Galatians 6:10.)

In short, all our prayers ought to bear reference to that community which our Lord has established in his kingdom and family.

39 We may pray specially for ourselves and certain others, provided we have in our mind a general reference to all.

This, however, does not prevent us from praying specially for ourselves and certain others, provided our mind is not withdrawn from the view of this community, does not deviate from it, but constantly refers to it. For prayers, though couched in special terms, keeping that object still in view, cease not to be common. All this may easily be understood by analogy. There is a general command from God to relieve the necessities of all the poor. Yet this command is obeyed by those who give succor to all they see or know to be in distress, although they pass by many whose wants are not less urgent, either because they cannot know or are unable to give supply to all. In this way, there is nothing repugnant to the will of God in those who, giving heed to this common society of the Church, yet offer up particular prayers, in which, with a public mind, though in special terms, they commend to God themselves or others with whose necessity He has been pleased to make them more familiarly acquainted.

It is true that prayer and the giving of our substance are not in all respects alike. We can only bestow the kindness of our liberality on those of whose wants we are aware, whereas in prayer we can assist the greatest strangers, no matter how wide the space may be that separates them from us. This is done by that general form of prayer, which includes all the sons of God and includes them. To this we may refer the exhortation which Paul gave to the believers of his age, to lift up "…holy hands without wrath and doubting" (1 Timothy 2:8). By reminding them that dissension is a bar to prayer, he shows it to be his wish that they should with one accord present their prayers in common.

40 In what sense God is said to be in heaven. A threefold use of this doctrine for our consolation. Three cautions. Summary of the preface to the Lord's Prayer.

The next words are, WHICH ART IN HEAVEN. From this we are not to infer that He is enclosed and confined within the circumference of heaven, as by boundaries. Hence, Solomon confesses, "The Heaven of heavens cannot contain thee" (1 Kings 8:27); and He himself says by the Prophet, "The heaven is my throne, and the earth is my footstool" (Isaiah 66:1); thereby intimating that his presence, not confined to any region, is diffused over all space. But as our gross minds are unable to conceive of His ineffable glory, it is designated to us by *Heaven*, nothing which our eyes can behold being so full of splendor and majesty. While, then, we are accustomed to regard every object as confined to the place where our senses discern it, no place can be assigned to God; and hence, if we would seek Him, we must rise higher than all corporeal or mental discernment. Again, this form of expression reminds us that He is far beyond the reach of change or corruption, that he holds the whole universe in his grasp, and rules it by His power. The effect of the expressions therefore, is the same as if it had been said, that He is of infinite majesty, incomprehensible essence, boundless power, and eternal duration. When we thus speak of God, our thoughts must be raised to their highest pitch; we must not ascribe to Him anything of a terrestrial or carnal nature, must not measure Him by our little standards, or suppose His will to be like ours. At the same time, we must put our confidence in Him, understanding that Heaven and Earth are governed by His providence and power.

In short, under the name of Father is set before us that God, who hath appeared to us in His own image, that we may invoke Him with sure faith; the familiar name of Father being given not only to inspire confidence, but also to curb our minds, and prevent them from going astray after doubtful or fictitious gods. We thus ascend from the only begotten Son to the supreme Father of angels and of the Church. Then, when his throne is fixed in Heaven, we are reminded that He governs the world, and, therefore, that it is not in vain to approach Him whose present care we actually experience. "He that cometh to God," says the apostle, "must believe that he is, and that he is a rewarder of them that diligently seek him" (Hebrews 11:6). Here Christ makes both claims for His Father, *first*, that we place our faith in Him; and, *secondly*, that we feel assured that our salvation is not neglected by Him, inasmuch as He condescends to extend His providence to us. By these elementary principles, Paul prepares us to pray aright; for before enjoining us to make our requests known unto God, He premises it in this way, "The Lord is at hand. Be careful for nothing" (Philippians 4:5, 6). Whence it appears that doubt and perplexity hang over the prayers of those in whose minds the belief is not firmly seated, that "The eyes of the Lord are upon the righteous" (Psalm 34:15).

41 The necessity of the first petition as proof of our unrighteousness, What is meant by the name of God. How it is hallowed. Parts of this hallowing. A deprecation of the sins by which the name of God is profaned.

he first petition is, HALLOWED BE THY NAME. The necessity for presenting it bespeaks our great disgrace. For what can be more unbecoming than that our ingratitude and malice should impair our audacity and petulance should as much as in them lies destroy the glory of God? But though all the ungodly should burst with sacrilegious rage, the holiness of God's name still shines forth. Justly does the Psalmist exclaim, "According to thy name, O God, so is thy praise unto the ends of the earth" (Psalm 48:10). For wherever God hath made himself known, His perfections must be displayed, His power, goodness, wisdom, justice, mercy, and truth, which fill us with admiration, and incite us to show forth His praise. Therefore, as the name of God is not duly hallowed on the Earth, and we are otherwise unable to assert it, it is at least our duty to make it the subject of our prayers.

The sum of the whole is: It must be our desire that God may receive the honor which is His due, that men may never think or speak of Him without the greatest reverence. The opposite of this reverence is profanity, which has always been too common in the world and is very prevalent in the present day. Hence, the necessity of the petition, which, if piety had any proper existence among us, would be superfluous. But if the name of God is duly hallowed only when separated from all other names, it alone is glorified; we are, in the petition, enjoined to ask not only that God would vindicate His sacred name from all contempt and insult, but also that He would compel the whole human race to reverence it. Then, since God manifests himself to us partly by His Word, and partly by His works, He is not sanctified unless in regard to both of these we ascribe to Him what is due, and thus embrace whatever has proceeded from Him, giving no less praise to His justice than to His mercy.

On the manifold diversity of His works, He has inscribed the marks of His glory, and these ought to call forth from every tongue an ascription of praise. Thus, Scripture will obtain its due authority with us, and no event will hinder us from celebrating the praises of God, in regard to every part of His government. On the other hand, the petition implies a wish that all impiety which pollutes this sacred name may perish and be extinguished, that everything which obscures or impairs His glory, all detraction and insult, may cease; that all blasphemy being suppressed, the divine majesty may be more and more signally displayed.

42 Distinction between the first and second petitions. What the Kingdom of God, is. How it is said to come. Special exposition of this petition. It reminds us of three things. The advent of the Kingdom of God in the world.

The second petition is, THY KINGDOM COME. This contains nothing new, and yet there is good reason for distinguishing it from the first. For, if we consider our lethargy in the greatest of all matters, we shall see how necessary it is that what ought to be in itself perfectly known should be inculcated at greater length. Therefore, after the injunction to pray that God would reduce to order, and at length completely efface every stain which is thrown on His sacred name, another petition, containing almost the same wish, is added— viz. Thy kingdom come. Although a definition of this kingdom has already been given, I now briefly repeat that God reigns when men, in denial of themselves and contempt of the world and this earthly life, devote themselves to righteousness and aspire to Heaven. (See Calvin, Harm. Matthew 6.) Thus, this kingdom consists of two parts: the first is when God by the agency of His Spirit corrects all the depraved lusts of the flesh, which in bands war against Him; and the second, when he brings all our thoughts into obedience to His authority. Only those who begin with themselves, therefore, duly present this petition; in other words, those who pray that they may be purified from all the corruptions which disturb the tranquility and impair the purity of God's kingdom. Then, as the Word of God is like His royal scepter, we are here enjoined to pray that He would subdue all minds and hearts to voluntary obedience. This is done when by the secret inspiration of His Spirit, He displays the efficacy of His Word, and raises it to the place of honor, which it deserves.

We must next descend to the wicked, who perversely and with desperate madness resist His authority. God, therefore, sets up His kingdom by humbling the whole world, though in different ways, taming the wantonness of some, and breaking the ungovernable pride of others. We should desire this to be done every day in order that God may gather churches to himself from all quarters of the world, may extend and increase their numbers, enrich them with His gifts, establish due order among them; on the other hand, that He may beat down all the enemies of pure doctrine and religion, dissipate their counsels, and defeat their attempts.

Hence, it appears that there is good ground for the precept, which enjoins daily progress, for human affairs are never so prosperous as when the impurities of vice are purged away, and integrity flourishes in full vigor. The completion, however, is deferred to the final advent of Christ, when, as Paul declares, "God will be all in all" (1 Corinthians 15:28). This prayer, therefore, ought to withdraw us from the corruptions of the world that separate us from God and prevent His kingdom from flourishing within us. Secondly, it ought to inflame us with an ardent desire for the mortification of the flesh. Lastly, it ought to train us to the endurance of the cross, since this is the way in which God would have His kingdom be advanced. It ought not to grieve us that the outward man decays, provided the inner man is renewed. For such is the nature of the Kingdom of God. While we submit to His righteousness, He makes us partakers of His glory. This is the case when continually adding to his light and truth, by which the lies and the darkness of Satan and His kingdom are dissipated, extinguished, and destroyed. Still, He protects his people, guides them aright by the agency of His Spirit, and confirms them in perseverance. At the same time, He frustrates the impious conspiracies of His enemies, dissipates their wiles and frauds, prevents their malice and curbs their petulance, until at length he consume Antichrist "with the spirit of his mouth," and destroys all impiety "with the brightness of his coming" (2 Thessalonians 2:8).

43 The distinction between the second and third petitions. The will here does mean not the secret will or good pleasure of God, but that which is manifested in the Word. The conclusion of the three first petitions.

The third petition is THY WILL BE DONE ON EARTH AS IT IS IN HEAVEN. Though this depends on His kingdom and cannot be disjoined from it, yet a separate place is not improperly given to it because of our ignorance, which does not at once or easily apprehend what God reigning in the world means. This, therefore, may not improperly be taken as the explanation that God will be King in the world when all shall subject themselves to His will. We are not here treating of that secret will by which He governs all things and destines them to their end. (See chapter 24, section 17.) For although devils and men rise in tumult against Him, He is able by His incomprehensible counsel to not only turn aside their violence, but also to make it subservient to the execution of His decrees.

What we here speak of is another will of God, namely, that of which voluntary obedience is the counterpart; and, therefore, Heaven is expressly contrasted with Earth, because, as is said in the Psalms, the angels "…do his commandments, hearkening unto the voice of his word" (Psalm 103:20). We are, therefore, enjoined to pray that as everything done in Heaven is at the command of God, and the angels are calmly disposed to do all that is right, so the Earth may be brought under His authority, all rebellion and depravity having been extinguished. In presenting this request, we renounce the desires of the flesh, because he who does not entirely resign his affections to God, does as much as in him lies to oppose the divine will, since everything, which proceeds from us, is vicious. Again, by this prayer, we are taught to deny ourselves, that God may rule us according to His pleasure. Also, having annihilated our own, He may create new thoughts and new minds so that we shall have no desire, save that of entire agreement with His will.

In short, we wish nothing of ourselves, but have our hearts governed by His Spirit, under whose inward teaching we may learn to love those things which please Him and hate those things which displease Him. Hence, also, we must desire that He would nullify and suppress all affections, which are repugnant to His will. Such are the three first heads of the prayer, in presenting which we should have the glory of God only in view, taking no account of ourselves, and paying no respect to our own advantage, which, though it is thereby greatly promoted, is not here to be the subject of request. Though all the events prayed for must happen in their own time, without being either thought of, wished, or asked by us, it is still our duty to wish and ask for them. And it is of no slight importance to do so, that we may testify and profess that we are the servants and children of God, desirous by every means in our power to promote the honor that is due to Him as our Lord and Father, and truly and thoroughly devoted to his service. Hence, if men, in praying that the name of God may be hallowed, that His kingdom may come and His will be done, are not influenced by this zeal for the promotion of His glory, they are not to be accounted among the servants and children of God. As all these things will take place against their will, so they will turn out to their confusion and destruction.

44 A summary of the second part of the Lord's Prayer. Three petitions. What is contained in the first. Declares the exceeding kindness of God, and our distrust. What is meant by bread. Why the petition for bread precedes that for the forgiveness of sins. Why it is called ours. Why it is to be sought this day, or daily. The doctrine resulting from this petition, illustrated by an example. Two classes of men sin in regard to this petition. In what sense it is called, our bread. Why we ask God to give it to us.

Now comes the second part of the prayer, in which we descend to our own interests, not that we are to lose sight of the glory of God, to which, as Paul declares, we must have respect even in meat and drink (see 1 Corinthians 10:31), and ask only what is expedient for ourselves. But the distinction, as we have already observed, is this: God, claiming the three first petitions as especially His own, carries us entirely to himself, that in this way He may prove our piety. Next he permits us to look to our own advantage, but still on the condition that when we ask anything for ourselves, it must be in order that all the benefits which He confers may show forth his glory, there being nothing more incumbent on us than to live and die to Him. By the first petition of the second part, GIVE US THIS DAY OUR DAILY BREAD, we pray in general that God would give us all things which the body requires in this sublunary state, not only food and clothing, but everything which He knows will assist us to eat our bread in peace. In this way we briefly cast our care upon Him and commit ourselves to His providence, that He may feed, foster, and preserve us. For our heavenly Father disdains not to take our body under His charge and protection, that he may exercise our faith in those minute matters, while we look to Him for everything, even to a morsel of bread and a drop of water.

Owing to some strange inequality, we feel more concern for the body than for the soul. Many, who can trust the latter to God, continue to be anxious about the former, still hesitate about what they are to eat and how they are to be clothed, and are in trepidation whenever their hands are not filled with corn, wine, and oil; so much more value do we set on this shadowy, fleeting life than on a blessed immortality. But those who, trusting to God, have once cast away that anxiety about the flesh, immediately look to Him for greater gifts, even salvation and eternal life. It is no slight exercise of faith, therefore, to hope in God for things, which would otherwise give us so much concern; nor have we made little progress when we are quit of this unbelief, which cleaves to our very bones.

The speculations of some concerning supersubstantial bread seem to be very little accordant with our Savior's meaning; for our prayer would be defective were we not to ascribe to God the nourishment even of this fading life. The reason which they give is heathenish—viz. that it is inconsistent with the character of sons of God, who ought to be spiritual, not only to occupy their mind with earthly cares, but to suppose God is also occupied with them. As if His blessing and paternal favor were not eminently displayed in giving us food, or as if there were nothing in the declaration that godliness hath "the promise of the life that now is, and of that which is to come" (1 Timothy 4:8). But although the forgiveness of sins is of far more importance than the nourishment of the body, yet Christ has set down the inferior in the prior place, in order that He might gradually raise us to the other two petitions, which properly belong to the heavenly life, in this providing for our sluggishness.

We are enjoined to ask for *our bread*, that we may be contented with the measure which our heavenly Father is pleased to dispense and not strive to make gain by illicit arts. Meanwhile, we must hold that the title by which it is ours is donation, because, as Moses says (Leviticus 26:20; Deuteronomy 8:17), neither our industry, nor labor, nor hands, acquire anything for us, unless the blessing of God be present; nay, not even would abundance of bread be of the least avail were it not divinely converted into nourishment. Hence, this liberality of God is not less necessary to the rich than to the poor, because, though their cellars and barns were full, they would be parched, and pine with want did they not enjoy His favor along with their bread. The terms *this day* (or, as it is in another evangelist, *daily*, and also the epithet *daily*) lays a restraint on our immoderate desire of fleeting good—a desire which we are extremely apt to indulge to excess, and from which other evils ensue.

When our supply is in richer abundance, we ambitiously squander it in pleasure, luxury, ostentation, or other kinds of extravagance. Wherefore, we are only enjoined to ask as much as our necessity requires, and for each day, confiding that our heavenly Father, who gives us the supply of today, will not fail us on the morrow. However great our abundance may be or how well filled our cellars and granaries, we must still always ask for daily bread, for we must feel assured that all substance is nothing, unless insofar as the Lord, by pouring out his blessing, makes it fruitful during its whole progress. Even that which is in our hand is not ours except insofar as he every hour portions it out, and permits us to use it.

As nothing is more difficult to human pride than the admission of this truth, the Lord declares that He gave a special proof for all ages, when He fed his people with manna in the desert. (See Deuteronomy 8:3.) In doing so, He reminds us, "Man shall not live by bread alone, but by every word that proceedeth out of the mouth of God" (Matthew 4:4). It is thus intimated, that by his power alone our life and strength are sustained, though He ministers supply to us by bodily instruments. In like manner, whenever it so pleases, he gives us a proof of an opposite description, by breaking the strength, or, as He himself calls it, the *staff* of bread (see Leviticus 26:26), and leaving us even while eating to pine with hunger, and while drinking to be parched with thirst. Those who, not contented with daily bread, indulge an unrestrained insatiable cupidity, or those who are full of their own abundance, and trust in their own riches, only mock God by offering up this prayer. For the former ask what they would be unwilling to obtain, nay, what they most of all abominate, namely, daily bread only, and as much as in them lies disguise their avarice from God, whereas true prayer should pour out the whole soul and every inward feeling before Him.

The latter again ask what they do not at all expect to obtain, namely, what they imagine that they in themselves already possess. In its being called *ours*, God, as we have already said, gives a striking display of His kindness, making that to be ours to which we have no just claim. Nor must we reject the view to which I have already adverted—viz. that this name is given to what is obtained by just and honest labor, as contrasted with what is obtained by fraud and rapine, nothing being our own which we obtain with injury to others.

When we ask God to *give us*, the meaning is that the thing asked is simply and freely the gift of God, whatever be the quarter from which it comes to us, even when it seems to have been specially prepared by our own art and industry, and procured by our hands. It is to His blessing alone that all our labors owe their success.

45 The close connection between this and the subsequent petition. Why our sins are called debts. This petition violated, A. By those who think they can satisfy God by their own merits or those of others. B. By those who dream of a perfection which makes pardon unnecessary. Why the elect cannot attain perfection in this life. Refutation of the libertine dreamers of perfection. Objection refuted. In what sense we are said to forgive those who have sinned against us. How the condition is to be understood.

The next petition is, FORGIVE US OUR DEBTS. In this and the following petition our Savior has briefly comprehended whatever is conducive to the heavenly life, as these two members contain the spiritual covenant, which God made for the salvation of His Church, "I will put my law in their inward parts, and write it on their hearts." "I will pardon all their iniquities" (Jeremiah 31:33; 33:8). Here our Savior begins with the forgiveness of sins and then adds the subsequent blessing—viz. that God would protect us by the power and support us by the aid of His Spirit, so that we may stand invincible against all temptations. To sins He gives the name of *debts*, because we owe the punishment due to them, a debt which we could not possibly pay were we not discharged by this remission. It is the result of His free mercy, when He freely expunges the debt, accepting nothing in return. It is of His own mercy, receiving satisfaction in Christ, who gave himself a ransom for us. (See Romans 3:24.)

Hence, those who expect to satisfy God by merits of their own or of others, or to compensate and purchase forgiveness by means of satisfactions, have no share in this free pardon, and while they address God in this petition, do nothing more than subscribe their own accusation, and seal their condemnation by their own testimony. For they confess that they are debtors, unless they are discharged by means of forgiveness. This forgiveness, however, they do not receive, but rather reject, when they obtrude their merits and satisfactions upon God, since by so doing they do not implore His mercy but appeal to His justice.

Let those who dream of a perfection which makes it unnecessary to seek pardon, find their disciples among those whose itching ears incline them to imposture. (See Daniel 9:20.) Only let them understand that those whom they thus acquire have been carried away from Christ, since He, by instructing all to confess their guilt, receives none but sinners, not that He may soothe and so encourage them in their sins, but because He knows that believers are never so divested of the sins of the flesh as not to remain subject to the justice of God. It is, indeed, to be wished—it ought even to be our strenuous endeavor—to perform all the parts of our duty, so as truly to congratulate ourselves before God as being pure from every stain. As God is pleased to renew His image in us by degrees, so that to some extent there is always a residue of corruption in our flesh, we ought by no means to neglect the remedy. But if Christ, according to the authority given to Him by his Father, enjoins us, during the whole course of our lives, to implore pardon, who can tolerate those new teachers who, by the phantom of perfect innocence, endeavor to dazzle the simple and make them believe they can render themselves completely free from guilt? This, as John declares, is nothing else than to make God a liar. (See 1 John 1:10.)

In like manner, those foolish men mutilate the covenant in which we have seen that our salvation is contained by concealing one head of it, and so destroying it entirely; being guilty not only of profanity in that they separate things which ought to be indissolubly connected, but also of wickedness and cruelty in overwhelming wretched souls with despair—of treachery also to themselves and their followers, in that they encourage themselves in a carelessness diametrically opposed to the mercy of God. It is excessively childish to object that when they long for the advent of the Kingdom of God, they at the same time pray for the abolition of sin. In the former division of the prayer, absolute perfection is set before us; but in the latter, our own weakness. Thus, the two fitly correspond to each other—we strive for the goal, and at the same time neglect not the remedies, which our necessities require.

In the next part of the petition we pray to be forgiven, "*as we forgive our debtors;*" that is, as we spare and pardon all by whom we are in any way offended, either in deed by unjust, or in word by contumelious treatment. Not that we can forgive the guilt of a fault or offense; this belongs to God only; but we can forgive to this extent: we can voluntarily divest our minds of wrath, hatred, and revenge, and efface the remembrance of injuries by a voluntary oblivion. Wherefore, we are not to ask the forgiveness of our sins from God, unless we forgive the offenses of all who are or have been injurious to us.

If we retain any hatred in our minds, if we meditate revenge, and devise the means of hurting; nay, if we do not return to a good understanding with our enemies, perform every kind of friendly office, and endeavor to effect a reconciliation with them, we by this petition beseech God not to grant us forgiveness. For we ask Him to do to us, as we do to others. This is the same as asking Him not to do unless we do also. What, then, do such persons obtain by this petition but a heavier judgment?

Lastly, the condition—being forgiven as we forgive our debtors—is not added because by forgiving others we deserve forgiveness, as if the cause of forgiveness were expressed. On the contrary, by the use of this expression, the Lord has been pleased partly to solace the weakness of our faith, using it as a sign to assure us that our sins are as certainly forgiven as we are certainly conscious of having forgiven others. Then our mind is completely purged from all envy, hatred, and malice; and partly using as a badge by which He excludes from the number of His children all who, prone to revenge and reluctant to forgive, obstinately keep up their enmity, cherishing against others that indignation, which they deprecate from themselves, so that they should not venture to invoke him as a Father. In the Gospel of Luke, we have this distinctly stated in the words of Christ.

46 The sixth petition reduced to three heads. A. The various forms of temptation. The depraved conceptions of our minds. The wiles of Satan, on the right hand and on the left. B. What it is to be led into temptation. We do not ask not to be tempted of God. What is meant by evil, or the evil one. Summary of this petition. How necessary it is. Condemns the pride of the superstitious. Includes many excellent properties. In what sense God may be said to lead us into temptation.

The sixth petition corresponds (as we have observed) to the promise of *writing the Law upon our hearts*; but because we do not obey God without a continual warfare, without sharp and arduous contests, we here pray that He would furnish us with armor and defend us by His protection, that we may be able to obtain the victory. By this we are reminded that we not only have need of the gift of the Spirit inwardly to soften our hearts and turn and direct them to the obedience of God, but also of His assistance to render us invincible by all the wiles and violent assaults of Satan.

The forms of temptation are many and various. The depraved conceptions of our minds provoking us to transgress the Law—conceptions which our concupiscence suggests or the devil excites, are temptations; and things which in their own nature are not evil, become temptations by the wiles of the devil, when they are presented to our eyes in such a way that the view of them makes us withdraw or decline from God.

These temptations are both on the right hand and on the left. On the right, when riches, power, and honors, which by their glare, and the semblance of good which they present, generally dazzle the eyes of men, and so entice by their blandishments, that, caught by their snares, and intoxicated by their sweetness, they forget their God: on the left, when offended by the hardship and bitterness of poverty, disgrace, contempt, afflictions, and other things of that description, they despond, cast away their confidence and hope, and are at length totally estranged from God. In regard to both kinds of temptation, which either enkindled in us by concupiscence or presented by the craft of Satan's war against us, we pray God the Father not to allow us to be overcome, but rather to raise and support us by his hand, that strengthened by His mighty power, we may stand firm against all the assaults of our malignant enemy, whatever be the thoughts which he sends into our minds; next we pray that whatever of either description is allotted us, we may turn to good, that is, may neither be inflated with prosperity, nor cast down by adversity. Here, however, we do not ask to be altogether exempted from temptation, which is very necessary to excite, stimulate, and urge us on, that we may not become too lethargic.

It was not without reason that David wished to be tried, nor is it without cause that the Lord daily tries his elect, chastising them by disgrace, poverty, tribulation, and other kinds of crosses. But the temptations of God and Satan are very different: Satan tempts, that he may destroy, condemn, confound, throw headlong; God, that by proving His people, He may make trial of their sincerity, and by exercising their strength, confirm it; may mortify, tame, and cauterize their flesh, which, if not curbed in this manner, would wanton and exult above measure. Besides, Satan attacks those who are unarmed and unprepared, that he may destroy them unawares; whereas, whatever God sends, He "…will with the temptation also make a way to escape, that ye may be able to bear it." Whether by the term evil we understand the devil or sin is not of the least consequence. Satan is indeed the very enemy who lays snares for our life, but it is by sin that he is armed for our destruction. Our petition, therefore, is, that we may not be overcome or overwhelmed with temptation, but in the strength of the Lord may stand firm against all the powers by which we are assailed; in other words, that we may not fall under temptation, that being thus taken under His charge and protection, we may remain invincible to sin, death, the gates of hell, and the whole power of the devil; in other words, that we would be delivered from evil.

Here it is carefully to be observed that we have no strength to contend with such a combatant as the devil, or to sustain the violence of His assault. Were it otherwise, it would be mockery of God to ask of him what we already possess in ourselves. Assuredly, those who in self-confidence prepare for such a fight do not understand how bold and well equipped the enemy is with whom they have to do. Now we ask to be delivered from his power, as from the mouth of some furious raging lion, who would instantly tear us with his teeth and claws, and swallow us up, did not the Lord rescue us from the midst of death; at the same time knowing that if the Lord is present and will fight for us while we stand by, through Him, "We shall do valiantly" (Psalm 60:12).

Let others, if they will confide in the powers and resources of their free will, which they think they possess; enough for us that we stand and are strong in the power of God alone. But the prayer comprehends more than at first sight it seems to do. For if the Spirit of God is our strength in waging the contest with Satan, we cannot gain the victory unless we are filled with Him and thereby freed from all infirmity of the flesh. Therefore, when we pray to be delivered from sin and Satan, we at the same time desire to be enriched with new supplies of divine grace until we are completely replenished with them, we triumph over every evil.

To some it seems rude and harsh to ask God not to lead us into temptation, since, as James declares (see James 1:13), it is contrary to His nature to do so. This difficulty has already been partly solved by the fact that our concupiscence is the cause, and, therefore, properly bears the blame of all the temptations by which we are overcome. All that James means is that it is vain and unjust to ascribe to God vices which our own consciousness compels us to impute to ourselves. But this is no reason that God may not when He sees it meet bring us into bondage to Satan, give us up to a reprobate mind and shameful lusts, and so by a just, indeed, but often hidden judgment, lead us into temptation. Though the cause is often concealed from men, it is well known to him. Hence, we may see that the expression is not improper, if we are persuaded that it is not without cause that He so often threatens to give sure signs of His vengeance by blinding the reprobate and hardening their hearts.

47 The three last petitions show that the prayers of Christians ought to be public. The conclusion of the Lord's Prayer. Why the word Amen is added.

These three petitions, in which we specially commend ourselves and all that we have to God, clearly show what we formerly observed (section 38, 39), that the prayers of Christians should be public and have respect to the public edification of the Church and the advancement of believers in spiritual communion. For no one requests that anything should be given to him as an individual, but we all ask in common for daily bread and the forgiveness of sins, not to be led into temptation and to be delivered from evil. Moreover, there is subjoined the reason for our great boldness in asking and confidence of obtaining (section 11, 36). Although this does not exist in the Latin copies, yet as it accords so well with the whole that we cannot think of omitting it.

The words are, THINE IS THE KINGDOM, AND THE POWER, AND THE GLORY FOREVER. Here is the calm and firm assurance of our faith. For were our prayers to be commended to God by our own worth, who would venture even to whisper before Him? Now, however wretched we may be, however unworthy, however devoid of commendation, we shall never want a reason for prayer, nor a ground of confidence, since the Kingdom, power, and glory, can never be wrested from our Father.

The last word is AMEN, by which is expressed the eagerness of our desire to obtain the things which we ask, while our hope is confirmed, that all things have already been obtained and will assuredly be granted to us, seeing they have been promised by God, who cannot deceive. This accords with the form of expression to which we have already adverted: "Grant, O Lord, for thy name's sake, not on account of us or of our righteousness." By this the saints not only express the end of their prayers, but confess that they are unworthy of obtaining if God did not find the cause in himself and were not their confidence, founded entirely on His nature.

48 The Lord's Prayer contains everything we can or ought to ask of God. Those who go beyond it sin in three ways.

All things that we ought, indeed, all that we are able to ask of God, are contained in this formula and rule of prayer delivered by Christ, our divine Master, whom the Father has appointed to be our teacher, and to whom alone He would have us listen. (See Matthew 17:5.) For He ever was the eternal wisdom of the Father, and being made man, was manifested as the Wonderful, the Counselor. (See Isaiah 11:2.) Accordingly, this prayer is complete in all its parts, it is so complete, that whatever is extraneous and foreign to it, whatever cannot be referred to it, is impious and unworthy of the approbation of God. For He has here summarily prescribed what is worthy of Him, what is acceptable to Him, and what is necessary for us; in short, whatever He is pleased to grant. Those, therefore, who presume to go further and ask something more from God, first seek to add of their own to the wisdom of God. This it is insane blasphemy to do. Secondly, they refuse to confine themselves within the will of God, and despising it, they wander as their cupidity directs. Lastly, they will never obtain anything, seeing that they pray without faith. For there cannot be a doubt that all such prayers are made without faith, because at variance with the Word of God, on which if faith does not always lean, it cannot possibly stand. Those who, disregarding the Master's rule, indulge their own wishes, not only do not have the Word of God, but also as much as in them lies, oppose it. Hence, Tertullian has not less truly than elegantly termed it *Lawful Prayer*, tacitly intimating that all other prayers are lawless and illicit.

49 We may, after the example of the saints, frame our prayers in different words, provided there is no difference in meaning.

By this, however, we would not have it understood that we are so restricted to this form of prayer as to make it unlawful to change a word or syllable of it. For in Scripture we meet with many prayers differing greatly from it in word, yet written by the same Spirit, and capable of being used by us with the greatest advantage. The same Spirit also continually suggests many prayers to believers, though in expression they bear no great resemblance to it. All we mean to say is that no man should wish, expect, or ask anything which is not summarily comprehended in this prayer. Though the words may be very different, there must be no difference in the sense. In this way, all prayers, both those which are contained in the Scripture and those which come forth from pious breasts must be referred to it;

certainly none can ever equal it, far less surpass it in perfection. It omits nothing which we can conceive in praise of God and nothing which we can imagine advantageous to man. The whole is so exact that all hope of improving it may well be renounced. In short, let us remember that we have here the doctrine of heavenly wisdom. God has taught what He willed and He willed what was necessary.

50 Some circumstances to be observed. Of appointing special hours of prayer. What is to be aimed at, and what is to be avoided. The will of God, the rule of our prayers.

It has been said above (see section 7, 27, etc.) that we ought always to raise our minds upwards towards God, and pray without ceasing. Yet such is our weakness, which requires to be supported, such our torpor, which requires to be stimulated, that it is requisite for us to appoint special hours for this exercise. The hours are not to pass away without prayer, and during them, the whole affections of our minds are to be completely occupied. Namely, when we rise in the morning, before we commence our daily work, when we sit down to food, when by the blessing of God we have taken it, and when we retire to rest. This, however, must not be a superstitious observance of hours, by which performing a task to God, we think we are discharged as to other hours; it should rather be considered as a discipline by which our weakness is exercised, and always stimulated. In particular, it must be our anxious care, whenever we are ourselves pressed, or see others pressed by any strait, instantly to have recourse to Him not only with quickened pace but with quickened minds; and again, we must not in any prosperity of ourselves or others omit to testify our recognition of His hand by praise and thanksgiving.

Lastly, in all our prayers we must carefully avoid wishing to confine God to certain circumstances or prescribe to Him the time, place, or mode of action. In like manner, we are taught by this prayer not to fix any law or impose any condition upon Him, but leave it entirely to Him to adopt whatever course of procedure seems to Him best in respect of method, time, and place. For before we offer up any petition for ourselves, we ask that his will may be done, and by so doing so, place our will in subordination to His, just as if we had laid a curb upon it, that, instead of presuming to give law to God, it may regard Him as the ruler and disposer of all its wishes.

51
Perseverance in prayer is especially recommended, both by precept and example. Condemnatory of those who assign to God a time and mode of hearing.

If, with minds thus framed to obedience, we allow ourselves to be governed by the laws of divine providence, we shall easily learn to persevere in prayer. Suspending our own desires, we wait patiently for the Lord, certain, however little the appearance of it may be, that He is always present with us, and will in His own time show how very far He was from turning a deaf ear to prayers, though to the eyes of men they may seem to be disregarded. This will be a very present consolation if, at any time, God does not grant an immediate answer to our prayers, preventing us from fainting or giving way to despondency, as those are wont to do who in invoking God are so borne away by their own fervor, that unless He yield on their first importunity and give present help, they immediately imagine that He is angry and offended with them and abandoning all hope of success, they cease from prayer.

On the contrary, deferring our hope with well-tempered equanimity, let us insist with that perseverance which is so strongly recommended to us in Scripture. We may often see in the Psalms how David and other believers, after they are almost weary of praying, and seem to have been beating the air by addressing a God who would not hear, yet cease not to pray because due authority is not given to the Word of God, unless the faith placed in it is superior to all events. Again, let us not tempt God, and by wearying Him with our importunity, provoke His anger against us.

Many have a practice of formally bargaining with God on certain conditions, and, as if He were the servant of their lust, binding Him to certain stipulations; with which if He does not immediately comply, they are indignant and fretful, murmur, complain, and make a noise. Thus offended, He often in His anger grants to such persons what in mercy He kindly denies to others. Of this we have a proof in the children of Israel, for whom it had been better not to have been heard by the Lord, than to swallow His indignation with their flesh. (See Numbers 11:18, 33.)

52
Of the dignity of faith, through which we always obtain in answer to prayer whatever is most expedient for us. The knowledge of this most necessary.

But if our sense is not able, until after long expectation, to perceive what the result of prayer is, or experience any benefit from it, still our faith will assure us of that which cannot be perceived by sense—viz. that we have obtained what was fit for us, the Lord having so often and so surely engaged to take an interest in all our troubles from the moment they have been deposited in His bosom. In this way, we shall possess abundance in poverty and comfort in affliction. For though all things fail, God will never abandon us, and he cannot frustrate the expectation and patience of His people. He alone will suffice for all, since in himself He comprehends all good, and will at last reveal it to us on the Day of Judgment, when His kingdom shall be plainly manifested.

We may add that although God complies with our request, He does not always give an answer in the very terms of our prayers, but while apparently holding us in suspense, yet in an unknown way, He shows that our prayers have not been in vain. This is the meaning of the words of John, "If we know that he hear us, whatsoever we ask, we know that we have the petitions that we desired of him" (1 John 5:15). It might seem that there is here a great superfluity of words, but the declaration is most useful, namely, that God, even when He does not comply with our requests, yet listens and is favorable to our prayers, so that our hope founded on His Word is never disappointed. But believers have always need of being supported by this patience, as they could not stand long if they did not lean upon it. For the trials by which the Lord proves and exercises us are severe, nay, He often drives us to extremes, and when driven allows us long to stick fast in the mire before He gives us any taste of His sweetness.

As Hannah says, "The Lord killeth, and maketh alive; he bringeth down to the grave, and bringeth up" (1 Samuel 2:6). What could they here do but become dispirited and rush on in despair, were they not, when afflicted, desolate, and half dead, comforted with the thought that they are regarded by God, and that there will be an end to their present evils. However secure their hopes may stand, they in the meantime cease not to pray, since prayer unaccompanied by perseverance leads to no result.

Chapter 21

OF THE ETERNAL ELECTION BY WHICH GOD HAS PREDESTINATED SOME TO SALVATION AND OTHERS TO DESTRUCTION

The divisions of this chapter are, I. The necessity and utility of the doctrine of eternal election is explained. Excessive curiosity restrained, sections 1, 2. II. Explanation to those who through false modesty shun the doctrine of predestination, sections 3, 4. III. The orthodox doctrine expounded.

Sections

1. *The doctrine of election and predestination. It is useful, necessary, and most sweet. Ignorance of it impairs the glory of God, plucks up humility by the roots, and begets and fosters pride. The doctrine establishes the certainty of salvation, peace of conscience, and the true origin of the Church. Answer to two classes of men: the first class being curious men.*

2. *A sentiment of Augustine confirmed by an admonition of our Savior and a passage of Solomon.*

3. *An answer to a second class—viz. those who are unwilling that the doctrine should be adverted to. An objection founded on a passage of Solomon, solved by the words of Moses.*

4. *A second objection—viz. That this doctrine is a stumbling block to the profane. Answer A. The same may be said of many other heads of doctrine. B. The truth of God will always defend itself. Third objection—viz. That this doctrine is dangerous even to believers. Answer. A. The same objection made to Augustine. B. We must not despise anything that God has revealed. Arrogance and blasphemy of such objections.*

5. *Certain cavils against the doctrine. Prescience regarded as the cause of predestination. Prescience and predestination explained. Not prescience, but the good pleasure of God is the cause of*

predestination. This is apparent from the gratuitous election of the posterity of Abraham and the rejection of all others.

6. Even of the posterity of Abraham some are elected and others are rejected by special grace.

7. The apostle shows that the same thing has been done in regard to individuals under the Christian dispensation.

I The doctrine of election and predestination. It is useful, necessary, and most sweet. Ignorance of it impairs the glory of God, plucks up humility by the roots, and begets and fosters pride. The doctrine establishes the certainty of salvation, peace of conscience, and the true origin of the Church. Answer to two classes of men: the first class being curious men.

The covenant of life is not preached equally to all, and among those to whom it is preached, does not always meet with the same reception. This diversity displays the unsearchable depth of the divine judgment and is without doubt subordinate to God's purpose of eternal election. But if it is plainly owing to the mere pleasure of God that salvation is spontaneously offered to some, while others have no access to it, great and difficult questions immediately arise, questions, which are inexplicable, when just views are not entertained concerning election and predestination. To many this seems a perplexing subject, because they deem it most incongruous that of the great body of mankind some should be predestinated to salvation, and others to destruction.

How ceaselessly they entangle themselves will appear as we proceed. We may add that in the very obscurity which deters them, we may see not only the utility of this doctrine, but also its most pleasant fruits. We shall never feel persuaded as we ought that our salvation flows from the free mercy of God as its fountain, until we are made acquainted with His eternal election, the grace of God being illustrated by the contrast—viz. that He does not adopt all promiscuously to the hope of salvation, but gives to some what He denies to others. It is plain how greatly ignorance of this principle detracts from the glory of God and impairs true humility.

Though thus necessary to be known, Paul declares that it cannot be known unless God, throwing works entirely out of view, elect those whom He has predestined. His words are, "Even so then at this present time also, there is a remnant according to the election of grace. And if by grace, then it is no more of works: otherwise, grace is no more grace. But if it be of works, then it is no more grace: otherwise work is no more work" (Romans 11:6). If to make it appear that our salvation flows entirely from the good mercy of God, we must be carried back to the origin of election, then those who would extinguish it, wickedly do as much as in them lies to obscure what they ought most loudly to extol and pluck up humility by the very roots. Paul clearly declares that it is only when the salvation of a remnant is ascribed to gratuitous election that we arrive at the knowledge that God saves whom He wills of His mere good pleasure and does not pay a debt, a debt which never can be due.

Those who preclude access, and would not have anyone to obtain a taste of this doctrine, are equally unjust to God and men, there being no other means of humbling us as we ought, or making us feel how much we are bound to Him. Nor, indeed, have we elsewhere any sure ground of confidence. This we say on the authority of Christ, who, to deliver us from all fear, and render us invincible amid our many dangers, snares, and mortal conflicts, promises safety to all that the Father has taken under His protection. (See John 10:26.)

From this we infer that all who know not that they are the peculiar people of God must be wretched from perpetual trepidation, and that those, therefore, who, by overlooking the three advantages which we have noted, would destroy the very foundation of our safety, consult ill for themselves and for all the faithful. What? Do we not here find the very origin of the Church, which, as Bernard rightly teaches, could not be found or recognized among the creatures, because it lies hid (in both cases wondrously) within the lap of blessed predestination, and the mass of wretched condemnation?

But before I enter on the subject, I have some remarks to address to two classes of men. The subject of predestination, which in itself is attended with considerable difficulty, is rendered very perplexed and hence perilous by human curiosity, which cannot be restrained from wandering into forbidden paths and climbing to the clouds, determined, if it could, that none of the secret things of God shall remain unexplored. When we see many, some of them in other respects not bad men, everywhere rushing into this audacity and wickedness, it is necessary to remind them of the course of duty in this matter. First, then, when they inquire into predestination, let them remember that they are penetrating into the recesses of the divine wisdom, where he who rushes forward securely and confidently, instead of satisfying his curiosity, will enter into an inextricable labyrinth. For it is not right that man should with impunity pry into things which the Lord has been pleased to conceal within himself, and scan that sublime eternal wisdom which it is His pleasure that we should not apprehend but adore, that therein also His perfections may appear. Those secrets of his will, which He has seen it meet to manifest, are revealed in His Word—revealed insofar as He knew to be conducive to our interest and welfare.

2 A sentiment of Augustine is confirmed by an admonition of our Savior and a passage of Solomon.

"We have come into the way of faith," says Augustine: "let us constantly adhere to it. It leads to the chambers of the king, in which are hidden all the treasures of wisdom and knowledge. For our Lord Jesus Christ did not speak invidiously to His great and most select disciples when He said, "I have yet many things to say unto you, but ye cannot bear them now" (John 16:12). We must walk, advance, increase, that our hearts may be able to comprehend those things,which they cannot now comprehend. But if the last day shall find us making progress, we shall there learn what here we could not." All presumption will be curbed and restrained if we give due weight to the consideration that the Word of the Lord is the only way to conduct us to the investigation of whatever is lawful for us to hold with regard to Him, and is the only light to enable us to discern what we ought to see with regard to Him. For it will show us that the moment we go beyond the bounds of the Word, we are out of the course, in darkness, and must every now and then stumble, go astray, and fall.

Let it, therefore, be our first principle that to desire any other knowledge of predestination than that which is expounded by the Word of God is no less infatuated than to walk where there is no path, or to seek light in darkness. Let us not be ashamed to be ignorant in a matter in which ignorance is learning. Rather, let us willingly abstain from the search after knowledge, to which it is both foolish as well as perilous, and even fatal to aspire. If an unrestrained imagination urges us, our proper course is to oppose it with these words, "It is not good to eat much honey: so for men to search their own glory is not glory" (Proverbs 25:27). There is good reason to dread a presumption, which can only plunge us headlong into ruin.

3 An answer to a second class—viz. those who are unwilling that the doctrine should be adverted to. An objection founded on a passage of Solomon, solved by the words of Moses.

There are others who, when they would cure this disease, recommend that the subject of predestination should scarcely if ever be mentioned, and tell us to shun every question concerning it as we would a rock. Although their moderation is justly commendable in thinking that such mysteries should be treated with moderation, yet because they keep too far within the proper measure, they have little influence over the human mind, which does not readily allow itself to be curbed. Therefore, in order to keep the legitimate course in this matter, we must return to the Word of God, in which we are furnished with the right rule of understanding. For Scripture is the school of the Holy Spirit, in which as nothing useful and necessary to be known has been omitted, so nothing is taught but what it is of importance to know. Everything therefore delivered in Scripture on the subject of predestination, we must beware of keeping from the faithful, lest we seem either maliciously to deprive them of the blessing of God, or to accuse and scoff at the Spirit, as having divulged what ought on any account to be suppressed.

Let us, I say, allow the Christian to unlock his mind and ears to all the words of God which are addressed to him, provided he do it with this moderation—viz. that whenever the Lord shuts His sacred mouth, He also desists from inquiry. The best rule of sobriety is, found in not only learning to follow wherever God leads, but also when He makes an end of teaching, to cease also from wishing to be wise. The danger, which they dread, is not so great that we ought because of it to turn away our minds from the oracles of God. There is a celebrated saying of Solomon, "It is the glory of God to conceal a thing" (Proverbs 25:2). However, since both piety and common sense dictate that this is not to be understood of everything, we must look for a distinction, lest under the pretense of modesty and sobriety, we be satisfied with a brutish ignorance.

This is clearly expressed by Moses in a few words, "The secret things belong unto the Lord our God: but those things which are revealed belong unto us, and to our children forever" (Deuteronomy 29:29). We see how he exhorts the people to study the doctrine of the Law in accordance with a heavenly decree, because God has been pleased to promulgate it, while He at the same time confines them within these boundaries, for the simple reason that it is not lawful for men to pry into the secret things of God.

4 A second objection—viz. That this doctrine is a stumbling block to the profane. Answer: A. The same may be said of many other heads of doctrine. B. The truth of God will always defend itself. Third objection—viz. That this doctrine is dangerous even to believers. Answer. A. The same objection made to Augustine. B. We must not despise anything that God has revealed. Arrogance and blasphemy of such objections.

I admit that profane men lay hold of the subject of predestination to carp or cavil or snarl or scoff. But if their petulance frightens us, it will be necessary to conceal all the principal articles of faith, because they and their fellows leave scarcely one of them unassailed with blasphemy. A rebellious spirit will display itself no less insolently when it hears that there are three persons in the divine essence, than when it hears that God, when He created man, foresaw everything that was to happen to him. Nor will they abstain from their jeers when told that little more than five thousand years have elapsed since the creation of the world. For they will ask, "Why did the power of God slumber so long in idleness?" In short, nothing can be stated that they will not assail with derision. To quell their blasphemies, must we say nothing concerning the divinity of the Son and Spirit? Must the creation of the world be passed over in silence? No! The truth of God is too powerful, both here and everywhere, to dread the slanders of the ungodly, as Augustine powerfully maintains in his treatise, *De Bono Perseverantiae* (chapters 14-20). For we see that the false apostles were unable, by defaming and accusing the true doctrine of Paul, to make him ashamed of it. There is nothing in the allegation that the whole subject is fraught with danger to pious minds, as tending to destroy exhortation, shake faith, disturb and dispirit the heart. Augustine disguises not that on these grounds he was often charged with preaching the doctrine of predestination too freely, but, as it was easy for him to do, he abundantly refutes the charge. As a great variety of absurd objections is here stated, we have thought it best to dispose of each of them in its proper place. (See Chapter 23.)

Only I wish it to be received as a general rule that the secret things of God are not to be scrutinized, and that those which He has revealed are not to be overlooked, lest we may, on the one hand, be chargeable with curiosity, and, on the other, with ingratitude. For it has been shrewdly observed by Augustine, that we can safely follow Scripture, which walks softly, as with a mother's step, in accommodation to our weakness. Those, however, who are so cautious and timid that they would bury all mention of predestination in order that it may not trouble weak minds, with what color, pray, will they cloak their arrogance, when they indirectly charge God with a want of due consideration, in not having foreseen a danger for which they imagine that they prudently provide? Whoever, therefore, throws obloquy on the doctrine of predestination openly brings a charge against God, as having inconsiderately allowed something to escape from Him, which is injurious to the Church.

5 Certain cavils against the doctrine. Prescience regarded as the cause of predestination. Prescience and predestination explained. Not prescience, but the good pleasure of God is the cause of predestination. This is apparent from the gratuitous election of the posterity of Abraham and the rejection of all others.

The predestination by which God adopts some to the hope of life and adjudges others to eternal death, no man who would be thought pious ventures simply to deny; but it is greatly caviled at, especially by those who make prescience its cause. We, indeed, ascribe both prescience and predestination to God, but we say that it is absurd to make the latter subordinate to the former. (See Chapter 22, section 1.) When we attribute prescience to God, we mean that all things always were and ever continue under His eye; that to His knowledge there is no past or future, but all things are, indeed, so present that it is not merely the idea of them that is before Him (as those objects are which we retain in our memory), but that He truly sees and contemplates them as actually under His immediate inspection. This prescience extends to the whole circuit of the world and to all creatures.

By predestination we mean the eternal decree of God, by which He determined with himself whatever He wished to happen with regard to every man. Not all are created on equal terms, but some are preordained to eternal life, others to eternal damnation; and, accordingly, as each has been created for one or other of these ends, we say that he has been predestinated to life or to death. This God has testified, not only in the case of single individuals. He has also given a specimen of it in the whole posterity of Abraham, to make it plain that the future condition of each nation lives entirely at His disposal: "When the Most High divided to the nations their inheritance, when he separated the sons of Adam, he set the bounds of the people according to the number of the children of Israel. For the Lord's portion is his people; Jacob is the lot of his inheritance" (Deuteronomy 32:8, 9).

The separation is before the eyes of all, in the person of Abraham, as in a withered stock, one people is specially chosen, while the others are rejected; but the cause does not appear, except that Moses, to deprive posterity of any handle for glorying, tells them that their superiority was owing entirely to the free love of God. The cause which He assigns for their deliverance is: "Because he loved thy fathers, therefore he chose their seed after them" (Deuteronomy 4:37). Or more explicitly in another chapter: "The Lord did not set his love upon you, nor choose you, because you were more in number than any people: for ye were the fewest of all people: but because the Lord loved you." (See Deuteronomy 7:7, 8.)

He repeatedly makes the same intimations, "Behold, the heaven, and the heaven of heavens is the Lord's thy God, the earth also, with all that therein is. Only the Lord had a delight in thy fathers to love them, and he chose their seed after them" (Deuteronomy 10:14, 15). Again, in another passage, holiness is enjoined upon them, because they have been chosen to be a peculiar people; while in another, love is declared the cause of their protection (Deuteronomy 23:5). This, too, believers with one voice proclaim, "He shall choose our inheritance for us, the excellency of Jacob, whom he loved" (Psalm 47:4). The endowments with which God had adorned them, they all ascribe to gratuitous love, not only because they knew that they had not obtained them by any merit, but that not even was the holy patriarch endued with a virtue that could procure such distinguished honor for himself and his posterity. And the more completely to crush all pride, He upbraids them with having merited nothing of the kind, seeing they were a rebellious and stiff-necked people. (See Deuteronomy 9:6.)

Often, also, do the prophets remind the Jews of this election by way of disparagement and opprobrium, because they had shamefully revolted from it. Be this as it may, let those who would ascribe the election of God to human worth or merit come forward. When they see that one nation is preferred to all others, when they hear that it was no feeling of respect that induced God to show more favor to a small and ignoble body, nay, even to the wicked and rebellious, will they plead against Him for having chosen to give such a manifestation of mercy? But neither will their obstreperous words hinder His work; nor will their invectives, like stones thrown against Heaven, strike or hurt His righteousness; nay, rather they will fall back on their own heads. To this principle of a free covenant, moreover, the Israelites are recalled whenever thanks are to be returned to God, or their hopes of the future are to be animated. "The Lord he is God," says the Psalmist; "it is he that has made us, and not we ourselves: we are his people, and the sheep of his pasture" (Psalm 100:3; 95:7). The negation which is added, "not we ourselves," is not superfluous, to teach us that God is not only the Author of all the good qualities in which men excel, but that they originate in himself, there being nothing in them worthy of so much honor.

In the following words, also, they are enjoined to rest satisfied with the mere good pleasure of God: "O ye seed of Abraham, his servant; ye children of Jacob, his chosen" (Psalm 105:6). And after an enumeration of the continual mercies of God as fruits of election, the conclusion is, that He acted thus kindly because He remembered His covenant. With this doctrine accords the song of the whole Church, "They got not the land in possession by their own sword, neither did their own arm save them; but thy right hand, and thine arm, and the light of thy countenance, because thou hadst a favor unto them" (Psalm 44:3).

It is to be observed that when the land is mentioned, it is a visible symbol of the secret election in which adoption is comprehended. To like gratitude David elsewhere exhorts the people, "Blessed is the nation whose God is the Lord, and the people whom he has chosen for his own inheritance" (Psalm 33:12). Samuel thus animates their hopes, "The Lord will not forsake his people for his great name's sake: because it has pleased the Lord to make you his people" (1 Samuel 12:22). And when David's faith is assailed, how does he arm himself for the battle? "Blessed is the man whom thou choosest, and causes to approach unto thee, that he may dwell in thy courts" (Psalm 65:4). But as the hidden election of God was confirmed both by a first and second election, and by other intermediate mercies, Isaiah thus applies the terms, "The Lord will have mercy on Jacob, and will yet choose Israel" (Isaiah 14:1). Referring to a future period, the gathering together of the Dispersion, which seemed to have been abandoned, He says that it will be a sign of a firm and stable election, notwithstanding of the apparent abandonment.

When it is elsewhere said, "I have chosen thee, and not cast thee away" (Isaiah 41:9), the continual course of His great liberality is ascribed to paternal kindness. This is stated more explicitly in Zechariah by the angel, the Lord "...shall choose Jerusalem again," as if the severity of His chastisements had amounted to reprobation, or the captivity had been an interruption of election, which, however, remains inviolable, though the signs of it do not always appear.

6 Even of the posterity of Abraham some are elected and others are rejected by special grace.

We must add a second step of a more limited nature, or one in which the grace of God was displayed in a more special form, when of the same family of Abraham, God rejected some, and by keeping others within His Church, showed that He retained them among His sons. At first Ishmael had obtained the same rank with his brother Isaac, because the spiritual covenant was equally sealed in him by the symbol of circumcision. He is first cut off, then Esau, at last an innumerable multitude, almost the whole of Israel. In Isaac was the seed called. The same calling held good in the case of Jacob. God gave a similar example in the rejection of Saul. This is also celebrated in the Psalm, "Moreover he refused the tabernacle of Joseph, and chose not the tribe of Ephraim: but chose the tribe of Judah" (Psalm 78:67, 68). This, the sacred history sometimes repeats: that the secret grace of God may be more admirably displayed in that change.

I admit that it was by their own fault that Ishmael, Esau, and others fell from their adoption; for the condition annexed was, that they should faithfully keep the covenant of God, whereas they perfidiously violated it. The singular kindness of God consisted in this, that He had been pleased to prefer them to other nations; as it is said in the Psalm, "He has not dealt so with any nation: and as for his judgments, they have not known them" (Psalm 147:20).

But I had good reason for saying that two steps are here to be observed. In the election of the whole nation, God had already shown that in the exercise of His mere liberality, He was under no law but was free, so that he was by no means to be restricted to an equal division of grace, its very inequality proving it gratuitous. Accordingly, Malachi enlarges on the ingratitude of Israel, in that being not only selected from the whole human race, but set peculiarly apart from a sacred household; they perfidiously and impiously spurn God their beneficent parent. "Was not Esau Jacob's brother? Saith the Lord: yet I loved Jacob, and I hated Esau" (Malachi 1:2, 3). God takes it for granted that as both were the sons of a holy father, and successors of the covenant—in short, branches from a sacred root, the sons of Jacob were under no ordinary obligation for having been admitted to that dignity. But when by the rejection of Esau the firstborn, their progenitor, though inferior in birth, was made heir, He charges them with double ingratitude, in not being restrained by a double tie.

7 The apostle shows that the same thing has been done in regard to individuals under the Christian dispensation.

Although it is now sufficiently plain that God by His secret counsel chooses whom He will, while He rejects others, His gratuitous election has only been partially explained until we come to the case of single individuals to whom God not only offers salvation, but so assigns it, that the certainty of the result remains not dubious or suspended. These are considered as belonging to that one seed of which Paul makes mention. (See Romans 9:8; Galatians 3:16, etc.) For, although adoption was deposited in the hand of Abraham, yet as many of his posterity were cut off as rotten members, in order that election may stand and be effectual, it is necessary to ascend to the head in whom the heavenly Father has connected His elect with each other and bound them to himself by an indissoluble tie. Thus, in the adoption of the family of Abraham, God gave them a liberal display of favor which He has denied to others; but in the members of Christ there is a far more excellent display of grace, because those engrafted into Him as their Head never fail to obtain salvation.

Hence, Paul skillfully argues from the passage of Malachi which I quoted (see Romans 9:13; Malachi 1:2), that when God, after making a covenant of eternal life, invites any people to himself, a special mode of election is in part understood, so that He does not, with promiscuous grace, effectually elect all of them. The words, "Jacob have I loved," refer to the whole progeny of the patriarch, which the prophet there opposes to the posterity of Esau. But there is nothing in this repugnant to the fact, that in the person of one man is set before us a specimen of election, which cannot fail in accomplishing its object.

It is not without cause that Paul observes, that these are called *a remnant* (Romans 9:27; 11:5); because experience shows that of the general body many fall away and are lost, so that often only a small portion remains. The reason that the general election of the people is not always firmly ratified, readily presents itself—viz. that on those with whom God makes the covenant, He does not immediately bestow the Spirit of regeneration, by whose power they persevere in the covenant even to the end. The external invitation, without the internal efficacy of grace, which would have the effect of retaining them, holds a kind of middle place between the rejection of the human race and the election of a small number of believers.

The whole people of Israel are called the Lord's inheritance, and yet there were many foreigners among them. Still, because the covenant which God had made to be their Father and Redeemer was not altogether null, he has respect to that free favor rather than to the perfidious defection of many; even by them His truth was not abolished, since by preserving some residue to himself, it appeared that His calling was without repentance. When God always gathered His Church from among the sons of Abraham rather than from profane nations, He had respect to his covenant, which, when violated by the great body, he restricted to a few, that it might not entirely fail. In short, that common adoption of the seed of Abraham was a kind of visible image of a greater benefit, which God deigned to bestow on some out of many. This is the reason why Paul so carefully distinguishes between the sons of Abraham according to the flesh and the spiritual sons who are called after the example of Isaac. Not that simply to be a son of Abraham was a vain or useless privilege (this could not be said without insult to the covenant), but that the immutable counsel of God, by which He predestinated to himself whomsoever He would, was alone effectual for their salvation. But until the proper view is made clear by the production of passages of Scripture, I advise my readers not to prejudge the question. We say, then, that Scripture clearly proves this much, that God by His eternal and immutable counsel, determined once for all those whom it was His pleasure one day to admit to salvation, and those whom, on the other hand, it was His pleasure to doom to destruction. We maintain that this counsel, as regards the elect, is founded on His free mercy, without any respect to human worth, while those whom He dooms to destruction are excluded from access to life by a just and blameless, but at the same time incomprehensible judgment.

Concerning the elect, we regard calling as the evidence of election, and justification as another symbol of its manifestation, until it is fully accomplished by the attainment of glory. But as the Lord seals His elect by calling and justification, so by excluding the reprobate either from the knowledge of His name or the sanctification of His Spirit, He by these marks, discloses the judgment, which awaits them. I will here omit many of the fictions, which foolish men have devised to overthrow predestination. There is no need of refuting objections which the moment they are produced abundantly betray their hollowness. I will dwell only on those points which either form the subject of dispute among the learned, or may occasion any difficulty to the simple, or may be employed by impiety as specious pretexts for assailing the justice of God.

Chapter 22

THIS DOCTRINE CONFIRMED BY PROOFS FROM SCRIPTURE

The divisions of this chapter are: I. A confirmation of the orthodox doctrine in opposition to two classes of individuals. This confirmation founded on a careful exposition of our Savior's words and passages in the writings of Paul, sections 1-7. II. A refutation of some objections taken from ancient writers, such as Thomas Aquinas, and more modern writers, sections 8-10. III. Of reprobation, which is founded entirely on the righteous will of God, section 11.

Sections

1. Some imagine that God elects or reprobates according to a foreknowledge of merit. Others make it a charge against God that He elects some and passes by others. Both refuted, A. By invincible arguments; B. By the testimony of Augustine.

2. Who are elected, when, in whom, to what, and for what reason.

3. The reason is the good pleasure of God, which so reigns in election that no works, either past or future, are taken into consideration. This proved by notable declarations of the Savior and passages of Paul.

4. Proved by a striking discussion in the Epistle to the Romans. Its scope and method explained. The advocates of foreknowledge refuted by the apostle, when he maintains that election is special and wholly of grace.

5. Evasion refuted. A summary and analysis of the apostle's discussion.

6. An exception, with three answers to it. The efficacy of gratuitous election extends only to believers, who are said to be elected according to foreknowledge. This foreknowledge or prescience is not speculative but active.

7. This proved from the words of Christ. Conclusion of the answer, and solution of the objection with regard to Judas.

8. An objection taken from the ancient fathers. Answer from Augustine, from Ambrose, as quoted by Augustine, and an invincible argument by an apostle. Summary of this argument.

9. Objection from Thomas Aquinas. Answer.

10. Objection of more modern writers. Answers. Passages in which there is a semblance of contradiction reconciled. Why many are called and few chosen. An objection founded on mutual consent between the word and faith. Solution confirmed by the Words of Paul, Augustine, and Bernard. A clear declaration by our Savior.

11. The view to be taken of reprobation. It is founded on the righteous will of God.

1 Some imagine that God elects or reprobates according to a foreknowledge of merit. Others make it a charge against God that He elects some and passes by others. Both refuted, A. By invincible arguments; B. By the testimony of Augustine.

Many controvert all the positions, which we have laid down, especially the gratuitous election of believers, which, however, cannot be overthrown. For they commonly imagine that God distinguishes between men according to the merits which He foresees that each individual is to have, giving the adoption of sons to those whom He foreknows will not be unworthy of His grace, and dooming those to destruction whose dispositions He perceives will be prone to mischief and wickedness. Thus, by interposing foreknowledge as a veil, they not only obscure election but also pretend to give it a different origin. Nor is this the commonly received opinion of the vulgar merely, for it has had great supporters in all ages. (See section 8.) This I candidly confess, lest anyone should expect greatly to prejudice our cause by opposing it with their names.

The truth of God is here too certain to be shaken, too clear to be overborne by human authority. Others who are neither versed in Scripture, nor entitled to any weight, assail sound doctrine with a petulance and improbity, which it is impossible to tolerate. Because

God of His mere good pleasure, while electing some, passes by others, and they raise a plea against Him. But if the fact is certain, what can they gain by quarreling with God? We teach nothing but what experience proves to be true—viz. that God has always been at liberty to bestow His grace on whom He would. Not to ask in what respect the posterity of Abraham excelled others if it were not in a worth, the cause of which has no existence out of God, let them tell why men are better than oxen or asses. God might have made them dogs when He formed them in His own image. Will they allow the lower animals to expostulate with God, as if the inferiority of their condition were unjust? It is certainly not more equitable that men should enjoy the privilege which they have not acquired by any merit, than that He should variously distribute favors as seems to Him meet. If they pass to the case of individuals where inequality is more offensive to them, they ought at least, concerning the example of our Savior, to be restrained by feelings of awe from talking so confidently of this sublime mystery. He is conceived as a mortal man of the seed of David; what, I would ask them, are the virtues by which He deserved to become in the very womb, the Head of angels, the only begotten Son of God, the image and glory of the Father, the light, righteousness, and salvation of the world?

It is wisely observed by Augustine that in the very Head of the Church we have a bright mirror of free election, lest it should give any trouble to us, the members—viz. that He did not become the Son of God by living righteously, but was freely presented with this great honor, that He might afterwards make others partakers of His gifts. Should anyone here ask why others are not what He was, or why we are all at so great a distance from Him, why we are all corrupt while He is purity, he would not only betray his madness, but his effrontery also. But if they are bent on depriving God of the free right of electing and reprobating, let them at the same time take away what has been given to Christ.

It will now be proper to attend to what Scripture declares concerning each. When Paul declares that we were chosen in Christ before the foundation of the world (see Ephesians 1:4), he certainly shows that no regard is had to our own worth. It is just as if he had said, "Since in the whole seed of Adam our heavenly Father found nothing worthy of his election, He turned His eye upon his own Anointed, that He might select as members of His body those whom He was to assume into the fellowship of life." Let believers, then, give full effect to this reason—viz. that we were adopted in Christ unto the heavenly inheritance, because in ourselves we were incapable of such excellence. This he elsewhere observes in another passage, in which he exhorts the Colossians to give thanks that they had been made meet to be partakers of the inheritance of the saints. (See Colossians 1:12.) If election precedes that divine grace by which we are made fit to obtain immortal life, what can God find in us to induce Him to elect us? My meaning is more clearly explained in another passage: God, says he, "...has chosen us in him before the foundation of the world, that we might be holy and without blame before him in love: having predestinated us unto the adoption of children by Jesus Christ to himself, according to the good pleasure of his will" (Ephesians 1:4, 5). Here he opposes the good pleasure of God to our merits of every description.

Holiness of life springs from election and is the object of it.

2 Who are elected, when, in whom, to what, for what reason.

That the proof may be more complete, it is of importance to attend to the separate clauses of that passage. When they are connected together, they leave no doubt. From giving them the name of elect, it is clear that he is addressing believers, as indeed he shortly after declares. It is, therefore, a complete perversion of the name to confine it to the age in which the gospel was published. By saying they were elected before the foundation of the world, he takes away all reference to worth. For what ground of distinction was there between persons who as yet existed not, and persons who were afterwards like them to exist in Adam? But if they were elected in Christ, it follows not only that each was elected on some extrinsic ground, but that some were placed on a different footing from others, since we see that not all are members of Christ. In the additional statement, that they were elected that they might be holy, the apostle openly refutes the error of those who deduce election from prescience, since he declares that whatever virtue appears in men is the result of election. Then, if a higher cause is asked, Paul answers that God so predestined and predestined according to the good pleasure of His will. By these words, he overturns all the grounds of election, which men imagine to exist in themselves. For he shows that whatever favors God bestows in reference to the spiritual life flow from this one fountain, because God chose whom He would, and before they were born, had the grace which he designed to bestow upon them set apart for their use.

3 The reason is the good pleasure of God, which so reigns in election that no works, either past or future, are taken into consideration. This is proved by notable declarations of one Savior and passages of Paul.

Wherever this good pleasure of God reigns, no good works are taken into account. The apostle, indeed, does not follow out the antithesis, but it is to be understood, as he himself explains it in another passage, "Who has called us with a holy calling, not according to our works, but according to his own purpose and grace, which was given us in Christ Jesus before the world began" (1 Timothy 2:9). We have already shown that the additional words, "That we might be holy," remove every doubt. If you say that He foresaw that they would be holy, and therefore elected them, you invert the order of Paul. You may, therefore, safely infer that if He elected us that we might be holy, He did not elect us because He foresaw that we would be holy. The two things are evidently inconsistent—viz. that the pious owe it to election that they are holy and yet attain to election by means of works. There is no force in the cavil to which they are ever recurring, that the Lord does not bestow election in recompense of preceding, but bestows it in consideration of future merits. For when it is said that believers were elected that they might be holy, it is at the same time intimated that the holiness, which was to be in them, has its origin in election.

Moreover, how can it be consistently said that things derived from election are the cause of election? The very thing which the apostle had said, he seems afterwards to confirm by adding, "According to his good pleasure which he has purposed in himself" (Ephesians 1:9). The expression that God "purposed in himself" is the same as if it had been said that in forming His decree, He considered nothing external to himself. Accordingly, it is immediately subjoined that the whole object contemplated in our election is, "We should be to the praise of His glory." Assuredly divine grace would not deserve all the praise of election, were not election gratuitous; and it would not be gratuitous did God in electing any individual pay regard to his future works. Hence, what Christ said to His disciples is found to be universally applicable to all believers, "Ye have not chosen me, but I have chosen you" (John 15:16). Here He not only excludes past merits, but declares that they had nothing in themselves for which they could be chosen except insofar as His mercy anticipated. And how are we to understand the words of Paul, "Who has first given to him, and it shall be recompensed unto him again?" (Romans 11:35). His meaning obviously is that men are altogether indebted to the goodness of God, there being nothing in them, either past or future, to conciliate His favor.

4 Proved by a striking discussion in the Epistle to the Romans. Its scope and method explained. The advocates of foreknowledge refuted by the apostle, when he maintains that election is special and wholly of grace.

In the Epistle to the Romans (Romans 9:6), in which he again treats this subject at greater length, he declares, "They are not all Israel which are of Israel;" for, though all were blessed in respect of hereditary rights, yet all did not equally obtain the succession. The whole discussion was occasioned by the pride and vain-glorying of the Jews, who, by claiming the name of the Church for themselves, would have made the faith of the gospel dependent on their pleasure; just as in the present day the papists would fain under this pretext substitute themselves in place of God. Paul, while he concedes that in respect of the covenant, they were the holy offspring of Abraham, yet contends that the greater part of them were strangers to it, not only because they were degenerate and so had become bastards instead of sons, but because the principal point to be considered was the special election of God, by which alone His adoption was ratified. If the piety of some established them in the hope of salvation, and the revolt of others was the sole cause of their being rejected, it would have been foolish and absurd in Paul to carry his readers back to a secret election. But if the will of God (no cause of which external to him either appears or is to be looked for) distinguishes some from others, so that all the sons of Israel are not true Israelites, it is vain for anyone to seek the origin of his condition in himself. He afterwards prosecutes the subject at greater length by contrasting the cases of Jacob and Esau. Both being sons of Abraham, both having been at the same time in the womb of their mother, there was something very strange in the change by which the honor of the birthright was transferred to Jacob, and yet Paul declares that the change was an attestation to the election of the one and the reprobation of the other.

The question considered is the origin and cause of election. The advocates of foreknowledge insist that it is to be found in the virtues and vices of men. For they take the short and easy method of asserting that God showed in the person of Jacob that He elects those who are worthy of His grace; and in the person of Esau, that He rejects those whom He foresees to be unworthy. Such is their confident assertion, but what does Paul say? "For the children being not yet born, neither having done any good or evil, that the purpose of God according to election might stand, not of works, but of him that calleth; it was said unto her [Rebecca] the elder shall serve the younger. As it is written, Jacob have I loved, but Esau have I hated" (Romans 9:11-13).

If foreknowledge had anything to do with this distinction of the brothers, the mention of time would have been out of place. Granting that Jacob was elected for a worth to be obtained by future virtues, to what end did Paul say that he was not yet born? Nor would there have been any occasion for adding that yet he had done no good, because the answer was always ready, that nothing is hid from God, and that therefore the piety of Jacob was present before Him.

If works procure favor, a value ought to have been put upon them before Jacob was born, just as if he had been of full age. But in explaining the difficulty, the apostle goes on to show that the adoption of Jacob proceeded not on works but on the calling of God. In works he makes no mention of past or future, but distinctly opposes them to the calling of God, intimating that when place is given to the one the other is overthrown; it is as if he had said, "The only thing to be considered is what pleased God, not what men furnished of themselves." Lastly, it is certain that all the causes which men are wont to devise as external to the secret counsel of God are excluded by the use of the terms *purpose* and *election*.

5 Evasion refuted. A summary and analysis of the apostle's discussion.

Why should men attempt to darken these statements by assigning some place in election to past or future works? This is altogether to evade what the apostle contends for—viz. that the distinction between the brothers is not founded on any ground of works, but on the mere calling of God, inasmuch as it was fixed before the children were born. Had there been any solidity in this subtlety, it would not have escaped the notice of the apostle, but, being perfectly aware that God foresaw no good in man, save that which He had already previously determined to bestow by means of his election, he does not employ a preposterous arrangement which would make good works antecedent to their cause.

We learn from the apostle's words that the salvation of believers is founded entirely on the decree of divine election, that the privilege is procured not by works but free calling. We have also a specimen of the thing itself set before us. Esau and Jacob are brothers, begotten of the same parents, within the same womb, not yet born. In them, all things are equal, and yet the judgment of God with regard to them is different. He adopts the one and rejects the other. The only right of precedence was that of primogeniture; but that is disregarded, and the younger is preferred to the elder. Nay, in the case of others, God seems to have disregarded primogeniture for the express purpose of excluding the flesh from all ground of boasting. Rejecting Ishmael, He gives His favor to Isaac; postponing Manasseh, He honors Ephraim.

6 An exception, with three answers to it. The efficacy of gratuitous election extends only to believers, who are said to be elected according to foreknowledge. This foreknowledge or prescience is not speculative but active.

Should anyone object that these minute and inferior favors do not enable us to decide with regard to the future life, that it is not to be supposed that he who received the honor of primogeniture was thereby adopted to the inheritance of Heaven; (many objectors do not even spare Paul, but accuse him of having in the quotation of these passages wrested Scripture from its proper meaning); I answer as before, that the apostle has not erred through inconsideration or spontaneously misapplied the passages of Scripture; but he saw (what these men cannot be brought to consider) that God purposed under an earthly sign to declare the spiritual election of Jacob, which otherwise lay hidden at His inaccessible tribunal. For, unless we refer the primogeniture bestowed upon him to the future world, the form of blessing would be altogether vain and ridiculous, inasmuch as he gained nothing by it but a multitude of toils and annoyances, exile, sharp sorrows, and bitter cares. Therefore, when Paul knew beyond a doubt that by the external, God manifested the spiritual and unfading blessings, which He had prepared for His servant in his kingdom, he hesitated not in proving the latter to draw an argument from the former. For we must remember that the land of Canaan was given in pledge of the heavenly inheritance, and that, therefore, there cannot be a doubt that Jacob was like the angels engrafted into the Body of Christ, that he might be a partaker of the same life. Jacob, therefore, is chosen, while Esau is rejected; the predestination of God makes a distinction where none existed in respect of merit. If you ask the reason, the apostle gives it, "For he saith to Moses, I will have mercy on whom I will have mercy, and I will have compassion on whom I will have compassion" (Romans 9:15). And what, pray, does this mean? It is just a clear declaration by the Lord that he finds nothing in men themselves to induce Him to show kindness, that it is owing entirely to His own mercy, and, accordingly, that their salvation is His own work. Since God places your salvation in himself alone, why should you descend to yourself? Since He assigns you His own mercy alone, why will you recur to your own merits? Since He confines your thoughts to His own mercy, why do you turn partly to the view of your own works?

We must, therefore, come to that smaller number whom Paul elsewhere describes as foreknown of God (see Romans 11:2); not foreknown, as these men imagine, by idle, inactive contemplations, but in the sense which it often bears. For surely when Peter says that Christ was "...delivered by the determinate counsel and foreknowledge of God" (Acts 2:23), he does not represent God as contemplating merely, but as actually accomplishing our salvation. Thus also Peter, in saying that the believers to whom he writes are elect "...according to the foreknowledge of God" (1 Peter 1:2), properly expresses that secret predestination by which God has sealed those whom He has been pleased to adopt as sons. In using the term *purpose* as synonymous with a term, which uniformly denotes what is called a fixed determination, he undoubtedly shows that God, in being the Author of our salvation, does not go beyond himself. In this sense, he says in the same chapters that Christ, as "a lamb," "was foreordained before the creation of the world" (1 Peter 1:19, 20).

What could have been more frigid or absurd than to have represented God as looking from the height of Heaven to see whence the salvation of the human race was to come? By a people foreknown, Peter means the same thing as Paul does by a remnant selected from a multitude falsely assuming the name of God. In another passage, to suppress the vain boasting of those who, while only covered with a mask, claim for themselves in the view of the world a first place among the godly, Paul says, "The Lord knoweth them that are his" (2 Timothy 2:19). In short, by that term he designates two classes of people, the one consisting of the whole race of Abraham, the other a people separated from that race, and though hidden from human view, yet open to the eye of God. No doubt, he took the passage from Moses, who declares that God would be merciful to whomsoever He pleased (although he was speaking of an elect people whose condition was apparently equal); just as if he had said that in a common adoption was included a special grace, which He bestows on some as a holier treasure, and that there is nothing in the common covenant to prevent this number from being exempted from the common order. God, being pleased in this matter to act as a free dispenser and disposer, distinctly declares that the only ground on which He will show mercy to one rather than to another is His sovereign pleasure.

When mercy is bestowed on him who asks it, though he indeed does not suffer a refusal, he, however, either anticipates or partly acquires a favor, the whole merit of which God claims for himself.

7 This is proved from the words of Christ. Conclusion of the answer and solution of the objection with regard to Judas.

Now, let the supreme Judge and Master decide on the whole case. Seeing such obduracy in His hearers that His words fell upon the multitude almost without fruit, He, to remove this obstacle, exclaims, "All that the Father giveth me shall come to me." "And this is the Father's will which has sent me, that of all which he has given me I should lose nothing" (John 6:37; 39). Observe that the donation of the Father is the first step in our delivery into the charge and protection of Christ. Someone, perhaps, will here turn round and object, that those only peculiarly belong to the Father who make a voluntary surrender by faith. But the only thing which Christ maintains is that, though the defections of vast multitudes should shake the world, yet the counsel of God would stand firm, more stable than Heaven itself, and that His election would never fail.

The elect are said to have belonged to the Father before He bestowed them on His only begotten Son. It is asked if they were his by nature. Nay, they were aliens, but He makes them His by delivering them. The words of Christ are too clear to be rendered obscure by any of the mists of caviling. "No man can come to me except the Father which has sent me draw him." "Every man, therefore, that has heard and learned of the Father comes unto me" (John 6:44, 45). Did all promiscuously bend the knee to Christ, election would be common, whereas now in the small number of believers a manifest diversity appears. Accordingly, our Savior, shortly after declaring that the disciples who were given to Him were the common property of the Father, adds, "I pray not for the world, but for them which thou hast given me; for they are thine" (John 17:9).

Hence, it is that the whole world no longer belongs to its Creator, except insofar as grace rescues from malediction, divine wrath, and eternal death, some, not many, who would otherwise perish, while he leaves the world to the destruction to which it is doomed. Meanwhile, though Christ interposes as a Mediator, yet He claims the right of electing in common with the Father, "I speak not of you all: I know whom I have chosen" (John 13:18). If it is asked whence He has chosen them, He answers in another passage "Out of the world;" which He excludes from His prayers when He commits His disciples to the Father (John 15:19). We must, indeed, hold, when He affirms that He knows whom he has chosen, first, that some individuals of the human race are denoted; and, secondly, that they are not distinguished by the quality of their virtues, but by a heavenly decree.

Hence, it follows that since Christ makes himself the Author of election, none excel by their own strength or industry. In elsewhere numbering Judas among the elect, though he was a devil (see John 6:70), he refers only to the apostolical office, which, though a bright manifestation of divine favor (as Paul so often acknowledges it to be in his own person), does not, however, contain within itself the hope of eternal salvation. Judas, therefore, when he discharged the office of apostle perfidiously, might have been worse than a devil; but not one of those whom Christ has once engrafted into His body will He ever permit to perish, for in securing their salvation, He will perform what he has promised; that is, exert a divine power greater than all. (See John 10:28.) For when He says, "Those that thou gavest me I have kept, and none of them is lost but the son of perdition" (John 17:12), the expression, though there is a catachresis in it, is not at all ambiguous. The sum is that God by gratuitous adoption forms those whom He wishes to have for sons, but that the intrinsic cause is in himself, because he is contented with His secret pleasure.

8 An objection taken from the ancient fathers. Answer from Augustine, from Ambrose, as quoted by Augustine, and an invincible argument by an apostle. Summary of this argument.

But Ambrose, Origen, and Jerome were of the opinion that God dispenses His grace among men according to the use which He foresees that each will make of it. It may be added that Augustine also was for some time of this opinion; but after he had made greater progress in the knowledge of Scripture, he not only retracted it as evidently false, but also powerfully confuted it. Nay, even after the retraction, glancing at the Pelagians who persisted in that error, he says, "Who does not wonder that the apostle failed to make this most acute observation? For after stating a most startling proposition concerning those who were not yet born, and afterwards putting the question to himself by way of objection, "What then? Is there unrighteousness with God?" he had an opportunity of answering that God foresaw the merits of both, he does not say so, but has recourse to the justice and mercy of God." And in another passage, after excluding all merit before election, he says, "Here, certainly, there is no place for the vain argument of those who defend the foreknowledge of God against the grace of God, and accordingly maintain that we were elected before the foundation of the world, because God foreknow that we would be good, not that He himself would make us good. This is not the language of one who says, "Ye have not chosen me, but I have chosen you" (John 15:16). For had He chosen us because He foreknow that we would be good, He would at the same time also have foreknown that we were to choose Him.

Let the testimony of Augustine prevail with those who willingly acquiesce in the authority of the Fathers: although Augustine allows not that he differs from the others, but shows by clear evidence that the difference, which the Pelagians invidiously objected to him, is unfounded. For he quotes from Ambrose, "Christ calls whom he pities." Again, "Had He pleased, He could have made them devout instead of undevout; but God calls whom He deigns to call and makes religious whom he will."

Were we disposed to frame an entire volume out of Augustine, it would be easy to show the reader that I have no occasion to use any other words than his; but I am unwilling to burden him with a prolix statement. But assuming that the fathers did not speak thus, let us attend to the thing itself. A difficult question had been raised—viz. Did God do justly in bestowing His grace on certain individuals? Paul might have disencumbered himself of this question at once by saying, that God had respect to works. Why does he not do so? Why does he rather continue to use a language, which leaves him exposed to the same difficulty? Why, but just because it would not have been right to say it? There was no obliviousness on the part of the Holy Spirit, who was speaking by his mouth. He, therefore, answers without ambiguity, that God favors His elect, because He is pleased to do so and shows mercy because He is pleased to do so. For the words, "I will be gracious to whom I will be gracious, and show mercy on whom I will show mercy" (Exodus 33:19), are the same in effect as if it had been said, God is moved to mercy by no other reason than that He is pleased to show mercy. Augustine's declaration, therefore, remains true. The grace of God does not find but makes persons fit to be chosen.

9 Objection from Thomas Aquinas. Answer.

Nor let us be detained by the subtlety of Thomas, that the foreknowledge of merit is the cause of predestination, not, indeed, in respect of the predestinating act, but that on our part it may in some sense be so called: namely, in respect of a particular estimate of predestination, as when it is said that God predestinates man to glory according to his merit, inasmuch as He decreed to bestow upon him the grace by which he merits glory. For while the Lord would have us to see nothing more in election than His mere goodness, for anyone to desire to see more is preposterous affectation. But were we to make a trial of subtlety, it would not be difficult to refute the sophistry of Thomas. He maintains that the elect are in a manner predestinated to glory because of their merits, because God predestines to give them the grace by which they merit glory. What if I should, on the contrary, object that predestination to grace is subservient to election unto life and follows as its handmaid, that grace is predestined to those to whom the possession of glory was previously assigned, the Lord being pleased to bring His sons by election to justification? For it will hence follow that the predestination to glory is the cause of the predestination to grace, and not the converse. But let us have done with these disputes as superfluous among those who think that there is enough of wisdom for them in the Word of God. For it has been truly said by an old ecclesiastical writer, Ambrose, "Those who ascribe the election of God to merits are wise above what they ought to be."

10 Objection of more modern writers. Answers. Passages in which there is a semblance of contradiction reconciled. Why many are called and few are chosen. An objection founded on mutual consent between the Word and faith. The solution is confirmed by the words of Paul, Augustine, and Bernard. A clear declaration by our Savior.

Some object that God would be inconsistent with himself in inviting all without distinction while He elects only a few. Thus, according to them, the universality of the promise destroys the distinction of special grace. Some moderate men speak in this way, not so much for suppressing the truth, as to be done with puzzling questions and curb excessive curiosity. The intention is laudable, but the design is by no means to be approved, dissimulation being at no time excusable. Again, in those who display their petulance, we see only a vile cavil or a disgraceful error.

The mode in which Scripture reconciles the two things—viz. that by external preaching all are called to faith and repentance, and that yet the Spirit of faith and repentance is not given to all, I have already explained and will again shortly repeat. But the point that they assume, I deny as being false in two respects. He who threatens that when it shall rain on one city, there will be drought in another (see Amos 4:7); and declares in another passage that there will be a famine of the Word (see Amos 8:11), does not lay himself under a fixed obligation to call all equally. And He who, forbidding Paul to preach in Asia and leading him away from Bithynia, carries him over to Macedonia (see Acts 16:6), shows that it belongs to Him to distribute the treasure in any way He pleases. But it is by Isaiah that He more clearly demonstrates how He destines the promises of salvation, specially to the elect (see Isaiah 8:16); for He declares that His disciples would consist of them only, and not indiscriminately of the whole human race. Whence it is evident that the doctrine of salvation, which is said to be set apart for the sons of the Church only, is abused when it is represented as effectually available to all.

For the present, let it suffice to observe, that though the word of the gospel is addressed generally to all, yet the gift of faith is rare. Isaiah assigns the cause when he says that the arm of the Lord is not revealed to all. (See Isaiah 53:1.) Had he said that the gospel is malignantly and perversely condemned, because many obstinately refuse to hear, there might perhaps be some color for this universal call. It is not the purpose of the prophet, however, to extenuate the guilt of men, when he states the source of their blindness to be that God deigns not to reveal His arm to them; he only reminds us that since faith is a special gift, it is in vain that external doctrine sounds in the ear. But I would fain know from those doctors whether it is mere preaching or faith that makes men sons of God. Certainly, when it is said, "As many as received him, to them gave he power to become the sons of God, even to them that believe on his name" (John 1:12), a confused mass is not set before us, but a special order is assigned to believers, who are "born not of blood, nor of the will of the flesh, nor of the will of man, but of God."

But it is said that there is a mutual agreement between faith and the Word. That must be wherever there is faith. But it is no new thing for the seed to fall among thorns or in stony places, not only because the majority appear in fact to be rebellious against God, but because all are not gifted with eyes and ears. How, then, can it consistently be said that God calls while He knows that the called will not come? Let Augustine answer for me: "Would you dispute with me? Wonder with me, and exclaim, O the depth! Let us both agree in dread, lest we perish in error." Moreover, if election is, as Paul declares, the parent of faith, I retort the argument and maintain that faith is not general, since election is special. For it is easily inferred from the series of causes and effects, when Paul says that the Father "...has blessed us with all spiritual blessings in heavenly places in Christ, according as he has chosen us in him before the foundation of the world" (Ephesians 1:3, 4), that these riches are not common to all, because God has chosen only whom He would. And the reason that in another passage he commends the faith of the elect is to prevent anyone from supposing that He acquires faith of his own nature; since to God alone belongs the glory of freely illuminating those whom he had previously chosen. (See Titus 1:1.)

For it is well said by Bernard, "His friend hear apart when he says to them, Fear not, little flock: to you it is given to know the mysteries of the Kingdom. Who are these? Those whom He foreknew and predestinated to be conformed to the image of his Son. He has made known his great and secret counsel. The Lord knoweth them that are his, but that which was known to God was manifested to men; nor, indeed, does He deign to give a participation in this great mystery to any but those whom He foreknew and predestinated to be his own." Shortly after he concludes, "The mercy of the Lord is from everlasting to everlasting upon them that fear Him; from everlasting through predestination, to everlasting through glorification: the one knows no beginning, the other no end."

But why cite Bernard as a witness, when we hear from the lips of our Master, "Not that any man has seen the Father, save he which is of God" (John 6:49)? By these words, he intimates that all who are not regenerated by God are amazed at the brightness of His countenance. And, indeed, faith is aptly conjoined with election, provided it holds the second place. This order is clearly expressed by our Savior in these words, "This is the Father's will which has sent me, that of all which he has given me I should lose nothing;" "And this is the will of him that sent me, that everyone which sees the Son, and believes on him, may have everlasting life" (John 6:39, 40). If He would have all to be saved, He would appoint His Son to be their guardian and would engraft them all into His body by the sacred bond of faith.

It is now clear that faith is a singular pledge of paternal love, treasured up for the sons whom He has adopted. Hence, Christ elsewhere says that the sheep follow the shepherd because they know his voice, but that they will not follow a stranger, because they know not the voice of strangers. (See John 10:4.) But whence that distinction, unless that their ears have been divinely bored? For no man makes himself a sheep, but is formed by heavenly grace.

And why does the Lord declare that our salvation will always be sure and certain, but just because it is guarded by the invincible power of God? (See John 10:29.) Accordingly, He concludes that unbelievers are not of his sheep (John 10:16). The reason is that they are not of the number of those who, as the Lord promised by Isaiah, were to be his disciples. Moreover, as the passages, which I have quoted, imply perseverance, they are also attestations to the inflexible constancy of election.

11 The view to be taken of reprobation. It is founded on the righteous will of God.

We come now to the reprobate, to whom the apostle at the same time refers. (See Romans 9:13.) For as Jacob, who yet had merited nothing by good works, is assumed into favor; so Esau, while yet unpolluted by any crime, is hated. If we turn our view to works, we do injustice to the apostle, as if he had failed to see the very thing that is clear to us. Moreover, there is complete proof of his not having seen it, since he expressly insists that when yet they had done neither good nor evil, the one was elected, the other rejected, in order to prove that the foundation of divine predestination is not in works. Then, after starting the objection, "Is God unjust?" Instead of employing what would have been the surest and plainest defense of his justice—viz. that God had recompensed Esau according to his wickedness, he is contented with a different solution—viz. that the reprobate are expressly raised up, in order that the glory of God may thereby be displayed. At last, he concludes that God has mercy on whom he will have mercy and whom He will, He hardeneth. (See Romans 9:18.) You see how he refers both to the mere pleasure of God. Therefore, if we cannot assign any reason for His bestowing mercy on His people, but just that it so pleases Him, neither can we have any reason for His reprobating others but His will. When God is said to visit in mercy or harden whom He will, men are reminded that they are not to seek for any cause beyond His will.

Chapter 23

REFUTATION OF THE CALUMNIES BY WHICH THIS DOCTRINE IS ALWAYS UNJUSTLY ASSAILED

This chapter consists of four parts, which refute the principal objections to this doctrine and the various pleas and exceptions founded on these objections. These are preceded by a refutation of those who hold election but deny reprobation, section 1. Then follows: I. A refutation of the first objection to the doctrine of reprobation and election, sections 2-5. II. An answer to the second objection, sections 6-9. III. A refutation of the third objection. IV. A refutation of the fourth objection, to which is added a useful and necessary caution, sections 12-14.

Sections

1. Error of those who deny reprobation. A. Election opposed to reprobation. B. Those who deny reprobation presumptuously plead with God, whose counsel even angels adore. C. They murmur against God when disclosing His counsels by the apostle. Exception and answer. Passage of Augustine.

2. First objection—viz. that God is unjustly offended with those whom He dooms to destruction without their own desert. First answer, from the consideration of the divine will. The nature of this will and how it is to be considered.

3. Second answer. God owes nothing to man. His hatred against those who are corrupted by sin is most just. The reprobates are convinced in their own consciences of the just judgment of God.

4. Exception—viz. that the reprobates seem to have been preordained to sin. Answer. Passage of the apostle vindicated from calumny.

5. Answer, confirmed by the authority of Augustine. Illustration. Passage of Augustine.

6. *Objection, that God ought not to impute the sins rendered necessary by His predestination. First answer by ancient writers. This is not valid. The second answer is also defective. The third answer, proposed by Valla, is well founded.*

7. *Objection, that God did not decree that Adam should perish by his fall, this is refuted by a variety of reasons. A noble passage of Augustine.*

8. *Objection, that the wicked perish by the permission, not by the will of God. Answer. A pious exhortation.*

9. *Objection and answer.*

10. *Objection that, according to the doctrine of predestination, God is a respecter of persons. Answer.*

11. *Objection that sinners are to be punished equally, or the justice of God is unequal. Answer. Confirmed by passages of Augustine.*

12. *Objection that the doctrine of predestination produces overweening confidence and impiety. Different answers.*

13. *Another objection, depending on the former. Answer. The doctrine of predestination is to be preached, not passed over in silence.*

14. *How it is to be preached and delivered to the people. Summary of the orthodox doctrine of predestination from Augustine.*

1 Error of those who deny reprobation. A. Election opposed to reprobation. B. Those who deny reprobation presumptuously plead with God, whose counsel even angels adore. C. They murmur against God when disclosing His counsels by the apostle. Exception and answer. Passage of Augustine.

The human mind, when it hears this doctrine, cannot restrain its petulance, but boils and rages as if aroused by the sound of a trumpet. Many professing a desire to defend the deity from an invidious charge admit the doctrine of election, but deny that anyone is reprobated. This they do ignorantly and childishly since there could be no election without its opposite reprobation. God is said to set apart those whom He adopts for salvation. It would be most absurd to say that He admits others fortuitously, or that they by their industry acquire what election alone confers on a few. Those, therefore, whom God passes by He reprobates, and that for no other cause but because He is pleased to exclude them from the inheritance which He predestines to his children. Nor is it possible to tolerate the petulance of men in refusing to be restrained by the Word of God, about his incomprehensible counsel, which even angels adore.

We have already been told that hardening is not less under the immediate hand of God than mercy. Paul does not, after the example of those whom I have mentioned, labor anxiously to defend God, by calling in the aid of falsehood, he only reminds us that it is unlawful for the creature to quarrel with its Creator. Then how will those who refuse to admit that any are reprobated by God explain the following words of Christ? "Every plant which my heavenly Father has not planted shall be rooted up" (Matthew 15:13).

They are plainly told that all whom the heavenly Father has not been pleased to plant as sacred trees in His garden are doomed and devoted to destruction. If they deny that this is a sign of reprobation, there is nothing, however clear, that can be proved to them. But if they will still murmur, let us in the soberness of faith rest contented with the admonition of Paul, that it can be no ground of complaint that God, "willing to show his wrath, and to make his power known, endured with much long-suffering the vessels of wrath fitted for destruction: and that he might make known the riches of his glory on the vessels of mercy, which he had afore prepared unto glory" (Romans 9:22, 23).

Let my readers observe that Paul, to cut off all handle for murmuring and detraction, attributes supreme sovereignty to the wrath and power of God; for it would be unjust that those profound judgments, which transcend all our powers of discernment, should be subjected to our calculation. It is frivolous in our opponents to reply that God does not altogether reject those whom in levity He tolerates, but remains in suspense with regard to them, if per adventure they may repent, as if Paul were representing God as patiently waiting for the conversion of those whom He describes as fitted for destruction.

For Augustine, rightly expounding this passage, says that where power is united to endurance, God does not permit, but rules. They add also, that it is not without cause that the vessels of wrath are said to be fitted for destruction, and that God is said to have prepared the vessels of mercy, because in this way the praise of salvation is claimed for God, whereas the blame of perdition is thrown upon those who of their own accord bring it upon themselves. But were I to concede that by the different forms of expression Paul softens the harshness of the former clause, it by no means follows, that he transfers the preparation for destruction to any other cause than the secret counsel of God. This, indeed, is asserted in the preceding context, where God is said to have raised up Pharaoh, and to harden whom He will. Hence, it follows that the hidden counsel of God is the cause of hardening. I at least hold with Augustine that when God makes sheep out of wolves, He forms them again by the powerful influence of grace, that their hardness may thus be subdued, and that he does not convert the obstinate, because He does not exert that more powerful grace, a grace which He has at His command, if He were disposed to use it.

2 First objection—viz. that God is unjustly offended with those whom He dooms to destruction without their own desert. First answer, from the consideration of the divine will. The nature of this will, and how it is to be considered.

These observations would be amply sufficient for the pious and modest and such as remember that they are men. But because many are the species of blasphemy, which these virulent dogs utter against God, we shall, as far as the case admits, give an answer to each. Foolish men raise many grounds of quarrel with God, as if they held Him subject to their accusations.

First, they ask why God is offended with His creatures who have not provoked Him by any previous offense; for to devote to destruction whomsoever He pleases, more resembles the caprice of a tyrant than the legal sentence of a judge; and, therefore, there is reason to expostulate with God, if at His mere pleasure men are, without any desert of their own, predestinated to eternal death. If at any time thoughts of this kind come into the minds of the pious, they will be sufficiently armed to repress them, by considering how sinful it is to insist on knowing the causes of the divine will, since it is itself, and justly ought to be, the cause of all that exists. For if His will has any cause, there must be something antecedent to it, and to which it is annexed; this it would be impious to imagine.

The will of God is the supreme rule of righteousness, so that everything which He wills must be held to be righteous by the mere fact of His willing it. Therefore, when it is asked why the Lord did so, we must answer, "Because He pleased." But if you proceed further to ask why he pleased, you ask for something greater and more sublime than the will of God, and nothing such can be found. Let human temerity then be quiet and cease to inquire after what exists not, lest perhaps it fails to find what does exist. This, I say, will be sufficient to restrain anyone who would reverently contemplate the secret things of God.

Against the audacity of the wicked, who hesitate not openly to blaspheme, God will sufficiently defend himself by His own righteousness without our assistance, when depriving their consciences of all means of evasion, He shall hold them under conviction and make them feel their guilt. We, however, give no countenance to the fiction of absolute power, which, as it is heathenish, so it ought justly to be held in detestation by us. We do not imagine God to be lawless. He is a law to himself; because, as Plato says, men laboring under the influence of concupiscence need law; but the will of God is not only free from all vice, but is the supreme standard of perfection, the Law of all laws. But we deny that He is bound to give an account of His procedure; and we deny that we are fit of our own ability to give judgment in such a case. Wherefore, when we are tempted to go further than we ought, let this consideration deter us, That thou shalt be "...justified when thou speakest, and be clear when thou judgest" (Psalm 51:4).

3 Second answer. God owes nothing to man. His hatred against those who are corrupted by sin is most just. The reprobate convinced in their own consciences of the just judgment of God.

God may thus quell His enemies by silence. But lest we should allow them with impunity to hold His sacred name in derision, He supplies us with weapons against them from His Word. Accordingly, when we are accosted in such terms as these, Why did God from the first predestine some to death, when, as they were not yet in existence, they could not have merited a sentence of death? Let us by way of reply ask in our turn, What do you imagine that God owes to man, if He is pleased to estimate him by His own nature? As we are all vitiated by sin, we cannot but be hateful to God and that not from tyrannical cruelty, but from the strictest justice. But if all whom the Lord predestines to death are naturally liable to a sentence of death, of what injustice, pray, do they complain? Should all the sons of Adam come to dispute and contend with their Creator, because by His eternal providence they were before their birth doomed to perpetual destruction, when God comes to reckon with them, what will they be able to mutter against this defense? If all are taken from a corrupt mass, it is not strange that all are subject to condemnation. Let them not, therefore, charge God with injustice, if by His eternal judgment they are doomed to a death to which they themselves feel that whether they will or not, they are drawn spontaneously by their own nature. Hence, it appears how perverse is this affectation of murmuring, when of set purpose they suppress the cause of condemnation, which they are compelled to recognize in themselves, that they may lay the blame upon God. But though I should confess a hundred times that God is the author (and it is most certain that He is), they do not, however, thereby efface their own guilt, which, engraved on their own consciences, is always presenting itself to their view.

4 Exception—viz. that the reprobates seem to have been preordained to sin. Answer. Passage of the apostle vindicated from calumny.

They again object, Were not men predestinated by the ordination of God to that corruption which is now held forth as the cause of condemnation? If so, when they perish in their corruptions, they do nothing else than suffer punishment for that calamity, into which, by the predestination of God, Adam fell, and dragged all his posterity headlong with him. Is not he, therefore, unjust in thus cruelly mocking His creatures? I admit that by the will of God all the sons of Adam fell into that state of wretchedness in which they are now involved; and this is just what I said at the first, that we must always return to the mere pleasure of the divine will, the cause of which is hidden in himself. But it does not forthwith follow that God lies open to this charge. For we will answer with Paul in these words, "Nay but, O man, who art thou that replies against God? Shall the thing formed say to him that formed it, Why hast thou made me thus? Has not the potter power over the clay, of the same lump to make one vessel unto honor, and another unto dishonor?" (Romans 9:20, 21). They will deny that the justice of God is thus truly defended, and will allege that we seek an evasion, such as those are wont to employ who have no good excuse. For what more seems to be said here than just that the power of God is such as cannot be hindered, so that He can do whatsoever He pleases? But it is far otherwise. For what stronger reason can be given than when we are ordered to reflect who God is? How could He who is the Judge of the world commit any unrighteousness? If it properly belongs to the nature of God to do judgment, He must naturally love justice and abhor injustice. Wherefore, the apostle did not, as if he had been caught in a difficulty, have recourse to evasion; he only intimated that the procedure of divine justice is too high to be scanned by human measure or comprehended by the feebleness of human intellect. The apostle, indeed, confesses that in the divine judgments there is a depth in which all the minds of men must be engulfed if they attempt to penetrate into it. But he also shows how unbecoming it is to reduce the works of God to such a law as that we can presume to condemn them the moment they accord not with our reason.

There is a well-known saying of Solomon (which, however, few properly understand), "The great God that formed all things both rewardeth the fool and rewardeth transgressors" (Proverbs 26:10). For he is speaking of the greatness of God, whose pleasure it is to inflict punishment on fools and transgressors, though He is not pleased to bestow His Spirit upon them. That a monstrous infatuation in men to seek to subject, has no bounds to the little measure of their reason. Paul gives the name of *elect* to the angels who maintained their integrity. If their steadfastness was owing to the good pleasure of God, the revolt of the others proves that they were abandoned. Of this, no other cause can be adduced than reprobation, which is hidden in the secret counsel of God.

5 Answer, confirmed by the authority of Augustine. Illustration. Passage of Augustine.

Now, should some Manes or Coelestinus come forward to arraign divine providence (see section 8), I say with Paul, that no account of it can be given, because by its magnitude it far surpasses our understanding. Is there anything strange or absurd in this? Would we have the power of God so limited as to be unable to do more than our minds can comprehend? I say with Augustine, that the Lord has created those who, as he certainly foreknow, were to go to destruction, and He did so because He so willed. Why He willed it is not ours to ask, as we cannot comprehend, nor can it become us even to raise a controversy as to the justice of the divine will. Whenever we speak of it, we are speaking of the supreme standard of justice. But when justice clearly appears, why should we raise any question of injustice? Let us not, therefore, be ashamed to stop their mouths after the example of Paul. Whenever they presume to carp, let us begin to repeat: Who are ye, miserable men who bring an accusation against God, and bring it because He does not adapt the greatness of His works to your meager capacity? As if everything must be perverse that is hidden from the flesh.

The immensity of the divine judgments is known to you by clear experience. You know that they are called "a great deep" (Psalm 36:6). Now, look at the narrowness of your own minds and say whether it can comprehend the decrees of God. Why, then, should you, by infatuated inquisitiveness, plunge yourselves into an abyss which reason itself tells you will prove your destruction? Why are you not deterred, in some degree at least, by what the Book of Job and the prophetical books declare concerning the incomprehensible wisdom and dreadful power of God?

If your mind is troubled, decline not to embrace the counsel of Augustine, "You, a man, expect an answer from me: I also am a man. Wherefore, let us both listen to Him who says, "O man, who art thou?" Believing ignorance is better than presumptuous knowledge. Seek merits; you will find nothing but punishment. O the height! Peter denies, a thief believes. O the height! Do you ask the reason? I will tremble at the height. Reason you, I will wonder; dispute you, I will believe. I see the height; I cannot sound the depth. Paul found rest, because he found wonder. He calls the judgments of God "unsearchable"; and have you come to search them? He says that His ways are "past finding out," and do you seek to find them out?" We shall gain nothing by proceeding further. For neither will the Lord satisfy the petulance of these men, nor does He need any other defense than that which He used by His Spirit, who spoke by the mouth of Paul. We unlearn the art of speaking well when we cease to speak with God.

6 Objection, that God ought not to impute the sins rendered necessary by His predestination. First answer, by ancient writers. This is not valid. Second answer also defective. Third answer, proposed by Valla, is well founded.

Impiety starts another objection, which, however, seeks not so much to criminate God as to excuse the sinner; though he who is condemned by God as a sinner cannot ultimately be acquitted without impugning the Judge. This, then, is the scoffing language, which profane tongues employ. Why should God blame men for things the necessity of which He has imposed by His own predestination?

What could they do? Could they struggle with his decrees? It would be in vain for them to do it, since they could not possibly succeed. It is not just, therefore, to punish them for things the principal cause of which is in the predestination of God.

Here I will abstain from a defense to which ecclesiastical writers usually recur, that there is nothing in the prescience of God to prevent Him from regarding man as a sinner, since the evils which He foresees are man's, not His. This would not stop the caviler, who would still insist that God might, if He had pleased, have prevented the evils which He foresaw, and not having done so, must with determinate counsel have created man for the very purpose of so acting on the earth. But if by the providence of God, man was created on the condition of afterwards doing whatever he does, then that which he cannot escape, and which he is constrained by the will of God to do, cannot be charged upon him as a crime. Let us, therefore, see what is the proper method of solving the difficulty.

First, all must admit what Solomon says, "The Lord has made all things for himself; yea, even the wicked for the day of evil" (Proverbs 16:4). Now, since the arrangement of all things is in the hand of God, since to Him belongs the disposal of life and death, He arranges all things by His sovereign counsel, in such a way that individuals are born, who are doomed from the womb to certain death and are to glorify Him by their destruction. If anyone alleges that no necessity is laid upon them by the providence of God, but rather that they are created by Him in that condition, because He foresaw their future depravity, he says something, but does not say enough. Ancient writers, indeed, occasionally employ this solution, though with some degree of hesitation. The Schoolmen, again, rest in it as if it could not be gainsaid. I, for my part, am willing to admit, that mere prescience lays no necessity on the creatures; though some do not assent to this, but hold that it is itself the cause of things. But Valla, though otherwise not greatly skilled in sacred matters, seems to me to have taken a shrewder and more acute view, when he shows that the dispute is superfluous since life and death are acts of the divine will rather than of prescience. If God merely foresaw human events, and did not also arrange and dispose of them at His pleasure, there might be room for agitating the question, how far His foreknowledge amounts to necessity. But since He foresees the things that are to happen, simply because He has decreed that they are so to happen, it is vain to debate about prescience, while it is clear that all events take place by His sovereign appointment.

7 Objection, that God did not decree that Adam should perish by his fall, refuted by a variety of reasons. A noble passage of Augustine.

They deny that it is ever said in distinct terms, God decreed that Adam should perish by his revolt. As if the same God, who is declared in Scripture to do whatsoever He pleases, could have made the noblest of His creatures without any special purpose. They say that, in accordance with free will, He was to be the architect of his own fortune, that God had decreed nothing but to treat him according to his desert. If this frigid fiction is received, where will be the omnipotence of God, by which, according to His secret counsel on which everything depends, He rules over all? But whether they will allow it or not, predestination is manifest in Adam's posterity. It was not owing to nature that they all lost salvation by the fault of one parent. Why should they refuse to admit with regard to one man that which against their will they admit with regard to the whole human race? Why should they in caviling lose their labor? Scripture proclaims that all were, in the person of one, made liable to eternal death. As this cannot be ascribed to nature, it is plain that it is owing to the wonderful counsel of God.

It is very absurd in these worthy defenders of the justice of God to strain at a gnat and swallow a camel. I again ask how it is that the Fall of Adam involves so many nations with their infant children in eternal death without remedy unless that it so seemed meet to God? Here the most loquacious tongues must be dumb.

The decree, I admit, is, dreadful; and yet it is impossible to deny that God foreknow what the end of man was to be before He made him, and foreknew, because He had so ordained by His decree. Should anyone here inveigh against the prescience of God, he does it rashly and unadvisedly. For why, pray, should it be made a charge against the heavenly Judge, that He was not ignorant of what was to happen? Thus, if there is any just or plausible complaint, it must be directed against predestination. Nor ought it to seem absurd when I say that God not only foresaw the fall of the first man, and in him the ruin of his posterity but also at His own pleasure, arranged it. For as it belongs to His wisdom to foreknow all future events, so it belongs to His power to rule and govern them by His hand.

This question, like others, is skillfully explained by Augustine: "Let us confess with the greatest benefit, what we believe with the greatest truth, that the God and Lord of all things who made all things very good, both foreknow that evil was to arise out of good, and knew that it belonged to His most omnipotent goodness to bring good out of evil, rather than not permit evil to be, and so ordained the life of angels and men as to show in it, first, what freewill could do; and, secondly, what the benefit of His grace and His righteous judgment could do."

8 Objection, that the wicked perish by the permission, not by the will of God. Answer. A pious exhortation.

Here, they recur to the distinction between will and permission, the object being to prove that the wicked perish only by the permission, but not by the will of God. But why do we say that He permits, but just because He wills? Nor, indeed, is there any probability in the thing itself—viz. that man brought death upon himself merely by the permission and not by the ordination of God, as if God had not determined what He wished the condition of the chief of His creatures to be.

I will not hesitate, therefore, simply to confess with Augustine that the will of God is necessity, and that everything is necessary which He has willed, just as those things will certainly happen which He has foreseen. Now, if in excuse of themselves and the ungodly, either the Pelagians, or Manichees, or Anabaptists, or Epicureans (for it is with these four sects that we have to discuss this matter), should object to the necessity by which they are constrained, in consequence of the divine predestination, they do nothing that is relevant to the cause. For if predestination is nothing else than a dispensation of divine justice, secret indeed, but unblamable, because it is certain that those predestinated to that condition were not unworthy of it, it is equally certain that the destruction consequent upon predestination is also most just.

Moreover, though their perdition depends on the predestination of God, the cause and matter of it is in themselves. The first man fell because the Lord deemed it meet that he should: why He deemed it meet, we know not. It is certain, however, that it was just, because He saw that His own glory would thereby be displayed. When you hear the glory of God mentioned, understand that His justice is included. For that which deserves praise must be just. Man, therefore, falls, divine providence so ordaining, but he falls by his own fault.

The Lord had a little before declared that all the things, which he had made, were very good. (See Genesis 1:31.) Whence then the depravity of man, which made him revolt from God? Lest it should be supposed that it was from His creation, God had expressly approved what proceeded from himself Therefore, man's own wickedness corrupted the pure nature which he had received from God, and his ruin brought with it the destruction of all his posterity. Wherefore, let us in the corruption of human nature contemplate the evident cause of condemnation (a cause which comes more closely home to us), rather than inquire into a cause that is hidden and almost incomprehensible in the predestination of God. Nor let us decline to submit our judgment to the boundless wisdom of God, so far as to confess its insufficiency to comprehend many of His secrets. Ignorance of things which we are not able, or which it is not lawful to know, is learning, while the desire to know them is a species of madness.

9 Objection and answer.

Someone, perhaps, will say that I have not yet stated enough to refute this blasphemous excuse. I confess that it is impossible to prevent impiety from murmuring and objecting, but I think I have said enough not only to remove the ground but also the pretext for throwing blame upon God. The reprobates would excuse their sins by alleging that they are unable to escape the necessity of sinning, especially because a necessity of this nature is laid upon them by the ordination of God. We deny that they can thus be validly excused, since the ordination of God, by which they complain that they are doomed to destruction, is consistent with equity, an equity, indeed, unknown to us, but most certain.

Hence, we conclude that every evil, which they bear, is inflicted by the most just judgment of God. Next, we have shown that they act preposterously when, in seeking the origin of their condemnation, they turn their view to the hidden recesses of the divine counsel, and wink at the corruption of nature, which is the true source. They cannot impute this corruption to God, because He bears testimony to the goodness of His creation. For, though, by the eternal providence of God, man was formed for the calamity under which he lies, he took the matter of it from himself, not from God, since the only cause of his destruction was his degenerating from the purity of his creation into a state of vice and impurity.

10 Objection, that, according to the doctrine of predestination, God is a respecter of persons. Answer.

There is a third absurdity by which the adversaries of predestination defame it. As we ascribe it entirely to the counsel of the divine will, that those whom God adopts as the heirs of His kingdom are exempted from universal destruction, they infer that He is an acceptor of persons, but this Scripture uniformly denies this, and, therefore, Scripture is either at variance with itself or respect is had to merit in election.

First, the sense in which Scripture declares that God is not an acceptor of persons, is different from that which they suppose: since the term *person* means not *man*, but those things which, when conspicuous in a man, either procure favor, grace, and dignity, or, on the contrary, produce hatred, contempt, and disgrace.

Among, these are, on the one hand, riches, wealth, power, rank, office, country, beauty, etc., and, on the other hand, poverty, want, mean birth, sordidness, contempt, and the like. Thus Peter and Paul say that the Lord is no acceptor of persons, because He makes no distinction between the Jew and the Greek, does not make the mere circumstance of country the ground for rejecting one or embracing the other. (See Acts 10:34; Romans 2:10; Galatians 3:28.) Thus, James also uses the same words when he would declare that God has no respect to riches in His judgment. (See James 2:5.) In another passage, Paul also says that in judging God has no respect to slavery or freedom. (See Ephesians 6:9; Colossians 3:25.) There is nothing inconsistent with this when we say, that God, according to the good pleasure of His will, without any regard to merit, elects those whom He chooses for sons, while He rejects and reprobates others. For fuller satisfaction, the matter may be thus explained.

It is asked how it happens that of two, between whom there is no difference of merit, God in His election adopts the one and passes by the other? I, in my turn, ask, "Is there anything in him who is adopted to incline God towards him?" If it must be confessed that there is nothing, it will follow that God looks not to the man, but is influenced entirely by His own goodness to do him good. Therefore, when God elects one and rejects another, it does owe not to any respect to the individual, but entirely to His own mercy, which is free to display and exert itself when and where He pleases. For we have elsewhere seen, that in order to humble the pride of the flesh,

"Not many wise men after the flesh, not many mighty, not many noble, are called" (1 Corinthians 1:26); so far is God in the exercise of His favor from showing any respect to persons.

11 Objection, that sinners are to be punished equally, or the justice of God is unequal. Answer. Confirmed by passages of Augustine.

Wherefore, it is false and most wicked to charge God with dispensing justice unequally, because in this predestination He does not observe the same course towards all. If (say they) He finds all guilty, let Him punish all alike: if He finds them innocent, let Him relieve all from the severity of judgment. But they plead with God as if He either were interdicted from showing mercy or were obliged, if He shows mercy, entirely to renounce judgment. What is it that they demand? That if all are guilty, all shall receive the same punishment. We admit that the guilt is common, but we say that God in mercy succors some. Let Him (they say) succor all. We object that it is right for Him to show by punishing that He is a just Judge. When they cannot tolerate this, what else are they attempting than to deprive God of the power of showing mercy; or, at least, to allow it to Him only on the condition of altogether renouncing judgment? Here the words of Augustine most admirably apply: "Since in the first man the whole human race fell under condemnation, those vessels which are made of it unto honor are not vessels of self-righteousness, but of divine mercy. When other vessels are made unto dishonor, it must be imputed not to injustice, but to judgment."

Since God inflicts due punishment on those whom He reprobates, and bestows unmerited favor on those whom He calls, He is free from every accusation, just as it belongs to the creditor to forgive the debt to one and exact it of another. The Lord, therefore, may show favor of whom He will, because He is merciful. He may not show it to all, because He is a just Judge. In giving to some that which they do not merit, He shows His free favor; in not giving to all, He declares what all deserve. For when Paul says, "God has concluded them all in unbelief, that he might have mercy upon all," it ought also to be added, that He is debtor to none; for "Who has first given to him and it shall be recompensed unto him again?" (Romans 11:32, 33).

12 Objection, that the doctrine of predestination produces overweening confidence and impiety. Different answers.

Another argument, which they employ to overthrow predestination, is that if it stands, all care and study of well doing must cease. For what man can hear (say they) that life and death are fixed by an eternal and immutable decree of God, without immediately concluding that it is of no consequence how he acts, since no work of his can either hinder or further the predestination of God? Thus, all will rush on, and as if desperate men plunge headlong wherever lust inclines. And it is true that this is not altogether a fiction; for there are multitudes of a swinish nature that defile the doctrine of predestination by their profane blasphemies and employ them as a cloak to evade all admonition and censure. "God knows what He has determined to do with regard to us: if He has decreed our salvation, He will bring us to it in His own time; if He has doomed us to death, it is vain for us to fight against it." But Scripture, while it enjoins us to think of this high mystery with much greater reverence and religion, gives very different instruction to the pious and justly condemns the accursed license of the ungodly. For it does not remind us of predestination to increase our audacity and tempt us to pry with impious presumption into the inscrutable counsels of God, but rather to humble and abase us, that we may tremble at His judgment and learn to look up to his mercy. This is the mark at which believers will aim.

The grunt of these filthy swine is duly silenced by Paul. They say that they feel secure in vices, because, if they are of the number of the elect, their vices will be no obstacle to the ultimate attainment of life. But Paul reminds us that the end for which we are elected is, "That we should be holy, and without blame before him" (Ephesians 1:4).

If the end of election is holiness of life, it ought to arouse and stimulate us strenuously to aspire to it, instead of serving as a pretext for sloth. How wide the difference between the two things, between ceasing from well-doing because election is sufficient for salvation, and its being the very end of election, that we should devote ourselves to the study of good works. Have done, then, with blasphemies, which wickedly invert the whole order of election. When they extend their blasphemies further, and say that he who is reprobated by God will lose his pains if he studies to approve himself to Him by innocence and probity of life, they are convicted of the most impudent falsehood. For whence can any such study arise but from election? As all who are of the number of the reprobate are vessels formed unto dishonor, so they cease not by their perpetual crimes to provoke the anger of God against them, and give evident signs of the judgment which God has already passed upon them; so far is it from being true that they vainly contend against it.

13 Another objection, depending on the former. Answer. The doctrine of predestination is to be preached, not passed over in silence.

Another impudent and malicious calumny against this doctrine is that it destroys all exhortations to a pious life. The great odium to which Augustine was at one time subjected on this head he wiped away in his treatise *De Correptione et Gratia*, to Valentinus, a perusal of which will easily satisfy the pious and docile. Here, however, I may touch on a few points, which will, I hope, be sufficient for those who are honest and not contentious. We have already seen how plainly and audibly Paul preaches the doctrine of free election: is he, therefore, cold in admonishing and exhorting? Let those good zealots compare his vehemence with theirs, and they will find that they are ice, while he is all fervor. And surely every doubt on this subject should be removed by the principles which he lays down, that God has not called us to uncleanness; that everyone should possess his vessel in honor; that we are the workmanship of God, "...created in Christ Jesus unto good works, which God has before ordained that we should walk in them" (1 Thessalonians 4:4, 7; Ephesians 2:10). In one word, those who have any tolerable acquaintance with the writings of Paul will understand, without a long demonstration, how well he reconciles the two things, which those men pretend to be contradictory to each other. Christ commands us to believe in Him, and yet there is nothing false or contrary to this command in the statement, which He afterwards makes: "No man can come unto me, except it were given him of my Father" (John 6:65).

Let preaching, then, have its free course, that it may lead men to faith, and dispose them to persevere with uninterrupted progress. Nor, at the same time, let there be any obstacle to the knowledge of predestination, so that those who obey may not plume themselves on anything of their own, but glory only in the Lord. It is not without cause that our Savior says, "Who has ears to hear, let him hear"

(Matthew 13:9). Therefore, while we exhort and preach, those who have ears willingly obey: in those again, who have no ears, is fulfilled what is written: "Hear ye indeed, but understand not" (Isaiah 6:9). "But why (says Augustine) have some ears, and others not? Who has known the mind of the Lord? Are we, therefore, to deny what is plain because we cannot comprehend what is hid?" This is a faithful quotation from Augustine; but because his words will perhaps have more authority than mine will, let us adduce the following passage from his treatise, *De Bone Persever:*

"Should some on hearing this turn to indolence and sloth, and leaving off all exertion, rush headlong into lust, are we, therefore to suppose that what has been said of the foreknowledge of God is not true? If God foreknew that they would be good, will they not be good, however great their present wickedness? And if God foreknow that they would be wicked, will they not be wicked, how great soever the goodness now seen in them? For reasons of this description, must the truth, which has been stated on the subject of divine foreknowledge, be denied or not mentioned? And more especially when, if it is not stated, other errors will arise?" In the sixteenth chapter he says, "The reason for not mentioning the truth is one thing, the necessity for telling the truth is another. It would be tedious to inquire into all the reasons for silence.

One, however, is, lest those who understand not become worse, while we are desirous to make those who understand better informed. Now such persons, when we say anything of this kind, do not indeed become better informed, but neither do they become worse. But when the truth is of such a nature, that he who cannot comprehend it becomes worse by our telling it, and he who can comprehend it becomes worse by our not telling it, what think ye ought we to do? Are we not to tell the truth, that he who can comprehend may comprehend, rather than not tell it, and thereby not only prevent both from comprehending, but also make the more intelligent of the two to become worse, whereas if he heard and comprehended, others might learn through him? And we are unwilling to say what, on the testimony of Scripture, it is lawful to say. For we fear lest, when we speak, he who cannot comprehend may be offended; but we have no fear lest while we are silent, he who can comprehend the truth be involved in falsehood.

In chapter twentieth, glancing again at the same view, he more clearly confirms it. "Wherefore, if the apostles and teachers of the

Church who came after them did both; if they discoursed piously of the eternal election of God, and at the same time kept believers under the discipline of a pious life, how can those men of our day, when shut up by the invincible force of truth, think they are right in saying that what is said of predestination, though it is true, must not be preached to the people? Nay, it ought indeed to be preached, that whoso has ears to hear may hear. And who has ears if he has not received them from Him who has promised to give them? Certainly, let him who receives not, reject. Let him who receives, take and drink, drink and live. For as piety is to be preached, that God may be duly worshipped, so predestination also is to be preached, that he who has ears to hear may, in regard to divine grace, glory not in himself, but in God."

14 How it is to be preached and delivered to the people. Summary of the orthodox doctrine of predestination from Augustine.

Yet, as that holy man had a singular desire to edify, he so regulates his method of teaching as carefully, and as far as in him lies, to avoid giving offense. He reminds us that those things, which are true, should be fitly spoken. If anyone were to address the people thus: "If you do not believe, the reason is that God has already doomed you to destruction," he would not only encourage sloth, but also give countenance to wickedness. Were anyone to give utterance to the sentiment in the future tense, and say, that those who hear will not believe because they are reprobates, it would be imprecation rather than doctrine. Wherefore, Augustine not undeservedly, orders such, as senseless teachers or ministers and ill-omened prophets, to retire from the Church. He, indeed, elsewhere truly contends, "A man profits by correction only when He who causes those whom He pleases to profit without correction, pities and assists. But why is it thus with some, and differently with others? Far be it from us to say that it belongs to the clay and not to the Potter to decide." He afterwards says, "When men by correction either come or return to the way of righteousness, who is it that works salvation in their hearts but He who gives the increase, whoever it be that plants and waters? When He is pleased to save, there is no free will in man to resist. Wherefore, it cannot be doubted that the will of God (who has done whatever He has pleased in Heaven and in Earth, and who has even done things which are to be) cannot be resisted by the human will, or prevented from doing what He pleases, since with the very wills of men He does so." Again, "When He would bring men to himself, does He bind them with corporeal fetters? He acts inwardly, inwardly holds, inwardly moves their hearts, and draws them by the will, which He has wrought in them." What He immediately adds must not be omitted: "...because we know not who belongs to the number of the predestinated, or does not belong, our desire ought to be that all may be saved; and hence every person we meet, we will desire to be with us a partaker of peace. But our peace will rest upon the sons of peace. Wherefore, on our part, let correction be used as a harsh yet salutary medicine for all, that they may neither perish, nor destroy others. To God it will belong to make it available to those whom He has foreknown and predestinated."

Chapter 24

ELECTION CONFIRMED BY THE CALLING OF GOD. THE REPROBATES BRING UPON THEMSELVES THE RIGHTEOUS DESTRUCTION TO WHICH THEY ARE DOOMED

The title of this chapter shows that it consists of two parts, I. The case of the elect, from sections 1-11. II. The case of the reprobates, from sections 12-17.

Sections

1. The election of God is secret, but is manifested by effectual calling. The nature of this effectual calling. How election and effectual calling are founded on the free mercy of God. A cavil of certain expositors refuted by the words of Augustine. An exception disposed of.

2. Calling proved to be free, A. By its nature and the mode in which it is dispensed. B. By the Word of God. C. By the calling of Abraham, the father of the faithful. D. By the testimony of John. E. By the example of those who have been called.

3. The pure doctrine of the calling of the elect misunderstood, A. By those who attribute too much to the human will. B. By those who make election dependent on faith. This error is amply refuted.

4. In this and the five following sections the certainty of election is vindicated from the assaults of Satan. The leading arguments are: A. Effectual calling. B. Christ apprehended by faith. C. The protection of Christ, the Guardian of the elect. We must not attempt to penetrate to the hidden recesses of divine wisdom, in order to learn what is decreed with regard to us at the judgment-seat. We must begin and end with the call of God. This is confirmed by an apposite saying of Bernard.

5. *Christ is the foundation of this calling and election. He who does not lean on Him alone cannot be certain of his election. He is the faithful interpreter of the eternal counsel in regard to our salvation.*

6. *Another security of our election is the protection of Christ, our Shepherd. How it is manifested to us. Objection. A. As to the future state. B. As to perseverance. Both objections refuted.*

7. *Objection, that those who seem elected sometimes fall away. Answer. A passage of Paul dissuading us from security explained. The kind of fear that is required in the elect.*

8. *An explanation of the saying, that many are called, but few are chosen. A twofold call.*

9. *Explanation of the passage, that none is lost but the son of perdition. Refutation of an objection to the certainty of election.*

10. *Explanation of the passages urged against the certainty of election. Examples by which some attempt to prove that the seed of election is sown in the hearts of the elect from their very births. Answer. A. One or two examples do not make the rule. B. This view is opposed to Scripture. C. It is expressly opposed by an apostle.*

11. *An explanation and confirmation of the third answer.*

12. *Second part of the chapter, which treats of the reprobate. Some of them God deprives of the opportunity of hearing His Word. Others He blinds and stupefies the more by the preaching of it.*

13. *Of this no other account can be given than that the reprobate are vessels fitted for destruction. This is confirmed by the case of the elect—of Pharaoh and of the Jewish people, both before and after the manifestation of Christ.*

14. *Question, Why does God blind the reprobate? Two answers. These are confirmed by different passages of Scripture. Objection of the reprobate. Answer.*

15. *Objection to this doctrine of the righteous rejection of the reprobate. The first is founded on a passage in Ezekiel. The passage is explained.*

16. *A second objection is founded on a passage in Paul. The apostle's meaning is explained. A third objection and fourth objection are answered.*

17. *A fifth objection—viz. that there seems to be a twofold will in God. Answer. Other objections and answers. Conclusion.*

1 The election of God is secret, but it is manifested by effectual calling. The nature of this effectual calling. How election and effectual calling are founded on the free mercy of God. A cavil of certain expositors refuted by the words of Augustine. An exception disposed of.

But that the subject may be more fully illustrated, we must treat both the calling of the elect, and the blinding and hardening of the ungodly. The former I have already in some measure discussed (see chapter 22, section 10, 11), when refuting the error of those who think that the general terms in which the promises are made place the whole human race on a level. The special election which otherwise would remain hidden in God, He at length manifests by His calling. "For whom he did foreknow, he also did predestinate to be conformed to the image of his Son."

Moreover, "Whom he did predestinate, them he also called; and whom he called, them he also justified," that He may one day glorify. (See Romans 8:29, 30.) Though the Lord, by electing His people, adopted them as His sons, we, however, see that they do not come into possession of this great good until they are called; but when they are called, the enjoyment of their election is in some measure communicated to them. For which reason the Spirit that they receive is termed by Paul both the "Spirit of adoption," and the "seal" and "earnest" of the future inheritance, because by his testimony he confirms and seals the certainty of future adoption on their hearts. For, although the preaching of the gospel springs from the fountain of election, yet being common to them with the reprobate, it would not be in itself a solid proof.

God, however, teaches his elect effectually when He brings them to faith, as we formerly quoted from the words of our Savior, "Not that any man has seen the Father, save he which is of God, he has seen the Father" (John 6:46). Again, "I have manifested thy name unto the men which thou gavest me out of the world" (John 17:6). He says in another passage, "No man can come to me, except the Father which has sent me draw him" (John 6:44).

This passage Augustine ably expounds in these words: "If (as truth says) everyone who has learned comes, then everyone who does not come has not learned. It does not, therefore, follow that he who can come does come, unless he have willed and done it; but everyone who has learned of the Father, not only can come, but also

501

comes; the antecedence of possibility, the affection of will, and the effect of action being now present."

In another passage, he says still more clearly, "What means, everyone that has heard and learned of the Father comes unto me, but just that there is no one who hears and learns of the Father that does not come to me? For if everyone who has heard and learned, comes; assuredly, everyone who does not come, has neither heard nor learned of the Father: for if he had heard and learned, he would come. Far removed from carnal sense is this school in which the Father is heard and teaches us to come to the Son." Shortly after, he says, "This grace, which is secretly imparted to the hearts of men, is not received by any hard heart; for the reason for which it is given is that the hardness of the heart may first be taken away."

Hence, when the Father is heard within, He takes away the stony heart and gives a heart of flesh. Thus, He makes them sons of promise and vessels of mercy, which He has prepared for glory. Why, then, does He not teach all to come to Christ, but just because all whom He teaches, He teaches in mercy, while those whom He teaches not, he teaches not in judgment? He pities whom he will, and hardens whom he will." Those, therefore, whom God has chosen He adopts as sons, while He becomes to them a Father. By calling, moreover, he admits them to His family, and unites them to himself, that they may be one with Him. When calling is thus added to election, the Scripture plainly intimates that nothing is to be looked for in it but the free mercy of God. For if we ask whom it is He calls, and for what reason, he answers that it is those whom He had chosen.

When we come to election, mercy alone everywhere appears; and, accordingly, in this the saying of Paul is truly realized, "So then, it is not of him that willeth, nor of him that runneth, but of God that showeth mercy" (Romans 9:16); and that not as is commonly understood by those who share the result between the grace of God and the will and agency of man. For their exposition is that the desire and endeavor of sinners are of no avail by themselves, unless they are accompanied by the grace of God, but that when aided by His blessing, they also do their part in procuring salvation.

This cavil I prefer refuting in the words of Augustine rather than my own: "If all that the apostle meant is that it is not alone of him that willeth, or of him that runneth, unless the Lord be present in mercy, we may retort and hold the converse, that it is not of mercy alone, unless willing and running be present." But if this is manifestly impious, let us have no doubt that the apostle attributes all to the mercy of the Lord and leaves nothing to our wills or exertions. Such were the sentiments of that holy man. I set not the value of a straw on the subtlety to which they have recourse—viz. that Paul would not have spoken thus had there not been some will and effort on our part. For he considered not what might be in man, but because certain persons ascribed a part of salvation to the industry of man, he simply condemned their error in the former clause, and then claimed the whole substance of salvation for the divine mercy. And what else do the prophets than perpetually proclaim the free calling of God?

2 Calling proved to be free, A. By its nature and the mode in which it is dispensed. B. By the Word of God. C. By the calling of Abraham, the father of the faithful. D. By the testimony of John. E. By the example of those who have been called.

Moreover, this is clearly demonstrated by the nature and dispensation of calling, which consists not merely of the preaching of the Word, but also of the illumination of the Spirit. Who those are to whom God offers His Word is explained by the prophet, "I am sought of them that asked not for me: I am found of them that sought me not: I said, Behold me, behold me, unto a nation that was not called by my name" (Isaiah 65:1). And lest the Jews should think that that mercy applied only to the Gentiles, He calls to their remembrance whence it was He took their father Abraham when He condescended to be his friend (Isaiah 41:8); namely, from the midst of idolatry, in which he was plunged with all his people. When He first shines with the light of His Word on the undeserving, He gives a sufficiently clear proof of His free goodness. Here, therefore, boundless goodness is displayed, but not to bring all to salvation, since a heavier judgment awaits the reprobate for rejecting the evidence of His love. God, also, to display His own glory, withholds from them the effectual agency of His Spirit. Therefore, this inward calling is an infallible pledge of salvation. Hence, the words of John, "Hereby we know that he abideth in us by the Spirit which he has given us" (1 John 3:24). And lest the flesh should glory, at least in responding to him, when He calls and spontaneously offers himself, He affirms that there would be no ears to hear, no eyes to see, did not He give them. And He acts not according to the gratitude of each, but according to His election. Of this, you have a striking example in Luke, when the Jews and Gentiles in common heard the discourse of Paul and Barnabas. Though they were all instructed in the same word, it is said, "As many as were ordained to eternal life believed" (Acts 13:48). How can we deny that calling is gratuitous, when election alone reigns in it even to its conclusion?

3 The pure doctrine of the calling of the elect is misunderstood, A. By those who attribute too much to the human will. B. By those who make election dependent on faith. This error is amply refuted.

Two errors are here to be avoided. Some make man a fellow-worker with God in such a sense that man's suffrage ratifies election, so that, according to them, the will of man is superior to the counsel of God. It is as if Scripture taught that only the power of being able to believe is given us and not, rather, faith itself. Others, although they do not so much impair the grace of the Holy Spirit, yet, induced by what means I know not, make election dependent on faith, as if it were doubtful and ineffectual until confirmed by faith. There can be no doubt, indeed, that concerning us it is so confirmed.

Moreover, we have already seen that the secret counsel of God, which lay concealed, is thus brought to light by this nothing more being understood than that which was unknown is proved and sealed. But it is false to say that election is then only effectual after we have embraced the gospel, and that it thence derives its vigor. It is true that we must there look for its certainty, because, if we attempt to penetrate to the secret ordination of God, we shall be engulfed in that profound abyss. But when the Lord has manifested it to us, we must ascend higher in order that the effect may not bury the cause. For what can be more absurd and unbecoming than while Scripture teaches that we are illuminated as God has chosen us, our eyes should be so dazzled with the brightness of this light as to refuse to attend to election?

Meanwhile, I deny not that in order to be assured of our salvation, we must begin with the Word, and that our confidence ought to go no further than the Word when we invoke God the Father. For some, to obtain more certainty of the counsel of God (which is nigh us in our mouth, and in our heart, Deuteronomy 30:14) is to absurdly desire to fly above the clouds. We must, therefore, curb that temerity by the soberness of faith and be satisfied to have God as the witness of His hidden grace in the external Word; provided always that the channel in which the water flows, and out of which we may freely drink, does not prevent us from paying due honor to the fountain.

4 In this and the five following sections the certainty of election vindicated from the assaults of Satan. The leading arguments are: A. Effectual calling. B. Christ apprehended by faith. C. The protection of Christ, the Guardian of the elect. We must not attempt to penetrate to the hidden recesses of the divine wisdom in order to learn what is decreed with regard to us at the Judgment Seat. We must begin and end with the call of God. This is confirmed by an apposite saying of Bernard.

Therefore, as those are in error who make the power of election dependent on the faith by which we perceive that we are elected, so we shall follow the best order, if, in seeking the certainty of our election, we cleave to those posterior signs which are sure attestations to it. Among the temptations with which Satan assaults believers, none is greater or more perilous, than when disquieting them with doubts as to their election, he at the same time stimulates them with a depraved desire of inquiring after it out of the proper way. By inquiring out of the proper way, I mean when puny man endeavors to penetrate to the hidden recesses of the divine wisdom, and goes back even to the remotest eternity, in order that he may understand what final determination God has made with regard to him. In this way, he plunges headlong into an immense abyss, involves himself in numberless inextricable snares, and buries himself in the thickest darkness. For it is right that the stupidity of the human mind should be punished with fearful destruction whenever it attempts to rise in its own strength to the height of divine wisdom. And this temptation is the more fatal, that it is the temptation to which of all others almost all of us are most prone. For there is scarcely a mind in which the thought does not sometimes rise, "Whence your salvation but from the election of God?" But what proof have you of your election? When once this thought has taken possession of any individual, it keeps him perpetually miserable, subjects him to dire torment, or throws him into a state of complete stupor.

I cannot wish a stronger proof of the depraved ideas, which men of this description form of predestination, than experience itself furnishes, since the mind cannot be infected by a more pestilential error than that which disturbs the conscience and deprives it of peace and tranquility in regard to God. Therefore, as we dread shipwreck, we must avoid this rock, which is fatal to everyone who strikes upon it. Though the discussion of predestination is regarded as a perilous sea, yet in sailing over it, the navigation is calm and safe, nay pleasant, provided we do not voluntarily court danger. For as a fatal abyss engulfs those who, to be assured of their election, pry into the eternal counsel of God without the Word, yet those who investigate it rightly, and in the order in which it is exhibited in the Word, reap from it rich fruits of consolation.

Let our method of inquiry then be to begin with the calling of God and to end with it. Although there is nothing in this to prevent believers from feeling that the blessings which they daily receive from the hand of God originate in that secret adoption, as they themselves express it in Isaiah, "Thou hast done wonderful things; thy counsels of old are faithfulness and truth" (Isaiah 25:1). For with this as a pledge; God is pleased to assure us of as much of His counsel as can be lawfully known. But lest any should think that testimony weak, let us consider what clearness and certainty it gives us. On this subject, there is an apposite passage in Bernard. After speaking of the reprobate, he says, "The purpose of God stands, the sentence of peace on those that fear Him also stands, a sentence concealing their bad and recompensing their good qualities; so that, in a wondrous manner, not only their good but their bad qualities work together for good. Who will lay anything to the charge of God's elect? It is sufficient for my justification to have Him propitious against whom only I have sinned. Everything which He has decreed not to impute to me is as if it had never been." A little after he says, "O the place of true rest, a place which I consider not unworthy of the name of inner-chamber, where God is seen, not as if disturbed with anger, or distracted by care, but where His will is proved to be good and acceptable and perfect. That vision does not terrify, but soothe, does not excite restless curiosity, but calms it, does not fatigue, but tranquilizes the senses. Here is true rest. A tranquil God tranquilizes all things; and to see him at rest, is to be at rest."

5 Christ, the foundation of this calling and election. He who does not lean on Him alone cannot be certain of his election. He is the faithful interpreter of the eternal counsel in regard to our salvation.

First, if we seek for the paternal mercy and favor of God, we must turn our eyes to Christ, in whom alone the Father is well pleased (Matthew 3:17). When we seek for salvation, life, and a blessed immortality, to Him also must we retake ourselves, since He alone is the fountain of life, the anchor of salvation, and the heir of the Kingdom of Heaven. Then, what is the end of election, but just that, being adopted as sons by the heavenly Father, we may obtain salvation and immortality by His favor? How much soever you may speculate and discuss, you will perceive that in its ultimate object it goes no further. Hence, those whom God has adopted as sons, he is said to have elected, not in themselves, but in Christ Jesus (see Ephesians 1:4); because He could love them only in Him, and only as being previously made partakers with Him, honor them with the inheritance of His kingdom. But if we are elected in Him, we cannot find the certainty of our election in ourselves; and not even in God the Father, if we look at Him apart from the Son. Christ, then, is the mirror in which we ought, and in which, without deception, we may contemplate our election. For since it is into His body that the Father has decreed to engraft those whom from eternity He wished to be His, that He may regard as sons all whom He acknowledges to be his members, if we are in communion with Christ, we have proof sufficiently clear and strong that we are written in the Book of Life. Moreover, He admitted us to sure communion with himself, when, by the preaching of the gospel, He declared that He was given us by the Father, to be ours with all His blessings. (See Romans 8:32.) We are said to be clothed with Him, to be one with Him, that we may live, because He himself lives.

The doctrine is often repeated, "God so loved the world, that he gave his only begotten Son, that whosoever believeth in him should not perish, but have everlasting life" (John 3:16). He who believes in Him is said to have passed from death unto life. (See John 5:24.) In this sense He calls himself the *bread of life*, of which if a man eat, he shall never die. (See John 6:35.)

He, I say, was our witness, that all by whom He is received in faith will be regarded by our heavenly Father as sons. If we long for more than to be regarded as sons of God and heirs, we must ascend above Christ. But if this is our final goal, how infatuated is it to seek out of Him what we have already obtained in Him, and can only find in Him? Besides, as He is the Eternal Wisdom, the Immutable Truth, the Determinate Counsel of the Father, there is no room for fear that anything which He tells us will vary in the minutest degree from that will of the Father after which we inquire. Nay, rather, He faithfully discloses it to us as it was from the beginning and always will be.

The practical influence of this doctrine ought also to be exhibited in our prayers. For, though a belief of our election animates us to involve God, yet when we frame our prayers, it would be preposterous to obtrude it upon God, or to stipulate in this way, "O Lord, if I am elected, hear me." He would have us to rest satisfied with his promises and not to inquire elsewhere whether or not He is disposed to hear us. We shall thus be disentangled from many snares, if we know how to make a right use of what is rightly written; but let us not inconsiderately wrest it to purposes different from that to which it ought to be confined.

6 Another security of our election is the protection of Christ, our Shepherd. How it is manifested to us. Objection. A. As to the future state. B. As to perseverance. Both objections refuted.

Another confirmation tending to establish our confidence is that our election is connected with our calling. For those whom Christ enlightens with the knowledge of His name and admits into the bosom of His Church, He is said to take under His guardianship and protection. All whom He thus receives are said to be committed and entrusted to Him by the Father, that they may be kept unto life eternal. What would we have? Christ proclaims aloud that all whom the Father is pleased to save, He has delivered into His protection. (See John 6:37-39, 17:6, 12.) Therefore, if we would know whether God cares for our salvation, let us ask whether He has committed us to Christ, whom He has appointed to be the only Savior of all His people. Then, if we doubt whether we are received into the protection of Christ, He obviates the doubt when He spontaneously offers himself as our Shepherd, and declares that we are of the number of His sheep, if we hear his voice. (See John 10:3, 16.)

Let us, therefore, embrace Christ, who is kindly offered to us, and comes forth to meet us: He will number us among His flock, and keep us within his fold. But anxiety arises as to our future state. For as Paul teaches, those are called who were previously elected, so our Savior shows that many are called, but few chosen. (See Matthew 22:14.) Nay, even Paul himself dissuades us from security, when he says, "Let him that thinketh he standeth take heed lest he fall" (1 Corinthians 10:12). Again, "Well, because of unbelief they were broken off, and thou standest by faith. Be not high-minded, but fear: for if God spared not the natural branches, take heed lest he also spare not thee" (Romans 11:20, 21).

In fine, we are sufficiently taught by experience itself that calling and faith are of little value without perseverance, which, however, is not the gift of all. But Christ has freed us from anxiety on this head; for the following promises undoubtedly have respect to the future: "All that the Father giveth me shall come to me, and him that comes to me I will in no wise cast out." Again, "This is the will of him that sent me, that of all which he has given me I should lose nothing; but should raise it up at the last day" (John 6:37, 39). Again, "My sheep hear my voice, and I know them, and they follow me: and I give unto them eternal life, and they shall never perish, neither shall any man pluck them out of my hand. My Father which gave them me is greater than all: and no man is able to pluck them out of my Father's hand" (John 10:27, 28). Again, when He declares, "Every plant which my heavenly Father has not planted shall be rooted up" (Matthew 15:13), He intimates conversely that those who have their root in God can never be deprived of their salvation. Agreeable to this are the words of John, "If they had been of us, they would no doubt have continued with us" (1 John 2:19).

Hence, also, the magnificent triumph of Paul over life and death, things present, and things to come. (See Romans 8:38.) This must be founded on the gift of perseverance. There is no doubt that he employs the sentiment as applicable to all the elect. Paul elsewhere says, "Being confident of this very thing, that he who has begun a good work in you will perform it until the day of Jesus Christ" (Philippians 1:6). David, also, when his faith threatened to fail, leant on this support, "Forsake not the works of thy hands." Moreover, it cannot be doubted, that since Christ prays for all the elect, He asks the same thing for them that he asked for Peter—viz. that their faith fail not. (See Luke 22:32.)

Hence, we infer that there is no danger of their falling away, since the Son of God, who asks that their piety may prove constant, never meets with a refusal. What then did our Savior intend to teach us by this prayer, but just to confide that whenever we are His, our eternal salvation is secure?

7 Objection, that those who seem elected sometimes fall away. Answer. A passage of Paul dissuading us from security explained. The kind of fear required in the elect.

But it daily happens that those who seemed to belong to Christ revolt from Him and fall away; nay, in the very passage where He declares that none of those whom the Father has given to Him has perished, He excepts the son of perdition. This, indeed, is true, but it is equally true that such persons never adhered to Christ with that heartfelt confidence by which I say that the certainty of our election is established, "They went out from us," says John, "but they were not of us; for if they had been of us, they would, no doubt, have continued with us" (1 John 2:19). I deny not that they have signs of calling similar to those given to the elect, but I do not at all admit that they have that sure confirmation of election, which I desire believers to seek from the word of the gospel. Wherefore, let not examples of this kind move us away from tranquil confidence in the promise of the Lord, when He declares that all by whom He is received in true faith have been given Him by the Father, and that none of them, while He is their Guardian and Shepherd, will perish. (See John 3:16; 6:39.)

Of Judas we shall shortly speak. (See section 9.) Paul does not dissuade Christians from security simply, but from careless, carnal security, which is accompanied with pride, arrogance, and contempt of others, which extinguishes humility and reverence for God, and produces a forgetfulness of grace received. (See Romans 11:20.) For he is addressing the Gentiles, and showing them that they ought not to exult proudly and cruelly over the Jews, in consequence of whose rejection they had been substituted in their stead. He also enjoins fear, not a fear under which they may waver in alarm, but a fear which, teaching us to receive the grace of God in humility, does not impair our confidence in it, as has elsewhere been said. We may add that he is not speaking to individuals, but to sects in general. (See Corinthians 10:12.) The Church, having been divided into two parties, and rivalry producing dissension, Paul reminds the Gentiles that their having been substituted in the place of a peculiar and holy people was a reason for modesty and fear. For there were many vainglorious persons among them, whose empty boasting it was expedient to repress. But we have elsewhere seen that our hope extends into the future, even beyond death, and that nothing is more contrary to its nature than to be in doubt as to our future destiny.

8 Explanation of the saying that many are called, but few are chosen. A twofold call.

The expression of our Savior, "Many are called, but few are chosen" (Matthew 22:14), is also very improperly interpreted. (See Book 3, chapter 2, sections 11, 12.) There will be no ambiguity in it if we attend to what our former remarks ought to have made clear—viz. that there are two species of calling; for there is a universal call, by which God, through the external preaching of the Word, invites all men alike, even those for whom He designs the call to be a savor of death, and the ground of a severer condemnation. Besides this there is a special call, which, for the most part, God bestows on believers only, when by the internal illumination of the Spirit He causes the Word preached to take deep root in their hearts. Sometimes, however, he communicates it also to those whom He enlightens only for a time and whom afterwards, in just punishment for their ingratitude, He abandons and smites with greater blindness. Now, our Lord seeing that the gospel was published far and wide, was despised by multitudes and justly valued by few, describes God under the character of a king, who, preparing a great feast, sends his servants all around to invite a great multitude, but can only obtain the presence of a very few, because almost all allege causes of excuse; at length, in consequence of their refusal, he is obliged to send his servants out into the highways to invite everyone they meet. It is perfectly clear, that thus far the parable is to be understood of external calling. He afterwards adds, that God acts the part of a kind entertainer, who goes round his table and affably receives his guests; but still if he finds anyone not adorned with the nuptial garment, he will by no means allow him to insult the festivity by his sordid dress.

I admit that this branch of the parable is to be understood of those who, by a profession of faith, enter the Church, but are not at all invested with the sanctification of Christ. Such disgraces to His Church, such cankers, God will not always tolerate, but will cast them forth as their turpitude deserves. Few, then, out of the great number of called are chosen; the calling, however, not being of that kind which enables believers to judge of their election. The former call is common to the wicked, the latter brings with it the spirit of regeneration, which is the earnest and seal of the future inheritance by which our hearts are sealed unto the day of the Lord. (See Ephesians 1:13, 14.)

In one word, while hypocrites pretend to piety, just as if they were true worshipers of God, Christ declares that they will ultimately be ejected from the place, which they improperly occupy, as it is said in the Psalm, "Lord, who shall abide in thy tabernacle? Who shall dwell in thy holy hill? He that walketh uprightly, and worketh righteousness, and speaketh the truth in his heart" (Psalm 15:1, 2). Again, in another passage, "This is the generation of them that seek him, that seek thy face, O Jacob" (Psalm 24:6). Thus, the Spirit exhorts believers to patience, and not to murmur because Ishmaelites are mingled with them in the Church since the mask will at length be torn off, and they will be ejected with disgrace.

9 Explanation of the passage, that none is lost but the son of perdition. Refutation of an objection to the certainty of election.

The same account is to be given of the passage lately quoted, in which Christ says that none is lost but the son of perdition. (John 17:12). The expression is not strictly proper; but it is by no means obscure; for Judas was not numbered among the sheep of Christ, because he was one truly, but because he held a place among them. Then, in another passage, where the Lord says that he was elected with the apostles, reference is made only to the office, "Have I not chosen you twelve," says He, "and one of you is a devil?" (John 6:70). That is, He had chosen him to the office of apostle. But when He speaks of election to salvation, He altogether excludes him from the number of the elect, "I speak not of you all: I know whom I have chosen" (John 13:18). Should anyone confound the term *election* in the two passages, he will miserably entangle himself, whereas if he distinguishes between them, nothing can be plainer.

Gregory, therefore, is most grievously and perniciously in error when he says that we are conscious only of our calling, but are uncertain of our election; and hence he exhorts all to fear and trembling, giving this as the reason, that though we know what we are today, yet we know not what we are to be. But in that passage, he clearly shows how he stumbled on that stone. By suspending election on the merit of works, he had too good a reason for dispiriting the minds of his readers, while, at the same time, as he did not lead them away from themselves to confidence in the divine goodness, he was unable to confirm them.

Hence, in some measure, believers may perceive the truth of what we said at the outset—viz. predestination duly considered does not shake faith, but rather affords the best confirmation of it. I deny not, however, that the Spirit sometimes accommodates His language to our feeble capacity, as when He says, "They shall not be in the assembly of my people, neither shall they be written in the writing of the house of Israel" (Ezekiel 13:9). As if God were beginning to write the names of those whom He counts among His people in the Book of Life; whereas we know, even on the testimony of Christ, that the names of the children of God were written in the Book of Life from the beginning. (See Luke 10:20.) The words simply indicate the abandonment of those who seemed to have a chief place among the elect, as is said in the psalm, "Let them be blotted out of the Book of the Living, and not be written with the righteous" (Psalm 69:28).

10 Explanation of the passages urged against the certainty of election. Examples by which some attempt to prove that the seed of election is sown in the hearts of the elect from their very birth. Answer. A. One or two examples do not make the rule. B. This view is opposed to Scripture. C. It is expressly opposed by an apostle.

For the elect are brought by calling into the fold of Christ, not from the very womb, nor all at the same time, but according as God sees it meet to dispense His grace. Before they are gathered to the supreme Shepherd, they wander dispersed in a common desert, and in no respect differ from others, except that by the special mercy of God they are kept from rushing to final destruction. Therefore, if you look to them, you will see the offspring of Adam giving token of the common corruption of the mass. That they proceed not to extreme and desperate impiety is not owing to any innate goodness in them, but because the eye of God watches for their safety and His hand is stretched over them.

Those who dream of some seed of election implanted in their hearts from their birth, by the agency of which they are ever inclined to piety and the fear of God, are not supported by the authority of Scripture, but refuted by experience. They, indeed, produce a few examples to prove that the elect, before they were enlightened, were not aliens from religion; for instance, that Paul led an unblemished life during his Pharisaism, that Cornelius was accepted for his prayers and alms, and so forth. (See Philippians 3:5; Acts 10:2.)

The case of Paul we admit, but we hold that they are in error as to Cornelius; for it appears that he was already enlightened and regenerated, so that all which he wanted was a clear revelation of the gospel. But what are they to extract from these few examples? Is it that all the elect were always endued with the spirit of piety? Just as well might anyone, after pointing to the integrity of Aristides, Socrates, Xenocrates, Scipio, Curios, Camillus, and others (see Book 2, chapter 4, section 4), infer that all who are left in the blindness of idolatry are studious of virtue and holiness. Nay, even Scripture is plainly opposed to them in more passages than one.

The description which Paul gives of the state of the Ephesians before regeneration shows not one grain of this seed. His words are, "You has he quickened, who were dead in trespasses and sins; wherein in time past ye walked according to the course of this world, according to the prince of the power of the air, the spirit that now worketh in the children of disobedience: among whom also we all had our conversation in times past in the lusts of our flesh, fulfilling the desires of the flesh and of the mind; and were by nature the children of wrath, even as others" (Ephesians 2:1-3). Again, "At that time ye were without Christ," "having no hope, and without God in the world" (Ephesians 2:12). Again, "Ye were sometimes darkness, but now are ye light in the Lord: walk as children of light" (Ephesians 5:8). But perhaps they will insist that in this last passage reference is made to that ignorance of the true God, in which they deny not that the elect lived before they were called. Though this is grossly inconsistent with the apostle's inference, that they were no longer to lie or steal. (See Ephesians 4:28.) What answer will they give to other passages; such as that in which, after declaring to the Corinthians that "neither fornicators, nor idolaters, nor adulterers, nor effeminate, nor abusers of themselves with mankind, nor thieves, nor covetous, nor drunkards, nor revilers, nor extortioners, shall inherit the kingdom of God," he immediately adds, "Such were some of you: but ye are washed, but ye are sanctified, but ye are justified in the name of the Lord Jesus, and by the Spirit of our God" (1 Corinthians 6:9-11)? Again, he says to the Romans, "As ye have yielded your members servants to uncleanness and to iniquity unto iniquity; even so now yield your members servants to righteousness unto holiness. For when ye were the servants of sin, ye were free from righteousness. What fruit had ye then in those things whereof ye are now ashamed?" (Romans 6:19-21).

11 An explanation and confirmation of the third answer.

S ay, then, what seed of election germinated in those who, contaminated in various ways during their whole lives, indulged as with desperate wickedness, in every kind of abomination? Had Paul meant to express this view, he ought to have shown how much they then owed to the kindness of God, by which they had been preserved from falling into such pollution. Thus, too, Peter ought to have exhorted his countrymen to gratitude for a perpetual seed of election. On the contrary, his admonition is, "The time past of our life may suffice us to have wrought the will of the Gentiles" (1 Peter 4:3). What if we come to examples? Was there any germ of righteousness in Rahab the harlot before she believed? (See Joshua 2:4.) In Manasseh when Jerusalem was dyed and almost deluged with the blood of the prophets? (See 2 Kings 23:16.) In the thief who only with his last breath, thought of repentance? (Luke 23:42).

Have done, then, with those arguments, which curious men of themselves rashly devise, without any authority from Scripture. But let us hold fast to what Scripture states—viz. that "All we like sheep have gone astray, we have turned everyone to his own way" (Isaiah 53:6); that is to perdition. In this gulf of perdition God leaves those whom He has determined one day to deliver until His own time arrives; He only preserves them from plunging into irremediable blasphemy.

12 Second part of the chapter, which treats of the reprobates. Some of them God deprives of the opportunity of hearing His Word. Others He blinds and stupefies the more by preaching it.

A s the Lord, by the efficacy of His calling, accomplishes towards His elect the salvation to which He had destined them by his eternal counsel, so He has judgments against the reprobates, by which He executes His counsel concerning them. Those, therefore, whom He has created for dishonor during life and destruction at death, that they may be vessels of wrath and examples of severity, in bringing to their doom, he at one time deprives of the means of hearing His Word, at another, by the preaching of it, blinds and stupefies them the more. The examples of the former case are innumerable, but let us select one of the most remarkable of all. Before the advent of Christ, about four thousand years passed away, during which he hid the light of saving doctrine from all nations. If anyone answers, that He did not put them in possession of the great blessing, because He judged them unworthy, then their posterity will be in no respect more worthy. Of this, in addition to experience, Malachi is a sufficient witness; for while charging them with mixed unbelief and blasphemy, he yet declares that the Redeemer will come. Why, then, is he given to the latter rather than to the former? They will in vain torment themselves in seeking for a deeper cause than the secret and inscrutable counsel of God. And there is no occasion to fear, lest some disciple of Porphyry with impunity arraign the justice of God, while we say nothing in its defense. For while we maintain that none perish without deserving it, and that it is owing to the free goodness of God that some are delivered, enough has been said for the display of His glory; there is not the least occasion for our caviling. The supreme Disposer then makes way for His own predestination, when depriving those whom He has reprobated of the communication of His light, He leaves them in blindness. Every day furnishes instances of the latter case, and many of them are set before us in Scripture.

Among a hundred to whom the same discourse is delivered, twenty, perhaps, receive it with the prompt obedience of faith; the others set no value upon it, or deride, spurn, or abominate it. If it is said that this diversity is owing to the malice and perversity of the latter, the answer is not satisfactory, for the same wickedness would possess the minds of the former, did not God in His goodness correct it. Hence, we will always be entangled until we call in the aid of Paul's question, "Who maketh thee to differ?" (1 Corinthians 4:7), intimating that some excel others, not by their own virtue, but by the mere favor of God.

13 Of this no other account can be given than that the reprobates are vessels fitted for destruction. This is confirmed by the case of the elect; of Pharaoh and of the Jewish people both before and after the manifestation of Christ.

Why, then, while bestowing grace on the one, does He pass by the other? In regard to the former, Luke gives the reason, Because they "...were ordained to eternal life" (Acts 13:48). What, then, shall we think of the latter, but that they are vessels of wrath unto dishonor? Wherefore, let us not decline to say with Augustine, "God could change the will of the wicked into good, because he is omnipotent. Clearly, He could. Why, then, does He not do it? Because He is unwilling. Why He is unwilling remains with himself."

We should not attempt to be wise above what is meet, and it is much better to take Augustine's explanation than to quibble with Chrysostom, "That He draws him who is willing, and stretching forth his hand," lest the difference should seem to lie in the judgment of God, and not in the mere will of man. So far is it, indeed, from being placed in the mere will of man, that we may add that even the pious, and those who fear God, need this special inspiration of the Spirit.

Lydia, a seller of purple, feared God, and yet it was necessary that her heart should be opened, that she might attend to the doctrine of Paul, and profit in it. (See Acts 16:14.) This was not said of one woman only, but to teach us that all progress in piety is the secret work of the Spirit.

Nor can it be questioned that God sends His Word to many whose blindness He is pleased to aggravate. For why does he order so many messages to be taken to Pharaoh? Was it because He hoped that he might be softened by the repetition? Nay, before He began, He both knew and had foretold the result: "The Lord said unto Moses, When thou goest to return into Egypt see that thou do all those wonders before Pharaoh, which I have put in thine hand: but I will harden his heart, that he will not let the people go" (Exodus 4:21). So when He raises up Ezekiel, He forewarns him, "I send thee to the children of Israel, to a rebellious nation that has rebelled against me." "Be not afraid of their words." "Thou dwellest in the midst of a rebellious house, which has eyes to see, and see not; they have ears to hear, and hear not" (Ezekiel 2:3, 6; 12:2). Thus, He foretells to Jeremiah that the effect of His doctrine would be, "To root out, and pull down, and to destroy" (Jeremiah 1:10).

But the prophecy of Isaiah presses still more closely; for he is thus commissioned by the Lord, "Go and tell this people, Hear ye indeed, but understand not, and see ye indeed but perceive not. Make the heart of this people fat, and make their ears heavy, and shut their eyes; lest they see with their eyes, and hear with their ears, and understand with their heart, and convert and be healed" (Isaiah 6:9, 10). Here He directs His voice to them, but it is that they may turn a deafer ear; He kindles a light, but it is that they may become more blind; He produces a doctrine, but it is that they may be more stupid; He employs a remedy, but it is that they may not be cured.

And John, referring to this prophecy, declares that the Jews could not believe the doctrine of Christ, because this curse from God lay upon them. It is also incontrovertible, that to those whom God is not pleased to illumine, He delivers His doctrine wrapped up in enigmas, so that they may not profit by it, but be given over to greater blindness.

Hence, our Savior declares that the parables in which he had spoken to the multitude He expounded to the apostles only, "Because it is given unto you to know the mysteries of the kingdom of heaven, but to them it is not given" (Matthew 13:11). What, you will ask, does our Lord mean, by teaching those by whom He is careful not to be understood? Consider where the fault lies, and then cease to ask. How obscure soever the Word may be, there is always sufficient light in it to convince the consciences of the ungodly.

14 Question, Why does God blind the reprobate? Two answers These are confirmed by different passages of Scripture. Objection of the reprobate. Answer.

It now remains to see why the Lord acts in the manner in which it is plain that He does. If the answer be given, that it is because men deserve this by their impiety, wickedness, and ingratitude, it is indeed well and truly said; but still, because it does not yet appear what the cause of the difference is, why some are turned to obedience and others remain obdurate, we must, in discussing it, pass to the passage from Moses, on which Paul has commented, namely, "Even for this same purpose have I raised thee up, that I might show my power in thee, and that my name might be declared throughout all the earth" (Romans 9:17).

The refusal of the reprobates to obey the Word of God, when it is manifested to them, will be properly ascribed to the malice and depravity of their hearts, provided it is at the same time added that they were adjudged to this depravity, because they were raised up by the just and inscrutable judgment of God, to show forth His glory by their condemnation.

In like manner, when it is said of the sons of Eli that they would not listen to salutary admonitions, "...because the Lord would slay them" (1 Samuel 2:25), it is not denied that their stubbornness was the result of their own iniquity; but it is at the same time stated why they were left to their stubbornness, when the Lord might have softened their hearts: namely, because His immutable decree had once for all doomed them to destruction.

Hence, the words of John, "Though he had done so many miracles before them, yet they believed not on him; that the saying of Esaias the prophet might be fulfilled which he spake, Lord, who has believed our report?" (John 12:37, 38); for though he does not exculpate their perverseness, he is satisfied with the reason that the grace of God is insipid to men, until the Holy Spirit gives it its savor.

And Christ, in quoting the prophecy of Isaiah, "They shall be all taught of God" (John 6:45), designs only to show that the Jews were reprobates and aliens from the Church, because they would not be taught; and he gives no other reason than that the promise of God does not belong to them. Confirmatory of this are the words of Paul, "Christ crucified" was "unto the Jews a stumbling block, and unto the Greeks foolishness; but unto them which are called, both Jews and Greeks, Christ the power of God, and the wisdom of God" (1 Corinthians 1:23). For after mentioning the usual result wherever the gospel is preached, that it exasperates some, and is despised by others, He says that it is precious to them only who are called. A little before, He had given them the name of believers, but He was unwilling to refuse the proper rank to divine grace, which precedes faith; or rather, He added the second term by way of correction, that those who had embraced the gospel might ascribe the merit of their faith to the calling of God. Thus, also, He shortly after shows that they were elected by God.

When the wicked hear these things, they complain that God abuses His inordinate power to make cruel sport with the miseries of His creatures. But let us, who know that all men are liable, on so many grounds, to the judgment of God, that they cannot answer for one in a thousand of their transgressions (Job 9:3), confess that the reprobate suffer nothing which is not accordant with the most perfect justice. When unable clearly to ascertain the reason, let us not decline to be somewhat in ignorance about the depths of the divine wisdom.

15 Objection to this doctrine of the righteous rejection of the reprobate. The first founded on a passage in Ezekiel. The passage is explained.

But since an objection is often founded on a few passages of Scripture in which God seems to deny that the wicked perish through His ordination, except as far as they spontaneously bring death upon themselves in opposition to His warning, let us briefly explain these passages and demonstrate that they are not adverse to the above view.

One of the passages adduced is, "Have I any pleasure at all that the wicked should die? saith the Lord God; and not that he should return from his ways and live?" (Ezekiel 18:23). If we are to extend this to the whole human race, why are not the very many whose minds might be more easily bent to obey urged to repentance, rather than those who by His invitations become daily more and more hardened? Our Lord declares that the preaching of the gospel and miracles would have produced more fruit among the people of Nineveh and Sodom than in Judea. (See Matthew 13:23.) Why is it, then, that if God would have all to be saved, He does not open a door of repentance for the wretched, who would more readily have received grace?

Hence, we may see that the passage is violently wrested, if the will of God, which the prophet mentions, is opposed to His eternal counsel by which He separated the elect from the reprobate.

Now, if the genuine meaning of the prophet is inquired into, it will be found that he only means to give the hope of pardon to them who repent. The sum is that God is undoubtedly ready to pardon whenever the sinner turns. Therefore, He does not will his death, as far as He wills repentance. But experience shows that this will, for the repentance of those whom He invites to himself, is not such as to make Him touch all their hearts. Still, it cannot be said that He acts deceitfully; for though the external Word only renders, those who hear its and do not obey it, inexcusable, it is still truly regarded as an evidence of the grace by which He reconciles men to himself.

Let us, therefore, hold the doctrine of the prophet, that God has no pleasure in the death of the sinner; that the godly may feel confident that whenever they repent, God is ready to pardon them; and that the wicked may feel that their guilt is doubled when they respond not to the great mercy and condescension of God. The mercy of God, therefore, will ever be ready to meet the penitent; but all the prophets, and apostles, and Ezekiel himself, clearly tell us to whom repentance is given.

16 A second objection is founded on a passage in Paul. The apostle's meaning is explained. A third objection and fourth objection answered.

The second passage adduced is that in which Paul says that "God will have all men to be saved" (1 Timothy 2:4). Though the reason here differs from the former, they have somewhat in common. I answer, first, That the mode in which God thus wills is plain from the context; for Paul connects two things, a will to be saved and a will to come to the knowledge of the truth. If by this they will have it to be fixed by the eternal counsel of God that they are to receive the doctrine of salvation, what is meant by Moses in these words, "What nation is there so great, who has God so nigh unto them?" (Deuteronomy 4:7).

Why are many nations deprived of that light of the Gospel which others enjoy? Why is it that the pure knowledge of the doctrine of godliness has never reached some, and others have scarcely tasted some obscure rudiments of it?

It will now be easy to extract the purport of Paul's statement. He had commanded Timothy that prayers should be regularly offered up in the Church for kings and princes, but as it seemed somewhat absurd that prayer should be offered up for a class of men who were almost hopeless (all of them being not only aliens from the Body of Christ, but doing their utmost to overthrow His kingdom), he adds, that it was acceptable to God, who will have all men to be saved. By this he assuredly means nothing more than that the way of salvation was not shut against any order of men; that, on the contrary, he had manifested His mercy in such a way, that He would have none debarred from it.

Other passages do not declare that which God, in His secret judgment, has determined with regard to all, but declare that pardon is prepared for all sinners who only turn to seek after it. For if they persist in urging the words, "God has concluded all in unbelief, that he might have mercy upon all" (Romans 11:32), I will, on the contrary, urge what is elsewhere written, "Our God is in the heavens: he has done whatsoever he has pleased" (Psalm 115:3). We must, therefore, expound the passage to reconcile it with another, I "... will be gracious to whom I will be gracious, and will show mercy on whom I will show mercy" (Exodus 33:19). He who selects those whom He is to visit in mercy does not impart it to all. But since it clearly appears that He is there speaking not of individuals, but of orders of men, let us have done with a longer discussion. At the same time, we ought to observe that Paul does not assert what God does always, everywhere, and in all circumstances, but leaves it free to him to make kings and magistrates partakers of heavenly doctrine, though in their blindness they rage against it.

A stronger objection seems to be founded on the passage in Peter; the Lord is "...not willing that any should perish, but that all should come to repentance" (2 Peter 3:9). But the solution of the difficulty is to be found in the second branch of the sentence, for His will that they should come to repentance cannot be used in any other sense than that which is uniformly employed.

Conversion is undoubtedly in the hand of God, whether He designs to convert all can be learned from himself, when He promises that He will give some a heart of flesh and leave to others a heart of stone. (See Ezekiel 36:26.) It is true that if He were not disposed to receive those who implore His mercy, it could not have been said, "Turn ye unto me, saith the Lord of Hosts, and I will turn unto you, saith the Lord of Hosts" (Zechariah 1:3); but I hold that no man approaches God unless previously influenced from above. And if repentance were placed at the will of man, Paul would not say, "If God peradventure will give them repentance" (2 Timothy 2:25). Nay, did not God at the very time when He is verbally exhorting all to repentance, influence the elect by the secret movement of his Spirit, Jeremiah would not say, "Turn thou me, and I shall be turned; for thou art the Lord my God. Surely after that I was turned, I repented" (Jeremiah 31:18).

17 A fifth objection—viz. that there seems to be a twofold will in God. Answer. Other objections and answers. Conclusion.

But if it is so (you will say), little faith can be put in the gospel promises, which, in testifying concerning the will of God, declare that He wills what is contrary to His inviolable decree. Not at all. For however universal the promises of salvation may be, there is no discrepancy between them and the predestination of the reprobate, provided we attend to their effect. We know that the promises are effectual only when we receive them in faith, but, on the contrary, when faith is made void, the promise is of no effect. If this is the nature of the promises, let us now see whether there be any inconsistency between the two things—viz. that God, by an eternal decree, fixed the number of those whom He is pleased to embrace in love, and on whom He is pleased to display His wrath, and that He offers salvation indiscriminately to all.

I hold that they are perfectly consistent, for all that is meant by the promise is, just that His mercy is offered to all who desire and implore it, and this none do, save those whom He has enlightened. Moreover, he enlightens those whom He has predestinated to salvation. Thus, the truth of the promises remains firm and unshaken, so that it cannot be said there is any disagreement between the eternal election of God and the testimony of His grace, which he offers to believers.

But why does He mention all men? Namely, that the consciences of the righteous may rest the more secure when they understand that there is no difference between sinners, provided they have faith, and that the ungodly may not be able to allege that they have not an asylum to which they may retake themselves from the bondage of sin, while they ungratefully reject the offer which is made to them. Therefore, since by the gospel the mercy of God is offered to both, it is faith, in other words, the illumination of God, which distinguishes between the righteous and the wicked, the former feeling the efficacy of the gospel, the latter obtaining no benefit from it. Illumination itself has eternal election for its rule.

Another passage quoted is the lamentation of our Savior, "O Jerusalem, Jerusalem, how often would I have gathered thy children together, even as a hen gathereth her chickens under her wings, and ye would not!" (Matthew 23:37); but it gives them no support. I admit that here Christ speaks not only in the character of man, but upbraids them with having, in every age, rejected His grace. But this will of God, of which we speak, must be defined. For it is well known what exertions the Lord made to retain that people, and how perversely from the highest to the lowest, they followed their own wayward desires, and refused to be gathered together. But it does not follow that by the wickedness of men, the counsel of God was frustrated. They object that nothing is less accordant with the nature of God than that He should have a double will. This I concede, provided they are sound interpreters. But why do they not attend to the many passages in which God clothes himself with human affections and descends beneath His proper majesty? He says, "I have spread out my hands all the day unto a rebellious people" (Isaiah 65:1), exerting himself early and late to bring them back. Were they to apply these qualities without regarding the figure, many unnecessary disputes would arise which are quashed by the simple solution that what is human is here transferred to God. Indeed, the solution which we have given elsewhere (see Book 1, chapter 18, section 3; and Book 3, chapter 20, section 43) is amply sufficient—viz. that, though to our apprehension, the will of God is manifold, yet He does not in himself will opposites, but, according to His manifold wisdom (so Paul styles it, Ephesians 3:10), transcends our senses, until such time as it shall be given us to know how He mysteriously wills what now seems to be adverse to His will.

They also amuse themselves with the cavil that since God is the Father of all, it is unjust to discard anyone before He by His misconduct has merited such a punishment as if the kindness of God did not extend even to dogs and swine. But if we confine our view to the human race, let them tell why God selected one people for himself and became their Father, and why, from that one people, He plucked only a small number as if they were the flower. But those who thus charge God are so blinded by their love of evil speaking, that they consider not that as God "...maketh his sun to rise on the evil and on the good" (Matthew 5:45), so the inheritance is treasured up for a few to whom it shall one day be said, "Come, ye blessed of my Father, inherit the kingdom" (Matthew 25:34).

They object, moreover, that God does not hate any of the things which He has made. This I concede, but it does not affect the doctrine which I maintain, that the reprobate are hateful to God and that with perfect justice, since those destitute of His Spirit cannot produce anything that does not deserve cursing. They add that there is no distinction between Jew and Gentile, and that, therefore, the grace of God is held forth to all indiscriminately: true, provided they admit (as Paul declares) that God calls Jews as Gentiles as well, according to His good pleasure, without being astricted to any. This disposes of their gloss upon another passage, "God has concluded all in unbelief, that he might have mercy upon all" (Romans 11:32); in other words, He wills that all who are saved should ascribe their salvation to His mercy, although the blessing of salvation is not common to all. Finally, after all that has been adduced on this side and on that let it be our conclusion to feel overawed with Paul at the great depth, and if petulant tongues will still murmur, let us not be ashamed to join in his exclamation, "Nay, but, O man, who art thou that replies against God?" (Romans 9:20). Truly does Augustine maintain that it is perverse to measure divine by the standard of human justice.

Chapter 25

OF THE LAST RESURRECTION

There are four principal heads in this chapter: I. The utility, necessity, truth, and irrefragable evidence of the orthodox doctrine of a final resurrection—a doctrine unknown to philosophers, sections 1-4. II. Refutation of the objections to this doctrine by atheists, Sadducees, Chiliasts, and other fanatics, sections 5-7. III. The nature of the final resurrection explained, sections 8, 9. IV. Of the eternal felicity of the elect and the everlasting misery of the reprobate.

Sections

1. For invincible perseverance in our calling, it is necessary to be animated with the blessed hope of our Savior's final advent.

2. The perfect happiness reserved for the elect at the final resurrection, unknown to philosophers.

3. The truth and necessity of this doctrine of a final resurrection. To confirm our belief in it we have: A. The example of Christ; and, B. The omnipotence of God. There is an inseparable connection between us and our risen Savior. The bodies of the elect must be conformed to the body of their Head. It is now in Heaven. Therefore, our bodies also must rise, and, reanimated by their souls, reign with Christ in Heaven. The Resurrection of Christ is a pledge of ours.

4. As God is omnipotent, He can raise the dead. Resurrection is explained by a natural process. The vision of dry bones.

5. The second part of the chapter, refuting objections to the doctrine of resurrection. A. Atheists. B. Sadducees. C. Chiliasts. Their evasion. Various answers. E. Universalists. Answer.

6. Objections continued. E. Some speculators who imagine that death destroys the whole man. Refutation. The condition and abode of souls from death until the last day. What is meant by the bosom of Abraham.

7. *Refutation of some weak men and Manichees, pretending that new bodies are to be given. Refutation confirmed by various arguments and passages of Scripture.*

8. *Refutation of the fiction of new bodies continued.*

9. *Shall the wicked rise again? Answer in the affirmative. Why the wicked shall rise again. Why resurrection is promised to the elect only.*

10. *The last part of the chapter, treating of eternal felicity; its excellence transcends our capacity. Rules to be observed. The glory of all the saints will not be equal.*

11. *Without rewarding questions which merely puzzle, an answer is given to some which are not without use.*

12. *As the happiness of the elect, so the misery of the reprobates, will be without measure and without end.*

1 For invincible perseverance in our calling, it is necessary to be animated with the blessed hope of our Savior's final advent.

Christ, the Sun of righteousness, shines upon us through the gospel, and as Paul declares, after conquering death, has given us the light of life. Hence, we believe that we have passed from "death unto life" and are no longer strangers and pilgrims, but fellow-citizens with the saints of the household of God, who has made us sit with His only begotten Son in heavenly places. We know that nothing is wanting to our complete felicity. Yet, lest we should feel it grievous to be exercised under a hard warfare, as if the victory obtained by Christ had produced no fruit, we must attend to what is elsewhere taught concerning the nature of hope. For since we hope for what we see not, and faith, as is said in another passage, is "...the evidence of things not seen," so long as we are imprisoned in the body we are absent from the Lord. For which reason Paul says, "Ye are dead, and your life is hid with Christ in God. When Christ, who is our life, shall appear, then shall ye also appear with him in glory."

Our present condition, therefore, requires us to "live soberly, righteously, and godly," "looking for that blessed hope, and the glorious appearing of the great God and our Savior Jesus Christ." Here there is need of no ordinary patience, lest, worn out with fatigue, we either turn backwards or abandon our post. Wherefore, all that has hitherto been said of our salvation, calls upon us to raise our minds towards Heaven, that, as Peter exhorts, though we now see not Christ, "yet believing," we may "rejoice with joy unspeakable and full of glory," receiving the end of our faith, even the salvation of our souls.

For this reason Paul says that the faith and charity of the saints have respect to the faith and hope which is laid up for them in Heaven. (See Colossians 1:5.) When we thus keep our eyes fixed upon Christ in Heaven, and nothing on Earth prevents us from directing them to the promised blessedness, there is a true fulfillment of the saying, "Where your treasure is, there will your heart be also" (Matthew 6:21).

Hence, the reason that faith is so rare in the world; nothing being more difficult for our sluggishness than to surmount innumerable obstacles in striving for the prize of our high calling. To the immense load of miseries, which almost overwhelm us, are added the jeers of profane men, who assail us for our simplicity, when spontaneously renouncing the allurements of the present life we seem, in seeking a happiness which lies hid from us, to catch at a fleeting shadow.

In short, we are beset above and below, behind and before, with violent temptations, which our minds would be altogether unable to withstand, were they not set free from earthly objects and devoted to the heavenly life, though apparently remote from us. Wherefore, he alone has made solid progress in the gospel who has acquired the habit of meditating continually on a blessed resurrection.

2 The perfect happiness reserved for the elect at the final resurrection unknown to philosophers.

In ancient times philosophers discoursed, and even debated with each other, concerning the chief good; none, however, except Plato, acknowledged that it consisted in union with God. He could not, however, form even an imperfect idea of its true nature; nor is this strange, as he had learned nothing of the sacred bond of that union. We, even, in this our earthly pilgrimage, know wherein our perfect and only felicity consists—a felicity which, while we long for it, daily inflames our hearts more and more, until we attain to full fruition. Therefore, I said that none participate in the benefits of Christ, save those who raise their minds to the resurrection. This, accordingly, is the mark which Paul sets before believers and at which he says they are to aim, forgetting everything until they reach it. (See

Philippians 3:8.) The more strenuously, therefore, must we contend for it, lest if the world engrosses us, we be severely punished for our sloth. Accordingly, he in another passage distinguishes believers by this mark, that their conversation is in heaven, from whence they look for the Savior. (See Philippians 3:20.) And that they may not faint in their course, he associates all the other creatures with them. As shapeless ruins are everywhere seen, he says that all things in Heaven and Earth struggle for renovation. For since Adam by his fall destroyed the proper order of nature, the creatures groan under the servitude to which they have been subjected through his sin; not that they are at all endued with sense, but that they naturally long for the state of perfection from which they have fallen. Paul therefore describes them as groaning and travailing in pain (see Romans 8:19), so that we who have received the first fruits of the Spirit may be ashamed to grovel in our corruption, instead of at least imitating the inanimate elements, which are bearing the punishment of another's sin. And in order that he may stimulate us the more powerfully, he terms the final advent of Christ our *redemption*. It is true, indeed, that all the parts of our redemption are already accomplished; but as Christ was once offered for sins (see Hebrews 9:28), so He shall again appear without sin unto salvation. Whatever, then, be the afflictions by which we are pressed, let this redemption sustain us until its final accomplishment.

3 The truth and necessity of this doctrine of a final resurrection. To confirm our belief in it we have, A. The example of Christ; and, B. The omnipotence of God. There is an inseparable connection between us and our risen Savior. The bodies of the elect must be conformed to the body of their Head. It is now in Heaven. Therefore, our bodies also must rise, and, reanimated by their souls, reign with Christ in Heaven. The Resurrection of Christ is a pledge of ours.

The very importance of the subject ought to increase our ardor. Paul justly contends, that if Christ rise not, the whole gospel is delusive and vain (see 1 Corinthians 15:14-17); for our condition would be more miserable than that of other mortals, because we are exposed to much hatred and insult and incur danger every hour; nay, are like sheep destined for slaughter; and hence the authority of the gospel would fail, not in one part merely, but in its very essence, including both our adoption and the accomplishment of our salvation. Let us, therefore, give heed to a matter of all others the most serious, so that no length of time may produce weariness.

I have deferred the brief consideration to be given of it to this place, that my readers may learn, when they have received Christ, the Author of perfect salvation, to rise higher, and know that He is clothed with heavenly immortality and glory in order that the whole body may be rendered conformable to the Head. For thus the Holy Spirit is ever setting before us in His person an example of the resurrection. It is difficult to believe that after our bodies have been consumed with rottenness, they sill rise again at their appointed time.

Hence, while many of the philosophers maintained the immortality of the soul, few of them assented to the resurrection of the body. Although in this they were inexcusable, we are thereby reminded that the subject is too difficult for human apprehension to reach it. To enable faith to surmount the great difficulty, Scripture furnishes two auxiliary proofs, the one the likeness of Christ's resurrection, and the other the omnipotence of God. Therefore, whenever the subject of the resurrection is considered, let us think of the case of our Savior, who, having completed his mortal course in our nature, which he had assumed, obtained immortality and is now the pledge of our future resurrection. For in the miseries by which we are beset, we always bear "...about in the body the dying of the Lord Jesus, that the life also of Jesus might be made manifest in our mortal flesh" (2 Corinthians 4:10). It is not lawful, it is not even possible, to separate Him from us without dividing Him.

Hence, Paul's argument, "If there be no resurrection of the dead, then is Christ not risen" (1 Corinthians 15:13). He assumes it as an acknowledged principle, that when Christ was subjected to death, and by rising gained a victory over death, it was not on His own account, but in the Head was begun what must necessarily be fulfilled in all the members, according to the degree and order of each. For it would not be proper to be made equal to Him in all respects. It is said in the Psalm, "Neither wilt thou suffer thine Holy One to see corruption" (Psalm 16:10). Although a portion of this confidence appertains to us according to the measure bestowed on us, yet the full effect appeared only in Christ, who, free from all corruption, resumed a spotless body.

Then, that there may be no doubt as to our fellowship with Christ in a blessed resurrection, and that we may be contented with this pledge, Paul distinctly affirms that he sits in the heavens, and will come as a judge on the last day for the express purpose of changing our vile body "...that it may be fashioned like unto his glorious body" (Philippians 3:21). He elsewhere says that God did not raise up His Son from death to give an isolated specimen of His mighty power, but that the Spirit exerts the same efficacy in regard to those who believe. Accordingly, He says that the Spirit, when He dwells in us, is life, because the end for which He was given is to quicken our mortal body. (See Romans 8:10, 11; Colossians 3:4.)

I briefly glance at subjects which might be treated more copiously, and deserve to be adorned more splendidly, and yet in the little I have said I trust pious readers will find sufficient materials for building up their faith. Christ rose again that He might have us as partakers with Him of future life. The Father raised Him up, inasmuch as He was the Head of the Church, from which He cannot possibly be dissevered. He was raised up by the power of the Spirit, who also in us performs the office of quickening. In fine, He was raised up to be the resurrection and the life. But as we have said that in this mirror we behold a living image of the resurrection, so it furnishes sure evidence to support our minds, provided we do not faint or grow weary at the long delay. It is not up to us to measure the periods of time at our own pleasure. We are to rest patiently until God in His own time renews His kingdom. To this Paul refers when he says, "But every man in his own order: Christ the first fruits; afterward they that are Christ's at his coming" (1 Corinthians 15:23).

But lest any question should be raised as to the Resurrection of Christ on which ours is founded, we see how often and in what various ways He has borne testimony to it. Scoffing men will deride the narrative, which is given by the evangelist as a childish fable. For what importance will they attach to a message which timid women bring and the disciples almost dead with fear, afterwards confirm? Why does not Christ rather place the illustrious trophies of His victory in the midst of the Temple and the forum? Why does He not come forth, and in the presence of Pilate strike terror? Why does He not show himself alive again to the priests and all Jerusalem? Profane men will scarcely admit that the witnesses whom he selects are well qualified. I answer that although their infirmity was contemptible at the commencement, yet the whole was directed by the admirable providence of God. Partly from love to Christ and religious zeal, partly from incredulity, those who were lately overcome with fear now hurry to the sepulcher, not only that they might be eyewitnesses of the fact, but also that they might hear angels announce what they actually saw.

How can we question the veracity of those who regarded what the women told them as a fable, until they saw the reality? It is not strange that the whole people and the governor, after they were furnished with sufficient evidence for conviction, were not allowed to see Christ or the other signs. (See Matthew 27:66; 28:11.) The sepulcher is sealed, sentinels keep watch, and on the third day, the body is not found. The soldiers are bribed to spread the report that His disciples had stolen the body. As if they had had the means of deforming a band of soldiers, or been supplied with weapons, or been trained to make such a daring attempt. But if the soldiers had not courage enough to repel them, why did they not follow and apprehend some of them by the aid of the populace? Pilate, therefore, in fact, put his signet to the Resurrection of Christ, and the guards who were placed at the sepulcher, by their silence or falsehood, became heralds of His resurrection.

Meanwhile, the voice of angels was heard, "He is not here, but is risen" (Luke 24:6). The celestial splendor plainly shows that they were not men but angels.

Afterwards, if any doubt remained, Christ himself removed it. The disciples saw Him frequently; they even touched His hands and His feet, and their unbelief is of no little avail in confirming our faith. He discoursed to them of the mysteries of the Kingdom of God, and at length, while they beheld, ascended to Heaven. This spectacle was exhibited not to eleven apostles only, but was seen by more than five hundred brethren at once. (See 1 Corinthians 15:6.) Then, by sending the Holy Spirit, He gave a proof not only of life but also of supreme power, as He had foretold, "It is expedient for you that I go away: for if I go not away, the Comforter will not come unto you" (John 16:7). Paul was not thrown down on the way by the power of a dead man, but felt that He whom he was opposing was possessed of sovereign authority. To Stephen He appeared for another purpose—viz. that he might overcome the fear of death by the certainty of life. To refuse assent to these numerous and authentic proofs is not diffidence, but depraved and, therefore, it is infatuated obstinacy.

4 As God is omnipotent, He can raise the dead. Resurrection is explained by a natural process. The vision of dry bones.

We have said that in proving the resurrection our thoughts must be directed to the immense power of God. This Paul briefly teaches, when he says that the Lord Jesus Christ, "...shall change our vile body, that it may be fashioned like unto his glorious body, according to the working of that mighty power whereby he is able even to subdue all things unto himself" (Philippians 3:21). Wherefore, nothing can be more incongruous than to look here at what can be done naturally when the subject presented to us is an inestimable miracle, which by its magnitude absorbs our senses. Paul, however, by producing a proof from nature, confutes the senselessness of those who deny the resurrection. "Thou fool, that which thou sowest is not quickened except it die," etc. (1 Corinthians 15:36). He says that in seed there is a species of resurrection, because the crop is produced from corruption. Nor would the thing be so difficult of belief were we as attentive as we ought to be to the wonders which meet our eye in every quarter of the world. But let us remember that none is truly persuaded of the future resurrection save he who, carried away with admiration gives God the glory.

Elated with this conviction Isaiah exclaims, "Thy dead men shall live, together with my dead body shall they arise. Awake and sing, ye that dwell in dust" (Isaiah 26:19). In desperate circumstances he rises to God, the Author of life, in whose hand are "the issues from death" (Psalm 68:20). Job, also, when more like a dead body than a living being, trusts the power of God and does not hesitate, as if in full vigor to rise to that day: "I know that my Redeemer liveth, and that He will stand at the latter day upon the earth." (That is, that he will there exert His power.) "...and though after my skin worms destroy this body, yet in my flesh shall I see God; whom I shall see for myself, and mine eyes shall behold, and not another" (Job 19:25-27). For though some have recourse to a more subtle interpretation, by which they wrest these passages, as if they were not to be understood of the resurrection, they only confirm what they are desirous to overthrow; for holy men, in seeking consolation in their misfortunes, have recourse for alleviation merely to the similitude of a resurrection.

This is better learned from a passage in Ezekiel. When the Jews scouted the promise of return, and objected that the probability of it was not greater than that of the dead coming forth from the tomb, there is presented to the prophet in vision a field covered with dry bones, which at the command of God recover sinews and flesh. Though under that figure he encourages the people to hope for return, yet the ground of hope is taken from the resurrection, as it is the special type of all the deliverances, which believers experience in this world. Thus Christ declares that the voice of the gospel gives life, but because the Jews did not receive it, he immediately adds, "Marvel not at this; for the hour is coming in which all that are in the grave shall hear his voice, and shall come forth" (John 5:28, 29). Wherefore, amid all our conflicts let us exult after the example of Paul, that he who has promised us future life "is able to keep that" which "is committed unto him," and thus glory that there is laid up for us "a crown of righteousness, which the Lord, the righteous judge, shall give" (2 Timothy 1:12; 4:8). Thus, all the hardships which we may endure will be a demonstration of our future life, "...seeing it is a righteous thing with God to recompense tribulation to them that trouble you; and to you who are troubled rest with us, when the Lord Jesus shall be revealed from heaven with his mighty angels, in flaming fire" (2 Thessalonians 1:6-8). But we must attend to what he shortly after adds—viz. that he "...shall come to be glorified in his saints, and to be admired in all them that believe," by receiving the gospel.

5 The second part of the chapter, refuting objections to the doctrine of resurrection. A. Atheists. B. Sadducees. C. Chiliasts. Their evasion. Various answers. E. Universalists. Answer.

Although the minds of men ought to be occupied perpetually with these pursuits, yet, as if they actually resolved to banish all remembrance of the resurrection, they have called death the end of all things, the extinction of man. For Solomon certainly expresses the commonly received opinion when he says, "A living dog is better than a dead lion" (Ecclesiastes 9:4). Again, "Who knoweth the spirit of man that goes upward, and the spirit of the beast that goes downward to the earth?"

In all ages a brutish stupor has prevailed, and, accordingly, it has made its way into the very Church; for the Sadducees had the hardihood openly to profess that there was no resurrection, nay, that the soul was mortal. (See Mark 12:18; Luke 20:27.) But that this gross ignorance might be no excuse, unbelievers, by natural instinct, have always had an image of the resurrection before their eyes. For why the sacred and inviolable custom of burying, but that it might be the earnest of a new life? Nor can it be said that it had its origin in error, for the solemnity of sepulture always prevailed among the holy patriarchs, and God was pleased that the same custom should continue among the Gentiles, in order that the image of the resurrection thus presented might shake off their torpor. But although that ceremony was without profit, yet it is useful to us if we prudently consider its end, because it is no feeble refutation of infidelity that all men agreed in professing what none of them believed. But not only did Satan stupefy the senses of mankind, so that with their bodies they buried the remembrance of the resurrection, but he also managed by various fictions so to corrupt this branch of doctrine that it at length was lost. Not to mention that even in the days of Paul he began to assail it (see 1 Corinthians 15), shortly after the Chiliasts arose, who limited the reign of Christ to a thousand years. This fiction is too puerile to need or to deserve refutation. Nor do they receive any countenance from the Apocalypse, from which it is known that they extracted a gloss for their error (see Revelation 20:4), since the thousand years there mentioned refer not to the eternal blessedness of the Church, but only to the various troubles which await the Church militant in this world.

The whole Scripture proclaims that there will be no end either to the happiness of the elect or the punishment of the reprobate. Moreover, in regard to all things, which lie beyond our sight, and far transcend the reach of our intellect, belief must either be founded on the sure oracles of God or be altogether renounced. Those who assign only a thousand years to the children of God to enjoy the inheritance of future life observe not how great an insult they offer to Christ and His kingdom. If they are not to be clothed with immortality, then Christ himself, into whose glory they shall be transformed, has not been received into immortal glory; if their blessedness is to have an end, the Kingdom of Christ, on whose solid structure it rests, is temporary.

In short, they are either most ignorant of all divine things, or they maliciously aim at subverting the whole grace of God and power of Christ, which cannot have their full effects unless sin is obliterated, death is swallowed up, and eternal life is fully renewed. How stupid and frivolous their fear that too much severity will be ascribed to God, if the reprobates are doomed to eternal punishment, even the blind may see. The Lord, forsooth, will be unjust if He excludes from His kingdom those who, by their ingratitude shall have rendered themselves unworthy of it. But their sins are temporary.

I admit it; but then the majesty of God, and also the justice which they have violated by their sins are eternal. Justly, therefore, the memory of their iniquity does not perish. But in this way, the punishment will exceed the measure of the fault. It is intolerable blasphemy to hold the majesty of God in so little estimation, as not to regard the contempt of it as of greater consequence than the destruction of a single soul. But let us have done with these triflers, that we may not seem (contrary to what we first observed) to think their dreams deserving of refutation.

6 Objections continued. E. Some speculators who imagine that death destroys the whole man. Refutation. The condition and abode of souls from death until the last day. What meant by the bosom of Abraham.

Besides these, other two dreams have been invented by men who indulge in a wicked curiosity. Some, under the idea that the whole man perishes, have thought that the soul will rise again with the body, while others, admitting that spirits are immortal, hold that they will be clothed with new bodies, and thus deny the resurrection of the flesh. Having already adverted to the former point when speaking of the creation of man, it will be sufficient again to remind the reader how groveling an error it is to convert a spirit, formed after the image of God, into an evanescent breath, which animates the body only during this fading life, and to reduce the temple of the Holy Spirit to nothing; in short, to rob of the badge of immortality that part of ourselves in which the divinity is most refulgent and the marks of immortality conspicuous, so as to make the condition of the body better and more excellent than that of the soul.

Very different is the course taken by Scripture, which compares the body to a tabernacle, from which it describes us as migrating when we die, because it estimates us by that part which distinguishes us from the lower animals. Thus, Peter, in reference to his approaching death, says, "Knowing that shortly I must put off this my tabernacle" (2 Peter 1:14). Paul, again, speaking of believers, after saying, "If our earthly house of this tabernacle were dissolved, we have a building of God," adds, "Whilst we are at home in the body, we are absent from the Lord" (2 Corinthians 5:1, 6). Did not the soul survive the body, how could it be present with the Lord on being separated from the body? But an apostle removes all doubt when he says that we go "…to the spirits of just men made perfect" (Hebrews 12:23); by these words meaning, that we are associated with the holy patriarchs, who, even when dead, cultivate the same piety, so that we cannot be the members of Christ unless we unite with them.

If the soul, when unclothed from the body, did not retain its essence and remain capable of beatific glory, our Savior would not have said to the thief, "Today shalt thou be with me in paradise" (Luke 23:43). Trusting to these clear proofs, let us doubt not, after the example of our Savior, to commend our spirits to God when we come to die, or after the example of Stephen, to commit ourselves to the protection of Christ, who, with good reason, is called, "The Shepherd and Bishop" of our souls. (See Acts 7:59; 1 Peter 2:25.) Moreover, to pry curiously into their intermediate state is neither lawful nor expedient. Many greatly torment themselves with discussing what place they occupy and whether or not they already enjoy celestial glory. It is foolish and rash to inquire into hidden things further than God permits us to know. Scripture, after telling that Christ is present with them, and receives them into paradise (see John 12:32), and that they are comforted while the souls of the reprobates suffer the torments, which they have merited, goes no further. What teacher or doctor will reveal to us what God has concealed?

As to the place of abode, the question is not less futile and inept, since we know that the dimension of the soul is not the same as that of the body. When the abode of blessed spirits is designated as the *bosom of Abraham*, it is plain that, on quitting this pilgrimage, they are received by the common Father of the faithful, who imparts to them the fruit of His faith. Still, since Scripture uniformly enjoins us to look with expectation to the advent of Christ, and delays the crown of glory until that period, let us be contented with the limits divinely prescribed to us—viz. that the souls of the righteous, after their warfare is ended, obtain blessed rest, where in joy they wait for the fruition of promised glory. Thus, the result is suspended until Christ the Redeemer appears. There can be no doubt that the reprobates have the same doom as that which Jude assigns to the devils; they are "...reserved in everlasting chains under darkness unto the judgment of the great day" (Jude 6).

7 Refutation of some weak men and Manichees, pretending that new bodies are to be given. Refutation confirmed by various arguments and passages of Scripture.

Equally monstrous is the error of those who imagine that the soul, instead of resuming the body with which it is now clothed, will obtain a new and different body. Nothing can be more futile than the reason given by the Manichees—viz. that it would be incongruous for impure flesh to rise again: as if there were no impurity in the soul; and yet this does not exclude it from the hope of heavenly life. It is just as if they were to say, that what is infected by the taint of sin cannot be divinely purified; for I now say nothing to the delirious dream that flesh is naturally impure as having been created by the devil.

I only maintain that nothing in us at present, which is unworthy of Heaven, is any obstacle to the resurrection. But, first, Paul enjoins believers to purify themselves from "...all filthiness of the flesh and spirit" (2 Corinthians 7:1). In the judgment which is to follow, everyone shall "...receive the things done in his body, according to that he has done, whether it be good or bad" (2 Corinthians 5:10). This accords with what he says to the Corinthians, "That the life also of Jesus might be made manifest in our body" (2 Corinthians 4:10). For which reason he elsewhere says, "I pray God your whole spirit and soul and body be preserved blameless unto the coming of our Lord Jesus Christ" (1 Thessalonians 5:23). He says "body" as well as "spirit and soul," and no wonder; for it would be most absurd that bodies which God has dedicated to himself as temples should fall into corruption without hope of resurrection. What? Are they not also the members of Christ? Does he not pray that God would sanctify every part of them, and enjoin them to celebrate His name with their tongues, lift up pure hands, and offer sacrifices? That part of man, therefore, which the heavenly Judge so highly honors, what madness is it for any mortal man to reduce to dust without hope of revival?

In like manner, when Paul exhorts, "Glorify God in your body, and in your spirit, which are God's," he certainly does not allow that that which he claims for God as sacred is to be adjudged to eternal corruption. Nor, indeed, on any subject does Scripture furnish clearer explanation than on the resurrection of our flesh. "This corruptible [says Paul] must put on incorruption, and this mortal must put on immortality" (1 Corinthians 15:53).

If God formed new bodies, where would be this change of quality? If it were said that we must be renewed, the ambiguity of the expression might, perhaps, afford room for cavil; but here, pointing with the finger to the bodies with which we are clothed, and promising that they shall be incorruptible, he very plainly affirms that no new bodies are to be fabricated. "Nay," as Tertullian says, "he could not have spoken more expressly, if he had held his skin in his hands." Nor can any quibbling enable them to evade the force of another passage, in which Christ is declared to be the Judge of the world; he quotes from Isaiah, "As I live, saith the Lord, every knee shall bow to me" (Romans 14:11; Isaiah 45:23). He openly declares that those whom he was addressing will have to give an account of their lives. This could not be true if new bodies were to be sisted to the tribunal.

Moreover, there is no ambiguity in the words of Daniel, "Many of them that sleep in the dust of the earth shall awake, some to everlasting life, and some to shame and everlasting contempt" (Daniel 12:2); since he does not bring new matter from the four elements to compose men, but calls forth the dead from their graves. The reason which dictates this is plain. For if death, which originated in the fall of man, is adventitious, the renewal produced by Christ must be in the same body, which began to be mortal. Certainly, since the Athenians mocked Paul for asserting the resurrection (Acts 17:32), we may infer what his preaching was: their derision is of no small force to confirm our faith.

The saying of our Savior, also, is worthy of observation, "Fear not them which kill the body, but are not able to kill the soul: but rather fear him which is able to destroy both soul and body in hell" (Matthew 10:28). Here there would be no ground for fear, were not the body which we now have liable to punishment. Nor is another saying of our Savior less obscure, "The hour is coming, in the which all that are in the graves shall hear his voice, and shall come forth; they that have done good, unto the resurrection of life; and they that have done evil, unto the resurrection of damnation" (John 5:28, 29).

Shall we say that the soul rests in the grave, that it may there hear the voice of Christ, and not, rather, that the body shall at His command resume the vigor which it had lost? Moreover, if we are to receive new bodies, where will be the conformity of the Head and the members? Christ rose again. Was it by forming for himself a new body? Nay, he had foretold, "Destroy this temple, and in three days I will raise it up" (John 2:19). The mortal body which He had formerly carried He again received, for it would not have availed us much if a new body had been substituted, and that which had been offered in expiatory sacrifice had been destroyed. Therefore, we must attend to that connection, which the apostle celebrates, that we rise because Christ rose (see 1 Corinthians 15:12); nothing being less probable than that the flesh in which we bear about the dying of Christ, shall have no share in the Resurrection of Christ. This was even manifested by a striking example, when, at the Resurrection of Christ, many bodies of the saints came forth from their graves. For it cannot be denied that this was a prelude, or rather earnest of the final resurrection for which we hope, such as already existed in Enoch and Elijah, whom Tertullian calls *candidates for resurrection*, because, exempted from corruption, both in body and soul, they were received into the custody of God.

8 Refutation of the fiction of new bodies continued.

I am ashamed to waste so many words on so clear a matter, but my readers will kindly submit to the annoyance, in order that perverse and presumptuous minds may not be able to avail themselves of any flaw to deceive the simple. The volatile spirits with whom I now dispute adduce the fiction of their own brains, that in the resurrection there will be a creation of new bodies. Their only reason for thinking so is that it seems to them incredible that a dead body, long wasted by corruption, should return to its former state. Therefore, mere unbelief is the parent of their opinion. The Spirit of God, on the contrary, uniformly exhorts us in Scripture to hope for the resurrection of our flesh. For this reason baptism is, according to Paul, a seal of our future resurrection; and in like manner the holy supper invites us confidently to expect it, when with our mouths we receive the symbols of spiritual grace. Certainly the whole exhortation of Paul, "Yield ye your members as instruments of righteousness unto God," (Romans 6:13), would be frigid, did he not add, as he does in another passage, "He that raised up Christ from the dead shall also quicken your mortal bodies" (Romans 8:11).

For what would it avail to apply feet, hands, eyes, and tongues to the service of God, did not these afterwards participate in the benefit and reward? This Paul expressly confirms when he says, "The body is not for fornication, but for the Lord; and the Lord for the body. And God has both raised up the Lord, and will also raise up us by his own power" (1 Corinthians 6:13, 14).

The words which follow are still clearer, "Know ye not that your bodies are the members of Christ?" "Know ye not that your body is the temple of the Holy Ghost?" (1 Corinthians 6:15, 19).

Meanwhile, we see how he connects the resurrection with chastity and holiness, as he shortly after includes our bodies in the purchase of redemption. It would be inconsistent with reason that the body, in which Paul bore the marks of his Savior, and in which he magnificently extolled him (see Galatians 6:17), should lose the reward of the crown. Hence, he glories thus, "Our conversation is in heaven; from whence also we look for the Savior, the Lord Jesus Christ: Who shall change our vile body, that it may be fashioned like unto his glorious body" (Philippians 3:20, 21). As it is true, "That we must through much tribulation enter into the kingdom of God" (Acts 14:22), so it would be unreasonable that this entrance should be denied to the bodies which God exercises under the banner of the cross and adorns with the palm of victory.

Accordingly, the saints never entertained any doubt that they would one day be the companions of Christ, who transfers to His own person all the afflictions by which we are tried, that He may show their quickening power. Nay, under the law, God trained the holy patriarch in this belief, by means of an external ceremony. For to what end was the rite of burial, as we have already seen, unless to teach that new life was prepared for the bodies thus deposited? Hence, also, the spices and other symbols of immortality, by which under the Law, the obscurity of the doctrine was illustrated in the same way as by sacrifices. That custom was not the offspring of superstition, since we see that the Spirit is not less careful in narrating burials than in stating the principal mysteries of the faith. Christ commends these last offices as of no trivial importance (see Matthew 16:10), and that, certainly, for no other reason than just that they raise our eyes from the view of the tombs, which corrupts and destroys all things, to the prospect of renovation. Besides, that careful observance of the ceremony for which the patriarchs are praised, sufficiently proves that they found in it a special and valuable help to their faith. Nor would Abraham have been so anxious about the burial of his wife (see Genesis 23:4, 19), had not the religious views and something superior to any worldly advantage, been present to his mind; in other words, by adorning her dead body with the insignia of the resurrection, he confirmed his own faith, and that of his family.

A clearer proof of this appears in the example of Jacob, who, to testify to his posterity that even death did not destroy the hope of the promised land, ordered his bones to be carried thither. Had he been to be clothed with a new body, would it not have been ridiculous in him to give commands concerning a dust which was to be reduced to nothing? Wherefore, if Scripture has any authority with us, we cannot desire a clearer or stronger proof of any doctrine. Even tyros understand this to be the meaning of the words, *resurrection*, and *raising up*. A thing which is created for the first time cannot be said to rise again; nor could our Savior have said, "This is the Father's will which has sent me, that of all which he has given me I should lose nothing, but should raise it up again at the last day" (John 6:39). The same is implied in the word *sleeping*, which is applicable only to the body. Hence, too, the name of cemetery, applied to burying-grounds.

It remains to make a passing remark on the mode of resurrection. I speak thus because Paul, by styling it as a mystery, exhorts us to soberness, in order that he may curb a licentious indulgence in free and subtle speculation. First, as we have already observed, we must hold that the body in which we shall rise will be the same as at present in respect of substance, but that the quality will be different; just as the Body of Christ, which was raised up, was the same as that which had been offered in sacrifice, and yet excelled in other qualities, as if it had been altogether different.

This Paul declares by familiar examples. (See 1 Corinthians 15:39.) The flesh of man and beasts is the same in substance, but not in quality. As all the stars are made of the same matter, but have different degrees of brightness, so he shows that though we shall retain the substance of the body, there will be a change by which its condition will become much more excellent. The corruptible body, therefore, in order that we may be raised, will not perish or vanish away, but, divested of corruption, will be clothed with incorruption. Since God has all the elements at His disposal, no difficulty can prevent Him from commanding the earth, the fire, and the water, to give up what they seem to have destroyed. This, also, though not without figure, Isaiah testifies, "Behold, the Lord comes out of his place to punish the inhabitants of the earth for their iniquity: the earth also shall disclose her blood, and shall no more cover her slain" (Isaiah 26:21).

But a distinction must be made between those who died long ago, and those who on that day shall be found alive. For as Paul declares, "We shall not all sleep, but we shall all be changed" (1 Corinthians 15:51). That is, it will not be necessary that a period should elapse between death and the beginning of the second life. In a moment of time, in the twinkling of an eye, the trumpet shall sound, raising up the dead incorruptible, and, by a sudden change, fitting those who are alive for the same glory. So, in another passage, he comforts believers who were to undergo death, telling them that those who are then alive shall not take precedence over the dead, because those who have fallen asleep in Christ shall rise first. (See 1 Thessalonians 4:15.) Should anyone urge the apostle's declaration, "It is appointed unto all men once to die" (Hebrews 9:27), the solution is easy. When the natural state is changed, there is an appearance of death, which is fitly so denominated. Therefore, there is no inconsistency in the two things—viz. that all when divested of their mortal body, shall be renewed by death; and yet that where the change is sudden, there will be no necessary separation between the soul and the body.

9 Shall the wicked rise again? Answer in the affirmative. Why the wicked shall rise again. Why resurrection is promised to the elect only.

But a more difficult question arises here, How can the resurrection, which is a special benefit of Christ, be common to the ungodly, who are lying under the curse of God? We know that in Adam all died. Christ has come to be the resurrection and the life. (See John 11:25.) Is it to revive the whole human race indiscriminately? But what could be more incongruous than that the ungodly in their obstinate blindness should obtain what the pious worshipers of God receive by faith only? It is certain, therefore, that there will be one resurrection to judgment, and another to life, and that Christ will come to separate the kids from the goats. (See Matthew 25:32.) I observe that this ought not to seem very strange, seeing that something similer happens every day. We know that in Adam we were deprived of the inheritance of the whole world, and that the same reason, which excludes us from eating of the tree of life, excludes us also from common food. How is it, then, that God not only makes His sun to rise on the evil and on the good, but that, in regard to the uses of the present life, His inestimable liberality is constantly flowing forth in rich abundance?

Hence, we certainly perceive, that things which are proper to Christ and His members, abound to the wicked also, not that their possession is legitimate, but that they may thus be rendered more inexcusable. Thus, the wicked often experience the beneficence of God, not in ordinary measures, but such as sometimes throw all the blessings of the godly into the shade, though they eventually lead to greater damnation.

Should it be objected that the resurrection is not properly compared to fading and earthly blessings, I again answer that when the devils were first alienated from God, the Fountain of Life, they deserved to be utterly destroyed; yet, by the admirable counsel of God, an intermediate state was prepared, where without life they might live in death. It ought not to seem in any respect more absurd that there is to be an adventitious resurrection of the ungodly which will drag them against their will before the tribunal of Christ, whom they now refuse to receive as their master and teacher. To be consumed by death would be a light punishment were they not, in order to the punishment of their rebellion, to be sisted before the Judge whom they have provoked to a vengeance without measure and without end.

We are to hold, as already observed and as is contained in the celebrated confession of Paul to Felix, "That there shall be a resurrection of the dead, both of the just and unjust" (Acts 24:15). Yet, Scripture more frequently sets forth the resurrection as intended, along with celestial glory and for the children of God only. Properly speaking, Christ does not come for the destruction, but for the salvation of the world. Therefore, in the creed the life of blessedness only is mentioned.

10 The last part of the chapter, treating of eternal felicity; its excellence transcends our capacity. Rules to be observed. The glory of all the saints will not be equal.

But since the prophecy that death shall be swallowed up in victory (see Hosea 13:14), will then only be completed, let us always remember that the end of the resurrection is eternal happiness, of whose excellence scarcely the minutest part can be described by all that human tongues can say. For though we are truly told that the kingdom of God will be full of light and gladness and felicity and glory, yet the things meant by these words remain most remote from sense, and as it would be involved in enigma, until the day arrives on which He will manifest His glory to us face to face. (See 1 Corinthians 15:54.) "Now," says John, "are we the sons of God; and it does not yet appear what we shall be: but we know that, when he shall appear, we shall be like him; for we shall see him as he is" (1 John 3:2).

Hence, as the prophets were unable to give a verbal description of that spiritual blessedness, they usually delineated it by corporeal objects. On the other hand, because the fervor of desire must be kindled in us by some taste of its sweetness, let us specially dwell upon this thought, If God contains in himself as an inexhaustible fountain all fullness of blessing, those who aspire to the supreme good and perfect happiness must not long for anything beyond Him. This we are taught in several passages, "Fear not, Abraham; I am thy shield, and thy exceeding great reward" (Genesis 15:1). With this accords David's sentiment, "The Lord is the portion of mine inheritance, and of my cup: thou maintainest my lot. The lines are fallen unto me in pleasant places" (Psalm 16:5, 6). Again, "I shall be satisfied when I awake with thy likeness" (Psalm 17:15). Peter declares that the purpose for which believers are called is that they may be "partakers of the divine nature" (2 Peter 1:4). How so? Because, "He shall come to be glorified in his saints and to be admired in all them that believe" (2 Thessalonians 1:10).

If our Lord will share His glory, power, and righteousness with the elect; nay, will give himself to be enjoyed by them, and what is better still, will, in a manner, become one with them, let us remember that every kind of happiness is herein included. But when we have made great progress in thus meditating, let us understand that if the conceptions of our minds were contrasted with the sublimity of the mystery, we are still halting at the very entrance. The more necessary is it for us to cultivate sobriety in this matter, lest unmindful of our feeble capacity, we presume to take too lofty a flight and be overwhelmed by the brightness of the celestial glory. We feel how much we are stimulated by an excessive desire of knowing more than is given us to know, and, hence, frivolous and noxious questions are always springing forth. By frivolous, I mean questions from which no advantage can be extracted. But there is a second class, which is worse than frivolous, because those who indulge in them involve themselves in hurtful speculations.

Hence, I call them noxious. The doctrine of Scripture on the subject ought not to be made the ground of any controversy, and it is that as God, in the varied distribution of gifts to His saints in this world, gives them unequal degrees of light, so when He shall crown His gifts, their degrees of glory in Heaven will also be unequal. When Paul says, "Ye are our glory and our joy" (1 Thessalonians 2:20), his words do not apply indiscriminately to all; nor do those of our Savior to His apostles, "Ye also shall sit on twelve thrones judging the twelve tribes of Israel" (Matthew 19:28). But Paul, who knew that as God enriches the saints with spiritual gifts in this world, He will in like manner adorn them with glory in Heaven, hesitates not to say, that a special crown is laid up for him in proportion to his labors.

Our Savior, also, to commend the dignity of the office, which He had conferred on the apostles, reminds them that the fruit of it is laid up in Heaven. This, too, Daniel says, "They that be wise shall shine as the brightness of the firmament; and they that turn many to righteousness as the stars forever and ever" (Daniel 12:3). Anyone who attentively considers the Scriptures will see not only that they promise eternal life to believers, but a special reward to each. Hence, the expression of Paul, "The Lord grant unto him that he may find mercy of the Lord in that day" (2 Timothy 1:18; 4:14). This is confirmed by our Savior's promise, that they "...shall receive a hundredfold and shall inherit everlasting life" (Matthew 19:29). In short, as Christ, by the manifold variety of His gifts, begins the glory of His body in this world, and gradually increases it, so He will complete it in Heaven.

11 **Without rewarding questions which merely puzzle, an answer is given to some which are not without use.**

While all the godly with one consent will admit this, because it is sufficiently attested by the Word of God, they will, on the other hand, avoid perplexing questions, which they feel to be a hindrance in their way, and thus keep within the prescribed limits. In regard to myself, I not only individually refrain from a superfluous investigation of useless matters, but also think myself bound to take care that I do not encourage the levity of others by answering them. Men puffed up with vain science are often inquiring how great the difference will be between prophets and apostles, and again, between apostles and martyrs; by how many degrees virgins will surpass those who are married; in short, they leave not a corner of Heaven untouched by their speculations. Next, it occurs to them to inquire to what end the world is to be repaired, since the children of God will not be in want of any part of this great and incomparable abundance, but will be like the angels, whose abstinence from food is a symbol of eternal blessedness.

I answer, that independent of use, there will be so much pleasantness in the very sight, so much delight in the very knowledge, that this happiness will far surpass all the means of enjoyment which are now afforded. Let us suppose ourselves placed in the richest quarter of the globe, where no kind of pleasure is wanting, who is there that is not always hindered and excluded by disease from enjoying the gifts of God? Who does not oftentimes interrupt the course of enjoyment by intemperance? Hence, it follows that fruition, pure and free from all defect, though it be of no use to a corruptible life, is the summit of happiness.

Others go further, and ask whether dross and other impurities in metals will have no existence at the restitution, and are inconsistent with it. Though I should go so far as concede this to them, yet I expect with Paul a reparation of those defects which first began with sin and on account of which the whole creation groaneth and travaileth with pain. (See Romans 8:22.)

Others go a step further, and ask, "What better condition can await the human race, since the blessing of offspring shall then have an end?" The solution of this difficulty also is easy. When Scripture so highly extols the blessing of offspring, it refers to the progress by which God is constantly urging nature forward to its goal, in perfection itself we know that the case is different. But, as such, alluring speculations instantly captivate the unwary, who are afterwards led farther into the labyrinth, until at length, everyone becoming pleased with his own views, there is no limit to disputation, the best and shortest course for us will be to rest contented with seeing through a glass darkly until we shall see face to face.

Few out of the vast multitude of mankind feel concerned about how they are to get to heaven; all would fain know before the time what is done in Heaven. Almost all, while slow and sluggish in entering upon the contest, are already depicting to themselves imaginary triumphs.

12 As the happiness of the elect, so the misery of the reprobate, will be without measure and without end.

Moreover, as language cannot describe the severity of the divine vengeance on the reprobates, their pains and torments are figured to us by corporeal things, such as darkness, wailing and gnashing of teeth, inextinguishable fire and the ever-gnawing worm. (See Matthew 8:12; 22:13; Mark 9:43; Isaiah 66:24.) It is certain that by such modes of expression, the Holy Spirit designed to impress all our senses with dread, as when it is said, "Tophet is ordained of old; yea, for the king it is prepared: he has made it deep and large; the pile thereof is fire and much wood; the breath of the Lord, like a stream of brimstone, does kindle it" (Isaiah 30:33). As we thus require to be assisted to conceive the miserable doom of the reprobate, so the consideration on which we ought chiefly to dwell is the fearful consequence of being estranged from all fellowship with God, and not only so, but of feeling that His majesty is adverse to us, while we cannot possibly escape from it.

First, His indignation is like a raging fire, by whose touch all things are devoured and annihilated. Next, all the creatures are the instruments of His judgment, so that those to whom the Lord will thus publicly manifest His anger will feel that Heaven and Earth and sea, all beings, animate and inanimate, are inflamed with dire indignation against them, and armed for their destruction. Wherefore, the Apostle made no trivial declaration, when he said that unbelievers shall be "... punished with everlasting destruction from the presence of the Lord, and from the glory of his power" (2 Thessalonians 1:9). And whenever the prophets strike terror by means of corporeal figures, although in respect to our dull understanding, there is no extravagance in their language, yet they give preludes of the future judgment in the sun and the moon and the whole fabric of the world.

Hence, unhappy consciences find no rest, but are vexed and driven about by a dire whirlwind, feeling as if torn by an angry God, pierced through with deadly darts, terrified by His thunderbolts and crushed by the weight of His hand, so that it would be easier to plunge into abysses and whirlpools than endure these terrors for a moment. How fearful it must be, then, to be thus beset throughout eternity! On this subject, there is a memorable passage in the ninetieth Psalm: "Although God by a mere look scatters all mortals, and brings them to nothing, yet as His worshippers are more timid in this world, He urges them the more, that He may stimulate them, while burdened with the cross to press onward until He himself shall be all in all."

Study Guide

CHAPTER ONE

1. In what sense is the Holy Spirit the bond that unites us to Christ?

2. What does the secret operation of the Holy Spirit produce in us?

3. Where may all the gifts of the Holy Spirit be seen in all their fullness? Why is this so?

4. Why is the Holy Spirit called the Spirit of the Father and the Son?

5. What are the titles of the Holy Spirit? What are their uses?

CHAPTER TWO

1. What is the necessity of the doctrine of faith?

2. In what does faith consist?

3. In what sense may our faith be said to be implicit?

4. What are some examples of faith in the Scriptures?

5. What is the source and basis of faith?

6. What is the relationship between the Word and faith?

7. What is Calvin's definition of faith?

8. In what ways are the elect to be distinguished from the reprobate?

9. How does the reprobate perceive faith?

10. What are the six principal heads under which faith falls?

11. What is the relationship between faith and knowledge?\

12. How does Calvin describe a true believer?

13. What is the victory of faith?

14. How are fear and faith connected?

15. What does Paul mean by working out our salvation with fear and trembling?

16. In what two ways is true fear caused?

17. What is the distinction between filial fear and servile fear?

18. In what way does faith have respect to the divine benevolence? What is meant by "divine benevolence"?

19. What is the foundation of faith?

20. What is the prop and root of faith?

21. What is the relationship between faith and the power of God?

22. How is faith revealed to our minds and sealed to our hearts?

23. What are the excellent qualities of faith?

24. Why is the Spirit called a seal, and earnest, and the Spirit of promise?

25. What is the inseparable attendant of true faith?

26. What is the connection between faith and hope?

CHAPTER THREE

1. What is the connection between faith and repentance?

2. Why is it incorrect to say that faith is produced by repentance?

3. What is Calvin's definition of repentance?

4. Why is the fear of God the first part of repentance?

5. How does Calvin explain the mortification of the flesh and the quickening of the Spirit?

6. What is Augustine's opinion regarding concupiscence in the regenerate?

7. What are the fruits of repentance?

8. What is the principal part of repentance?

9. What distinction does Calvin make between ordinary and special repentance?

10. When does Christian repentance end?

11. What is the origin of repentance?

12. What is the sin against the Holy Ghost?

13. Why is the sin against the Holy Ghost unpardonable?

CHAPTER FOUR

1. What, according to Calvin, is true and genuine contrition?

2. What is meant by auricular confession?

3. Should auricular confession be practiced in the Church?

4. What kind of confession is enjoined by the Word of God?

5. What are the two kinds of private confession?

6. What is meant by absolution?

7. To whom is the office of loosing and binding committed?

8. Are priests successors of the apostles?

9. Is there a difference between venial and mortal sins?

10. What is the distinction between guilt and its punishment?

11. Why are all people subjected to chastisement?

CHAPTER FIVE

1. What is the true nature of indulgences?

2. What is the doctrine of indulgences?

3. What, according to Calvin, is the origin of indulgences?

4. Is Purgatory fictitious?

5. What does the passage about paying the last farthing mean?

6. What is the fire that will try every person's work?

CHAPTER SIX

1. What five special inducements or exhortations to a Christian life are given by Calvin?

2. Why should Christians not grow despondent?

CHAPTER SEVEN

1. What, according to Calvin, is the beginning and sum of the Christian life?

2. What are three things that are to be followed in the Christian life? What are two things that should be shunned?

3. What should the attendants of charity be?

CHAPTER EIGHT

1. Why was the cross necessary?

2. Why does God permit our infirmities and correct our past faults?

CHAPTER NINE

1. What is the purpose of affliction in our lives?

2. What are the disadvantages of prosperity?

3. What are two reasons why Christians should not tremble at the fear of death?

CHAPTER TEN

1. What are the remedies for impatience and immoderate desire?

2. Why is the doctrine related to God's calling a source of comfort for us?

CHAPTER ELEVEN

1. What is the connection between the doctrine of justification and that of regeneration?

2. What does it mean to be justified in the sight of God?

3. What is meant by being justified by works?

4. What is meant by being justified by faith?

5. In what sense is Christ our righteousness?

CHAPTER TWELVE

1. Contrast the perfection of God with the imperfection of man.

2. In what does Christian humility consist?

3. What does the Parable of the Publican tell us?

CHAPTER THIRTEEN

1. How is the peace of conscience obtained?

2. What happens to faith, according to the Apostle Paul, if righteousness comes by the Law.

CHAPTER FOURTEEN

1. By what are all human virtues corrupted?

2. What is the natural condition of men as described in the Scriptures?

3. What, according to Augustine, are two reasons why no believer will presume to boast before God of his works?

CHAPTER FIFTEEN

1. Do good works merit favor with God?

2. Do good works please God?

3. What benefits are derived from good works?

CHAPTER SIXTEEN

1. What establishes the necessity of good works?

2. What do the apostles refer us to when they exhort us to good works?

CHAPTER SEVENTEEN

1. How is one exempted from the power of the Law?

2. What is the primary difference between the legal promise and the evangelical promise?

3. What are the causes and effects of justification?

4. What is meant by the perfection of saints?

CHAPTER EIGHTEEN

1. What does Calvin mean by "works" and "working"?

2. What is our inheritance as believers?

3. Do works lead to salvation?

4. What is the way to the Kingdom of God?

5. Why should we lay up treasures in Heaven? How can we do so?

6. Is faith a work?

CHAPTER NINETEEN

1.   What does Calvin mean by Christian liberty?

2.   What does Christian liberty do for us?

3.   What are the three parts of Christian liberty?

4.   What enables us to answer the call of God?

5.   What kinds of people are regarded as weak and Pharisaical?

6.   What is Calvin's definition of conscience?

7.   What is the relationship between the conscience and external obedience?

CHAPTER TWENTY

1.   What is the connection between prayer and faith?

2.   What is Calvin's definition of prayer?

3.   Why is prayer necessary?

4.   How should the mind be composed during prayer?

5.   Who guides us in prayer?

6.   How often should we pray?

7.   What is the advantage that comes from the suppression of pride?

8.   From what does true prayer spring?

9.   What is the role of confidence in prayer?

10. What is the role of faith in prayer?

11. What kinds of people, according to Calvin, are no better than idolaters?

12. What are the rules for right prayer?

13. Through whom is God to be invoked?

14. Upon whom does the wrath of God lie?

15. What is the nature of Christ's intercession?

16. Do the saints in Heaven intercede for us?

17. What are the effects of invoking saints in prayer?

18. What different kinds of prayer does Calvin discuss?

19. What are the rules regarding supplication and thanksgiving?

20. What does Calvin mean by "secret prayer"?

21. How should singing be done?

22. What does the form of prayer employed by Christ display?

23. What six petitions are found within the Lord's Prayer?

24. Why is God called "our Father"?

25. What does the phrase "Hallowed by thy name" mean?

26. What is the Kingdom of God?

27. How does the Kingdom come?

28. Where do we find the will of God manifested?

29. What does the word "bread" in the Lord's Prayer mean?

30. Why should we ask God to give us our daily bread?

31. Why are our sins called "debts"?

32. What are the various forms of temptation cited by Calvin?

33. In what sense may it be said that God leads us into temptation?

34. What is the purpose of the word "Amen" at the end of a prayer?

35. Why is perseverance in prayer important?

CHAPTER TWENTY-ONE

1. What is the doctrine of election and predestination?

2. What does ignorance of this doctrine cause?

CHAPTER TWENTY-TWO

1. Who are the elect?

2. For what reason are some elected?

3. Why does the Scripture say that many are called, but few are chosen?

CHAPTER TWENTY-THREE

1. What does God owe to human beings?

2. Did God decree that Adam should perish as a result of the Fall?

3. Is God a respecter of persons?

4. How should the doctrine of predestination be preached?

CHAPTER TWENTY-FOUR

1. In what sense are election and effectual calling founded upon the free mercy of God?

2. Why does God blind the reprobate?

CHAPTER TWENTY-FIVE

1. With what must we be animated for invincible perseverance in our calling?

2. Why is a final resurrection necessary?

3. How is the vision of dry bones connected to the Last Resurrection?

4. Does death destroy the whole man?

5. What is meant by "the bosom of Abraham"?

6. Shall the wicked rise again?

7. Will the glory of all the saints be equal?

One Hundred Aphorisms

CONTAINING, WITHIN A NARROW COMPASS,
THE SUBSTANCE AND ORDER OF THE
FOUR BOOKS OF THE

Institutes of the Christian Religion

Book 1

1. The true wisdom of man consists in the knowledge of God the Creator and Redeemer.

2. This knowledge is naturally implanted in us, and the end of it ought to be the worship of God rightly performed, or reverence for the Deity accompanied by fear and love.

3. But this seed is corrupted by ignorance, whence arises superstitious worship; and by wickedness, whence arise slavish dread and hatred of the Deity.

4. It is also from another source that it is derived namely, from the structure of the whole world, and from the Holy Scriptures.

5. This structure teaches us what are the goodness, power, justice, and wisdom of God in creating all things in heaven and earth, and in preserving them by ordinary and extraordinary government, by which his Providence is more clearly made known. It teaches also, what are our wants, that we may learn to place our confidence in the goodness, power, and wisdom of God, to obey his commandments, to flee to him in adversity, and to offer thanksgiving to him for the gifts, which we enjoy.

6. By the Holy Scriptures, also, God the Creator is known. We ought to consider what these Scriptures are; that they are true, and have proceeded from the Spirit of God; which is proved by the testimony of the Holy Spirit, by the efficacy and antiquity of the Scriptures, by the certainty of the Prophecies, by the miraculous preservation of the Law, by the calling and writings of the Apostles, by the consent of the Church, and by the steadfastness of the martyrs, whence it is evident that all the principles of piety are overthrown by those fanatics who, laying aside the Scripture, fly to revelations.

7. Next, what they teach; or, what is the nature of God in himself and in the creation and government of all things.

8. The nature of God in himself is infinite, invisible, eternal, almighty; whence it follows that they are mistaken who ascribe to God a visible form. In his one essence, there are three persons, the Father, the Son, and the Holy Spirit.

9. In the creation of all things there are chiefly considered, A. Heavenly and spiritual substances, that is, angels, of which some are good and the protectors of the godly, while others are bad, not by creation, but by corruption; B. Earthly substances, and particularly man, whose perfection is displayed in soul and in body.

10. In the government of all things, the nature of God is manifested. Now his government is, in one respect, universal, by which he directs all the creatures according to the properties, which he bestowed on each when he created them.

11. In another respect, it is special; which appears in regard to contingent events, so that if any person is visited either by adversity or by any prosperous result, he ought to ascribe it wholly to God; and with respect to those things which act according to a fixed law of nature, though their peculiar properties were naturally bestowed on them, still they exert their power only so far as they are directed by the immediate hand of God.

12. It is viewed also with respect to time past and future. *Past*, that we may learn that all things happen by the appointment of God, who acts either by means, or without means, or contrary to means; so that everything which happens yields good to the godly and evil to the wicked. *Future*, to which belong human deliberations, and which

shows that we ought to employ lawful means; since that Providence on which we rely furnishes its own means.

13. Lastly, by attending to the advantage, which the godly derive from it. For we know certainly, A. That God takes care of the whole human race, but especially of his Church. B. That God governs all things by his will, and regulates them by his wisdom. C. That he has most abundant power of doing good; for in his hand are heaven and earth, all creatures are subject to his sway, the godly rest on his protection, and the power of hell is restrained by his authority. That nothing happens by chance, though the causes may be concealed, but by the will of God; by his secret will which we are unable to explore, but adore with reverence, and by his will which is conveyed to us in the Law and in the Gospel.

Book 2

14. The knowledge of God the Redeemer is obtained from the fall of man, and from the material cause of redemption.

15. In the fall of man, we must consider what he ought to be, and what he may be.

16. For he was created after the image of God; that is, he was made a partaker of the divine Wisdom, Righteousness, and Holiness, and, being thus perfect in soul and in body, was bound to render to God a perfect obedience to his commandments.

17. The immediate causes of the fall were—Satan, the Serpent, Eve, the forbidden fruit; the remote causes were—unbelief, ambition, ingratitude, and obstinacy. Hence, followed the obliteration of the image of God in man, who became unbelieving, unrighteous, and liable to death.

18. We must now see what he may be, in respect both of soul and of body. The understanding of the soul in divine things, that is, in the knowledge and true worship of God, is blinder than a mole; good works it can neither contrive nor perform. In human affairs, as in the liberal and mechanical arts, it is exceedingly blind and

variable. Now the will, so far as regards divine things, chooses only what is evil. So far as regards lower and human affairs, it is uncertain, wandering, and not wholly at its own disposal.

19. The body follows the depraved appetites of the soul, is liable to many infirmities, and at length to death.

20. Hence, it follows that redemption for ruined man must be sought through Christ the Mediator; because the first adoption of a chosen people, the preservation of the Church, her deliverance from dangers, her recovery after dispersions, and the hope of the godly, always depended on the grace of the Mediator. Accordingly, the law was given, that it might keep their minds in suspense until the coming of Christ; which is evident from the history of a gracious covenant frequently repeated, from ceremonies, sacrifices, and washings, from the end of adoption, and from the law of the priesthood.

21. The material cause of redemption is Christ, in whom we must consider three things; A. How he is exhibited to men; B. How he is received; C. How men are retained in his fellowship.

22. Christ is exhibited to men by the Law and by the Gospel.

23. The Law is threefold: Ceremonial, Judicial, and Moral. The use of the Ceremonial Law is repealed; its effect is perpetual. The Judicial or Political Law was peculiar to the Jews, and has been set aside, while that universal justice which is described in the Moral Law remains. The latter, or Moral Law, the object of which is to cherish and maintain godliness and righteousness, is perpetual, and is incumbent on all.

24. The use of the Moral Law is threefold. The first use shows our weakness, unrighteousness, and condemnation; not that we may despair, but that we may flee to Christ. The second is that those who are not moved by promises may be urged by the terror of threatening. The third is, that we may know what is the will of God; that we may consider it in order to obedience; that our minds may be strengthened for that purpose; and that we may be kept from falling.

25. The sum of the Law is contained in the Preface, and in the two Tables. In the Preface we observe, A. The power of God, to constrain the people by the necessity of obedience; B. A promise of

grace, by which he declares himself the God of the Church; C. A kind act, on the ground of which he charges the Jews with ingratitude, if they do not requite his goodness.

26. The first Table, which relates to the worship of God, consists of four commandments.

27. The design of the First Commandment is that God alone may be exalted in his people. To God alone, therefore, we owe adoration, trust, invocation, and thanksgiving.

28. The design of the Second Commandment is that God will not have his worship profaned by superstitious rites. It consists of two parts. The former restrains our licentious daring, that we may not subject God to our senses, or represent him under any visible shape. The latter forbids us to worship any images on religious grounds, and, therefore, proclaims his power, which he cannot suffer to be despised, —his jealousy, for he cannot bear a partner, —his vengeance on children's children, —his mercy to those who adore his majesty.

29. The Third Commandment enjoins three things: A. That whatever our mind conceives, or our tongue utters, may have a regard to the majesty of God; B. That we may not rashly abuse his holy word and adorable mysteries for the purposes of ambition or avarice; C. That we may not throw obloquy on his works, but may speak of them with commendations of his Wisdom, Long-suffering, Power, Goodness, Justice. With these is contrasted a threefold profanation of the name of God, by perjury, unnecessary oaths, and idolatrous rites; that is, when we substitute in the place of God saints, or creatures animate or inanimate.

30. The design of the Fourth Commandment is that, being dead to our own affections and works, we may meditate on the kingdom of God. Now there are three things here to be considered: A. A spiritual rest, when believers abstain from their own works, that God may work in them; B. That there may be a stated day for calling on the name of God, for hearing his word, and for performing religious rites; C. That servants may have some remission from labor.

31. The Second Table, which relates to the duties of charity towards our neighbor, contains the last Six Commandments. The design of the Fifth Commandment is, that, since God takes pleasure in

the observance of his own ordinance, the degrees of dignity appointed by him must be held inviolable. We are therefore forbidden to take anything from the dignity of those who are above us, by contempt, obstinacy, or ingratitude; and we are commanded to pay them reverence, obedience, and gratitude.

32. The design of the Sixth Commandment is that, since God has bound mankind by a kind of unity, the safety of all ought to be considered by each person; whence it follows that we are forbidden to do violence to private individuals, and are commanded to exercise benevolence.

33. The design of the Seventh Commandment is that, because God loves purity, we ought to put away from us all uncleanness. He therefore forbids adultery in mind, word, and deed.

34. The design of the Eighth Commandment is that, since injustice is an abomination to God, he requires us to render to every man what is his own. Now men steal, either by violence, or by malicious imposture, or by craft, or by sycophancy, etc.

35. The design of the Ninth Commandment is, that, since God, who is truth, abhors falsehood, he forbids calumnies and false accusations, by which the name of our neighbor is injured, —and lies, by which anyone suffers loss in his fortunes. On the other hand, he requires every one of us to defend the name and property of our neighbor by asserting the truth.

36. The design of the Tenth Commandment is, that, since God would have the whole soul pervaded by love, every desire averse to charity must be banished from our minds; and therefore every feeling, which tends to the injury of another is forbidden.

37. We have said that Christ is revealed to us by the Gospel. In addition, first, the agreement between the Gospel, or the New Testament, and the Old Testament is demonstrated: A. Because the godly, under both dispensations, have had the same hope of immortality; B. They have had the same covenant, founded not on the works of men, but on the mercy of God; C. They have had the same Mediator between God and men—Christ.

38. Next, five points of difference between the two dispensations are pointed out. A. Under the Law the heavenly inheritance was held out to them under earthly blessings; but under the Gospel, our minds are led directly to meditate upon it. B. The Old Testament, by means of figures, presented the image only, while the reality was absent; but the New Testament exhibits the present truth. C. The former, in respect of the Law, was the ministry of condemnation and death; the latter, of righteousness and life. D. The former is connected with bondage, which begets fear in the mind; the latter is connected with freedom, which produces confidence. E. The word had been confined to the single nation of the Jews; but now it is preached to all nations.

39. The sum of evangelical doctrine is, to teach, A. What Christ is; B. Why he was sent; C. In what manner he accomplished the work of redemption.

40. Christ is God and man: *God*, that he may bestow on his people righteousness, sanctification, and redemption; *Man*, because he had to pay the debt of man.

41. He was sent to perform the office, A. Of a Prophet, by preaching the truth, by fulfilling the prophecies, by teaching and doing the will of his Father; B. Of a King, by governing the whole Church and every member of it, and by defending his people from every kind of adversaries; C. Of a Priest, by offering his body as a sacrifice for sins, by reconciling God to us though his obedience, and by perpetual intercession for his people to the Father.

42. He performed the office of a Redeemer by dying for our sins, by rising again for our justification, by opening heaven to us through his ascension, by sitting at the right hand of the Father whence he will come to judge the quick and the dead; and, therefore, he procured for us the grace of God and salvation.

Book 3

43. We receive Christ the Redeemer by the power of the Holy Spirit, who unites us to Christ; and, therefore, he is called the Spirit

of sanctification and adoption, the earnest and seal of our salvation, water, oil, a fountain, fire, the hand of God.

44. Faith is the hand of the soul, which receives, through the same efficacy of the Holy Spirit, Christ offered to us in the Gospel.

45. The general office of faith is, to assent to the truth of God, whenever, whatever, and in what manner soever he speaks; but its peculiar office is, to behold the will of God in Christ, his mercy, the promises of grace, for the full conviction of which the Holy Spirit enlightens our minds and strengthens our hearts.

46. Faith, therefore, is a steady and certain knowledge of the divine kindness towards us, which is founded on a gracious promise through Christ, and is revealed to our minds and sealed on our hearts by the Holy Spirit.

47. The effects of faith are four: A. Repentance; B. A Christian life; C. Justification; D. Prayer.

48. True repentance consists of two parts: A. Mortification, which proceeds from the acknowledgment of sin, and a real perception of the divine displeasure; B. Quickening, the fruits of which are—piety towards God, charity towards our neighbor, the hope of eternal life, holiness of life. With this true repentance is contrasted false repentance, the parts of which are, Contrition, Confession, and Satisfaction. The two former may be referred to true repentance, provided that there be contrition of heart because of the acknowledgment of sin. It must not be separated from the hope of forgiveness through Christ. The confession must be either *private* to God alone or made to the pastors of the Church willingly and for the purpose of consolation, not for the enumeration of offenses, and for introducing a torture of the conscience; or *public*, which is made to the whole Church, or to one or many persons in presence of the whole Church. What was formerly called Ecclesiastical Satisfaction, that is, what was made for the edification of the Church on account of repentance and public confession of sins, was introduced as due to God by the Sophists; whence sprung the supplements of Indulgences in this world, and the fire of Purgatory after death. But that Contrition of the Sophists, Auricular Confession (as they call

it), and the Satisfaction of actual performance are opposed to the free forgiveness of sins.

49. The two parts of a Christian life are laid down: A. The love of righteousness; that we may be holy, because God is holy, and because we are united to him, and are reckoned among his people; B. That a rule may be prescribed to us, which does not permit us to wander in the course of righteousness, and that we may be conformed to Christ. A model of this is laid down to us, which we ought to copy in our whole life. Next are mentioned the blessings of God, which it will argue extreme ingratitude if we do not requite.

50. The sum of the Christian life is denial of ourselves.

51. The ends of this self-denial are four. A. That we may devote ourselves to God as a living sacrifice. B. That we may not seek our own things, but those which belong to God and to our neighbor. C. That we may patiently bear the cross, the fruits of which are—acknowledgment of our weakness, the trial of our patience, correction of faults, more earnest prayer, and more cheerful meditation on eternal life. D. That we may know in what manner we ought to use the present life and its aids, for necessity and delight. Necessity demands that we possess all things as though we possessed them not; that we bear poverty with mildness, and abundance with moderation; that we know how to endure patiently fullness, and hunger, and want; that we pay regard to our neighbor, because we must give account of our stewardship; and that all things correspond to our calling. The delight of praising the kindness of God ought to be with us a stronger argument.

52. In considering Justification, which is the third effect of faith, the first thing that occurs is an explanation of the word. He is said to be justified who, in the judgment of God, is deemed righteous. He is justified by works, whose life is pure and blameless before God; and no such person ever existed except Christ. They are justified by faith who, shut out from the righteousness of works, receive the righteousness of Christ. Such are the elect of God.

53. Hence follows the strongest consolation; for instead of a severe Judge, we have a most merciful Father. Justified in Christ, and having peace, trusting to his power, we aim at holiness.

54. Next follows Christian liberty, consisting of three parts. A. That the consciences of believers may rise above the Law, and may forget the whole righteousness of the Law. B. That the conscience, free from the yoke of the Law, may cheerfully obey the will of God. C. That they may not be bound by any religious scruples before God about things indifferent. But here we must avoid two precipices. A. That we do not abuse the gifts of God. B. That we avoid giving and taking offense.

55. The fourth effect of faith is Prayer; in which are considered its fruits, laws, faults, and petitions.

56. The fruit of prayer is fivefold. A. When we are accustomed to flee to God, our heart is inflamed with a stronger desire to seek, love, and adore him. B. Our heart is not a prey to any wicked desire, of which we would be ashamed to make God our witness. C. We receive his benefits with thanksgiving. D. Having obtained a gift, we more earnestly meditate on the goodness of God. E. Experience confirms to us the Goodness, Providence, and Truth of God.

57. The laws are four. A. That we should have our heart framed as becomes those who enter into converse with God; and therefore the lifting up of the hands, the raising of the heart, and perseverance, are recommended. B. That we should feel our wants. C. That we should divest ourselves of every thought of our own glory, giving the whole glory to God. D. That while we are prostrated amidst overwhelming evils, we should be animated by the sure hope of succeeding, since we rely on the command and promise of God.

58. They err who call on the Saints that are placed beyond this life. A. Because Scripture teaches that prayer ought to be offered to God alone, who alone knows what is necessary for us. He chooses to be present, because he has promised. He can do so, for he is Almighty. B. Because he requires that he is addressed in faith, which rests on his word and promise. C. Because faith is corrupted as soon as it departs from this rule. But in calling on the saints, there is no word, no promise; and therefore there is no faith; nor can the saints themselves either hear or assist.

59. The summary of prayer, which has been delivered to us by Christ the Lord, is contained in a Preface and two Tables.

60. In the Preface, the Goodness of God is conspicuous, for he is called *our Father*. It follows that we are his children, and that to seek supplies from any other quarter would be to charge God either with poverty or with cruelty; that sins ought not to hinder us from humbly imploring mercy; and that a feeling of brotherly love ought to exist amongst us. The power of God is likewise conspicuous in this Preface, for he is *in Heaven*. Hence, we infer that God is present everywhere, and that when we seek him, we ought to rise above perceptions of the body and the soul; that he is far beyond all risk of change or corruption; that he holds the whole universe in his grasp, and governs it by his power.

61. The First Table is entirely devoted to the glory of God, and contains three petitions. A. That the *name* of God, that is, his power, goodness, wisdom, justice, and truth, *may be hallowed*; that is, that men may neither speak nor think of God but with the deepest veneration. B. That God may correct, by the agency of his Spirit, all the depraved lusts of the flesh; may bring all our thoughts into obedience to his authority; may protect his children; and may defeat the attempts of the wicked. The use of this petition is threefold. (1). It withdraws us from the corruptions of the world. (2). It inflames us with the desire of mortifying the flesh. (3). It animates us to endure the cross. C. The Third petition relates not to the secret will of God, but to that which is made known by the Scriptures, and to which voluntary obedience is the counterpart.

62. The Second Table contains the three remaining petitions, which relate to our neighbors and ourselves. A. It asks everything, which the body needs in this sublunary state; for we commit ourselves to the care and providence of God, that he may feed, foster, and preserve us. B. We ask those things which contribute to the spiritual life, namely, the *forgiveness of sins*, which implies satisfaction, and to which is added a condition, that when we have been offended by deed or by word, we nevertheless forgive them their offenses against us. C. We ask *deliverance from temptations*, or, that we may be furnished with armor and defended by the Divine protection, that we may be able to obtain the victory. *Temptations* differ in their *causes*, for God, Satan, the world, and the flesh *tempt*; in their *matter*, for we are tempted, on the right hand, in respect of riches, honors,

beauty, etc., and on the left hand, in respect of poverty, contempt, and afflictions: and in their *end*, for God tempts the godly for good, but Satan, the flesh, and the world, tempt them for evil.

63. Those Four effects of faith bring us to the certainty of election, and of the final resurrection.

64. The causes of election are these. The *efficient* cause is—the free mercy of God, which we ought to acknowledge with humility and thanksgiving. The *material* cause is—Christ, the well-beloved Son. The *final* cause is—that, being assured of our salvation, because we are God's people, we may glorify him both in this life and in the life which is to come, to all eternity. The effects are, in respect either of many persons, or of a single individual; and that by electing some, and justly reprobating others. The elect are called by the preaching of the word and the illumination of the Holy Spirit, are justified, and sanctified, that they may at length be glorified.

65. The final resurrection will take place. A. Because on any other supposition we cannot be perfectly glorified. B. Because Christ rose in our flesh. C. Because God is Almighty.

Book 4

66. God keeps us united in the fellowship of Christ by means of Ecclesiastical and Civil government.

67. In Ecclesiastical government, three things are considered. A. What is the Church? B. How is it governed? C. What is its power?

68. The Church is regarded in two points of view; as Invisible and Universal, which is the communion of saints; and as Visible and Particular. The Church is discerned by the pure preaching of the word, and by the lawful administration of the sacraments.

69. As to the government of the Church, there are five points of inquiry. A. Who rule? B. What are they? C. What is their calling? D. What is their office? E. What was the condition of the ancient Church?

70. They that rule are not Angels, but Men. In this respect, God declares his condescension towards us: we have a most excellent training to humility and obedience, and it is singularly fitted to bind us to mutual charity.

71. These are Prophets, Apostles, Evangelists, whose office was temporary; Pastors and Teachers, whose office is of perpetual duration.

72. Their calling is twofold: *internal* and *external*. The *internal* is from the Spirit of God. In the *external*, there are four things to be considered. A. What sort of persons ought to be chosen? Men of sound doctrine and holy lives. B. In what manner? With fasting and prayer. C. By whom? Immediately, by God, as Prophets and Apostles. Mediately, with the direction of the word, by Bishops, by Elders, and by the people. D. With what rite of ordination? By the laying on of hands, the use of which is threefold. (1). That the dignity of the ministry may be commended. (2). That he who is called may know that he is devoted to God. (3). That he may believe that the Holy Spirit will not desert this holy ministry.

73. The duty of Pastors in the Church is, to preach the Word, to administer the Sacraments, to exercise Discipline.

74. The condition of the ancient Church was distributed into Presbyters, Elders, Deacons, who dispensed the funds of the Church to the Bishops, the Clergy, the poor, and for repairing churches.

75. The power of the Church is viewed in relation to Doctrine, Legislation, and Jurisdiction.

76. Doctrine respects the articles of faith, none of which must be laid down without the authority of the word of God, but all must be directed to the glory of God and the edification of the Church. It respects also the application of the articles, which must agree with the analogy of faith.

77. Ecclesiastical laws, in precepts necessary to be observed, must be in accordance with the written word of God. In things indifferent, regard must be had to places, persons, times, with a due attention to order and decorum. Those constitutions ought to be avoided which have been laid down by pretended pastors instead of the pure worship

of God, which bind the consciences by rigid necessity, which make void a commandment of God, which are useless and trifling, which oppress the consciences by their number, which lead to theatrical display, which are considered to be propitiatory sacrifices, and which are turned to the purposes of gain.

78. Jurisdiction is twofold. (A). That which belongs to the Clergy, which was treated of under the head of Provincial and General Synods. (B). That which is common to the Clergy and the people, the design of which is twofold that scandals may be prevented, and that scandal which has arisen may be removed. The exercise of it consists in private and public admonitions, and likewise in excommunication, the object of which is threefold. (1). That the Church may not be blamed; (2). That the good may not be corrupted by intercourse with the bad; (3). That they who are excommunicated may be ashamed, and may begin to repent.

79. With regard to Times, Fasts are appointed, and Vows are made. The design of Fasts is, that the flesh may be mortified, that we may be better prepared for prayer, and that they may be evidences of humility and obedience. They consist of three things, the time, the quality, and the quantity of food. But here we must beware lest we rend our garments only, and not our hearts, as hypocrites do, lest those actions be regarded as a meritorious performance, and lest they be too rigorously demanded as necessary to salvation.

80. In Vows we must consider; A. To whom the vow is made—namely, to God. Hence, it follows that nothing must be attempted but what is approved by his word, which teaches us what is pleasing and what is displeasing to God. B. Who it is that vows—namely, a man. We must, therefore, beware lest we disregard our liberty, or promise what is beyond our strength or inconsistent with our calling. C. What is vowed. Here regard must be had to time; to the *past*, such as a vow of thanksgiving and repentance; to the *future*, that we may afterwards be more cautious, and may be stimulated by them to the performance of duty. Hence, it is evident what opinion we ought to form respecting Popish vows.

81. In explaining the Sacraments, there are three things to be considered. A. What a sacrament is—namely, an external sign, by

which God seals on our consciences the promises of his good will towards us, in order to sustain the weakness of our faith. We in our turn testify our piety towards him. B. What things are necessary—namely, the Sign, the Thing signified, the Promise, and the general Participation. C. What is the number of them—namely, Baptism and the Lord's Supper.

82. The Sign in Baptism is water; the Thing Signified is the blood of Christ; the Promise is eternal life; the Communicants or Partakers are, adults, after making a confession of their faith, and likewise infants; for Baptism came in the place of Circumcision, and in both the mystery, promise, use, and efficacy, are the same. Forgiveness of sins also belongs to infants, and therefore it is likewise a sign of this forgiveness.

83. The end of Baptism is twofold. (A). To promote our faith towards God. For it is a sign of our washing by the blood of Christ, and of the mortification of our flesh, and the renewal of our souls in Christ. Besides, being united to Christ, we believe that we shall be partakers of all his blessings, and that we shall never fall under condemnation. (B). To serve as our confession before our neighbor, for it is a mark that we choose to be regarded as the people of God, and we testify that we profess the Christian religion, and that our desire is, that all the members of our body may proclaim the praise of God.

84. The Lord's Supper is a spiritual feast, by which we are preserved in that life into which God hath begotten us by his word.

85. The design of the Lord's Supper is threefold. (A). To aid in confirming our faith towards God. (B). To serve as a confession before men. (C). To be an exhortation to charity.

86. We must beware lest, by undervaluing the signs, we separate them too much from their mysteries, with which they are in some measure connected; and lest, on the other hand, by immoderately extolling them, we appear to obscure the mysteries themselves.

87. The parts are two. (A). The *spiritual truth* in which the meaning is beheld consists in the promises; the *matter*, or substance, is Christ dead and risen; and the *effect* is our redemption and justification. (B). The visible signs are, bread, and wine.

88. With the Lord's Supper is contrasted the Popish Mass. A. It offers insult and blasphemy to Christ. B. It buries the cross of Christ. C. It obliterates his death. D. It robs us of the benefits, which we obtain in Christ. E. It destroys the Sacraments in which the memorial of his death was left.

89. The Sacraments, falsely so-called, are enumerated, which are Confirmation, Penitence, Extreme Unction, Orders [which gave rise to the (seven) less and the (three) greater], and Marriage.

90. Next comes civil government, which belongs to the external regulation of manners.

91. Under this head are considered Magistrates, Laws, and the People.

92. The Magistrate is God's vicegerent, the father of his country, the guardian of the laws, the administrator of justice, the defender of the Church.

93. By these names, he is excited to the performance of duty. A. That he may walk in holiness before God, and before men may maintain uprightness, prudence, temperance, harmlessness, and righteousness. B. That by wonderful consolation it may smooth the difficulties of his office.

94. The kinds of Magistracy or Civil Government are Monarchy, Aristocracy, and Democracy.

95. As to Laws, we must see what is their constitution in regard to God and to men: and what is their equity in regard to times, places, and nations.

96. The People owe to the Magistrate, A. Reverence heartily rendered to him as God's ambassador. B. Obedience or compliance with edicts, or paying taxes, or undertaking public offices and burdens. C. That love which will lead us to pray to God for his prosperity.

97. We are enjoined to obey not only good magistrates, but all who possess authority, though they may exercise tyranny; for it was not without the authority of God that they were appointed princes.

98. When tyrants reign, let us first remember our faults, which are chastised by such scourges; and, therefore, humility will restrain

our impatience. Besides, it is not in our power to remedy these evils, and all that remains for us is to implore the assistance of the Lord, in whose hand are the hearts of men and the revolutions of kingdoms.

99. In Two ways God restrains the fury of tyrants; either by raising up from among their own subjects open avengers, who rid the people of their tyranny, or by employing for that purpose the rage of men whose thoughts and contrivances are totally different, thus overturning one tyranny by means of another.

100. The obedience enjoined on subjects does not prevent the interference of any popular Magistrates whose office it is to restrain tyrants and to protect the liberty of the people. Our obedience to Magistrates ought to be such, that the obedience, which we owe to the King of kings, shall remain entire and unimpaired

A Defense of Calvinism

by
Charles Haddon Spurgeon
Author of *Morning by Morning* and *Evening by Evening*

The old truth that Calvin preached, that Augustine preached, and that Paul preached is the truth that I must preach today, or else be false to my conscience and my God. I cannot shape the truth; I know of no such thing as paring off the rough edges of a doctrine. John Knox's Gospel is my Gospel. That which thundered through Scotland must thunder through England again.

It is a great thing to begin the Christian life by believing good solid doctrine. Some people have received twenty different "gospels" in as many years; how many more they will accept before they get to their journey's end, it would be difficult to predict. I thank God that He early taught me the Gospel, and I have been so perfectly satisfied with it, that I do not want to know any other. Constant change of creed is sure loss. If a tree has to be taken up two or three times a year, you will not need to build a very large loft in which to store the apples. When people are always shifting their doctrinal principles, they are not likely to bring forth much fruit to the glory of God. It is good for young believers to begin with a firm hold upon those great fundamental doctrines, which the Lord has taught in His Word. Why, if I believed what some preach about the temporary, trumpery salvation which only lasts for a time, I would scarcely be at all grateful for it; but when I know that those whom God saves He saves with an everlasting salvation, when I know that He gives to them an everlasting righteousness, when I know that He settles them on an everlasting foundation of everlasting love, and that He will bring them to His everlasting kingdom, oh, then I do wonder, and I am astonished that such a blessing as this should ever have been given to me!

Pause, my soul! adore, and wonder!
Ask, "Oh, why such love to me?"
Grace hath put me in the number
Of the Saviour's family:
Hallelujah!
Thanks, eternal thanks, to Thee.

I suppose there are some persons whose minds naturally incline towards the doctrine of free will. I can only say that mine inclines as naturally towards the doctrines of sovereign grace. Sometimes, when I see some of the worst characters in the street, I feel as if my heart must burst forth in tears of gratitude that God has never let me act as they have done! I have thought, if God had left me alone, and had not touched me by His grace, what a great sinner I should have been! I should have run to the utmost lengths of sin, dived into the very depths of evil, nor should I have stopped at any vice or folly, if God had not restrained me. I feel that I should have been a very king of sinners, if God had let me alone. I cannot understand the reason why I am saved, except upon the ground that God would have it so. I cannot, if I look ever so earnestly, discover any kind of reason in myself why I should be a partaker of Divine grace. If I am not at this moment without Christ, it is only because Christ Jesus would have His will with me, and that will was that I should be with Him where He is, and should share His glory. I can put the crown nowhere but upon the head of Him whose mighty grace has saved me from going down into the pit.

Looking back on my past life, I can see that the dawning of it all was of God, of God effectively. I took no torch with which to light the sun, but the sun enlightened me. I did not commence my spiritual life—no, I rather kicked, and struggled against the things of the Spirit: when He drew me, for a time I did not run after Him: there was a natural hatred in my soul of everything holy and good. Wooings were lost upon me-warnings were cast to the wind- thunders were despised; and as for the whispers of His love, they were rejected as being less than nothing and vanity. But, sure I am, I can say now, speaking on behalf of myself, "He only is my salvation." It was He who turned my heart, and brought me down on my knees before Him. I can in very deed, say with Doddridge and Toplady:

Grace taught my soul to pray,
And made my eyes o'erflow.

And coming to this moment, I can add:

Tis grace has kept me to this day,
And will not let me go.

Well can I remember the manner in which I learned the doctrines of grace in a single instant. Born, as all of us are by nature, an Arminian, I still believed the old things I had heard continually from the pulpit, and did not see the grace of God. When I was coming to Christ, I thought I was doing it all myself, and though I sought the Lord earnestly, I had no idea the Lord was seeking me. I do not think the young convert is at first aware of this. I can recall the very day and hour when first I received those truths in my own soul-when they were, as John Bunyan says, burnt into my heart as with a hot iron, and I can recollect how I felt that I had grown on a sudden from a babe into a man-that I had made progress in Scriptural knowledge, through having found, once for all, the clue to the truth of God. One weeknight, when I was sitting in the house of God, I was not thinking much about the preacher's sermon, for I did not believe it. The thought struck me, How did you come to be a Christian? I sought the Lord. But how did you come to seek the Lord? The truth flashed across my mind in a moment- I should not have sought Him unless there had been some previous influence in my mind to make me seek Him. I prayed, thought I, but then I asked myself, How came I to pray? I was induced to pray by reading the Scriptures. How came I to read the Scriptures? I did read them, but what led me to do so? Then, in a moment, I saw that God was at the bottom of it all, and that He was the Author of my faith, and so the whole doctrine of grace opened up to me, and from that doctrine I have not departed to this day, and I desire to make this my constant confession, "I ascribe my change wholly to God."

I once attended a service where the text happened to be, "He shall choose our inheritance for us;" and the good man who occupied the pulpit was more than a little of an Arminian. Therefore, when he commenced, he said, "This passage refers entirely to our temporal inheritance, it has nothing whatever to do with our everlasting destiny, for," said he, "we do not want Christ to choose for us in the matter of Heaven or hell. It is so plain and easy, that every man who has a grain of common sense will choose Heaven, and any person would know better than to choose hell. We have no need of any superior intelligence, or any greater Being, to choose Heaven or hell for us. It is left to our own free- will, and we have enough wisdom given us, sufficiently correct means to judge for ourselves," and therefore, as he very logically inferred, there was no necessity for Jesus Christ, or anyone, to make a choice for us. We could choose the inheritance for ourselves without any assistance. "Ah!" I thought, "but, my good brother, it may be very true that we could, but I think we should want something more than common sense before we should choose aright."

First, let me ask, must we not all of us admit an over-ruling Providence, and the appointment of Jehovah's hand, as to the means whereby we came into this world? Those men who think that, afterwards, we are left to our own free-will to choose this one or the other to direct our steps, must admit that our entrance into the world was not of our own will, but that God had then to choose for us. What circumstances were those in our power, which led us to elect certain persons to be our parents? Had we anything to do with it? Did not God Himself appoint our parents, native place, and friends? Could He not have caused me to be born with the skin of the Hottentot, brought forth by a filthy mother who would nurse me in her "kraal," and teach me to bow down to Pagan gods, quite as easily as to have given me a pious mother, who would each morning and night bend her knee in prayer on my behalf? Or, might He not, if He had pleased have given me some profligate to have been my parent, from whose lips I might have early heard fearful, filthy, and obscene language? Might He not have placed me where

I should have had a drunken father, who would have immured me in a very dungeon of ignorance, and brought me up in the chains of crime? Was it not God's Providence that I had so happy a lot, that both my parents were His children, and endeavored to train me up in the fear of the Lord?

John Newton used to tell a whimsical story, and laugh at it, too, of a good woman who said, in order to prove the doctrine of election, "Ah! sir, the Lord must have loved me before I was born, or else He would not have seen anything in me to love afterwards." I am sure it is true in my case; I believe the doctrine of election, because I am quite certain that, if God had not chosen me, I should never have chosen Him; and I am sure He chose me before I was born, or else He never would have chosen me afterwards; and He must have elected me for reasons unknown to me, for I never could find any reason in myself why He should have looked upon me with special love. So I am forced to accept that great Biblical doctrine. I recollect an Arminian brother telling me that he had read the Scriptures through a score or more times, and could never find the doctrine of election in them. He added that he was sure he would have done so if it had been there, for he read the Word on his knees. I said to him, "I think you read the Bible in a very uncomfortable posture, and if you had read it in your easy chair, you would have been more likely to understand it. Pray, by all means, and the more, the better, but it is a piece of superstition to think there is anything in the posture in which a man puts himself for reading: and as to reading through the Bible twenty times without having found anything about the doctrine of election, the wonder is that you found anything at all: you must have galloped through it at such a rate that you were not likely to have any intelligible idea of the meaning of the Scriptures."

If it would be marvelous to see one river leap up from the earth full-grown, what would it be to gaze upon a vast spring from which all the rivers of the earth should at once come bubbling up, a million of them born at a birth? What a vision would it be! Who can conceive it. And yet the love of God is that fountain, from which all the rivers of mercy, which have ever gladdened our race-all the rivers of grace in time, and of glory hereafter-take their rise. My soul, stand thou at that sacred fountainhead, and adore and magnify, forever and ever,

God, even our Father, who hath loved us! In the very beginning, when this great universe lay in the mind of God, like unborn forests in the acorn cup; long ere the echoes awoke the solitudes; before the mountains were brought forth; and long ere the light flashed through the sky, God loved His chosen creatures. Before there was any created being-when the ether was not fanned by an angel's wing, when space itself had not an existence, when there was nothing save God alone-even then, in that loneliness of Deity, and in that deep quiet and profundity, His bowels moved with love for His chosen. Their names were written on His heart, and then were they dear to His soul. Jesus loved His people before the foundation of the world-even from eternity! and when He called me by His grace, He said to me, "I have loved thee with an everlasting love: therefore with loving kindness have I drawn thee."

Then, in the fullness of time, He purchased me with His blood; He let His heart run out in one deep gaping wound for me long ere I loved Him. Yea, when He first came to me, did I not spurn Him? When He knocked at the door, and asked for entrance, did I not drive Him away, and do despite to Ms grace? Ah, I can remember that I full often did so until, at last, by the power of His effectual grace, He said, "I must, I will come in;" and then He turned my heart, and made me love Him. But even till now I should have resisted Him, had it not been for His grace. Well, then since He purchased me when I was dead in sins, does it not follow, as a consequence necessary and logical, that He must have loved me first? Did my Saviour die for me because I believed on Him? No; I was not then in existence; I had then no being. Could the Saviour, therefore, have died because I had faith, when I myself was not yet born? Could that have been possible? Could that have been the origin of the Savior's love towards me? Oh! no; my Saviour died for me long before I believed. "But," says someone, "He foresaw that you would have faith; and, therefore, He loved you." What did He foresee about my faith? Did He foresee that I should get that faith myself, and that I should believe on Him of myself) No; Christ could not foresee that, because no Christian man will ever say that faith came of itself without the gift and without the working of the Holy Spirit. I have met with a great many believers, and talked with them about this matter; but I never knew one who could put his hand on his heart, and say, "I believed in Jesus without the assistance of the Holy Spirit."

I am bound to the doctrine of the depravity of the human heart, because I find myself depraved in heart, and have daily proofs that in my flesh there dwelleth no good thing. If God enters into covenant with unfallen man, man is so insignificant a creature that it must be an act of gracious condescension on the Lord's part; but if God enters into covenant with sinful man, he is then so offensive a creature that it must be, on God's part, an act of pure, free, rich, sovereign grace. When the Lord entered into covenant with me, I am sure that it was all of grace, nothing else but grace. When I remember what a den of unclean beasts and birds my heart was, and how strong was my unrenewed will, how obstinate and rebellious against the sovereignty of the Divine rule, I always feel inclined to take the very lowest room in my Father's house, and when I enter Heaven, it will be to go among the less than the least of all saints, and with the chief of sinners.

The late lamented Mr. Denham has put, at the foot of his portrait, a most admirable text, "Salvation is of the Lord." That is just an epitome of Calvinism; it is the sum and substance of it. If anyone should ask me what I mean by a Calvinist, I should reply, "He is one who says, Salvation is of the Lord." I cannot find in Scripture any other doctrine than this. It is the essence of the Bible. "He only is my rock and my salvation." Tell me anything contrary to this truth, and it will be a heresy; tell me a heresy, and I shall find its essence here, that it has departed from this great, this fundamental, this rock-truth, "God is my rock and my salvation." What is the heresy of Rome, but the addition of something to the perfect merits of Jesus Christ-the bringing in of the works of the flesh, to assist in our justification? And what is the heresy of Arminianism but the addition of something to the work of the Redeemer? Every heresy, if brought to the touchstone, will discover itself here. I have my own Private opinion that there is no such thing as preaching Christ and Him crucified, unless we preach what nowadays is called Calvinism. It is a nickname to call it Calvinism; Calvinism is the Gospel, and nothing else. I do not believe we can preach the Gospel, if we do not preach justification by faith, without works; nor unless we preach the sovereignty of God in His dispensation of grace; nor unless we exalt the electing, unchangeable, eternal, immutable, conquering love of Jehovah; nor do I think we can preach the Gospel, unless we base it upon the special and particular redemption of His elect and chosen people which Christ wrought out upon the cross; nor can I comprehend a Gospel which lets saints fall away after they are called, and suffers the children of God to be burned in the fires of damnation after having once believed in Jesus. Such a Gospel I abhor.

If ever it should come to pass,
That sheep of Christ might fall away,
My fickle, feeble soul, alas!
Would fall a thousand times a day.

If one dear saint of God had perished, so might all; if one of the covenant ones be lost, so may all be; and then there is no Gospel promise true, but the Bible is a lie, and there is nothing in it worth my acceptance. I will be an infidel at once when I can believe that a saint of God can ever fall finally. If God hath loved me once, then He will love me forever. God has a mastermind; He arranged everything in His gigantic intellect long before He did it; and once having settled it, He never alters it, 'This shall be done," saith He, and the iron hand of destiny marks it down, and it is brought to pass. "This is My purpose," and it stands, nor can earth or hell alter it. "This is My decree," saith He, "promulgate it, ye holy angels; rend it down from the gate of Heaven, ye devils, if ye can; but ye cannot alter the decree, it shall stand for ever." God altereth not His plans; why should He? He is Almighty, and therefore can perform His pleasure. Why should He? He is the All Wise, and therefore cannot have planned wrongly. Why should He? He is the everlasting God, and therefore cannot die before His plan is accomplished. Why should He change? Ye worthless atoms of earth, ephemera of a day, ye creeping insects upon this bay leaf of existence, ye may change your plans, but He shall never, never change His. Has He told me that His plan is to save me? If so, I am forever safe.

My name from the palms of His hands
Eternity will not erase;

Impress'd on His heart it remains,
In marks of indelible grace.

I do not know how some people, who believe that a Christian can fall from grace, manage to be happy. It must be a very commendable thing in them to be able to get through a day without despair. If I did not believe the doctrine of the final perseverance of the saints, I think I should be of all men the most miserable, because I should lack any ground of comfort. I could not say, whatever state of heart I came into, that I should be like a well- spring of water, whose stream fails not; I should rather have to take the comparison of an intermittent spring, that might stop on a sudden, or a reservoir, which I had no reason to expect would always be full. I believe that the happiest of Christians and the truest of Christians are those who never dare to doubt God, but who take His Word simply as it stands, and believe it, and ask no questions, just feeling assured that if God has said it, it will be so. I bear my willing testimony that I have no reason, nor even the shadow of a reason, to doubt my Lord, and I challenge Heaven, and earth, and hell, to bring any proof that God is untrue. From the depths of hell I call the fiends, and from this earth I call the tried and afflicted believers, and to Heaven I appeal, and challenge the long experience of the blood-washed host, and there is not to be found in the three realms a single person who can bear witness to one fact which can disprove the faithfulness of God, or weaken Ms claim to be trusted by His servants. There are many things that may or may not happen, but this I know shall happen:

He shall present my soul,
Unblemish'd and complete,
Before the glory of His face,
With joys divinely great.

All the purposes of man have been defeated, but not the purposes of God. The promises of man may be broken-many of them are made to be broken, but the promises of God shall all be fulfilled. He is a promise-maker, but He never was a promise-breaker; He is a promise-keeping God, and every one of His people shall prove it to be so. This is my grateful, personal confidence, "The Lord will perfect that which concerneth me"-unworthy me, lost and ruined me. He will yet save me; and ...

I, among the blood-wash'd throng,
Shall wave the palm, and wear the crown,
And shout loud victory.

I go to a land, which the plough of earth hath never upturned, where it is greener than earth's best pastures, and richer than her most abundant harvests ever saw. I go to a building of more gorgeous architecture than man hath ever built; it is not of mortal design; it is "a building of God, a house not made with hands, eternal in the Heavens." All I shall know and enjoy in Heaven, will be given to me by the Lord, and I shall say, when at last I appear before Him-

Grace all the work shall crown
Through everlasting days;
It lays in Heaven the topmost stone,
And well deserves the praise.

I know there are some who think it necessary to their system of theology to limit the merit of the blood of Jesus: if my theological system needed such a limitation, I would cast it to the winds. I cannot, I dare not allow the thought to find a lodging in my mind, it seems so near akin to blasphemy. In Christ's finished work I see an ocean of merit; my plummet finds no bottom, my eye discovers no shore. There must be sufficient efficacy in the blood of Christ, if God had so willed it, to have saved not only all in this world, but all in ten thousand worlds, had they transgressed their Maker's law. Once admit infinity into the matter, and limit is out of the question. Having a Divine Person for an offering, it is not consistent to conceive of limited value; bound and measure are terms inapplicable to the Divine sacrifice. The intent of the Divine purpose fixes the application of the infinite offering, but does not change it into a finite work. Think of the numbers upon whom God has bestowed His grace already. Think of the countless hosts in Heaven: if thou wert introduced there today, thou wouldst find it as easy to tell the stars, or the sands of the sea, as to count the multitudes that are before the throne even now. They have come from the East, and from the West, from the North, and from the South, and they are sitting down with Abraham, and with Isaac, and with Jacob in the Kingdom of God; and beside those in Heaven, think of the saved ones on earth. Blessed be God, His elect on earth are to be counted by millions, I believe, and the days are coming, brighter days than these, when there shall be multitudes upon multitudes brought to know the Saviour, and to rejoice in Him. The Father's love is not for a few only, but for an exceeding great company. "A great multitude, which no man could number," will be found in Heaven. A man can reckon up to very high figures; set to work your Newtons, your mightiest calculators, and they can count great numbers, but God and God alone can tell the multitude of His redeemed. I believe there will be more in Heaven than in hell. If anyone asks me why I think so, I answer, because Christ, in everything, is to "have the pre-eminence," and I cannot conceive how He could have the pre-eminence if there are to be more in the dominions of Satan than in Paradise. Moreover, I have never read that there is to be in hell a great multitude, which no man could number. I rejoice to know that the souls of all infants, as soon as they die, speed their way to Paradise. Think what a multitude there is of them! Then there are already in Heaven unnumbered myriads of the spirits of just men made perfect-the redeemed of all nations, and kindred, and people, and tongues up till now; and there are better times coming, when the religion of Christ shall be universal; when ...

He shall reign from pole to pole,
With illimitable sway,

... when whole kingdoms shall bow down before Him, and nations shall be born in a day, and in the thousand years of the great millennial state there will be enough saved to make up all the deficiencies of the thousands of years that have gone before. Christ shall be Master everywhere, and His praise shall be sounded in every land. Christ shall have the pre-eminence at last; His train shall be far larger than that which shall attend the chariot of the grim monarch of hell.

Some persons love the doctrine of universal atonement because they say, "It is so beautiful. It is a lovely idea that Christ should have died for all men; it commends itself," they say, "to the instincts of humanity; there is something in it full of joy and beauty." I admit there is, but beauty may be often associated with falsehood. There is much, which I might admire in the theory of universal redemption, but I will just show what the supposition necessarily involves. If Christ on His cross intended to save every man, then He intended to save those who were lost before He died. If the doctrine is true, that He died for all men, then He died for some who were in hell before He came into this world, for doubtless there were even then myriads there that had been cast away because of their sins. Once again, if it was Christ's intention to save all men, how deplorably has He been disappointed, for we have His own testimony that there is a lake which burns with fire and brimstone, and into that pit of woe have been cast some of the very persons who, according to the theory of universal redemption, were bought with His blood. That seems to me a conception a thousand times more repulsive than any of those consequences, which are said to be associated with the Calvinistic and Christian doctrine of special and particular redemption.

To think that my Saviour died for men who were or are in hell, seems a supposition too horrible for me to entertain. To imagine for a moment that He was the Substitute for all the sons of men, and that God, having first punished the Substitute, afterwards punished the sinners themselves, seems to conflict with all my ideas of Divine justice. That Christ should offer an atonement and satisfaction for the sins of all men, and that afterwards some of those very men should be punished for the sins for which Christ had already atoned, appears to me to be the most monstrous iniquity that could ever have been imputed to Saturn, to Janus, to the goddess of the Thugs, or to the most diabolical heathen deities. God forbid that we should ever think thus of Jehovah, the just and wise and good! There is no soul living who holds more firmly to the doctrines of grace than I do, and if any man asks me whether I am ashamed to be called a Calvinist, I answer- I wish to be called nothing but a Christian; but if you ask me, do I hold the doctrinal views which were held by John Calvin, I reply, I do in the main hold them, and rejoice to avow it. But far be it from me even to imagine that Zion contains none but Calvinistic Christians within her walls, or that there are none saved who do not hold our views.

Most atrocious things have been spoken about the character and spiritual condition of John Wesley, the modern prince of Arminians. I can only say concerning him that, while I detest many of the doctrines which he preached, yet for the man himself I have a reverence second to no Wesleyan; and if there were wanted two apostles to be added to the number of the twelve, I do not believe that there could be found two men more fit to be so added than George Whitefield and John Wesley. The character of John Wesley stands beyond all imputation for self-sacrifice, zeal, holiness, and communion with God; he lived far above the ordinary level of common Christians, and was one "of whom the world was not worthy." I believe there are multitudes of men who cannot see these truths, or, at least, cannot see them in the way in which we put them, who nevertheless have received Christ as their Saviour, and are as dear to the heart of the God of grace as the soundest Calvinist in or out of Heaven.

I do not think I differ from any of my Hyper-Calvinistic brethren in what I do believe, but I differ from them in what they do not believe. I do not hold any less than they do, but I hold a little more, and, I think, a little more of the truth revealed in the Scriptures. Not only are there a few cardinal doctrines, by which we can steer our ship North, South, East, or West, but as we study the Word, we shall begin to learn something about the Northwest and Northeast, and all else that lies between the four cardinal points. The system of truth revealed in the Scriptures is not simply one straight line, but two; and no man will ever get a right view of the Gospel until he knows how to look at the two lines at once. For instance, I read in one Book of the Bible, "The Spirit and the bride say, Come. And let him that heareth say, Come. And let him that is athirst come. And whosoever will, let him take the water of life freely." Yet I am taught, in another part of the same inspired Word, that "it is not of him that willeth, nor of him that runneth, but of God that sheweth mercy." I see, in one place, God in providence presiding over all, and yet I see, and I cannot help seeing, that man acts as he pleases, and that God has left his actions, in a great measure, to his own free-will. Now, if I were to declare that man was so free to act that there was no control of God over his actions, I should be driven very near to atheism; and if, on the other hand, I should declare that God so over-rules all things that man is not free enough to be responsible, I should be driven at once into Antinomianism or fatalism.

That God predestines, and yet that man is responsible, are two facts that few can see clearly. They are believed to be inconsistent and contradictory to each other. If, then, I find taught in one part of the Bible that everything is foreordained, that is true; and if I find, in another Scripture, that man is responsible for all his actions, that is true; and it is only my folly that leads me to imagine that these two truths can ever contradict each other. I do not believe they can ever be welded into one upon any earthly anvil, but they certainly shall be one in eternity. They are two lines that are so nearly parallel, that the human mind which pursues them farthest will never discover that they converge, but they do converge, and they will meet somewhere in eternity, close to the throne of God, whence all truth doth spring.

It is often said that the doctrines we believe have a tendency to lead us to sin. I have heard it asserted most positively, that those high doctrines which we love, and which we find in the Scriptures, are licentious ones. I do not know who will have the hardihood to make that assertion, when they consider that the holiest of men have been believers in them. I ask the man who dares to say that Calvinism is a licentious religion, what he thinks of the character of Augustine, or Calvin, or Whitefield, who in successive ages were the great exponents of the system of grace; or what will he say of the Puritans, whose works are full of them? Had a man been an Arminian in those days, he would have been accounted the vilest heretic breathing, but now we are looked upon as the heretics, and they as the orthodox. We have gone back to the old school; we can trace our descent from the apostles. It is that vein of free-grace, running through the sermonizing of Baptists, which has saved us as a denomination. Were it not for that, we should not stand where we are today. We can run a golden line up to Jesus Christ Himself, through a holy succession of mighty fathers, who all held these glorious truths; and we can ask concerning them, "Where will you find holier and better men in the world?"

No doctrine is so calculated to preserve a man from sin as the doctrine of the grace of God. Those who have called it "a licentious doctrine" did not know anything at all about it. Poor ignorant things, they little knew that their own vile stuff was the most licentious doctrine under Heaven. If they knew the grace of God in truth, they would soon see that there was no preservative from lying like a knowledge that we are elect of God from the foundation of the world. There is nothing like a belief in my eternal perseverance, and the immutability of my Father's affection, which can keep me near to Him from a motive of simple gratitude. Nothing makes a man so virtuous as belief of the truth. A lying doctrine will soon beget a lying practice. A man cannot have an erroneous belief without by-and-by having an erroneous life. I believe the one thing naturally begets the other. Of all men, those have the most disinterested piety, the most sublime reverence, the most ardent devotion, who believe that they are saved by grace, without works, through faith, and that not of themselves, it is the gift of God. Christians should take heed, and see that it always is so, lest by any means Christ should be crucified afresh, and put to an open shame.

The Five Points of Calvinism

With the possible exception of Martin Luther, no man has had greater influence on the theology of the Protestant Churches today than John Calvin. It's impossible to condense countless volumes of Biblical commentary of John Calvin down to a short summary, it is true that Calvin's most well-know teachings, set forth in *The Institutes of Christian Religion* are the often-quoted "Five Points of Calvinism."

The acronym used to help remember them is "**T.U.L.I.P.**" They are:

TOTAL DEPRAVITY OF MAN: That man's nature is basically evil, not basically good. Apart from the direct influence of God, man will never truly seek God or God's will, though he may seek the benefits of association with God.

UNCONDITIONAL ELECTION: That God sovereignly chooses or "elects" his children from before the foundation of time. God does not "look down the corridors of time to see what decision people will make"... rather, God causes them to make the decision to seek him.

LIMITED ATONEMENT: That the death and resurrection of Christ is a substitutionary payment for the sins of only those who are God's elect children... not the entire world.

IRRESISTIBLE GRACE: That when God calls a person, his call cannot ultimately be ignored.

PERSEVERANCE OF THE SAINTS: That it is not possible for one to "lose his salvation.

Index

schism xxxiv, 121
schismatics xxxv
Schoolmen 27, 29, 31, 36, 37,
　　54, 65, 69, 74, 114, 116,
　　130, 132, 141, 157, 246,
　　286, 287, 335, 487
scribes xxxiv
searcher of hearts 417
self-denial 87, 185, 186, 188,
　　189, 193, 567
Seneca 201
Servetus 3, 4
Socrates 514
sophism 267, 272
Sophist 235
Sophists 112, 139, 161, 180,
　　244, 245, 249, 252, 258,
　　286, 302, 303, 305, 306,
　　315, 320, 342, 343, 403,
　　566
Sorbonne 1, 306, 347
sorcerer xxvi
Spirit xxxiv
Spurgeon, Charles Haddon ix,
　　577
Stoics 205

T

Tertullian 443, 538, 539
Theodore Beza 6
Trinity 3
true Church xxxiii
truth xii, xv, xx, xxi, xxv,
　　xxvii, xxxi, xxxii, xxxiii,
　　xxxvi, xxxviii, xl, 3, 5,
　　8, 21, 22, 28, 30, 31, 32,
　　34, 35, 36, 38, 40, 42,

48, 51, 55, 57, 62, 64,
66, 67, 68, 73, 75, 76,
93, 101, 103, 104, 106,
131, 147, 158, 163, 170,
171, 200, 203, 204, 207,
211, 226, 229, 252, 258,
263, 271, 272, 282, 284,
301, 319, 321, 324, 330,
336, 340, 346, 352, 353,
363, 377, 382, 385, 386,
393, 403, 420, 427, 433,
443, 445, 446, 447, 452,
458, 462, 474, 489, 495,
496, 501, 506, 507, 512,
521, 522, 525, 528, 564,
566, 568, 569, 573, 577,
579, 583, 589, 591

V

Valentinus 494
vows 372, 413, 572

W

Wesley, John 589
Whitchurch, Edward xii
Whitefield, George 589
Wisner, Rev. Dr. xlii
Wolfe, Reginald xii
works of God 62, 279, 308,
　　485
works of supererogation 288,
　　289, 291

Z

Zion 101, 102, 265, 415, 418,
　　589
Zuinglians 238

Pure Gold Classics
Timeless Truth in a
Distinctive, Best-Selling Collection

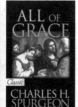

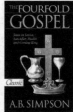

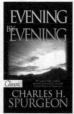

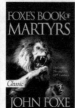

GOD OF ALL **COMFORT**

Classic

HANNAH WHITALL SMITH

The **GREATEST THING** IN THE **WORLD**

Classic

HENRY DRUMMOND

THE **IMITATION** OF **CHRIST**

Classic

THOMAS à KEMPIS

IN **HIS** STEPS

Classic

CHARLES M. SHELDON

INTERIOR CASTLE

Classic

TERESA OF AVILA

THE **HOLY SPIRIT POWER**

10 Includes Timeless Messages

Classic

JOHN WESLEY

R. A. TORREY

Classic

THE **HOLY SPIRIT** WHO HE IS AND WHAT HE DOES

HUMILITY

Classic

ANDREW MURRAY

JEWELS FROM E.M. BOUNDS

Classic

E.M. BOUNDS

THE **KNEELING CHRISTIAN**

Classic

AN UNKNOWN CHRISTIAN

MADAME JEANNE GUYON

Classic

EXPERIENCING UNION WITH GOD THROUGH INNER PRAYER & THE WAY AND RESULTS OF UNION WITH GOD

MORNING BY MORNING

Classic

CHARLES H. SPURGEON

THE **OVERCOMING LIFE**

Classic

D.L. MOODY

THE **PILGRIM'S PROGRESS** IN MODERN ENGLISH

Classic

JOHN BUNYAN

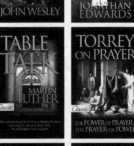
POWER, PASSION & **PRAYER**

Finney's Greatest Sermons on Revival through Prayer

Classic

CHARLES G. FINNEY

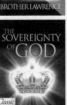
THE **PRACTICE** OF THE **PRESENCE** OF **GOD**

Classic

BROTHER LAWRENCE

SECRET POWER

Classic

D.L. MOODY

A SERIOUS CALL TO A **DEVOUT** & **HOLY LIFE**

Classic

WILLIAM LAW

THE **SERMON** ON THE **MOUNT**

Classic

JOHN WESLEY

SINNERS IN THE **HANDS** OF AN **ANGRY GOD**

Classic

JONATHAN EDWARDS

THE **SOVEREIGNTY** OF **GOD**

Classic

A.W. PINK

SPURGEON ON THE **HOLY SPIRIT**

Classic

CHARLES H. SPURGEON

SPURGEON ON PRAYER HOW TO CONVERSE WITH GOD

Classic

CHARLES H. SPURGEON

TABLE TALK MARTIN LUTHER

Classic

TORREY ON PRAYER

Classic

THE POWER OF PRAYER & THE PRAYER OF POWER

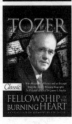
TOZER

Classic

FELLOWSHIP OF THE BURNING HEART

TOZER: MYSTERY OF THE **HOLY SPIRIT**

Classic

A.W. TOZER

WALKING WITH **GOD**

Classic

THE ANDREW MURRAY TRILOGY ON SANCTIFICATION

WILLIAM WILBERFORCE

Classic

GREATEST WORKS

WITH **CHRIST** IN THE **SCHOOL** OF **PRAYER**

ANDREW MURRAY